P9-DFR-022

MONOPOLY AND FREE ENTERPRISE

BY

GEORGE W. STOCKING
AND
MYRON W. WATKINS

With the Report and Recommendations of the
Committee on Cartels and Monopoly

GREENWOOD PRESS, PUBLISHERS
NEW YORK 1968

First Greenwood reprinting, 1968

LIBRARY OF CONGRESS catalogue card number: 68-54439

Printed in the United States of America

FOREWORD

EVER SINCE the activities of the early "trusts" aroused the American public to fury in the late 1880's the monopoly problem has ranked high in terms of controversy and low in terms of the vast factual knowledge needed to deal with it. Even to define what is a monopoly—much less to apply the definition to specific industries and companies—has baffled both economists and legislators for many years.

The authors of this study make no pretense at taking the full measure of monopoly in the various areas of American economic life. They have focussed their efforts on four less ambitious, but most important, major objectives. First, they have attempted to throw into sharp perspective the relation of the concentration of economic power to the theory and practice of "free enterprise"—and to its future as well. Second, the authors have sought to show in detail and by specific instances how the free play of competitive forces has actually been limited by American business concerns and, in certain fields, by legislation. Third, they have tried to assess the economic and social effects of these developments. Finally, they have given special attention to governmental action to curb monopolistic practices, but they have not overlooked governmental actions that sometimes deliberately sanction such practices and sometimes unwittingly foster them.

These objectives have, of course, forced the authors to concentrate their attention on business practices that are undesirable, rather than on the accomplishments of those companies that have well served the competitive ideal. Nor have they attempted to cast up a balance of debits and credits. Consequently, the book affords no basis for an inference as to how common are the restrictive practices it describes or as to whether the companies involved in such practices have, on net balance, done more good than harm to the economy, from the point of view of the national welfare. But the limitations on competition—potential as well as actual, direct and indirect, public as well as private—with which this report is concerned do pose critical problems for the people of the United States.

The international situation that has developed in 1950, with its ominous threat to the United States and to all free nations, increases the urgency of coming to grips with the monopoly problem. To keep a vast program of rearmament free of monopoly abuses has now become an important matter of national security as well as of sound economic policy. While monopoly practices are most common in slack times, activities designed to suppress technological improvements, to raise the cost of war contracts, or to increase the price of necessities to the civilian population in periods of mobilization reduce the nation's power to stop aggression and to build an adequate defense.

This volume is the third in a series of reports growing out of a major Fund survey in the field of monopoly—both international and domestic.

The first volume, *Cartels in Action,* published in 1946, is a "case book." It reviews the development, describes the methods, and analyzes the results of international cartels in eight important fields: sugar, rubber, nitrogen, iron and steel, aluminum, magnesium, electric lamps, and chemicals.

The second volume, *Cartels or Competition?,* published in 1948, gives the general reader an objective appraisal of the international cartel movement as a whole and supplements *Cartels in Action* with factual material on other industries than those covered in the first volume. It includes an estimate of the extent to which cartels affect the foreign trade and the domestic markets of the United States, and also an analysis of the influence of cartels on industrial stability, volume of employment, technological advance, and the rate of investment.

Following its usual procedure, the Fund set up a special research staff for the Cartels and Monopoly survey headed by two leading authorities on the subject—George W. Stocking and Myron W. Watkins. Messrs. Stocking and Watkins are responsible for the factual findings contained in all these reports—in this volume, Chapters 1-15 inclusive.

The Fund also appointed a Special Committee on Cartels and Monopoly, under the chairmanship of James M. Landis, formerly Dean of the Harvard Law School and Chairman of the Civil Aeronautics Board. The Committee was invited to explore the issues that the research findings disclose and to draw up a program of action to meet these challenging problems. In selecting the distinguished members of this Committee, listed opposite the title page, the Trustees of the Fund sought to give unofficial representation to the points of view of business, labor, and agriculture, as well as to those of the economic and legal professions. The Committee also represents wide experience in government administration.

Chapter 16 of this book contains the Committee's analysis of the monopoly problem in the United States with constructive suggestions for more effectively safeguarding and promoting free competitive enterprise in the domestic economy. Chapter 12 of *Cartels or Competition?* gave the Committee's report and recommendations as to international cartels. We believe that, taken together, these two contain a valuable and most timely contribution to the formation of a wise and effective policy toward business and governmental actions that limit competition in home markets and foreign trade.

The Fund's appreciation goes, in full measure, to the members of the Committee who have given so much of their time and effort in formulating these policy reports. It acknowledges with thanks, also, the editorial assistance of Ferdinand Lundberg. Finally, the Fund is gratefully conscious of the outstanding contribution the research directors have made, through their factual findings and analyses, to a more intelligent public understanding of the ways in which coercive control of markets has been exercised—whether contrived by private interests or imposed by government authority—and of the effects of these controls.

EVANS CLARK, *Executive Director*
The Twentieth Century Fund

330 WEST 42D STREET
NEW YORK 18, N. Y.
SEPTEMBER 1, 1950

PREFACE

THIS BOOK deals with certain aspects of the problem of industrial government in a democratic society. The problem itself is perennial and inescapable in any society. How to organize and control economic activities so as to insure willing cooperation, adequate livelihood, and progressive improvement in the ratio of real income to productive effort has always been a vital social issue. For on its success in solving this problem depends a community's survival. But in a democratic society the problem is exceptionally acute, because the distinctive goal of such a society is to maximize free choice and minimize coercion.

Of the many aspects of the problem of industrial government, this study focuses primarily on the relation of business organization to the structure and behavior of markets. How can enterprise be fostered and freedom of choice preserved without sacrificing efficiency or tolerating inequity? Experience both at home and abroad shows that unless private enterprise is free—free alike from bureaucratic and from monopolistic domination—it cannot safely be relied on to allocate resources, organize production, distribute income, and promote technological progress. Society can afford to entrust these basic economic functions to private enterprise only if it is genuinely free. And enterprise can be free only when it is competitive. That is the mark of its freedom, just as monopoly is a sign of arbitrary control.

But the lesson of history is clear: Business will not long remain competitive, if left to its own devices. Laissez faire promotes monopoly, not competition. To keep business enterprise healthy and free it is necessary to provide a legal and economic environment hospitable to competition. This is not easy. For an essential condition of creating and maintaining such an environment is restriction of *some* business privileges, *some* business practices. The question is where to draw the line: What specific privileges shall be withdrawn or withheld to safeguard the basic right of freedom of enterprise and its distinctive quality of initiative?

The problem is complicated by the fact that the increasing size of business units (achieved in substantial part through combination) and the increasing scope of trade cooperation have upset the customary "checks and balances" (both external and internal) of business policy. Neither businessmen nor lawmakers have yet shown any clear realization of the implications of this fact. But economic theory teaches, and business practice confirms, that in markets where sellers are few and large they are apt to behave like monopolists—though of course such behavior is not invariably or in all respects pernicious.

Nevertheless, people tend to identify bigness and efficiency and to assume that one cannot be had without the other. Obviously in many areas of the economy modern technology severely limits the number of business rivals. Mass production and pure competition are incompatible. It may be less obvious, but it is no less true, that competition may be effective even though the conditions of pure competition are not fulfilled. In many industries no loss of efficiency would necessarily attend an increase in the number of firms.

Because businessmen have more to gain than any other group from a private enterprise regime—and more to lose by its suppression—once the issues are clearly drawn, if they are farsighted, they will support a program designed to implement such a regime. In general terms, such a program would provide an economic environment favorable to freedom of enterprise and would insure in every market as many sellers as are consistent with the economies of large-scale production and distribution. As to the specific elements of such a program we invite the reader to examine the book itself.

Much of the analysis of this study is based on patterns of industrial organization and business conduct prevailing before World War II. This is partly because the survey was begun several years ago. But in any event the wartime and postwar periods have been quite abnormal. Prewar experience furnishes a better clue to the basic tendencies implicit in American business practice and public economic policy. During the war, the economy was government-regulated. Since the war, business firms and whole industries have been vying with each other to supply a huge pent-up demand, foreign as well as domestic, occasioned by the extraordinary, war-generated dearth of goods and surplus of purchasing power. When the business to be done exceeds the capacity of the facilities for doing it, competition permits nearly everybody to prosper. So businessmen, big and little, are all for it.

The test of free enterprise will come with a return to more normal conditions—if "normal" any longer has meaning. When competition means lower profits for most firms and bankruptcy for some, businessmen are apt again to seek security through mergers or through concerted action. Of course World War III, if it comes, and even the global commitments of the United States in helping to prevent it, may lead to a devastating inflation and a permanently regimented economy. In that event, the problem of monopoly will give way to the problem of survival. If, however, by grace of fate or by virtue of heroic courage and rare statesmanship, a genial era for a free society follows these anxious times, this survey may prove useful in formulating public economic policy.

Monopoly and Free Enterprise is to an uncommon degree a joint product, as were the two preceding studies in this series. While the co-directors of the survey have taken account of the advantages of division of labor, they have also been mindful of the axiom that two heads are better than one. Consequently, they share responsibility equally for every chapter.

In bringing this survey to a close, we again acknowledge our grateful appreciation of the unfailing courtesy of Evans Clark and J. Frederic Dewhurst, Director and Economist, respectively, of the Fund, of the unstinted cooperation of the survey staff and the Fund staff, and of the many helpful criticisms and suggestions made by members of the advisory Committee.

GEORGE W. STOCKING
MYRON W. WATKINS

CONTENTS

MONOPOLY AND FREE ENTERPRISE

Chapter 1

THE SIGNIFICANCE OF ECONOMIC ORGANIZATION

ECONOMIC ACTIVITY is purposeful. It must be controlled, therefore, whether the avowed purpose is to provide subsistence, to accumulate riches, to gain power, to build civilization, or to achieve some other end. And control requires organization. Without discipline and order, economic activity could not accomplish its purpose—for the individual or the group, for the primitive tribe or for the large and wealthy nation. However diligent, resourceful, and skillful men may be, their activities, if uncoordinated, could hardly fail to end in confusion and mutual frustration.

Increasing Complexity of Economic Organization

As a society becomes more populous, as people learn to make and do things in more complex ways, individual goals become greatly diversified and the ways of attaining them more varied. The task of harmonizing individual economic activities becomes more difficult. The problem of economic organization and control grows ever more complex. A solution adapted to the needs of the past does not necessarily fit the circumstances of the present. For no special method of organization and control is "best" for all peoples and all times. But some method of organizing the multifarious activities that provide the material basis for civilized life is obviously necessary.

The perennial question is: What is the best way of organizing economic activity for *this* society *now?* On that question, today as always, men are divided. But the division of opinion is exceptionally sharp in our times. For the traditional system of economic organization has been subjected to extraordinary strains—World War I, the Great Depression of the 1930's, and World War II. Yet, despite the disruption wrought by mass unemployment and total war, the American economy, organized predominantly by private enterprise, has survived in good working order. Evidently Adam Smith's remark about England's losses in the American Revolution—that "there is a great deal of ruin in a nation" [1]—could be applied also to a going economic system. For the private enterprise system in America, whatever its shortcomings, has not only withstood disintegrating forces of unprecedented violence since 1914 but has proved its power of adaptation by raising real income per capita to a level never before reached.

The Issue: Extent of Authoritative Direction of the Economy

The basic issue of economic organization in the United States, or for that matter in most modern states, is not between laissez faire and totalitarianism. These are unreal extremes, alike in the context of history and of contemporary experience.

Nor is the issue one between unified and diffused control of economic activity. An economy organized with a maximum of authoritative control may be either dictatorial or socialistic. If it is dictatorial, as in Soviet Russia, those who have captured the machinery of government directly or indirectly make all the vital decisions on what shall be produced, methods of production, and distribution of income. If it is genuinely socialistic, the responsibility for making these decisions may rest immediately with those at the head of a democratically chosen government but ultimately, in theory at least, with the electorate.

Similarly, in an economy such as ours, organized with a minimum of authoritative control, power to make decisions—and to make them effective—may also be either highly concentrated or highly diffused. In short, the actual economic organization may be either monopolistic or competitive.

But none of these is the fundamental issue.

The fundamental issue is between more or less governmental control. Under the private enterprise system as it has developed here, the need for a certain measure of governmental control is recognized. The law forbids unlicensed traffic in some goods, such as narcotics and alcoholic beverages. In many jurisdictions it restricts the choice of working personnel, as in forbidding child labor. It limits entry to some industries and regulates investment and prices therein, as with telephone service. The government itself may supply

1. *The correspondence of . . . Sir John Sinclair*, Edinburgh, 1831, Vol. 1, p. 391.

certain goods, such as water, electricity, highways, and education. In short, the accepted functions of government in respect to economic organization under a free private enterprise system extend far beyond mere protection of property, enforcement of contracts, and prevention of fraud. Yet, much is left to private control.

Meaning of Free Private Enterprise System

Perhaps the easiest way to grasp the fundamental issue—more governmental control or less—is to set down the distinctive elements of a free private enterprise system. While such a system cannot be precisely defined, because it embraces a great number and variety of institutions, customs, and divergent patterns of thought and behavior that are in constant flux, certain major aspects persist and may be singled out.

First, such a system is private in the sense that individuals or voluntary associations have the right to produce, buy, and sell whatever goods or services they choose, and in whatever way, except as they may be limited by due process of law. In short, private persons acting on their own responsibility—not government officials—determine what shall be produced, where investments shall be made, how goods shall be distributed, and how much shall be saved.

Secondly, such a system is free in the sense that anyone may enter any lawful industry or occupation. Individuals or voluntary groups who can assemble the necessary resources are free to engage in most businesses without let or hindrance from government and free from molestation or obstruction by private persons with an adverse interest at stake.

Thirdly, a free private enterprise system requires a competitive market. Free competition is, so to speak, the price of freedom of enterprise. It is the basic condition on which society, for its own protection, permits private enterprisers to assume the responsibility and exercise the power of organizing the productive activities on which the life of the community depends.

All these features of a free private enterprise system are closely interrelated. Its private aspect may, indeed, be described broadly as freedom from government direction. And its competitive feature may be characterized simply as freedom from control by private power groups—which is a corollary of freedom of entry.

When a government undertakes to uphold in general the rights of private producers and sellers to act on their own responsibility, and commits itself not to direct them, it assumes that enough enterprisers will have the will and the means to go into business to assure effective competition in the markets. If it did not assume this, it would merely be conferring monopolistic privileges by indirection, as did the Tudors and Stuarts directly. In America, Congress in 1890 gave statutory recognition to the idea that a free private enterprise system requires effective competition as a safeguard for the public interest. But long before the enactment of the Sherman Antitrust Act the courts had developed a body of common-law doctrine based on the same principle: that free competition is the price of free enterprise. The aim of the doctrine of restraint of trade was to prevent private monopoly, to assure free enterprise.

Economists' Model of Free Private Enterprise System

During the nineteenth century economists perfected a theory to explain how a free-enterprise economy organizes and directs the voluntary activities of independent businessmen and free laborers and coordinates them in a system for supplying the members of a society with the goods and services they want.

In a free private enterprise economy, according to this theory, businessmen make decisions on a basis of price-cost relationships. They can make money only by making goods or supplying services people want. By their free choices in spending their incomes in a competitive market, consumers guide the production process. Businessmen independently decide what to produce and in what amounts, but always in response to consumer demand. If they turn out goods in the wrong proportions, or the wrong goods, the market quickly reflects those facts. The prices of things in relative shortage will rise above costs, the prices of things in relative surplus will fall below costs. Productive resources will gradually shift from those uses wherein they are slightly valued to those wherein they are more highly valued. In this way resources are allocated in an economical way among the many uses to which they might be put.

In organizing production to meet consumer demands, the theory continues, businessmen bid against each other for the limited supply of productive resources—land, labor, and capital—and combine them in the economically and technically proper proportions to produce what consumers want. In thus organizing production, they not only produce what consumers want, but they provide the members of society with their monetary incomes. For in organizing production businessmen buy raw materials, hire laborers and managers, rent land, and borrow capital. For these they pay the market price.

Functions of an Economic System

By this circular process the price mechanism performs the functions which must somehow, in some way, be performed in any economic organization. It allocates limited productive facilities among the alternative uses to which they might be put in accordance with the ends that have been determined; it organizes production; it rations in the short run a limited stock of goods; and, over the longer period, it distributes the national income among the members of society.

Moreover, it distributes income in accordance with a principle which on its face seems equitable. The owners of property and the sellers of labor are paid in accordance with the impersonal evaluation that society makes of their relative importance. Justice in such a society does not require that every man receive an equal share of the social income but that every man has as nearly equal an opportunity as is consistent with the free-enterprise system. The theory of free enterprise recognizes that the state must play an important role in insuring fair play and an equal chance. It must provide free public schools. It must promote public health. It must prevent fraud and enforce contracts. It must fix employment standards. It must prevent all practices that tend to undermine the system itself. In short, it must provide an appropriate framework of legal sanctions, rights, and privileges within which a free-enterprise system can survive and thrive.

Decentralized Decision Making

The voluntary organization of production and distribution of goods and services in response to anticipated demand is the essence of a free private enterprise regime. But voluntary organization is not enough. Neoclassical economic theory premises individual behavior conforming to a universal principle—utilitarianism—and molded by strong social pressures. The neoclassicists' model of a free-enterprise economy serving the public interest is an economy of large numbers. There is no room in it for private monopoly. According to the theory, only competitive markets can harness the selfish and diverse interests of business rivals and bend their activities to social goals. The essence of competitive markets is the diffusion of power. In perfectly competitive markets buyers and sellers are so numerous and so small that none can appreciably affect price by varying his output.

Although the neoclassicists' competitive market is a mental construct with no objective counterpart, some actual markets closely approximate it. For example, a farmer with 500 acres in wheat might either double his acreage or give up raising wheat entirely without exerting any appreciable effect on prices. The 10,000 to 20,000 bushels he might raise is so trifling in comparison with the billion bushels American farmers together pile up in a year that his output cannot appreciably affect the price. A wheat farmer, therefore, has no price policy. He may switch his land from a less to a more important use, or he may change his occupation, but, in the absence of governmental controls, as long as he sells wheat he must accept the "bloodless verdict of the market," whether he likes the price or not.

Competitive Pricing

In both competitive and monopolistic markets, according to neoclassical theory, sellers will try to regulate their output so as to make as much money as possible. In both kinds of market each seller will increase his production as long as he can add more to his revenues than to his costs. But while monopoly and competitive markets are alike in their motivation, they differ in their consequences. Since each seller in a competitive market produces so little that he cannot appreciably affect price, when he increases output by any given percentage he increases his total revenues in a similar proportion. Other things being equal, a 10 per cent increase in output means a 10 per cent increase in gross income. But while a change in one seller's output will bring no change in price, it may bring a change in cost. Each seller in a competitive market increases production until marginal costs (additional costs incurred by increasing output) equal marginal revenues (additional revenues gained by increasing output). Because each additional unit of output adds to gross revenue the price obtained for it, and because the market fixes this price for all sellers, under competition each seller increases production until marginal cost equals market price.

All costs are variable in the long run, because any industry can increase or decrease its total productive resources, given sufficient time. But within a period not long enough to permit increase (or decrease) of *some* of the available facilities, part of the costs are fixed. These so-called fixed costs, as everyone knows, are those such as rent, interest, and property taxes that remain the same in total amount whether a firm produces much or nothing at all. The proportion of total fixed costs chargeable to each unit produced varies, however, with the rate of output, becoming progressively smaller as output approaches the capacity of given facilities. Therein is one of the "secrets" of mass production.

Costs commonly termed variable are those the total of which changes with changes in output. They consist of wages, cost of materials, and similar items. Over the "short run" in competitive markets marginal unit cost on the one hand and price on the other may be more or less than total unit cost (variable cost plus fixed cost per unit). If price persists below total cost, firms must either discontinue business or find ways of lowering their costs. If price persistently exceeds total unit cost, abnormal profits will attract into the industry enough additional productive factors, perhaps including additional firms, to reduce price to total unit cost. Because price equals cost in competitive markets—marginal unit cost in the short run, total unit cost in the long run—the independent decisions of producers, if they are rational, are theoretically consistent with public interest. While producers might prefer to price above costs, they cannot so long as they act independently. And while they might prefer never to sell for less than cost, they cannot avoid doing so at times unless they cease to act independently.

Monopolistic Pricing

The essence of monopoly is the concentration of economic power. A perfect monopoly market is one with only a single seller.[2] A monopolist, like every seller in a competitive market, according to

2. Economists call a market with many sellers and only one buyer "monopsony." Such a market operates like a monopolistic market.

accepted theory, ordinarily tries to make as much money as possible. He does this by adjusting output so that marginal cost equals marginal revenue. That is, he will increase output as long as he adds more to his revenue than he adds to his cost. But in determining his most profitable output he must take account of two major variables as he varies his output—cost and price.

Since a monopolist is the only seller of a particular product in the market, his production policy exerts a decisive influence on price. If he increases output by 10 per cent, it is as though all producers in a competitive market had increased their output by 10 per cent. Ordinarily the monopolist can sell the larger output only by taking a lower price for each unit. The amount he receives from the sale of the additional units is not a net addition to gross revenue. To sell more he must take a lower price on all units, including those he might have sold at a higher price. To calculate the marginal revenue (addition to gross revenue) that increased output would bring in, he must deduct from the sum obtained from the sale of additional units the sum foregone on the former sales volume because of the reduced price. A monopolist's marginal unit revenue is always less than his average unit revenue or market price.[3]

A monopolist, like a competitor, will tend to increase production until marginal cost equals marginal revenue. But, unlike a competitor's, a monopolist's marginal revenue is less than price. He will therefore stop increasing his production at a point where marginal cost is less than price. That is to say, less will be produced by an industry controlled by a monopolist, other things being equal, than would have been produced were the industry competitively controlled. By restricting output a monopolist is able to keep his price above his marginal cost—and in the long run perhaps above his total unit cost. The difference between price and cost—marginal

3. To illustrate: Suppose a monopolist is selling 1,000,000 packages of cigarettes at 20 cents each and that he can sell 1,200,000 at 18 cents. The revenue from 200,000 packages at 18 cents each totals $36,000. But this is not a net addition to gross revenues, for to sell the additional 200,000 packages he must accept 2 cents less on each of 1,000,000 packages he might have sold at 20 cents. His loss of revenue from the decrease in price on the 1,000,000 packages is $20,000. His marginal revenue amounts to $36,000 minus $20,000, or $16,000. Reduced to a unit basis his marginal revenue is $16,000 divided by 200,000, or 8 cents. Suppose, further, that to increase his output by 200,000 units it has also cost him 8 cents a package. His marginal cost thus equals his marginal revenue, but marginal cost is less by 10 cents than average revenue or market price.

cost in the short run and total unit cost in the long run—measures his monopoly gain.[4]

These, then, are the significant differences in the consequences of rational behavior by competitors and monopolists as neoclassical economists have analyzed them. Competitors in trying to make as much money as they can will produce all they can sell at a price that covers cost; monopolists will restrict output to make more money. Under a competitive organization of the economy, other things being equal, society gets more goods and pays less for them.[5]

Monopoly Makes for Inequities and Retards Progress

But not only does monopoly tend to supply society with fewer goods than competition would provide; it leads to an inequitable distribution of income. While society gets fewer goods under monopoly than under competition, the monopolist gets a larger share than he could obtain under a competitive system. If only a portion of the economy is monopolistically controlled, the social costs of monopoly will be borne largely by the competitive sector of the economy. Rates of return to capital will be abnormally high in the monopoly sectors, abnormally low in the competitive sectors. When too little of the community's resources is employed in some sectors and too much in others, society as a whole would benefit by a shift in production facilities from one to the other. Not only would a redistribution of resources increase the total income, but it would promote its more equitable distribution.

Moreover, according to neoclassical doctrines, competition facilitates progress, monopoly tends to retard it. The businessman, whether operating as a monopolist or as a competitor, wants to make as much money as he can. In competitive markets the most promising way open to him to do so is through decreasing his costs. Not only are all enterprisers persistently driven to devise more efficient ways of doing things, but when some are faster in achieving greater

4. Costs in general terms include all the resistances that must be overcome in order to insure that a product will be produced. In the long run they include all the payments that must be made to the several factors of production: land, labor, capital, managerial services.

5. Neoclassical theorists recognize that in diminishing-cost industries a monopolist can produce more cheaply than competitors. The problem then becomes one of regulating monopoly. They also recognize that a monopolist's conception of rational behavior may differ from that assumed in the theorists' model. For a discussion of these qualifying factors, see Chaps. 4 and 12.

efficiency and lower costs all must meet the lower price that the lower costs of one enterprise bring. In freely competitive markets it will always pay some person to introduce new processes when by doing so he can reduce the unit cost of producing a commodity. If the new techniques are freely available, they will be introduced promptly by all and price will tend to fall to the total unit cost of the most efficient producer. It will not pay a monopolist, however, to introduce a new process immediately unless it reduces his total cost per unit of producing a commodity below the variable cost per unit under the old process. This is so because to substitute the new technique for the old will make the investment in the old process worthless.[6] To maximize his earnings a monopolist must so regulate the inflow of new capital as not to impair the value of the old, whether it is a question of new processes or of new products that will compete with old. Where a monopolist can realize profits from a new product only by accepting smaller revenues from an old, he will be reluctant to introduce the new. Unless he can expect a monopoly return from the new that more than offsets the losses of monopoly revenue from the old, he will not put the new product on the market.[7] A monopolist restricts not only output but new investment as well. In this way monopoly tends to block innovation and change, to retard technological progress and to deprive society of its benefits.

Private Enterprise Defined

Such, in brief, is the indictment that nineteenth-century neoclassical economists brought against private monopoly. Such is the ideology that shaped public policy in the English-speaking nations from Adam Smith's day until the first quarter of the twentieth century.

In summary, a private enterprise system is one in which individuals or groups of their own initiative voluntarily organize and direct economic activities. Such a system is always private and always free in the equivocal sense that the government does not assume direct responsibility for determining, positively, who shall produce this or that and when, how, and where production shall take place. But a

6. A single competitor is in the same position as a monopolist in this respect. It will be costly for any firm to substitute new equipment for old unless the old has been fully depreciated, or to lower price to the average cost under the new process, but the competitor has no choice if outsiders are free to enter the market.

7. For a fuller discussion and an illustration of this principle, see *Cartels or Competition?*, Chap. 7, especially pp. 222-25.

free private enterprise system requires more than the absence of governmental coercion or control. It requires that no individuals or private groups in any field legally open to private enterprise shall subvert the system itself and injure society by exercising monopolistic power. Whenever private economic power becomes so concentrated that the decisions of a few individuals or groups can substantially determine investment, employment, output, and price policies in whole branches of industry, then and there business enterprise ceases to be really free and it may even cease to be truly enterprising.

Crux of the Current Debate on Economic Policy

Fortunately, the issue that confronts every democratic country in the organization of its economic life is not between pure monopoly and pure competition. Pure competition can scarcely be realized in a machine age. But competition need not be pure in order to be effective.[8] Obviously, something in between must do, or the private enterprise system is doomed. For no responsible democratic statesman and no reputable economist favors private monopoly as such. If industrial monopolies are unavoidable, sooner or later the public

8. See Chap. 4 for a discussion of this idea. Economists make much finer distinctions than that between perfect competition and pure monopoly, but unfortunately they have not standardized their terms. Between the extremes of perfect competition and pure monopoly they generally recognize pure competition, imperfect competition, oligopoly, and monopolistic competition.

As used in this study, perfect competition presupposes (1) a homogeneous commodity, (2) many sellers and buyers, all acting independently and with full information of market conditions, (3) mobility of productive factors, and (4) no artificial barriers to entering or leaving an industry. Pure competition comes close to the ideal of perfection—it requires many buyers and sellers of a homogeneous product, but admits lack of information, as well as the influence of custom and friction impeding economic adjustments. Imperfect competition is a broad term that includes all market situations between pure competition and pure monopoly. It embraces both oligopoly (price making in markets in which only a few firms sell a standardized product) and monopolistic competition (price making in markets in which few or many business rivals sell similar products, differentiated by location, trade names, advertising, and the like). Under monopolistic competition, quality differences in the rival products may be real or imaginary. But in any event, the difference must not be so great that one product cannot be readily substituted for another, nor so little that each is a perfect substitute for the other. The American Tobacco Company and Reynolds engage in monopolistic competition in selling cigarettes. Some smokers prefer Camels, but if a Lucky Strike were nearer at hand, few would literally walk a mile for a Camel, as Reynolds' old slogan suggested.

Pure monopoly means a single seller of a product for which no substitute is available. But, like perfect competition, such a monopoly is a theoretical ideal. In modern markets it is true of most products that even though a seller engrosses the whole supply he must compete with sellers of products closely similar or performing a similar service. Moreover, even a pure monopolist must always compete for consumers' dollars with sellers of other kinds of products.

will insist on the government's controlling or running them in the general interest. For believers in private enterprise, then, the problem is how to keep business enterprise sufficiently free to enjoy the benefits of competition, how to avoid that concentration of private economic power which is incompatible with genuine free enterprise and leads, unless checked, inexorably to the extensive substitution therefor of governmental control.

To what extent have monopolistic elements penetrated the business enterprise system and limited the effectiveness of free markets as regulators of economic activities? To what extent are rates of investment, employment and output, and changes of prices in various parts of the economy, the outcome of spontaneous adjustments through the independent action of a large number of self-interested producers? And to what extent are all these phenomena, on which the livelihood of the community depends, the outcome of decisions by a few business leaders occupying strategic positions of great power?

To answer these questions requires, first, a review of the evolution of the American economy, for only in historical perspective can the present position of private enterprise be fairly appraised; and, second, a consideration of the significance of departures from the competitive ideal in the light of recent developments in economic theory and business practice.

Chapter 2

THE CHANGING STRUCTURE OF THE AMERICAN ECONOMY

THE AMERICAN ECONOMY has never conformed exactly to any of the economists' theoretical models positing particular patterns or degrees of competition—perfect, pure, imperfect, oligopolistic, or monopolistic. In a strictly legal sense, however, it has for the most part remained private and free throughout its history. And during much of its history large sections of it have been genuinely free and effectively competitive, as this study uses these phrases.[1]

From colonial times until the final quarter of the nineteenth century, the *commercial* drift was from market control to market freedom. In the eighteenth century, chartered plantation companies and colonial trade monopolies gave way to independent settlers and privateering merchants. Later, as technology advanced and transportation facilities improved, local monopolies based on geographic isolation were displaced in various trades by large-scale producers competing actively with one another in a much wider market, regional and sometimes national.

This early trend away from commercial concentration is all the more striking because *industrial* organization in America followed the evolutionary rule: from the simple to the complex. In the beginning household industry and family self-sufficiency prevailed. But even in colonial times shipbuilding and privateering were organized and conducted on a fairly large scale. The common techniques were the simple ones of husbandry: tilling the soil and raising domestic animals. These supplemented the primitive techniques of collecting nature's bounty, as in logging, hunting, and fishing. By such means early Americans, on the settled seaboard or on the frontier, provided themselves with the essentials of livelihood. Most

1. See Chaps. 1 and 4.

households grew their own food, made their own clothing and soap, built their own shelter, and provided their own fuel.

This mode of production, although now gone, is more than a memory. It left an indelible mark on the American character. It shaped habits of thought and behavior that still persist. It made for independence, self-assertion, self-reliance, and respect for equality of opportunity. It fitted Americans for the exercise of individual initiative in a competitive economy. If Americans as a people are uncommonly vigorous, aggressive, blustering, if their ambitions focus mainly on material advancement, if they generally have at least one eye on the main chance, the experience of their forefathers in subduing a continent and wresting a living from the wilderness helps explain these traits. Good or bad, they are part of the American heritage. The urge to get things done and the aversion to everything that smacks of privilege, favoritism, or social stratification are rooted in the harsh conditions of life on the frontier.[2]

The Settlement Era

Along the Atlantic during the Revolutionary period and even earlier, and in the Mississippi Valley somewhat later, new forms of industrial organization appeared as the frontier receded. Specialized handicraft trades supplied local markets with such services as blacksmithing, printing, and milling and such products as shoes, hats, furniture, and harness.[3] These trades were often village monopolies from the strictly economic standpoint. But they were also institutions closely woven into the social fabric of the community. Both custom and the frontiersman's varied skills set limits to what the local wagon maker and miller might charge for their services. The consumer at first usually patronized the craftsman directly.

2. Other factors, to be sure, also helped mold the national character. Three important ones were (1) the wealth of the virgin resources awaiting exploitation here (as compared, for example, with those that drew colonists to Australia), (2) the heterogeneity of racial stocks and cultural antecedents among the waves of immigrants, and (3) the humanistic empiricism and natural-rights dogma that formed the background, the point of departure, for "the American enterprise." Without Locke and Hume, Rousseau and Voltaire, frontier conditions might have spawned a very different breed of frontiersman—as they did, in fact, in Portuguese Brazil and Spanish Peru.

3. On the early organization of American manufacturers, consult: J. R. Commons, *A Documentary History of American Industrial Society,* 11 vols., Clark, Chicago, 1910–1911; V. S. Clark, *History of Manufactures in the United States,* 3 vols., McGraw-Hill, New York, 1926–1929; and T. C. Cochran and W. Miller, *The Age of Enterprise,* Macmillan, New York, 1943, Chaps. 1-4.

Their relation was personal as well as commercial. As long as difficulties of transport limited exchange of products to an area of a few square miles, intermediaries were unnecessary. Gradually, as people and wealth multiplied and the area of settlement widened, improved roads and waterways joined distant settlements.

As markets widened and came to embrace whole regions instead of village communities, the scope of enterprise and the need for capital increased.[4] But competition also intensified. Merchant capitalists operating over a wide area replaced the single seller of local markets. They bought goods in localities previously isolated and sold them in others in competition with rivals. Wholesale trade required a certain standardization of products and dependable sources of supply. To meet this need, merchant capitalists began buying up raw materials and putting them out to artisans to work upon in their own shops.[5] With no superintendence of the actual work process, the difficulties of scheduling and the risks of fraudulent conversion or careless damaging of materials soon led to introduction of the factory system. And the factory system, initially at least, intensified competition.

Rise of Factory System and Business Corporations

The development of power-driven machinery made it more convenient and profitable to concentrate work processes under one roof.[6] Neither water power, which came first, nor steam power, which followed after the middle of the nineteenth century, could be transmitted far from its source without great loss. Moreover, the cost of the power-generating equipment and the fabricating machines was beyond the reach of individual craftsmen. The equipment and machinery were, in fact, often too costly for even a merchant capitalist. Only groups like the Boston Associates or the Pennsylvania Society

4. Cf. Robert A. East, *Business Enterprise in the American Revolutionary Era*, Columbia University Press, New York, 1938; and Joseph S. Davis, *Essays in the Earlier History of American Corporations*, Harvard University Press, Cambridge, 1917, Vol. 1.

5. This "putting-out" practice was especially common in the shoe trade in New England. Besides trained craftsmen, farmers often took on piece work of this kind to earn cash during the winter months. They developed the necessary skills in making their own shoes; and neither guild regulations nor trade-union restrictions stood in the way of their employment as cobblers. See B. E. Hazard, *The Organization of the Boot and Shoe Industry in Massachusetts Before 1875*, Harvard University Press, Cambridge, 1921, pp. 50-55.

6. The textile industry seems to have been the trail blazer in developing the factory system in the United States. See, for example, C. F. Ware, *Early New England Cotton Manufacture*, Houghton Mifflin, Boston, 1931.

for the Encouragement of Manufactures and Useful Arts, by combining the funds of several rich merchants, made possible large-scale production.[7] But to tap wider sources of capital, some limitation of liability for absentee investors was necessary. Only corporation charters could give this advantage, but state legislatures were at first reluctant to grant such a privilege except to enterprises formed to promote some recognized public interest.[8] Toll roads, bridges, canals, and railroads fell readily into the category of "internal improvements." Even though constructed for private profit, they seemed to the contemporary mind to have more public utility than plants for producing ordinary goods, wares, and merchandise. This attitude probably reflected the desperate need for transportation facilities in opening up a new country.[9] At any rate, industrial corporation

7. The capital requirements of the earliest manufacturing concerns were not large enough to make necessary an appeal for funds from scattered investors. Up to 1830 apparently only two industrial corporations in the United States had received charters authorizing a capital subscription of as much as a million dollars. "The amount of capital necessary to establish a manufacturing industry was not large, and could be easily supplied by a few men. The stock . . . was usually owned by the men directly interested in [i.e., managing] the enterprise, and was rarely bought and sold." G. S. Callender, "The Early Transportation and Banking Enterprises of the States in Relation to the Growth of Corporations," *Quarterly Journal of Economics,* November 1902, p. 150. Ware (*op. cit.,* pp. 128-49) notes that this situation had changed noticeably by 1845.

8. Popular antagonism to incorporation of private business enterprises was widespread. The author of America's first systematic treatise on economics expressed this viewpoint forcibly. "Wealth, of itself, gives the possessor artificial and unnatural power enough, when exerted singly and individually, and quite too much when combined and cloathed with artificial advantage.

"People are not usually aware of the immense advantage, a company of monied men acquire in consequence of an act of incorporation. It gives them a much greater influence and power, than the same amount of property would do, divided among the individual members of the corporation. It enables them to control in a great degree, the operations and industry of a whole community. . . .

* * *

"Every money corporation, therefore, is *prima facie,* injurious to national wealth, and ought to be looked upon by those who have no money, with jealousy and suspicion. They are, and ought to be considered, as artificial engines of power, contrived by the rich, for the purpose of increasing their already too great ascendancy, and calculated to destroy that natural equality among men, which no government ought to lend its power in destroying. The tendency of such institutions is to cause a more unequal division of property, and a greater inequality among men, than would otherwise take place." Daniel Raymond, *Elements of Political Economy,* 2d edition, Lucas and Coale, Baltimore, 1823, Pt. 2; the first part of the quotation is from p. 123, the second from pp. 121-22. Callender quoted the last paragraph of this passage in his brilliant article cited above.

9. The English common law had for centuries, of course, recognized common carriers as special enterprises. But though they were subject to exceptional obligations and sometimes received special privileges, incorporation, with limited liability, was not a legal right even for them. Nor could banks and insurance companies, which frequently obtained special legislative charters, claim either incorporation or limited liability as a right.

For a summary review of the early position of corporations in American law, see charters were few in the early decades of the nineteenth century.[10] Moreover, charters for manufacturing enterprises were much less liberal in the privileges granted to promoters than charters for banks, land companies, and transportation agencies.[11]

The widespread adoption of general incorporation laws around the middle of the nineteenth century opened the gates to large-scale speculative enterprise. This statutory development signalized a radical change in public sentiment toward private business corporations. The reasons for the change are obscure but were probably intertwined with (1) the growth of a sense of national destiny and an accompanying urge to hasten its fulfillment at whatever cost, (2) the rapid expansion of the domestic market as turnpikes, canals, and railroads opened up the West and gave opportunities for domestic manufacture on a scale far exceeding that of establishments geared to local demands, and (3) revulsion against the corruption that frequently attended solicitation of legislative charters for particular groups and, perhaps even more, against the special privileges such groups sometimes obtained.

The Birth of a Nation

Once law and public opinion severed the ties that bound industry to individual enterprise, the way was open to big business. But manufacture did not at once displace agriculture as the nation's primary means of livelihood. The bulk of the labor force was not suddenly divorced from its tools and regimented in factories under a strict discipline. Nor did the increase in the size of business units portend,

---

E. Merrick Dodd, Jr., "The First Half Century of Statutory Regulation of Business Corporations in Massachusetts," in R. Pound (Ed.), *Harvard Legal Essays*, Harvard University Press, Cambridge, 1934, pp. 65-132.

10. Resort to incorporation became much more frequent in the second quarter of the century than it had been in the first, as a result of the adoption of general incorporation statutes in many states. But in both periods, as nowadays, the number of charters issued annually to manufacturing enterprises fluctuated directly with the ups and downs of business. The three periods of greatest activity were immediately after the War of 1812, the years preceding the panic of 1837, and during the Mexican War boom and the gold rush in the late 1840's. See Dodd, *op. cit., passim;* W. C. Kessler, "A Statistical Study of the New York General Incorporation Act of 1811," *Journal of Political Economy*, 1940, p. 877; and W. C. Miller, "A Note on the History of Business Corporations in Pennsylvania, 1800–1860," *Quarterly Journal of Economics*, 1940, p. 150.

11. Cf. Shaw Livermore, "Unlimited Liability in Early American Corporations," *Journal of Political Economy*, 1935, pp. 674-87; and J. G. Blandi, *Maryland Business Corporations, 1783–1852*, Johns Hopkins University Studies, Vol. 52, No. 3, Baltimore, 1934.

initially at least, the disappearance of competition. On the contrary, the introduction of large-scale production of standardized goods and the development of a railway network binding together a continent appear at the outset to have intensified competition.

But the American economy had started on a road that led eventually to a destination quite different from that originally contemplated. The goal of spontaneous self-direction in productive activities had never, of course, been even closely approached, and thenceforth it became more and more illusory. Strive as men might, and did, for economic independence, the obstacles to its achievement became ever more formidable for the great majority. In the half century from 1840 to 1890 industry in America underwent a basic transformation which, more than any other single influence, set the problems, shaped the development, and molded the character of the nation in the next half century. This transformation in the structure of industry had two main features: the growth of large-scale operations—big plants—and the increase in size of business units—big companies (which may operate no plant, one plant, or many plants).

Technology Fosters Large-Scale Production

Before the Civil War manufacturing was generally carried on in small shops, using handicraft techniques, employing few workers, and requiring little capital. Application of the machine technique in manufacture made it possible to bring together in single plants a larger number of workers and more equipment, thereby increasing capital requirements. To keep specialized labor busy, and expensive single-purpose machines in steady use, required continuous processing of a large volume of materials, which also increased the capital needed.

The direct influence of technology on the scale of manufacturing production was unquestionably real and potent, though it has often been exaggerated. The indirect influence of technology through the application of the machine technique to transportation was certainly no less potent.

Railroad construction opened up a big market in the agricultural West. With a continent of unrivalled resources awaiting exploitation, the impulse to expansion was strong. In the quarter century following the Civil War railroad mileage increased more than fourfold. As extension of railway lines and improvement in their operating efficiency reduced long-distance transportation costs, a national market for many products emerged.

In general, widening of the market preceded and called forth enlargement of the scale of output, though to some extent the two developments stimulated one another.[12] The Civil War itself also stimulated expansion. Not only was it the immediate occasion for building transcontinental railroads, but government contracts for supplying the armies gave impetus to the organization of industry in larger units. Before 1860, vehicles, clothing, shoes, meat, and other consumers' goods that were also military supplies were mainly produced for local markets by small shops. Civil War contractors, like the meat firms of Armour, Morris, and Dold, could not rely on scattered small units. They built their own plants to a size proportioned to their large government orders and to a civilian market rapidly becoming nation-wide.

Concentration in Iron and Steel

The iron and steel industry exemplifies the trend toward concentration. Before the Civil War pig and wrought iron were produced by hundreds of local bloomeries, scattered through Massachusetts, Connecticut, New York, New Jersey, Pennsylvania, and Virginia. Ironmongers bought up the output of these bloomeries and distributed it, mostly as "merchant bars," to the blacksmith trade and small local stove foundries. Though in the 1850's, when steelmaking really began,[13] a score of ironmongers in the Pittsburgh district had built their own rolling mills, it was not until 1859 that an enterprising ironmaster set the industry on the road to large-scale production by integrating in one plant the successive operations from blast furnaces to rolling mills.[14] In that year the Great Bend Iron Works was organized with a capital of a million dollars, making it

12. The gains from selling more goods are ordinarily more certain than the gains from reducing cost by making more goods. An accumulation of unfilled orders, or an opportunity to tap a virgin market, is more apt to persuade a manufacturer to enlarge his plant than a belief that by producing on a larger scale he could cut his costs and make more profits.

13. U.S. Census Office, 8th Census, 1860, *Manufactures,* p. cxcii.

14. Louis M. Hacker, *The Triumph of American Capitalism,* Simon & Schuster, New York, 1940, p. 258.

the largest in the industry.[15] The organization forty-two years later of the United States Steel Corporation with a capitalization of $1.4 billion suggests how rapid was the evolution of big business in basic steel.

Though the Carnegie Steel Company was the largest enterprise entering the consolidation and was more highly integrated than any other, especially in the first two stages of production—blast furnace operations and steelmaking—not even all the Carnegie plants were technically and managerially a single unit. Nevertheless, by and large the growth of the Carnegie business gives a fair picture of the increasing scale of production in this industry from the Civil War to 1900.

Growth of the Carnegie Business

Joining the Kloman Iron Works in 1861 as a silent partner, Andrew Carnegie first became a full-time ironmaster in 1865, when he gave up his job as a division superintendent of the Pennsylvania Railroad. In that year he reorganized and incorporated the Kloman works as the Union Iron Mills, with a capital of $500,000, and organized the Keystone Bridge Company, with a capital of $500,000. These firms had an assured market, thanks to Carnegie's close associations with Pennsylvania Railroad officials, and they prospered accordingly.

Carnegie built his first blast furnace in 1870. Three years later, in the midst of a panic, he started making Bessemer steel. For this bold venture he organized Carnegie, McCandless & Company, with a capital of $700,000. So successful was the steelmaking enterprise and so ingenious was its promoter in squeezing out the majority stockholders that in 1878 the company changed its name to the Carnegie Company and increased its capital to $1.25 million, of which Andrew Carnegie obtained 59 per cent.

In 1881, with the steel plant (called J. Edgar Thomson Works) earning more than 100 per cent on the capital invested, Carnegie merged his three principal enterprises—Union, Keystone, and Thomson Works—in Carnegie Bros. & Co., Ltd. This company had an initial capitalization of $5 million. After paying liberal dividends the

15. See Myron W. Watkins, "Large Scale Production," *Encyclopaedia of the Social Sciences*, Macmillan, New York, 1933, Vol. 9, pp. 170-81.

capitalization was increased, partly out of profits, and partly through a merger with the Frick coal interests, to $12.5 million in 1889. With profits steadily rising ($5.4 million in 1890), the company doubled its outstanding capital in 1891.

But this was only the beginning. During the 1890's Carnegie steel output increased tenfold—from about 300,000 tons annually to 3 million tons—and profits rose apace. In 1900 Carnegie recapitalized his company for $300 million, a conservative figure based on earning power, as proved by the terms on which the House of Morgan acquired the properties for the Steel Corporation the following year. Thus in a third of a century the size of the Carnegie enterprise had increased, chiefly through internal expansion and integration, about three hundred times.[16]

Slow Increase in Scale of Operations

But this four-decade growth in the capitalization of the biggest unit in iron and steel did not bring about a comparable increase in the scale of operations. At least half of the Steel Corporation's capitalization was "water." [17] The Census Bureau estimated that the excess of the par value of the Steel Corporation's securities over the current (1901) market value of the assets acquired ranged, on various bases of valuation, from $609 million to $726 million.

Moreover, the corporation combined more than a score of separate plants, most of which continued to operate as distinct manufacturing units with no radical change in the scale of operations. Nevertheless, a radical change had occurred in the size of manufacturing plants, and also in the complexity of their equipment. American industry had been extensively mechanized and the country largely industrialized in little more than a generation. According to the Census the value of products for all branches of manufacture increased 184 per cent between 1860 and 1880, while the number of wage earners increased only 108 per cent. By 1900, the total value of manufactured products had again more than doubled, the increase amounting to 142 per cent, while the number of wage earners had not quite doubled, increasing 94 per cent.

16. See John K. Winkler, *Incredible Carnegie*, Vanguard Press, New York, 1931, Chaps. 6-11; Hacker, *op. cit.*, pp. 421 ff.; and U.S. Bureau of Corporations, *Report on the Steel Industry*, Washington, 1911, Pt. 1.
17. *Ibid.*, p. 239.

In certain heavy industries the increase in value of products was much greater. From 1860 to 1880, the value of the annual output of iron and steel increased from $21.6 million to $296.5 million, or nearly fourteen times. In the same period the increase amounted to 300 per cent in agricultural implements, and a like increase took place in the manufacture of nonagricultural machinery. In these three branches of heavy industry, the increase in value of products continued over the next two decades, though the rate of growth was not so rapid. The value of the 1899 output of iron and steel ($802.9 million) was 2.7 times that of 1880; that of agricultural implements ($101.2 million), 50 per cent greater; and that of machinery of all other kinds ($644.9 million), three times what it was in 1880.[18]

The predominantly agricultural economy of 1850, with 80 per cent of all Americans living on farms, had been transformed by 1900 into an urban-industrial economy, with only 50 per cent of the people directly dependent on farming or residing in rural communities.[19]

Corporation Finance and the Rise of Big Business

In manufacturing generally, as in iron and steel, the enormous widening of the market caused by the spreading network of railroads and the technical advantages of mass machine production stimulated a remarkable increase in the size of industrial plants. Larger-scale operations led to the conduct of business on a larger scale. But the growth in the size of business units eventually far

18. See U.S. Census Office, 8th Census, 1860, *Manufactures,* pp. cxcii, ccxvii, and 737-38; 10th Census, 1880, *Manufactures,* Table II and pp. 446-47; 12th Census, 1900, *Manufactures,* Pt. 1, Table I. The financial data are unadjusted for changes in the price level, but by 1880 the Civil War inflation had been largely corrected, and 1880 and 1900 prices were on substantially the same level. A qualification on comparisons arises from inclusion of hand and neighborhood trades in the census of manufactures before 1900. With due allowance for this fact, the evidence of the phenomenal growth of American manufactures in the latter part of the nineteenth century is clear. The data suggest, moreover, that the increase in capital invested in manufacturing industry had much to do with increasing output. Some of this new capital undoubtedly went into new industries: bicycles, electrical apparatus, aluminum, chemicals. But most of it was probably used in the mechanization and enlargement of old industries, like cotton textiles and iron and steel.

19. The Census Office has used various standards from time to time for dividing the population between rural and urban. Defining "urban" as centers of 4,000 population and upward, the 12th Census found that in 1900, 36.6 million, or 48.1 per cent of the total population (76.1 million), were urban residents and 51.9 per cent were rural residents. See U.S. Census Office, 12th Census, 1900, *Population,* Vol. 1, Pt. 1, pp. lxxiii-lxxxix.

Using the same criterion, a computation made from a table in the 7th Census (1850, *Population,* pp. 338-93) shows that only 4.7 million, or 20.5 per cent, of a total population in 1850 of 23.1 million were urban residents.

outstripped the increase in the scale of operations. The capital requirements of large-scale industry encouraged incorporation of business enterprises. The steady liberalization of corporation laws also encouraged replacement of partnerships and individual proprietorships.

As the size of business units increased and corporations multiplied, corporate securities absorbed more and more of the people's savings. Clerks and artisans, who in an earlier period had used their small means to set up shop for themselves, to an ever-increasing extent retained their salaried status and became absentee owners of intangible property—stocks and bonds, life insurance policies, and bank deposits. More and more of the tangible assets—power plants, machines, inventories of materials in process of manufacture—were concentrated in large corporations that drew their capital from many stockholders. Corporation executives increasingly became the managers of other people's property.

The upshot was that business enterprise became more and more speculative, not only from the viewpoint of those who managed large corporations that they did not own but also from the viewpoint of those who invested in those corporations and who, in the vast majority of cases, exercised no control over their operations. The rise of corporate capitalism provided many opportunities for inside manipulation, stock jobbing, and similar abuses, and lax incorporation laws frequently abetted such malpractices. A new type of business leader appeared, the security speculator, and the formation and conduct of corporations to suit the ends of such leaders tended to disrupt competitive markets.[20] They were not so much concerned

20. The exploits of Daniel Drew and Jim Fisk in Erie, of Cornelius Vanderbilt in New York Central, of Jay Gould in Kansas Pacific, Union Pacific, and Missouri Pacific, of Collis P. Huntington in Central Pacific and Southern Pacific, and of Jay Cooke in Northern Pacific proved that greater personal stakes could be won in security speculation, account juggling, market rigging, and political intriguing than in the efficient operation of railroads.

For detailed accounts of the records of specific railroads or of individual financiers, see: Charles F. Adams, Jr., and Henry Adams, *Chapters on Erie and Other Essays,* Osgoods, Boston, 1871; Matthew Josephson, *The Robber Barons,* Harcourt, Brace, New York, 1934; Edwin H. Mott, *Between the Ocean and the Lakes,* Ticker, New York, 1908; Stuart Daggett, *Chapters on the History of the Southern Pacific,* Ronald, New York, 1922; and Frederick C. Hicks, *High Finance in the Sixties,* Yale University Press, New Haven, 1929.

On railroad finance generally, consult: F. A. Cleveland and F. W. Powell, *Railroad Finance,* Appleton, New York, 1912; S. L. Miller, *Railroad Transportation,* Shaw, Chicago, 1924; William Z. Ripley, *Railroads: Finance and Organization,* Longmans, Green, New York, 1920; and R. E. Riegel, *The Story of the Western Railroads,* Macmillan, New York, 1926.

with reducing costs, improving the quality of products, and building up good will as they were with manipulation of the prices of their companies' securities in stock market speculation. Their operations generally made competition more convulsive and less effective than it would have been otherwise—alternately cutthroat and quiescent. In sum, the temper of the times encouraged economic expansion, even rash venturesomeness, and brooked little legislative regulation of corporate management. And, of course, the lure of quick and easy wealth through corporate financial manipulation was not calculated to foster sober business management and effective competition.

Fiscal and Monetary Policies

Other phases of public policy also reflected—and helped to stimulate—the highly speculative temper of the times. The government's policy of financing the Civil War largely by greenbacks and afterward retiring a large part of this unsecured currency without regard to the effects of a declining price level on business commitments discouraged economic individualism and effective competition. Similarly, the creation of a national banking system without strong central control promoted economic instability by providing the means for reckless credit expansion and no means for corrective contraction except by wholesale bankruptcy.[21]

Of course, the spasmodic advance of technology and the tendency of business enterprise alternately to overexpand and to curtail production excessively also promoted economic instability. But the government's fiscal and monetary policies added to these unsettling forces instead of counteracting them, and so contributed to the growing concentration of private economic power. Caught in the turbulent cycle of boom and bust, businessmen found competition increasingly distasteful.

The erratically fluctuating price level for fifty years after the Civil War was poison to a competitive business system. It added to ordinary commercial risks a subtle but nonetheless vital hazard of intermittent changes in the buying power of money. It made business

21. Nevins notes that from 1870 to 1877 no fewer than twenty-eight life insurance companies went out of business in New York alone. These failures brought losses of $139 million to policyholders. Allan Nevins, *The Emergence of Modern America,* Macmillan, New York, 1927, p. 193.

hardly more than a gamble. Small businesses were especially demoralized by the continually fluctuating value of money. Loaded, as a rule, with relatively heavy short-term liabilities, they had only a narrow margin of net worth on which to fall back when trouble came. The panic of 1873 and the long depression that followed it ruined thousands of small manufacturers who could not withstand the rigors of deflation.[22] In the ups and downs that kept recurring at irregular intervals, the mortality of small business firms was extremely high. In the wild scramble alternately to take advantage of easy credit and skyrocketing prices and then to save what could be saved from tight credit and falling prices, the control of much of American industry passed into fewer and richer hands.[23] But from the standpoint of technical efficiency, commercial acumen, and general ability, unquestionably many of these victims of insolvency were as "fit" to survive as their more fortunate fellows with favorable financial connections, and the disappearance of the victims contributed still further to the concentration of economic power.

Role of Financiers in Industrial Organization

As large-scale corporate capitalism replaced small-scale capitalism of self-employed enterprisers, and as general economic convulsions became more acute, the influence of financiers in shaping the industrial structure came more and more to supplement commercial and technical factors. The McCormicks, Armours, Clarks, Fricks, and Carnegies were primarily interested in making money by making and selling goods. Some of them were apparently vigorous advocates of free enterprise and forthright competition. According to report, Carnegie advised his partners:

> Put your trust in the policy of attending to your own business in your own way and running your mills full, regardless of prices and very little trust

22. See T. E. Burton, *Financial Crises and Periods of Industrial and Commercial Depression,* Appleton, New York, 1902, p. 344; and Willard L. Thorp, *Business Annals,* National Bureau of Economic Research, New York, 1926, pp. 131-33. Now, as then, small businessmen are preoccupied with day-to-day problems of management, technical problems in the plant, and commercial developments. Only the head of a big concern can afford to delegate such responsibilities and so find time to study the forces making for instability and fortify his business against their impact.

23. As to the rise of American millionaires in the late nineteenth century, the sources of their fortunes, and the social and economic implications of these accumulations, see the arresting study by George P. Watkins, "Growth of Large Fortunes," *Publications of the American Economic Association,* November 1907, Third Series Vol. 8, No. 4, especially (for estimates of the number of millionaires) pp. 141-47.

in the efficacy of artificial arrangements with your competitors, which have the serious result of strengthening them if they strengthen you.[24]

Initially, industrialists of this type were the prime movers in transforming little business into big business. As a business grew, its proprietor, seeing good chances of gain from increasing output, might take in partners. It was in this way that, in the 1870's and 1880's, Carnegie built his steel business.[25] But the partners he took in were men already interested in some phase of the industry. Possibilities of real growth by this means were limited, partly because competitors, if they were growing, were frequently reluctant to give up undivided control of their own businesses, and partly because amalgamation brought little new capital into the industry. The times called for rapid expansion of capacity. Even though the profits "plowed back" were large, owners of most lines of industry found profits as a source of capital inadequate for their needs. They therefore looked to outsiders for additional funds to finance the construction of new plants or the purchase and rebuilding of old ones.

Many people with money to invest either were not qualified to take part actively in business management or had no liking for such activity. The scions of old mercantile or maritime shipping families—the Neals, Girards, Aspinwalls, Griswolds, Astors, and Schuylers—had come to prefer a life of ease and the security of a rentier status. To obtain sizable funds from outside, a mining or manufacturing enterprise had to attract more venturesome capital, and this was usually widely scattered in comparatively small holdings.

Railroad Financing

Railroad finance was another matter; the huge capital requirements and the pre-eminent position of railway construction in programs of internal improvement determined the financing problem in this field quite apart from that of corporation finance in general. Government provided much of the railroad capital, a fact usually

24. Ida M. Tarbell, *The Life of Elbert H. Gary,* Appleton, New York, 1925, p. 114.

25. Carnegie did not form a partnership in the strict legal sense when he joined forces with other businessmen. He admitted his "partners," who increased from two or three in 1868 to a score in 1891, to membership in a limited-liability company the stock of which was closely held and could be transferred only with the consent of the owners of a majority of the stock. In practical effect, this arrangement was similar to a partnership agreement, particularly in respect to limitations on the right of withdrawal or transfer.

slurred over by those inclined to exaggerate the historic role of individual enterprise. The federal government alone subsidized railway construction between 1850 and 1875 by grants of 180 million acres out of the public domain. Much of this endowment consisted of fertile farm lands. These federal land-grant subsidies alone had an estimated current value of at least $500 million. States and municipalities were relatively not less generous.

With such substantial government aid promoters generally found it unnecessary to address themselves to a horde of scattered petty savers; they obtained adequate additional assistance from wealthy men on the Atlantic seaboard, in England, or in Holland. Indeed, these were frequently the principals of the promoters who obtained land grants from Congress. For example, Rantoul, who was the chief lobbyist for the Illinois Central, was an agent of Boston and British capitalists. Manufacturers, even established firms with a market for more goods than they had facilities to make, could offer the monied interests no such margin of safety as these government subsidies provided the railroads. They had to depend for capital mainly on local sources, where it was available as a rule only in small lots.[26]

The Investment Banker Steps to the Front

Investment bankers were the intermediaries for assembling venture capital and distributing corporation securities. Investment banking was primarily an outgrowth of railroad finance. The business developed rapidly after the middle of the nineteenth century and was greatly accelerated by energetic promotion of government bond sales during the 1860's, under the leadership of Jay Cooke. The war-bond-selling campaigns widened tremendously the clientele of investment bankers.[27]

As investment is based on confidence, the investment banker, unlike the security speculator, had a continuing interest in the value of the securities in which he dealt. It was to his presumed advantage to protect the market for the securities he distributed. In his role as stabilizer, he developed a technique for making railroad securities less of a football for speculators. To this end, the House of Morgan

26. See Hacker, *op. cit.*, p. 233; Riegel, *op. cit.*, pp. 41 ff.; and A. M. Sokolsky, *The Great American Land Bubble,* Harper, New York, 1932, pp. 295 ff.
27. See H. Parker Willis and Jules I. Bogen, *Investment Banking,* Harper, New York, 1929, Chap. 7.

not only assumed leadership in railroad financial reorganizations but also undertook to safeguard the roads from competition. In January 1889 Morgan made the following announcement to a group of leading railroad presidents assembled in his home:

> I am authorized to say, I think, on behalf of the banking houses represented here that if an organization can be formed practically upon the basis submitted by the committee, and with an executive committee able to enforce its provisions, upon which the bankers shall be represented, they are prepared to say that they will not negotiate, and will do everything in their power to prevent the negotiation of, any securities for the construction of parallel lines, or the extension of lines not approved by that executive committee. I wish that distinctly understood.[28]

Using a similar technique for the same purpose, stabilization, the investment banker became a powerful force behind the combination movement of the late 1890's that remodelled the structure of American industry and transferred control from the captains of industry to the financiers.[29]

The Era of Consolidation

Though the captains of industry themselves engineered most of the combinations before 1890, the bankers and financiers soon ceased to be mere intermediaries. They became the promoters. In organizing large consolidations they soon took the place of the roving professional promoters who had for a time offered the investing public corporate securities with a strong speculative appeal.[30] It was under their auspices, and spurred by their encouragement, that the combination movement rose to flood tide around the turn of the century.

The pioneer in industrial consolidation was John D. Rockefeller. He organized the first Standard Oil Trust in 1879 after experimenting with pooling agreements to quell competitors, waging local price wars to smash rivals, and negotiating surreptitious railway rebates and pipeline freeze-outs to gain ascendancy in the richest markets.[31]

In law, trusts are an ancient device of equity for the separation

28. Quoted in George W. Edwards, *The Evolution of Finance Capitalism,* Longmans, Green, New York, 1938, p. 174.

29. Cf. Thorstein Veblen, *The Theory of Business Enterprise,* Scribner's, New York, 1904, Chaps. 5, 6, and 7.

30. See Myron W. Watkins, article on "Promotion," *Encyclopaedia of the Social Sciences,* Macmillan, New York, 1934, Vol. 12, pp. 518-21.

31. *Report of the Commissioner of Corporations on the Petroleum Industry,* Washington, 1907, Pts. 1 and 2.

of control from ownership, in the interests, mainly, of widows and minors. Their use to aggrandize and control business gave the consolidation movement its popular name: the trust movement. Either through the trustee device, as in the sugar, whiskey, and white-lead industries; through long-term lease contracts, as in matches and cordage; or through merger, some half-dozen important industries in the 1880's followed the lead of Standard Oil in unifying control of the principal plants.

States Give a Boost to Bigness

The outlawing of trust agreements for this purpose in certain state jurisdictions and the enactment of the Sherman Antitrust Act by Congress in 1890 brought to an abrupt end the organization of formal trusts.[32] It did not, however, end the "trust" movement. Industrial combination thenceforth usually took the form of either an outright merger or a holding company. In 1889 New Jersey gave carte blanche to the use of these expedients by liberalizing its general incorporation law so that incorporators obtained the widest possible latitude in defining corporate powers and the rights and responsibilities of directors, officers, and stockholders.[33] This legislation let down the bars to intercorporate stockholding.

Mead interpreted the significance of this move from the standpoint of its effect on the policy of preserving competition as follows:

> For momentous consequences, this statute of New Jersey is hardly to be equaled in the annals of legislation. . . . the little State of New Jersey, containing two per cent of the population and one and three-tenths [per cent] of the wealth of the United States, by the simple act of amending its corporation law, nullified the antitrust laws of every State which had passed them.[34]

Other states soon followed suit; one by one they relaxed the restrictions in their general incorporation laws that limited the size and privileges of corporations.[35] The belief became common that the

32. Henry R. Seager and Charles A. Gulick, *Trust and Corporation Problems,* Harper, New York, 1929, pp. 51-58.

33. Commenting on this development, Seager and Gulick observe: "It has been said, with some exaggeration, that . . . the United States Steel Corporation may do everything but coin money." *Ibid.,* p. 39.

34. Edward S. Mead, *Trust Finance,* Appleton, New York, 1903, p. 39.

35. Seager and Gulick, *op. cit.,* Chap. 4. See also Eliot Jones, *The Trust Problem in the United States,* Macmillan, New York, 1921, pp. 30-31; Paul T. Homan and Myron W. Watkins, article on "Trusts," *Encyclopaedia of the Social Sciences,* Mac-

exercise of corporate powers which sovereign states had freely granted was immune from the prohibitions of the federal antitrust law—even though the exercise of those powers to effect industrial combination might lead to monopoly.[36] Acting on this belief, industrialists and financiers pushed consolidations in industry after industry.

The Heyday of Trusts

From 1890 to 1904 no fewer than 237 corporate consolidations took place, each of regional or national compass and capitalized for more than a million dollars. Together they covered practically every important manufacturing industry and represented a gross capitalization of $5.96 billion.[37] The movement reached its peak in 1899, when 78 combinations were launched which issued $1.88 billion (par value) of securities.

However, the decision of the Supreme Court in the Northern Securities case in 1904,[38] condemning a holding company that put an end to competition among three large railroad systems, cast doubt on the lawfulness of this device even for industrial combinations. For the next few years the consolidation movement subsided.[39] But it had already transformed the structure of American industry.

By 1905 few important lines of manufacture were free of domination by a giant corporation or by two or three such giants, operating perhaps in distinct but related branches of the industry. Combinations had taken place not only in such important industries as steel,

millan, New York, 1935, Vol. 15, pp. 111-21; and Alfred L. Bernheim (Ed.), *Big Business: Its Growth and Its Place,* Twentieth Century Fund, New York, 1937, pp. 25 ff.

For a painstaking and persuasive review of the evidence on charter mongering among the states, see Mr. Justice Brandeis' dissenting opinion in *Liggett Co.* v. *Lee,* 288 U.S. 517 (1933), in particular pp. 541-59. On the growing laxity of incorporation law after the 1880's, see E. Merrick Dodd, Jr., "American Business Association Law a Hundred Years Ago and Today," in *Law: A Century of Progress,* New York University Press, New York, 1937, Vol. 3, pp. 254-93.

36. In the first case under the Sherman Act to reach the Supreme Court, *U.S.* v. *E. C. Knight Co.,* 156 U.S. 1 (1895), the decision of the Court, vindicating the American Sugar Refining Company, appeared to confirm this belief and certainly gave it wide currency. See Chap. 9, pp. 265-67.

37. See Myron W. Watkins, *Industrial Combinations and Public Policy,* Houghton Mifflin, Boston, 1927, App. II; and Bernheim, *op. cit.,* pp. 28 ff. See also John Moody, *The Truth About the Trusts,* Moody Publishing Co., New York, 1904.

38. *Northern Securities Co.* v. *U.S.,* 193 U.S. 197 (1904).

39. Seager and Gulick (*op. cit.,* pp. 66-67) suggest that another reason for the suspension of the trust movement was that promoters had just about exhausted the field of potential consolidation.

nonferrous metals, oil, chemicals, textiles, paper, rubber, and agricultural, industrial, office, and household machinery but also in many minor industries such as chewing gum, oatmeal, and sewing thread.

Small Units Still Important

It is easy, of course, to exaggerate the extent of the concentration of control brought about by the combination movement, and perhaps even easier to exaggerate the significance of this development to the decline of competition. First, few combinations acquired a 100 per cent monopoly and still fewer held their initial advantage. Out of the 237 industrial consolidations formed between 1890 and 1904 no fewer than 48, or almost a fifth, had been in receivership or reorganized by 1914.[40] Many others lost ground to rivals. Secondly, although a reduction in the number of sellers tends to make competition less effective, it does not always or certainly do so.[41] Thirdly, even though a large part of American manufacturing and mining came under the domination of great corporate consolidations, some important sectors of the American economy remained outside the combination movement. For example, agriculture (including forestry and fisheries), wholesale and retail trade, repair shops, personal and household service trades, clothing manufacture, and the construction industry were in 1910 almost wholly organized in small, independent units, for the most part locally owned and producer-controlled. Since then, consolidation has directly affected many of these.

No less than 68.2 per cent of the entire gainfully occupied population, according to the census of 1910, were engaged in economic activities carried on mainly in small units.[42] Satisfactory data are not

40. See National Industrial Conference Board, *Mergers in Industry,* New York, 1929, pp. 38-40 and App. C.

41. See Chaps. 4 and 5 of this study.

42. U.S. Department of Commerce, *Statistical Abstract of the United States,* 1920, pp. 273 ff. The comparable figure for 1940 was nearly identical, 67.7 per cent. See *Statistical Abstract,* 1943, pp. 116 ff.

The construction industry was lumped with "Manufacturing and Mechanical Trades" before the 16th Census (1940). Building crafts were easily identifiable in the census list of occupations, however, and the number of persons engaged in such work was subtracted from the "Manufacturing" total. Construction laborers, however, were not enumerated separately from common laborers in other "Manufacturing" industries before 1930. See *Statistical Abstract,* 1937, p. 58. So the proportion of general laborers in all "Manufacturing" industries employed in construction work in 1930 was applied to the 1910 total of general laborers in "Manufacturing and Mechanical Trades" to find the number of construction laborers in that year. This figure (330,401) was added to the number of building craftsmen in 1910, and the sum (2,100,154) was subtracted

available on the proportion of national income these occupations produced at that time. But in 1929 they produced 53.6 per cent of total income paid out. The market territory of most service trades and of the construction industry is generally rather limited. However, a few small concerns may dominate a local market as effectively as a few large ones may dominate a national market. Moreover, restrictive agreements among local merchants and tradespeople are and always have been common, and they frequently throttle competition, even if only temporarily.

In sum, even after the post-World War I resurgence of the industrial combination movement, those branches of the national economy directly under the sway of big business—chiefly mining, manufacturing, transportation and public utilities, and finance—accounted directly for less than half the national income. And not all parts of these branches of the economy conformed to the big-business pattern; outstanding exceptions were bituminous coal in the mining branch and the motor-carrier business in the transportation branch.[43]

Progressive Movement a Check to Economic Concentration

Despite the onward surge of the combination movement, small enterprise was still characteristic of broad areas of the economy before World War I. But the tremendous growth of big business had more radical effects on the development of the structure of the American economy than any measure of its scope indicates.

First, the degree of concentration of industrial control was greater than appeared on the surface because of the strategic position of large-scale manufacturing industry. Big business was closely allied

---

from the number of persons gainfully occupied in manufacturing industries in that year. Out of a total gainfully occupied population of 38,167,336 in 1910, only 12,161,232, or 31.8 per cent, were engaged in mining, manufacturing, or transportation and public utilities—the major fields of big-business employment.

43. Even in these branches of industry, however, recent years have witnessed striking developments toward concentration of control. In bituminous coal, the Island Creek–Thacker merger in 1941 and the formation of Pittsburgh Consolidation in 1945 gave the industry two $25 million companies. One of the country's 200 largest corporations, M. A. Hanna & Co., controls Pittsburgh Consolidation. Furthermore, captive mines of the giant steel companies and the railroads produce about a quarter of the total output.

Among motor carriers combinations were frequent in the 1930's and banker representation on the boards of directors of the large fleets became common. The consolidation movement was perhaps more conspicuous in the motorbus field, but it also extended to trucking companies.

with big finance; and finance, in directing the flow of capital and credit, occupied the very center of the economic complex. Investment and pricing decisions of the executives of giant corporations and their banker associates are immensely important because of their direct effect on the volume of disposable income and the pace of business activity. Beyond that, indirectly, what the leaders of the business world do and what they think tend to set the fashion and mold the ideas of businessmen generally.[44] In terms of effective power the men at the helm of big business generally exert a pervasive influence, an influence far greater than that directly stemming from the productive assets they control.

In other ways, too, the rapid growth of big business around the turn of the century affected the course of American economic development. It aroused grave apprehensions among farmers and small shopkeepers. Though somewhat disillusioned by the developments of the 1890's, they had not lost the faith in individual initiative and the aspiration for equality of opportunity that are the bone and sinew of the American tradition. The increasing concentration of private economic power was a personal challenge to which they reacted strongly.

Antimonopoly sentiment was one of the main elements in the Progressive movement that colored American public life in the decade before World War I. The establishment of the Bureau of Corporations in 1903 to track down the "malefactors of great wealth," the talk about the "Big Stick" by President Theodore Roosevelt, and the trust-busting campaigns of the Taft and the first Wilson Administrations were responses to popular agitation over the threat of big business to the independence and prosperity of "little men." [45]

But the attempt to preserve competitive opportunity in trade by a direct attack on monopoly was only one aspect of the Progressive movement. Essentially the forces represented by it found expression in a number of measures designed to protect consumers, to preserve

44. Other elements of the community come under the sway of opinions and habits of thought that successful businessmen find congenial. It requires no crude supposition of venality in the press to recognize that newspapers and other organs shaping public opinion are solicitous of the good will of advertisers. Most publishers, like other men, are loath to bite the hand that feeds them.

45. Cf. John D. Clark, *Federal Trust Policy,* Johns Hopkins University Press, Baltimore, 1931, Chap. 4.

competition, and where this seemed futile, to regulate monopoly. The pure food and drug laws, stricter railroad and public utility regulation, conservation laws, and reinforcement of the antitrust laws with investigational agencies were among such measures.

The Rule of Reason

This storm of protest boded ill for big business. The Standard Oil and American Tobacco decisions in 1911, dissolving two of the largest and most ruthless of the "trusts," signalized the strength of the antimonopoly forces.[46] But out of a tactical setback big business won a strategic victory. For at the same time that the Supreme Court condemned these giant corporations for flagrant violation of the antitrust law it introduced the tempering "rule of reason" as a standard for determining the lawfulness of industrial consolidation. Concretely, this meant that "good trusts" had little to fear from the law. Its prohibitions, under the rule of reason, would apply only to the abuse of power, not to the power to abuse.

Leadership and Good Will

While the courts were reinterpreting the antitrust laws, Congress revising them, and the country changing its attitude toward the concentration of economic power, business was itself developing a new code of behavior. A new generation of business leaders arose who shunned the bludgeoning tactics of their predecessors. But few of the new business leaders abandoned the effort to stabilize markets. They simply followed a policy of live and let live rather than one of driving out or absorbing business rivals. They joined in promoting trade associations and fostering good will through their cooperative activities. They relied more and more on leadership—in pricing, technical research, advertising. The antitrust legislation of 1914, outlawing the use of "unfair methods of competition," no doubt contributed to the development of the new pattern of business behavior.

The Clayton Act and the Federal Trade Commission Act were the

46. *Standard Oil Co.* v. *U.S.*, 221 U.S. 1 (1911); *U.S.* v. *American Tobacco Co.*, 221 U.S. 106 (1911). On the meaning and implications of these decisions, see R. L. Raymond, "The Standard Oil and American Tobacco Cases," *Harvard Law Review*, 1911, p. 31; and W. H. Taft, *The Antitrust Act and the Supreme Court*, Harper, New York, 1914.

statutory embodiment of President Wilson's "New Freedom." [47] The Clayton Act specifically condemned price discrimination, tying contracts, intercorporate stockholding, and interlocking directorates among trade competitors. The Federal Trade Commission Act sweepingly forbade all unfair methods of competition and charged the Commission with the duty of preventing them.

This new approach to the problem of industrial stability did not sharply reverse the trend toward concentration, although from 1905 to 1920 few new consolidations took place and some old ones disintegrated or their position in the market weakened. The combination movement, however, took a new form. For with increasing frequency business rivals relied on trade associations rather than outright consolidation as a means of tightening control of the market. The Department of Commerce estimated that the number of active trade associations, national in scope, increased from 100 in 1900 to about 1,000 in 1920.[48]

Trade Associations

Trade associations multiplied rapidly after the introduction of the rule of reason in 1911 and the inauguration about the same time of the "open-competition" plan for association activity.[49] This plan called for the exchange of extensive data on output, costs, orders, stocks, shipments, and prices among competitors.[50] However sin-

47. These acts were, respectively, Act of October 15, 1914, U.S. Code, Title 15, c. 1, Secs. 12-27, and Act of September 26, 1914, U.S. Code, Title 15, c. 2, Secs. 41-51. For a detailed analysis of the provisions of these statutes and a review of the administrative record of their enforcement, see Myron W. Watkins, *Public Regulation of Competitive Practices*, 3d edition, National Industrial Conference Board, New York, 1940.

48. See U.S. Department of Commerce, *Selected Trade Associations of the United States*, Market Research Series, No. 1, Washington, 1937, p. 1.

Another estimate for 1920 by a qualified student of trade association activities placed the number closer to 800; but in view of the paucity of authentic information on the subject, the discrepancy is not very great. See E. H. Naylor, *Trade Associations: Their Organization and Management*, Ronald Press, New York, 1921, p. 24. The scope, activity, specific objectives, and practical achievements of trade associations have varied greatly. See Chap. 8 of this study.

49. A. J. Eddy, a Chicago lawyer, appears to have been the originator of this plan. He set forth his ideas on trade cooperation in a book entitled *The New Competition* (Appleton, New York, 1911) that had a great vogue among businessmen. See Leverett S. Lyon and Victor Abramson, *The Economics of Open Price Systems*, The Brookings Institution, Washington, 1936, Chap. 2.

50. Significantly, the first application of the "open-competition" plan was in the iron and steel industry, where in 1911 it replaced the Gary dinners. *Ibid.*, p. 11. The Gary dinners were periodic social gatherings of steel magnates at the house of Judge

cerely some businessmen may have subscribed to the plan as a pathway to enlightened yet genuine competition, in practice it frequently served as a route to collective control of the market. Though the War Industries Board in 1917–1918 encouraged the organization and work of trade associations and many new converts swelled the ranks of the movement immediately after the war, two adverse decisions in the early 1920's on the "open-competition" plan of trade cooperation gave it a severe setback.[51] Under the energetic sponsorship of Herbert Hoover as Secretary of Commerce, however, trade associations won many new adherents in the 1920's and even obtained in 1925 judicial approval for certain types of statistical work.[52] But two years later the Supreme Court severely limited the license accorded in these cases by its condemnation of price fixing in the Trenton Potteries case.[53] In the 1930's, under stimulus of the National Industrial Recovery Act, the trade association movement revived and, like the trade-union movement, reached unprecedentedly large proportions.

Corporate Consolidation Revived

In the early 1920's the way was again open for resumption of the more effective route to concentration: through outright corporate consolidation. Two Supreme Court decisions near the end of World War I made it plain that under the rule of reason, however comprehensive a merger of competing corporations was, it did not, by itself, violate the antitrust laws.[54] In both decisions the Court found that the defendants had combined in a single corporation the control of 80 per cent or more of some lines of business in which they were engaged. Exonerating the shoe machinery trust, the Court declared (p. 56): "The company indeed has magnitude, but it is at once the result and cause of efficiency, and the charge that it has been

Gary, chairman of the board of U.S. Steel. These occasions afforded an opportunity for discussion of business conditions no less than for conviviality.

51. *American Column & Lumber Co.* v. *U.S.*, 257 U.S. 377 (1921); *U.S.* v. *American Linseed Oil Co.*, 262 U.S. 371 (1923).

52. *Maple Flooring Manufacturers Association, et al.* v. *U.S.*, 268 U.S. 563 (1925); *Cement Manufacturers Protective Association* v. *U.S.*, 268 U.S. 588 (1925). On the increase in the number of trade associations in the 1920's, see U.S. Department of Commerce, *Trade Association Activities*, Washington, 1923, App. A; and Federal Trade Commission, *Open Price Trade Associations*, Washington, 1929, pp. 30-31.

53. *U.S.* v. *Trenton Potteries Co.*, 273 U.S. 392 (1927).

54. *U.S.* v. *United Shoe Machinery Co.*, 247 U.S. 32 (1918); and *U.S.* v. *United States Steel Corp.*, 251 U.S. 417 (1920).

oppressively used is not sustained." Vindicating the defendant, in the Steel Corporation case, the Court said (p. 441): "The Corporation did not at any time abuse the power or ascendancy it possessed . . ."

The Return to Normalcy: Increasing Concentration

Though mergers were common in the 1920's no official tabulation of them exists, so it is difficult to determine readily the scale and scope of the movement.[55] Also, in the absence of a generally accepted definition of business mergers, statistics on their number and size are apt to be misleading. For example, when one neighborhood bakery buys out another in an adjoining city block, does that constitute a merger? Should the acquisition by the Ward Baking Company of a 15 per cent stock interest in a local chain of such bakeries be classified as a merger? If an individual purchases a controlling stock interest in two corporations, one a printing concern turning out soap wrappers along with labels for numerous other products, and the other making soap, is the transaction a merger?

According to data compiled by Willard Thorp, no fewer than 1,179 manufacturing and mining consolidations took place from 1920 to 1928 inclusive.[56] The number declined from 173 in 1920 to 67 in 1923 and rose steadily thereafter to 221 in 1928. The number of enterprises disappearing in this manner declined from 760 in 1920 to 311 in 1923 and then increased to 1,058 in 1928. Mergers in public utilities in this period set the pace for the movement elsewhere, and the volume of capital involved was enormous. According to Thorp, the number of mergers and merger acquisitions in public utilities rose from 15 in 1920 to 1,029 in 1926, declining slightly thereafter.[57]

A similar survey that carried forward the statistical study of trust formation in 1890–1904 reported in *Industrial Combinations and Public Policy,* using the same definition and standards, makes pos-

55. The Twentieth Century Fund's study, *Big Business: Its Growth and Its Place* (pp. 31-33), used Willard L. Thorp's estimates from President's Conference on Unemployment, *Recent Economic Changes in the United States,* McGraw-Hill, New York, 1929.

56. See President's Conference on Unemployment, *op. cit.,* p. 184. For a continuation of this computation through 1939, see Willard L. Thorp, "The Merger Movement," in *The Structure of Industry,* TNEC Monograph No. 27, Washington, 1941, Pt. 3, pp. 227-34.

57. See Thorp's estimates in President's Conference on Unemployment, *op. cit.,* pp. 185-87.

sible a direct comparison of the magnitude of the merger movement before and after World War I. The prewar peak of 78 primary mergers and merger acquisitions in 1899 contrasts with a postwar peak of 232 in 1928.[58]

In a 1925 report from its extensive investigation of utility corporations the Federal Trade Commission declared that "During the last ten years electric power operating companies have been acquired by holding companies *at an accelerating rate*" and that "at the end of 1924, 20 large holding company interests controlled 61 per cent of the total operating capacity of commercial electric power plants."[59] The next five years saw 228 holding company mergers and 2,851 merger acquisitions in this field. Those in 1925 alone, as reported in *Electrical World,* absorbed 407 companies with a capitalization of almost $2 billion, or about one quarter of the total capitalization of the electric power industry.

In banking, also, the merger movement attained large proportions, though it did not attract so much public attention as the pyramiding of public utilities. According to estimates of Edwin F. Gay and Leo Wolman, more than 4,000 bank mergers took place in the decade 1920–1929. The number rose from 172 in 1920 to 601 in 1929.[60]

Nature of Merger Movement of the 1920's

A number of features distinguished this merger movement of the 1920's from the earlier combination movement.

First, its field was broader. Instead of being confined largely to manufacturing and mining industries, it took in public utilities, banking, distributive trade (dairies, chain stores, department stores), and amusement and personal service trades (hotels, theatres, restaurants, laundries).

Second, the method of consolidation changed. Instead of launching at one stroke a comprehensive amalgamation of all or most of the competing enterprises in an industry, piecemeal absorption in

58. See Myron W. Watkins, "A New Way to Sound Mergers," *Forbes Magazine,* May 15, 1929. Watkins used a narrower definition of "merger" than Thorp, one which places more emphasis on the relation of the combination or acquisition to the establishment or extension of unified control in the industry concerned.

59. Quoted from Carl D. Thompson's summary and analysis of the FTC report, *Confessions of the Power Trust,* Dutton, New York, 1932, p. 103.

60. See President's Research Committee on Social Trends, *Recent Social Trends in the United States,* McGraw-Hill, New York, 1933, Vol. 1, p. 246.

response to specific contingencies and opportunities was the typical procedure. Moreover, the mergers frequently involved moderate-sized rather than giant corporations.

In the third place, most of the pre-1917 consolidations embraced only competing enterprises in the same line of business, or at most enterprises operating in successive phases of a single industry, but many of the mergers effected in the 1920's combined noncompeting concerns. For example, in the food industries makers of several different kinds of packaged groceries often joined hands in a single corporate combine. In the public utility field it was common for gas, electric, and traction properties to be brought under a single management. In the chemical industries producers of various heavy chemicals (alkalies and acids), industrial gases, coal-tar intermediates, dyestuffs, fertilizers, pharmaceuticals, insecticides, explosives, solvents, finishes, plasticizers, and a host of other items amalgamated their several interests in four or five giant companies.

Economists disagree about the significance of this merger movement to the effectiveness of competition, particularly as mergers sometimes have intensified interindustry competition, for instance among the various branches of the nonferrous metals and the fuel industries. Nevertheless, in many fields mergers reduced to a mere handful the number of sellers whose policies really mattered in shaping the market.

Big Business in the Great Depression

The sudden collapse of the febrile prosperity of the 1920's at the end of the decade did not bring about decentralization of industrial control. In the long depression that followed, big business suffered reverses, as did every other part of the economy.[61] But with few exceptions (mostly among the labyrinthine corporate structures put together by public utility empire builders like Insull and Hopson) the giant corporations weathered the storm better than small business. The "compiled net profit" of the 200 largest nonfinancial corporations decreased almost 90 per cent as the depression deepened, or

61. For example, net total assets of the 200 largest nonfinancial corporations (industrials, public utilities, and railroads, each with total assets over $67 million) declined nearly $7 billion between 1929 and 1933, or from $84.8 billion to $77.8 billion. See National Resources Committee, *The Structure of the American Economy*, Washington, 1939, Pt. 1, Table VII, p. 107.

from $5,293 million in 1929 to $533 million in 1933. But the "compiled net profit" of all nonfinancial corporations declined even more precipitately: from $9,323 million in 1929 to only $140 million in 1933. On the average, therefore, the group of giant corporations still operated profitably in 1933 while the group of smaller corporate enterprises operated in the red, because the profits of the former group exceeded the combined profits of the two groups.[62]

Tied closely as they were to great banking houses in the financial centers, the credit resources of the giant companies were greater, and in the general stringency were impaired less, than those of small concerns.[63] Also, they were in a better position than the numerous producers in fully competitive industries to protect their markets from the pressure of deflation, by restricting supply and supporting prices.[64] All in all, big business came out of the depression with its relative position strengthened.

The proportion of net assets of all nonfinancial corporations held by the 200 largest of these business units increased from 47.9 per cent in 1929 to 54.8 per cent in 1933.[65] The proportion of net assets of all manufacturing corporations held by the group of largest manufacturing corporations (82 in 1929, 78 in 1933, each with more than $67 million of total assets) increased in the same period from 37.1 per cent to 40.5 per cent. Reflecting the relatively strengthened market position of these giant manufacturing corporations, the increase in the proportion of their reported net profits to those of all manufacturing corporations was much greater: from 48.2 per cent to 69.4 per cent.[66]

62. *Ibid.*, p. 284.

63. The Reconstruction Finance Corporation, founded in the Hoover Administration, brought federal funds to the relief mainly of large banks and railroads, while many small firms were forced out of business. See J. F. Ebersole, "One Year of the Reconstruction Finance Corporation," *Quarterly Journal of Economics*, May 1933, pp. 464-92.

64. The more determined resistance to price reduction on the products of industries in which sellers are few than on those of industries in which no producer is large enough to influence the market is now a generally recognized fact. Differences of opinion persist, however, on its explanation and its significance. Cf. Gardiner C. Means, *Industrial Prices and Their Relative Flexibility*, S.Doc. 13, 74th Cong., 1st sess., Washington, 1935; *The Structure of the American Economy*, Pt. 1, Chap. 8; and Saul Nelson and Walter G. Keim, *Price Behavior and Business Policy*, TNEC Monograph No. 1, Washington, 1940, especially Chap. 2.

65. *The Structure of the American Economy*, p. 284.

66. *Ibid.*, p. 285. These computations are based on *Statistics of Income*, the U.S. Treasury's annual summary of corporation income-tax returns. They leave out of account, therefore, the operations of unincorporated business. Though the omission

Nevertheless, the progressive disintegration of the national economy, with falling prices, declining production, dwindling employment, and disappearing profits, reaching an acute stage in the banking crisis of 1932–1933, shook all business, big and little, to its foundations. With the entire nation in the grip of fear, neither big corporations nor national trade associations could reverse the trend.

Not only businessmen, but wage earners, farmers, the whole public, sought relief from economic insecurity. With the coming of the Roosevelt Administration the tide turned. But the experiments that ensued did not satisfy expectations. They did not, after all, reconstruct the American economy on a new model. They reinforced the power of organized groups (labor, farmers, businessmen) and sharpened the divisions of interest among them, while providing no effective procedure or standards for their mutual adjustment.

New Deal Agencies

The New Deal program for overcoming depression had three main elements: NRA, AAA, and NLRB. All three were based on a common double-barreled assumption. The first was that the special interests of specific groups—businessmen, farmers, wage earners—were fundamentally in harmony with the public interest. The second was that if all members of each specific group were coerced into following a common policy, that is to say, were subjected to the rule of the majority, it would bring about the greatest advance to each individual group, to the combined group interest, and hence most effectively promote the interests of society.

---

of data on partnerships and individual proprietorships engaged in manufacture undoubtedly raises the concentration ratio, it probably does not seriously distort the *trend* of developments or result in a *substantial* exaggeration of the over-all ratio. The Bureau of the Census compiled for the National Resources Committee returns covering the operations in 1935 of the 200 largest manufacturing *enterprises.* The Bureau assembled these data according to size, in groups of five. The first 16 groups, comprising the 80 largest manufacturing enterprises, had a total value product of $13.1 billion, amounting to 28.6 per cent of the total value product of all manufacturing enterprises ($45.7 billion). *The Structure of the American Economy,* App. 9, p. 270.

No similar compilation is available for 1933. But the 78 largest manufacturing corporations making income-tax returns to the Treasury in 1933 reported "Gross Receipts from Sales and Services" of $11.4 billion. This amounted to 33.8 per cent of the "Gross Receipts from Sales and Services" of all manufacturing corporations. *Ibid.,* App. 11, p. 285. The conclusion seems warranted that the position of large manufacturing corporations among all manufacturing corporations, as shown by *Statistics of Income,* corresponds fairly closely to the position of large manufacturing enterprises among all manufacturing enterprises (as the Bureau of the Census defines manufacturing).

Self-government in industry, by majority rule, was the gist of NRA. This prescription for industrial recovery represented, manifestly, a reaffirmation of the thesis on which big business had been built up—that competition is bad for business. In fact, Congress suspended the antitrust laws in authorizing the formation of industry-wide syndicates under so-called "codes of fair competition." [67]

The 557 basic codes that blanketed American industry and trade from the spring of 1933 to the spring of 1935 varied much in their terms and in their administration.[68] But with few exceptions the codes applying to manufacturing industries "stabilized" business by subordinating the interests and opportunity for growth of small-scale independents to the vested interests of large corporations.[69]

With the failure of NRA to bring the desired recovery, criticism from small business and consumers became open and vehement. As problems of enforcement of the will of code-membership majorities (usually measured by productive capacity, never simply by counting heads) became more difficult, even big business began to see in the codes more of a nuisance than a help. Few mourned the end of the Blue Eagle when the Supreme Court eventually killed it with the Schechter decision.[70] The AAA and the NLRA (the Wagner Act) still survive,[71] but charges of one-sided operation of the Wagner Act led to the enactment, over the President's veto, of the Taft-Hartley Act in mid-1947.

The American Economy on the Eve of World War II

The outlawing of the NIRA resulted in restoration of the antitrust laws, but it left the basic structure of industry undisturbed. Moreover, the codes had greatly stimulated trade association organi-

67. U.S. Code, Title 15, c. 15, Secs. 701-12.

68. See Leverett S. Lyon and Associates, *The National Recovery Administration,* The Brookings Institution, Washington, 1935, especially Pts. 2 and 5.

69. Cf. Theodore J. Kreps, *Business and Government Under the National Recovery Administration,* Institute of Pacific Relations, New York, 1936; and *Report of the President's Committee on Industrial Analysis,* Washington, 1937.

70. *Schechter Poultry Corp.* v. *U.S.,* 295 U.S. 495 (1935).

71. The Supreme Court held unconstitutional certain parts of the first Agricultural Adjustment Act in the Hoosac Mills case, *U.S.* v. *William Butler, et al.,* 297 U.S. 1 (1935). Congress then revamped its program in the Soil Conservation and Domestic Allotment Act of 1936 (49 Stat.L. 1148), which embodies similar basic principles but relies on different methods. By the Agricultural Adjustment Act of 1938 (52 Stat.L. 31) Congress further extended and strengthened the conservation program. It provided for crop loans to supplement benefit payments (for acreage limitation) and in this way sought to effectuate the "ever-normal-granary" plan that Secretary Wallace had championed.

zation; and many of the new associations survived, frequently under the disarming name of "institutes." Voluntary trade cooperation continued to limit effective competition throughout much of the American economy.[72] Lacking the element of compulsion that made the codes so appealing to apostles of "self-government in industry," trade confederation nevertheless went a long way to supplement big-business leadership in fostering concerted control of the market. In spite of the clear and unequivocal condemnation of collusive trade agreements in the only two tests of their legality that reached the Supreme Court after NRA and before World War II,[73] the evidence suggests that they flourished underground.[74]

Before the United States entered World War II, concentration of control in giant corporations, either through outright consolidation or through pyramiding (the holding company device), had gone far in many industrial areas. The process of amalgamation had perhaps gone furthest in the public utilities field. The American Telephone and Telegraph Company, with a virtual monopoly of the telephone business, was the apotheosis of big business. Its net total assets of $4 billion, its 300,000 employees and 600,000 stockholders made it the mightiest business enterprise anywhere.[75]

In transportation, a few big railroad systems exercised, through voluntary rate bureaus, an unofficial but pervasive influence on the rate structure, and thereby on the economic development, of whole sections of the country. Through the establishment of an independent

72. Clair Wilcox has compiled "a partial list of the instances . . . in which it has appeared . . . that [at some time between 1920 and 1940, exclusive of the NRA period] a trade association, industrial institute, or other common agency was exercising some form of control over production, price, and terms of sale in national or regional markets." Clair Wilcox, *Competition and Monopoly in American Industry,* TNEC Monograph No. 21, Washington, 1940, p. 234. The list (pp. 235-40) includes 135 different trades ranging all the way from candy wholesaling and jewelry merchandising to copper refining and water-gate valve and hydrant manufacture.

73. See the Sugar Institute case, *Sugar Institute, Inc.* v. *U.S.*, 297 U.S. 553 (1936), and the Socony-Vacuum (gasoline-buying pool) case, *U.S.* v. *Socony-Vacuum Oil Co., Inc.*, 310 U.S. 150 (1940).

74. See footnote 72, also the discussion of trade association activities in Chap. 8. Cf. Charles A. Pearce, *Trade Association Survey,* TNEC Monograph No. 18, Washington, 1941, especially Chap. 3.

75. Cf. N. R. Danielian, *A.T. & T.*, Harper, New York, 1940. Other nation-wide utility systems also showed the results of concentration. In radio communication RCA was the colossus, in the telegraph business Western Union. A triumvirate—NBC, CBS, and Mutual—held a dominant position in radio broadcasting. The express business was completely unified in the Railway Express Agency; Pullman had a sleeping-car monopoly; and two companies, Union Tank Car and General American Transportation, owned most of the tank cars.

Federal Power Commission in 1930 and the Securities and Exchange Commission in 1934, and particularly through the enactment of the Public Utility Holding Company and the Federal Power Acts in 1935, the further pyramiding of control of local public utilities, especially among electric power companies, had been stopped.[76] But the reorganization of the crazy-quilt holding companies that the 1920's spawned to bring them into line with something approaching a rational system of integration, as the law authorized SEC to do, encountered formidable obstacles and proceeded slowly.[77]

Though concentration of control in the public utility field was far advanced, this development was not generally considered ominous. Common carriers and other utilities had long been subject to public regulation. They were recognized as natural monopolies, with a legal duty to serve the public, at fair rates, without discrimination. It was only in so far as monopolistic control in private hands escaped regulation by public authority in these fields that its propriety or legitimacy was questioned.[78]

Areas of Increased Concentration

In manufacturing, mining, and mercantile trade, the situation was quite different. The public relied here primarily on competition to keep prices down, quality up, and techniques constantly improving. Yet the periodic laxity in antitrust-law enforcement, notably in the late 1890's and the 1920's, the virtual emasculation of the law as applied to mergers under the judicially established rule of reason, the popular indifference to the aggrandizement of big business in the period of general apathy that followed World War I, and the complaisant attitude of Congress as shown in the grant of a long series of exemptions from antitrust prohibitions,[79] all combined to

76. The FPC organic act is 46 Stat.L. 797; that of SEC, 48 Stat.L. 881. The 1935 laws mentioned form, in fact, Titles 1 and 2, respectively, of a single statute: 49 Stat.L. 803.

77. Securities and Exchange Commission, Fifth Annual Report, Washington, 1939, pp. 69-72. See also Leverett S. Lyon and Associates, *Government and Economic Life*, The Brookings Institution, Washington, 1940, Vol. 2, pp. 653-55 and 725-28.

78. For example, the Department of Justice has challenged AT & T's control of the telephone equipment business through its ownership of Western Electric Company, a manufacturing enterprise exclusively. See *U.S.* v. *Western Electric Co.*, Civil Action No. 17-49, in U.S. District Court for the District of New Jersey, complaint filed January 14, 1949.

79. See National Industrial Conference Board, *Mergers and the Law*, New York, 1929, Chap. 5; and Myron W. Watkins, "Present Position and Prospects of Antitrust Policy," *American Economic Review*, June 1942, Supplement, p. 111.

concentrate economic power in an economy that had traditionally relied on decentralized decision making for the protection of the public interest.

For example, in each of the following industries one corporation was either the sole seller or controlled the entire supply: virgin aluminum, shoe machinery, bottle machinery, optical glass, nickel, magnesium, and molybdenum.[80] Four producers or less accounted for from 75 to 100 per cent, by value, of the product of industries producing one third, by value, of all manufactured products. Fifty-seven per cent of the value of all manufactured products was accounted for by industries in which the four largest producers, when there were that many, turned out half the total value.

Patents or the control of raw materials accounted for the strong market position of some of these companies. Most of them, however, had grown to commanding size through corporate mergers or acquisition of the assets of rival concerns. The American Can Company, for example, brought together in one huge combine "over a hundred" separate plants previously operated by independent can manufacturers.[81] Few industries experienced such a spectacular reduction in the number of producers as tin can manufacture, but corporate consolidations had greatly transformed the markets for many manufactured products. In general, buyers confronted a few big sellers instead of many small sellers.

Areas of Less Concentration

Not all manufacturing industry had experienced such a high degree of concentration, however. The concentration movement had gone furthest in the heavy-goods industries, in industries making light standardized products or complex products subject to moving belt assembly techniques, and in industries using patented or intricate technical processes. In industries whose products were subject to fickle fashion, whose capital requirements were small, whose processes were simple and unpatented, ownership remained more decentralized. The four largest concerns produced less than a fourth and the eight largest concerns produced less than a third of the

80. See Wilcox, *op. cit.*, pp. 68-82. For source of the data given in the last part of this paragraph, see *ibid.*, pp. 98-116.

81. *U.S.* v. *American Can Co.*, 230 Fed. 859 (1916), at p. 868.

total output in some fifty manufacturing industries.[82] A survey of all lines of manufacture in which the concentration ratio was low [83] shows that they produced in 1939 nearly 45 per cent of the total value product of all manufacturing industry.

In mining, geography and geology largely determined the extent of concentration of ownership. Where the product was widely scattered and chance played an important role in discovery, control was generally decentralized. Thousands of firms accounted for the domestic output of bituminous coal and petroleum, whereas control of production of anthracite coal, sulphur, and nonferrous metals was highly centralized.

Decentralization of ownership was most marked, however, outside the areas of finance, public utilities, manufacturing, and mining. In agriculture, construction, wholesale and retail distribution, and service trades (amusements, barber and beauty shops, filling stations, and so forth), ownership was decentralized and the scale of production had remained small.

The average size of American farms has not increased significantly in the last eighty years; the typical farm remains a family-sized production unit. In the construction industry the 1,075 largest companies, doing an annual business of more than $500,000 each in 1939, accounted for only 27.4 per cent of all construction. Even adding the share of construction work (28.5 per cent) that went to the 13,568 medium-sized firms (those with an annual business of more than $50,000 and less than $500,000) to that of the largest companies raises the level of business done by fairly large units to not quite 56 per cent.[84]

In most lines of retail trade the share of chain stores did not increase appreciably during the 1930's and remained moderate.[85]

82. Wilcox, *op. cit.*, p. 29.

83. This short-cut term means the percentage of the total business in a given industry that a specified number of large firms handle. No standard number of firms or basis for measuring size exists. These are matters for definition in each study. Cf. *Big Business: Its Growth and Its Place*, pp. 41-43.

Specifically, as used in the text, "concentration ratio" means the percentage of the total value product of an industry produced by the four largest firms, measured by value product. See *The Structure of the American Economy*, pp. 248-59.

84. Bureau of the Census, Census of Business, 1939, Vol. 4, *Construction, 1939*, Washington, 1940, Table VII, p. 17.

85. In all branches of trade, chains did 20.3 per cent of the total business in 1929 and 21.7 per cent in 1939; in groceries, 45.7 per cent in 1929 and 32.4 per cent in 1939; in shoes, 38 per cent in 1929 and 49.7 per cent in 1939; in drugs, 28.8 per cent

Though ten of the 200 largest nonfinancial corporations in the United States were primarily retail merchandising enterprises (mail-order houses, department stores, or chain store organizations), their total sales represented less than 8 per cent of total retail sales in 1935.[86]

Retail service trades require relatively small amounts of capital and they serve local communities. This accounts primarily for their decentralized ownership and the small size of individual establishments. But many local communities can boast only a few suppliers of products or services, and among these price agreements are not uncommon, though they frequently break down. In one or two of these service trades, however, conditions are exceptional. The five giant corporations that dominate motion-picture production have entered the exhibition field, some of them on a large scale, and by 1945 together they owned more than 70 per cent of the first-run theatres in cities of more than 100,000 population and 17 per cent of all motion-picture theatres (18,076) in the United States.[87] Moreover, because of restrictive trade practices and certain features of their contracts with exhibitors, their control over exhibition extends well beyond their ownership interests in theatres.[88]

The Picture as a Whole

Although economists do not agree on the extent to which competition ruled American industry, it is obvious that its pattern of organization on the eve of World War II, fifty years after the passage of the Sherman Act, did not conform to the economists' model of pure competition.[89] In large sectors of the economy rela-

---

in 1935 (data for 1929 not available) and 27.1 per cent in 1939. Chain filling stations sold 33.8 per cent of all gasoline sold at retail in 1929; but their share of the business in 1939 was only 10.2 per cent. *Ibid.*, Vol. 1, *Retail Trade, 1939,* Washington, 1940, Table 3A, pp. 63-64.

86. See *The Structure of the American Economy,* p. 103. But the large chains undoubtedly handle a higher percentage of total sales in some lines. The variety chains, for example, together did 86.8 per cent of the retail business in notions in 1939. See *Retail Trade, 1939,* pp. 63-64. Probably a few large chains, such as Woolworth and Kresge, handle more than half the trade.

87. See *U.S.* v. *Paramount Pictures, Inc., et al.,* 334 U.S. 131 (1948). In this antitrust suit, the government won a victory on the major points at issue.

88. *Ibid.*

89. Economists agree that industry affords no example of pure competition or of pure monopoly. They also agree that in virtually every industry some producers exercise some degree of monopoly power, but that in many industries monopoly power may be inappreciable. They do not agree on a precise definition of effective or workable competition and, even if they did, they do not have enough information to classify unequivocally all industries as monopolistic or competitive.

Using a classification similar to that of Wilcox (*op. cit.,* p. 12), Stigler finds 55.2

tively few corporation executives immediately determined price and production policies. Though in doing so they could ignore neither the policies that their rivals adopted nor the response of consumers to the policies they pursued, they obviously did not make their decisions in response to the automatic forces of an uncontrolled market. On the contrary, many of them produced such a large part of the total output that their production policies and pricing policies exerted a significant influence on the market itself.

---

per cent of national income produced in 1939 to have been derived from competitive industries, 24.4 per cent from monopolized industries, 2.5 per cent from cartelized industries, and 17.9 per cent from industries "not allocable" to one or another of these categories. Or, disregarding the nonallocable group, about two thirds of the national income in 1939 is traced to competitive industries and one third to industries monopolized in one way or another. George J. Stigler, *Five Lectures on Economic Problems,* London School of Economics, Longmans, Green and Co., London, 1949, p. 50.

Stigler does not break down his calculations by the major branches of industry, agriculture (including fisheries and lumbering), mining and manufacturing. Had he done so, his results would have been more significant. Those results show that 94.4 per cent of income from agriculture, fisheries, and lumbering was derived from competition, only 5.6 per cent from monopoly. But they show far larger percentages derived from monopoly in mining (58.4 per cent) and in manufacturing (43.2 per cent). Moreover, his study indicates how precarious is his procedure. Thus, in mining he classifies petroleum production as competitive, despite the tight output controls that administrative agencies have established in their conservation-stabilization programs. (See Chap. 12 of this study.) Shifting petroleum from the competitive to the compulsory cartel category, where it obviously belongs, results in a showing that 89.8 per cent of mining income was derived from monopoly, only 10.2 per cent from competition. Stigler makes what seems to be a similarly indefensible classification of all agriculture except dairying as competitive, despite the control over production established under the AAA and the Soil Conservation Act. Shifting the income derived from the production of the crops that in 1939 were under the rigid control of the Department of Agriculture would show a quite contrary picture to that which Stigler presents.

While in the nature of things no one could make a precise and generally acceptable classification of industries as competitive or noncompetitive, few will dispute the fact that industrial concentration weakens competition. But only by an intensive study of the changing scope of markets, changes in the mechanism of supply and demand adjustment, and changes in price behavior in every specific industry could it be determined whether there has occurred an over-all trend toward monopoly, a decline in competition. Edward S. Mason and others question that industry is any less competitive today than it was in the nineteenth century, and Stigler makes calculations that support this view.

Stigler's method is to compare the percentage of allocable labor force employed in industries which *today* he classifies as monopolistic with the percentage employed in these *same* industries *identically* classified in 1870 and in succeeding decades. In short, he assumes the nonexistence of what he set out to measure, the trend toward monopolization in industry. Accepting his methods, his findings are neither surprising nor convincing, viz., that there has been no trend toward monopoly—22.5 per cent of the 1870 labor force were in sectors monopolized in 1939; 23.8 per cent of the 1940 labor force. Changes in the percentage of the total labor force that the employees in any particular industry constitute are apt to reflect primarily the effect of unequal rates of technological improvement or of changes in the relative consumption of different products.

Stigler's analysis indicates that mathematical calculations of the extent of monopoly, however accurate the arithmetic, are worth no more than the assumptions on which they rest.

But structural patterns may be deceptive. On the one hand, an industry may be tightly monopolized despite a low concentration ratio, with no single company producing more than a small fraction of the total output. A price-fixing agreement may accomplish this trick. On the other hand, in some industries in which two, three, or four large companies produce and sell a preponderant part of the total output, their investment, operating, and pricing policies may all be determined not only independently but substantially in accordance with the standards of effective competition. Such a condition may reflect the competitive weakness of overgrown giants. Size does not invariably give market power, either on economic or strategic grounds. And the advantages of size may slip through the fingers of an aging giant and be firmly grasped by younger rivals on the make, as in the chewing gum and the leather industries. During such a transitional period—and the displacement process may, for a variety of reasons, be long drawn out—effective competition may prevail. Or the rather unusual condition of a high degree of concentration coexistent with unrestricted competition may reflect simply the influence of forceful personalities and vigorous traditions of independent management in a particular industry. Unreconstructed rebels constitute an American type that did not disappear entirely in a generation or two after the Civil War, and good examples of such personalities can be found in business on either side of the Mason and Dixon line.

Moreover, whether the concentration ratio be high or low, such data take no account of the intangible but nevertheless often decisive influence of communities of interests, interlocking directorates, voting trusts, the whole pervasive network of controls that derive from common dependence on a capital market in which a few highly cohesive investment banking houses exercise great power.[90] The syndicates that the leading banking houses organize to underwrite security issues are extremely exclusive. Of the entire volume of new securities floated in the New York market during 1934–1939, Morgan Stanley & Company acted as the syndicate manager for one third, and of the first-grade bonds, for four fifths.[91] The lines of con-

90. See *The Structure of the American Economy,* Chap. 9 and Apps. XI and XIII.
91. See Wilcox, *op. cit.,* pp. 176-77. The precise period covered by this survey was January 1, 1934 to June 30, 1939. Between these dates new issues registered with SEC amounted to $9.6 billion.

trol that ran out from this highly unified credit mechanism reached into virtually every segment of the national economy.

Perhaps President Roosevelt was not far wrong when, in asking Congress to institute a comprehensive inquiry into industrial organization, he said:

> We have witnessed the merging-out of effective competition in many fields of enterprise. We have learned that the so-called competitive system works differently in an industry where there are many independent units, from the way it works in an industry where a few large producers dominate the market. . . .
>
> If private enterprise left to its own devices becomes half-regimented and half-competitive, half-slave and half-free, as it is today, it obviously cannot adjust itself to meet the needs and the demands of the country. . . .
>
> The power of a few to manage the economic life of the Nation must be diffused among the many or be transferred to the public and its democratically responsible government. If prices are to be managed and administered, if the Nation's business is to be allotted by plan and not by competition, that power should not be vested in any private group or cartel, however benevolent its professions profess to be.[92]

Though the quotation may be more the clarion call of a political crusader than the sober factual summary of an economic analyst, it recognizes the basic problem that industrial concentration raises and strikingly portrays the great gulf that separates the modern American economy from its theoretical prototype, Adam Smith's obvious and simple system of natural liberty.

92. S.Doc. 173, 75th Cong., 3d sess. This document, the President's Message of April 29, 1938, is reproduced in *Investigation of the Concentration of Economic Power*, Temporary National Economic Committee, Hearings pursuant to Pub.Res. 113 (75th Cong.), Pt. 1, "Economic Prologue," Appendix, Ex. 1, pp. 185-91. The passages quoted in the text above are not in the order in which they appear in the message.

Chapter 3

BASIC FACTORS IN INDUSTRIAL CONCENTRATION

AN OUTSTANDING FEATURE of American industrial history has been the increase in size and, in many fields, the decline in number of business enterprises relative to national output. More significant than the growth in the average size of business units is the disparity that has developed in the scale of enterprise in various fields, sometimes even in the same field. The pattern of industrial organization, in short, is remarkably varied. In some lines relatively small-scale business is still characteristic. But in most branches of American industry the representative form of business enterprise is the giant corporation.

Increased Productivity

The productivity of American industry as a whole has steadily increased and now vastly surpasses that of other countries. Considering this fact in the light of the transformation of the American industrial structure, one might be led to infer that the primary cause of the rise of big business was a quest for industrial efficiency. But this interpretation ignores other factors no less important.

Many forces have contributed to the increase in productivity. The progress of science, the discovery of new resources, the accumulation of capital, the increase and refinement of special skills, the improvement in transport and communication, invention, the gradual adjustment of diversities in law, custom, language, and education—these and similar influences have played important roles in promoting productive efficiency. Undoubtedly the per capita output of American industry would have increased greatly during the past half century had business units remained much smaller and more numerous.

The question remains whether the industrial efficiency of America arose and persists in spite of, or because of, the degree to which concentration has reshaped the industrial structure of the nation. An analysis of the forces that stimulated the growth of big business should illuminate this question. The trend toward centralization of industrial power in the United States is primarily a business phenomenon. As such, industrial transformation along this line presumably afforded opportunities for making greater profits than could be made by conducting business on a smaller scale in a larger number of separate enterprises.

Obviously the extent and attractiveness of these opportunities for making profit depended partly on political and legal factors. Both the action and inaction of government, as well as public policy as construed by the courts, plainly had much to do with industrial concentration. Ultimately, however, the reorganization of industry in fewer units operating on a vastly larger scale was unquestionably in response primarily to business forces as distinct from political ones. Businessmen, not government officials, were the prime movers. And basically they acted for self-centered business reasons, though they presumably had as much regard for broad national interests and the general welfare as other men.

From the purely economic standpoint, the forces that have fostered industrial concentration can be classified under four main heads—technical, commercial, financial, and strategic. Briefly, the technical forces that have pushed and pulled industry toward organization into bigger units work out their effects on the physical processes of production—the refining, fabricating, assembly, or delivery of goods. The commercial forces relate to the buying and selling of goods. The financial forces are those affecting the provision of capital and the distribution of income. The strategic forces have to do with the maintenance or strengthening of a firm's market position, in relation both to other producers and to consumers.

Efficiency and Size: What the Terms Mean

The quest for greater productive efficiency was undoubtedly one of the influences that fostered big business. Efficiency depends, in part, on the scale of production. No productive process can ever be 100 per cent efficient. Manufacturing always involves some loss of materials. Labor and equipment will be idle part of the time. Some of the available floor space and the mechanical power supplied will go unutilized. Management and workers will now and then loaf on the job or, worse, make mistakes. But it is often possible under unified direction in a single organization to reduce these losses—and raise the output-input ratio—by increasing the volume of goods being worked up, the number of employees working together, and the amount of equipment used.

Large-scale production is an ambiguous term. Sometimes it refers to the size of an industry, but this use is infrequent and its meaning when so used is generally evident from the context. More troublesome is the ambiguity that arises from using the term to refer sometimes to the size of the business unit and sometimes to the size of the manufacturing plant. Large-scale production is an appropriate term for either purpose, but it is important to distinguish between these two senses.[1]

To avoid confusion the term "large-scale organization" will be used in this study when referring solely to the great size of a business unit, firm, or corporation, and the term "large-scale operation" when referring simply to the great size of a factory, mill, refinery, or "works." As these are but two aspects of industrial size, a single term is useful to cover both large-scale organization and large-scale operation. "Large-scale production" will here be used for that purpose.

1. The term is appropriate for either purpose because "production" has two meanings. If one views manufacturing, for example, strictly as a physical transformation of materials into products, then only the operations that directly change the shape, color, composition, or some other property of things are significant. The scale of production, then, is the magnitude of the actual fabricating, refining, milling, or assembling processes carried on in a single manufacturing unit, or plant. But if one views manufacture from the broad standpoint of "production" as an economic category complementary to "consumption," it includes, in addition to the actual working up of materials, all those auxiliary or supplementary activities—such as designing the product, scheduling, routing, and supervising the work processes, and keeping records—that indirectly contribute to the effectiveness of the physical transformation processes. The scale of production, from this latter standpoint, is the magnitude of the whole business organization that under unified command turns out something to sell, and sells it. To measure the scale of production, so conceived, it is necessary not only to take account of the number of employees and the amount of equipment used in drafting rooms, research laboratories, accounting offices, and other departments of the business not directly engaged in making something to sell, but also, if the business operates more than one plant, to add together the resources of both kinds employed in different plants.

For discussions of the various meanings of large-scale production, and in particular of the importance of the distinction between size of business unit and size of factory, or plant, see: E. A. G. Robinson, *The Structure of Competitive Industry,* Harcourt, Brace, New York, 1932, especially Chap. 2; P. Sargant Florence, *The Logic of Industrial Organization,* Kegan Paul, Trench, Trubner & Co., London, 1933, Chap. 1; and Myron W. Watkins, article on "Large Scale Production," *Encyclopaedia of the Social Sciences,* Macmillan, New York, 1933, Vol. 9, pp. 170-81.

Technical Forces Behind Industrial Concentration

Large-scale operations afford technical advantages of two basic sorts. First, they permit greater specialization and, secondly, they open the way to better coordination, closer integration. Specialization of labor and equipment involves repetitive performance of the same operation, and practice makes perfect. Doing the same thing over and over again puts less strain on a worker's attention and helps him develop superior muscular coordination. Specialization of labor, therefore, of itself speeds up the work and, if not carried too far, reduces fatigue.

An operation steadily repeated may become almost automatic. When specialization has been carried so far that in a particular operation or sequence of operations the need for human judgment has been eliminated, a machine can take over the work. A machine makes only routine movements, though such a complicated machine as a mechanical calculator can make an incredibly vast number of such movements and even many different sequences—under the control of an operator. Machines vary greatly, of course, in degree of specialization of function.[2] A general-purpose lathe, for example, is adaptable to many different turning operations, but an automatic glass-bottle-blowing machine produces only a single type and size of bottle unless a new set of molds is installed. The more completely

2. Some authors have suggested that increasing mechanization need not involve increasing specialization. (See, for example, Robinson, *op. cit.,* Chap. 2.) This view appears incorrect. It may be true, as Robinson points out, that a complex machine, such as an automatic screw machine, will perform in a single "operation" what would be, without such a machine, a whole series of "specialized tasks." So it will. But it does not follow that the use of the machine lowers the degree of specialization. The mere fact that, for example, the tapering operation, the head-slot operation, and the threading operation are all combined in a single mechanism, instead of being performed on three different screw machines, does not mean that the processes are less specialized. Indeed, quite the contrary. For the greater the number of cutting operations a single machine tool performs, regardless of whether it performs these different operations simultaneously or in sequence, the more essential is a high degree of standardization in the depth, speed, and pressure of each cutting operation. Moreover, and this is not less important, the more complex the machine the more exacting are the requirements—the lower the margin of tolerance, as the engineers say—with respect to timing and spatial movements *in each operation.*

The view that introduction of a highly complex machine to replace two or more machines performing distinct operations decreases specialization appears to spring from a false analogy. If one man performs three tasks that formerly were divided among three men, one can say quite rightly that the change has been toward less specialization. But machines are not men, nor men machines. In the case of machinery, increased specialization of function *within mechanical equipment* is possible and, in fact, is the direct counterpart of a reduction in the number of "specialized" machines, or operations.

products are standardized, the more routine are productive processes. And the more routine the productive processes, the more readily are they mechanized.

Because specialization, whether of labor or equipment, reduces the time required to perform a given operation, the greater the degree of specialization the larger must be the scale of operations. To keep specialized units busy, to avoid wasting by idleness the increase in efficiency that their routine character makes possible, a continuous flow of work materials must be provided. Similarly, ensuing processes—of which there are often many—must be on a large enough scale to absorb the increased output of specialized workers and machines. Otherwise the whole productive process would be jammed up and the increase in technical efficiency through specialization would be self-defeating.

Better Coordination With Increasing Size

The second basic advantage of large-scale operation is that it facilitates coordination of various productive processes. Down-the-line efficiency in a manufacturing plant requires that the various specialized processes be synchronized, their rates of output so adjusted that no slack or surplus occurs anywhere along the line. Suppose, for example, the complex of productive facilities in process A that achieves greatest efficiency and lowest cost can turn out enough of certain parts or materials for 1,000 product units a day, that of process B enough for 750 product units a day, and that of process C enough for 500 product units a day. If such a hypothetical plant were equipped with only a single set of productive facilities for each process, part of its facilities would lie idle a good part of the time; for the speed of the slowest process would govern the rate of operation of the plant. By installing two sets of facilities for process C it could be synchronized with process A, because each could turn out daily enough parts for 1,000 units of finished product. But process B, with a daily capacity of only 750 units, would still be a laggard.

To synchronize the operations of all three processes a plant would have to turn out 3,000 units of finished product or some multiple thereof. Three sets of facilities for process A, each of the optimum size, would provide parts for 3,000 (3 × 1,000) units of the finished product; four sets of such facilities for process B would supply parts for 3,000 (4 × 750) product units; and six sets of facilities for process C would turn out parts for 3,000 (6 × 500) product units. For any capacity less than that represented by the lowest common multiple of the potential output of the three specialized processes some part of the capacity of one or more of them will go to waste.

If an enterpriser in such a situation is obliged, perhaps because of lack of capital, to limit his scale of production to, say, 2,000 units of finished product a day, he could synchronize processes A and C by providing two sets of facilities for process A (2 × 1,000 = 2,000) and four sets of facilities for process C (4 × 500 = 2,000). But he could not synchronize process B with the other processes. Two sets of facilities for process B would yield parts for only 1,500 finished units; and three sets, parts for 2,250 units. If he installs only two sets of facilities for process B he must limit his total output of finished products to 1,500 units and let some of his facilities for processes A and C lie idle part of the time, unless perchance he can obtain enough process B parts for 500 product units from an outside supplier. If he installs three sets of facilities for process B he must let some of these facilities lie idle part of the time.

He may prefer to take a loss of potential output (parts for about 250 product units) from an installation of additional process B facilities rather than run the risk of not getting prompt delivery and acceptable terms from an outside supplier. But the enterprise can plainly reduce its unit cost by expanding to a capacity of 3,000 product units a day if the necessary capital funds are available and an assured demand appears for output at that rate. Thus technical advantages in the form of better coordination of processes prompt enlargement of plant operations up to a point that permits full use of all the facilities necessary for efficient production in every department.

Technical Advantages From Large-Scale Organization

Large size may bring advantages by permitting greater specialization and better coordination in a big company as well as in a big plant. If a company merges two similar newsprint mills each equipped to produce annually 500,000 tons of paper with minimum input of materials, labor, power, and capital per ton of output, greater productive efficiency may result without any alteration in the technological pattern. If the operation of two or more mills by one executive staff requires less managerial service per unit of output, the merger will have a higher efficiency ratio than either of its constituents, other factors remaining the same. Moreover, operating several plants of similar type and size in different locations may enable a big company to hold down delivery costs if it sells in a geographically extensive market or to reduce the costs of assembling raw materials.

But quite apart from all this, a multi-plant company may be able to use more fully the managerial capacities necessary for efficient operation of even a single large plant. The opportunity to select men of special skills for particular managerial functions and to utilize those skills continuously on the types of executive work for which they are exceptionally well adapted is, indeed, one of the clearest illustrations of the advantages that division of labor gives to a large organization.

Advantages for Research

Large-scale organization also permits the use of better and more extensive research services than a company could afford if the advantages of "large-scale operation," alone, determined its size. With the growing importance of chemistry and biology as supplements to physics in solving the problems of modern technology, the equipment and staff requirements of an industrial research laboratory adequate to keep a company abreast of new technical developments have greatly increased.[3] Moreover, the fruits of research in such laboratories are likely to be applicable over a much wider field than is provided in the large-scale operations of a single specialized plant.

In order to get full benefits, a company that maintains a research staff and laboratory big enough to serve well one large plant may need to operate several similar plants or plants in closely related lines.[4] General Electric probably could not afford to conduct technical

3. See National Resources Planning Board, *Research—A National Resource,* Pt. 2, "Industrial Research," Washington, 1940, pp. 221-67; and George Perazich and Philip M. Field, *Industrial Research and Changing Technology,* Works Progress Administration, Report M, No. 4, Philadelphia, 1940, Chap. 1.

4. Experience confirms logic here. Only the very large, multi-plant companies support extensive basic research. Of the 90,000-odd manufacturing corporations in the

research on its present scale unless it could use many of the discoveries and improvements in a score of manufacturing plants. Similarly, by spreading the cost of its centralized research organization over the output of Chevrolets, Pontiacs, Oldsmobiles, Cadillacs, Yellow Trucks, Delco equipment, and Frigidaires, General Motors unquestionably has lower overhead research costs per unit of output than it would have if each of these manufacturing divisions provided its own technical research facilities. Again, if the Aluminum Company of America could use the technical achievements of its Kensington Laboratories only in a single large plant instead of in a dozen or more, it would probably be uneconomical for the company to spend as much on research as it now does, either in the aggregate or per unit of output. And almost certainly, even if it did, the fruitfulness of such expenditures—measured by technical achievements per dollar of research cost—would be substantially less. Conducting research work on a scale that permits a high degree of specialization is advantageous, more so today perhaps than ever before.

While research may be more economical if its fruits are made available throughout a large-scale organization, extensive and intensive research need not depend on large-scale organization. Industrial research laboratories may and do operate independently, serving many companies, sometimes in the same industry, sometimes in different industries. Some such laboratories are endowed; others are run as a business. In either case, if such laboratories could more readily sell their services to business generally, they might operate on an even larger scale than the private laboratory of any single corporation. If there were no monopoly incentives to supplement ordinary competitive incentives for giant corporations to finance their own technical research, the opportunities for independent research laboratories selling their services in the open market would no doubt be much greater.

Nevertheless, in some industries economies in those parts of overhead expense that relate directly to operating efficiency may be achieved by an enterprise that embraces more than one plant of the optimum size. In other words, strictly from the technical standpoint,

United States before World War II, only 2 per cent (fewer than 2,000) carried on any formal research work at all. Furthermore, the laboratories of 45 big companies employed half of the country's industrial research workers. See Perazich and Field, *op. cit.*, Chap. 2, especially pp. 9-11; and National Resources Planning Board, *op. cit.*, pp. 37-87.

the most advantageous size of an enterprise may sometimes be greater than it would be if the factors bearing on the optimum size of plant alone were considered.

Limits to Advantages of Size

Conceivably, specialization might be carried too far. It is a question whether, apart from the problem of effective coordination of extremely specialized operations, disadvantages in the performance of specialized functions themselves accumulate the more they are split up and routinized until the disadvantages offset the advantages. In the case of labor, monotony and ennui may set in at an earlier stage when specialization reduces tasks too near to a mechanical routine, with resulting decline in efficiency. On the other hand, psychological studies in recent years point to emotional strains and nervous tensions originating outside the shop—in domestic situations, living conditions, etc.—as the principal sources of workers' ennui and attendant lack of diligence. The factors mainly responsible for a sense of the monotony of work apparently have no close relationship to the degree of specialization—and therefore repetition—of the task assigned.[5]

But it is possible that the psychologists have their noses too close to the grindstone in their studies of industrial fatigue and the direct effects of specialization. Deterioration of labor morale may be an insidious, long-run development connected with overspecialization of work in huge industrial organizations. Part, and perhaps not the least part, of the disadvantages of repressing spontaneity and creative impulses among factory workers and of impressing on them too close a resemblance to cogs in a machine finds expression in noneconomic spheres—in civic attitudes and social relations.[6]

But in industry the decisive factor limiting the scale of operations and size of organization is probably the increasing difficulty, beyond a certain point, of effecting smooth coordination among all phases of the enterprise. The problem of keeping all the specialized depart-

5. See Elton Mayo, *Human Problems of an Industrialized Civilization,* Macmillan, New York, 1933, Chaps. 2 and 7; *idem, Social Problems of an Industrial Civilization,* Harvard University Press, Cambridge, 1945, Chap. 6; and Flanders Dunbar, *Emotions and Bodily Changes,* 3d edition, Columbia University Press, New York, 1946.

6. See Charles S. Myers, *Mind and Work,* University of London Press, London, 1929, pp. 162-70; Lewis Mumford, *Technics and Civilization,* Harcourt, Brace, New York, 1934, especially pp. 411 ff.; Thorstein Veblen, *The Instinct of Workmanship,* Huebsch, New York, 1918, especially Chap. 7.

ments working in balance, or in unison, when business organization goes beyond a certain size becomes too great for efficient management. Even Henry Ford, great exponent of large-scale production that he was and surely a managerial genius if ever there was one, apparently overreached his capacity.[7] At any rate, his successors have modified his policy of integrating under one management all the productive processes involved in turning out a finished automobile.

The managerial capacity of executive staffs varies. And it always has a limit. The more minutely managerial functions are split up, the more difficult it becomes to keep the whole executive hierarchy working smoothly together. In setting work schedules, estimating costs, passing on the suitability of materials, and making many other decisions, a production manager is apt to use different criteria from those a sales manager would use. Department heads often have different notions of how much time and expense a change-over from one product style to another would involve. Someone must reconcile these conflicting judgments. As Robinson observes:

> It has been proved by experience that no individual can effectively control more than four or five subordinate department heads. If he attempts to manage more he must either cause endless delays, or else become no more than a rubber stamp. And so the big firm is a series of wheels within wheels, an elaborate hierarchy, in which every decision requires the consulting of this man, the referring to that man, the permission of a third, the agreement of a fourth, so that decisions become endlessly delayed.[8]

7. The costly blunder of sticking too long to the extremely standardized Model T probably reflected in part Ford's preoccupation with the advantages of mass production. This mistake may well have influenced his change of outlook in later years, when he became a strong advocate—and an active practitioner—of industrial decentralization. Compare the passage in Henry Ford, *My Life and Work,* Doubleday, Page, Garden City, 1923, pp. 71 ff., and the scarcely reconcilable statement seven years later that "The eventual ideal is a complete decentralization in which most plants will be so small and so situated that the workers will be both farmers and industrialists" (in *Moving Forward,* Doubleday, Page, Garden City, 1930, p. 157).

8. Robinson, *op. cit.,* p. 49. A critic might answer that huge business organizations do, nevertheless, exist and even thrive, so that experience disproves Robinson's contention. The answer is not convincing. Undoubtedly, study and experimentation have enabled the executive groups that manage such large organizations as General Electric, General Motors, U.S. Steel, and Standard Oil of New Jersey to overcome many of the handicaps of size. But that does not prove that in these and similar cases the organization of production in smaller-scale enterprises might not result in more efficient management. It is at least as plausible an inference from the known facts that some giant corporations survive in spite of a lack of efficiency. Their success may depend more on their power over markets than on efficiency in production and management. This apparently has been true of the United States Steel Corporation. See Chap. 5, pp. 117-18, of this study; also, Hearings on Study of Monopoly Power before the Subcommittee of the Committee on the Judiciary, House of Representatives, 81st Cong.

Alfred P. Sloan, Jr., in discussing the advantages of decentralized management of General Motors' several enterprises expressed a similar idea:

> We realized that in an institution as big as General Motors . . . any plan that involved too great a concentration of problems upon a limited number of executives would limit initiative, would involve delay, would increase expense, and would reduce efficiency and development. Further it would mean an autocracy, which is just as dangerous in a great industrial organization as it is in a government; aside from the question as to whether any limited number of executives could deal with so many diversified problems, in so many places, promptly and effectively.[9]

Problems Increase With Size

Problems of managerial efficiency are, of course, inescapable in any business organization, whatever the scale of production. But apparently they grow progressively more difficult as the size of the business increases. Committee systems may help iron out differences of opinion among management specialists. But conferences are time-consuming and often lead to a sacrifice of dispatch in a vain quest for agreement. To quote Robinson again:

> Anyone who has ever done business with committees knows that five people can reach a decision, fifteen people can be persuaded by a man who has made up his mind, and twenty-five people are a debating society.[10]

Improved factory records and accounting systems may help keep every executive, however narrow his particular field of responsibility, better informed about what the whole organization is doing. But much of the information may be useless for the specialist's own work, serving only to prevent his isolation; and in any event paper work is costly. To counteract the benumbing effect of a top-heavy bureaucracy wrapped in red tape, decentralized management schemes are sometimes tried.[11] They may help to restore initiative; but to the

(popularly known, from the name of its chairman, as the Celler Committee), April 26-28, 1950; and Myron W. Watkins, *Industrial Combinations and Public Policy,* Houghton Mifflin, Boston, 1927, especially p. 139.

9. Alfred P. Sloan, Jr., *Adventures of a White-Collar Man,* Doubleday, Doran, New York, 1941, pp. 134-35.

10. Robinson, *op. cit.,* pp. 48-49. On reflection, Robinson's figures seem too high. Substituting three for five, five for fifteen, and ten for twenty-five would probably be more realistic, in most cases.

11. See Donaldson Brown, *Decentralized Operations and Responsibilities With Coordinated Control,* American Management Association, New York, 1927; J. D.

extent that they do, they obviously increase the risk of divergent policies and discordant action. Though big business has many privileges, that of having its cake and eating it too is not one of them.

Limits to "External Economies"

The technical forces fostering large-scale production, particularly as they affect the size of business organization, tend to bring under unified control not only large groups of productive agents operating in a given processing stage or branch of an industry but also productive agents operating in successive processing stages. In the automobile industry, for example, forces similar to those that made it advantageous for Ford to produce motors on a large scale favored, and eventually led to, production by the same organization of the steel and other products from which the automobiles were made. It is immaterial whether such integration is advantageous because it eliminates unnecessary handling of materials or steps in their preparation—as happens when blast furnaces and steel furnaces are integrated—or because it permits more effective coordination of operations.[12] In either case, integration may make possible greater productive efficiency up to a certain point.[13]

The classic illustration of the technical advantages of integration is the steel industry. From the extraction of the iron ore through the

---

Mooney and A. C. Reilly, *Onward Industry!*, Harper, New York, 1931; and Peter F. Drucker, *Concept of the Corporation*, Day, New York, 1946, Chap. 2.

The terms "bureaucracy" and "red tape" in common usage carry a certain derogatory implication, probably justly so. But as used here, bureaucracy means simply a multiplication of offices, or officeholders, and red tape means a multiplication of procedural rules. The tendency for bureaucrats each to be jealous of his authority within the field assigned him and to defend it against encroachments from outside, even at the expense of effective "government" or "management," may be avoidable, but it is certainly common. Likewise, as procedural rules multiply with the growth of an official hierarchy, conceivably they may remain flexible. In practice, however, they often become cut and dried, thus affording a ready means of "passing the buck" and otherwise obstructing the accomplishment of the basic purposes of the organization as a whole.

12. Professor Frank A. Fetter takes a different position on this particular matter. See his paper on "The Fundamental Principle of Efficiency in Mass Production," reproduced in Federal Trade Commission, *Relative Efficiency of Large, Medium-Sized, and Small Business*, TNEC Monograph No. 13, Washington, 1941, pp. 398-415. The present study leads to conclusions on the relation of size and efficiency generally similar to those of Fetter. The difference on this particular point appears to reflect a difference in definitions, specifically in the meaning of "productive efficiency."

13. Ford's integration program was actuated in part by a desire to free his firm from dependence on outsiders. In achieving this goal Ford apparently transgressed the limits of economy. At any rate, Henry Ford II's management of the company seems to be reversing the policy of complete self-containment that the founder inaugurated.

transport of the ore to the blast furnace, its reduction to molten iron, its conversion to steel ingots, its tempering and rolling, up to the stage at which semifinished steel is ready for fabrication, production can be organized as practically a continuous process. An integrated company carrying on all these successive operations can avoid the accumulation of excessive working inventories at various stages, avoid heat losses and reduce handling costs in moving materials from stage to stage, utilize the power or byproducts of one stage in preceding or succeeding operations; in short, it can reduce to a minimum the total unit cost of production.

But as the scale of organization increases in response to these forces it meets counterforces. Whenever industrial specialization offers advantages from the organization and operation of a particular processing stage—say the B stage—on a scale well in excess of that necessary for the industry's other processing stages organized and operating on an optimum scale—say the C and D stages—then the integration of the B, C, and D branches of the industry does not promote productive efficiency. Integration is then wasteful. Large as many cotton and rayon textile mills are, few of them engage in dyeing and finishing.[14]

Though they are industrial giants, none of the Big Three automobile companies makes its own paint and finishes, and only one makes its own steel. The advantages of specialization in making paints and finishes apparently outweigh the advantages of coordinating all the processes that feed an automobile assembly line. To give a new turn to a technical term, the external economies of paint manufacturing favor a scale of production adapted, not to the requirements of one automobile manufacturer, however large, but to the demands of the whole automobile trade, the railway car trade, homeowners, shipowners, and a host of other paint users.

Another illustration of how the advantages of specialization set definite limits to the extension of the scale of organization through integration of processes is the increasing tendency to divorce power generation from industrial production. The optimum scale of operation of steam plants for generating electricity has increased so much that manufacturing plants are coming more and more to

14. More do so since the recent merger movement in textiles than previously. But it appears that strategic rather than technical factors were primarily responsible for the development.

rely on public utilities as a source of power.[15] Even some of the largest automobile companies now find it cheaper to buy than to generate electric power. If public utility regulation prevents rate discrimination, this development tends to put large and small manufacturing companies on the same level as far as power costs are concerned. Taken together with the greater range of electrical energy distribution that high-voltage transmission permits, it points toward an effective long-run check on industrial concentration. The external economies of power generation for a whole industrial district are now so great as to alter very much the role that the quest of cheap power played in the historic development of large-scale production.

Relation of Size to Efficiency

The limitations of available data make it impossible to measure directly the influence of the scale of production on technical efficiency. Economists have attempted, therefore, to determine the relationship of size to efficiency by indirect means. One method of attacking the problem is to study the profit rates of large and small companies.[16] But results of such analyses are inconclusive and contra-

15. See John M. Blair, *Technology in Our Economy,* TNEC Monograph No. 22, Washington, 1941, p. 203.

16. W. L. Crum in his *Corporate Size and Earning Power* (Harvard University Press, Cambridge, 1939, p. 230) concluded after an analysis of income-tax data for all corporations (that is, both those reporting losses and those reporting net earnings) that, starting from the smallest size class (the "lowest" class, in Crum's terminology), "(1) rate of return increases unmistakably in the low and moderately large size classes; (2) the advance in rate may continue in all size classes; or may disappear or even be replaced by a moderate reduction in the high size classes; (3) even in cases for which rate declines in the highest size classes, rates for those classes remain emphatically above those for the lowest classes."

Joseph Steindl in *Small and Big Business* (Blackwell, Oxford, 1945, pp. 40-42) accepts Crum's conclusions without qualification. Yet two National Bureau of Economic Research studies and a Twentieth Century Fund study point to a quite different conclusion. See William A. Paton, *Corporate Profits as Shown by Audit Reports,* National Bureau of Economic Research, New York, 1935; R. C. Epstein, *Industrial Profits in the United States,* National Bureau of Economic Research, New York, 1934. Compare Alfred L. Bernheim (Ed.), *How Profitable Is Big Business?,* Twentieth Century Fund, New York, 1937, pp. 57 ff. and Chap. 14.

Because the turnover among small companies is much higher than among big ones, it makes a great deal of difference whether the comparison of profitability of different size classes is based on all reporting corporations or solely on those reporting a *positive* net income. New enterprises are commonly small and hazardous. Their high mortality is at least as likely to be due to other factors as to technical inefficiency and high cost of production. If one excludes the unprofitable companies from all size classes, the evidence suggests that profit rates, and presumably costs, remain at about the same level over a considerable range of size classes between—and above—the very small and the very large. See Charles L. Merwin, Jr., *Characteristics of American Manufacturing Corporations,* TNEC Monograph No. 15, Washington, 1940, pp. 23-33; and K. C. Stokes, "Financial Trends of Large Manufacturing Corporations, 1939–1946," *Survey of Current Business,* November 1947, p. 22.

dictory. High earning rates may reflect monopoly power rather than productive efficiency. Moreover, the accounting treatment of income and expense items, especially in respect to compensation of executives, varies greatly among different companies.[17] Differences of this kind are particularly marked between large and small enterprises.

Another indirect method of testing the bearing of size on efficiency is to compare unit costs of production of large and small companies.[18] But the difficulties are great in finding suitably standardized products subject to fairly uniform cost accounting rules and practices. And the scattered, scanty data that have from time to time been assembled have led to conflicting conclusions. After analyzing data from various government agencies on unit costs of production for companies of all sizes in a score of industries the Federal Trade Commission concluded that "the largest companies made, on the whole, a very poor showing. . . . medium size in itself did not insure a low cost . . . But certain efficient medium-sized units . . . generally made the best showing." [19]

The Commission's study has been severely criticized; [20] and, if the imperfect data it assembled would support any inference at all, it would probably be that other factors are at least as important as size (beyond a certain minimum) in determining productive efficiency.[21]

Several students, working independently, have reached the con-

17. For a criticism of Crum's procedure from this standpoint, see J. L. McConnell, "Corporate Earnings by Size of Firms," *Survey of Current Business,* May 1945, pp. 6-12. See also Merwin, *op. cit.,* pp. 34-43.

18. Such studies might be even more significant if adequate data were available to permit a comparison of costs in a fair-sized sample of both large and small plants in a wide range of industries. Such comparisons would go a long way toward determining the optimum scale of *operations*—instead of *organization*—in various industries. But giant multi-plant companies do not ordinarily divulge operating data on their separate plants. John M. Blair has pointed out that OPA files contain much data of this kind, the systematic organization and analysis of which should yield findings of great value. See his review of Steindl's book in *American Economic Review,* March 1947, pp. 237-40.

19. Federal Trade Commission, *op. cit.,* pp. 10-11. See also Kemper Simpson, *Big Business, Efficiency, and Fascism,* Harper, New York, 1941, especially Chap. 5; and the Preface (p. vii), where the author claims credit for the FTC study, which he regards as providing conclusive evidence of the inefficiency of big business.

20. See, for example, Robert N. Anthony, "Effect of Size on Efficiency," *Harvard Business Review,* Spring 1942, pp. 290-306; John Scoville and Noel Sargent, *Fact and Fancy in TNEC Monographs,* National Association of Manufacturers, New York, 1942, pp. 190-200; and John M. Blair, "The Relation Between Size and Efficiency," *Review of Economic Statistics,* August 1942, pp. 125-35.

21. German experience appears to support this conclusion. See H. W. Singer, "The German War Economy," *Economic Journal,* December 1943, pp. 370-80, particularly pp. 371-73.

clusion, on the basis partly of observation and partly of still very slight statistical evidence, that the optimum scale of production for manufacturing industries generally falls within a broad range, rather than at a single point.[22] More specifically, the conclusion to which recent studies appear to point is that unit costs decline with increasing size of plant up to a certain point, then level off until, in some industries at least, a scale of operations is reached beyond which increasing size is attended with rising unit costs.

Generalization in this field is obviously more than ordinarily hazardous. On a priori grounds the great differences among industries in complexity of techniques employed and intensity of the use of capital strongly suggest that scale of operations exerts a very uneven influence on productive efficiency. At any rate—until more reliable, standardized, and comprehensive cost data are made available—the only safe conclusion is a negative one: that it has not been proved that there is a direct and continuous correlation between industrial plant size and efficiency.

Role of Technical Forces in Industrial Concentration

Though the quest for greater technical efficiency unquestionably helps explain the development of industrial concentration, it has evidently not been the sole or even the decisive influence. If other forces had not been at work, both logic and the available facts suggest that the movement toward combination of industry into bigger and fewer units would have stopped far short of the stage it has reached. But the economies of large-scale production probably played a major role among motivating forces in the early stages of industrial concentration in the United States, say in the quarter century after the Civil War. Among the newer industries, of course, the effort to achieve a mass-production scale has continued during the past half century to influence profoundly the shape of the industrial structure.

But the persistence of the tendency toward concentration of control in the older industries during the past fifty years strongly suggests that something more than—and different from—a search for greater

22. See John M. Blair, "Technology and Size," *American Economic Review,* May 1948, pp. 121-52; John M. Clark, "Toward a Concept of Workable Competition," *American Economic Review,* June 1940, pp. 241-56, especially p. 248; cf. Joe S. Bain, *Economics of the Pacific Coast Petroleum Industry,* University of California Press, Berkeley, 1940, Pt. 1, pp. 99-114, and Pt. 2, pp. 182 ff., and Pt. 3, pp. 71 ff.

efficiency and lower costs of production has prompted business mergers. If technical forces were mainly responsible for the continuing concentration, if increasing plant capacity continued indefinitely to yield lower and lower unit costs, one would expect a giant combine to center in one plant its entire output of a specific product—or at least the entire output salable within the limits of a market area defined by transportation costs.

Yet almost none of the great consolidations has found such a policy desirable. General Motors operates six different automobile plants within a radius of eighty miles from Detroit. United States Steel operates four separate steelworks in the Pittsburgh district alone. A similar pattern of manufacturing operations holds for American Sugar Refining, National Lead, International Harvester, and scores of other consolidations.[23] And if multi-plant organization yields substantial technical advantages, these economies do not show up in the available cost of production data. A satisfactory explanation of the continuing tendency toward industrial concentration therefore requires consideration of other factors.

Commercial Forces Behind Industrial Concentration

One of the greatest sources of waste in an industrial system made up of a large number of relatively small-scale, independent business units in each branch of trade is in buying and selling. Competition presupposes such a multiple-unit industrial structure. Moreover, the pressure of competition encourages, if it does not compel, each producer to devote much time and effort to making purchases and sales—on advantageous terms. He must canvass various possible sources of supply for materials, continually scrutinize his selling methods, investigate the possibility of new market outlets, and compare prices all along the line. This preoccupation with commercial affairs not only interferes with efficient management of manufacturing operations but also leads to considerable duplication, and an unnecessary amount of fact finding, account keeping, inventory storing, and advertising.

23. Rare exceptions are United Shoe Machinery's concentration of all machinery-manufacturing operations in its Beverly plant and Reynolds Tobacco's concentration of all its manufacturing operations in its Winston-Salem plant. Special circumstances account for both of these industrial "sports." In the case of shoe machinery, one factor is the comparatively narrow market for most of the specific types of machines. In the case of cigarettes, the origin and traditions of the Reynolds company appear to have played a prominent part in its localization.

Analyzing the economic significance of industrial consolidation in the early stages of the movement, Veblen observed half a century ago that:

> In great measure the saving effected is a saving of the costs of business management and of the competitive costs of marketing products and services, rather than a saving in the prime costs of production. . . . The amount of "business" that has to be transacted per unit of product is much greater where the various related industrial processes are managed in severalty than where several of them are brought under one business management. . . . The greater the parcelment in point of ownership, the greater the amount of business work that has to be done in connection with a given output of goods and services . . . It is in doing away with unnecessary business transactions and industrially futile maneuvering on the part of independent firms that the promoter of combinations finds his most telling opportunity.[24]

On the other hand, under conditions of imperfect competition or oligopoly some of the commercial activities that make up a large part of the final cost of goods in a freely competitive market tend to be still further intensified. As a substitute for cost reduction and price competition an oligopolist usually finds it expedient to redouble his selling efforts. Even a full monopolist seldom finds it advantageous to trim his advertising outlays; quite the contrary, because his unique position makes the cultivation of consumer good will peculiarly urgent. Moreover, some of the bargaining and market-probing efforts that Veblen decries find their economic justification through uncovering low-cost sources of supply that might otherwise remain unknown and neglected.

Although Veblen exaggerates "the saving effected" by industrial consolidation, reduction in bargaining activities is a real advantage. It is particularly great when consolidation results in industrial integra-

24. Thorstein Veblen, *The Theory of Business Enterprise,* Scribner's, New York, 1915, pp. 45-48. This book was first published in 1905.

Veblen was an acute critic, rather than a careful analyst, of contemporary economic institutions. His mordant satire tended to obscure the real economic benefits from competitive buying and selling activities in so far as they provide an effective means of so distributing productive resources and adjusting the output of various goods and services as to meet the changing wants of consumers and maintain a sort of equilibrium of economic forces. Lumping all business activities under the epithet "pecuniary employments," and in effect ignoring the value problem by treating production as if it were a simple engineering problem of turning out a maximum of "things" measured by weight and tale, Veblen never came to grips with the basic economic problem.

Nevertheless, the point he makes in the passage quoted has a good deal of merit. A freely competitive business regime probably tends to carry specialization—the splitting up of the productive process into separate commercial segments—further than strict economy would warrant.

tion; but, as previously shown, some sacrifice of the advantages of specialization accompanies every extension of integration. If the Corn Products Refining Company were to extend integration back to the growing of corn, it could eliminate a great deal of commercial trafficking in its raw material. It is at least questionable, however, that "the saving effected" by such an extension of industrial consolidation would outweigh the advantages the company could obtain by "sticking to its last."

Advantages of Horizontal Combination

Horizontal combination—bringing together a number of formerly rival firms engaged in the same stages of an industrial process—can also effect commercial savings. A single selling organization can often solicit orders in a given market territory as effectively as, and with much lower cost per dollar of sales than, the separate staffs of the several constituent companies that it replaces. It may lack the competitive spirit that stimulates salesmen where rivalry is keen, but it is less likely to "oversell" the market.

A closely related source of potential saving from horizontal combination (alike to society and the businessman) is the opportunity it affords to buy materials and supplies in larger quantities. But apart from the bargaining leverage a consolidation may obtain as a dominant seller or buyer in raw materials markets, the possible gains from larger-scale purchasing have apparently been a minor factor in industrial concentration. In meat packing and cigarette manufacture, power to rig the market against scattered, small-scale farmers appears to have fostered consolidation.[25] In most cases, however, the same sources of raw materials serve more than one industry and the socially defensible advantages of purchasing on a larger scale than minimum carload lots (or similar conventional units) are probably negligible. If National Cash Register or United Shoe Machinery obtained any advantage from buying iron and steel in large quantities, it is not recorded. If Owens-Illinois Glass or International

25. On the manipulation of tobacco prices by the Big Three cigarette manufacturers, see Chap. 6; also *U.S.* v. *American Tobacco Co., et al.,* 328 U.S. 781 (1946), and Federal Trade Commission, *Prices of Tobacco Products,* Washington, 1922. On similar practices in meat packing, see *U.S.* v. *Swift & Co., et al.,* 196 U.S. 375 (1905); *Swift & Co.* v. *U.S.,* 276 U.S. 311 (1928); *U.S.* v. *Swift & Co.,* 286 U.S. 106 (1932); and *U.S.* v. *Swift & Co.,* 318 U.S. 442 (1943). See also Federal Trade Commission, *The Meat Packing Industry,* Washington, 1919, Pt. 2, *passim.*

Paper are able to buy soda ash or caustic soda cheaper than their constituents could have, there is no evidence that it is because of any economy in larger-scale transactions.

Again, industrial combinations may be able to eliminate a good deal of crosshauling. With scattered plants run by independent producers, each seller is likely to be shipping substantially identical products at about the same time to customers in areas adjacent to the plants of other producers. By supplying every customer, as far as possible, from the plant located nearest him, a consolidation can reduce delivery costs. A similar saving is possible for dressed meats, bread and other bakery products, milk and other dairy products requiring an extensive network of local warehousing and delivery facilities. Such combinations as National Biscuit, Continental Baking, Armour, and Borden avoid much costly duplication of distributive facilities. This has undoubtedly been an important factor stimulating the growth of consolidation in certain fields.[26] But to obtain these savings in distribution costs, a combine may have to forego some part, at least, of whatever technical advantages could be realized from concentrating manufacturing operations in one or a few big plants. To some extent the economies of mass production and those of mass distribution limit one another.

Industrial Concentration in Relation to Advertising

Perhaps the greatest potential source of cost saving to society in commercial (buying and selling) operations is in advertising. A frequent indictment of competitive capitalism is that it encourages wasteful expenditure in sales promotion.[27] Of course, advertising

26. The possibility of effecting savings in delivery and servicing costs is not confined to perishable products. The extensive distributive organizations of National Lead in bearing metals, Standard Sanitary and American Radiator in plumbing supplies, Eastman Kodak in photographic materials, and International Harvester in farm equipment would have been duplicated many times over without consolidation. Probably in all these and other instances prospective commercial economies were more important than prospective gains in technical efficiency in fostering combination. But this is not to say that either commercial or technical forces provided the main spur to industrial consolidation, here or elsewhere.

27. See, for example, Stuart Chase and F. J. Schlink, *Your Money's Worth,* Macmillan, New York, 1927. For a more penetrating analysis and discriminating evaluation of advertising, see Frederic W. Taylor, *The Economics of Advertising,* G. Allen & Unwin, London, 1934.

Part of the wastes of competitive advertising consists of the promotion of what Ruskin, and later Hobson, called "illth"—the opposite of wealth. On the vulgarity and misleading character of much contemporary advertising, see B. Clark, *The Advertising Smoke Screen,* Harper, New York, 1944, in which the author draws heavily on

has a legitimate economic function. Basically, it is a means of acquainting buyers with the composition, specifications, properties, and uses of available goods and where and on what terms they may be obtained. In so far as advertising serves this informational function it enables buyers to use their purchasing power more discriminatingly and sellers to realize the volume of sales that their products can win on their merits.

Under the pressure to expand sales, however, rival traders sometimes lose sight of the fundamental purposes of advertising. As in an armament race, the more one company spends the more others feel impelled to spend. Cajoling buyers, rather than giving them information, becomes a business in itself—the tail wags the dog. So a legitimate method of spreading information is transformed into a strenuous, and costly, campaign of insistent appeals for patronage.

Far from checking the occasional overemphasis on aggressive selling that develops in a freely competitive market, the growth of giant combines with quasi-monopolistic power appears to be closely associated with the spread of wasteful selling practices. Their relationship is reciprocal: each leads to the other. Two important types of advertising media have exerted a strong pull toward industrial concentration, especially in consumers' goods fields: radio and magazines. They provide a nation-wide coverage. To reap where he has sown—to get the full benefit of his advertising expenditures—the radio or magazine advertiser must have a nation-wide distribution system. And, in some lines, the most effective way to provide it appears to be through a giant multi-plant organization.[28]

A strong monopoly, for example one holding an irrevocable public franchise, has little incentive to spend more on advertising than is necessary to keep consumers informed of prices, qualities, and the uses of its products.[29] But the same cannot be said of giant cor-

---

FTC investigations. See also Peter Hood, *Ourselves and the Press*, John Lane, London, 1939, pp. 175-215; and Joseph Jastrow, *The Betrayal of Intelligence*, Greenberg, New York, 1938, pp. 59-66 and 87-88.

28. General Foods, for example, could hardly afford to use radio and magazine advertising media on anything like the scale it does unless its factories and warehouses were sufficiently numerous and dispersed to enable it to supply the potential demand for its products in all parts of the country. In the oil industry the Texas Company appears to have been one of the first units to appreciate the reciprocal advantages of a nation-wide marketing organization and the use of radio and magazine advertising.

29. With or without monopoly power, companies making producers' goods are not likely to spend large sums on advertising. The maxim that it pays to advertise

porations and their satellites operating under conditions of imperfect competition. When for any reason industrial consolidation stops short of complete monopoly, leaving perhaps two or three big companies in the field, as frequently happens, the scale of advertising expenditures is likely to increase rather than diminish.

No Reduction in Selling Expense

An industrial consolidation is unlikely for two main reasons to reduce selling and advertising expenditures in such circumstances. First, under imperfect competition, price cutting is taboo. Blocked either by rational calculation of self-interest or by the concerted pressure of alert trade rivals from that method of going after new business, each of a few large sellers will ordinarily redouble his efforts to get and hold customers by other means. He may emphasize the quality and dependability of his products through direct demonstrations, educational programs, and personal solicitation of orders, all of which call for heavy expenditures on—and usually by—the sales force. But in most cases an "imperfect competitor" finds a large-scale advertising campaign the surest way of holding his customers or attracting new buyers.

Businessmen themselves recognize that the development of stabilization programs and an *esprit de corps* among a few large producers operating in imperfectly competitive markets tends to divert the pressure of competition from prices to service and salesmanship. For example, when the Big Brothers of the cement industry finally prevailed on those in ultimate control of the Aetna Portland Cement Company, represented by an absentee-president, Mr. F. R. Johnson, to discharge its general manager and sales manager because they had been persistent "chiselers," the more cooperative manager who replaced them frankly declared that keeping up sales volume under

applies more particularly to consumers' goods industries. The reason is that impulse, habit, and emulation greatly influence consumer purchases. Producers, on the other hand, ordinarily buy on the basis of certified technical information, careful tests, or detailed specifications.

Of late years some giant industrial consolidations in producers' goods fields have started to advertise on a fairly extensive scale, both on the radio and in general circulation magazines. But an increase of sales is not the primary aim of such programs; rather it is to develop smoother public relations, a public opinion more hospitable to big business. Moreover, the scale of expenditures on such programs is dwarfed by the huge sums spent by manufacturers of cosmetics, cigarettes, and automobiles to cultivate consumer good will.

the new dispensation entailed larger selling costs. The Federal Trade Commission reports the incident as follows:

> In a report to Mr. Johnson dated May 7, 1937, Mr. Calvin [the new manager] stated: '. . . we are now merchandising our cement according to the ethics of the industry' and explained that this involved the employment of additional salesmen because he was 'in the process of getting business on a new basis . . .' [30]

The second reason for reliance on advertising and sales promotion campaigns by imperfect competitors is that in this way they can most effectively keep out potential new competitors. The comparatively high prices and large profits that result from imperfect competition tend to attract new enterprises. Direct obstruction of them is legally risky and, if discovered, is likely to generate popular sympathy for the interloper and obloquy for the vested interests. But a less dangerous and equally effective way of making entrance to the industry difficult, and therefore unattractive, is to bind consumers to established brands. By liberal advertising appropriations the giant consolidations build consumer good will, channelize consumer tastes, make buying habits inflexible; in short, they place practically insurmountable hurdles before a new small-scale enter-

30. *In re Cement Institute, et al.,* 37 FTC Decisions 87 (1943), at pp. 190-91. "Big Brothers" is a term members of the industry use to refer to the five exceptionally large companies of which control is centered in eastern financial circles. These companies are: Universal, Lehigh, Lone Star, Penn-Dixie, and Alpha. *Ibid.,* pp. 142 and 190.

For further discussion of the way monopolistic competition works in the cement industry, see Chap. 7.

Economists use a variety of less colorful terms to describe industry members occupying a position comparable to that of the cement industry's Big Brothers, e.g., "cooperating oligopolists" or "conforming imperfect competitors." To avoid such cumbersome terms, this study will sometimes use "monopoly partners" as a rough equivalent. This term describes a market relationship among a small, compact group of sellers working together or along parallel lines with or without express mutual commitments to do so. Though no formal partnership agreement binds together the few big sellers in such groups, they act with the mutual consideration that partners tend to show toward one another. As the gist of the partnership is subordination of the separate interests of the several members to the interests of the firm as a unit, so the essence of an oligopolistic consortium is the subordination of competitive interests to group interests. In both cases the "binder" is *collective* long-run advantage; the pursuit of maximum short-run gain by *any one* of the partners, or by any one of the oligopolists, would upset the applecart.

While the analogy is not perfect, in their basic features the two relationships are so similar that the term "monopoly partners" is clearly appropriate for concerting oligopolists. Actual situations in many manufacturing industries conform closely to the partnership pattern, frequently with one big company occupying the position of senior partner, two or three others acting as junior partners, and a few smaller producers playing the role of silent partners.

prise.[31] So, in practice, industrial concentration offers little prospect of abating wasteful advertising and high-cost distribution.

Financial Forces Behind Industrial Concentration

The possibilities of obtaining financial advantages from the consolidation of independent enterprises in giant corporations are of two main kinds, and both have fostered the concentration movement. The first is the profits, fees, or commissions that financiers get for launching such consolidations and for serving thereafter as their financial agents, advisers, or even rulers. The second is the genuine economic saving that comes from the ability of a very large enterprise to obtain funds on favorable terms in the capital market.

Size itself is one factor influencing the acceptability of a company's securities in the financial markets. The securities of a big, well-known company appeal more strongly to investors than those of a small, obscure enterprise, partly at least because investors are more familiar with its record and so in a better position to estimate the risk.

The difference in the ease of access of big companies and small companies to the capital market is reflected in the terms accorded them. One computation covering registered security flotations in the first half of 1937 shows that preferred stock issues amounting each to less than a million dollars bore an expense ratio averaging 16.5 per cent, while for issues amounting each to a million dollars or more the average expense ratio was 7.7 per cent.[32] Bond issues amounting each to less than a million dollars cost the borrowers, on the average, 8.8 per cent of the proceeds of the loan, while for those amounting to a million dollars or more the average flotation cost was only 3.7 per cent. Economy in obtaining funds is an incentive to grow big and a means of remaining big.

The first kind of financial advantage is of doubtful benefit to either the large company or the national economy. It is largely a matter of pecuniary gain to the financial interests concerned. But it serves,

31. Cf. E. A. G. Robinson, *Monopoly,* Nisbet & Co., London, 1941, p. 140.

32. See J. L. Nicholson, "The Fallacy of Easy Money," *Harvard Business Review,* Autumn 1938, pp. 31-34. See also Securities and Exchange Commission, Tenth Annual Report, *A Ten Year Survey, 1934-1944,* Washington, 1945, p. 21 and Table 2, p. 225. The Commission publishes annually data on costs of *equity* security flotations, arranged according to assets-size of issuer. But these official compilations omit issues by companies with total assets of more than $5 million. Hence they are not directly comparable with the figures cited in the text.

nevertheless, as a highly effective stimulus to industrial concentration. The prospect of a promoter's fee, limited—because of secrecy of negotiations—only by what the traffic will bear and his modesty in assessing the value of his own services, has been the main incentive behind the merger movement in many an industry. The heads of long-established family businesses are often reluctant to sell out, and the promoter may have to work hard in many cases to persuade them to do so. Still, the scale of remuneration for merger promoters frequently looks excessive.

Financing Fees

J. P. Morgan & Company may have earned its fee of some $12.5 million for organizing United States Steel. The even greater profit that Dillon Read & Company presumably made on the Dodge-Chrysler merger may have been little enough in view of the substantial business success of the resultant consolidation.[33] But the fact remains that the services rendered, however onerous on the one hand or conducive to higher profits on the other, were not priced in a free and open market.

Again, an investment banking house that has fathered an industrial consolidation usually manages to maintain close links with its offspring, whether by contract, by voting trust agreement, by the reservation of stock with special voting privileges, or simply by cultivation of mutuality of interests through representation on the board of directors.[34] Once a banking house has established a prior claim to act as financial counsellor and agent for a big merger, it is in a position to arrange the terms of refunding operations, new stock

33. See U.S. Bureau of Corporations, *Report on the Steel Industry,* Washington, 1911, Pt. 1, p. 244. In the Dodge reorganization in 1925 Dillon Read & Company retained for itself as part of its compensation 650,000 out of 1,500,000 shares of Class A stock and all the Class B stock (500,000 shares), which alone had voting power. The Class B stock had no market, of course, but as it gave control of the company it undoubtedly provided the leverage which resulted in highly favorable terms of exchange—for its holders, i.e., for Dillon Read—in the Dodge-Chrysler merger three years later.

If Dillon Read continued until the merger to hold the Dodge Class A stock it received in 1925 as well as all the Class B stock, by selling immediately after the merger in July 1928 the Chrysler stock issued in exchange for these securities it could have realized a profit of roughly $13.5 million. If it held the Chrysler stock until the end of the year and then sold it, its profit was $22.5 million. On these transactions, see W. Z. Ripley, *Main Street and Wall Street,* Little, Brown, Boston, 1927, pp. 87 ff. and 200 ff.; and *Moody's Manual of Investments,* 1929, pp. 1133-35.

34. See National Resources Committee, *The Structure of the American Economy,* Washington, 1939, Pt. 1, Chap. 9 and Apps. XI and XIII.

issues, reorganization plans, and the like without effective check or hindrance.[35] Although the Securities and Exchange Commission has since April 1941 required competitive bidding on all securities issued by companies subject to the Public Utility Holding Company Act and in recent years the Interstate Commerce Commission has stipulated competitive marketing of railroad bonds, noncompetitive bidding is still the general rule in financing large industrial corporations.[36]

The commissions that investment bankers obtain under such circumstances are likely to be liberal. Since 1906 the House of Morgan has had an exclusive, or "proprietary," interest in American Telephone and Telegraph financing.[37] From 1905 to 1940, its gross commissions for marketing the security issues of this single company amounted to $45,991,766.[38] It grossed even more from launching one of the biggest mergers in the 1920's. A Senate committee described the deal thus:

> J. P. Morgan & Co. received 1,514,200 option warrants on United Corporation stock for which they paid $1 each. Within 60 days thereafter, J. P. Morgan & Co. was in a position to sell these warrants in the market at a minimum price of $40 for a total profit of over $68,000,000.[39]

The Influence of Complexity

Apparently no comprehensive study has ever been made of the costs, either direct or indirect, of banker management of American industrial consolidations. But the evidence amassed by the Pecora investigation of stock exchange practices shows plainly that these costs have been great.[40] Within the labyrinthine corporate structure

35. See Securities and Exchange Commission, *Report on the Study and Investigation of the Work Activities and Personnel of Protective and Reorganization Committees,* Washington, 1938, Pt. 7; and *Investigation of the Concentration of Economic Power,* Temporary National Economic Committee, Hearings pursuant to Pub.Res. 113 (75th Cong.), Pt. 24, "Investment Banking," pp. 12343-681. (These hearings will hereinafter be cited: TNEC Hearings, Pt. —.)

36. *Ibid.,* pp. 12536-38 and p. 12639; and SEC, Tenth Annual Report, p. 105. In the three years ending June 30, 1944, the average underwriting spread on public utility bond issues floated in accordance with SEC Rule U-50 (the competitive-bidding rule) was reduced to $1.21 per $100. This figure was less than half the average underwriting spread on such issues in the five years prior to the adoption of Rule U-50. *Ibid.,* pp. 106-07.

37. See TNEC Hearings, Pt. 23, pp. 11829-994, especially pp. 11875 ff.

38. *Ibid.,* p. 12218.

39. *Stock Exchange Practices,* Report of the Committee on Banking and Currency, S.Rept. 1455, 73d Cong., 2d sess., Washington, June 16, 1934, p. 115.

40. See *Stock Exchange Practices,* Hearings before the Committee on Banking and

of giant combines, with holding company piled on holding company, and the whole overlaid by a complex network of investment banking tie-ups, "insiders" can play hide and seek with other people's money. The opportunities for financial manipulation and other malpractices are many.

The testimony of Owen D. Young on this point is conclusive.[41] The chairman of the board of the General Electric Company was asked about the organization of the Insull group of companies, one of the public utility "empires" that were so prominent a part of the merger movement of the 1920's. He replied:

> Well, I confess to a feeling of helplessness as I began to examine . . . the complicated structure of that organization. . . . Great numbers of operating utilities, with holding companies superimposed on those holding companies, investment companies and affiliates, which made it, as I thought then and think now, impossible for any man however able really to grasp the real situation. . . . I would say it was so set up that it was impossible really for anyone to comprehend its entire aspect; and it was so set up that you could not possibly get an accounting system which would not mislead even the officers themselves of that complicated structure.

While corporate pyramiding was carried further among public utilities than in almost any other field,[42] the development of huge consolidations in manufacturing industries gave opportunities for inside manipulation on a scale hardly less spectacular.[43] Before he became a member of the Supreme Court, Mr. Justice Douglas listed

---

Currency, U.S. Senate, 73d Cong., 1st and 2d sess., on S.Res. 84 (72d Cong.), and S.Res. 56 and S.Res. 97 (73d Cong.), Pts. 1-20, Washington, 1933–1934. (The Committee's counsel was Mr. Ferdinand Pecora, and the hearings will hereinafter be cited: Pecora Investigation, Pt. —.)

41. See *Stock Exchange Practices,* Hearings before a Subcommittee of the Committee on Banking and Currency, U.S. Senate, 72d Cong., 2d sess., on S.Res. 84 and S.Res. 239, Pt. 5, Washington, 1933, pp. 1515-16. These hearings, in six parts, were on the same subject as the Pecora Investigation; but in the 72d Congress the Committee had a different counsel, Mr. William A. Gray. (The hearings in the 72d Congress will hereinafter be cited: Gray Investigation, Pt. —.)

42. An outstanding exception was the match industry. On the Kreuger & Toll setup and the astounding frauds to which it led, see *ibid.,* Pt. 4. The Federal Trade Commission assembled a mass of authentic information on public utility consolidations and the evils that resulted therefrom. See *Utility Corporations,* Report of the Federal Trade Commission pursuant to S.Res. 83, 70th Cong., 1st sess., S.Doc. 92, Pts. 1-84C, Washington, 1928–1935. Parts 72A and 73A of this report contain summary descriptions and analyses of the "questionable practices" that the investigation uncovered.

43. See, for example, the record of undercover deals and inside manipulation in Anaconda Copper and Fox Films, Gray Investigation, Pt. 3, and in Radio Corporation of America and Warner Bros. Pictures, *ibid.,* Pt. 2. Also, on the disregard of investors' interests by banking interests, in the Hoe & Co. and the Cuban Cane Sugar reorganizations, see SEC, *Report on . . . Protective and Reorganization Committees,* previously cited, Pt. 6, pp. 83-100.

some of the more common types of chicanery that flourish behind the corporate veil when industrial enterprises are amalgamated in giant combines with diffused ownership and highly concentrated control.

> Recent court records and Senate hearings are replete with specific and illustrative material—secret loans to officers and directors, undisclosed profit-sharing plans, timely contracts unduly favorable to affiliated interests, dividend policies based on false estimates, manipulations of credit resources and capital structures to the detriment of minority interests, pool operations, and trading in securities of the company by virtue of inside information, to mention only a few.[44]

Such abuses were so common and so flagrant in public utility mergers that Congress in 1935 passed the Public Utility Holding Company Act to stop them.[45] The law required simplification of the corporate structure of the sprawling combinations that had developed in this field. It also subjected all their loan, engineering and management service, and construction contracts to the scrutiny of the Securities and Exchange Commission, which was empowered to establish and enforce suitable standards for such transactions. But outside this special field the formation and administration of mergers has proceeded, by and large, according to the decisions of small groups of financial interests that control the merging corporations though they provide, as a rule, no more than a small fraction of the investment.[46] The discretion of these "control groups" remains very wide in practice, despite the Securities and Exchange Act of 1934 regulating security flotations and imposing formal curbs on manipulation of security prices through self-interested transactions of officers and directors with inside information.[47]

44. William O. Douglas, "Directors Who Do Not Direct," *Harvard Law Review*, June 1934, p. 1306.

45. 49 Stat.L. 803 (1935).

46. See Chap. 13; also Marshall E. Dimmock, *Bureaucracy and Trusteeship in Large Corporations*, TNEC Monograph No. 11, Washington, 1940, especially Pt. 1.

47. 48 Stat.L. 881 (1934). On the broad powers of "control groups" in large corporations with widely diffused stockholdings, see R. A. Gordon, *Business Leadership in the Large Corporation*, The Brookings Institution, Washington, 1945, especially Chaps. 5-9. The American Ice Company's recent dividend record provides an example of the sorts of practices that the directors of big industrial combines can indulge in, apparently with impunity. This consolidation, formed in 1899 in the heyday of the trusts, has never been very successful and from 1932 to 1947 paid no dividends on its common stock. In the eight years before 1947 it paid altogether only $19 a share on its $6 noncumulative preferred stock, though its annual average earnings during these years amounted to $10 a share on the preferred. On January 2, 1947 the directors declared a dividend of 50 cents a share on the common stock, and three

Plainly, the organization of huge industrial consolidations with an inarticulate mass of scattered, small stockholders created many opportunities for gain by insiders through manipulation of accounts, stock-trading pools, bonus schemes, underwriting deals, and the like. It would be naive to assume that the prospect of such attractive opportunities for easy gain has had no influence in fostering the merger movement. Financiers, like other men, aspire to increase their incomes by lawful means. Since the law has placed no effective barrier to the creation of these opportunities for large profits or to their exploitation, the investment bankers have done what comes naturally. These financial forces for a half century were among the most powerful stimuli promoting concentration of industrial control.

Strategic Forces Behind Industrial Consolidation

Probably the most persistent and pervasive influence fostering growth in the size of business units has been the quest for power to control the market. The fewer the sellers the greater is the possibility of stabilizing prices, restricting output, curtailing investment—and maximizing profits. In the heyday of "trust" formation monopoly gains in one form or another were an avowed purpose of most consolidations. Though the architects who have been busily adding more floors and new wings to the big-business structure since World War II may speak in terms of "expansion" and "rounding out the picture," the primary objective of industrial consolidation remains the same. It is market power.

The urge to achieve a strong strategic position in the market has many roots. Personal prestige may accrue to the promoter of a giant merger and his successors are prone to emulate the founder. In some fields such considerations carry more weight than in others. The Shuberts may stay backstage in the theatre, perhaps recalling Shakespeare's question, "What's in a name?" But the motion-picture industry glamorizes its business titans no less than its stars. Not big money alone accounts for the operations of the Warners, the Mayers, and the Foxes. The erection of pyramids, modern as well as ancient, is partly just monument building.

---

months later passed the dividend on the preferred. See *Standard and Poor's Corporation Records,* 1947, and comment in the *New York Sun,* April 23, 1947.

On the other hand, the evidence suggests that while the search for strategic advantage has been a powerful stimulus to consolidation in the distilling industry, the thirst for personal prestige has played little part in prompting that search. Here, as elsewhere commonly, the consolidation movement apparently owes more to a strictly business calculation of profit-making possibilities.[48]

In most lines of industry modern technology entails large fixed-capital investment. This increases the risks of competitive pricing. Price cuts are likely to lead to price wars. And price wars are not conducive to high profits. Mergers reduce the likelihood of price cutting by reducing the number of sellers. A merger big enough to influence prices can exercise a stabilizing influence in the market. Rational behavior on the part of consolidated enterprises counsels against "weak selling"; it calls for shunning price cuts and encouraging price increases.

"Big-Brother" Leadership

The bigger the business, the wider and more effective will be its influence as a pacemaker in the industry. Smaller rivals have many good reasons for following its leadership in restricting supply and holding up prices. First and foremost, it pays. Though it means renouncing aggressive ambitions, it promises a more dependable share in a more profitable market. If consolidation continues, bringing together in three or four giant corporations a preponderant part of the productive facilities in an industry, the advantage of following identical pricing policies becomes plainer still. The merging of business competitors need not go so far as complete unification, 100 per cent monopoly, to reduce competitive pressures—and yield extra profits. Power to restrict supply and raise prices need not be absolute to be worth while. It helps to insure profits if the number of sellers is so small that each will recognize the benefits of following a live-and-let-live policy.[49]

Another good reason for general acceptance of "big-brother" leadership, thus reinforcing the ability of a giant corporation to

48. On the rise of National Distillers Products Corporation, for example, see Pecora Investigation, Pt. 14, pp. 6247-74.

49. For a more detailed discussion of these practices and the principles involved, see the next two chapters.

stabilize its markets, is the police power that size confers. Though the gloved hand has long since displaced the mailed fist as the symbol of industrial discipline, the fist is still there, and no small-scale producer is likely to be left unaware of its presence if he rashly adopts an independent course, that is to say, a vigorously competitive policy. The power that a large combination, operating in the whole breadth and length of the market, possesses to harass and, it may be, destroy a recalcitrant producer is still formidable. Its ability to get secret rebates or preferential favors from the railroads, like those on which Standard Oil rose to unchallenged mastery, has been checkmated by the Interstate Commerce Commission; but discriminatory discounts and allowances to big buyers, unrelated to demonstrable cost savings, still persist despite their prohibition by the Robinson-Patman Act.[50] Exclusive dealing arrangements, such as those by which United Shoe Machinery, Corn Products Refining, and International Harvester drove out competitors, have been outlawed by the Clayton Act; but after thirty-five years exclusive dealerships were still common in the oil industry.[51]

Although local price cutting, which American Tobacco and National Cash Register used so ruthlessly in their march to monopoly, was forbidden more than thirty years ago by the Clayton Act, geographic price discrimination survived under various types of delivered-price systems. And even exclusionary local price cutting has been used in some quarters apparently, for example in the practice of the Big Five cement companies of imposing punitive bases on independent mills that failed to follow the rules of the industry's basing point system.[52]

Certain other predatory tactics are even less susceptible of effective suppression by direct attack. By flimsy charges of patent infringement, leading to expensive litigation, a large combination with ample financial reserves can severely handicap a small independent strug-

50. See, for example, *U.S.* v. *New York Great Atlantic & Pacific Tea Co.,* 67 Fed. Supp. 626 (1946); affirmed, 173 Fed. *2d* 79 (1949).

51. See *U.S.* v. *Standard Oil Co. (Calif.)*, 78 Fed.Supp. 850 (1948); affirmed, 337 U.S. 293 (1949). For earlier cases condemning exclusive dealing contracts, see *Standard Fashion Co.* v. *Magrane-Houston Co.,* 258 U.S. 346 (1922); and *Butterick Co.* v. *FTC,* 4 Fed. *2d* 910 (1925); certiorari denied, 267 U.S. 602 (1925).

52. See *In re Cement Institute, et al.,* 37 FTC Decisions 87 (1943), at pp. 178-91; and *FTC* v. *Cement Institute,* 333 U.S. 683 (1948). For a discussion of this case, see Chap. 7.

gling to get established.[53] Cutting off supplies of essential materials is another device that industry leaders, backed by close affiliations with related industries through investment banking tie-ups, can employ to hinder uncooperative rivals.[54]

By and large, however, the resort to disciplinary tactics is seldom necessary. If the leading firms of an industry avoid aggressiveness and show suitable self-restraint on their own part, they may be able to count on the active cultivation of like-mindedness among organized trade groups to maintain noncompetitive prices in the market. This is the kernel of the strategic advantage that industrial consolidation gives, and beyond doubt the lure of such market power goes far to explain the scope and persistence of the consolidation movement.

53. On the use of such tactics by Hartford Empire Co. in the glass container industry, see TNEC Hearings, Pt. 2, pp. 419-569. See also *General Electric Co.* v. *Wabash Appliance Corp.*, 304 U.S. 364 (1938); and *General Electric Co.* v. *Jewel Incandescent Co.*, 146 Fed. *2d* 414 (1944); affirmed, 326 U.S. 242 (1945). For further evidence of practices of this kind, see Chap. 14.

54. On Henry J. Kaiser's difficulties in obtaining steel for Kaiser-Frazer and his allegation of a surreptitious "squeeze," see *New York Times*, March 6, 1946, p. 1.

Chapter 4

COMPETITION IN MARKETS OF FEW SELLERS: THE THEORY

THE COMBINATION MOVEMENT wrought three significant changes in the American economy between 1890 and 1940: (1) it vastly increased the size of business firms; (2) it increased the extent of the market within which each sold; and (3) it greatly reduced the number of sellers in many markets. Whatever the relative importance of the forces behind the movement, whether the chief impetus came from a drive for the economies of mass production or from a quest for control of markets, the movement led to the giant corporation that typically achieved its dominant position by combining business rivals under a single corporate control.

Although somewhat similar developments took place simultaneously in other industrial countries,[1] economists generally continued for a long time to accept without further analysis the theory of neoclassical economics as an explanation of market behavior and as a guide to public policy. They generally wrote as though competition were the normal market situation, monopoly the exception, and as though both competition and monopoly were always pure. For a considerable interval price theorists were undisturbed by economic realities.

Economists Re-examine Price Theory

Within the past twenty-five years, however, all this has changed. As students of industrial organization threw more light on the structure of the modern economy and the role of the big business unit in it,[2] price theorists re-examined the assumptions of neoclassical economics and tried to harmonize theory with industrial facts. As

1. For a brief discussion of developments elsewhere, particularly in England and Germany, see *Cartels or Competition?*, Chaps. 1 and 2.
2. See particularly Adolf A. Berle, Jr., and Gardiner C. Means, *The Modern Corporation and Private Property*, Macmillan, New York, 1932.

early as 1926 Sraffa argued that monopoly, not free competition, was the normal market situation and indicated the significance of this alleged fact for pricing policies.[3] A decade later Burns contended that "Elements of monopoly . . . can no longer be regarded as occasional and relatively unimportant aberrations from competition." [4] Meanwhile, Chamberlin [5] and Mrs. Robinson,[6] independently but on a basis of similar assumptions, restated and refined neoclassical theory. In doing so they made an important contribution to the methodology of economics by focussing analysis on the conduct of the individual firm rather than the industry and in their use of the marginal revenue curve (expressing the additional revenue derived from successive increments of output, or sales).[7] Chamberlin, in analyzing the significance of product differentiation, also brought merchandising and advertising within the scope of price theory, and focussed attention on the economic forces tending to maintain equilibrium within a group of competing quasi-monopolists. It was his analysis of pricing in markets of few sellers (usually referred to in the literature as oligopoly), however, that brought to light significant aspects of the growth of big business that had not previously been noticed or, at any rate, aroused public concern.

3. Piero Sraffa, "The Laws of Returns Under Competitive Conditions," *Economic Journal*, December 1926, pp. 535-50. So remote from reality were the theorists' conceptions that Sraffa said of price theory (pp. 535-36): "It is essentially a pedagogic instrument, somewhat like the study of the classics, and, unlike the study of the exact sciences and law, its purposes are exclusively those of training the mind, for which reason it is hardly apt to excite the passions of men, even academic men—a theory, in short, in respect to which it is not worth while departing from a tradition which is finally accepted."

4. Arthur R. Burns, *The Decline of Competition*, McGraw-Hill, New York, 1936, p. 3.

5. Edward Chamberlin, *The Theory of Monopolistic Competition*, Harvard University Press, Cambridge, 1933.

6. Joan Robinson, *The Economics of Imperfect Competition*, Macmillan, London, 1933.

7. Both Chamberlin's and Mrs. Robinson's theoretical views are frequently referred to as "the theory of imperfect competition." Chamberlin protests this, and on good grounds. (See Chamberlin, *op. cit.*, 5th edition, Chap. 9.) Mrs. Robinson treats monopoly and competition as mutually exclusive. Chamberlin, on the other hand, thinks elements of monopoly and competition are intermingled in all modern business. He regards oligopoly, with or without product differentiation, and product differentiation, with many or few sellers, as constituting monopolistic competition. However, theoretical economics while abandoning the old dichotomy of competition and monopoly is recognizing a new one: (1) few sellers of a standardized product (oligopoly); and (2) sellers of differentiated products, whether few or many (monopolistic competition). This study uses "imperfect competition" to cover both these categories. See footnote 8, Chap. 1.

Many Kinds of Markets

Between the theoretical poles of pure competition and pure monopoly are many real kinds of industrial markets. In 1939 Westinghouse Air Brake made three out of every four air brakes in America; New York Air Brake made the fourth. International Business Machines made 85 per cent of the electrically driven card-punching, sorting, and accounting machines; Remington Rand made the rest. In 1935, Pittsburgh Plate Glass and Libbey-Owens-Ford Glass made 95 per cent of the plate glass; only two other companies made plate glass for sale. From 1924 to World War II the Texas Gulf Sulphur Company and the Freeport Sulphur Company produced 90 per cent of the domestic sulphur sold in the American market.[8]

On the other hand, 545 manufacturers in 1937 made one-piece dresses to retail for $2 or more and the four largest producers made only 3.1 per cent of the total; 1,256 mills produced corn meal and the four largest made only 19.5 per cent of the total. Among the manufacturing industries making products valued at more than $10 million, there were 48 in which the four largest companies produced less than one quarter of the total output.[9]

The New Doctrines

No industry conforms fully to either the competitive or the monopolistic model. In many American industries, ordinarily regarded as competitive, competition is far from pure; and in others, commonly regarded as monopolistic, monopoly is far from complete. Recognizing this fact, Chamberlin expressed his dissatisfaction with the "perfection and refinement of a separate body of theory" for monopoly and competition, and argued that "association of the theory of competition with facts which it does not fit has not only led to false conclusions about the facts; it has obscured the theory as well." [10] Believing that a "condition of monopoly shades gradually into one of pure competition as the sellers increase in number," [11] Chamberlin undertook to develop more realistic and adequate

8. Clair Wilcox, *Competition and Monopoly in American Industry,* TNEC Monograph No. 21, Washington, 1940, pp. 103-09.
9. *Ibid.,* p. 30.
10. Chamberlin, *op. cit.,* p. 3.
11. *Ibid.,* p. 8.

theories of price determination in markets intermediate between pure monopoly and pure competition, the theories of oligopoly and monopolistic competition. His distinctive contribution to the theory of oligopoly is that each seller of a standardized commodity, when rational and fully informed, must "take account of his *total* influence upon the price, indirect as well as direct,"[12] if he is to maximize his profit. Assuming that he does take account of his total influence, Chamberlin concluded that a "monopoly price" will result. "Independence of the producers and the pursuit of their self-interest are not sufficient to lower it. Only if the number is large enough to render negligible the effect of an adjustment by any one upon each of the others is the equilibrium price the purely competitive one."[13]

Textbook writers soon incorporated Chamberlin's analysis in their "principles" and all too easily drew the uncritical conclusion that, so far as price was concerned, as between oligopoly and pure monopoly it was "six of one and half a dozen of the other."[14] This was the aspect of Chamberlinian doctrine expounded to undergraduates throughout the land. But it was another aspect that interested the legal fraternity: its emphasis on the sufficiency of self-interest among oligopolists to insure a stable price above the purely competitive level, *without collusion.* This phase of Chamberlin's theory became a standard defense in antitrust proceedings where price leadership,

12. *Ibid.,* p. 46.

13. *Ibid.,* p. 54. Though not explicitly so stated, the implication is that the equilibrium price under the conditions postulated will be that of a complete (single-seller) monopoly. At best, this result could obtain only on the rigid assumptions specified, including the one that each of the few sellers possesses perfect knowledge of the market—is "*fully* informed." A theory built on the assumption that sellers are omniscient obviously has a very tenuous relation to reality. Actually, Chamberlin himself (*ibid.,* pp. 50-53) recognizes qualifications that are sufficient to suggest that in actual markets of few sellers the perfect monopoly solution is likely to be rare *if sellers act independently.*

In discussing the "Elements of Uncertainty" that confront each of a few sellers acting independently, he notes, among others, uncertainty as to the degree of intelligence and farsightedness of rivals and as to how promptly the rivals will react to a move as they rationally should. Concerning the latter element of uncertainty, Chamberlin acknowledges that "Under these circumstances, no assumption as to the intelligence which the sellers apply to the pursuit of their maximum gain, *short of omniscience,* would render the outcome determinate." *Ibid.,* p. 53. Italics supplied.

14. See, for example, M. J. Bowman and G. L. Bach, *Economic Analysis and Public Policy,* Prentice-Hall, New York, 1943; John Ise, *Economics,* Harper, New York, 1946; F. R. Fairchild, E. S. Furniss, and N. S. Buck, *Elementary Economics,* Macmillan, New York, 1943. Perhaps Triffin has not greatly exaggerated in saying that "the most revolutionary feature of the monopolistic competition theories will probably be the unprecedented pace at which they conquered their audience." Robert Triffin, *Monopolistic Competition and General Equilibrium Theory,* Harvard University Press, Cambridge, 1940, p. 17.

basing point practices, trade association activities, and the like were challenged as indications of restraint of trade.

In several such cases economists were found who testified that common pricing policies followed by business rivals were consistent with complete independence of action and afforded no basis for the conclusion that defendants had conspired to restrain trade or to monopolize markets within the meaning of the antitrust laws. However, these witnesses used only part of the Chamberlinian argument.[15] While contending that conspiracy is not essential to common pricing policies in markets where sellers are few (oligopoly), they failed to point out that according to the theory of oligopoly the results in price terms tended to approach those of pure monopoly. A summary of the Chamberlin theory of oligopolistic pricing is necessary to make clear its policy implications.

Price Making in Oligopoly Markets

Where sellers are few and relatively large, each has power over the market similar to that of a monopolist but different in degree. Like a monopolist, each can influence price by increasing or decreasing output. If each of two sellers in a market shared equally reduces or increases his output by 10 per cent, for example, they can exert the same influence on price that a monopolist might exert by a like reduction or increase of output. Moreover, on a change in market conditions that would indicate to a pure monopolist the profitability of reducing or increasing output by a certain percentage, self-interest

15. As witnesses for the defense they had no other choice. After his experience as a consultant in the Cement Institute case, Clark recognized the practical impossibility of avoiding the compromising effect of testimony thus elicited. He said:

"I agree that the state of the economist as expert witness wants improving, whichever side he testifies for, . . .

"Aside from any warping of the personal attitude of the witness, there is the fact that his testimony is limited by the highly selective list of questions he is asked. For this there is no easy antidote.

"But perhaps the clinching difficulty is that if a witness employed by one side should somehow manage to include in his testimony a balanced array of points favorable to both sides, it would have the effect of testifying for the opposing side in the most damaging possible way. This is because whatever he said favorable to his own side would be discounted as not impartial, while whatever he said favorable to the other side would tend to be regarded as conclusive, being in a sense an 'admission contrary to interest.' For this reason the most impartial-minded witness accepts the fact that his testimony must inevitably be limited to answering questions aimed to bring out those portions of his sincere convictions which fit his employer's case. If a code of ethics should be completely successful so far as the witness's personal attitude is concerned, this difficulty would remain." J. M. Clark, "Imperfect Competition Theory and Basing-Point Problems," *American Economic Review*, June 1943, pp. 299-300.

would lead each of the two sellers to reduce or increase his output in the same proportion.[16]

In markets where sellers are few, each in trying to determine his most profitable volume of output must, as would a monopolist, consider the probable effects of various possible rates of production not only on costs, but also on prices. Indeed, each seller will ordinarily decide on the price at which he will sell and adjust his output accordingly, just as a monopolist does. Each oligopolist, however, in determining his price must consider not merely his own cost-price relationships, but also how his rivals will react to his prices. Any one of a few sellers, if fully informed and perfectly rational, when selling a completely standardized product will realize that if he reduces his price his rivals will meet the lower price promptly.

If the total demand for the product is relatively inelastic,[17] it would be unprofitable for any seller to reduce the price. For with consumers buying so little more at the lower price that they spend less for the product than they had been spending at the old price, the price cutter will find himself sharing with his rivals a smaller dollar volume of business in about the same proportions as before the price reduction. Reducing the price under such circumstances does not pay. When sellers know this, as in Chamberlin's hypothetical model they are presumed to know it, they will refrain from price reductions, making such reductions in output during periods of slack demand as may be necessary to forestall lower prices.

In theory, then, where a few sellers share a market each will seek to maximize his net revenue and a monopoly price will tend to result. In trying to make as much money as possible each will increase output as long as doing so adds more to his revenues than to his costs. But each will stabilize production at the point where marginal cost and marginal revenue are equalized.

According to this logic, from the standpoint of consumers there is

16. The possibility that the two sellers might react differently to the change in market conditions is ruled out by the rigid assumptions of Chamberlin's theoretical model. In practice, of course, different interpretations of the same basic data would be quite conceivable.

17. Elasticity of demand is a technical concept. It refers to the extent to which all buyers will change the amount they spend for a product with changes in its price. If consumers so respond to price changes for a particular product that their total expenditures for it remain constant regardless of price, demand has an elasticity of unity. If with price decreases they together spend more and with price increases they spend less, demand is elastic; if with price decreases they spend less and with price increases they spend more, demand is inelastic.

little to choose between oligopolistic price policies and those of a monopolist. As can a monopolist, so each of a few sellers in a market can appreciably affect price by varying output. Each, of course, must not only take account of his rivals' probable reactions to price changes; each must recognize as well that lowering prices and selling more units may not increase total revenues proportionately to the greater number of units sold—or at all.[18] He therefore tends to keep his marginal cost below his average revenue (price) by restricting output. By doing so he may make a monopoly profit. But even if demand is insufficiently inelastic to permit the price to be raised—without substantially affecting the volume of sales—to a point above average costs, he will get a noncompetitive return.

To the extent that they behave as they are presumed to behave in the Chamberlinian model, oligopolists will always get a price above marginal cost. They will always restrict output below the competitive, cost-indemnifying level. Other things being equal, society gets less and pays more for what it gets than it would were oligopolists to follow the policy, "irrational" for them, of carrying production to a point where the cost of producing additional units of output equalled the price received for them.[19] In this respect, oligopoly works adversely to the general welfare.

18. Chamberlin does not explain precisely how oligopolists will react to price increases, but he implies that through a series of moves they will settle on a uniform price that will maximize the profits of each. He says (*op. cit.*, p. 46): "When a move by one seller evidently forces the other to make a counter-move, he is very stupidly refusing to look further than his nose if he proceeds on the assumption that it will not." Paul Sweezy has argued that oligopolists will follow price cuts, but may not follow price advances. Uncertainty about this creates a "kink" in the demand curve confronting an oligopolist and makes for stable prices somewhat below the monopoly level. See Paul Sweezy, "Demand Under Conditions of Oligopoly," *Journal of Political Economy*, August 1939.

19. The above is a simplified summary of the theory of oligopolistic pricing as developed by Chamberlin and his followers. It sacrifices precision for simplicity. Chamberlin recognized, as indicated above, that uncertainty by one oligopolist about the reactions of his principal rivals would upset the theoretical solution. "If now he does not know what assumption to make [regarding rivals' reactions], the conclusion must be that price may be anything between these limits" ("all the way from the equilibrium price" of pure monopoly to that of pure competition). *Op. cit.*, p. 51.

So far as concerns the practical significance of oligopolistic pricing, this appears to be a pretty broad—and damaging—concession. In any event, economists now rather generally agree with the view, to which Chamberlin presumably would subscribe as do the authors of this study, that in practice the solution to pricing in markets supplied by a few large sellers depends on the assumptions each makes regarding the reactions of the others to his moves. Uncertainty about rivals' conduct, be it noted, is a problem that does not trouble a monopolist at all—a consideration that by itself suffices to impede severely the "approach" to monopoly pricing by oligopolists. In the absence of concerted action, oligopolists may make price adjustments very similar to those competitors would make. See Chap. 5.

The New Doctrines and Public Policy

Such, in brief, was the theory of price making in markets with only a few sellers. The theory obviously had significant implications for public policy toward the organization and control of industry. Some economists, assuming that the concentration of output in only a few firms was primarily a quest for the economies of mass production, concluded that the antitrust laws were obsolete. Burns, bluntly stating that monopoly elements "are such an organic part of the industrial system that it is useless to hope that they can be removed by law," [20] advocated such an extensive system of investment control and management regulation that his most vigorous critic characterized his program as planning for a totalitarian economy.[21] Less fearful of private power and more fearful of what might be the outcome of unrestrained competition among industrial giants are some other economists. For the protection of the public interest, they look in part to the development of a sense of social responsibility among those who possess some power over the market, to the sedulous cultivation of a long-run calculation of the most advantageous pricing policy by these strategically placed businessmen, or to the educational influence of autonomous industry-wide organizations of a quasi-professional character.[22]

But not all students of industrial organization and price making in markets of imperfect competition have acknowledged so readily the inevitability of the concentration of economic power. President Roosevelt reflected the opinion of those who reject this notion when in his message to Congress in April 1938 recommending the creation of the Temporary National Economic Committee he said:

> Private enterprise is ceasing to be free enterprise and is becoming a cluster of private collectivisms . . . One of the primary causes of our present difficulties lies in the disappearance of price competition in many industrial

20. Burns, *op. cit.*, p. 3. For Burns' program, see *ibid.*, Chaps. 11 and 12.

21. Frank A. Fetter, "Planning for Totalitarian Monopoly," *Journal of Political Economy*, 1937, pp. 95-110.

22. See, for example, J. M. Clark, *Alternative to Serfdom*, Knopf, New York, 1948, especially pp. 125-44, Chap. 5; *idem, Guideposts in Time of Change*, Harper, New York, 1949, especially pp. 59-63 and pp. 199-201; and the following publications of The Brookings Institution, Washington: Harold G. Moulton, *Income and Economic Progress* (1935); Edwin G. Nourse and Horace B. Drury, *Industrial Price Policies and Economic Progress* (1938); Edwin G. Nourse, *Price Making in a Democracy* (1944). For a criticism of Nourse's analysis, see the review by George W. Stocking in *American Economic Review*, September 1944, pp. 618-24.

fields, particularly in basic manufacture where concentrated economic power is most evident—and where rigid prices and fluctuating pay rolls are general.[23]

Thurman Arnold, as Assistant Attorney General in charge of the Antitrust Division of the Department of Justice, while striking out against all unreasonable restraints of trade, directed antitrust policy also against the power of bigness. In magazine articles, in public speeches, in radio addresses, and in his *The Bottlenecks of Business,* he tirelessly proclaimed the economic philosophy behind his antitrust campaign.

You may grow as big as you can provided that you can justify the extent of your organized power by showing that it contributes to the efficiency of mass production and distribution. We will protect you against organized groups of small business which attempt to prevent you from giving cheaper goods to the public. We will, on the other hand, attack you if you seek to maintain your system of distribution by using your organized power to prevent experimental developments by others either in production or in distribution or in price policies. Size in itself is not an evil, but it does give power to those who control it. That power must be constantly watched by an adequate enforcement organization to see that it does not destroy a free market.[24]

Arnold would not merely watch big business, he would destroy it if necessary to prevent its exploiting the consumers.[25] And his ideas not only caught the public fancy, they influenced administrative agencies and the courts. The courts eventually accepted the notion that harmonious market behavior, parallel action, price leadership, and the like may afford circumstantial evidence that large concerns have violated Sections 1 and 2 of the Sherman Act.[26]

Economists Challenge the New Doctrines

This attack on bigness brought a prompt reaction among economists. While some, influenced by the theories of imperfect competition, expounded the notion that bigness per se constituted a threat to competitive markets and free enterprise, others re-examined and

23. See *Investigation of the Concentration of Economic Power,* Temporary National Economic Committee, Hearings pursuant to Pub.Res. 113 (75th Cong.), Pt. 1, "Economic Prologue," Appendix, Ex. 1, pp. 186-87.

24. Thurman W. Arnold, *The Bottlenecks of Business,* Harcourt, Brace, New York, 1940, p. 125.

25. Taking the automobile industry as an example, he said, "A free market does mean, however, that Henry Ford's combination should be dissolved or curbed the moment it is not giving consumers the savings which his more efficient methods are capable of producing." *Ibid.,* p. 130.

26. See Chap. 9.

re-evaluated the Chamberlinian doctrines. Among the latter, Galbraith challenged their basic assumptions, alleging that no one can safely generalize about the behavior of oligopolists. As he put it:

> . . . the competitive market only yields to generalization because of the predictability of mass behavior—we have an acceptable and probably quite accurate theory of the competitive market because of the comparative certainty of mass responses to given stimuli . . . motivations to individual behavior, unlike the motivations to mass behavior, are infinitely various . . . When economists came to the market of small numbers from the market of large numbers, with few exceptions they failed to recognize that they had moved into a new world.[27]

Force of Profit-Making Motive

Galbraith is perhaps correct in holding that no one can predict the market behavior of oligopolists. But presumably an oligopolist's market behavior is rational in the sense of being guided primarily by ordinary business calculations of profit and loss. It is recognized, of course, that other considerations frequently have a role in managerial decisions and help to shape business policy. But such motives as paternal solicitude for employees and fiduciary concern for the interests of consumers, however strong they may be in certain individuals or prevalent in certain trades, are hardly comparable to motives of gain in universality and persistence. They are too sporadic, inconstant, and unpredictable to be taken into account in a systematic formulation of basic economic forces.

Moreover, the men who make price and production policies in markets of imperfect competition have been exceptionally conditioned in their responses by a business environment. They live in a society where money making counts for much, and in a sector of that society where it counts for even more. Furthermore, they are frequently linked by a community of interest through investment bankers, lawyers, and accountants who render services to them. Finally, they are at least legally responsible to tens and even hundreds of thousands of stockholders who, as such, have a single aim—the maximization of profits. Although directors are frequently remote from their "bosses," they cannot utterly ignore them. When a vege-

27. J. K. Galbraith, "A Retrospect on Monopoly," an unpublished lecture delivered at the University of Illinois Graduate Seminar, November 1948. See also Galbraith, "Monopoly and the Concentration of Economic Power," in Howard S. Ellis (Ed.), *A Survey of Contemporary Economics*, Blakiston, Philadelphia, 1948, Chap. 3.

tarian director of a leading chain of restaurants sought to cultivate vegetarianism among the restaurants' patrons at the expense of the chain's earnings, indignant stockholders dismissed him. Corporate directors, in determining output and pricing policies, are seldom unresponsive to the will of those who own the business when an occasion arises that stimulates the formation and expression of such a collective "will." [28]

But in any event, to say that policy makers in giant corporations are concerned solely with maximization of earnings is to oversimplify. Business rivalry has some of the qualities of a game of strategy, a battle in a military campaign. The object is to win.[29] Winning in business does not, however, consist merely in getting the better of rivals—that is, making more money or getting a bigger share of the market than any of the others—but in making as much money as possible over the long run.[30]

Inadequate Empirical Basis for the New Doctrines

Other economists question the factual foundations for the theory of oligopoly. They point out that Chamberlin has left out of account characteristics of such markets other than fewness of sellers and differentiation of products. Market structure and behavior in the real world are highly diversified. As Bain contends:

> Oligopoly is an extremely broad category, and within it numerous important differences with respect to characteristics of market structure other

28. Whether Galbraith is right or wrong in questioning the predictability of motives when sellers are few, it does not follow that their actions are predictable. Even though the managers of large firms, like the managers of small, are interested in maximizing earnings, they may not agree on how to do it. Galbraith recognizes this.

29. See John von Neumann and Oskar Morgenstern, *The Theory of Games and Economic Behavior,* Princeton University Press, Princeton, 1944; more to the point, see Oskar Morgenstern, "Oligopoly, Monopolistic Competition, and the Theory of Games," *American Economic Review,* Papers and Proceedings, May 1948, pp. 10-18.

30. Not all economists will agree with this statement. Adelman concludes from his study of the Great Atlantic and Pacific Tea Company that "maximization" of profits in the usual sense has played no role in A & P's pricing policies. As he puts it: "It is then as clear as daylight that they [top management] are striving not for the largest possible profits over the planning period, but for the best possible position at the end of it." M. A. Adelman, *The Dominant Firm* (unpublished doctoral dissertation, Harvard University, 1948), p. 422. Despite Adelman's vigorous contention to the contrary, for the long run this seems to be a distinction without a difference. For a discussion of nonfinancial incentives motivating businessmen, see Robert A. Gordon, *Business Leadership in the Large Corporation,* The Brookings Institution, Washington, 1945, pp. 305-12. See also Frank H. Knight, *The Ethics of Competition,* Harper, New York, 1935, pp. 32 ff.

than numbers may exist. . . . [These structural differences] are very probably associated in one fashion or another with the price behavior which emerges from a particular market. It is not at all impossible that this association is regular and systematic.[31]

But the theorists alone cannot solve the problem of market behavior, according to these critics. Wallace, for instance, declares that:

Existing theory provides few norms of desirable results for work in this field. Such norms can be developed only by giving content and particularity to broad value judgments through further theoretical work and extensive factual study. Study of actual conditions in the market and of policies is imperative . . .[32]

Meanwhile, according to Wallace, we know too little about the character and behavior of industrial markets "to support a comprehensive program of public policy of *any* sort" toward them.[33]

Mason, from whom some of these ideas seem to stem, views all markets as compounds of competition and monopoly and regards some features of both elements as socially advantageous. He argues that the formulation of public policy requires a distinction between situations and practices, whether competitive or monopolistic, that are in the public interest and those that are not.[34]

31. And in Bain's view it is the theorists' job to "elicit this association and to propound an adequate system of hypotheses describing it." Joe S. Bain, "Market Classifications in Modern Price Theory," *Quarterly Journal of Economics,* August 1942, p. 568. See also Bain's "Price and Production Policies," in Ellis, *op. cit.,* p. 4.

32. Donald H. Wallace, "Industrial Markets and Public Policy: Some Major Problems," in C. J. Friedrich and Edward S. Mason (Eds.), *Public Policy,* 1940 Yearbook of the Graduate School of Public Administration, Harvard University Press, Cambridge, 1940, p. 98. See also Wallace's "Monopolistic Competition and Public Policy," *American Economic Review,* Supplement, 1936, pp. 77-87, reprinted in *Readings in the Social Control of Industry,* Blakiston, Philadelphia, 1942, pp. 262-79. (This volume, a collection of articles selected by a committee of the American Economic Association, will hereinafter be cited: *Readings.*)

33. From the article in *Public Policy* cited above, p. 99.

34. Edward S. Mason, "Monopoly in Law and Economics," *Yale Law Journal,* November 1937, pp. 34-49; reprinted in *Readings,* pp. 25-47 (see especially p. 47). For somewhat similar ideas, see Theodore O. Yntema, "Competition as the Norm of Economic Behavior," *Journal of Business,* 1941, pp. 270-83.

Although Mason recognizes some practical benefits from antitrust policy, he regards the policy as inadequate, if not at times mischievous. He is particularly doubtful that the problem of oligopoly can "be effectively handled by a reshaping of the anti-trust acts, or by any conceivable reinterpretation of the meaning of restraint of trade." See his "Methods of Developing a Proper Control of Big Business," *Proceedings of the Academy of Political Science,* 1939, pp. 40-49; reprinted in *Readings,* pp. 215-25 (see p. 218). Despite this skepticism, Mason believes that, on the whole, "the American economy is in fact substantially more 'workably competitive' than it would have been without the existence of the antitrust acts." He thinks this is "due . . . not so much to

Chamberlin recognizes that oligopolistic behavior is not standardized and doubtless would agree that factual studies of a variety of specific industrial situations are necessary to a more complete understanding of the problem. But it does not follow that, because public policy makers do not fully understand market behavior, they should do nothing about the concentration of economic power. Those who countenance doing nothing, because too little is known, fail to recognize that inaction is as definitely a policy as is a positive program designed to insure the largest number of sellers in industrial markets consistent with the economies of mass production.

Workable Competition

Some economists, convinced that neither theories of imperfect competition nor those of pure competition afford a solid basis for public policy, have tried to develop a more realistic theory, based on a concept of workable competition. No one has defined the concept very precisely, and as Mason has stated, "Whether a given industry is judged to be workably competitive will depend to a very substantial extent on the 'ideology' of the judges." [35]

"Workable competition" refers to some market situations intermediate between pure monopoly and perfect competition. But that proposition covers virtually all actual market situations, and in particular every species of imperfect competition. The question is: How imperfect may competition be and still be "workable"? The core of the concept has two elements. Competition is workable in the sense (1) that it is preferable to the best alternative "competitive" arrangement practically attainable; (2) that such market control as

---

the contribution that particular [court] judgments have made to the restoring of competition as it is to the fact that the consideration of whether a particular course of business action may or may not be in violation of the antitrust acts is a persistent factor affecting business judgment, at least in large firms." From his contribution to a symposium on "The Effectiveness of the Federal Antitrust Laws," organized by Dexter M. Keezer, *American Economic Review,* June 1949, pp. 689-724. (Hereinafter referred to as "Symposium.") It is not clear whether Mason was suggesting that business executives are dissuaded by the fear of prosecution from making specific agreements with business rivals that might violate the law, or that the fear of prosecution keeps them from using in a specific fashion such power as they may have over the market. For a more recent statement of Mason's position, see "The Current Status of the Monopoly Problem in the United States," *Harvard Law Review,* 1949, pp. 1265-85.

35. Edward S. Mason, in "Symposium," p. 713.

sellers can exert is slight and, under the particular circumstances, does more good than harm.[36]

Economists who believe it impracticable to change greatly the structure of American industry count on potential competition and the competition of substitute products to make the existing structure of industry workably competitive by curbing monopoly power over the long run.[37] They believe that most businessmen in a strong strategic position will recognize that it is "good business" to maintain and expand sales "even at some sacrifice of immediate profits." And in view of the limitations that the availability of substitutes imposes on the price-making power of sellers in imperfectly competitive markets, the contention that their prices are apt in the long run to differ only slightly, if at all, from those in a purely competitive market is not wholly implausible. For one of the most remarkable achievements of modern technology is the continual multiplication of new

36. These are the elements emphasized by Clark, who is both a pioneer and an able expounder of the idea. See J. M. Clark, "Toward a Concept of Workable Competition," *American Economic Review,* June 1940, pp. 241-56; reprinted in *Readings,* pp. 452-75. Others who have contributed to the concept include Mason (*op. cit.*); Joe S. Bain ("Workable Competition in Oligopoly," a paper read before the American Economic Association in New York, at the December 1949 meeting); Adelman (*op. cit.*); Jesse Markham ("An Alternative Approach to the Concept of Workable Competition," *American Economic Review,* June 1950, pp. 349-61). See also Corwin Edwards, *Maintaining Competition* (McGraw-Hill, New York, 1949), not only for a realistic analysis of the implications of workable competition (Chap. 1) but also for a penetrating study of the whole problem of regulating industrial organization so as to vitalize competition. In summarizing significant aspects of the concept of workable competition, this study does not imply that they are the particular ideas of any individual economist unless it links his name with them.

37. See Clark, in *Readings,* pp. 460-64. Clark does not believe that either potential competition or substitutes is a perfect check, but "both together may come near it under favorable conditions." *Ibid.,* p. 460. He also believes that "The long-run [demand] schedule might in numerous cases approach the horizontal so closely that the slope would not be a matter of material moment, in the light of all the uncertainties involved." Pp. 462-63. He believes, too, that long-run cost curves tend toward the horizontal. Therefore he considers relatively unimportant such imperfections of competition as attend the long-run slopes of the curves. "So far as immediate price policies are governed by long-run demand curves, or behave as if they were so governed, they are likely not to differ materially from those of perfect competition . . . And even if the long-run scale of production is somewhat restricted, cost of production, as distinct from selling, is not likely to be thereby materially increased." Pp. 463-64. See also Clark's *Alternative to Serfdom,* where (p. 65), speaking of monopoly, he says: ". . . what is sacrificed by a grasping price-policy is not just a given amount of sales next year, but indefinite possibilities of future growth, which might be turned into a shrinkage if 'potential competition' were to materialize, as is always possible in the long run. And most business men, whether they have something approaching a monopoly position or not, recognize clearly that it is bad business to sacrifice future growth to an exorbitant rate of present profit, even if the curves on paper would permit it." Despite the checks which the market imposes on a monopolist, Clark recognizes that "It is not exactly safe to let him be the sole judge of reasonableness in his own case; in fact, it is thoroughly unsound—he can do plenty of harm if he uses only a third or a quarter of his monopoly power." *Ibid.,* pp. 65-66.

products made from familiar materials and of familiar products made of new materials. The variety of products available for satisfying any particular want is constantly growing. And therewith opportunities for relentless exploitation of whatever monopolistic power a seller may possess are appreciably narrowed.

Public Policy Implications

The public policy implications of this line of reasoning are fairly obvious. It leads readily to acquiescence in the status quo and to a low estimate of the value of remedial action designed to increase the number of sellers and reduce the monopoly elements in industrial markets.[38] If the object of policy is to insure the preservation of a private enterprise economy, accelerating and accentuating the forces that in a dynamic society tend to undermine monopoly power—whether that power rests in the hands of a few sellers or of a single seller—might help to attain it.

As for the short run, those who are bent on transforming imperfect competition into workable competition find the problem less urgent than a consideration of the "bare bones" of oligopolistic pricing theory might lead one to infer. They admit a general tendency in markets of few sellers for prices to be held at relatively stable levels somewhat below the price level of pure monopoly.[39] But they find an extenuating circumstance for such patterns of pricing policy in that they prevent prices from falling to marginal costs. Wherever fixed costs play an important role, as they generally do in modern industry, it would be disastrous, in the view of those seeking a solid basis for workable competition, if prices always conformed to short-run marginal costs. So here again, though doubtless without premeditation or design, elaboration of the workable competition concept leads to complacency. The persistence of monopolistic elements in industrial structure and market pricing serves a useful purpose, forsooth, because it prevents ruinous competition.[40]

38. Clark, for example, cautiously expresses the "hope that government need not assume the burden of doing something about *every* departure from the model of perfect competition." *Readings*, p. 475. Italics supplied. In his more recent writings (see *Guideposts in Time of Change*, p. 143) he gives less restrained approval of antitrust policies, and says: "We may take for granted that antitrust policy will be maintained."

39. Otherwise expressed, at levels somewhat above the level of purely competitive prices.

40. Clark recognizes the function of bankruptcy, but fears that price competition

Most economists would readily admit that the interests of society are best served by prices that cover *long-run* unit cost of production. But many will deny that a degree of competition so "imperfect," so lacking in vigor, that it prevents prices from ever falling to the level of short-run marginal cost is required to assure recovery of total production costs in the long run.[41]

Workable Competition and Price Flexibility

In truth, the chief objection to the attempt to clothe with respectability under the name of "workable" such restricted competition as that which has frequently prevailed in markets for manufactured goods is that it leads to ignoring or slighting the function of price in an enterprise economy. The price system is a mechanism by which resources are allocated among the myriad uses to which they may be put.[42] To the extent that competitive conditions prevail, they tend

---

may make whole industries "sick." See *Readings,* p. 454. He thinks, however, that industry can be healthy with from 10 to 15 per cent of its output produced at a loss. *Guideposts in Time of Change,* p. 144.

41. See, for example, George Stigler's comments on Clark's discussion of "workable competition," in *American Economic Review,* Supplement, 1940, p. 402. Clark argues that many industries meet rising demand by bringing into use stand-by equipment so slightly obsolescent that cost will rise only slightly with an increase in output. If in such industries short-run marginal costs remain constant up to full utilization of plant and are well below total costs—as Clark believes them to be—short-run profits from a rise in price in times of abnormal demand cannot be expected to compensate for short-run losses in times of slack demand. This argument is not altogether convincing. Rational enterprisers who recognize that fluctuating demand may at times reduce prices below total unit cost will ordinarily not launch a business venture unless prices promise at other times to be above costs so as to cover them in the long run. In truth, they may well demand as a condition of investment a larger rate of return in the long run than they would be content with if prices were more stable. (The issue that this argument raises is: How can prices, stable in the short run, perform their long-run function? See pp. 101-03 below.) But a higher rate of return need not mean a higher average price over a cyclical upswing and downswing. Yntema, after analyzing the factors tending to raise prices under both perfect and imperfect competition, concludes: "On balance, the average price under pure competition would probably be somewhat lower." *Op. cit.,* p. 281.

42. Clark denies that price changes are necessary to allocate resources economically. He says: "One idea of the functions of the price-cost structure which will stand deflating is the very common conception that it 'allocates the country's resources between different uses.' This has a basis of truth; but is often wrongly used to support the idea that it takes a change in prices to change the allocation of resources; or the idea that when something is scarce, production will not be stimulated *to make good the scarcity* unless the price is allowed to go to the full height that supply and demand would dictate. Those in control of large industries do not believe this, and do not practice it, though it has been used as a club to belabor wartime price controls. A moderate shift in resources, increasing the production of this and reducing the production of that, can commonly be brought about simply by changes in the volume of sales, *without any change in price.* Ultimately, if one of the products is a large factor in the demand for some raw material, the price of this material may change. But, to stimulate an increase in the output of a particular product, a moderate premium

to facilitate the supplying of consumers with what they want. But even though the market often operates haltingly and noncompetitively, it is still the only means on which peacetime America relies to bring into balance an intricately intermeshed economy, to make an integrated system out of the vast complex of economic activity.

The price system is also the mechanism by which adjustments are made in a dynamic economy—an economy in which consumers' wants are forever changing, technology forever advancing, centers of population and production forever shifting, the rate of industrial activity forever fluctuating. If, despite the pressures created by ceaseless change, sellers—either severally through the market power their size and small number give them or jointly through concerted action (with or without government aid)—can keep prices always close to total unit cost, they deprive the price system of its self-adjusting qualities.

Competition that is workable in any acceptable sense must protect the interests of society as a whole. If those interests are in conflict with the interests of persons who have assumed the risks of free enterprise by venturing their capital for gain in an industry, as they sometimes are, the latter should obviously give way. Competition

---

above cost is generally sufficient to do all that *can usefully be done,* and a decrease in output requires *no reduction in price.*" *Guideposts in Time of Change,* pp. 119-20. Italics supplied.

This represents a serious challenge to a basic principle underlying neoclassical economics. A chief justification of a private enterprise economy is that it relies on the democratic and impersonal forces of free markets to so organize economic activity as to meet economically the needs of consumers as expressed in the market place and to promote progress. See Chap. 1 and text below. Price-cost relationships, price movements, relative prices, are responses to consumer choices and guides to business decisions. Clark suggests that economists have overemphasized the role of prices in bringing about economic readjustments. He implies that in a private enterprise economy where there is no authoritarian determination of the use of resources, a socially desirable allocation of resources can be had in response to changes in demand and in the conditions of supply with no changes in price, or at any rate with relatively insignificant changes.

But his discussion raises more questions than it answers. How can production be stimulated to "make good the scarcity" without allowing price to go to the "full height that supply and demand" dictate? Who is to judge what constitutes *making good* the scarcity? Is the benevolent discretion of oligopolists to be relied on as a substitute for the judgment of buyers? Can any factor of production be moved from one industry to another, or from use to idleness, or from idleness to use, in a free-enterprise economy without affecting the price of the factor? Will not stable prices for a product of any single industry confronted with declining demand necessitate a lower price for some factor used in producing it? Can stable prices for products insure an economical use of resources? In the face of declining demand, even if some firms were content to maintain prices while business dwindled, is there fair reason to believe that without concerted action they can do so? Or that concerted action will insure a desirable use of resources?

must be workable in recession as well as in boom times. It must be workable in declining industries as well as in growing industries. Competitive private enterprise promises great gains to the fortunate and the sagacious. Even to those who are not exceptionally farsighted or lucky it promises prices that in the long run will cover total costs of a prudently and efficiently managed enterprise.

But competition does not always fulfill its promises to producers. Inevitably in a dynamic economy some producers will not realize their expectations and whole industries must eventually decay. Price serves as both guide and monitor to businessmen. Its job is both that of the carrot and the stick. To protect society's interests, at times competition must be ruinous in a very real sense in some industries and to some enterprisers.

Sick Industries and a Sick Economy

Economists are agreed on the need for short-run price adjustments as a means of prompting long-run adjustments in the use of resources and of insuring industrial progress in at least two situations. When the economic importance of an industry is declining because of a shift in consumers' tastes, and when radically new techniques have outmoded established ways of making a given product, price adjustments are plainly in order. A decline in demand that reflects a change in consumers' evaluations of a product must, if competition is to serve its social function, drive prices below total unit cost. Similarly, when new techniques that entail lower average costs than do the old have outmoded older techniques of production, the prices of the goods made by obsolete methods must in the long run fall below their cost of production. Established firms can prevent this only if they can block the introduction of new techniques.[43]

43. Producers may have a similar interest in blocking the introduction of substitutes. This was well illustrated when the Standard Oil Company of New Jersey found its pour-point depressant, Paraflow, threatened by a superior and more economical product, Santopour. On what to do about it, a Standard Oil official reasoned as follows in an October 1936 interoffice memorandum:

"If Santopour of present quality is continued on the market as a competitor of Paraflow and at the same price, there will be a substantial shift in business from Paraflow to a smaller volume of Santopour due to the greater potency of the latter in many oils. This will result in a very substantial decrease in the total volume of pour depressants sold and a proportionate decrease in gross dollar income. . . .

"If Paraflow and Santopour are both to be marketed without loss of total income it is apparent that Santopour would have to be adjusted to the same cost per unit of pour reduction as Paraflow. This could be done by either making a substantial increase in the price of Santopour or diluting it to a considerable extent . . .

"We would have to tell a rather embarrassing story to explain the marked change

If the new technique is so radical that it cannot be used by established firms, they, as high-cost producers, will be forced to write down the value of their productive facilities. If total unit cost of the new technique should be lower than marginal cost of the old, established producers may be driven into bankruptcy.[44]

Either a decline in demand or technological innovations may make an industry "sick." But in a dynamic society there are always apt to be some sick industries. Paradoxically, sickness of segments of the economy may evidence the soundness of the economy as a whole. The processes of bankruptcy work hardship on segments of labor and capital, but that is the price someone must pay for industrial progress in a private enterprise economy. Society's problem is to facilitate the shift of resources to more economical uses in response to shifts in demand or the introduction of technological innovations (and to alleviate suffering while doing so), not to subsidize excessive or inefficient capacity for making goods no longer so keenly wanted or so costly to produce as they once were.

As to whether in cyclical declines of general business activity price flexibility is everywhere desirable, economists are not agreed. Some argue that price flexibility tends to accelerate and accentuate the processes of deflation once a downward spiral of prices has begun.[45]

This is not the place for an adequate discussion of this issue.[46] However, what constitutes sound policy toward specific industrial situations during a general depression will depend somewhat on the

---

in either price or potency of Santopour, and the real reason for the change would be obvious to the trade.

"Our conclusion is, therefore, that the best policy is to retire Santopour as quickly and as quietly as possible and to market only Paraflow of present potency."

See *Patents,* Committee on Patents, U.S. Senate, 70th Cong., 2d sess., Hearings pursuant to S. 2303 and S. 2491, Pt. 4, p. 1824. For Standard Oil's explanation of the Paraflow-Santopour incident, see Pt. 9, pp. 5204-09. The final upshot of the negotiations was that Monsanto Chemical Company continued to make, and Socony-Vacuum continued to sell, Santopour, but they agreed to reduce its potency to the equivalent of Paraflow. Antitrust records contain many similar illustrations of the effort of vested interests to retard the introduction of new techniques or new products. See *Cartels or Competition?,* Chap. 7.

44. If a firm manufactures a variety of products, bankruptcy is, of course, not inevitable.

45. See particularly K. E. Boulding, "In Defense of Monopoly," *Quarterly Journal of Economics,* August 1945, p. 532; Abraham Bergson, "Price Flexibility and the Level of Income," *Review of Economic Statistics,* February 1945, pp. 2-5; John R. Hicks, *Value and Capital,* Clarendon Press, Oxford, 1939, pp. 265 ff.; Alfred C. Neal, *Industrial Concentration and Price Inflexibility,* American Council on Public Affairs, Washington, 1942; Joseph A. Schumpeter, *Capitalism, Socialism, and Democracy,* Harper, New York, 1942, Chap. 8; Clark, *Alternative to Serfdom,* Chap. 5.

46. See *Cartels or Competition?,* Chap. 7.

policy adopted with regard to the economy as a whole. When the whole economy is sick, an attempt to cure it by curing one industry at a time is futile. Output restriction and price control, industry by industry, when the entire economy is suffering from inadequate demand is likely to add to its troubles. What is needed in time of general business recession is expansion of demand, thereby increasing output and employment, not reduction of output, industry by industry (and discharge of workers, thereby further reducing effective demand), merely in order to prevent below-cost selling. To cure a sick economy one cannot systematically starve it.

The Perennial Gale of Creative Destruction

Schumpeter has made a brilliant criticism of the theory of oligopoly, while at the same time recognizing the necessity for continual readjustment of prices in response to the "perennial gale of creative destruction" that shakes the monopolistic positions producers sometimes achieve.[47] Schumpeter's chief quarrel with the theory of oligopoly is that it is a static concept concerned primarily with the problem of allocating resources economically in the matrix of a "specious present" and ignoring the more important problem of economic progress.[48] He emphasizes that "The essential point to grasp is that in dealing with capitalism we are dealing with an evolutionary process." [49] The theorists of oligopoly are concerned

47. For an original and perhaps more realistic expression of a somewhat similar thesis, see Oswald W. Knauth, *Managerial Enterprise,* Norton, New York, 1948. Knauth brings to his discussion the combined experience of a scholar and a man of affairs. He recognizes a transition in our economy from "free enterprise" to "managerial enterprise." Modern business managers continually seek trade advantages—"the foundation stones for the stability and the continuity which distinguish managerial from free enterprise." P. 91. But business rivalry continually undermines preferred positions. "An apparently secure monopoly is subject to erosion. It requires such an extensive organization and capital equipment that it cannot help becoming frozen. It cannot always utilize or adjust itself to new methods or processes. With a shift in demand or some new device, the monopoly of last year with power to exploit, reverts to a strong trade position without power to exploit." P. 179.

48. See Schumpeter, *op. cit.,* especially Chaps. 7 and 8. Schumpeter is only partly justified in challenging conventional theory on the ground that it deals exclusively with static phenomena. It is true that recent price theorists, and more particularly the contemporary texts, have been primarily concerned with the problem of economically distributing limited productive resources among their alternative uses in accordance with the free choice of consumers. But neoclassical theorists of the past generation were thoroughly aware of the twin problems of economic progress and economy in the use of resources. We have forgotten or ignored much that the earlier economists learned. See, for example, John Bates Clark, *Essentials of Economic Theory,* Macmillan, New York, 1907, particularly Chaps. 12 through 17.

49. Schumpeter, *op. cit.,* p. 82.

primarily with how capitalism administers existing structures, "whereas the relevant problem is how it creates and destroys them." [50]

Schumpeter claims that what really counts is not the competition among going concerns, following rigid patterns and with stable methods of production and unchanging forms of organization. Rather it is the competition of the new technology, the new product, the new source of supply, the new form of business organization. These "competitors" strike not at profit margins of existing firms but at their very foundations.[51] Moreover, this type of competition may be powerful even though it is only potential, for "The businessman feels himself to be in a competitive situation even if he is alone in his field." Schumpeter, like Clark, believes that potential competition may "in the long run enforce behavior very similar to the perfectly competitive pattern." [52] But as for the short run, he advances a quite different ground for viewing with toleration fewness of sellers—and their attendant quasi-monopolistic power over prices. He thinks that the monopoly elements in such a situation may perform a basic function that otherwise would be left unperformed, in which case capitalism would not work at all. Modern industry calls for extraordinarily large amounts of capital. Temporary monopoly advantages may be the bait essential to lure capital into costly and very risky undertakings.

Of short-run price rigidity, Schumpeter says:

> What the business strategy in question really aims at—all, in any case, that it can achieve—is to avoid seasonal, random and cyclical fluctuations in prices and to move only in response to the more fundamental changes in the conditions that underlie those fluctuations. Since these more fundamental changes take time in declaring themselves, this involves moving slowly by discrete steps . . .[53]

50. *Ibid.*, p. 84.
51. *Ibid.* According to Schumpeter (pp. 84-85), "This kind of competition is as much more effective than the other as a bombardment is in comparison with forcing a door, and so much more important that it becomes a matter of comparative indifference whether competition in the ordinary sense functions more or less promptly; the powerful lever that in the long run expands output and brings down prices is in any case made of other stuff."
52. *Ibid.*, p. 85.
53. *Ibid.*, p. 93. Schumpeter says (p. 95) that price rigidity and output reductions may in the downswing of the business cycle make "fortresses out of what otherwise might be centers of devastation." He recognizes, however, "plenty of cases of genuine price rigidity" as a matter of business policy, but holds that "There are no major instances of long-run rigidity of prices." The accuracy of the latter statement depends obviously on the definitions of "long run" and "major." Molybdenum was priced at 95

Economic Dynamism From Monopoly Elements Questioned

Schumpeter's arguments, like Clark's, possess merit, but they can obviously be carried too far.[54] Big business, like big labor or big agriculture, is struggling not merely to advance its position but also to make it more secure. This struggle may involve the blocking of innovation—which creates wealth for society only by destroying it for certain individuals. Efforts to keep out the new may not be so futile as Schumpeter's analysis suggests.

The outcome of the conflict between economic security and economic progress is not always certain. It is the struggle among rivals, big or little, that produces price-reducing innovations. Victory by any one, or peace among the lot, may retard, conceivably even stop, economic progress. And even when progress wins at the expense of security, there is no guarantee that the progress elements of monopoly power vouchsafe will be as rapid as that which competition would insure.[55]

The long-run readjustments that industrial innovation entails must have their beginnings in the short run. Economic progress

---

cents a pound from 1931 to 1940. Steel rails sold for $28 a ton through good times and bad in the first fifteen years after the United States Steel Corporation was organized.

For other illustrations of price rigidity see *Cartels or Competition?,* Chap. 7. For a further discussion of flexible and inflexible prices, consult: Gardiner C. Means, *Industrial Prices and Their Relative Flexibility,* S.Doc. 13, 74th Cong., 1st sess., Washington, 1935; Don Humphrey, "The Nature and Meaning of Rigid Prices, 1890–1933," *Journal of Political Economy,* October 1937; Rufus S. Tucker, "The Reasons for Price Rigidity," *American Economic Review,* March 1938, pp. 41-56; Ralph C. Wood, "Tucker's 'Reason' for Price Rigidity," *American Economic Review,* December 1938, pp. 663-73; J. K. Galbraith, "Monopoly Power and Price Rigidities," *Quarterly Journal of Economics,* May 1936; Donald H. Wallace, "Monopoly Prices and Depression," in *Explorations in Economics, Essays in Honor of F. W. Taussig,* McGraw-Hill, New York, 1936; Edward S. Mason, "Price and Production Policies of Large-Scale Enterprise," *American Economic Review,* Supplement, 1939, discussion, *ibid.,* p. 100; *idem,* "Price Policies and Full Employment," in Friedrich and Mason, *op. cit.;* Vernon A. Mund, "Prices Under Competition and Monopoly," *Quarterly Journal of Economics,* February 1934; Clark, *Guideposts in Time of Change* and *Alternative to Serfdom, passim.*

54. Neither the references to Clark nor those to Schumpeter do their arguments complete justice. Readers should consult their works cited above. On policy, Schumpeter's position is similar to Clark's, and both differ only in emphasis from the policy implications of this study. Schumpeter states his position as follows (*op. cit.,* p. 91): "It is certainly as conceivable that an all-pervading cartel system might sabotage all progress as it is that it might realize, with smaller social and private costs, all that perfect competition is supposed to realize. This is why our argument does not amount to a case against state regulation. It does show that there is no general case for *indiscriminate* 'trust-busting' or for the prosecution of *everything* that qualifies as a restraint of trade." Italics supplied.

55. See Chap. 1.

necessitates constant shifts in the use of resources. But recognition of the role of new techniques, new products, new forms of business organization, new sources of supply, and other innovations in raising living standards and advancing the general welfare must be accompanied by recognition of the fact that progress involves readjustments often painful to established interests.

To transform technical progress into economic progress upsets the industrial status quo. The search for improved techniques, more attractive products, more efficient business forms, or better sources of supply, if successful, necessitates constant readjustment within firms, within industries, within the whole economy. The new devices mean profits for some firms in some industries, in some localities. They mean losses for other firms in other industries, in other localities. A private enterprise economy depends on the price system to spur the necessary readjustments.

Quasi-monopolistic controls may protect the interests of particular groups by retarding readjustment, but only at the expense of society. Equally important, restrictive controls of this kind in the industrial segments to which the displaced resources might move will make more difficult the readjustments that innovations necessitate. The problem of readjustment is seldom easy to solve, and as A. G. B. Fisher has aptly said of it:

> The gratuitous addition to its magnitude, through the influence of monopoly controls, whether in the industries directly affected by technical change or [in] those into which displaced resources should move, is a powerful reason, quite apart from anything else, for regarding counter-monopoly measures as an important task for modern economic policy.[56]

When Is Competition Workable?

Because the critics of imperfect competition have not developed a wholly acceptable concept of "workable competition," does it follow that none is available? Probably none is, but these critics in seeking standards and rules for workable competition seem to have

56. A. G. B. Fisher, *Economic Progress and Social Security,* Macmillan, London, 1946, p. 59. Fisher further observes (p. 81): "It has become fashionable in many quarters in recent years to take a favourable view of 'controlled' monopoly as a factor making for 'stability,' but when we consider the immense power of monopoly influences in checking the structural adjustments necessary both for raising income levels and for assuring steady growth to an economy as a whole, the weight of the argument seems to be on the other side."

erred in rejecting too completely the neoclassical concepts in setting up their standards of workable competition.[57]

The fact that contemporary patterns of industrial organization and market behavior conform neither to the conventional concept of perfect competition nor to concepts of pure monopoly or imperfect competition does not justify abandoning completely the theories of competitive and monopolistic price making. Neoclassical theories of price determination may still be useful both in understanding market behavior and in shaping public economic policy. For they establish in the first place, if not a norm for market behavior, at least useful limiting cases, and in the second place standards by which to appraise the actual and probable effects of intermediate patterns, types, or situations.

Critics of imperfect-competition theory are correct, however, in the contention that competition may be workable without being pure. But to be "workable" in any proper sense, competition must surely be effective. Effective competition means doing those things that facilitate economic progress and economize the use of scarce resources. If competition does not do these things, a private enterprise economy cannot endure. If they are done, prices in the short run must be flexible enough to start the readjustments that innovations require. Inevitably, the readjustments will lag behind the price changes. But retarding the price changes will only retard still more the industrial readjustments, and this is likely to make them more cataclysmic when they come. If competition works, it does not merely alleviate the ill consequences of change; it speeds the benefits of change. Above all, it prevents the freezing of the status quo. The downward pressure that competition exerts on price converts the short-run gains that technological advance brings to the innovator into the long-run improvements in living standards that it promises for everyone.

The effectiveness of competition is apt to vary directly with the number of sellers up to the maximum consistent with the economies of scale. Though this maximum varies with different industries and at different times in the same industry, on the basis of existing informa-

57. Mason and his followers may be correct in holding that workability can be determined only on a case-by-case basis. Even so, that requires no innovation in public policy. Congress has laid down a general policy in the antitrust laws but it can be applied only on a case-by-case basis.

tion it is indeterminate. But the lack of a precise goal need not prevent determination of the direction in which to travel. If society wants to preserve a private enterprise economy, public policy must keep the market free from monopolistic controls, whether they rest on size alone or on conspiracy.

To define in more precise terms a policy aimed at fostering effective competition requires further examination of the conventional theory of imperfect competition and of actual market behavior in markets where sellers are few. What is the real significance of bigness and fewness of sellers for the effectiveness of competition in the short run and—since the long run is made up of a series of short runs—in the long?

Chapter 5

IMPERFECT COMPETITION IN PRACTICE

AS THE CRITICS CONTEND, there is indeed a discrepancy between the facts of industrial life and the theory of imperfect competition. For the theory does not sufficiently explain price behavior in markets of few sellers. Nevertheless, an understanding of the theories of imperfect and perfect competition is indispensable to the development of public policy designed to preserve a private enterprise system.

Two producers selling identical products, each with 50 per cent of the business, each behaving rationally, and each interpreting market data in precisely the same way, might well behave like monopolists, quite in accord with Chamberlinian theory.[1] To maximize earnings each might increase production only to the point where marginal cost equalled marginal revenue (with marginal revenue, and hence cost, below average revenue or price). Each might realize that his rival would immediately meet a price cut or match a price increase. Under such unique circumstances two sellers could control price as effectively as one, and they could do so without collusion. But such circumstances are never encountered in real life. The merger movement, however, has brought into being conditions closely approximating the theorists' model.

Cooperation in Markets of Few Sellers

Two factors make for sluggish competition in markets of few sellers. First, sellers in such markets tend to behave like monopolists. Experience may teach them that price cutting, at best, will not pay; at worst, may lead to price wars and ruinous competition.[2] Secondly, the fewer the sellers the easier it is for them to reap the fruits of

1. See Chap. 4.

2. Competition always tends to ruin high-cost producers, and this tendency serves the public interest. In economics, as in nature, every life-sustaining process involves destruction.

conspiracy without actually entering into what the courts say is conspiracy.

With only two companies in a market, the normal business and social contacts of their chief policy makers afford ample opportunity for imparting information, exchanging views, and cultivating good will—in short, laying the groundwork for the independent, unsolicited adoption by each of price and production policies consistent with mutual interest. Adam Smith long ago remarked: "People of the same trade seldom meet together, even for merriment and diversion, but the conversation ends in a conspiracy against the public, or in some contrivance to raise prices." [3]

If the conversation were among only a few sellers supplying the whole market, however, it might achieve the same results as conspiracy without leading to definite commitments by any of them and without infringing the law. In truth, such a conversation might be nothing more than an exercise of the constitutional right of freedom of speech. American courts recognize that an exchange of views among business rivals may influence price and output without constituting an agreement to restrain trade.[4]

Identical conclusions may follow an exchange of views by business executives. Judge Gary recognized this fact in steel pricing over a third of a century ago, when at his famous "dinners" he exhorted rival steel magnates like an evangelist at an old-fashioned revival meeting to hit the sawdust trail to business salvation.[5]

3. Adam Smith, *The Wealth of Nations,* Methuen & Co., London, 1904, Vol. 1, p. 130.

4. The Supreme Court has said: "It was not the intention of the Sherman Anti-Trust Law to inhibit the intelligent conduct of business operations, nor do we conceive that its purpose was to suppress such influences as might affect the operations of interstate commerce through the application to them of the individual intelligence of those engaged in commerce, enlightened by accurate information as to the essential elements of the economics of a trade or business, however gathered or disseminated. . . . Sellers of any commodity who guide the daily conduct of their business on the basis of market reports would hardly be deemed to be conspirators engaged in restraint of interstate commerce. . . . We do not conceive that the members of trade associations become such conspirators merely because they gather and disseminate information such as is here complained of, bearing on the business in which they are engaged and make use of it in the management and control of their individual businesses." *Maple Flooring Manufacturers Association* v. *U.S.,* 268 U.S. 563 (1925), at pp. 583-84.

But a "contrivance to raise prices" is another matter. Justice Douglas declared in *U.S.* v. *Socony-Vacuum Oil Co.,* 310 U.S. 150 (1940), at p. 221, "Any combination which tampers with price structures is engaged in an unlawful activity."

5. Of the Gary dinners *Fortune* has aptly said: "When the steel masters got up from the table, everyone somehow or other had a pretty clear idea of what prices he was going to charge for his steel. The earnest homily delivered by the Judge over the coffee cups was specially helpful in clearing up his listeners' minds." *Fortune,* April 1936, p. 129.

Diversity Among Producers Makes for Competition

The fewer the producers, the greater the likelihood of their independently behaving like pure monopolists, and the easier it is for them to act in concert on prices and output without conspiring. The more numerous the producers, the more likely they are to behave like competitors and the more difficult it is for them to collaborate effectively without violating the antitrust statutes. With only two or three producers in a market neither economists nor courts can always be certain to what extent price uniformity reflects collusion and to what extent it is the result of independent, but identical, judgments. Just how many producers are necessary to insure effective competition, no one can say precisely. But if society relies on effective competition to protect—and promote—its interests, policy should aim at as many firms as is consistent with the economies of scale.

The more producers there are operating in an industry, the greater the probability that they will differ about the pricing policy best adapted to their several situations, even though all may be seeking single-mindedly to maximize profits. No seller large enough to influence the market can afford to ignore his rivals' reactions to his own decisions, but he must also take account of other factors. At least six factors may cause each of a few sellers to act in pricing as though he were a competitor instead of a monopoly partner: (1) differences in interpretation of the elasticity of demand; (2) differences in position in the market; (3) differences in financial needs; (4) differences in the scope and character of operations; (5) differences in cost accounting methods; and (6) differences in production processes.

Estimates of Elasticity of Demand and Price Policies

In markets of imperfect competition, when a few large firms operate alongside many smaller firms, it is rare that all sellers interpret market signs and portents in the same way or, if they do, that they make identical decisions about output or prices. Both of these contingencies bear decisively on price behavior. For if they act independently, policy-making executives are apt to differ more in their estimates of the probable response of buyers to price changes than on anything else.

It is virtually impossible for them, proceeding independently, to reach a common judgment on these matters; for no one has developed a technique for measuring accurately and quickly the elasticity of demand for a product, nor is anyone likely to do so. To isolate the effect of price changes on a particular product from the complex bundle of factors affecting its consumption is no easy task. Price is only one of many variables that determine how much of any commodity consumers will buy at any given time. The state of business, changes in the amount or distribution of consumer purchasing power, the prices of substitute or complementary products, changes in consumer tastes and habits—all these and many other factors at times exert a greater influence on the sales of a commodity than do changes in price.

Factors Affecting Consumer Demand

If business activity is declining and consumers' incomes diminishing, a price reduction may be less effective in stimulating demand for any particular product, say automobiles, than it would were business more stable. The per capita consumption of grapefruit among middle-class income groups is far greater than among low-income groups, who probably eat more potatoes than do the middle classes. Raising incomes generally would no doubt exert a far greater influence on the consumption of grapefruit than any moderate reduction in its price.

People with different incomes apportion their expenditures differently among the major groups of commodities and services—food, clothing, housing, education, medicine, and recreation—as the classic study by Ernst Engels showed. A change in the amount or distribution of income will, accordingly, affect differently the sales of different products. Economists refer to the effect of changes in the average income of buyers on the total demand for a given product as the income elasticity of demand.

Consumer response to price changes varies with income groups. Rich people may ignore changes in the price of a luxury, buying about as much at one price as at another. Poor people respond more quickly to price changes in anything they buy except sheer necessities. If a commodity has close substitutes, a change either in its price or in the prices of its substitutes may greatly affect its sales. When commodities complement one another—gasoline, oil, tires, garage rents, repair costs, and automobiles—consumer response to a change in the price of one will depend on many factors, but chiefly on the demand for the whole complex of complementary goods—in this case automobile transportation.

The many varied factors affecting consumer demand make it impossible with known techniques to isolate the influence of any one. Studies of consumer response to price changes are therefore inconclusive.[6] Only by experimenting can businessmen find out how consumers will respond at any particular time to price changes. Even when there are only a few sellers in a market, if they act independently some will experiment with price cutting because all will seldom interpret demand alike. In brief, where the number of sellers falls far short of the number required to force all to accept market price passively, as an objective datum of business management, if each follows his independent judgment prices may well be competitive. They may change frequently and hover around cost. But the likelihood of their doing so increases with an increase in the number of firms and the diversity of their needs and judgments.

Market Position and Price Policy

Because reducing prices is one method of attracting customers, a small firm is more apt to be a price cutter than a large one. An ambitious, aggressive manager of a relatively small firm may conclude that price cutting rather than a follow-the-leader policy is his most profitable procedure, particularly if he can cut prices without the fact becoming immediately known to his rivals. Seeking the economies of mass production, he may undersell his rivals in order to expand his business.

6. For an excellent analysis of the problem, see Edwin G. Nourse, *Price Making in a Democracy,* The Brookings Institution, Washington, 1944, Chap. 7. Henry L. Moore (*Economic Cycles: Their Law and Cause,* Macmillan, New York, 1914), Henry Schultz (*The Theory and Measurement of Demand,* University of Chicago Press, Chicago, 1938), and Mordecai Ezekiel (*Methods of Correlation Analysis,* Wiley, New York, 1941) were pioneers in the study of elasticity of demand. But no one has devised a technique for determining a coefficient of price elasticity on which business executives can rely in shaping price policy. Nourse has pointed out (pp. 205-06) that a coefficient of price elasticity isolated from other conditions turns the price executive's "attention away from rather than toward the questions of greatest significance. It is likely to become a new rule-of-thumb less realistic and sound than the rules intuitively arrived at by the purely 'practical' business manager. These statistical and theoretical 'isolationists' in abstracting a single factor from a complex total situation are not giving the businessman a safe or useful tool of management."

Even if he cannot long keep his prices secret, he may believe that his larger rivals will tolerate his price cuts rather than meet them. He may reason that, because of the scale on which they operate, whatever deflection of patronage his lower price can effect will be no more than a trivial annoyance, or that they will ignore his prices because of their belief that their advertising has made their customers immune to lower offers—if they are not too much lower—from a less well known producer. The price cutter may proceed on the assumption that the most profitable course for his giant rivals will be to lose some customers to him rather than to sacrifice profits on the bulk of their business, even if only temporarily, by meeting his lower price. He may conclude that larger firms will prefer to sell a little less for a little more rather than to experiment with selling a little more for a little less; because the little less of goods for a little more of price might, if the seller had a large sales volume to begin with, increase net earnings substantially, and the little more of goods for a little less of price might greatly reduce them.[7]

Depending on the tolerance of the industry's leaders, several small firms may follow a similar policy of cutting prices. If they do, and particularly if some make deeper cuts than others, they may eventually force an all-round price reduction—or at any rate provoke the leaders to retaliate.

The petroleum-refining industry illustrates these contingencies. As long as the smaller refiners have been content to retail their gasoline at not more than about 1.5 or 2 cents a gallon less than the major companies charge, the latter have for long periods tolerated the situation.[8] But when some necessitous or aggressive independent overreaches the "limits of tolerance," the gasoline price structure may collapse, permitting cost-price relationships to reflect more accurately changes in supply or demand. Because the smaller refiners find it difficult to expand their business without cutting prices, every now and then one of them takes a chance, even though he is aware that eventually the major companies will probably meet or beat his price cuts.

7. See George J. Stigler, "The Kinky Oligopoly Demand Curve and Rigid Prices," *Journal of Political Economy,* October 1947, pp. 432-49, particularly his discussion of price leadership by the dominant firm, at pp. 444-45.

8. See Myron W. Watkins, *Oil: Stabilization or Conservation?,* Harper, New York, 1937, pp. 163 ff. and 232 ff.

Steel Prices

The steel industry affords another example of how latent competition persists even under conditions of quasi-monopoly, or imperfect competition. A specific episode in its recent history shows the strength of the temptation for relatively small firms to cut prices in order to improve their market position.

The National Steel Company, a relatively small but efficient producer, began business in 1929 with an independent price policy. It was a merger of Weirton Steel of Weirton, West Virginia, Great Lakes Steel of Detroit, and the ore and coal reserves and freighters of the M. A. Hanna firm of Cleveland, and became the sixth largest producer in the industry. Its chairman and guiding spirit, Ernest P. Weir, was a rugged individualist and an aggressive innovator, apparently more interested in lowering costs and competing for business than in stabilizing prices. National Steel was the first integrated company to use American Rolling Mills' patented continuous sheet-rolling process, the first to introduce the Steckel mill, an improved sheet-rolling process that turns out thinner sheets with a finer finish, and the first to acquire a steel plant in the Detroit area.[9] Known among its rivals as a price cutter, National Steel apparently went after business at prices buyers were willing to pay.[10] Its policy of shading prices paid. National Steel, steel consumers, and the public were gainers. And National Steel made money.

Operating its up-to-date equipment at a larger percentage of capacity than its rivals, National Steel kept its costs low.[11] It was the only major steel company to show a profit throughout the depression of the 1930's. More striking, in 1931 it earned more than all its

9. George R. Fink, later National Steel's president, built the Michigan Steel Corporation's finishing plant at Detroit in 1922 and began the construction of the Great Lakes steel plant before the National Steel merger. The Great Lakes plant when finished was the latest in steel plants, wholly electrified and using fuel oil in its open-hearth furnace. See *Bradstreet's* (New York), November 14, 1931, p. 904. According to *Fortune,* it was commonly believed that the older, larger companies had an unwritten agreement not to locate in the Detroit area. Mr. Fink "as a steel outsider . . . was not bound by any consensus of established steel opinion." "National Steel: A Phenomenon," *Fortune,* June 1932, p. 36.

10. *Ibid.,* p. 89. See also March 1936, p. 191. "Not for nothing was Mr. Weir for years the industry's leading price cutter, and expert at the undignified but lucrative practice of 'chiseling.' "

11. Its cheap water transportation, well-planned integration (National Steel had an excess of finishing capacity that could be more economically shut down in periods of slack demand than could plants for the manufacture of crude and semifinished steels), and its modern equipment, all contributed to its financial success.

competitors combined. Not only was it more prosperous, but it grew faster, moving from sixth to fifth place within a decade.[12] Whether National Steel was responsible for the break in steel prices that came during the depression is not clear, but price shading eventually became a general practice, and, more accurately than before, steel prices reflected demand-supply relationships.[13]

Old Firms Seldom Price Cutters

Age as well as size affect a corporation's price policies. Other things being equal, old well-established concerns tend to be more hostile to price cutting than younger concerns. Economic maturity frequently leads to the conservatism characteristic of old age. Old concerns, particularly those that have grown large through consolidation, may have so much to conserve that they lose the venture spirit without which small, young firms cannot grow.[14]

The steel industry provides a striking case in point. Both in its organization and in its subsequent concern with price stability the United States Steel Corporation illustrates how big business may try to prevent the "perennial gale of creative destruction" from working havoc on vested interests. Bankers promoted the Steel Corporation to stabilize investments in an industry threatened by a battle of the giants. They were apparently more concerned with the protection of property values than with the production of steel. In the words of *Fortune:*

> The fact that the Corporation, simply because of the magnitude of its conception, had from the beginning so many hundreds of millions of its dollars in plant worked strongly against change. And so the chief energies

12. *Annalist* (New York), November 9, 1939, p. 605.

13. In 1936 *Fortune* characterized pricing in the steel industry as follows: "There are, in effect, two price systems in steel. One is open, public, unyielding. This is the bleak prospect that the average consumer faces. But the big consumers buy their steel under another system, an unofficial and undercover business of concessions from the published basing-point prices." *Fortune,* April 1936, p. 132.

14. Counsel for Liggett & Myers Tobacco Company expressed the idea as follows: "The management of Liggett & Myers is responsible for the savings and investment of thousands of shareholders, many of them estates and institutions, and for the security of thousands of employees. It has assets of almost $200,000,000. It enjoys enormous good will. The management of a company so situated is likely to be cautious and conservative, to take the courses involving the least risk." *Liggett & Myers Tobacco Co., et al.* v. *U.S.,* in the Circuit Court of Appeals, Sixth Circuit, Brief on behalf of Appellants, p. 263. In the reports this case appears under the title of a parallel antitrust action: *U.S.* v. *American Tobacco Co., et al.,* 39 Fed.Supp. 957 (1941); affirmed, 147 Fed. *2d* 93 (1944); affirmed, 328 U.S. 781 (1946).

of the men who guided the Corporation were directed to preventing deterioration in the investment value of the enormous properties confided to their care. To achieve this they consistently tried to freeze the steel industry at present, or better yet, past levels.[15]

The Steel Corporation's interest in stabilizing steel markets apparently stifled its interest in cost reduction. When the Great Depression hit the iron and steel trade, the Steel Corporation had achieved the unenviable reputation of being one of the most inefficient steel producers. When Myron C. Taylor became board chairman in 1932, his job, in the language of *Fortune,* was to "revitalize the Corporation's enormous, inert bulk." [16] Under his direction young and vigorous men replaced old ones and the whole organization underwent a thorough overhauling. The Corporation built new mills, scrapped old ones, reduced its funded debt, consolidated its production operations, and coordinated its selling activities. It gave no convincing evidence, however, of having abandoned its interest in stabilizing the steel market; indeed, it continued to use the basing point system and to collaborate with rivals on a schedule for extras.

Influence of Financial Position on Price Policies

In markets of few sellers, differences in their corporate structure, credit position, working capital, and inventories may lead to different price policies. Even though all members of the group may believe that restricting output to maintain prices will advance their long-run mutual interests, some firm may decide to cut prices because of immediate financial need. The price-making executives of a corporation confronted with an interest payment on bonded debt, with overdue bank loans, or with large inventories and little working capital may feel that sufficient unto the day is the evil thereof. That restriction of output and maintenance of price might pay, in the long run, is irrelevant. The last lap is of no interest to contestants who may fall out on the first. Diversity of immediate financial interests therefore makes for diversity in price policies. The real markets of imperfect competition do not always behave like the Chamberlinian model. Without collusion, they may operate more like competitive markets.

15. *Fortune,* March 1936, p. 170.
16. *Ibid.,* p. 59.

Difference in Scope and Character of Operations

The scope and character of a firm's operations may influence its attitude toward price cutting. The manufacturer of nationally advertised products views the price problem differently from the maker of standardized, undifferentiated products. The one in maintaining prices, the other in shading them, does what seems most profitable. Mass retail distributors who rely on small profit margins and large sales volume are notorious price cutters.[17]

Even in markets of few sellers, differences in cost lead to differences in judgment on cost-remunerative prices and hence to price competition. Costs are not the same for all firms. Some may use more labor, some more machinery. While the highly mechanized firm, operating at capacity, may be able to produce more cheaply than the firm using relatively more labor, machine overhead in times of slack demand is heavy. The urge to reduce prices then may be overwhelming.

Cost Accounting and Price Making

Differences in accounting methods among the several firms in an industry of imperfect competition may lead to different judgments on prices and different price policies. Differences in handling depreciation and obsolescence charges are particularly significant. A firm that writes off the book value of its productive facilities rapidly in good times may look with less disfavor on price cutting in bad times than a rival firm that has been less farsighted in its accounting policy.

Uniformity in cost accounting methods is particularly unlikely in the absence of agreement among firms producing several joint-cost products. It is impossible to determine accurately the costs of producing one of two or more such products produced jointly. Only an arbitrary decision can divide between mutton and wool the costs of raising sheep. Where two or more products are produced jointly in unvarying proportions and without special costs peculiarly applicable to any one, allocation of costs among the several products must be wholly arbitrary. If each producer acts independently, all

17. Such companies as Sears, Roebuck and R. H. Macy frequently buy products from manufacturers and sell them under their own house brands in competition with the manufacturers' branded merchandise.

may allocate costs differently and hence adopt different pricing policies. Because an increase in demand for one product increases the supply of others, price cutting may quickly develop unless producers join forces to prevent it.

Where the output of each can be varied, one at the expense of the other—for example, gasoline at the expense of kerosene or fuel oil in refining petroleum—special costs may be encountered. A producer can readily calculate the addition to cost of increasing the output of one product if the output of others is fixed. But when facilities are used in common and are operating at capacity, the plant manager can increase the output of one only by decreasing the output of another. Under such circumstances it may require some experimentation to determine the best combinations of output because it is difficult to estimate accurately demand and costs for each under the several possible alternatives. With several producers in the field, each operating under slightly different conditions, identical estimates of proper prices are unlikely. In periods of slack demand the prospect of price cutting is particularly great.

Differences in Production Processes

The problem of insuring identical price policies among rival sellers in markets of imperfect competition if the sellers do not actively collaborate is even more difficult where several producers make substantially the same products under wholly different conditions and by different processes. The production of nitrogen illustrates this problem.

From natural deposits in which the nitrate salt is mixed with common salt and smaller amounts of magnesium, calcium, iodine, and the like, Chilean nitrate of soda is produced by a relatively simple mining and refining process. It competes in world markets with synthetic nitrogen produced under a variety of processes and with byproduct nitrogen—chiefly ammonia derived from the distillation of coal in the manufacture of coke and artificial gas.

The conditions under which synthetic nitrogen is produced vary greatly among the different producers. Not only do processes differ, but the immediate aims of the several producers in entering the synthetic field have differed. Some companies seek a market for a chemical byproduct, others a raw material for use in related manufacturing operations. Allied Chemical & Dye Corporation as a producer of sodium assured itself of an immediate market for soda by making sodium nitrates; E. I. du Pont de Nemours & Company by entering the nitrogen field freed itself from dependence on foreign sources of a raw material for its lacquers and explosives; Pennsylvania Salt Manufacturing Company by producing nitrogen got an outlet for the byproduct hydrogen from its electrolytic chlorine plant. The cost of nitrogen produced under these widely diverse conditions varies greatly. No two of the several sellers in the market acting independently are apt to arrive at precisely the same pricing policies.[18]

The Glass Industry: Deficiencies of Imperfect-Competition Theory

Both the early and the more recent history of the flat-glass industry illustrate the influence of number and diversity of sellers on market price policies and the industry's collaborative effort to prevent the readjustments that effective competition would entail.[19] The American Window Glass Company, organized in 1899 as a consolidation of the leading manufacturers of window glass, produced about 85 per cent of all domestic output. It early acquired the Lubbers patent for blowing glass cylinders by machine. Although enjoying a virtual monopoly of the product, it encountered the vigorous competition of the hand-blown window-glass producers. The National Window Glass Workers, a union of skilled craftsmen fighting for survival, agreed with their employers to extend working time and to base wage rates on the price of window glass. Despite the company's dominant position in the market, competition forced down the price of single-strength window glass from $2.39 a box in 1904 to $1.70 a box in 1909. Wage rates for hand blowers meanwhile had dropped precipitously.[20]

Competition was briefly suspended in 1909 when 50 of the 56 hand-blowing establishments organized the Imperial Window Glass Company as sole selling agent for their combined output. But the

18. For a discussion of concerted effort by the nitrogen industry to restrain competition, see *Cartels in Action,* Chap. 4.

19. For a detailed discussion of the early development, see Myron W. Watkins, *Industrial Combinations and Public Policy,* Houghton Mifflin, Boston, 1927, Chap. 4.

20. Bureau of Foreign and Domestic Commerce, *The Glass Industry,* Miscellaneous Series, No. 60, Washington, 1917, p. 193.

company was dissolved in 1910 as a result of a federal antitrust suit. Window-glass prices promptly dropped to a new low of $1.30 a box. Competition, having apparently forced prices below cost,[21] brought a change in the policies of both the high-cost hand-blown window-glass manufacturers and American Window Glass with its lower-cost machine techniques. Both chose the immediate security of "live and let live" to a continuance of a competitive struggle that had brought severe losses to all. If not checked, it would have hastened the liquidation of the manufacturers using the hand-blowing process, which was quite obsolete.

The new policy, restricting output, was followed at once by a rise in price. By 1914 single-strength window glass sold at $2.26 and by 1916 at $3.06 a box. O. C. Teague, president of the National Association of Window Glass Manufacturers, speaking before that body in 1915, described the situation in the industry in this way:

> The window-glass industry during the past year has operated at 50 per cent capacity . . .
>
> Most producers have recognized the fundamental law of supply and demand and *demonstrated a willingness to exact* [*their*] *share and be satisfied.* Unfortunately, however, there are still a few manufacturers who propose to operate full capacity for a full year, furnace conditions permitting. This last-named factor is the dangerous element in our largely overbuilt industry. Unless we can convince these free lances of their mistaken policy our future business life is indeed short.[22]

The general manager in 1918 stated the policy of the American Window Glass Company before the Tariff Commission as follows:

> As a matter of policy we have had no desire to drive the hand blower off the map. There is no other machine on the market today that can drive them out, other than our machine, and we probably could; but in driving anybody out of a line of business you have to take some of the medicine that you administer to them, and from a business standpoint we thought it was much more profitable for us to be satisfied with a reasonable share of the country's business rather than to drive out operatives from an industry that had existed as long as this one had existed. The policy of live and let live has been our policy throughout, not only in production but in prices.[23]

21. American Window Glass Company did not pay dividends on either its common or preferred stock for many years.
22. Quoted in *The Glass Industry*, p. 202. Italics supplied.
23. U.S. Tariff Commission, *The Glass Industry as Affected by the War*, Washington, 1918, p. 79.

A vice-president of Pittsburgh Plate Glass Company, which had become an important manufacturer of window glass, recognized the stabilizing influence under which the industry then operated. He said:

> During the past year . . . the consumption of window glass was greatly limited. The hand manufacturers have met this condition in a way which I think is very creditable; they have provided for six or seven months' blast. The American Window Glass Company . . . also recognized the situation, and instead of indulging in ruinous competition they have been broad enough and sensible enough to materially curtail production.[24]

Trade Cooperation Needed to Supplement Rational Self-Interest

The abatement of competition under the new policy reflected something more than independent rational behavior in a market of imperfect competition by sellers each of whom realized that all would profit by a policy of self-restraint. It reflected the behavior of monopoly partners, not genuine competitors, even though it may not have violated the antitrust statutes as the courts interpreted them. American Window Glass as the dominant producer was no doubt in a position, by regulating its output, to affect the price at which window glass sold. But it was apparently unwilling to restrict output rigorously unless producers by the outmoded hand process did the same.

With about fifty producers, it was difficult to assure a consistent policy unless they collaborated. This they did, however, first through the use of a common selling agency, secondly through their collective bargaining contracts with the hand blowers. Under the new policy the National Association of Window Glass Manufacturers negotiated a collective bargaining contract with the National Window Glass Workers that not merely provided for a standard wage scale but held down the production of window glass by limiting the operations of each of the companies to four and a half months a year and even fixed the operating dates for each plant.[25]

24. Watkins, *Industrial Combinations and Public Policy,* p. 159. American Window Glass's restraint paid off. With window glass selling at $3.06 a box in 1916, the company paid 54.5 per cent accumulated dividends on its preferred stock.

25. The Supreme Court in 1923 set aside a finding of a lower court that this arrangement violated the antitrust statutes. See *National Association of Window Glass Manufacturers* v. *U.S.,* 263 U.S. 403 (1923). The decision rested partly on the reasonableness of the restrictions on production in view of the depressed condition of the hand-blown window-glass industry, partly on the special status of trade unions and collective bargaining agreements under the antitrust laws. The Court's opinion

During the 1920's the window-glass industry experienced a minor revolution that eventually eliminated the hand blowers. In 1916 the Libbey-Owens Sheet Glass Company was organized to manufacture flat glass by a sheet-drawing process under the Colburn patents.[26] Within the next decade a number of American producers introduced the Fourcault process, developed in Belgium. Shortly afterward the Pittsburgh Plate Glass Company developed a third process. During the building boom of the 1920's glass manufacturers built new and larger plants, remodelled old plants, and generally introduced continuous-process machines. In brief, they placed the whole flat-glass industry on a mass-production basis.

By 1926 hand production of window glass represented only 2 per cent of the total. American Window Glass's machine cylinder process accounted for 59 per cent, Libbey-Owens' sheet-drawing process for 29 per cent, the Fourcault process for 10 per cent.[27] By 1929 all producers had abandoned the hand process. The machine cylinder process accounted for only 20 per cent and newer, more efficient, lower-cost sheet-drawing processes accounted for the remainder. This development reduced the number of producers and increased the scale of operation. In 1929, sixteen plants and fifteen companies accounted for all domestic production; three companies—Pittsburgh Plate Glass, Libbey-Owens, and American Window Glass—accounted for about 75 per cent.

Despite the dominance of the three big producers, the decline in demand during the Great Depression brought a sharp drop in prices. The price of single-strength Grade B glass dropped from about $2.50 a box in 1929 to about $1.45 a box by the middle of 1931. After a slight temporary increase in 1932 and 1933, by the middle of 1934 it was selling at a new low of about $1.40. Most of the smaller companies suspended operations; some temporarily, some because they were bankrupt.

---

barely hinted at the question of the relationship between the arrangement under attack (which involved directly only the hand-blown branch of the industry) and the market policy of American Window Glass.

26. Its name was changed to Libbey-Owens Glass Company in 1929 and in 1930, with the acquisition of the Edward Ford Plate Glass Company, to Libbey-Owens-Ford Glass Company.

27. See U.S. Tariff Commission, *Flat Glass and Related Products*, Report No. 123, Second Series, Washington, 1937, p. 32. The peak window-glass output was reached early in the business boom. From a high of 567 million square feet in 1925, output had fallen to about 400 million square feet in 1929. *Ibid.*

A Merger Comes to the Rescue

But even bankruptcy did not lead to permanent abandonment of facilities. A reorganized company or a purchaser at a forced sale commonly took over the properties at a lower capitalization, and with fixed costs thus reduced the plant could be held in readiness for resuming operations when market conditions improved. Moreover, it pays to operate in the short run even though the price may not cover total unit cost. As long as sale of the output will yield prices greater than variable costs, a firm will lose less by producing than by closing down. Any contribution to fixed costs is better than none. Only when variable expenses cannot be met will it pay better to quit than to go on. Apparently the smaller plants, by opening and closing whenever it paid to do so, prevented the larger producers from exacting monopoly prices.

From a business viewpoint the industry was demoralized. Demand was slack, capacity far in excess of production, profits for most producers had disappeared. Nevertheless, stubborn nonconformists with an eye on their own immediate needs jeopardized the interests of the large producers who otherwise might have controlled the market. Competition in the window-glass industry, although imperfect, was nonetheless effective. Consumers were the beneficiaries.[28]

Out of this situation a merger program developed, apparently designed to "stabilize" the window-glass industry. Eugene Rolland, president of the Rolland Glass Company, a small company using the Fourcault process, led in organizing the Fourco Glass Company to act as a sales agent for the small companies. With funds borrowed from the Michigan Alkali Company, controlled by the Edward Ford family, which had heavy investments in Libbey-Owens-Ford, and from the Diamond Alkali Company, suppliers to American Window Glass, Mr. Rolland bought out the smaller plants or arranged for a common selling agency for them. To bring all independent output under its control, Fourco spent about $1,250,000 for operating properties and about a million dollars for plants temporarily out of

28. There is no reason to believe that the long-run interests of the industry were jeopardized. With a surplus of capacity, prices had fallen below total unit cost for some producers. If the situation were permanent, society would benefit by a transfer of production facilities to lines where they were more highly valued or by a permanent writing down of the value of the less efficient window-glass plants. If the situation were temporary, a rising demand would remedy it.

production. Altogether Fourco acquired twelve plants, of which it closed eight permanently.

Price Reflects Market Control

When the plan took form in 1935, twelve companies with twenty-one plants, not all of which were operating, sold window glass in the domestic market.[29] After execution of the plan, four companies—Pittsburgh Plate Glass, Libbey-Owens-Ford, American Window Glass, and Fourco—sold all the window glass produced in the United States. Pittsburgh Plate Glass did about 25 per cent of the business, Libbey-Owens-Ford about 30 per cent, American Window Glass about 20 per cent, Fourco about 25 per cent.

Probably some economists would defend this merger on the ground that it converted twelve weak, relatively inefficient companies into a single strong company able to hold its own in competition with the Big Three. Actually, it transformed a market of effective competition into a market more closely approaching monopoly. It made it easier for the several sellers to reach common judgments about market conditions without formal collusion. More important, it also made it easier for them to collaborate on market policies without violating the antitrust statutes or without being discovered if they should violate them.

The price of window glass soon reflected the increase in sellers' control of the market. During the merger negotiations the price of single-strength window glass (B quality) increased in two steps from about $1.40 to about $2 a box. Higher prices brought greater earnings. The companies whose selling was merged through Fourco had experienced heavy losses in 1931, 1932, 1934, and 1935, but their merged operations during 1936–1939 yielded earnings on the capital and surplus of the combination ranging from a low of 9 per cent in 1938 to a high of 24 per cent in 1937. Although after formation of Fourco they collectively made and sold less window glass, they made more money.

Pricing in the Sulphur Industry

The sulphur industry also illustrates how, even in a market of few sellers, business rivals may behave like competitors unless they

29. Libbey-Owens-Ford had two plants; Pittsburgh Plate Glass, three; American Window Glass, four; and Fourco Glass, four. Eight smaller companies had one each. See *Flat Glass and Related Products*, p. 24.

collaborate. It also illustrates how the gale of creative destruction may be effectively prevented through concerted action without running afoul of the law. Between 1913 and 1922 three sulphur companies—Texas Gulf, Freeport Texas, and Union—produced the entire American output of natural sulphur. During this time the three producers apparently competed actively for available business, and with the decline in demand after World War I prices fell steadily from $22 a ton to $12.50 a ton by 1922.[30] In that year the American producers organized the Sulphur Export Corporation under the Webb-Pomerene Act and the Corporation made a price-fixing agreement with Sicilian producers covering sales in foreign markets.[31] The Webb-Pomerene Act authorized agreements among American exporters, provided they did not restrain trade within the United States nor restrain the foreign trade of any domestic competitor. But it did not specifically authorize such agreements as the Sulphur Export Corporation made with the Sicilian producers. A Department of Justice investigation in the late 1930's revealed no evidence, however, of the Corporation members' having violated the law by conspiring to restrain trade in domestic markets.

Nevertheless, the price of sulphur in the American market rose steadily after the domestic producers began cooperating in foreign markets. It was $16 a ton in 1924, $17 in 1925, and $18 in 1926. Despite a sharp decline in consumption during the Great Depression the price remained at $18 for more than a decade. This may not have been precisely a pure monopoly price, but it was not an effectively competitive one. It aimed at higher profits than effective competition would have permitted. It tended to prevent an economical use of resources.[32]

The stability of sulphur prices during the Great Depression contrasts dramatically with their decline during the 1920–1922 depression. Apparently the two American companies, having collabo-

30. *Investigation of the Concentration of Economic Power,* Temporary National Economic Committee, Hearings pursuant to Pub.Res. 113 (75th Cong.), Pt. 5, p. 1991.

31. *Ibid.,* Ex. 381-A, pp. 2214-17. The agreement (officially dated March 14, 1923 but effective October 4, 1922) provided that "The prices, terms, and conditions of sale of all sulphur . . . shall be fixed from time to time by the parties in such manner as best to serve their mutual interest." The agreement extended to 1932, and was renewed in 1934. *Ibid.,* Ex. 381, pp. 2208-12.

32. After World War I Union Sulphur rapidly exhausted its deposits and in 1924 it stopped producing. After it had disposed of its inventories in 1928, Union sold its stock in the Export Corporation to Texas Gulf Sulphur and Freeport Sulphur and quit business. *Ibid.,* p. 1992.

rated to fix prices in foreign markets, found it unnecessary to conspire in order to insure stable prices in domestic markets. That $18 a ton was a noncompetitive price is indicated not merely by its fixity over a long period but by its relation to production costs and the rate of return that it yielded. Freeport's average cost, from 1926 to 1938, exclusive of royalties, was $6.13 a ton; Texas Gulf's was $5.64. In 1929 Freeport earned $5 million on an investment of $11.5 million, or 43.72 per cent. Texas Gulf earned $13 million in 1927 on an investment of $17.5 million, a return of 74.12 per cent. During the twenty years ending with 1938 Texas Gulf averaged 28.75 per cent on its investment. Freeport's net income during the same period averaged 13.31 per cent after deductions for property taxes, capital losses, and adjustment of depreciation reserves.[33]

The Evolution of Esprit de Corps in Business

Business leaders have recognized that a diversity of interests among rival sellers may lead to effective competition even in markets in which there are only a few sellers, particularly if some of them are relatively small.[34] Recognizing that competition may lower profits and in periods of slack demand become ruinous, they have frequently sought security in concerted action. In an effort to stabilize markets they have resorted to a variety of devices. In doing so they have, of course, tried to avoid violating the law. They have sought the fruits of conspiracy while trying to avoid its penalties.

Programs for stabilizing markets in such industries have included tangible and intangible elements. Industrial leaders have tried to develop a business morality that makes price cutting taboo. They have tried to lead their associates to see the futility of unrestrained competition. They have tried to inculcate throughout the business community the doctrine of live and let live. The intimate intercorporate relationships they have built up over the years have greatly aided them in their quest for economic security.

33. Clair Wilcox, *Competition and Monopoly in American Industry,* TNEC Monograph No. 21, Washington, 1940, p. 110.

34. A one-time executive of a defunct trade association in explaining its demise stated the case as follows: "Manufacturers and installers have tried to establish fair business rules that would benefit both the consumer and the industry but have found, by years of experience, that the chiseling 10 percent who operate in every business will not abide by any rules unless enforced by State or National laws." Quoted in Charles A. Pearce, *Trade Association Survey,* TNEC Monograph No. 18, Washington, 1941, p. 18.

Through interlocking directorates, 91 of the 107 industrial corporations in the group of 250 largest American corporations in 1935 had a direct link with one or more other companies among the 250.[35] Intercorporate stockholdings amounting to at least 10 per cent (but less than 50 per cent) of the equity brought 27 of these 250 largest corporations into alliance with another (sometimes two others) of the group.[36] Common agencies rendering financial, legal, engineering, and accounting services to industrial corporations operating in the same field may also help temper their rivalry. In 1935, ten investment banking houses managed the sale of 56 per cent of all new corporate security issues, and ten auditing firms certified the accounts of 52 per cent of the registered companies reporting to the Securities and Exchange Commission.[37]

But perhaps the most pervasive influence in fostering a recognition of solidarity of interests and creating an atmosphere of mutual forbearance in the major fields of industry has stemmed from the steadily widening ramifications of the great financial institutions and

35. See National Resources Committee, *The Structure of the American Economy*, Washington, 1939, Pt. 1, p. 159. By itself, such a compilation shows little about the community of interest among the companies thus linked. A particular director may exercise much or little influence on the business policies of the companies on whose boards of directors he serves. On the other hand, the compilation may seriously understate the degree to which the existence of common directors reflects and fosters an abiding harmony in the general lines of business strategy in the industries in which these 91 giant industrials operate.

First, the compilation ignores similar ties, not to mention other types of interconnection, with smaller companies than those in the group of 250 giants, which smaller companies may, nevertheless, be important factors in the industry in which a given industrial giant is predominantly interested. Thus this compilation takes no account of the close links between General Motors and Bendix Aviation, or between Pittsburgh Plate Glass and Southern Alkali, because Bendix and Southern Alkali each had assets of less than $65 million.

Second, it ignores the *indirect* ties, not only through common directors but otherwise, between two or more of the larger industrial corporations, each of which may have a close connection with the same financial group. For example, International Paper and Brown Bros. (both operating in the same field and both included in the list of 107 large industrials) each has close ties with the "Boston group" of financial interests, and thus they are not likely to tread on one another's toes even though they may have no common directors and neither may own any stock in the other.

These two observations concerning the deficiencies of the National Resources Committee's data on interlocking directorates apply also, after making the necessary changes, to each of the other measures of interconnection or community of interest among the 250 largest American corporations.

36. *Ibid.* In its study the National Resources Committee treated as a subsidiary any company, no matter how large, of which another corporation held more than 50 per cent of the voting stock. For example, the Committee excluded Western Electric from the list of 107 largest industrial corporations because AT & T owns more than 50 per cent of its voting stock. Western Electric has far greater assets, however, than some of the 107 "largest" industrials.

37. *Ibid.*

family interest groups. The National Resources Committee reported in 1939 that "A careful study of the interrelationships between the [250] large corporations disclosed eight more or less clearly defined interest groups which . . . overshadowed" all others.[38] Out of this network of financial interconnection, commercial interdependence, and social cohesion has evolved a climate of opinion in American business that is hostile to a genuinely free market. However eager the captains of industry may be to display their prowess in forthright competition, the generals of finance set the outlines of strategy. Competition is a disturbing factor, opposed to their interests.

Many Means, Many Devices

This tempering of the competitive spirit is not a new development. In 1911 Eddy used the term "new competition" to describe the new attitude.[39] A decade later trade association leaders called it "open competition," or "trade cooperation." In the early 1930's it found expression in the "Swope Plan" and later, under NRA, business hailed it as "industrial self-government." [40] But under whatever name it passed current, the new order signified a growing distaste for forthright rivalry and a quickening sentiment of brotherly solidarity.

As the Great Depression dried up purchasing power and left plant capacity unused, the price cutter became the "chiseler"—a violator of the new business mores. Finally Congress, driven by lobbyists to heroic measures, made him a law breaker subject to fine and imprisonment for violating an industrial code. The demise of NRA, moreover, did not kill its spirit.[41]

38. *Ibid.,* p. 161. These groups included the Morgan, Rockefeller, Mellon, and du Pont interests.

39. A. J. Eddy, *The New Competition,* Appleton, New York, 1912.

40. The Swope Plan, of course, was far broader than a mere price stabilization program. It was designed to give security to the workers under a privately administered social insurance program. This was the price business was to pay to free itself from the restrictions of the antitrust laws. The key to prosperity was cooperative action of business rivals through trade associations. By standardizing its accounting and trade practices within a particular industry, business was to stabilize prices and employment. See Gerard Swope, "Stabilization of Industry," an address delivered before the National Electrical Manufacturers Association, New York, September 16, 1931; and J. George Frederick (Ed.), *The Swope Plan,* Business Bourse, New York, 1931, Chap. 2.

41. Industrial developments during World War II and since may make some forget the lessons of the interwar period. The abnormal expansion of demand for goods and services during the war and postwar inflation lessened, if it did not eliminate, the need for restrictive practices. When firms are able to sell all they can produce at steadily advancing prices, the incentive to restrict output is small. But as American business passes from a sellers' to a buyers' market a reversion to prewar practices may well occur.

The new canons of business behavior approved a variety of specific devices designed to prevent price competition and standardize business practices. Business groups resorted to price leadership, resale price maintenance, competitive advertising, trade association activities, basing point and other delivered pricing systems, and the like in an effort to prevent the readjustments that economic progress entails and effective competition compels. Whether legal or illegal, these practices tended to free business from the control of the automatic forces of the market and to subject the market to the deliberate guidance of businessmen. Between World Wars I and II American business became less enterprising and less free. Competition was not always and everywhere effective.

Chapter 6

PRICE LEADERSHIP

IN MARKETS OF relatively few sellers where one or more are large enough to make or break prices by independent action, all sellers usually follow the price leaders. Price leadership is most common in industries producing standardized or nearly standardized goods. Unless the products of rival sellers are approximately alike, identical prices have no special significance and price leadership is out of the question.

Companies often achieve leadership by consolidating rival enterprises. Many of the historic "trusts," although they may not now dominate the market as effectively as they once did, have continued to exercise price leadership. United States Steel, Pittsburgh Plate Glass, and American Woolen are cases in point. Leadership may change hands from time to time, however, as when the Archer-Daniels-Midland consolidation displaced American Linseed Oil in the role of price leader in the linseed oil industry.

Moreover, in different regions different firms may take the lead. The several Standard Oil companies, each in a particular area of operations, generally initiate price changes both in the purchase of crude oil and in the sale of gasoline. But other companies, such as Sinclair, have taken the lead in posting buying prices in certain regions where their crude-oil production is relatively great. In gasoline marketing as a rule, former constituents of the old Standard Oil Trust continue to point the way in the areas they dominated before dissolution of the trust in 1911. Thus Standard Oil of New Jersey is the recognized price leader for gasoline in most of the Middle Atlantic states, but in New York and New England its subsidiaries take their cue from the largest marketer, Socony-Vacuum —also a member of the Standard Oil group. Similarly, Socony-Vacuum recognizes the leadership of Standard Oil of Indiana in the Midwest. On the Pacific Coast, Standard Oil of California takes the lead; in the Southwest, Humble Oil and Refining, a subsidiary of Standard Oil of New Jersey.

Price Leadership as Standard Practice

Companies not only frankly admit the practice of price leadership but they sometimes provide for it in dealer contracts. For example, a contract between Pennzoil Company, a manufacturer of petroleum products, and the New Deal Oil Company, a jobber and broker, made these provisions:

> Price on PENNZIP Gasoline to be that published in Platt's Oilgram on date of each shipment, as quoted by the Standard Oil Company of Ohio, for 65 Octane gasoline in tank cars, with freight allowed to Ohio destination. It being further agreed that if such price does not allow a margin of six (6¢) cents under the state wide retail price for X-70 gasoline, as posted by the Standard Oil Company of Ohio, the Buyer is to be billed at a price which will give such margin.[1]

The president of the Riverside Metal Company, a manufacturer of alloys, testified before TNEC that his industry had "a well crystallized practice of price leadership" and that the American Brass Company was the leader.[2]

Sometimes, as in the glass industry, nominally competing producers recognize a division of product fields, within each of which a different company acts as price leader. According to a Hazel-Atlas Glass official, "Hazel-Atlas . . . initiates the prices covering wide-mouthed container ware, and the Hazel-Atlas price list for ware of this class constitutes the recognized market price of the industry." [3] Hazel-Atlas also initiates prices on opal ware for the cosmetic and drug trade. But in pricing proprietary and prescription ware it adopts

1. *Investigation of the Concentration of Economic Power,* Temporary National Economic Committee, Hearings pursuant to Pub.Res. 113 (75th Cong.), Pt. 16, Ex. 1231, p. 9221. (These hearings will hereinafter be cited: TNEC Hearings, Pt. —.)

2. *Ibid.,* Pt. 5, pp. 2085-86. A vice-president of American Brass in his testimony before TNEC at first categorically denied that the company was a price leader or that price leadership prevailed in the industry. Under questioning he admitted that "to some extent we have been the leader"; but he also insisted that at times American Brass had followed the price changes of other companies. *Ibid.,* p. 2094. The company's general sales manager testified, however, that competitors customarily changed their prices within eight to twelve hours after American Brass announced a price change. *Ibid.,* p. 2125. Moreover, American Brass regularly sent price lists to its competitors when announcing price changes to its customers. *Ibid.,* p. 2130.

3. *Ibid.,* Pt. 2, p. 547. The witness was vice-president and general manager of the company.

the price schedules of Owens-Illinois Glass, and on fruit jars and jelly glasses those of Ball Brothers.[4]

In iron and steel United States Steel has been the leader. As the president of the Steel Corporation put it: "I would say we generally make the prices."[5] Eugene Grace, president of Bethlehem Steel, professed an old-fashioned confidence in "that old law of supply and demand," but he admitted that in making price decisions the Bethlehem management found the Steel Corporation prices a "good guide" and on certain occasions welcomed "the opportunity to follow the Corporation's lead in the publishing of new base prices."[6] Among other industries in which price leadership has been standard practice are anthracite coal, tin cans, corn products, salmon, biscuits and crackers, agricultural implements, fertilizers, industrial alcohol, copper, lead, newsprint, sulphur, plaster, and bananas.[7]

Conflicting Opinions on Price Leadership

Economists, businessmen, and lawyers interpret the legal and economic significance of price leadership differently.

Burns, an economist, says:

> Leadership is merely a relation between sellers and, in this respect, resembles a trade association . . . both types of relation may, and do, occur in the same industry, the trade association administering and perfecting the policy of leadership. The large firm may stand outside the trade association in its industry, the association circulating information concerning the prices of the leader, or it may be a member of the trade association which facilitates the acceptance of its lead.[8]

Lynch, also an economist, writing more recently, says:

> The practice is similar to the price pool, but there is no overt evidence of its existence, and it often represents nothing more than a tacit understanding among producers to "follow the leader" in price policy.[9]

4. *Ibid.*, p. 548. The witness testified that the quality of the same products sold by different glass companies differed very little, but he thought those of his company were as good as any. *Ibid.*, p. 549.
5. Quoted in *ibid.*, Pt. 27, p. 14250, from testimony before the Senate Committee on Interstate Commerce in 1936.
6. *Ibid.*, Pt. 19, pp. 10586-87, 10592.
7. See Clair Wilcox, *Competition and Monopoly in American Industry*, TNEC Monograph No. 21, Washington, 1940, p. 123; and George J. Stigler, "The Kinky Oligopoly Demand Curve and Rigid Prices," *Journal of Political Economy*, October 1947, pp. 432-49.
8. Arthur R. Burns, *The Decline of Competition*, McGraw-Hill, New York, 1936, p. 76.
9. David Lynch, *The Concentration of Economic Power*, Columbia University Press, New York, 1946, p. 174.

Both Burns and Lynch apparently hold that price leadership implies deliberate collaboration. Handler, a lawyer, takes the opposite view, implicitly following the theorists of imperfect competition. He says that:

> . . . the object and effect of the practice is the establishment of a non-competitive market price. This end, however, is achieved without any agreement or understanding. . . . There need be no meetings, no discussions, no direct interchange of price information, no exchange of assurances, no commitments to adhere to any announced price for the practice to take root in an industry.[10]

Businessmen more or less unanimously defend price leadership as an expression of free competition. They argue: Someone must initiate price changes. It is logical that the largest company do so. If the leader reduces prices, rivals must meet the reduction if they are to get business. If the leader raises prices, rivals find it profitable to do likewise. If the state of the market justifies higher prices for the leader, it justifies them for the whole industry. Failure of rivals to follow a price advance in response to market conditions would be to forego needlessly an opportunity to make money. Impersonal market forces in the long run determine prices; the market leader, like a barometer, merely measures such forces. Rivals compete by meeting the leader's prices. Competition thus forces prices to a common level.

The controversy over price leadership turns around two important questions: Is the public interest adequately protected in industries in which price leadership prevails? If not, is price leadership beyond

10. See Milton Handler, *A Study of the Construction and Enforcement of the Federal Antitrust Laws,* TNEC Monograph No. 38, Washington, 1941, pp. 40-41. Handler is not entirely consistent in his position. For he also says: "The price announcement of one of the companies in the field, typically the dominant concern, or principal producer, is *loyally* followed by most of its competitors." *Ibid.* Italics supplied.

Stigler has classified price leadership under two categories: the dominant and the barometric firm. The dominant firm is larger than any rival and perhaps as large as all rivals combined. According to Stigler, the dominant firm sets the price so as to maximize its earnings, and permits the smaller firms to sell as much as they can at that price. To maximize its earnings it must know the total market demand and the marginal cost of its rivals. The barometric firm merely interprets supply-demand relationships and adjusts its prices to conform to them. Others follow its lead "because, and to the extent that," its "price reflects market conditions with tolerable promptness." Stigler, *op. cit.,* p. 446. See also Stigler, *The Theory of Price,* Macmillan, New York, 1947, pp. 226-27. Like other theoretical models, the dominant firm finds few precise counterparts in industry. In practice, prices of a barometric firm may be followed not merely because it interprets market conditions accurately but because rivals prefer price stability to price competition. It sometimes requires concerted action to achieve the goal.

reach of the antitrust laws? A description of the operation of price leadership in two quite different industries—cigarette and tin can manufacture—may aid in answering these questions.

Price Making in the Cigarette Industry

After the dissolution of the tobacco trust in 1911,[11] four successor companies dominated the industry—American Tobacco, Liggett & Myers, R. J. Reynolds, and P. Lorillard—and in recent years, the first three alone.[12] Under the dissolution decree American Tobacco retained control of about 33 per cent of the domestic trade in ciga-

11. *U.S.* v. *American Tobacco Co.,* 221 U.S. 106 (1911). In this opinion and the one handed down the same day in the Standard Oil case (221 U.S. 1), the Supreme Court announced the so-called "rule of reason" in applying the Sherman antitrust statute. This doctrine in effect distinguished between "good" and "bad" trusts.

The tobacco trust was very bad indeed. Its history was replete with acts that showed "the existence from the beginning of a purpose to acquire dominion and control of the tobacco trade, not by the mere exertion of the ordinary right to contract and to trade, but by methods devised in order to monopolize the trade by driving competitors out of business, which were ruthlessly carried out upon the assumption that to work upon the fears or play upon the cupidity of competitors would make success possible." 221 U.S., pp. 181-82. In its struggle to monopolize the tobacco industry American Tobacco had resorted to ruinous competition by cutting prices locally, using "fighting" brands and bogus independents to draw trade away from real competitors without the need of reducing prices on the trust's well-established products outside the limited territory in which genuine competitors customarily operated. It also made extensive use of exclusive dealer contracts, and sometimes imitated its rivals' products.

James B. Duke organized the original American Tobacco Company in 1890 as a merger of five leading smoking tobacco companies. Thomas Fortune Ryan and associates formed a rival combine, Union Tobacco, in 1898. The rival groups came to terms the following year and in 1904 merged their interests in various companies in a single corporation, American Tobacco. The most important of the merged companies were Continental Tobacco (the plug trust) and Consolidated Tobacco, mainly a holding company. To distinguish the "trust" that was dissolved by court order in 1911 from the American Tobacco Company that survived, though stripped of more than half its assets, the former will hereinafter be identified as American Tobacco I.

12. American Tobacco as a "successor" company retained, after the dissolution, assets equal to the combined assets of the two principal "new" successor companies formed pursuant to the dissolution decree: Liggett & Myers and P. Lorillard. But American Tobacco was also required to dispose of its interests in eleven other successor companies, including R. J. Reynolds. Neither Liggett & Myers nor P. Lorillard were new names in the tobacco trade. Indeed, their businesses and that of R. J. Reynolds had developed on a large scale long before the trust took them over. The American Tobacco I interests acquired control of P. Lorillard in 1898 and of Liggett & Myers and R. J. Reynolds in 1899. At the time of the dissolution, Reynolds was one of the smaller companies, with a business confined almost wholly to plug tobacco. Its market was mainly in the South. See Eliot Jones, *The Trust Problem in the United States,* Macmillan, New York, 1921, Chap. 7; and W. H. S. Stevens, *Industrial Combinations and Trusts,* Macmillan, New York, 1914, pp. 440-61.

As a result of the transfer of American Tobacco I assets in the dissolution, Lorillard became the third largest tobacco manufacturer. But its sales volume did not keep pace with sales of the other principal successor companies, and by 1940 it was not even in fourth place in the industry. Therefore, references hereinafter to the Big Three mean: American Tobacco, Liggett & Myers, and Reynolds.

rettes, 40 per cent in smoking tobacco, 25 per cent in plug tobacco, and about 14 per cent in fine-cut tobacco. The decree allotted Liggett & Myers about 21 per cent of the trade in cigarettes, 16 per cent in smoking tobacco, 38 per cent in plug tobacco, and 36 per cent in fine-cut tobacco. Lorillard got about 26 per cent of the cigarette trade, 19 per cent of smoking tobacco, 5 per cent of plug, and 30 per cent of fine cut. R. J. Reynolds obtained none of the cigarette or fine-cut business. It received about 3 per cent of the smoking tobacco business and 15 per cent of the plug business. Together those four companies immediately after the dissolution produced about 80 per cent of all cigarettes, smoking tobacco, plug tobacco, and fine cut sold in the United States.[13]

Despite the fact that the dissolution did not immediately remove control of the American tobacco industry from the small group that had built the trust, competition revived with astonishing rapidity.[14] It was the old story of a relatively small concern not being content with its position in the industry and willing to sacrifice the interests of the group to promote its individual welfare. Reynolds became the disturbing element.[15] It showed its independence of the old line-up in two ways.

13. *American Tobacco Co.* v. *U.S.*, 147 Fed. *2d* 93 (1944), in the Circuit Court of Appeals, Sixth Circuit, Record on Appeal, Exhibits, Vol. 5, p. 2509, Defendants' Exhibit No. 696. This was a criminal proceeding under the antitrust statutes, charging conspiracy in restraint of trade in leaf tobacco and tobacco products and attempts to monopolize. The Department of Justice filed a Criminal Information on July 24, 1940 in the U.S. District Court for the Eastern District of Kentucky against American Tobacco Co., Liggett & Myers Tobacco Co., R. J. Reynolds Tobacco Co., P. Lorillard Co., The Imperial Tobacco Co. (of Great Britain), British-American Tobacco Co., Ltd., Philip Morris & Co., Ltd., and Universal Leaf Tobacco Co. as principal defendants, and against 26 subsidiaries of the principal defendants and 33 individuals, officers of the parent and subsidiary companies. The charges were later dropped against all the defendants except the Big Three—American Tobacco, Liggett & Myers, and Reynolds—and certain of their officers. The jury found the defendants guilty and the court levied fines of $255,000. The Circuit Court of Appeals sustained the verdict and the Supreme Court affirmed this decision, 328 U.S. 781 (1946). Hereinafter the proceedings will be referred to as *ATC* v. *U.S.* and the various documents will be identified with appropriate symbols, e.g., Transcript of Record as Rec., Government Exhibits as GX, Defendants' Exhibits as DX, etc.

14. Under the dissolution decree the holders of American Tobacco I stock acquired pro rata shares in the stocks of successor companies. This left the same group that controlled the trust in control of about the same proportion of the industry. For a history of the tobacco trust, see *Report of the Commissioner of Corporations on the Tobacco Industry,* Washington, Pt. 1 (1909), Pt. 2 (1911), and Pt. 3 (1915). On the effects of the dissolution, see Reavis Cox, *Competitive Conditions in the American Tobacco Industry,* Columbia University Press, New York, 1933. The briefs for the government and for the several defendants in *ATC* v. *U.S.* summarize the story and the Record develops it in detail.

15. Some evidence suggests that Reynolds was never thoroughly integrated into the trust. No officer of Reynolds was ever a member of American Tobacco's board

First, it undertook to get Reynolds stock out of the hands of the "New York crowd" and into the hands of its employees and North Carolinians generally.[16] Then, it enlarged the scope of its activities in order to become a full-line company. In 1913 it aggressively elbowed its way into the cigarette market by introducing its now famous Camel cigarette—the first popular brand of burley blend cigarettes on the American market.[17] In doing so it disdained the use of premiums as a means of attracting customers—the generally accepted competitive device among the old trust members. Reynolds advertised on each Camel package: "Don't look for premiums or coupons, as the cost of the tobaccos blended in Camel cigarettes prohibits the use of them." It still uses this slogan. Reynolds priced Camels at $4 a thousand, wholesale, less a trade discount of 2 per cent and a cash discount of 10 per cent. This permitted retail sales at 10 cents a package of 20, compared with retail prices on quality brands of American Tobacco, Liggett & Myers, and Lorillard ranging from 15 cents to 20 cents.[18]

Appearance of Popular-Brand Cigarettes

Camels caught on at once. Within two years after putting them on the market Reynolds sold 2.4 billion out of a total national consumption of 18 billion cigarettes. The next year, sales of Camels nearly tripled, and the following year they doubled. Though cigarette sales of all the principal manufacturers increased rapidly during World War I, within five years of the introduction of Camels

---

of directors. *ATC* v. *U.S.*, Rec., Vol. 4, p. 2489. After 1905 no representative of American Tobacco sat on Reynolds' board, and in 1907 American Tobacco opposed Reynolds' introduction of Prince Albert smoking tobacco. The conflict of interests became so sharp that Reynolds' management offered American Tobacco the alternative of selling its interest in the Reynolds company to the Reynolds management or of buying out the Reynolds interests. *Ibid.*, Vol. 6, pp. 4800-66.

16. *Ibid.*, Vol. 6, p. 4871.

17. Turkish and Turkish blends had been the market favorites. Even the cheaper cigarettes masqueraded as Turkish. George W. Hill, president of American Tobacco, described it thus: "It was not really Turkish, but they were oval in shape, in imitation of the higher grade Turkish . . . and their boxes had minarets and designs of Turkish scenes . . . and their names were Turkish in atmosphere, like Mecca and Hasson." *Ibid.*, Vol. 5, p. 3849.

18. Liggett & Myers' Fatima, American Tobacco's Omar, and Lorillard's Zubelda all retailed for 15 cents a package of 20. American Tobacco's Pall Mall, Lorillard's Egyptian Deities, and Liggett & Myers' Condax sold at 25 cents for 10. American Tobacco's Egyptian Straights, Lorillard's Helmar and Turkish Trophies sold for 10 cents for 10. These companies also sold several brands of lower quality at 10 for 5 cents. *Ibid.*, Vol. 5, p. 3851.

Reynolds had captured more than one third of the entire domestic market. By the end of 1923 Reynolds was selling 45 per cent of all cigarettes in the domestic market.[19]

Liggett & Myers responded by introducing a burley blend cigarette—Chesterfields—to sell in Camels' price class. Shortly afterward American Tobacco brought out Lucky Strikes, also a burley blend, and, adopting Reynolds' strategy, concentrated sales effort on the single brand.

During the decade following the dissolution of the trust, competition, while not conforming to the economists' ideal model, apparently was effective. Reynolds' aggressive and successful effort to capture a large part of the cigarette market was an independent decision. By popularizing a "quality" cigarette at a low price, Reynolds forced its rivals to follow suit. With the exception of Lorillard, which was tardy in recognizing the trend, the leading producers organized elaborate and expensive sales campaigns for promoting popular-priced cigarettes, which swept the field. Rivalry among the cigarette manufacturers was not merely keen; it was frequently bitter.[20] American Tobacco and Liggett & Myers pushed Lucky Strikes and Chesterfields in an effort to stem Reynolds' inroads into the expanding cigarette market.[21]

19. *ATC* v. *U.S.*, Exhibits, Vol. 6, DX 1236, p. 3219; Vol. 5, DX 689, p. 2489; GX 376-77, pp. 1514-15.

20. Reynolds accompanied the introduction of Camels by an aggressive and effective advertising campaign using the slogan "The Camels are coming." George W. Hill, president of American Tobacco, testified that at first he thought it a joke. He soon learned differently. As he said, "It was not any joke. In town after town, when they introduced Camels, other cigarette brands were swept to one side." *ATC* v. *U.S.*, Rec., Vol. 5, pp. 3853-54.

As Camels forged ahead, they encountered an undercover campaign of vilification and slander. In response, Reynolds published full-page advertisements under the caption "The Stench of Contemptible Slander Is Repulsive Even to the Nostrils of a Buzzard." The advertisements condemned the alleged tactics of undesignated competitors who hired agents to slander the Camel cigarette on crowded streetcars by suggesting that it was peculiarly injurious to the smoker's health. See Cox, *op. cit.*, pp. 232-33. But Reynolds' major competitors—if, indeed, they were responsible—did not rely mainly on such tactics.

21. Reynolds entered the cigarette market opportunely. American smoking habits were changing rapidly. When the tobacco trust was dissolved in 1911 the cigarette habit was confined to comparatively few persons. In 1910 about 48 per cent of the tobacco leaf used in the United States went into smoking tobacco, cigars, and snuff, about 45 per cent into chewing tobacco, and only 7 per cent into manufactured cigarettes. Provincial moralists regarded the use of tobacco as a dirty habit, and cigarette smoking was thought to be particularly evil. In the parlance of the day, each cigarette smoked was a "nail driven into your coffin." World War I changed all this, transforming cigarettes from a vile evil to a comforting necessity. Between the outbreak of the war and its end, domestic sales of cigarettes increased about 200 per cent. *ATC* v. *U.S.*, Exhibits, Vol. 5, DX 680, p. 2489.

The Big Three Compete

Not only were the Big Three striving vigorously to capture and hold the lead through advertising and competitive sales effort; they apparently also resorted to price competition.[22] During the ten years following the introduction of Camels no price leader dominated the field. The Big Three neither generally charged identical prices nor changed them simultaneously. Liggett & Myers brought out Chesterfields at $3.75 a thousand, wholesale, less 2 per cent for cash, or $3.675 net,[23] in contrast with Reynolds' introductory price on Camels of $4 a thousand less discounts of 2 per cent trade and 10 per cent cash, or $3.528 net.[24] American Tobacco introduced Lucky Strikes at $4 a thousand less discounts of 5 per cent trade and 2 per cent cash, or $3.724 net.[25]

The Big Three revised prices frequently. In the seven years after Lucky Strikes came out the Big Three charged identical prices only about one third of the time. In nine months Chesterfields sold at a higher price than either Lucky Strikes or Camels, in four months at a lower. The price of Chesterfields was higher than that of Lucky Strikes but lower than that of Camels in four and a half months, identical with Lucky Strikes but lower than Camels in one month, identical with Camels but lower than Lucky Strikes in eleven months, the same as Lucky Strikes but higher than Camels in seven and a half months, the same as Camels but higher than Lucky Strikes in two months.[26] Not only did the list prices of the Big Three generally differ, but so did their standard discounts. Moreover, one or the other of the Big Three occasionally granted special and confidential discounts and more frequently made "free deals" that lowered the net price to jobbers.[27] According to the Federal Trade Commission, American Tobacco gave secret rebates to jobbers at various times between 1916 and 1921.[28]

22. Lorillard did not introduce Old Gold, its competing burley blend cigarette, until 1926. It has never overcome the lead of its rivals.

23. *Ibid.*, Vol. 3, GX 412, p. 1602. This was the price as of April 30, 1912. Chesterfields actually appeared before Camels, but were a relatively insignificant brand until Camels blazed the way.

24. Liggett & Myers' Brief on Appeal (p. 155) incorrectly states that the Camel discounts were 10 and 2 rather than 2 and 10. Cf. *ATC* v. *U.S.*, Exhibits, Vol. 3, GX 389, p. 1527.

25. *Ibid.*, Vol. 4, GX 568, p. 2077.

26. *ATC* v. *U.S.*, Liggett & Myers' Brief on Appeal, pp. 265-66.

27. *ATC* v. *U.S.*, Exhibits, Vol. 5, GX 568, pp. 2091-92.

28. Federal Trade Commission, *Prices of Tobacco Products*, Washington, 1922, pp. 85-88.

With the general decline of prices during the business recession in 1921 the Big Three engaged in a price war. Cigarettes had reached a peak wholesale price of about $8 a thousand in 1919, when the popular brands retailed for 20 cents.[29] In 1921 American Tobacco reduced Lucky Strikes to $7.75; Reynolds lowered Camels to $7.50. When the prices of other brands dropped to this level, Reynolds reduced prices still further, first to $6.80 and then to $6.40 a thousand. Retailers passed the reductions on to consumers and the prices of popular brands fell from 20 cents to 15 cents a package.

Price Stabilization Follows Price Competition

But, as has frequently happened in other fields, the leaders of the industry soon learned that price competition as a matter of tactics did not pay. Reynolds' rivals apparently recognized that its newly achieved pre-eminence in the industry was no passing phenomenon. And the Big Three apparently realized that their separate interests were dependent on their collective welfare and that a prolonged price war presaged mutual defeat and frustration. They accordingly concluded they could best promote their several interests by charging identical prices in accordance with the price leadership principle. Counsel for Liggett & Myers said that "in making price decisions the management of Liggett & Myers has acted in response to a long experience of non-identical prices as well as identical prices." [30]

Reynolds as the largest producer was the natural leader. Between February 1923 and July 1940, when the government began its antitrust suit, Camels and Chesterfields sold continuously at the same price. During the first five years of this period Lucky Strikes sold for a nickel a thousand more, a differential too small to affect their retail price.[31]

29. An increase in the internal revenue tax from $1.25 a thousand before the war to $3 was responsible for much of the increase. *ATC* v. *U.S.*, Rec., Vol. 6, p. 4580.

30. See *ATC* v. *U.S.*, Liggett & Myers' Brief, p. 264; see also pp. 251-61; Reynolds' Brief, p. 390; and American Tobacco's Brief, pp. 94-95.

31. In 1925 Lucky Strikes ran a poor third to Camels and Chesterfields in national sales. American Tobacco decided on the 5 cent differential mainly as a means of getting revenue for an intensive advertising campaign. See testimony of George W. Hill, in *ATC* v. *U.S.*, Rec., Vol. 5, pp. 3876-77.

The program paid. Annual sales of Lucky Strikes increased from 13.72 billion in 1925 to 36.99 billion in 1929, drawing up to the sales volume of Camels. Lucky Strikes passed Camels the next year and held the lead until 1934. *ATC* v. *U.S.*, Exhibits, Vol. 3, p. 1848, and Vol. 4, p. 2412; also *ATC* v. *U.S.*, Rec., Vol. 2, pp. 1629-30.

As to this development Mr. Hill testified as follows: "In 1928, Mr. Reynolds' company cut his price to $6 per thousand. I have always felt that he was deliberately

During the remainder of the period Lucky Strikes, Camels, and Chesterfields sold at the same price. Except briefly in 1928 when Old Golds sold at 10 cents a thousand more than competing brands, the prices of the Big Four were identical from 1928 to 1940. During the seventeen years from 1923 to 1940 the manufacturers' list prices of Camels, Chesterfields, Lucky Strikes, and Old Golds changed eight times. Reynolds initiated six changes and American Tobacco two. In every instance the other companies quickly followed the price leader.

Although the relative sales of the Big Three changed from time to time as the public responded to the advertising appeals of one or the other, the combined power of the Big Three over the market steadily increased during the 1920's.[32] Whereas the trust members sold about 80 per cent of the cigarettes marketed in 1910, the Big Three sold about 91 per cent of all the cigarettes sold in this country in 1929. Including Lorillard they sold 98 per cent. With the market so neatly in their hands they used their power as monopoly partners to exploit it to the limit.[33]

---

trying to stop my advertising money, to stop those advertising campaigns. At any rate, my volume had grown to a point where I felt I was able to meet him, so, when he dropped from $6.40 to $6, we dropped from $6.45 to $6." *Ibid.,* Vol. 5, p. 3877. For the next decade, according to the record, Camels and Lucky Strikes had identical list prices.

32. Lorillard remained a poor fourth, with only about 7 per cent of total national sales. *ATC* v. *U.S.,* Exhibits, Vol. 5, GX 677, p. 2473.

During the period American Tobacco's advertising of Lucky Strikes was remarkably successful. Mr. Hill was an advertising expert. His basic idea in selling was not to "give the customer what he wants," but to "give him something you and he know he can use" and make him want it.

Among the several successive themes of Lucky Strike advertising were "Lucky Strike, It's Toasted," "The Cream of the Crop," "The Precious Voice," "Coming Events Cast their Shadows Before," and "Reach for a Lucky Instead of a Sweet." The last made advertising history. The program "really went to town," as Mr. Hill expressed it.

Mr. Hill's account of how he hit on this happy slogan reveals something of the working of the huckster mind. "The way I got that campaign, I was riding out to my home. I got to 110th Street and Fifth Avenue; I was sitting in the car and I looked at the corner, and there was a great big stout negro lady chewing on gum. And, there was a taxicab,—it was in the summertime,—coming the other way. I thought I was human and I looked, and there was a young lady sitting in the taxicab with a long cigarette holder in her mouth, and her skirts were pretty high, and she had a very good figure. I didn't know what she was smoking; maybe she was smoking a Camel.

"But, right then and there it hit me; there was the colored lady that was stout and chewing, and there was the young girl that was slim and smoking a cigarette,—'Reach for a Lucky Instead of a Sweet.' " *ATC* v. *U.S.,* Rec., Vol. 5, p. 3863. For a more detailed account of American Tobacco's advertising campaigns and sales strategy, see *ibid.,* pp. 3853-79.

33. On the meaning of "monopoly partners," see p. 75, footnote 30.

Prices Up Again

On October 5, 1929 Reynolds raised Camels from $6 to $6.40. Lorillard and Liggett & Myers followed suit the same day. American Tobacco followed on October 11. On June 24, 1931, with farmers receiving for tobacco leaf the lowest price in a quarter of a century, manufacturing costs declining, and cigarette company profits at an all-time peak, Reynolds raised the price of Camels to $6.85 a thousand—its peak since December 1921.[34] American Tobacco, Liggett & Myers, and Lorillard promptly followed. S. Clay Williams, board chairman of Reynolds, justified this increase because Reynolds had planned an expensive advertising campaign to popularize Camels' new moisture-proof cellophane wrapper and as an expression of "our own courage for the future and our own confidence in our industry." [35]

American Tobacco gave a more realistic explanation for following Reynolds' lead. Mr. Hill admitted frankly: "I naturally saw the opportunity to make some money." [36] Liggett & Myers' management thought the price increase a mistake, but nevertheless followed Reynolds' lead.[37] Mr. Hill's hope of making money for his stockholders was immediately realized. American Tobacco's 1931 profits rose about 7 per cent above its record 1930 profits, despite a decrease

34. American Tobacco's net profits in 1930 exceeded its 1929 profits by about 43 per cent; Reynolds and Liggett & Myers each had profits about 10 per cent greater than in 1929. The combined net earnings of the Big Three in 1930 were about 20 per cent above the amount earned in 1929. *ATC* v. *U.S.,* Exhibits, Vol. 5, GX 694, pp. 2507-08.

35. *ATC* v. *U.S.,* Rec., Vol. 7, pp. 5233-34. ". . . there was quite a clamor for somebody to show confidence enough in the future to go in and handle his business as if there were going to be business in the future." *Ibid.,* p. 5233.

36. *Ibid.,* Vol. 5, p. 3879. Mr. Hill expressed "the view that my duty is to the public primarily, then to my consumers of my products, and lastly, to my stockholders." While he placed his obligation to his stockholders last, he apparently did not regard it as least. For he added, "I am not unmindful that I am employed to make money for the American Tobacco Company." Since Mr. Hill was a beneficiary, under Article XII of the company's by-laws, which allotted him an annual bonus of 2.5 per cent of net earnings in excess of $8,222,245.20 (its 1910 net profits), by serving his stockholders he also served himself well. *ATC* v. *U.S.,* Exhibits, Vol. 4, GX 478, p. 1979. His bonus for 1931 under this arrangement was $891,570.45. *ATC* v. *U.S.,* Rec., Vol. 3, p. 1864. A stockholders' suit to upset this arrangement and recover some of the bonus money for the company was finally settled out of court [see *Rogers* v. *Hill,* 34 Fed.Supp. 358 (1940)] after the Supreme Court had suggested that such large "extra compensation" might be excessive. See *ibid.,* 289 U.S. 582 (1933). For further discussion of these arrangements, see p. 433, footnote 38.

Officers of Reynolds, Liggett & Myers, and Lorillard were also beneficiaries of profit-sharing plans.

37. *ATC* v. *U.S.,* Rec., Vol. 6, p. 4592.

in its cigarette sales.[38] The Big Three's combined net earnings in 1931 reached the incredible amount of $105,707,939—an annual profit volume more than double that gained in 1923, on approximately the same price level, when they first called a halt to the cigarette price war.[39]

The Advent of Ten Cent Cigarettes

The Big Three had overreached themselves, however. In their exploitation of the market they had not reckoned with potential competition. Low prices for raw tobacco and high prices for cigarettes, together with a decline in consumer purchasing power, paved the way for the introduction of 10 cent cigarettes by small independents. In 1929 Continental Tobacco introduced Paul Jones selling at a list price of $4.75 a thousand to retail for 10 cents. Larus & Brother followed in 1931 with White Rolls, Brown & Williamson with Wings, and Axton-Fisher with Twenty Grand in 1932.

In the first half of 1931 these four companies, the Little Four, produced about 1.5 per cent of all the cigarettes produced in this country, the Big Four about 97.5 per cent.[40] After the Big Four raised prices in June 1931 the Little Four's output increased rapidly. Within three months their percentage of the combined Big Four–Little Four output doubled. Within a year it multiplied more than seven times. By December 1932 the four independents together were producing and selling approximately 22 per cent of the combined output of the entire Big Four–Little Four group.

All of the increase in sales of 10 cent cigarettes was at the expense of the Big Four. Between 1930 and 1932 Reynolds' annual sales of Camels decreased from 35.3 billion to 23.9 billion; American Tobacco's sales of Lucky Strikes from 43.2 billion to 36.6 billion; Liggett & Myers' sales of Chesterfields from 26.4 billion to 20.9 billion; Lorillard's sales of Old Golds from 8.5 billion to 5.5 billion.[41] Obviously the Little Four with their 10 cent cigarettes were a serious threat to Big Four domination of the market.

38. *ATC* v. *U.S.*, Exhibits, Vol. 5, GX 677, p. 2475.
39. *Ibid.*, Vol. 5, GX 693-94, pp. 2507-08.
40. *ATC* v. *U.S.*, Rec., Vol. 3, pp. 2403 ff., and Digest of Government's Testimony, Vol. 1, pp. 285 ff. Reed Tobacco Co. replaced Larus & Brother about this time.
41. *ATC* v. *U.S.*, Exhibits, Vol. 3, GX 428, p. 1848, GX 294, p. 1295; and Vol. 4, GX 638, p. 2412; and *ATC* v. *U.S.*, Rec., Vol. 2, p. 1630.

The Big Four Counterattack

The Big Four reacted to the threat energetically. American Tobacco reduced Lucky Strikes from $6.85 to $6 a thousand on January 2, 1933.[42] Reynolds, Liggett & Myers, and Lorillard followed immediately. On February 11 American Tobacco cut the price to $5.50—the lowest since 1918—and held it unchanged for a year. The other three notified their customers of a similar reduction, effective the same day.[43]

Having reduced their list prices, the Big Three took steps to see that the reductions were carried forward to the retail level. After the January price cut, American Tobacco announced over the radio a retail price of two packages for a quarter.[44] Although it announced the second price cut to the trade by night letter of February 10, effective the next day, the Great Atlantic & Pacific Tea Company sent night letters from its New York office to its 15,000 local stores the same night—that is, the night before A & P received formal notice of the reduction in the wholesale price—authorizing retail sales at a dime a pack the next day.[45] With A & P selling popular, or "standard," brands at this record low price, the Big Three tried

42. Mr. Hill contended that in deciding to reduce the price of Lucky Strikes he was not concerned with the increase in the sale of 10 cent cigarettes. In 1933 the sales of all cigarettes had declined more than 10 billion from 1931 sales. Although the Big Three had lost more than 20 per cent of the smaller total to the 10 cent brands, this did not particularly bother Mr. Hill. What worried him to death was the general decline in the production curve.

As a matter of fact, American Tobacco's own Bull Durham had been a beneficiary of the decline in cigarette sales as impoverished Americans again rolled their own. This proved to Mr. Hill that the American public still appreciated a good burley cigarette. "While the public liked the price of 10-cent cigarettes," he said, "we in the cigarette business . . . knew they did not like the taste of the 10-cent cigarettes." Aware of his obligation to the consuming public, he decided to "change the curve" by reducing the price of Lucky Strikes. "I am not changing that curve because of 10-cent cigarettes; I am changing it in spite of the 10-cent cigarette." *Ibid.*, Vol. 5, pp. 3866 ff. Mr. Hill evidently decided that a price inducement would be more effective in increasing sales than some such slogan as "Love that smoke."

43. *ATC* v. *U.S.*, Exhibits, Vol. 5, DX 894, p. 2725; Vol. 4, GX 587, p. 2257; and Vol. 3, GX 412, p. 572, GX 299, p. 1299, GX 385, p. 1522. See also *ATC* v. *U.S.*, Rec., Vol. 5, pp. 3321-22.

44. *Ibid.*, Vol. 5, pp. 3918 ff. Mr. Hill testified: "What we tried to do was to get the 2.5 cent price reduction through to the consumer." On January 7, 1933, V. Riggio, vice-president of American Tobacco, wrote one of the company's Pacific Coast representatives: "In the East in cities as well as in rural districts the 2 for 25¢ price is to be found everywhere but we are now endeavoring to get retailers to sell *Lucky Strikes* at 2 for 23¢, or 12¢ per package, and in special places we are endeavoring to get an 11¢ price." *ATC* v. *U.S.*, Exhibits, Vol. 5, GX 819, p. 2643.

45. *ATC* v. *U.S.*, Rec., Vol. 5, pp. 3304-06 and 3314-15. A & P was even ready on the morning of February 11 with printed posters announcing the sale of Camels, Lucky Strikes, Chesterfields, and Old Golds at 10 cents a package.

to get other dealers to fall in line. As an inducement, their salesmen sold cigarettes in certain localities directly to retailers, with truck delivery, at less than jobber prices and subject to allowances for window displays.[46] Thus assisted, retailers generally lowered the price from two packs for a quarter to two packs for 23 cents. In some special cases, to induce retailers to sell Lucky Strikes at a dime a package, American Tobacco took 10 per cent off the list price and allowed an additional 10 per cent in free goods.[47]

Outcome of the Price War

In competition with old popular brands on a more nearly equal price basis, the 10 cent newcomers could not hold their own. Their sales declined. From 22.78 per cent of all domestic sales in November 1932, they sank to 16.76 per cent in January 1933. With the second price reduction they declined to 7 per cent in March and to a low of 6.4 per cent in May. By the end of the year the 10 cent brands' share of the market had risen slightly to 9 per cent of total sales.[48] Thereafter they levelled off at about 10 per cent.

Meanwhile sales of the Big Four brands increased. Camels' sales rose from 23.9 billion in 1932 to 25.5 billion in 1933 and, despite a price increase to $6.10 a thousand in January 1934, continued to increase until they reached a new record of 47.7 billion in 1937. Chesterfields' sales increased from 20.9 billion in 1932 to 29.2 billion in 1933 and the upswing continued through 1937, when 34.6 billion were sold. Sales of Lucky Strikes reached a low for the decade of 30.7 billion in 1935, and then rose gradually to 38.3 billion in 1939, a volume 15 per cent below this brand's 1931 peak. Sales of Old Golds declined slightly in 1933 and 1934, when they reached 5 billion annually. They then rose to 7.9 billion in 1937.[49]

46. *Ibid.,* Vol. 4, pp. 3095-96.

47. *Ibid.,* Vol. 4, pp. 2835-45. Mr. Hill testified that after the second price reduction Lucky Strikes sold generally for 11 cents a pack. *Ibid.,* Vol. 5, p. 3920. Camels, Chesterfields, and Old Golds usually sold at the same price.

48. An even sharper decline in production accompanied the decline in sales. Production of Wings in December 1932 exceeded a billion, in March 1933 was only 256 million. In the same interval, production of Twenty Grand fell from 586 million to 286 million, of Paul Jones from 93 million to 29.7 million, and of White Rolls from 20 million to only 400—two cartons! See *ATC* v. *U.S.,* Exhibits, Vol. 5, GX 673, pp. 2453-60, and GX 676, p. 2491.

49. During this period Philip Morris became a contender for fourth place. Since 1938 its annual sales have exceeded Old Golds'. *Ibid.,* Vol. 3, GX 437, p. 1896.

Although the lowering of prices by the large companies in 1933 retarded the sales of 10 cent cigarettes, it also affected adversely the profits of the Big Three. From a record of $105,707,000 in 1931 their combined net earnings declined to $55,286,000 in 1933.[50] In the latter part of 1933 Reynolds actually sold Camels below cost.[51] By drastic pruning of salaries and advertising expenses Liggett & Myers kept its cigarette division "in the black," but its total profits shrank from $23.1 million in 1931 to $16.7 million in 1933.[52]

The Big Three had apparently had enough. At any rate, in January 1934 each raised its price to $6.10 a thousand. In renouncing hara-kiri, however, they did not abandon their fight against the 10 cent cigarettes. They changed weapons and selected new points of attack. According to the government, they attempted to squeeze the manufacturers of 10 cent brands between the prongs of higher leaf tobacco prices and slighter differences between the retail prices of standard and 10 cent brands.

Alleged Strategy of Manipulating Leaf Prices

The government alleged that, beginning about 1934, American Tobacco, Liggett & Myers, and Reynolds began buying more of the cheaper grades of tobacco in order to increase the cost, and raise the prices, of 10 cent cigarettes.[53] The government also alleged that the Big Three simultaneously lowered the prices they paid for higher-

50. *Ibid.*, Vol. 5, GX 694, p. 2508. American Tobacco was hardest hit, its profits shrinking from $46,189,741 to $17,401,207, a decline of about 63 per cent.

51. According to the testimony of a Reynolds vice-president. See *ATC* v. *U.S.*, Rec., Vol. 6, p. 4912. Marketing agreements with the Department of Agriculture, covering purchases of flue-cured and burley, raised leaf prices, and a processing tax effective October 1, under the Agricultural Adjustment Act, also increased costs.

52. A vice-president of Liggett & Myers testified that it was "a very bad position, a very bad—well, it just curtailed all activities and all promotion and advertising—cut everything to the bone." *Ibid.*, Vol. 6, p. 4524.

53. See *ibid.*, Vol. 1, p. 21, reproducing par. 26, subpar. (a), of the Information; *ibid.*, Vol. 1, pp. 293-94, part of the government's opening statement; and *ibid.*, Vol. 1, pp. 360 ff., part of the Government's Brief. The Circuit Court of Appeals, sustaining the verdict of the trial court, did not pass judgment on each of the separate allegations. It limited its review to the question of whether there was substantial evidence to support the verdict of guilty. Without making a detailed analysis of the evidence, the court upheld the government's contention that after the 10 cent cigarettes came on the market the defendants, to harass the newcomers, began buying large amounts of the cheaper grades of tobacco. In affirming the judgment below, the Supreme Court confined itself largely to the issue whether actual exclusion of competitors, or merely the power to exclude them, was essential to a violation of the antitrust statute. The Court found sufficient evidence, however, to justify the jury in convicting the defendants on the several counts of the Information.

grade tobaccos and that in this way they raised the leaf costs of manufacturers of 10 cent brands without any over-all increase in their own costs.

To illustrate its contention, the government introduced into evidence charts showing the annual average prices per pound that American Tobacco and Liggett & Myers paid during 1931–1939 for the various cigarette grades of flue-cured tobacco, and a chart showing similar data on prices paid by Reynolds, over a longer period, for cigarette grades of burley tobacco. While the evidence is not conclusive, it tends to support the government's position. Crop yields affected the relative supply of tobacco of different grades, hence the price differentials, during the period under review. The margin between the low-grade and the high-grade tobacco bought by American Tobacco and Liggett & Myers was greatest in 1934, a short crop year. Thereafter margins declined, except in 1936, another short crop year. Reynolds' margin remained unchanged from 1928 to 1936, and thereafter declined sharply. The margins for all three companies were just about halved between 1934 and 1939.[54]

In trying to refute the government's contention that the Big Three had deliberately rigged prices of the lower-grade tobaccos to handicap the manufacturers of 10 cent cigarettes, Liggett & Myers presented data on its purchases of the several grades of leaf between 1927 and 1939. The three-year average price Liggett & Myers paid for its best grade of cigarette tobacco in 1927–1929 was 31.11 cents a pound, as compared with a three-year average in 1937–1939 of 29.19 cents. The three-year average it paid for its poorest grade in 1927–1929 was 14.99 cents, as compared with a three-year average in 1937–1939 of 15.86 cents. Thus on average the margin between the prices of the two grades declined in the ten-year interval from 16.12 cents to 13.33 cents, or by 2.79 cents.[55]

On the whole, the additional data covering Liggett & Myers' purchases in earlier years tend to confirm the trend shown by the data presented by the government.[56] Measuring the change in the relation-

54. *ATC* v. *U.S.*, Exhibits, Vol. 5, GX 880, 881, 882, pp. 2700, 2701, 2702.

55. *ATC* v. *U.S.;* computed from data presented in Brief for Appellants, Liggett & Myers, *et al.*, in the Circuit Court of Appeals, Sixth Circuit, p. 179.

56. The testimony of three tobacco experts supported the government's interpretation of the price data shown on these charts. One warehouseman testified that, since 1934, prices of the "better grades of tobacco have been lowered while the lower grades of tobacco have remained about where they were"; another that prices of the common

ship of high-grade and low-grade leaf prices from a pre-1930 base instead of from a 1934 base results in a narrower margin but it does not greatly alter the main outlines of the situation.

Cigarette Manufacturers Deny Collusion

The defendants contended that the price movements for the several grades of cigarette tobacco they bought failed to prove the government's charge of conspiracy to raise the prices of the grades bought by manufacturers of 10 cent cigarettes. They stressed that the government had introduced no evidence on the grades of tobacco used in 10 cent cigarettes or on the prices the makers of such cigarettes paid for leaf. They argued that if in their own purchases of lower-grade tobacco they competed with the manufacturers of 10 cent cigarettes, this competition would of itself explain the relatively strong upward price trend for such tobacco. As the demand for the lower grades increased with the growing sales of 10 cent brands, the prices of those grades of leaf would naturally tend to rise.[57]

The logic of the defense is unassailable, but certain facts of record raise doubts that their explanation of the changing price relationship between the better and poorer grades of tobacco is sufficient. The evidence indicates clearly that as the 10 cent brands made serious inroads into the cigarette market the Big Three greatly increased their purchases of lower grades of tobacco. Liggett & Myers' purchases of its lowest two grades of flue-cured cigarette tobacco increased from 20.6 million pounds in 1931 to 57.9 million in 1934, or by about 180 per cent, while its total purchases of all grades combined increased only 73 per cent, from 62.4 million pounds to 108.2 million. In 1931 its purchases of the lowest two grades represented only 33.1 per cent of total purchases; in 1934, 53.5 per cent. By 1938 the percentage had risen to 57.75.[58]

---

grades "have gotten higher and the top, better grades had a tendency to get cheaper; in other words, they come closer together"; and a third that the common grades "have been higher" and "I think the higher grades have not gained any." *ATC* v. *U.S.*, Rec., Vol. 2, pp. 1230, 1264, and 1378.

57. See Liggett & Myers' Brief, pp. 176-85; see also American Tobacco's Brief, pp. 69-71 and Appendix; and Reynolds' Brief, pp. 335-40.

58. *ATC* v. *U.S.*, Exhibits, Vol. 6, GX 1275, p. 3325. Liggett & Myers' purchases of the lowest grade alone increased from 10.58 per cent of total purchases in 1931 to 25.29 per cent in 1939. Furthermore, in 1939 the company began buying another low-grade leaf, Grade C-2. If purchases of this grade are included with its purchases of its previous lowest two grades, the combined purchases represented 60 per cent of its entire flue-cured purchases in 1939.

As the 1930's advanced, American Tobacco also bought more of the cheaper grades. In 1932 it began buying a new low-grade leaf, Grade 66.[59] In 1932 American Tobacco bought 17.1 million pounds of flue-cured tobacco of Grade 66 or lower, amounting to 32.9 per cent of its total purchases of all grades of such tobacco.[60] The percentage of its total purchases represented by these cheaper grades remained about the same each year through 1934. Thereafter it rose sharply, to 37.7 per cent in 1935, to 42.8 per cent in 1937, and to 61.5 per cent in 1939.

Reynolds' purchases of the lower grades followed a similar course. In 1933 Reynolds bought 12.2 million pounds of its lowest two grades of flue-cured cigarette tobacco, and these purchases represented 16.6 per cent of its total auction purchases of all grades of flue-cured tobacco.[61] The percentage of its total purchases represented by these cheaper grades rose to 31.7 in 1935, and to no less than 53.4 in 1938.[62]

An explanation, only superficially plausible, of the increased buying of the cheaper grades of cigarette tobaccos by the Big Three might be that it reflected their increased need for such grades of leaf as their cigarette production increased. But the facts as here reviewed make such an explanation implausible. For the increase in their purchases of the cheaper grades of cigarette tobacco far outstripped the increase in their total cigarette production, which rose merely from 86.7 billion in 1932 and 96.3 billion in 1933 to 121.9 billion in 1938 and 122.9 billion in 1939. Another possible explanation is that to meet competition of cheaper brands, the majors had to use a higher proportion of cheaper tobacco in their cigarettes. However, representatives of the Big Three testified that leaf blends of their popular brands of cigarettes had not been changed in the meantime.

59. *ATC* v. *U.S.*, Rec., Vol. 5, p. 3717.

60. *ATC* v. *U.S.*, Exhibits, Vol. 1, GX 41-43, pp. 229-48.

61. *Ibid.*, Vol. 1, GX 39, pp. 167-82. Reynolds' purchases of these lowest two grades in 1932 apparently amounted to less than half a million pounds, or only 2.2 per cent of its purchases of all grades of flue-cured leaf. The year 1933 was probably more representative of Reynolds' operations in the leaf tobacco market before the alleged "squeeze play" on the 10 cent cigarette manufacturers began.

62. *Ibid.* The amount of these cheaper grades bought in 1935 was 27.7 million pounds; by 1938 such purchases had increased to 39.5 million pounds, or more than three times the amount bought in 1933. Yet during these six years Reynolds' sales of Camels had increased only 90 per cent, or from 25.5 billion to 47.7 billion. See *ibid.*, Vol. 3, GX 428, p. 1848.

What became, then, of the greatly increased amount of the cheaper grades of cigarette tobacco bought by the Big Three in the latter half of the 1930's? The record unfortunately does not show what use, if any, they made of such tobacco. It is obvious, however, that the dramatic change in the leaf tobacco buying programs of the Big Three forced the 10 cent manufacturers to pay higher prices for the grades of tobacco they bought than they otherwise would have paid.[63] The Big Three apparently applied a squeeze to their upstart rivals.

Top Side of the "Pincers"—Retail Pricing

The Big Three also tried to standardize price differences between their popular brands and the so-called 10 cent brands. In this way they sought to limit the marketing advantages of manufacturers of 10 cent brands. It was the policy of both Liggett & Myers and Reynolds to require retailers to sell Chesterfields and Camels at the same markup from list as they sold the 10 cent brands. The president of Liggett & Myers stated his company's policy as follows:

> And, so we say to our sales organization: If you find a retail store where the differential is greater than 3 cents a package between Chesterfield and the so-called 10-cent brands, try to persuade . . . first, point out to the retail dealer the unfairness to Chesterfield of a greater differential than 3 cents and try to persuade him to change it; other than that, do nothing.[64]

If a retailer sold Chesterfields for more than 3 cents above the 10 cent brands, Liggett & Myers did not care whether he reduced the margin by raising the price of 10 cent cigarettes or by lowering

63. The circumstance that the record does not indicate the specific grades of leaf bought by the manufacturers of 10 cent cigarettes in no way weakens this conclusion. For the market prices of the lower grades of cigarette tobacco would certainly have been lower than they in fact were if the Big Three had not suddenly become such heavy buyers of those grades.

64. *ATC* v. *U.S.*, Rec., Vol. 6, p. 4599. Liggett & Myers arrived at the 3 cent differential by subtracting the list price of 10 cent cigarettes from the list price of Chesterfields and dividing the difference by 50—the number of packages per thousand cigarettes. For example, with Chesterfields selling at $6.53 a thousand and the 10 cent brands at $5.05 (the prices in 1940) the difference in list is $1.48, or about 3 cents a package. "The list price of those brands would be two and a fraction cents difference, and the retailer could not hardly be expected to split a penny, so that he should not make a larger profit on them, in even money prices, than he should on ours, on our price." *Ibid.*, Vol. 6, pp. 4453-54. This statement shows that the pricing policy Liggett & Myers sought to impose on its dealers was one involving a higher percentage of profit on the 10 cent brands than on Chesterfields. An identical markup in cents per package would, of course, have that result.

Reynolds' policy on retail markup was similar to Liggett & Myers'. *Ibid.*, Vol. 7, pp. 5024-25.

the price of Chesterfields. The president of Liggett & Myers expressed it this way:

It doesn't make any difference to us whether he reduces the price of Chesterfields from 14 to 13 and leaves the other at 10, or increases the price of the 10 cents to 11 cents. The sole idea there is to eliminate any differential exceeding 3 cents.[65]

It was an equally important part of Liggett & Myers' policy to require retailers to sell Chesterfields at precisely the same prices that they sold Lucky Strikes and Camels. A vice-president of Liggett & Myers in charge of sales in the New York territory stated his company's policy as follows:

We do not want any of the best of it or any of the worst of it in wholesale or retail prices. It is reasonable—thoroughly so, to expect any customer to sell our products which are billed at the same price as competitors' products, at the same price at which he sells the competitive products. Anything different from that is not right or fair, and any person who discriminates for or against us is not a good customer in our judgment. The same principle applies to the retail trade. We cannot stand a discrimination against us at retail. This being so, then we should not seek or tolerate a discrimination in our favor at retail. It follows that no deal is to be operated to reduce a retail price.[66]

Reynolds likewise insisted that retailers sell Camels for no higher price than Lucky Strikes and Chesterfields.[67] American Tobacco stated its policy on identical pricing in a reference book for salesmen as follows: "Never allow a price differential to stand against Lucky Strike cigarettes or any of our other products." [68] The company

65. *Ibid.*, Vol. 6, p. 4613. Reynolds' attitude was the same. *Ibid.*, Vol. 7, p. 5026.

66. *ATC* v. *U.S.*, Exhibits, Vol. 4, GX 994, p. 2899. The quotation is an excerpt from an interoffice memorandum. See also *ATC* v. *U.S.*, Rec., Vol. 6, pp. 4458-59. The same official testified further that "it is the fixed policy of Liggett & Myers Tobacco Company to maintain the same prices on its brands as the other companies do for corresponding brands." He said, "Our instructions to our organization . . . are that they positively must never seek a price advantage." He added that Liggett & Myers had followed this policy of identical pricing "for 18 years or more." *Ibid.*, pp. 4500-01. Since the witness was testifying in 1940, this indicated that Liggett & Myers inaugurated its follow-the-leader policy at about the time the Big Four stopped their price war in the early 1920's. See also *ibid.*, p. 4505.

67. The sales manager for Reynolds testified: "I would like to make it clear that our salesmen always, when they go into a dealer's store and find a price discrimination, endeavor to get the dealer to eliminate it by persuasion, and pointing out to him the advantage of selling our brand on a comparable basis." *Ibid.*, Vol. 7, p. 4976. He added that the company tried to prevent discrimination when a group of distributors collectively practiced it.

68. *Ibid.*, Vol. 5, p. 3993. The booklet added: "Remember this business is always competitive and that you must protect the consumers of your brands." Company

characterized its policy as solely one of antidiscrimination. However, the policy was also apparently intended to contribute to identical pricing by the Big Three. At any rate, after having cancelled a recommendation that the company remove a dealer from its "direct list" for having maintained a price differential against Lucky Strikes, American Tobacco's assistant sales manager explained the cancellation in a letter to a fellow executive: "I found that the differential had been created unintentionally. This concern is new in the jobbing business and *did not realize the importance of selling all brands at the same price.*" [69]

How It Was Done

Each of the Big Three denied that it coerced dealers into following its pricing policy. But possessing as they did some monopoly power over the market, each of the Big Three generally found it easy to persuade a dealer to follow its suggestions. Their brands were the most popular cigarettes on the market. Consumers smoked more of each than of all the 10 cent brands combined.[70] While Camel smokers might not "walk a mile" for their favorite cigarette, retailers no doubt realized they might go across the street. Similarly, they no doubt recognized that consumer preference for Lucky Strikes and Chesterfields was great enough so that unless they kept these brands in stock they would lose trade, and hence it would be a mistake to antagonize the suppliers of these brands.

Each of the Big Three had the power to reward distributors who followed its pricing policy and to punish those who did not. Each followed the practice of making direct shipments at wholesale prices, of granting advertising allowances, and of making drop shipments and free deals to selected retailers.[71] Such a favored retailer would

---

officials "felt that it was a discrimination against consumers of our products if consumers were charged a higher price than consumers of other products selling at the same list price and discounts." *Ibid.*, Vol. 5, p. 4106.

69. *ATC* v. *U.S.*, Exhibits, Vol. 5, GX 865, p. 2693. Italics supplied. The "direct list" included dealers to whom American Tobacco sold tobacco products direct at its list prices. The Big Three maintained almost identical "direct lists." Of a total of 6,567 customers in the direct lists of the Big Three, 5,336 were common to all three.

70. Cf. *ibid.*, Vol. 6, GX 1271, p. 3311, and data on Big Three cigarette sales cited earlier in this chapter.

71. The Big Three's advertising allowances were sometimes very large. Between 1930 and 1933 American Tobacco, Liggett & Myers, and Reynolds together paid A & P more than $1,800,000 for window and counter displays. *Ibid.*, Vol. 5, GX 892, p. 2723. Some distributors regarded advertising allowances as cash rebates. David Gross, a wholesaler at Buffalo, New York, testified: "Cash allowance, regardless of

hesitate to follow a price policy that worked against the interests of his benefactor. Common sense and experience taught him that it would not pay—that suppliers might cancel these favorable arrangements. He could generally be counted on, therefore, to use his influence to correct any local pricing practice that one of the Big Three suppliers found "discriminatory."

Although it was rarely necessary for any of the Big Three to use the power it possessed to make retailers conform to its pricing policy, neither Reynolds nor American Tobacco refrained from using it or threatening to use it when in its judgment the occasion warranted. For example, when Tulsa retailers agreed on a price differential between the 10 cent cigarette and the standard brands that Reynolds regarded as discriminatory, its sales manager wrote to a field representative, on November 29, 1938, as follows:

> No doubt you are familiar with the price situation on cigarettes in Tulsa . . . This is not a satisfactory condition, and we cannot continue to stand for such discrimination.
>
> On your next trip to Tulsa, we want you to handle with Colonial Stores, with whom we have an advertising arrangement, and let them know that if they are not willing to increase the price of $4.75 brands to 14¢, 2 for 27¢, so as to put them on a comparable basis with $6.25 brands, it will be necessary to discontinue advertising arrangement they now enjoy.[72]

In describing his efforts to persuade an Atlanta dealer to stop "discriminating" in favor of 10 cent cigarettes, another Reynolds field representative reported to the sales manager:

> I then mentioned that we had at times in the past been forced to use rather unpleasant, as well as drastic, methods in order to protect ourselves against discrimination against our brands in the way of retail prices on the part of *direct* buyers.[73]

---

what it is for, is a cash allowance, to my way of thinking." *ATC* v. *U.S.*, Rec., Vol. 4, p. 2874.

A free deal is a combination order under which a manufacturer offers a retailer a batch of free goods if he buys a specified quantity of other goods at regular prices. A drop shipment is one shipped directly to the retailer but financed through customary wholesale channels.

72. *ATC* v. *U.S.*, Exhibits, Vol. 5, GX 1066, pp. 2986-87. In reporting, ten days later, the success of his efforts, the Reynolds field representative wrote that "Tulsa is lined up on Camels at 15¢ . . . *Of course, they will sell Chesterfields, Lucky Strikes, and Old Golds at the same price.* For your information, the Colonial Stores do not handle the $4.75 brands, and they were glad to get in the buggy on Camels *and assured me that nobody would know anything about my talking to them.*" *Ibid.*, Vol. 5, GX 1067, p. 2988. Italics supplied.

73. *Ibid.*, Vol. 5, GX 1039, p. 2947. Italics supplied. The date of this letter was September 7, 1938.

American Tobacco over a period of years dropped six important retailers from its direct list because they sold Lucky Strikes for higher prices than they charged for Camels and Chesterfields.[74]

Monopoly Power in the Cigarette Market

The record evidently justifies the conclusion that after the early 1920's the Big Three refrained from competing on a price basis among themselves and that they used their power over the market to promote their monopoly interests. When the Great Depression threatened profits throughout industry generally, the Big Three used their monopoly power to exploit consumers of cigarettes. When they overreached themselves and lost markets to 10 cent cigarettes, they reduced prices severely. When they found price cutting disadvantageous to themselves, they revised their campaign against the 10 cent cigarettes. Thereafter they tried to handicap the manufacturers of 10 cent brands by forcing up the prices of cheaper tobaccos, thus narrowing the difference between their prices and those of 10 cent cigarettes.

If their objective was to eliminate the 10 cent brands, they did not wholly achieve it. After 1933 the 10 cent brands, despite vicissitudes, held their own. In 1932, 10 cent cigarettes represented 11.9 per cent of all cigarettes sold in the United States; in 1939 they were 14.1 per cent.[75] Meanwhile Big Three sales declined from

74. President Hill testified as follows on his policy of insisting that every retailer charge no more for Lucky Strikes than for other brands selling at wholesale on the same basis: "Q. You undertake to persuade him first? A. Yes, sir. Q. And, if he does not respond to persuasion, you cut him off your direct list? A. Just as I have described." *ATC* v. *U.S.*, Rec., Vol. 5, p. 3912.

Apparently Reynolds representatives tried to conceal from outsiders the role they played in "correcting" local "price discriminations" against Camel cigarettes. Thus, in reporting on his activities of this kind in several Arizona towns, a Reynolds representative wrote to his superior in part as follows: "Of course, this work has been done in a very careful manner so as not to involve us in any way in the matter of price reduction, however, the work has been most gratifying and will result in a large increase in the sale of Camels." *ATC* v. *U.S.*, Exhibits, Vol. 5, GX 1046, pp. 2958-59. Another Reynolds interoffice report, dealing with the correction of an unsatisfactory price situation in the San Francisco Bay region in October 1937, stated: "This break down in price has been done strictly on the quiet and you may rest assured R.J.R. Co. will not be mentioned as being responsible." *Ibid.*, Vol. 5, GX 1059, p. 2978. See also footnote 72 of this chapter.

75. The figure for 1932 is the simple average of the monthly percentages shown in *ibid.*, Vol. 5, GX 685, p. 2500.

The estimated total sales of all 10 cent brands in 1939 were 25.5 billion. See *ibid.*, Vol. 6, DX 1271, p. 3311. According to Liggett & Myers' Brief (p. 150), total sales of all cigarettes in the United States in that year were 180.6 billion, citing *ibid.*, Vol. 5, GX 677, p. 2473—a tabulation of *production* statistics 1929–1939. The evident assumption is that no changes occurred in inventory from year to year.

81.4 per cent of the total in 1932 to 68 per cent in 1939.[76] Philip Morris replaced Old Golds as the fourth largest seller. In 1939 the five most popular cigarettes accounted for only 80.9 per cent of all cigarettes sold in the United States, whereas ten years earlier the Big Three alone had accounted for 90 per cent. Although the Big Three so abused their monopoly power in the cigarette market that they weakened it, they did not lose it entirely. It was still great enough to make price leadership workable and to force retailers generally to conform to Big Three pricing policies.

Big Three's Power to Manipulate Leaf Tobacco Prices

According to the finding of the Supreme Court, the Big Three also had the power to control prices of leaf tobacco. They used this power to fix ceiling prices for standard grades above which none of them would bid at tobacco auctions, and to refrain from buying the distinctive grades of tobacco for which a rival had made a special classification.[77] They determined the communities in which tobacco auctions would be held.[78]

It is beyond the scope of this study to analyze in detail the influence that the monopoly power of the Big Three exerted on leaf tobacco prices and the welfare of the farmer. The defendants introduced evidence to show that tobacco prices customarily responded

76. *Ibid.*, Vol. 5, GX 677, p. 2473. These figures relate to production, but the text adopts the assumption implicit in Liggett & Myers' Brief (p. 150), namely, that sales and output followed pretty much the same course.

77. Before the opening of the annual auction markets, officials of each of the Big Three customarily instructed their buyers on the ceiling prices they might pay. In practice a common ceiling developed above which no buyer would bid. "In case of tie bids the auctioneer awarded the sale customarily to the buyer who bid first. Under this custom the buyers representing the petitioners often made bids on various baskets before the opening price could be announced so that they might have their claim to the tobacco recognized at the understood ceiling price in the case of tie bids." *ATC* v. *U.S.*, 328 U.S. 781 (1946), at p. 802.

While each of the Big Three refrained from buying certain grades customarily bought by another of the Big Three, each customarily bid on these distinctive grades to insure that none of the Big Three would get its tobacco at a lower price than any other. In the language of the Circuit Court of Appeals: "Appellants are more concerned that each pays the same than with the amount paid." *ATC* v. *U.S.*, 147 Fed. *2d* 93 (1944), at p. 102.

78. Each of the Big Three refused to take part in auctions at which the others were not represented. As farmers were generally unwilling to sell to speculators for resale to the major buyers, auctions were established only on approval of the Big Three. ". . . the new tobacco markets and their locations were determined by the unanimous consent of the petitioners and, in arriving at their determination, the petitioners consulted with each other as to whether or not a community deserved a market." *ATC* v. *U.S.*, 328 U.S. 781 (1946), at p. 801.

to fluctuating crop yields and to changes in the purchasing power of the dollar very much as did the prices of other agricultural products. They argued, that is, that the forces of demand and supply set leaf tobacco prices. Prices were high enough, of course, to insure a supply adequate, in the long run, to meet demand at the prices charged for tobacco products.

The Big Three customarily held in storage about a three-year supply of leaf tobacco. Because of the heavy expense of drying and storing, tobacco in the hands of the farmer is, in effect, a perishable crop. Together the Big Three bought annually about one third of the flue-cured crop and about two thirds of the burley crop. Imperial Tobacco, British-American Tobacco, and Universal Leaf Tobacco bought most of the remainder. With a three-year supply on hand, the Big Three as purchasers of the bulk of supplies in a market of few buyers obviously were in a position temporarily to exploit tobacco growers.[79]

Effective Competition in Cigarettes

Business rivalry in the sale of cigarettes has apparently not resulted in effective competition. Cigarette prices have not shown the response to changing supply-demand relationships that consumer interest has required. During 1929–1932 when costs were declining and farmer and consumer incomes generally shrinking, an increase in cigarette prices was clearly incompatible with general economic welfare, and as subsequent developments indicated, was probably incompatible also with the Big Three's own business interests.[80] The Big Three have apparently used their power over the market to exploit both consumers of cigarettes and producers of tobacco. Although they have run afoul of the antitrust laws in doing so, the evidence on

79. See T. J. Woofter, Jr., *The Plight of Cigarette Tobacco,* University of North Carolina, Chapel Hill, 1931.

80. Earnings of the Big Three during 1926–1946 reflect monopoly power. American Tobacco's net income expressed as a percentage of net worth less good will varied in this period from a high of 20.8 per cent in 1930 to a low of 7.7 per cent in 1933. In only one year did it fall below 10.5 per cent. It averaged 13.6 per cent for the twenty-one years. Liggett & Myers' earnings varied from 20.3 per cent in 1929 to 9.1 per cent in 1945, and averaged 13.1 per cent for the entire period. Reynolds' earnings varied from 22.4 per cent in 1931 to 9.3 per cent in 1945, and averaged 13.9 per cent for the entire period. Omitting the years of price control, Reynolds never earned at a rate less than 13.5 per cent; Liggett & Myers never less than 12 per cent; and in only three years did American Tobacco fall below 13.5 per cent. See the forthcoming book by William H. Nicholls, *The American Cigarette Industry: A Study of Oligopoly and Its Social Control.*

which they were convicted was circumstantial. There was no direct evidence of conspiracy.

Price making in the cigarette market corresponds rather clearly to the Chamberlinian theory of oligopoly. Apparently the experience of the Big Three was that price competition in the sale of cigarettes was disadvantageous to them. Since 1923, except for a brief period when fighting the manufacturers of 10 cent cigarettes, each of the Big Three relied primarily on advertising rather than price to win customers. Reynolds increased its advertising expenditures from $6.3 million in 1923 to $19.5 million in 1927. In only one year in the period 1923 to 1939 did Reynolds' advertising expenditures fall below the 1923 level. American Tobacco increased its advertising expenditures from $8.8 million in 1925 to $24.8 million in 1932. In only one year did its advertising expenditures fall as low as the 1925 figure. Liggett & Myers increased advertising expenditures from approximately $12 million in 1930 to $16.9 million in 1937.[81]

Mr. S. Clay Williams, chairman of Reynolds' board, in discussing the significance of advertising to cost-price relationships in the cigarette industry, said:

> . . . the line of cost in cigarette manufacture that is related to price is not, as in steel to some much greater extent, the manufacturing cost line.
>
> If you are manufacturing a product, in the merchandising of which a high volume of advertising expenditure is unnecessary, price naturally is related to the factory cost line and will follow it very closely. If you are manufacturing a product in which advertising . . . in enormous amounts is necessary to keep the consumers on that product instead of some other . . . then your price line is much more . . . closely . . . related to a line that represents factory cost plus advertising expenditure than it is to the line that represents simply factory cost.[82]

Big Three Retain Monopoly Power

The Supreme Court's judgment that the Big Three possessed a significant degree of monopoly power over the market for leaf tobacco and cigarettes was simply a recognition of the economic implications of imperfect competition as attested by both theory and experience. But the Court left that power undisturbed.

81. For data on Reynolds, see *ATC* v. *U.S.*, Exhibits, Vol. 6, DX 1260, pp. 3253-54; for data on American, Rec., Vol. 4, p. 2522; for data on Liggett & Myers, Rec., Vol. 6, p. 4593, and Rec., Vol. 3, p. 1634.

82. *ATC* v. *U.S.*, Rec., Vol. 7, pp. 5211-12.

Chapter 5 of this study has indicated that in markets where sellers are few and informed they *may* behave like monopolists. As Chamberlin has contended, when such sellers take account of the indirect as well as the direct consequences of their price decisions, they are apt to recognize that to serve their own interests they must harmonize their behavior with that of their rivals. Whether or not the Big Three agreed among themselves to follow the price lead of Reynolds after 1923 and, if not, whether Liggett & Myers and American Tobacco, acting independently, each disciplined by its own experience with price competition, deliberately decided to accept the currently largest and the most aggressive seller as its leader may to the skeptical never be fully established.

The Court uncovered no direct evidence of agreement.[83] And some economists testified that the pricing practices of the Big Three were consistent with independent competitive rivalry, as indeed they were on the strict theory of oligopolistic competition. For such collaboration as is necessary to insure common pricing policies that will promote the interest of each by promoting the interest of all may at most be only tacit, that is, not an overt agreement but an informal procedure based on a mutual recognition of the facts.

Since the Court left the structure of the industry undisturbed, its judgment does not show the Big Three how they can "live within the law." [84] Nor does the judgment give any assurance that henceforth the public interest in the sale of cigarettes will be adequately

83. The Court pointed out that the Information charged the defendants with conspiracy and that the jury had found that a conspiracy existed. But the Court acknowledged that this finding rested "entirely on circumstantial evidence." *ATC* v. *U.S.*, 328 U.S. 781 (1946), at p. 793. It is an unresolved question whether, without the historic background of the monopolistic activities of the tobacco trust, the Court would sustain a verdict of guilty against one, two, or three giant corporations, operating under conditions of monopolistic competition, that merely met each other's prices.

84. Counsel for Reynolds claimed that a finding of guilt would leave defendants "entirely without a guide as to how they may lawfully avoid the creation of evidence of future Sherman Act violations . . . unless they close business altogether." (In the Supreme Court, October Term, 1944, No. 840, *Reynolds* v. *U.S.*, Petition for Writ of Certiorari, pp. 12-13.)

Counsel for Liggett & Myers took a similar position: "What are the specific policies and practices we must abandon, modify, or adopt in order to conduct our business according to law? . . . presumably, the appellants were convicted of agreement, not of the particular operations alleged to constitute agreement. Yet, on the Government's theory, continuation by more than one of the appellants of the operations alleged is evidence of a further Sherman Act agreement . . . If this is so, how is Liggett & Myers to carry on? Must it start all over again with new management, a new system? Is everything that appellants do illegal, or evidence of illegality, if done by more than one of them?" *ATC* v. *U.S.*, Brief on Behalf of Liggett & Myers, p. 27.

protected. While some of the defendants' conduct strongly suggested deliberate conspiracy, even if they scrupulously avoid conspiracy in the future the Big Three can scarcely avoid using the monopoly power they severally possess in the market position they collectively occupy. They may use it well, but use it they will.[85]

Greater Prudence Likely in Future

While the Big Three are unlikely to abandon price leadership, they may use it with greater discretion. The Circuit Court of Appeals declared that changes in the Big Three's list prices had "no relationship to cost of production or to economic conditions generally." [86] As long as the Big Three have monopoly power—in their collective market position—they run the risk of investigation and prosecution by the government. They are also constantly subject to potential competition. Each has probably learned by experience that, regardless of any governmental action, it may lose such monopoly power as it possesses if it does not use it judiciously. In the future, cigarette prices are likely either to be more stable than in the past or to vary more nearly in harmony with economic conditions. Each of the Big Three must find more reasonable explanations than those given in the recent proceedings for promptly meeting a price change by either of the others.[87] They may continue to charge what the traffic will bear, but

85. Some scholars suggest that judicial construction of the Sherman Act is veering toward the view that the power of a great corporate merger to fix its own prices may be enough, without any proof of abuse of that power, to constitute a violation of Section 2. See Edward H. Levi, "The Antitrust Laws and Monopoly," *University of Chicago Law Review*, February 1947, pp. 157-83.

Reasoning from the accepted legal doctrine applicable to price-fixing combinations among competitors, Judge Hand argued in the Alcoa case that giant corporations controlling a preponderant part of output should be held to be within the provisions of the law, regardless of how they exercise their market power. He said: "Starting, however, with the authoritative premise that all contracts fixing prices are unconditionally prohibited, the only possible difference between them and a monopoly is that while a monopoly necessarily involves an equal, or even greater, power to fix prices, its mere existence might be thought not to constitute an exercise of that power. That distinction is nevertheless purely formal; it would be valid only so long as the monopoly remained wholly inert; it would disappear as soon as the monopoly began to operate; for, when it did—that is, as soon as it began to sell at all—it must sell at some price and the only price at which it could sell is a price which it itself fixed. Thereafter the power and its exercise must needs coalesce. Indeed it would be absurd to condemn such contracts unconditionally, and not to extend the condemnation to monopolies; for the contracts are only steps toward that entire control which monopoly confers: they are really partial monopolies." *U.S.* v. *Aluminum Co. of America*, 148 Fed. *2d* 416 (1945), at pp. 427-28. The Supreme Court quoted this passage with approval in *ATC* v. *U.S.*, 328 U.S. 781 (1946), at p. 813.

86. *ATC* v. *U.S.*, 147 Fed. *2d* 93 (1944), at p. 103.

87. The Circuit Court of Appeals made an acute observation on defendants' ex-

experience has probably taught them that it will bear less than they formerly thought.[88]

The course of cigarette prices since 1940 bears out this conjecture. The wholesale price of one or all of the three leading brands of cigarettes increased seven times between January 1940 and July 1948. Two increases, totalling 53 cents a thousand, slightly more than compensated for corresponding increases in the federal excise tax. Two—one initiated by American Tobacco Company on December 27, 1941 and one by Liggett & Myers on July 30, 1946[89]—failed to carry through and were rescinded. Of the other three increases, OPA authorized one of 28 cents on April 26, 1946; American initiated one of 29 cents on October 7, 1946, which Liggett & Myers met promptly and which Reynolds followed within four days to the extent of 26 cents; and American initiated another of 40 cents on July 28, 1948, which all major companies followed within twenty-four hours.

These three increases raised the price of Chesterfields and Lucky Strikes by 97 cents a thousand, and of Camels by 94 cents. Between January 1940 and July 1948 cigarette prices, exclusive of federal

---

planation of how identical prices come about: "All appellants gave the same reason for being obliged to follow a price rise inaugurated by any one of them—that if they do not follow it, the others will have more money to spend on advertising. But all of them also explain that they must similarly follow a price cut or will lose business through sales, as otherwise the cheaper priced cigarettes would completely outsell their product . . . These explanations are patently inconsistent." *Ibid.*, p. 114. The court was obviously correct. The record in the tobacco case indicates rather clearly that none of the Big Three was able by its heavy advertising expenditures to insulate its product from the cigarette market. Each was forced to follow price cuts or to lose business. By the same logic each would have gained business, temporarily at any rate, by refusing to follow a price advance. If any one of the three had failed to follow, however, a price advance would not have carried through, and so the gain from not following would have been short-lived. It probably would not have been equal to the gain of holding relative sales constant, and selling at higher prices. At any rate each of the Big Three has generally chosen to follow when, on occasion, one of the others has advanced its price. In technical language, price behavior in the cigarette market indicates that teamwork may eliminate the "kink" in the demand curve confronting an oligopolist. See Paul M. Sweezy, "Demand Under Conditions of Oligopoly," *Journal of Political Economy,* August 1939, pp. 568-73.

88. While the Big Three are unlikely to forego all monopoly gains, they may follow more closely the principles in accordance with which the president of American Tobacco professed to shape its policy. "My first duty is to the American public in my job, the American public as a whole. My second duty is to the consumers of my brand, my Lucky Strike consumers. My third duty is to my stockholders, but I can't serve my stockholders if I don't serve the public and if I don't serve the consumers of my brand." *ATC* v. *U.S.,* Rec., Vol. 5, pp. 3869-70.

89. OPA froze prices as of December 26, 1941 when American refused to rescind a 57 cent price advance made December 27, 1941, and authorized no increase for the standard brands until April 26, 1946 when it approved a 28 cent increase.

tax and trade discounts, had increased by only about 30 per cent. When one compares this with a 112.5 per cent increase over the same period in the Bureau of Labor Statistics index of wholesale prices, it suggests that the Big Three were exercising self-restraint in pricing cigarettes—a restraint that contrasts strikingly with the pricing policy they pursued during the early 1930's.

But those who share the Supreme Court's view "that possession of unchallenged economic power deadens initiative, discourages thrift and depresses energy; that immunity from competition is a narcotic, and rivalry a stimulant to industrial progress; that the spur of constant stress is necessary to counteract an inevitable disposition to let well enough alone," [90] may not be content to rely on a prudent exercise of monopoly power. Brief consideration of what would be required to break down the monopoly power of the Big Three seems called for.

How to Restore Cigarette Competition

The strategic power of the three largest cigarette manufacturers originated in a combination to restrain trade—in a persistent policy of eliminating by fair means or foul all competition in the sale of tobacco products, a policy pursued by the promoters of the tobacco trust for two decades. The dissolution of the trust in 1911 was enough to revive competition but not to preserve it. However, experience in the cigarette market does not warrant generalization about the likelihood of a few firms that dominate a market behaving like monopolists without overt collaboration. The cigarette industry is unusual, if not unique, as an example of the Chamberlinian model. It therefore raises an unusually complex question of social control.

If the manufacture and sale of cigarettes were decentralized, price leadership would hardly survive. And if it did, it would be unlikely to survive for long. But decentralization of the manufacture of cigarettes presents a difficult problem. Reynolds manufactures Camel cigarettes in a single group of plants at Winston-Salem, North Carolina. The facilities include leaf-handling, stemming, and processing plants, as well as cigarette, smoking, and chewing tobacco plants.[91]

90. From Judge Learned Hand's opinion in *U.S.* v. *Aluminum Co. of America*, previously cited, p. 427. Quoted with approval by Mr. Justice Burton, speaking for a unanimous Court, in *ATC* v. *U.S.*, 328 U.S. 781 (1946), at p. 813.

91. See *Moody's Manual of Investments* (Industrials), 1946.

These plants have been built and operated as a unit and their segregation under separate ownership would be difficult and probably inexpedient. American Tobacco's and Liggett & Myers' cigarette-manufacturing operations are less centralized. American Tobacco makes Lucky Strikes in three plants—at Durham and Reidsville, North Carolina, and at Richmond, Virginia. Liggett & Myers also makes Chesterfields in three plants—at Durham, Richmond, and San Francisco. American Tobacco and Liggett & Myers both produce several brands of cigarettes. The production of their leading brands is already decentralized and the ownership of these plants might likewise be decentralized. But a dissolution decree that separated the ownership of each of the plants from that of any of the others is not enough. The monopoly power that the Big Three possess rests on trade good will—the popularity of Camels, Lucky Strikes, and Chesterfields. A concern controlling any of these brands could quickly expand its manufacturing facilities and sell at going prices all that consumers wanted—probably as many as are currently sold under the particular brand. Therefore an effective dissolution would require either some curb on the use of these brand names by the successor companies allotted them, or a transfer of the names to the public domain—permitting anyone to use them. Precedent for the latter remedy is provided by decrees making available for royalty-free licenses patents that an antitrust offender has used to restrain trade.

Limitations on Advertising

Because such monopoly power as American Tobacco, Reynolds, and Liggett & Myers have in the cigarette market is largely based on prestige, depending on steady and enormous expenditures for advertising,[92] a direct attack on this facet of the monopoly might be an effective way to break it up. Without advertising, consumer preference for Camels, Lucky Strikes, and Chesterfields would probably end.[93] Even a limitation of advertising expenditures would to

92. During the 1930's American Tobacco spent $153,265,288.88 on advertising; and Reynolds $144,142,505.54. Its advertising cost Liggett & Myers $81,856,631.69 in the last half of the decade. The average annual advertising expenditure of the three companies combined during 1935–1939 was $42,955,550.64. *ATC* v. *U.S.*, Digest of Government's Testimony, Vol. 1, p. 113.

93. Evidence presented by the government in the recent suit indicates how insubstantial is the basis for consumer preference. Professor Carl I. Hovland, Director of Graduate Studies in Psychology at Yale University, organized and supervised two series of tests at the request of the government. The first showed that seasoned smokers

some extent dispel that large part of their good-will values resting on the costly reiteration of unverified claims of superior quality. In this way it would lower the biggest barrier to potential competition in the industry and would open the cigarette market to new enterprises.

But the economic validity of a direct limitation on advertising is debatable. In a complex industrial society advertising plays an important role in acquainting consumers with new products. In some cases it is doubtless essential to insure purchases on a scale large enough to permit the economies of mass production. How to penalize uneconomic advertising without penalizing economic advertising presents an administrative and probably a constitutional problem. An indirect approach through the exercise of the taxing power might solve the administrative difficulties. The amount of advertising expenditures deductible as business expense under the corporation income-tax law might be limited. Or a graduated excise tax might be imposed on advertising.

Either procedure would encourage price competition in the sale of cigarettes. But any limitation on advertising as a means of increasing the effectiveness of competition would no doubt be politically inexpedient. For the bare proposal alone would arouse the vehement opposition of practically every newspaper and periodical in the country. Editors and publishers as well as national advertisers generally would defend the cigarette manufacturers and fight their battle for them, probably under the slogan of "freedom of the press." So the idea of curbing the cigarette monopoly by limiting advertising expenditures must be dismissed as quixotic.

---

could not recognize their "favorite" brand of cigarettes among seven nonidentified brands smoked under controlled conditions. The second showed that they could not distinguish between their favorite brand and the brand they declared beforehand that they liked the least.

On the first test smokers identified their favorite cigarette 20 times out of 100. In short, they were wrong 80 per cent of the time. With seven cigarettes to choose from, had they guessed, they would on the average have been right about 14 per cent of the time. In the second test they had a fifty-fifty chance of identifying their "favorite" by guessing. Actually they did only a little better than that. Out of 16 smokes distributed equally between their favorite and the cigarette they liked least, under the law of averages each should have got 8 correct. Actually they averaged 8.66 correct identifications.

From these tests Professor Hovland concluded that "typical average subjects" are unable "to tell either their favorite from their non-preferred cigarette or to correctly identify and distinguish between the common brands." *ATC* v. *U.S.*, Rec., Vol. 3, p. 2265; see also pp. 2238-320. Similar tests made by Consumers Union gave similar results. See also *ATC* v. *U.S.*, Exhibits, Vol. 4, GX 661 and 662, p. 2444, and Vol. 5, GX 665 and 666, pp. 2447-48.

At least two other ways are open to weaken the monopoly power that the Big Three have built up on the prestige values of their leading brands. The government might grade cigarettes, as is now done with leaf tobacco. If cigarette manufacturers were required to label every package with a simple formula showing the proportions of the tobacco ingredients of various specified grades, consumers might make judicious selection among rival brands. If they did, the effectiveness of advertising would thereby be reduced. But as was shown by the strenuous opposition to the OPA proposal to introduce compulsory grading of canned fruits and vegetables, this kind of check on cigarette monopoly power is also probably politically impractical at this time.[94]

Graduated Tax to Encourage Price Competition

The most promising way to dissipate monopoly power in the cigarette market would be to substitute a graduated tax for the present federal excise tax of $3.50 a thousand on all "small" cigarettes.[95] The present tax in effect discriminates against the lower-priced brands because they bear the same excise duty as the higher-priced brands—7 cents on a package of twenty. Thus the federal excise levy represents only about one third of the price of a brand retailing for 20 cents, but two thirds of the retail price of a 10 cent brand.

An excise tax that progressively graduated the tax rate on the basis of the manufacturer's list price would make the cheaper cigarettes relatively a better "buy" than the more expensive brands. For example, the tax on a cigarette brand retailing at two packages for a quarter could be reduced to, say, $2 a thousand. Then the brand could be sold at 10 cents straight. And the tax on a brand retailing at two packages for 35 cents could be raised to, say, $5 a thousand. Then retailers could hardly afford to sell the brand for less than 20 cents straight. As a result, the price appeal of the cheaper brand would in some measure offset the market leverage the higher-

94. See, for example, Hearings before a Subcommittee of the Committee on Interstate and Foreign Commerce, House of Representatives, 78th Cong., 1st sess., pursuant to H.Res. 98, A Resolution to Investigate Federal Grade Labeling, etc.; see especially Pt. 1, pp. 435 ff.

95. A bill introduced in the Eightieth Congress embodying such a proposal had the support of the Department of Agriculture and the Federal Trade Commission. See *New York Times,* October 10, 1947, p. 44.

priced brand gets from its high-pressure advertising. Such an excise-tax revision would encourage price competition in the sale of cigarettes almost as effectively as a measure directed specifically at the limitation of advertising expenditures. And from the political point of view it might very well have the considerable advantage of active support from millions of cigarette consumers.[96]

Without legislative action along one or another of the lines suggested, the government can do little to insure that consumers will get the benefits of competitive pricing of cigarettes. But it can do something. Constant surveillance by the Department of Justice of the market practices of the Big Three would help. Supplied with adequate funds to maintain a competent field staff, which it does not now have, the Department could go a long way toward keeping giant corporations toeing the mark. Vigilant supervision of their activities by antitrust officials would at least reduce the likelihood of abuse of power. By encouraging the development of vigorous competition from the smaller producers and from new enterprises, such supervision might check the further development of concentration.

Another Case of Price Leadership

When a few large companies about equal in size produce most of the output of an industry, they *may* avoid price competition, as we have seen, without visible signs of collusion—perhaps even without collusion. Though price changes may be simultaneous and uniform, as in cigarettes, no obvious follow-the-leader pattern need be evident. Singly, none of the Big Three cigarette manufacturers dominates the industry; dominance is tripartite, but nonetheless effective. Sometimes one, sometimes another, takes the initiative in setting prices.[97] But whichever moves first, it can generally count on the self-interest of the others to keep standard-brand prices the same. Thus, in spite of a mixed pattern, price leadership prevails.

But it would be a mistake to base generalizations about the certainty of monopolistic behavior in markets of few sellers, and more particularly about the difficulty of reorganizing an industry so as to

96. William Nicholls arrives independently at somewhat similar conclusions about the usefulness of a revision of the excise tax as a means of stimulating competition in cigarettes. See his "Tobacco Case of 1946," *American Economic Review,* Papers and Proceedings, May 1949, pp. 284-96.

97. As indicated earlier, Reynolds has generally taken the lead, although occasionally American Tobacco and Liggett & Myers have done so.

foster effective competition, on price behavior in the cigarette industry. That price leadership has worked so well in the sale of cigarettes is due largely to two factors in addition to fewness of sellers: first, competitive advertising affords a less disturbing means of getting business than price competition; secondly, the bargaining power of individual cigarette dealers is negligible.

Where the bargaining power of buyers and sellers is more evenly balanced and the product is bought on specification, effective competition would seem, on theoretical grounds, to be more likely. But in practice it may not be safe to rely on such conditions alone. For, as pointed out in Chapter 5, the fewer the sellers in a market the greater the likelihood that noncollusive rational behavior will result in monopoly pricing and, of equal importance, the greater the likelihood that rivals will collaborate without being guilty of legal conspiracy. These basic tendencies are more important than the special qualifying conditions. In any event, where advertising counts for little in the sale of a product, decentralization of control may be a feasible remedy if price leadership renders competition ineffective.

The tin can industry is an illustration in point. The American Can Company is the acknowledged price leader in the purchase of tin plate as well as in the sale of tin cans. But while American Can, with the help of Continental Can Company, rules its field as the Big Three cigarette companies collectively rule theirs, its dominance does not rest, as does theirs, on a monopoly of prestige created through advertising. It rests, in fact, on a monopoly of productive capacity achieved through consolidation.

The Dominance of American Can

American Can did not attain its eminence by greater efficiency. Its towering size derives from the activities of promoters in combining about a hundred separate can companies in 1901. Though most of these constituents operated only a single plant each, together they represented more than 90 per cent of domestic can-making capacity. Promoting American Can was an enterprise in corporate finance, not an industrial undertaking. Its sponsors were manufacturers of can companies, not of cans.[98] Apparently their primary

98. After organizing American Can the same promoters put Continental Can together. See *U.S.* v. *American Can Co.*, 230 Fed. 859 (1916).

purpose was to obtain large promoters' profits by creating a monopoly, and in 1913 the government brought suit under the antitrust laws.[99] The District Court declared that American Can had "sought to emancipate itself from the restraints of competition." [100]

Nevertheless the court, impressed by the services that American Can had rendered the canning industry, was "reluctant to destroy so finely adjusted an industrial machine." [101] Expressing the hope that "all potential restraints upon free competition now imposed by the size and power of the defendant will pass away as speedily without as with dissolution"—and the fear that "dissolution will cause far more loss and business disturbance than will attend the gradual reestablishment of competitive conditions by the play of economic forces"—the court decided to leave the structure of American Can undisturbed.[102]

Court's Hope Not Fully Realized

The structure of the can industry has changed considerably since the birth of the American Can Company. In truth even by 1913 American Can had lost ground. At that time it made about 63 per cent of all the tin cans made in the United States, as compared with 90 per cent when organized. Continental made about 12 per cent. Nine other firms made the rest. By 1941 American Can made only 55 per cent of all tin cans sold in the United States. Continental made

99. *Ibid.* See also *U.S.* v. *American Can Co.*, 234 Fed. 1019 (1917). The court withheld the decree of dissolution sought by the government, but offered to retain the case on its docket and keep the company under surveillance. The government appealed to the Supreme Court but withdrew the appeal on June 6, 1921, after the decision in *U.S.* v. *United States Steel Corp.*, 251 U.S. 417 (1920).

100. 230 Fed., at p. 903. The court recognized that "one of the designs of the framers of the Antitrust Act was to prevent the concentration in a few hands of control over great industries. They preferred a social and industrial state in which there should be many industrial producers. . . . The law wishes that industrial and trading corporations shall operate under the checks and balances imposed by free and unrestrained competition." *Ibid.*, pp. 901-02. Despite its clear conception of the objectives of the Sherman Act and despite the fact that the evidence indicated that American Can was organized to eliminate competition in the sale of cans, the court concluded that the combination did not unreasonably restrain trade.

This conclusion rested mainly on a finding that the company had reformed its ways. A decade after its formation the company's activities showed no "continued intent," according to the court, "to dominate and restrain trade *by the use of methods which interfered more or less obviously with the reasonable freedom of their customers or their competitors.*" *Ibid.* Italics supplied. In brief, the court found that American Can was a "good trust." It recognized that bigness may sin, but found no sin in bigness per se.

101. *Ibid.*, p. 903.

102. 234 Fed., at p. 1021. Italics omitted.

about 30 per cent. But these two concerns dominated the industry. Continental, like American Can, had been put together by professional promoters. It was organized by combining independent can makers in 1904. Unlike American Can, which since 1913 has grown primarily from within, Continental has continued to buy out independent can companies. Between 1927 and 1930 Continental absorbed seventeen competitors.[103]

In 1941, fifty-five relatively small can companies shared domestic markets with their two large trade rivals. Only four of these—Crown Can, National Can, Owens-Illinois Can, and Heekin Can—did as much as 2 per cent of the total business in tin cans. The rest of the group together sold only about 3.5 per cent of the total. None of the smaller companies did business throughout the nation. In many areas canners looked exclusively to American Can or Continental for their cans.[104] But while two large companies dominate the sale of cans, many small companies buy cans. In 1942 an estimated 1,600 firms canned fruit and vegetables for the American market. None was large enough to have much, if any, influence on the price of cans. The three largest—California Packing Corporation, Libby, McNeill & Libby, Minnesota Valley Canning Company—are estimated to have packed only 13 per cent of the country's canned vegetables and 30 per cent of its canned fruit in 1937.[105]

Tin Can Prices Geared to Tin Plate

In selling cans American Can is the price leader. In announcing the price of packers' cans, it links the price of cans to the price of tin plate.[106] Before 1939 its contracts with its packers' can customers stated the price for each standard size and provided a scale of "differentials" for increasing or decreasing can prices whenever

103. Charles H. Hession, *Competition in the Metal Food Container Industry, 1916–1946,* Edwards Bros., Ann Arbor, 1949, pp. 51-55.

104. In 1940 some forty-one can-using firms made their own cans. *Ibid.,* p. 42. Their output is not available. As they did not sell cans, their production affected the market only indirectly.

105. *Ibid.,* p. 75.

106. TNEC Hearings, Pt. 26, pp. 14018-19. Tin cans fall into two broad classes: packers' cans (for food) and general-line cans. Before World War II packers' cans represented about 55 per cent of the value of all tin cans sold. Since packers' cans come in a few standard sizes, pricing under the leadership principle is easy. General-line cans are of many sizes and shapes, varying from small tin pill boxes to large oil cans, and are used for a great variety of commodities not requiring heat treatment in packaging. It is more difficult to make price leadership an effective stabilizing device in this field.

Carnegie-Illinois changed its "official" price of tin plate by 10 cents or more a box.[107] After the TNEC investigation began in 1939, American Can altered its contracts so that can prices should be adjusted annually on a basis of the average price the company paid for tin plate during the contract year.[108] Other can manufacturers generally followed suit, linking can prices to the price of tin plate in the same way.[109]

Although Continental has customarily followed American Can's leadership in prices, in doing so it has not always acted as an independent fellow duopolist who realized the futility of price cutting. At any rate, American Can and Continental did not contest an antitrust suit charging them with having criminally conspired to fix prices over a ten-year period in their California can sales. They simply entered pleas of *nolo contendere* and paid fines.[110]

107. Specifically the contracts provided that "The official price of the Carnegie-Illinois Steel Corporation for tin plate per base box 100 lb. Coke Plate, 14″ x 20″, 112 sheets per box, F.O.B. Mill, Pittsburgh, Pa., shall be the standard by which all readjustments of prices of cans covered hereby shall be determined." *Ibid.*, Pt. 20, p. 10763.

For every change of 10 cents in the price of tin plate, the price of standard cans was adjusted in accordance with the following table of "differentials."

Standard Size of Cans	*Differential Per M*
No. 1	18 cents
No. 2	26 cents
No. 2½	33 cents
No. 3-4⅞ inches	38 cents
No. 10	74 cents

For a fractional change beyond 10 cents or a multiple thereof, a proportionate adjustment was made. *Ibid.*

108. The president of American Can intimated that the TNEC investigation was one factor prompting the change in the company's method of pricing tin cans. *Ibid.*, p. 10771.

Under the new form of contract, American Can's customers benefited from any price reductions on tin plate it obtained from any supplier. In 1938 Carnegie-Illinois' official price was undercut so frequently and notoriously that American Can granted rebates to all its customers. These rebates reflected the advantages the can company got from buying plate at less than the official price.

The new method of adjusting the price of cans based on changes in tin plate prices during the period of the contract would result in substantial differences in the net prices realized by various can manufacturers if the price of plate fluctuated widely, or varied greatly among different suppliers. Apparently American Can assumed that the instability of the plate market in 1938 would not often recur. And with good reason. See text below.

109. According to Hession, most of the smaller concerns have regularly sold cans at slightly lower prices than American Can and Continental. *Op. cit.*, pp. 203-05. However, *Fortune* says the small can company is "likely to go along under the price umbrella held jointly by American and Continental." "Profits in Cans," *Fortune*, April 1934, p. 78.

110. *U.S.* v. *American Can Co., et al.*, 87 Fed.Supp. 18 (1949).

How Tin Plate Prices Are Set

The principal cost of making cans is the materials cost. Between 1931 and 1939 the cost of the tin plate in a No. 2 can varied from 55.9 per cent to 63.9 per cent of the selling price of the can.[111]

Price leadership has been the rule in the market for tin plate, as in that for tin cans. The United States Steel Corporation through a subsidiary, Carnegie-Illinois Steel, is by far the largest seller of tin plate, and American Can is the largest buyer. These two companies generally negotiate the price of tin plate each year in November or December.[112] The price on which they agree becomes the announced market price at which the Steel Corporation offers to sell tin plate to all other buyers.

American Can buys the rest of its tin plate—from 25 to 35 per cent of its requirements—from some ten independent mills. By a judicious apportionment of its purchases American Can is able to influence the prices of these suppliers. In practice, they have generally duplicated the prices negotiated by American Can and the Steel Corporation. When these smaller suppliers sell tin plate to can manufacturers, the contract has generally provided that the price shall be that announced by Carnegie-Illinois—that is, by United States Steel.[113]

Are Tin Plate Prices Competitive?

When the president of Bethlehem Steel, testifying before the Temporary National Economic Committee, was asked why his company had "adopted a policy of using the officially announced price of Carnegie-Illinois as the standard for the sale of its tin plate," he replied: "That in our judgment sets the competitive price for us for tin plate." [114] The chairman of the board of National Steel was

111. Hession, *op. cit.*, p. 87.

112. This account is based primarily on the practice between the two world wars. No evidence is at hand to indicate that price leadership has been abandoned. Before World War II American Can bought about $100 million worth of tin plate every year—from 65 per cent to 75 per cent of its requirements—from United States Steel. This was more than half of the Steel Corporation's entire output.

113. National Steel's contracts with Continental Can constitute the single recorded exception to the rule that contracts of other tin plate suppliers stipulate that the price will be that charged by Carnegie-Illinois on its sales. TNEC Hearings, Pt. 19, p. 10683. National Steel has not generally sold to American Can. American Can's contracts with all its suppliers except Bethlehem Steel have provided that if the supplier sells tin plate to anyone below the "official" price, he will lower his price to American Can proportionately.

114. *Ibid.*, p. 10625.

less laconic. His answer to the question whether he thought that it was a good policy for the industry to follow the officially announced price of Carnegie-Illinois was:

> Well, you have an unusual situation in the tin-plate and the tin-can industry, in that the price is really set by the Corporation [U.S. Steel] in their dealings with the American Can Co., the Corporation being the largest producer of tin plate and the American Can Co. the largest consumer of tin plate. I think that that price is set on a competitive basis, because as a buyer of tin plate the American Can Co. is interested in buying as cheaply as it can, and naturally uses all factors to that effect in its dealings with the Corporation in getting a price which it thinks is a proper and fair price, taking all conditions into consideration.
>
> That results, as I say, in a price, in my opinion, originally being set through competition, strictly competition between a large buyer and a large seller which, after all, is what produces the price. Then the American Can Co., the largest producer of cans, the largest buyer of tin plate, is willing to pay that price. It would be assumed throughout the balance of the industry that that would be a fair price.[115]

Economists certainly do not generally recognize these practices as competitive. American Can, selling as it does more cans than all the rest of the industry together, has some monopoly power over the market. The Steel Corporation as the largest seller of tin plate and the recognized price leader has similar power in the plate market. Its strength as a seller is matched by American Can's as a buyer. If there were no other buyers or sellers of tin plate the price would be indeterminate; it would depend on the bargaining skill of the opposing monopolists—assuming that no overriding power, such as some investment banking house, exercises remote control over both companies. If the companies, alone in the field, eventually agreed on some definite price it would no doubt be a compromise. But it is extremely unlikely that it would be either a short-run competitive price, merely covering the seller's marginal costs, or a long-run competitive price that gave the seller no more than his total unit costs. Were the several sellers and buyers in the tin plate market each to act independently, diversity of judgment and of need might drive prices to competitive levels.[116]

Their own sworn testimony shows that, actually, neither the sellers nor the buyers of tin plate bargain independently. They customarily

115. *Ibid.*, p. 10681.
116. See Chap. 5 for a discussion of the principle.

accept the prices privately agreed on by American Can and United States Steel.[117] Evidence indicates, moreover, that United States Steel has in the past consulted with its rivals before opening annual negotiations with American Can. A letter of March 24, 1938 from a vice-president of American Can to its president refers to a "conference" in 1937 of the "leading officials" of all the steel companies regarding the price of tin plate for 1938.[118] Although the president of Bethlehem Steel denied knowledge of such a conference, he said:

I would feel free to tell any of my tin-plate competitors at any time if I thought the price of tin plate was too low, and try to encourage them in some way or other to get a higher price for it; of course I would. I would be foolish if I didn't.[119]

American Can Wants Stable Prices

Although American Can has an interest in buying tin plate as cheaply as possible, it also has an interest in stabilizing the price of tin cans, presumably at a level that will maximize its earnings.[120] Negotiating an annual price for tin plate and linking the price of tin cans to the price of tin plate helps accomplish this. If other sellers of tin plate follow the price lead of Carnegie-Illinois, as they say they do, and if other sellers of cans follow American Can's lead, as they have done, that will stabilize prices all along the line.

The inelastic demand for packers' cans has made it urgent, from the strictly business point of view, to stabilize their prices. Moreover, it has permitted stabilization at a high level without greatly reducing sales.[121] The demand for packers' cans stems, ultimately,

117. It could, of course, be argued that these two, at least, act independently. Considering the preferential treatment that American Sheet and Tin Plate, one of the original constituents of United States Steel and a predecessor of Carnegie-Illinois, accorded American Can in its early years, such an argument would appear unsound. At any rate, if they do act independently, each does so in order to increase its share in monopoly gains. The prices they set are certainly not competitive by any standards known to economics.

118. TNEC Hearings, Pt. 20, Ex. 1407, pp. 10992-93.

119. *Ibid.*, Pt. 19, p. 10629.

120. The president of American Can pointed out that under the company's annual contract with Carnegie-Illinois specifying the price of tin plate "we were protected and our customers were protected by a uniform price throughout the year, which has been the method necessary to process agricultural products in as varying a climate as from Utah to Florida for tomatoes, for instance. They wanted a uniform price throughout the year. They wanted to be able to sell futures; they wanted an important element of their canned-foods cost, the container, to be at a stable price throughout the year, and that system was devised to enable that to be done by the use of a so-called official price of tin plate." *Ibid.*, Pt. 20, pp. 10761-62.

121. The following evidence indicates that can prices have been relatively high. (1) During the prosperous 1920's (1922–1928 inclusive) American Can and Con-

from the demand for preserved food. The number of cans used in any one season depends more on weather conditions, that is, on crop yields, than on the amount people are willing to spend on food: with a large fruit and vegetable crop, demand for cans is large; a smaller crop correspondingly restricts demand. But consumer incomes and food consumption habits exert a greater influence on the use of canned foods, particularly in the long run, than does the price of cans.[122]

When purchases of a product do not alter greatly in response to changes in its price, producers are strongly impelled to control its output and stabilize its price.

American Can's Stabilization Program Fairly Successful

American Can has been fairly successful in its price stabilization program. Between 1929 and 1939 the contract price of No. 2 plain packers' cans ranged from about 1.9 cents a can to about 2.2 cents. In only four years did the price change by as much as 10 per cent from that of the preceding year. From 1934 through 1937 it did not change at all.

The price of tin plate was equally stable. Between 1925 and 1939 Carnegie-Illinois' official price for tin plate at Pittsburgh ranged from about $4.25 a base box to $5.50. In only three years did it change by as much as 10 per cent from the preceding year. During two three-year periods it did not change at all.[123]

---

tinental earned slightly higher rates of return on invested capital (10.1 per cent for American; 11.5 per cent for Continental) than the average for 2,046 manufacturing corporations (9.7 per cent). (2) Neither American nor Continental earned less than 6 per cent during the worst years of the Great Depression, when most corporations were operating at a loss. (3) Between 1922 and 1929, despite a "veritable technological revolution" (American doubled its production per minute of No. 2 cans during the 1920's and increased its output per man-hour 26.7 per cent), American's gross margin between the cost of tin plate and the price of its No. 2 can declined only about 8 per cent. Hession, *op. cit.*, pp. 242-67.

122. In the past a reduction of, say, 5 per cent in can prices would probably have had little effect on the price of canned foods and even less on their consumption. Hence it would have had no appreciable effect on the demand for cans. But such a price cut would have greatly reduced the profits of can manufacturers. Similarly, if competition in the production of cans increased output even a little above customary requirements, it might have engendered "ruinous" price competition without appreciably increasing the use of cans.

Today the demand for cans is probably more elastic than it was before the war. In the past consumer habits and housewife preferences limited the use of substitutes for tin containers. Existing equipment and distribution facilities also delayed the use of substitutes. With the development of quick-freezing and the enforced use of paper and glass containers during the war, the obstacles to substitution have apparently been reduced.

123. *Ibid.*, pp. 120-25. It was very different with pig tin prices. They fluctuated

But neither American Can's nor United States Steel's control of the market was perfect. With the great shrinkage of business in 1938, price cutting on tin plate became so common that the Steel Corporation reduced its published price from $5.35 a box (of 100 pounds) to $5.10 to make it harmonize more closely with the actual market price.[124] Tin plate mills have occasionally departed from the "official" price, but the "official" price has been the generally recognized market price. By linking the price of tin cans to that of tin plate—a practice followed generally by American Can's rivals—American Can has made the price of tin cans relatively stable. It has given rival can manufacturers a formula by which they have been able to fix their prices for packers' cans. Prices made in this way respond to only a single element of cost—and that is a price-fixed element. The result is relatively stable, noncompetitive prices.

Discrimination in Tin Plate Prices

Although American Can has aimed to stabilize the "official" price of tin plate to its rivals and to link the price of tin cans to the "official" price of plate, it has not hesitated to use its monopoly power to obtain secret price concessions—concessions that its less powerful rivals have not enjoyed, nor its customers shared. Before NRA, American Can, under its contracts with the Steel Corporation subsidiary, customarily got a secret $7\frac{1}{2}$ per cent discount from the "official" price.[125] Competitors generally paid the official price.

These rebates were, of course, prejudicial to rival can companies.

---

between 20 cents and 63 cents a pound between 1929 and 1937. In 1933, when the tin cartel became effective, the price doubled within six months. Thereafter it fluctuated around 50 cents a pound, with a maximum annual variation of about 20 per cent.

124. TNEC Hearings, Pt. 20, p. 10766. According to the president of American Can, tin plate prices were also unstable during 1919 and 1920 and his company made voluntary adjustments in its tin can prices, ". . . and then there were questions about the stability of the price after 1930, and '31, '32, '33, with rather confused conditions." *Ibid.*, p. 10767.

125. Apparently the Steel Corporation, through its subsidiaries (Carnegie-Illinois or a predecessor company, American Sheet and Tin Plate), continually granted rebates to American Can from about the time of its formation until 1936. From 1902 to 1913 these totalled $9 million. During this period the Steel Corporation billed American Can at the published price and paid rebates monthly. Only two officials of American Can were aware of the rebates and they took great precautions to prevent anyone else from learning of them. For example, they set up the Steel Corporation subsidiary's account on American Can's books under the heading "secretary's account." In 1921 when American Can began buying tin plate from Bethlehem Steel it set up a similar account entitled "secretary No. 2." American Can carried its accounts with all other suppliers under the supplying company's name. *Ibid.*, pp. 10788-90.

And as both American Can's and its rivals' prices for tin cans were tied to the official price for plate, canners received none of the benefits of the rebate-reduced price that American Can paid for its tin plate. It follows, of course, that retail buyers of canned goods received no benefits.

In the negotiation of the NRA steel code knowledge of this rebate became public and the code made the discount of 7½ per cent applicable to the trade generally. Because its contract with the Steel Corporation provided that American Can should get tin plate for 7½ per cent less than the Corporation's "lowest net selling schedule," American Can contended that it was entitled to a further discount of 7½ per cent. The Steel Corporation rejected this interpretation and American Can filed suit. The case was settled out of court by Carnegie-Illinois' paying American Can $2,250,000.[126]

In 1936, while the Steel Corporation was negotiating a settlement with American Can, under a pledge of secrecy it offered a schedule of additional discounts if American Can would buy 90 per cent of its requirements from Carnegie-Illinois instead of 75 per cent. After bringing suit, American Can used the Steel Corporation's proposed new schedule of discounts "as a club to conclude contracts with Bethlehem, J & L [Jones & Laughlin], Republic and Youngstown" according to a vice-president of the Steel Corporation. These contracts were to run for ten years and the terms were similar to those the Steel Corporation had proposed in lieu of American Can's claim of a second 7½ per cent discount. They provided for a discount of *25 cents* a box on annual purchases of a million boxes or more, beyond the 7½ per cent that had become part of the regular terms of trade after NRA.[127]

126. *Ibid.*, pp. 10778-79. On October 15, 1935, while the suit was pending, a vice-president of the Steel Corporation explained the matter as follows to the president of the Corporation: "In connection with the American Can Company claim, I think an important point, which is perhaps not fully realized by Mr. Wheeler and other members of the Executive Committee, is that before we assented to the Steel Code containing this provision we submitted the actual wording to Mr. Phelps [president of American Can] for his comment. Unfortunately for us this was done verbally and not in writing. Mr. Phelps had no comment to make, the reason being that *it accomplished the very purpose that he has been seeking for several years, namely, no cutting of the American Can price.*" *Ibid.*, Ex. 1403, p. 10989. Italics supplied. As the authors interpret this ambiguous statement, the last clause refers to American Can's price (schedule) for tin cans, not to the price American Can paid for tin plate.

127. *Ibid.*, Ex. 1404, pp. 10989-90. This exhibit is a letter of June 5, 1936 from a vice-president to the president of the Steel Corporation. It indicates not only how great is American Can's power but also how, by obtaining preferential treatment, it

After the passage of the Robinson-Patman Act in 1936, tightening the Clayton Act prohibition of price discrimination, these contracts proved so embarrassing to the tin plate companies that they negotiated cash settlements with American Can, under which they paid it about $3.3 million. Asked if the differential of 25 cents a box to American Can under these contracts was embarrassing to the tin plate companies "because the difference in price could not be justi-

---

was undermining the very market stability for which it had so valiantly struggled. The first sentence refers to the contracts American Can had made with other tin plate suppliers.

"These contracts completely change the situation. It would seem to leave us with but two courses of action—

1—to stand on our present contract and fight the case in the courts if they dare to go there. The danger to us in this course lies not so much in the possible result of the case in the courts as in the damage that the American Can Company would be able to do us during the period of probably two years before the case could get into court. They could offer [*sic:* to buy from?] us cold reduced plate far beyond our capacity to supply and thus reduce substantially the corresponding amount of tonnage due us under the contract. They could be unreasonable in their rejections of plates and claims for damages. They could refuse to cooperate in the scheduling of tonnage at our various plants and could hurt our mill people and make it costly for them in a number of ways.

2—to revise immediately our contract with them giving them an additional 25¢ per box beyond the 7½% discount on all the plate they take. This would cost us about two and one-half million dollars per year. It would meet the contracts already concluded with Bethlehem, J & L, Republic and Youngstown.

"In following the second course the seriousness of the situation pricewise in the tin plate market is pronounced. All four companies who have made contracts with American would have to give Continental the same price—in fact one at least has already done so. The news would spread within 24 hours, concessions would be made by all not only to Continental and American but to all other can makers. Wheeling, McKeesport and Weirton would not stand on present prices for a minute. They could not do so and keep their can producing customers in business. The practical result would be that the net price of tin plate to everybody would be reduced from $4.66 per base box to $4.41 per base box. While there might be a temporary gain by the can makers in profit equivalent to approximately 25¢ per box it is my opinion that eventually nothing would be gained by the can makers either. The price of cans would decline in the same proportion as 25¢ per box on tin plate.

"The trouble does not stop there—the price of sheet bars of course cannot be maintained at $30. with a $5. reduction in tin plate. A similar reduction would have to be made on the 100,000 tons of black plate that we annually supply to Continental Can Co. These particular price reductions inevitably follow. But it is conceivable that the reduction also will extend to flat rolled products generally.

"If we should follow the second course, we are further confronted with the possibility that we may be charged with collusion by the F.T.C. or other governmental agency. This is a very serious aspect of the case.

"At present we publish a price on tin plate of $5.25 per base box but actually sell that plate at $4.76 per base box, a spread of 49¢ per box, made up of the 7½% contract differential and 10¢ for 10 Pkg. containers.

"At present therefore there is 49¢ fiction in our published price and it is to our published price that the can companies generally tie their selling price of cans. This spread is already too much. The addition of another 25¢ discount would increase the fiction in our published price from 49¢ to 74¢ per box. A situation which must inevitably be aired by the can user or somebody else.

"It is to be noted that the Corporation is the only tin plate producer on the spot in this connection. The others do not publish tin plate prices in the first instance and their names are not used in contracts for the sale of cans, as is ours."

fied on the basis of a quantity discount," the vice-president of American Can in charge of tin plate purchases replied, "That is right." [128] But while these settlements may have relieved the tin plate companies of liability under the antitrust laws, they gained for American Can continuing benefits from the price favors it had received. For the lump-sum payments represented a sort of calculation of the present worth of the anticipated benefits over the unexpired term of the contracts.

Discrimination in Tin Can Prices

In building up its monopoly position, American Can obtained great advantages from preferential prices in buying tin plate. But it also used price discrimination as a lever for increasing its sales. In the 1920's it granted to one of its larger customers, the Van Camp Packing Company, a secret rebate on tin cans.[129] This special discount amounted to an 18 per cent reduction from its published price list, and brought the net prices paid by Van Camp substantially below those paid by any other canner, whatever the volume of its purchases. In a suit for treble damages under the antitrust laws by a competitor of Van Camp's, the court declared:

> Defendant's [American Can Co.'s] efforts to secure or obtain business were limited by the statute. It could not rebate or discriminate in price save as a purchaser gave an order, the size of which justified the price reduction. Ordinarily a manufacturer, in fixing prices based on volume of business, would publish a price list from which all customers would learn the amount of purchases necessary to secure the best prices. Defendant published a price list, but it was a false one. Defendant showed favoritism to Van Camp, and the jury, upon the evidence before it, was justified in finding that such favoritism was not dependent on the volume of the latter's business.[130]

Thus, in the tin can market as in the tin plate market American Can, while exerting strong pressure for price stabilization, was not averse to taking advantage of the system behind the backs of its collaborators. So secure was its monopoly position during the period between the wars that it has not hesitated to play both ends against the middle.

128. *Ibid.,* p. 10780. Perhaps because of the doubtful legality of contracts specifying such preferential treatment, this same official testified that the company "settled for about 30 cents on the dollar." *Ibid.,* p. 10779.

129. See *Van Camp* v. *American Can Co.,* 278 U.S. 245 (1929).

130. *American Can Co.* v. *Ladoga Canning Co.,* 44 Fed. *2d* 763 and 768 (1930); certiorari denied, 282 U.S. 899 (1930).

Does Price Control Benefit the Public?

American Can has obviously gained by its program for stabilizing tin can prices, but not all the benefits were passed on to the public. In truth, such monopoly profits as it has enjoyed in the sale of cans have been at the expense of the buyers and sellers of foodstuffs. Although a decline in the price of packers' cans might not greatly increase their use, it would tend to increase either the monetary income of farmers who sell the raw foods that go into cans or the real income of consumers of canned foods.[131]

A study made for the Steel Corporation shows that for only four out of eleven major canned fruits and vegetables was the cost of tin plate more than 10 per cent of the final retail price.[132] For seven fruits and vegetables the cost of tin plate ranged from 3.4 to 10 per cent. The study concludes that "Even a ten percent reduction in the price of tin plate, if passed on to the consumer, would by itself lower the retail price of most canned food products by less than 1 percent, or approximately only one-tenth of one cent per can." [133] The plain implication of this statement is that a reduction in the price of tin plate is not of much importance to the public. But the implication is unwarranted.

The Steel Corporation study ignores the significance of can manufacturers' linking can prices to the price of tin plate and thereby stabilizing the price of cans. While tin plate costs may represent only from 3.4 to 13.9 per cent of the retail price of eleven selected canned fruits and vegetables, the cost of tin cans represents a far larger percentage. In truth, out of every dollar spent at wholesale for canned tomatoes, corn, and peas in No. 2 cans from 1934 to 1939, from 22.5 to 40.6 cents went to the can manufacturer.[134] If the follow-

131. Relief of farmers was more important during the 1930's than during the 1940's. Farmers were so badly off during the depression that the government came to their rescue with various subsidy programs. Relief of consumers was also more important in the 1930's than in the 1940's, for national income was shrinking until 1933—and stayed shrunk thereafter to the end of the decade. So millions of persons were unemployed. If consumers had paid less for canned goods they would have had more money for other things. This would have tended, however slightly, to increase business activity and employment.

132. TNEC Hearings, Pt. 26, Ex. 1415, p. 14022. Dr. Theodore O. Yntema directed this study. He was at that time a University of Chicago professor, a post he later resigned to join the Ford Motor Co. as vice-president in charge of finance.

133. *Ibid.*, p. 14023.

134. *Ibid.*, Pt. 20, Ex. 1402, p. 10989. Data from "The Almanac of the Canning Industry," published annually by the Canning Trade Publishing Co., Baltimore, Md. Assuming a 20 per cent markup by retailers, this would indicate that the percentage

the-leader pricing system in the tin can market were responsible for can prices being no more than, say, 3 per cent higher than they would otherwise have been, the added cost to consumers would amount to more than $6 million a year.[135]

What Should Be Done About It?

This brief account of American Can's influence over the market indicates that the hope expressed by the court (in the 1915 antitrust case) that competition would become effective in the sale of cans has not been fully realized. What, if anything, should now be done about it?

The problem is to decentralize power in buying tin plate and selling cans. And this obviously involves both American Can and Continental, as well as Carnegie-Illinois. American's and Continental's position in the market stems basically from two factors: (1) the power got by consolidating rivals; and (2) the use of monopoly earnings to bulwark their position. The latter has two aspects. Monopoly earnings have supplied both American Can and Continental with large sums for conducting research for improving can making and canning. This has enabled them to furnish services to fruit and vegetable packers that smaller firms cannot furnish. Since each can spread research costs over a far larger output than can their smaller rivals, each has a big advantage in this field. Research is a factor of production not quickly subject to diminishing returns.

Both American Can and Continental have used their control over the technology of can making and canning to control the sale of cans. Although the basic patents on can-making machinery have long since expired, American Can in January 1944 owned 1,100 patents and Continental owned 497, mostly covering improvements.[136] American Can in 1937 had ten types of vacuum machines for closing cans. No other company had more than two. The government has charged both American Can and Continental with violation of Sections 1

---

of the retail price representing the cost of the tin can ranged from 19 per cent to 33 per cent.

135. Computed from data in U.S. Department of Commerce, *Statistical Abstract of the United States,* 1943, pp. 648 and 695. The wholesale value of canned foods produced in 1939 amounted to, roughly, $700 million. Assuming on the basis of data cited in the preceding footnote that 30 per cent of this sum represented the cost of cans, then a 3 per cent reduction in the price of cans would be equal to nine tenths of one per cent of the $700 million expenditure on canned foods.

136. Hession, *op. cit.,* p. 168.

and 2 of the Sherman Act and Section 3 of the Clayton Act by leasing can-closing machinery to canning companies on condition that they buy their cans exclusively from the lessor.[137] On November 10, 1949 the court filed its opinion in the American Can suit, upholding the government's main contentions.[138] It condemned the use of the tying contract by defendant but indicated that the remedies granted must recognize the legality of total requirements contracts for a reasonable period. This ruling should afford small manufacturers of cans better opportunities for growth, but it is doubtful that it will make competition in this industry really effective.

Is Dissolution the Remedy?

The dissolution problem today is similar to that which confronted the court in 1916. Can you dissolve so "finely adjusted an industrial machine" without serious repercussions on the whole industry and perhaps on the whole economy? Any acceptable dissolution decree would have to be designed to avoid this contingency. To suggest the details of such a decree obviously is not the task of this study. But it should be pointed out that the separation of ownership of American Can's scattered plants apparently presents no serious problem.

In 1946 American Can had fifty-eight can factories and eight machine shops located in the United States, Canada, and the Hawaiian Islands. Although they had been greatly improved and expanded, forty-seven of these can-making plants were the same plants that the company owned when the government brought suit in 1913. Despite the fact that each of these plants is designed primarily to serve consumers in a particular geographic area, a breakdown of American Can into a half-dozen or more separate firms would no doubt eventually lead to an intensification of competition. Rival producers would be likely to enter the more attractive markets by building new plants or by absorbing freight on sales to such markets.

If the government should elect to intensify competition by dissolving American Can, its efforts might prove futile unless it also

137. Complaints filed August 27, 1946, *U.S.* v. *American Can Co.* (Civil No. 26345 H), and *U.S.* v. *Continental Can Co.* (Civil No. 26346 R), in U.S. District Court for the Northern District of California. Commerce Clearing House, *The Federal Antitrust Laws, Summary of Cases* (Blue Book), cited above, p. 337.

138. *U.S.* v. *American Can Co., et al.,* 87 Fed.Supp. 18 (1949).

dissolved Continental and unless it took whatever steps were necessary to insure more effective competition in the sale of tin plate. An effective dissolution program might start a small chain reaction. And this no doubt deters government agencies from experimenting with it. The willingness to experiment is apt to vary with confidence in a free-enterprise system. Risk taking is the essence of such a system. Achieving effective competition may necessitate risk taking by the government as well as by enterprisers.

If dissolution were undertaken, what to do with Continental's and American Can's research facilities might present a more serious problem. To transfer all of them to any one of the dissolved units would handicap all the others. If their physical layout permits, they might be distributed among the several successor firms. The resulting intensification of rivalry in research might compensate for any possible immediate loss of efficiency. If the organization of research makes it impractical to dissolve the research facilities, they might be put under the separate ownership of a research company required to serve all can-making and canning companies on a basis of equality. American ingenuity in business organization could no doubt devise a way to make research serve the can industry without making it the monopoly of one or two firms.

Conclusions

These surveys of price leadership in the cigarette and the tin can industries show how this trade practice tends to prevent effective competition. Detailed studies of other industries might, of course, reveal some cases of effective competition in industries in which sellers are relatively few.[139] But it could scarcely refute the general principle that an increase in the number and diversity of sellers as far as is consistent with the economies of scale will tend to make competition more effective. Though in many lines of manufacture, modern technology will not permit a market pattern that conforms even approximately to the economists' model of perfect competition, a dissolution program applied through a case-by-case procedure, as the facts may warrant, should produce results more closely resembling those that public policy contemplates. The resultant flexibility of price relationships would encourage a more economical use of

139. See, for example, Jesse W. Markham, *Price and Output Behavior in the Domestic Rayon Industry* (unpublished doctoral dissertation, Harvard University).

limited resources and bring more promptly to consumers the fruits of technological advance.

At best, however, vigorous enforcement of the antitrust laws alone does not promise an early resolution of the problems posed by the rise of semimonopolistic giant corporations with their strong bias in favor of price stabilization and "orderly marketing." Legislation supplementary to the antitrust laws is plainly required if more effective competition is to be achieved. Even with a resolute use of the taxing power, the power to establish federal standards of corporate organization, the power "To promote the Progress of Science and useful Arts," and indeed every other power that has any bearing on the conduct of trade—all for the deliberate purpose of fostering competition—the outcome would still fall far short of the economists' model of perfect competition. But from the standpoint of the public interest, the resultant increased opportunity for independent enterprise would contribute to a more nearly effective competition than that which through such practices as price leadership subtly eliminates the substance, leaving only the empty form.

Chapter 7

BASING POINT PRICING AND MONOPOLY

THE BASING POINT SYSTEM is a way of quoting delivered prices. It is used mostly in sales by manufacturers to other producers or to dealers. Such prices so quoted are composed of the factory price plus a transportation charge. But the transportation charge does not always correspond to actual cost, being generally the cost from some designated production center known as a "basing point." Such a system may use one or more points in calculating delivered prices.

Though this system is the most common way of calculating delivered prices, variations such as zone-pricing and freight equalization systems have developed. TNEC investigators listed sixty industries that used one or another of these pricing methods.[1] The list ranged from alcohol and asbestos roofing to turbine generators and zinc. The method of classification was not uniform, however, and some overlapping appears in the list; for example, the woodpulp and paper industry was listed and then there was a separate listing for newsprint. Also, some of the "industries" listed really represent a score or more lines of manufacture—for example, "builders' supplies." On the whole, the evidence indicates widespread use of delivered-price systems in the so-called heavy industries.

Steel Adopts Pittsburgh Plus

After experimenting with zone pricing and simple price agreements in the 1880's and 1890's, steelmakers eventually resorted to a basing point system and followed it until 1948.[2] When this method of

1. See Clair Wilcox, *Competition and Monopoly in American Industry,* TNEC Monograph No. 21, Washington, 1940, pp. 147-48.

Zone-pricing systems set a uniform price for delivery of products within extensive regions, such as west or east of the Mississippi River. Under freight equalization systems a producer quotes a price made up of the f.o.b. price plus an adjusted freight charge that will make the delivered price equal to the lowest delivered price offered by competitors.

2. The Federal Trade Commission in 1924 ordered the United States Steel Corporation to discontinue selling at prices based solely on Pittsburgh. The Corporation

pricing was devised, Pittsburgh produced more steel than all other districts combined and was the only center that regularly shipped steel to all parts of the country. Pittsburgh, therefore, was made the single basing point from which steel prices were generally quoted. Because steelmakers, wherever located, quoted as their delivered prices the price at Pittsburgh plus the cost of rail shipment from Pittsburgh to the delivery point, the system was called "Pittsburgh Plus." Under Pittsburgh Plus all steelmakers generally quoted identical delivered prices on any particular steel product for delivery to any part of the United States.

Under a multiple basing point system each manufacturer, wherever located, will ordinarily quote as his price in any city the lowest delivered price from any basing point. For example, if Pittsburgh, Chicago, and Birmingham are all basing points, and if steel bars at Pittsburgh are $60 a ton, at Chicago $61, and at Birmingham $62; and if rail freight charges from Pittsburgh to Nashville are $5 a ton, from Chicago to Nashville $4, and from Birmingham to Nashville $2, then steel manufacturers, wherever located, including those at Pittsburgh and Chicago, quote a delivered price at Nashville of $64.

Plants at basing points are known as base mills, others as non-base mills. In both the single and multiple systems manufacturers operating base mills and those operating non-base mills quote identical delivered prices.

Freight Absorption and Phantom Freight

Only when the manufacturer is located at the basing point that governs the delivered price does the buyer pay the actual charge of rail shipment. As both the Chicago and the Pittsburgh mills in the above illustration sell at a delivered price one dollar less than their own mill base price plus freight to Nashville, in effect they absorb one dollar of the freight charges.

A manufacturer, even though located at a basing point, absorbs the freight differential when he sells to a buyer in a city where the delivered price is governed by some basing point other than his

---

thereupon increased the number of its basing points. By announcing prices at the new bases somewhat higher than those at Pittsburgh, the Corporation "froze" some phantom freight into the price structure. In 1938 it eliminated many of these price differentials. See *The Basing Point Problem,* TNEC Monograph No. 42, Washington, 1941, pp. 42-43.

own. Only when he sells in a city where his base mill governs the delivered price does his delivered price equal his mill price plus freight. The practice of absorbing freight differentials varies the net yields for a plant on sales made to buyers in different cities. A Chicago manufacturer who sold steel bars for delivery in Chicago would have a mill net equal to his base price—in the example used, $61 a ton. If he sold for delivery in Birmingham, as he occasionally might, his mill net would be Birmingham's base price, $62, minus freight to Birmingham, say $6, or $56.

Assuming rail shipment, when base mills deliver to points where their base price governs the delivered price, their mill net equals their base price. But when they deliver to points where another base governs the price, they absorb differential freight charges and their mill net is reduced correspondingly.

"Phantom freight" is the name applied to transportation charges (included in the delivered price) in excess of actual cost thereof. The most common sources of phantom freight are in sales by a non-base mill delivered to a destination nearer its plant than the basing point, and in sales by either a base or a non-base mill delivered by cheaper means of transport than rail—for example, truck or ship. When a non-base mill making deliveries in its own city incurs no actual transportation cost, the freight charge included in the delivered price is wholly "phantom." [3]

Conditions Favorable to Basing Point Pricing

A basing point system is essentially a means of assuring identical delivered prices to all customers located in the same place, no matter where they buy. Obviously rival sellers can use it to stabilize prices and eliminate price competition. Some economists hold that it is prima facie evidence of noncompetitive selling, even of collusion, and they suggest that the government outlaw it.[4] Others argue with

3. A manufacturer not located at a basing point may deny that he charges phantom freight, contending that he merely takes advantage of his location by charging more to buyers the more distant they are from a rival seller. According to this view he merely exploits a monopoly of location.

4. See Frank Fetter, *The Masquerade of Monopoly,* Harcourt, Brace, New York, 1931, especially Pt. 5; Vernon A. Mund, "Monopolistic Competition Theory and Public Price Policy," *American Economic Review,* December 1942, pp. 727-43; and Fritz Machlup, *The Basing Point System,* Blakiston, Philadelphia, 1949. Machlup's is the most penetrating and exhaustive study yet made of basing point pricing. While his conclusions on the role of conspiracy in the practice and on public policy toward it agree with Fetter's and Mund's, his arguments are more sophisticated.

equal vigor that the basing point system is a normal manifestation of noncollusive business rivalry in industries of imperfect or monopolistic competition, and that forbidding it by law is likely to bring even less desirable marketing practices.[5]

Economists who favor the system point to six characteristics of industries using a basing point system: (1) standardized products; (2) relatively constant per unit variable costs as output increases until plants are operating at full capacity; (3) relatively large fixed costs; (4) products subject to heavy transportation charges; (5) widely separated single plants or clusters of plants; and (6) inelastic demand. The steel and cement industries are cases in point.

Favorable Factors Operating in Steel and Cement

Although most Portland cement exceeds the standard specifications of the American Society for Testing Materials and of the National Bureau of Standards, a barrel of standard Portland cement is for all practical purposes a barrel of cement.[6] Buyers apparently will not knowingly pay a penny more for one brand than for another. Quality variations in steel are many and great, but the different steels generally conform to standard specifications. Customers usually know what they want, and for steels of a specified quality one seller can get no more than another.

When a steel mill or a cement plant operates below capacity, variable costs increase at an almost constant rate as output increases, until operations approach capacity. The United States Steel Corporation has estimated that under the operating conditions of 1938, when its ingot output was about 36 per cent of capacity, every additional

5. See J. M. Clark, "Basing Point Methods of Price Quoting," *Canadian Journal of Economics and Political Science,* November 1938, pp. 477-89; *idem,* "Imperfect Competition Theory and Basing Point Problems," *American Economic Review,* June 1945, pp. 283-300; C. R. Daugherty, M. G. de Chazeau, and S. S. Stratton, *The Economics of the Iron and Steel Industry,* McGraw-Hill, New York, 1937, Vol. 1, Chap. 12, and Vol. 2, Chap. 22; and *Investigation of the Concentration of Economic Power,* Temporary National Economic Committee, Hearings pursuant to Pub.Res. 113 (75th Cong.), Pt. 26, pp. 13893 ff., and Pt. 27, pp. 14619-79. (The hearings will hereinafter be cited: TNEC Hearings, Pt. —.) The citations from TNEC Hearings refer to parts of a study that a group of economists prepared for the United States Steel Corporation for submission to TNEC.

6. In Federal Trade Commission proceedings against the Cement Institute and its members, respondents offered evidence to support this statement. According to them, "cement is cement." The record indicated, however, that "in the interest of eliminating competition," respondents had "suppressed information as to the variations in quality that sometimes exist in different cements." *FTC* v. *Cement Institute, et al.,* 333 U.S. 683 (1948), at pp. 714-15.

ton of steel it might have produced up to about 90 per cent of capacity would have cost it, in direct outlays, $55.75.[7] Apparently the direct cost for each additional unit of output (marginal cost) in both steel and cement is not only constant over a wide range of output, but is substantially less than the average total cost, including a return on capital. In the cement industry, Clark found that the marginal cost was about one half the average cost (minimum long-run supply price). He estimates that if the long-run average cost of cement is $1.50 a barrel and if the investment is not increased, the increase in direct costs for each additional barrel produced would be not more than 80 cents.[8]

While marginal cost remains relatively constant as output increases, fixed cost per unit decreases sharply as output increases. The Steel Corporation calculated its 1938 fixed costs at $182 million for any operating rate between 18 per cent and 90 per cent of annual ingot capacity.[9]

Buyers More Widely Dispersed Than Sellers

Cement and steel products are cumbersome and heavy. Transportation charges therefore represent a relatively large part of the delivered price.[10]

7. TNEC Hearings, Pt. 26, p. 13773.

8. This is apparently Clark's estimate of the minimum long-run supply price including normal return on investment with less-than-capacity operations. Clark, "Basing Point Methods of Price Quoting," p. 478.

9. TNEC Hearings, Pt. 26, p. 13775. One third of the fixed costs were payrolls and one sixth depreciation and depletion. Of the costs that vary with volume, payrolls accounted for more than half, and materials and services for about 40 per cent.

10. On cement, freight charges of from 30 to 60 cents a barrel are quite usual, and they average about a fifth or a quarter of the delivered price. See *Aetna Portland Cement Co., et al.* v. *FTC,* 157 Fed. *2d* 533 (1946), Petitioner's Brief, App. A, Vol. 1, p. 176. This case was an appeal from an FTC order requiring the Cement Institute and its members (of which Aetna was one) to cease and desist from following through concerted action the trade practice of pricing cement according to the basing point method. *In re Cement Institute, et al.,* 37 FTC Decisions 87 (1943). The complaint was issued July 2, 1937. Hearings before the trial examiner, beginning in 1940, lasted three years and filled 49,000 pages of testimony and 50,000 pages of exhibits. The Circuit Court of Appeals vacated the Commission's order. The Commission appealed, and on April 26, 1948 the Supreme Court reversed the lower court. *FTC* v. *The Cement Institute,* 333 U.S. 683 (1948).

Because of frequent reference in the present chapter to documents in this case, citations will be abbreviated as follows: *In re Cement Institute, et al.* to 37 FTC; hearings before the trial examiner to FTC Rec.; Commission Exhibit to Comm.Ex.; Respondents' Exhibit to Resp.Ex.; *Aetna Portland Cement Co.* v. *FTC* to *Aetna* v. *FTC;* Opinion in *Aetna* v. *FTC* to 157 Fed. *2d;* and in *Aetna* v. *FTC,* Brief for Petitioners to Pet.Br. and Brief for Respondent to Comm.Br.; *FTC* v. *The Cement Institute* to *FTC* v. *Institute;* Opinion in *FTC* v. *Institute* to 333 U.S.

To produce a ton of finished steel from ore of high metallic content requires about four tons of raw materials—coal for power and heat, lime for fluxing, and iron ore. Steel mills are generally located near the needed raw materials or where the raw materials can be assembled economically. In the United States most steel products are made in the Pittsburgh-Youngstown, Buffalo, Sparrows Point (Maryland), Philadelphia-Bethlehem, Chicago-Gary, or Birmingham districts. Producers in each of these districts sell throughout the United States.[11]

Availability of raw materials and accessibility of markets have mainly determined the location of cement plants.[12] Of the 163 cement plants in the United States in 1937, the Lehigh Valley of eastern Pennsylvania contained 21; western Pennsylvania 6; Michigan 11. The remaining 125 plants were scattered in thirty-four states, with clusters in northern Ohio, southeastern Kansas, central Alabama, and central California. Five New England states, three southern, one north central, and three western states were without any.

Demand for steel and for cement varies with the rate of business activity. And the demand for cement fluctuates both seasonally and geographically with the rise and fall of construction activity. From 1930 to 1938 annual steel output never exceeded 75 per cent of rated capacity and cement output never exceeded 60 per cent.[13] In 1932 the monthly average output of steel dwindled to less than 20 per cent of capacity, and that of cement to 23 per cent.

The tendency for their marginal cost to remain relatively constant and for their fixed cost per unit to decline as output increases, the tendency for buyers to be more widely dispersed than sellers, and the fluctuating character of demand for their products stimulate steel and cement producers to reach out for business in relatively distant markets.[14] The difference between added cost per unit on the extra

11. Colorado and the Pacific Coast region produced a small amount of steel before World War II. Plants built by the government, particularly the Geneva plant in Utah, may have shifted the center of production slightly westward, but the prewar centers east of the Mississippi are still dominant.

12. Cement is made by burning limestone and grinding the resulting "clinkers," mixed together with gypsum or calcium sulphate, to a fine powder.

13. TNEC Hearings, Pt. 26, p. 13860; *Aetna* v. *FTC,* Pet.Br., App., Vol. 1, p. 70.

14. Steel producers reach farther than cement producers. Cement manufacturers ordinarily sell most of their output that is distributed through dealers (i.e., indirectly) within a radius of 200 to 300 miles, but they occasionally ship substantial amounts much greater distances when supplying contractors on large construction jobs.

George Stigler regards geographical instability in demand as the fundamental

output and the net mill price received for it limits the distances over which they can afford to reach for business.

Elasticity of Demand and Basing Point Practices

When producers sell a standardized product ordinarily none can obtain a higher price than any other. As all sellers with plants in the same vicinity, or selling in a common market, will quickly meet any open price reduction, a seller is reluctant to quote a lower price unless he believes that sales will increase sufficiently to more than compensate for the price reduction.

Producers of steel and cement apparently believe that the total demand for their products is relatively constant, whatever the prices may be. In this belief they have the support of many economists.[15] Believing that demand is inelastic, cement and steel producers are reluctant to reduce prices, especially in those regions where they sell most. When demand near his plant is insufficient to permit capacity operation, the producer has a strong incentive to reach out for business. In doing so, he must sell at a delivered price no higher than mills nearer the customer receive. He must, therefore, either absorb freight or reduce his base price.[16] But to reduce his base price would lower his profit margin on the bulk of business done in his "home" market, and by inviting a like reduction by any near-by competitor might well prevent any increase in his sales volume. To absorb freight on the sales made at a distance is likely to be more profitable and to involve less risk of a price war.

---

requirement for a uniform delivered-price system. See "A Theory of Delivered Price Systems," *American Economic Review,* December 1949, pp. 1143-57. Stigler's theory throws new light on basing point pricing, but it exaggerates the influence of a single factor. The statistical data that he presents to support his theory—contract awards for reinforcing steel bars in 1936 by quarters for seven widely scattered states and a comparison of price movements for steel billets before the adoption of basing point pricing in steel (1898–1899) with price movements for steel bars after the adoption of basing point pricing (1939–1940)—are consistent with his theory but also consistent with other explanations of basing point pricing. Moreover, uniform, delivered pricing is not confined to industries characterized by geographical fluctuations in demand—crown corks, ice cream cans, and crepe paper, for example.

15. See Clark, "Basing Point Methods of Price Quoting," p. 481; TNEC Hearings, Pt. 27, p. 14635; FTC Rec., p. 44119, testimony of Roland S. Vaile; pp. 42991-92, testimony of Clare E. Griffin; p. 45810, testimony of Ewald T. Grether; and p. 44742, testimony of Fred R. Fairchild.

16. One critic thinks this statement arbitrary. He argues that the seller merely reduces his delivered price. In his view, it would be just as logical to hold that the seller "absorbs" the cost of material or the fuel or any other expense. This is a highly unrealistic view and one that not even the industry sponsors.

Defenders of basing point pricing contend, therefore, that prices for products like steel and cement fall naturally into this pattern. Prices of such products tend to become rigid. Base mills are price leaders, non-base mills price followers. A base mill or group of base mills determines the base price and enlightened self-interest (or mutual restraint founded simply thereon) tends to hold the price firm. The stability of prices is claimed to be advantageous not only to the industry but also to the economy. The system stabilizes prices, so the argument runs, without any need of formal agreement or concerted action among the producers.

Setting Base Prices

In setting their base prices, say supporters of this method of pricing, base mills take account both of what the traffic will bear and of what will yield them a "reasonable" rate of return.[17] In selling in markets where they are at a freight disadvantage, price leaders find it profitable to accept delivered prices as set by other base mills.[18] To cut prices might precipitate a disastrous price war without bringing an increase in dollar volume of business proportional to the price decline. Producers would do about the same volume of business but at much lower prices.[19] Bankruptcies would be inevitable.[20]

Thus, according to many economists and businessmen, collusion is unnecessary to stabilize delivered prices under the basing point system. The system reflects the independent rational behavior of business firms anxious to maximize their earnings and to avoid losses. Such, in brief, is the argument.[21]

17. Clark, "Basing Point Methods of Price Quoting," pp. 481-82.

18. In the FTC hearings F. M. Coogan of Alpha Portland Cement Co. testified in part as follows: "Q. You say you quote delivered prices because it enables you to meet competition. Aren't you interested in beating competition, or just in meeting it? A. I am interested in meeting the lowest price I find in any given market. Q. You are not interested in beating the lowest price that any competitor offers? A. No sir. I am not." Quoted in 37 FTC, p. 145. Lone Star's pamphlet on "Trade Ethics and Marketing Policies" states the case as follows: ". . . as we cannot get more than our competitors' price, we quote a price which we *expect will be identical* with that asked by the competitor whose lower freight rate gives his product the advantage at that point. . . . It is equally simple to anticipate the competitive price at any definite point, just as it is for the competitor to anticipate ours. This usually results in *identical* quotations being submitted by several manufacturers at a given time and place." Quoted, with italics, in *ibid.*, pp. 145-46.

19. Marginal costs would set the lower limit to which prices might fall.

20. As Blaine S. Smith, president of Pennsylvania-Dixie, said: "It is quite true that any deviation from the uniform price structure works in cumulative fashion and cannot be limited to a few isolated cases without doing serious harm." *Ibid.*, p. 146.

21. The cement and steel industries hired a large number of economists to explain

Economists Disagree

The argument is logical, but to some students of business practice it is not entirely convincing. They doubt that a basing point system could be inaugurated and successfully maintained without concerted action among the producers.[22] Like the defenders of the basing point system, they rely both on logic and on industry practices to support their position. A brief summary of their argument follows.

Under a basing point system mills persistently reach out for business in territory that can be more economically served by rival firms. On business done outside the area where it has a freight advantage each mill accepts a lower mill net price than on business done within that area. It also realizes a lower mill net price than the rival base mill gets from the same delivered price. This practice increases the cost of selling cement and deprives buyers in areas adjacent to base mills of the natural advantage of their location. It forces them to pay more for cement than more remote buyers pay.[23] The mills, in effect, discriminate among buyers. When buying from non-base mills, buyers to whom it costs the mills the least to deliver the product pay the highest mill net prices; buyers to whom it costs the mills the most to deliver the product pay the lowest mill net prices. When buying from base mills, the more remote buyers frequently pay a lower mill net price than near-by buyers.

Critics of the basing point system hold that such practices are inconsistent with competition. They argue that sellers of standardized goods in a competitive market cannot exact more of one buyer than

---

the basing point method of pricing in terms of accepted price theory. However, industry has had no monopoly of economists' services. Economists with different convictions testified for the government in the same proceedings. See TNEC Hearings, Pt. 26, pp. 13586-87 and 13676 ff., and *passim;* and FTC Rec., pp. 42976 ff., 44246 ff., 45485 ff., and *passim.*

22. The Circuit Court of Appeals (157 Fed. *2d* 554) censured FTC's consistent reference to the basing point practice as a "system," rather than simply as a method of pricing. The distinction is important and FTC's terminology appears well justified. It is one thing for a firm that customarily sells f.o.b. to treat all rival plants as basing points from which to calculate delivered prices when trying to sell in territory closer to a rival's plant and to absorb freight when necessary to get the business. That might properly be called a basing point method of pricing. It is quite another thing for all producers to quote delivered prices exclusively, to use a common freight rate book they have collaborated in compiling, to use a limited number of identical basing points from which to compute delivered prices, and to standardize all charges so that all rivals will be certain to quote identical prices at any point. Such practices transform a basing point method of pricing into a basing point system.

23. The more remote buyers may pay the same or higher delivered prices, because of the greater freight charge, but that part of their delivered price representing payment for cement is in many cases lower than that charged buyers nearer the mill.

of any other buyer at the same time—in conformity with what economists call the "principle of indifference." They contend that the persistent violation of this principle by producers selling under a basing point system reflects a monopolistic situation. While critics of the system do not insist that conspiracy as legally defined is always essential to the operation of the basing point system, they argue that the system involves something more than a rational choice of marketing strategy by each of several producers acting independently.

The critics also point out that when plants operate at partial capacity, as they did in the cement industry during the 1930's, producers are obviously greatly tempted to compete for business. The pressure is especially strong to make "concessions" at such times in order to get near-by business, even if in particular transactions a seller must shade his regularly quoted prices. In the absence of collusion sellers cannot be expected to resist such pressure.

Defenders of the system concede much of this. But they point out that the "principle of indifference" is applicable only to perfectly competitive markets and that modern technology makes such markets impossible. In markets of few sellers, they contend, each must take account of the probable reaction of his business rivals to his price policies. Independent rational behavior will simply by itself result, so the argument runs, in a live-and-let-live policy. Individual sellers will rely on salesmanship—not price—to get business. The critics dispute this; moreover, they insist that even if the system is free of collusion it would still reflect monopolistic pricing.

Cement: A Sample Case

The controversy sketched raises important questions of law and business practice. The main issues were brought into sharp focus in the Federal Trade Commission proceeding against the Cement Institute.[24] The respondents were, besides the Institute and its officers, seventy-five cement-manufacturing corporations. The complaint charged that the respondents had maintained "a combination . . . to hinder . . . and restrain competition in price, . . . made effective by . . . what is known as a multiple basing-point system of pricing."[25] After extensive hearings, the Commission ordered discon-

24. 37 FTC 87.
25. *Ibid.*, p. 102.

tinuance of the practice on two grounds: first, because the respondents' pricing system and their concerted action to make it effective constituted an "unfair method of competition" in violation of Section 5 of the Federal Trade Commission Act; and, second, because the varying mill nets realized by the respondents in selling cement under the basing point system constituted price discrimination resorted to for the purpose of destroying competition in price, in violation of Section 2 of the Clayton Act as amended by the Robinson-Patman Act.[26]

The litigation that followed eventually brought before the Supreme Court the controversy among economists regarding the collusive or noncollusive nature of basing point pricing.[27]

Economists clearly are not of one mind on the question of whether in the cement case the Commission's application of the law to the facts and the Supreme Court's decision upholding the Commission's order constitute sound public policy. But economists on both sides of the question, and laymen, too, will find the proceedings instructive. The record contains much material helpful in evaluating the theory of those economists who hold that rational business behavior alone, deriving from independent decisions, adequately explains the adherence to a basing point system of pricing in such an industry as cement. The record shows how the system grew, how it was enforced, how it was weakened and strengthened from time to time, and how it worked in terms of business rivalry. It indicates clearly that collaborative action was essential to the effective operation of the basing point system.

26. *Ibid.*, pp. 259-62. On the first count, FTC directed respondents to "cease and desist from entering into, . . . or carrying out any planned common course of action, . . . or conspiracy . . . for selling cement at prices calculated or determined pursuant to or in accordance with the multiple basing-point delivered price system." On the second count, FTC ordered respondents to cease and desist from "discriminating in price . . . among . . . customers by systematically charging . . . mill net prices which differ by the amounts necessary to produce" identical delivered prices.

27. The Court took cognizance of it in its opinion, stating: "Respondents introduced the testimony of economists to the effect that competition alone could lead to the evolution of a multiple basing-point system of uniform delivered prices and terms of sale for an industry with a standardized product and with relatively high freight costs. These economists testified that for the above reasons no inference of collusion, agreement or understanding could be drawn from the admitted fact that cement prices of all United States producers had for many years almost invariably been the same in every given locality in the country. There was also considerable testimony by other economic experts that the multiple basing-point system of delivered prices . . . contravened accepted economic principles and could have been maintained only through collusion." 333 U.S., p. 715.

Self-Discipline as a Possible Explanation

Though the Supreme Court held that the kind and extent of collaboration among cement manufacturers in maintaining this pricing system violated the law, this study is not concerned at this point with that particular issue. Its immediate object is to shed critical light on the thesis that, in conditions such as those characteristic of cement production, the development of basing point pricing is "automatic" in the sense of requiring no deliberate, concerted action.

Conceivably, at least, businessmen may strive to achieve the economic consequences of a conspiracy in restraint of trade without being guilty of that offense. In closely controlled markets their refusal to engage in price competition may, as some economists contend, be the product simply of self-discipline. But the exceptional power of self-control displayed by sellers where they are large and few may be the result of an "educational process" conducted by the group of which they are a part. A set of business rules, written or unwritten, serving as a guide to sellers' behavior may aid them in cultivating the almost invaluable attribute of self-restraint. Such collective rule making may approach so close to conspiracy that even a court cannot determine conclusively whether it really is or is not.

As John Treanor, president of the Riverside company, frankly said, cooperation cannot always "be left to the mutual, spontaneous adoption of considerate policies on the part of each and every competitor . . . The practical need for argument, persuasion, conference, exchange of assurances, soon appears. By gradual steps even the most righteous upholder of the law, finding himself in a competitive industry, may also find himself drawn into the realm of law evasion, or even of downright law violation in the form of deliberate price fixing." [28]

Background of Association in Cement Industry

The record of collective activity in developing "sound business practices" among cement manufacturers dates back at least to December 1904. At a meeting then of the Association of American Portland Cement Manufacturers (AAPCM), members expressed perturbation

28. Quoted in 37 FTC, pp. 144, 160, and 248.

over the lack of uniformity in prices and urged the Association to do something about it.[29] The following resolution recorded the sentiment of the meeting: "Resolved . . . that it is the sense of this meeting that the price should not be less than $1.00 per barrel at the mill for the Lehigh District." [30]

At an AAPCM meeting in April 1905 members indicated that, although conditions had improved, further collective action was desirable.[31] The group unanimously adopted a proposal for the appointment of "a special committee to take charge of the matter of prices and business methods." The following September the committee submitted a program, which the Association adopted, forty-six members signing up and only three refusing to go along.[32] Apparently the program worked. At any rate, a year later, at the September 1906 meeting, the committee chairman reported that:

> Having passed through both the demoralizing and unbusinesslike methods of one year ago, and now experiencing and enjoying the very opposite, viz., a very healthy condition of our trade, there should be no question which method should govern the management of our business in the future. It may be well, however, at this time to caution the members of our Association not to permit the present favorable conditions to lead them into a false position by adopting more stringent and uncalled-for methods, or unreasonably high prices, and thereby create the false impression that a Trust has secured control of our common industry.[33]

29. *Ibid.*, p. 151. AAPCM was organized in 1902 and at the time of the 1904 meeting its membership represented approximately 90 per cent of productive capacity in the United States. The Association changed its name in 1916 to Portland Cement Association (PCA) and has continued under that title to date. Since 1919, PCA has engaged exclusively in research and advertising activities designed to increase the use of cement.

Other trade associations in this industry that will be mentioned in the text below were of more limited scope or more specialized functions. These included the Association of Licensed Cement Manufacturers (ALCM), organized in 1907 and disbanded in 1911. *Ibid.*, p. 153. Also in this group were: the Cement Manufacturers Protective Association (CMPA), organized in 1916 and dissolved in 1922, and the Cement Institute, organized in 1929 and not dissolved until June 1946.

30. 37 FTC, pp. 151-52.

31. *Ibid.*, p. 145. As a Michigan member stated, "We are trying to follow our Eastern friends in the Lehigh Valley, and we will be very well satisfied if they keep up their 'nerve.'"

32. Of the three nonsubscribing members, only one, Atlas, was an important producer. Apparently Atlas' noncooperation did not mean it was holding out for free competition. It owned a patent through which it appeared possible to get singlehanded control of the industry. Atlas at the time was prosecuting numerous infringement suits against other cement companies, and about a year later (November 1906) the parties settled out of court and organized ALCM. See *Aetna* v. *FTC*, Pet.Br., App. A, Vol. 3, pp. 1792-93.

33. 37 FTC, p. 153.

Nonconformance to Cooperative Program a Problem

The industry's self-discipline at this stage, however, was a fair-weather cloak. During the business depression after the 1907 panic, many cement producers apparently preferred to go it alone in search of business.[34]

In this period of uncertainty and disorder the proposal for industry-wide cooperation in quoting only delivered prices was put forward, to wit: that "All prices quoted for Portland Cement shall be prices for delivery at the point required by the purchaser." [35]

AAPCM did not itself act on this suggestion. But a new organization had been set up the year before that had among its primary aims the strict enforcement of a uniform basing point system. The ALCM was an association of sixteen of the larger cement companies operating in the East and Northeast, which agreed to take licenses under an Atlas patent, later invalidated.[36] Each license agreement stipulated that:

> . . . all prices quoted for Portland Cement covered by the License Agreement . . . shall be prices for delivery at the point required by the purchaser . . . Prices in Territory A shall not be less than $1.20 in wood and cotton and 95 cents in paper plus the Northampton all-rail freight rate with the following exceptions . . .[37]

Thus at its inception it appears the standardized basing point system was anything but a spontaneous development. The pressure of infringement suits gave rise to ALCM; only the refusal of the courts to enforce the scheme prompted its dissolution.

34. The committee chairman wrote to the president of AAPCM in 1908 in part as follows: "I think it fair to assume that the consensus of opinion of the Association is that the lack of unity and cooperation on the part of all manufacturers in their respective territories is the only lucid explanation of the unwarranted and unfortunate condition which our business has drifted into." *Ibid.*, p. 153.

35. *Ibid.*, p. 153. Since the turn of the century several individual cement producers had apparently been using their own mill locations (mostly in the Lehigh Valley district) as basing points, and selling partly on a delivered-price basis. See *Aetna* v. *FTC*, Pet.Br., App. A, Vol. 1, pp. 104-34. But the lack of uniformity in the bases used and in the freight rates added thereto apparently made this crude "delivered-price" system ineffective. At any rate, vigorous competition cropped out in 1908.

36. 37 FTC, pp. 154 ff., and *U.S.* v. *CMPA*, 294 Fed. 390 (1923), at pp. 395 ff. The patent in question covered a method of using pulverized coal in cement kilns. It was invalidated in 1910, two years before the Supreme Court in the famous Bathtub Pool case condemned a similar licensing scheme because it was a mere subterfuge—an effort to escape the penalties of the antitrust statutes by cloaking unlawful action in a lawful costume. See *Standard Sanitary Manufacturing Co.* v. *U.S.*, 226 U.S. 20 (1912).

37. *Aetna* v. *FTC*, Pet.Br., App. A, Vol. 1, pp. 135-36.

Extension of Basing Point System

But as fair weather succeeded foul, cooperative action again became more effective, enabling AAPCM to extend the basing point system to the Midwest. A Wabash representative reported at the 1910 meeting:

> The situation in Michigan is very satisfactory and growing more so. There was no unity of action at all among the mills until they formed a little association which comprises all the Michigan mills and one or two across the border. This has resulted in a free interchange of views and an understanding to the effect that the Lehigh prices would govern the prices out here. This understanding has been observed. The price today, based upon the Lehigh price of 80 cents, makes Detroit a price of $1.25 delivered.[38]

According to the Federal Trade Commission, the basing point system was extended farther west in 1915 by agreement among competitors.[39] In support of this finding the Commission cited certain letters from the sales manager of Colorado Portland Cement instructing its affiliate, Three Forks, to use as a basing point a certain town in Washington, where International Portland Cement had a mill, and to quote only delivered prices determined by adding to the $1.50 base price the freight rate from that point to destination:

> . . . as shown in list sent you by our Chicago friends. . . . No deviation or exception to the above price will be considered in any instance and any salesman, or employee, deviating one iota, will be discharged at once . . . We will give every salesman, and every employee, every assistance possible . . . and we will see that our prices are as low as our legitimate competitors are naming, *but no lower if we know it,* and on this basis we expect them to secure for us practically all of the business in our territory.[40]

Another letter set forth the grounds for the sales manager's confidence that prices computed according to his instructions would hold firm. He stated that Lehigh, its principal competitor, was cooperating in the basing point program described.

> You need have no fear, whatever, of the Lehigh people taking any business except on this basis, as their Chicago office is now in complete charge of their Spokane factory, and will be responsible for every action of every one of their employees. . . . Mr. Gowan gave me his personal guarantee of this,

38. 37 FTC, p. 152.
39. *Ibid.,* pp. 153 ff. FTC said that "this extension was not the result of independent action."
40. Letter of January 25, 1915. *Ibid.,* p. 154. Italics supplied.

and I in turn gave him my guarantee of our strict adherence to this . . . While on this subject I want to call your attention to the fact of not letting any one know that any understanding, whatsoever, has been agreed upon, and especially never mention this to any of our customers, but simply say to them, that we have reasons to believe, that no lower prices will be named than we are quoting. . . . Please caution your salesmen particularly in this regard.[41]

By 1916, except on the Pacific Coast, the basing point system was apparently in general use in the cement industry.[42] The growth of the system was no more spontaneous than its inception. Cement producers recognized it as an aid in stabilizing prices and encouraged and promoted its use. They also adopted common trade practices to make it work.[43]

Without collective discussion of their pricing problems and culti-

41. *Ibid.*, p. 155.

42. According to the Federal Trade Commission, the system was extended to western Washington in 1931 after a price war that started when two new mills began operations in 1928 and 1929. An upshot of the price war was that Superior, a long-established company, took over one of the new mills, and shortly thereafter, according to the Commission, the basing point practice was introduced. The record does not indicate the date or manner of its extension to California. But it was already in use there when the War Industries Board fixed cement prices during World War I. In southern California an elaborate zone-pricing system was used. *Ibid.*, p. 156.

43. The above account of the growth of this basing point system is based primarily on the findings of the Federal Trade Commission in 37 FTC, pp. 143-61, but also on the opinion in *U.S.* v. *CMPA,* previously cited. J. M. Clark, who with A. R. Burns conducted for the industry an extensive inquiry on price making in cement, gives a wholly different account of the practice as a spontaneous development in industries with the economic characteristics described heretofore. See Clark, "Basing Point Methods of Price Quoting," p. 480. Clark relies largely on abstract reasoning to support this view. Either he was not familiar with the documents the Federal Trade Commission used or he did not think them significant. Confronted with nearly 100,000 pages of exhibits and testimony (much of it conflicting), an analyst must choose and evaluate. Respondents introduced considerable testimony to indicate that the transition from f.o.b. to delivered pricing accompanied the disappearance of the wholesale distributor and the assumption of his function by the manufacturers. See *Aetna* v. *FTC,* Pet.Br., App. A, Vol. 1, pp. 97-167. In the absence of other facts this testimony might offer an adequate explanation of the origins of delivered pricing. But it does not invalidate the facts on which the present analysis rests.

The conflict between Clark's account and that of this study is not so great as might appear. Clark is probably correct in concluding that in periods of slack demand rival sellers of cement will reach out to get business in regions other sellers can supply more economically and that in doing so they must quote a delivered price at least as low as that of their rivals. Experience may also teach that price cutting doesn't pay. The practice of using basing points may develop spontaneously. But basing point pricing does not guarantee price stability; it only facilitates stabilization. It promptly signals any price deviations, and provides a starting point for "missionary efforts." Group action appears necessary to convert basing point pricing into a system for stabilizing prices.

Clark merely analyzes the conditions that tend to result in basing point pricing. The present study describes the collective efforts of the industry to insure that the practice is general and to make it an effective device for stabilizing prices.

vation of widespread acceptance of certain basic rules of the game, cement manufacturers knew from experience that some sellers would profit by the forbearance of others. Hence they developed formal codes of sound business practice and less formal devices for enforcing them. Recognizing the necessity for such cooperation, the Report of the Executive Committee of AAPCM at its December 1915 meeting stated:

A shoulder-to-shoulder movement is what this industry needs, and its future success depends on . . . co-operation.

It should also be applied, and at once, to our commercial methods. At a recent conference of businessmen representing various industries it was the consensus of those present that "the salvation of the manufacturer and the safety of the public lies in the development of co-operative competition, of competition in the open, and that unintelligent price-cutting must cease."[44]

Supplementary Business Rules

A producer may cut prices directly, or he may indirectly accomplish much the same result by granting more favorable terms of payment than other producers. Indirect price cutting may be more troublesome to rival producers than direct price cutting. It is almost impossible to conceal outright price cuts, and competitors can promptly meet them. But rebates, discounts, special concessions on credit terms, advertising allowances, sales-help services, guarantees, and similar bargaining adjustments leave competing sellers groping in the dark, uncertain of what they must offer to attract business. To stabilize the structure of prices in an industry like cement, sellers as a body must have certain rules and comply with them.

An agreement on such rules is a necessary supplement even to a price agreement, and still more so to a mechanical pricing formula like the basing point system.[45] While cement producers were trying

44. FTC Rec., Vol. 67, Comm.Ex. 3236-Z86. A little later the committee added: "We need not blush to acknowledge that our main object in business is to acquire a competence, and that those whose property we administer may receive a fair return on their investment.

". . . Hence the best thing to do is to get together and help the weaker brothers.

* * *

"The help for this must come from within. When it was a case of filling orders at our own price, we did not need help, but that day is past. We must now get down to the hard facts of business and practice the same thoroughness as is used in trade in Europe." *Ibid.*, Comm.Ex. 3236-Z88.

45. Although the pricing system may properly be called a "mechanical pricing formula," it does not relieve businessmen of the necessity of keeping constantly in touch with the market. Certainly in the cement industry producers were not so well-

to standardize the methods of quoting prices, therefore, they also found it expedient to standardize business practices that indirectly affect the price structure. Thus as early as 1906 AAPCM adopted an "Agreement to Standardize the Customs and Usages in the Cement Trade," which covered uniform terms of payment and allowances for returned bags.[46]

The Association of Licensed Cement Manufacturers in its brief career played an important role in standardizing trade practices. Its license agreements, in addition to stipulating uniform delivered prices computed on a basing point formula, required licensees to grant only standard trade discounts, to place a uniform limit on the effective period of quotations or bids, and to conform to uniform rules in crediting buyers for returned bags. A federal district court observed that among cement manufacturers generally these rules and standards seemed to be "regarded as helpful, if not essential, in an endeavor to maintain prices and to apportion territory." [47]

An AAPCM booklet published in 1915 listed the recommendations of the Committee on Trade Conditions, as approved by the Association.[48] Among other things, members were advised to assume no responsibility for damage to shipments in transit; to sell no cement conforming to other specifications than the recognized official standards or those of the American Society for Testing Materials; to charge three cents a barrel for testing and storing cement for a purchaser; to use standard forms for specific job contracts,[49] dealer contracts,

---

disciplined in the use of this pricing system that they could ignore what their rivals did. Eternal vigilance seems to have been, from the sellers' standpoint, the cost of identical pricing.

46. 37 FTC, p. 207. The members agreed "that all cotton sacks be charged at the rate of 10 cents each, and . . . that each company repurchase the cotton sacks at 7½ cents each."

47. *U.S.* v. *CMPA,* p. 395.

48. The Association urged that "the sale and distribution of the product be conducted upon firm and definite fixed principles, and that doubt and uncertainty be eliminated. . . . Uniform observance of the best practices will promptly eliminate many abuses and irregularities now prevalent." 37 FTC, p. 208; and *Aetna* v. *FTC,* Pet.Br., App. A, Vol. 4, p. 2560. PCA, successor to AAPCM, published a similar pamphlet in 1919.

49. Specific job contracts are drawn to meet the cement requirements for a particular construction job. Since the contractor, at least during the period here in question, ordinarily got the benefit of any reduction in the cement manufacturer's quoted prices while the contract was in force, and since his contract protected him against a price advance, he frequently took an option, so to speak, on more cement than the job called for. Apparently, also, some cement producers encouraged this practice among dealers as well as contractors, despite the fact that it obviously created a threat to the price structure. The 1915 report of the Committee on Trade Conditions of AAPCM

and orders; to grant credit for returned bags only in accordance with AAPCM rules; to grant no rebates in any form to any buyer; and to add at least 5 cents a barrel to the dealer price on sales to contractors.

Exchange of Trade Data as a Stabilizing Device

In 1916 the industry adopted a more formal program for stabilizing prices and standardizing business practices. Besides reorganizing AAPCM as PCA, nineteen leading cement manufacturers in the Northeast organized an open price association, CMPA.[50] The CMPA program centered mainly on the exchange of detailed trade statistics, and its founders were careful to emphasize that the organization did not in any way bind its members to a common course of action. According to Article III of the CMPA constitution:

> The objects of the Association are the collection and dissemination of such accurate information as may serve to protect each manufacturer against misrepresentation, deception, and imposition and enable him to *conduct his business exactly as he pleases in every respect and particular,* free from misdirection by false or insufficient information . . .[51]

But the spirit behind the whole project was expressed by the chairman of the first meeting of the group.

> The idea of this thing is cooperation . . . We all agree that the necessity of cooperation is acknowledged by everybody in the industry. The only question now we have to determine is how we can best make use of cooperation . . .[52]

CMPA performed four major services for its members. (1) It collected from each and distributed to all its members monthly

---

recognized this as a serious danger. It stated that "Urging dealers to place orders for extended delivery for specific work, and permitting such dealers, at their option, to take more or less cement on such orders than actual quantity used in the work, has been one of the most objectionable devices and practices known, and has done more than any other one thing to bring about demoralization." 37 FTC, p. 203.

50. See *U.S.* v. *CMPA,* p. 391. Other agencies performed somewhat similar functions in other parts of the country. The Southeastern Portland Cement Association and the Kansas City Cement Bureau furnished freight rate information to their members. 37 FTC, pp. 143 and 162.

51. *U.S.* v. *CMPA,* p. 391. Italics supplied. Article VIII made even more explicit the industry's determination to avoid illegal agreements in restraint of trade. "No member of the Association shall enter into any arrangement, agreement, or understanding of any nature or kind whatsoever, the object of which is to restrain trade, limit competition, or accomplish any purpose contrary to the spirit or letter of the law . . ."

52. *Ibid.*

information on specific job contracts, showing for each such contract the price, the maximum amount of cement called for and the amount still to be delivered, the name of the contractor, the location of the job, and other details. (2) Similarly, it collected, compiled, and distributed monthly statistics on production, shipments, and stocks on hand, and quarterly statistics on returned bags. (3) It compiled and distributed among its members books giving the freight rate from the nearest basing point to each of the numerous delivery points in the area. (4) It acted as a credit clearinghouse, collecting and distributing information on members' outstanding accounts receivable, showing the name and address of debtor, total amount unpaid, and the time overdue, if any.

Supreme Court Upholds Statistical Interchange Plan

The activities of CMPA, whatever the primary objectives of the group and however innocent of conspiracy its members may have been, obviously helped stabilize prices. In 1921 the Department of Justice sued under the antitrust laws to enjoin these activities. A federal district court held CMPA an unlawful combination, but the Supreme Court reversed this ruling.[53] The Supreme Court sharply distinguished between agreement among competitors to collect and disseminate trade statistics and agreement to act upon such statistics in concert. It declared:

> Agreements or understandings among competitors for the maintenance of uniform prices are of course unlawful . . ., but the Government does not rely upon agreement or understanding, and this record wholly fails to establish, either directly or by inference, any concerted action other than that

53. *Ibid.*, reversed in 268 U.S. 588 (1925).

The District Court found that, though the arrangements involved no outright agreement on prices or output, the statistics interchanged disclosed to each member any lack of uniformity among sellers in so adjusting their operations and policies as to support the market. The court observed that "since the Association began to operate, there has been a uniformity and stability in . . . quotations that previously did not exist." 294 Fed., p. 398. It then cited with approval the Supreme Court's opinion in the hardwood lumber case, 257 U.S. 377 (1921): ". . . members do naturally follow their most intelligent competitors, if they know what those competitors have actually been doing."

The District Court also viewed the CMPA freight rate book as a convenient device for making certain that each seller would quote precisely the same price for cement delivered to any designated point. The Federal Trade Commission later shared this view and cited, in support, certain correspondence in 1918 between a member and CMPA. A Lehigh representative inquired: "Have you an extra West Virginia price book?" CMPA replied: "In your letter you request a price book, which is no doubt a typographical error, inasmuch as you are aware of the fact that this Association does not issue books in any way connected with price matters." 37 FTC, pp. 163-64.

involved in the gathering and dissemination of pertinent information with respect to the sale and distribution of cement . . ., and it fails to show any effect on price and production except such as would naturally flow from the dissemination of that information in the trade and its natural influence on individual action.[54]

On CMPA activities concerned with specific job contracts the Supreme Court took the position that their primary purpose was simply to prevent buyers from fraudulently taking advantage of sellers by obtaining more cement—at a favorable price—than was actually required in the construction work specified in the contract. The preparation and distribution of the freight rate book amounted, in the view of the Court, to nothing more than an economical method of doing collectively what some of the companies had previously done individually.

With this judicial approval of their association activities, cement manufacturers continued generally to use the basing point method of pricing, though in the course of the litigation the defendants had voluntarily dissolved CMPA. The industry continued, also, to follow recognized rules and practices governing terms and conditions of sale. Of course, some exceptions were recognized in the application of these so-called customs of the trade.[55] But, by and large, cement manufacturers had adjusted their operations to a uniform pricing pattern and to rules of conduct that helped stabilize cement prices.

Nevertheless, after 1929, departures from the customary way of doing business became more frequent. Evidently CMPA was missed when a declining market let loose disorganizing forces too powerful for a less compact and cohesive organization to resist. At any rate, in the Great Depression, price cutting, either directly or through special concessions, became general. The cement industry tried to

54. 268 U.S., pp. 604-05. The Court apparently was influenced by "A great volume of testimony . . . given by distinguished economists in support of the thesis that, in the case of a standardized product sold wholesale to fully informed professional buyers, as were the dealers in cement, uniformity of price will inevitably result from active, free and unrestrained competition . . ." *Ibid.*, p. 605. For a discussion of this issue see above, pp. 191-93.

55. For example, in southern California zone pricing was generally used. In other areas manufacturers sold cement at what the trade called arbitrary prices, that is, delivered prices not equal to the sum of the governing basing point's price and freight to points of destination. Such departures from general practice were apparently designed to meet special competitive situations—for example, the competition of imported cement along the Atlantic Coast—or to make the basing point system more acceptable to dealers by eliminating inequities that would have resulted from its rigid application. *Aetna* v. *FTC*, Pet.Br., App. A, Vol. 1, pp. 557 ff.

stem the tide, and at times the federal government encouraged these efforts. The producers first adopted a "Code of Ethics" (1929) and later, under NRA, a code of law to guide them.

Cement Institute Formed

Cement manufacturers, with the approval of the federal government, organized the Cement Institute in August 1929.[56] The articles of association thus set forth the purposes of the Institute:

> To promote the best interests of the cement industry by providing facilities for collecting, through voluntary action, information with respect to trade and commerce therein, and disseminating such information among the members of the Institute and the public generally.
>
> To adopt and promulgate a Code of Ethics for the Government of the members.
>
> To establish and maintain all such lawful trade customs and usages for the protection of the members as the Institute may deem desirable.[57]

One of the vexations of the industry at this period was diversion of shipments. The Institute promptly addressed itself to the correction of this "evil." This activity was an essential part of its program for stabilizing prices and shows the relation of its activities to the defense of the multiple basing point system. As previously explained, under such a system, when a base mill (mill A) sells in a locality in which the price is governed by another base mill (mill B), mill A absorbs freight in order to sell at a delivered price no higher than that of mill B. Dealers learned to circumvent the system by ordering cement from mill A for delivery to some designated point at which mill B's base price governed and then diverting the shipment to a point nearer mill A where its own base price governed. After adjusting the delivered price to take account of the cancelled rail transport (and lower freight cost), mill A's customer would obtain his cement at a reduction amounting to the difference between mill A's normal base price and the mill net that mill A normally realized on deliveries to the designated point in mill B's market territory. By doing this

56. At an unofficial meeting of the Federal Trade Commission in May 1929, a commissioner invited members of the industry to form an association, draft rules for governing the trade, and submit them to the Commission for approval. Mr. Coogan, vice-president of Alpha, testified that in his opinion this was the "controlling reason" for the formation of the Institute. *Ibid.*, Vol. 3, p. 1798. The organizers, apparently trying scrupulously to keep the Institute and its activities within the law, proceeded only on advice of counsel. *Ibid.*, p. 1826.

57. *Ibid.*

dealers could obtain cement for less, and by passing their gains on to consumers they could upset the price structure.[58] The Institute's Code of Ethics forbade this practice.[59]

On many subjects, such as commercial bribery, the Code of Ethics followed the terminology then in common use in framing the provisions of trade practice conferences. These sections evidently were considered less urgent than the provisions defining offenses in terms specifically applicable to the cement industry. Compliance with the Code was entirely voluntary. It was the Institute's practice, however, to rebuke members for violating its provisions.[60]

Perhaps the Institute's most important work was operating two freight rate bureaus, one in the Lehigh Valley and one in Chicago. The bureaus computed and distributed to Institute members freight books for nearly every state east of the Rockies showing rail rates from mills and ports of entry to all destinations. The Commission found that these books "were intended . . . to provide common freight rate factors for pricing purposes, avoid differences in delivered price quotations resulting from errors in rate calculations or failure to keep abreast of rate changes, and thus enable the corporate respondents to quote identical delivered prices for cement at all destinations; and they were in fact used for that purpose." [61]

58. This practice was, of course, very much resented by dealers who did not resort to it, for they lost business, and they apparently protested to manufacturers who permitted the practice. It is not evident that any cement manufacturers connived at this method of doing business, but some backsliders may have done so in their zeal to get orders when demand was shrinking.

59. 37 FTC, p. 199. The Code of Ethics also condemned as unfair trade practices: the guarantee of finished cement work; discrimination "in price, or terms and conditions of sale, as between purchasers or users in the same class, except as provided by the Clayton Act"; failure to make "prices and all terms and conditions of sale public by broadcast quotations to the trade so that interested members of the trade and buying public may at all times have accurate information"; payment of secret rebates and allowance of unearned refunds; and many other business practices. See *Aetna* v. *FTC,* Pet.Br., App. A, Vol. 3, pp. 1835-44, where the Code of Ethics is reproduced in full.

60. *Ibid.,* pp. 1844-46.

To standardize terms and conditions of sale, the Institute considered recommending to its members a uniform sales contract and its counsel prepared a preliminary draft of such a contract. Because "certain provisions" presented "some doubtful questions of legality," counsel thought "it would be wiser for the Institute to . . . simply prepare a bulletin recommending . . . the provisions which should be embodied" in such a contract. The Institute followed this advice. *Ibid.,* Vol. 4, pp. 2597-98.

61. 37 FTC, p. 164. According to FTC, "The rate books lack information that a genuine rate service would be expected to supply: they give no information which would assist in routing shipments; they give no information concerning minimum carload weights; and they give no information respecting switching charges." *Ibid.,* p. 166.

The Institute's first freight books contained a conversion table for changing the

The Circuit Court of Appeals took a contrary view of this as of other activities of the Institute and, after pointing out that "there was no exchange of prices or price data among the members and [that] the Institute . . . did not receive . . . or send out any information as to basing-points, base prices, change of mills from non-base to base, or vice versa," concluded that the Institute's entire program came "within the legal sphere of a trade association, as held in the old Cement case." [62] As previously indicated, the Supreme Court reversed the lower court on all the principal issues.

Institute Encounters Difficulties

The Institute's membership increased from fourteen to forty companies in ten months, but a year later (June 1931) half the members had dropped out.[63] After a change of official policy, doubt arose regarding the Federal Trade Commission's attitude toward the industry's Code of Ethics and it was not submitted for approval. Lacking official support for its program, the Institute was unable to get full compliance with the rules. These rules provided a satisfactory guide to business behavior in fair weather, but as the depression deepened competition sharpened and the crust of custom crumbled under the pressure of idle capacity, rising overhead, and shrinking demand. Although the basing point system was not abandoned, departures from identical delivered prices were common; and the price structure disintegrated.

The NRA program put the government behind the industry's efforts to standardize and stabilize the marketing of cement. Cement manufacturers responded promptly to the opportunity NRA afforded them to develop an effective program of industrial self-government.[64]

---

freight rates from cents per hundred pounds, the basis on which railroads quoted rates, to cents per barrel, the basis on which the cement companies quoted prices. Since the conversion tables dropped fractions of a cent, the converted freight rates did not always correspond to the actual freight rates. So the table was dropped from the Chicago Bureau books after 1933 and from all books after 1937. As a result the delivered prices quoted by different producers were not identical.

62. 157 Fed. *2d*, p. 545.

63. *Ibid.*, p. 543. According to the Institute's counsel, "Lehigh, the oldest and one of the largest companies, resigned in March 1931 because it felt that the Institute no longer held any possibility for the execution of the purposes for which it had been formed, due to the resignation of a great many companies and because, in view of the low prices prevailing at the time, it desired to avoid all items of cost which it could." *Aetna* v. *FTC*, Pet.Br., App. A, Vol. 3, pp. 1810-11.

64. When the Institute submitted its code of fair competition for NRA approval,

The Institute revised its articles of association and enlarged its board of trustees to make the organization more "truly representative" of the industry.[65]

NRA Reinforces Cement Institute Program

The industry's code of fair competition as finally approved contained many provisions similar to those of the Institute's Code of Ethics. But for several reasons it was far more effective in standardizing business practices and stabilizing prices. First, the code of fair competition was the law. Second, it went further in controlling elements affecting price than did the Code of Ethics.

The more important provisions of the NRA code not paralleled in the Institute's Code of Ethics were Articles VI, VII, VIII, and IX and paragraph (g) of Article X. The first three are important not primarily because they helped greatly in stabilizing the industry but because they reflected the industry's attitude toward the problem of stabilization and because they encouraged collaboration among producers in attacking that problem. Article VI authorized the Institute's board to formulate a plan for dividing available business among the members of the industry. The board was unable to agree on a plan acceptable to the industry and none was adopted.[66]

Article VII authorized the Institute to petition the President of the United States to prohibit the construction of any new cement plants if "such new plant will result in further increasing the prob-

---

its membership included 96 per cent of the nation's cement producers and about 98 per cent of its productive capacity. 37 FTC, p. 157.

Some manufacturers contended that they felt compelled to join. The president of Keystone testified: "Well, the NRA legislation was an effective thing. General Johnson said you were not much of an American if you did not have a blue eagle up, and it was our impression at that time that unless you did function through the Trade Institute or trade association provided for you that you could not share in Government business that might be coming out, and that was more reason for joining the Cement Institute." *Aetna* v. *FTC,* Pet.Br., App. A, Vol. 3, p. 1815.

65. Though it does not appear that NRA formally named the Institute as the cement code authority, the code provided that the Institute's board of trustees should elect the code authority and the Federal Trade Commission found that the Institute "controlled the administration of the Code for the Cement Industry, subject to such limitations as were imposed" by NRA. 37 FTC, p. 143.

66. *Aetna* v. *FTC,* Pet.Br., App. A, Vol. 3, pp. 2126 ff. The Federal Trade Commission found that "substantially all members of the industry desired a proration plan, but there was difficulty in agreeing upon a basis for proration." 37 FTC, p. 215. According to FTC, representatives of the industry had tried, unsuccessfully, to formulate a plan for balancing production and shipments long before NRA.

lem of overproduction or overcapacity . . ." [67] Before the collapse of NRA the Institute protested the proposed construction of four plants. One was completed over its protest. Three were never placed in operation, although the Reconstruction Finance Corporation granted a $50,000 loan for the completion of one of them, a plant at Foreman, Arkansas. The industry, both through the Institute and through PCA, continued its collective opposition to RFC's granting this loan for almost a year after the death of NRA.[68]

Article VIII prohibited less-than-cost sales of cement, except to meet the competition of producers with lower costs. To enforce this provision the code directed the code authority to adopt "a standard method or system of uniform cost accounting which shall specify all items and include all elements of manufacturers' cost." [69] This the code authority did on approval by the NRA administrators.

Article IX helped more directly to stabilize prices. It required each member company to file its prices with the code authority and "make same public by broadcast quotations to the trade, so that competitors, the trade, and the buying public may at all times have accurate information relative thereto." It also forbade changes in prices until five days after the filing.[70] Such open price filing may have tended to eliminate price discrimination but it also discouraged

67. This was not an entirely new policy. Before NRA some of the more important cement companies had bought up plants to prevent their being operated. *Aetna* v. *FTC,* Pet.Br., App. A, Vol. 3, p. 2152.

68. 37 FTC, pp. 220-22. Vice-President Morse of Ideal expressed a point of view common in the industry when he said, ". . . this loan is apparently a menace to the entire cement industry as it will constitute the entry of the United States Government in the manufacture of cement." *Ibid.,* p. 222.

69. *Aetna* v. *FTC,* Pet.Br., App. A, Vol. 3, pp. 2124-25.

70. The code was amended on May 21, 1935, six days before the Schechter decision, to provide for filing prices "with a confidential and disinterested agent of the Code Authority," instead of with the code authority itself. But code members were to be notified immediately of any price change by any member. *Ibid.,* Vol. 2, p. 619.

Price filing requirements were quite common in NRA codes for manufacturing industries and in general had a cramping effect on competition. See *Experience With Open Price Provisions of Approved Codes,* Hearings before the Committee on Finance, U.S. Senate, 74th Cong., 1st sess., Vol. 1, pp. 923 ff.; and Enid Baird, *Price Filing Under NRA Codes,* Work Materials No. 76, Division of Industrial Economics, U.S. Department of Commerce, Washington, April 1936.

The cement code's pricing provisions apparently were a compromise. Institute members suggested various standards for fixing prices. At the outset the committee on pricing provisions recommended that: "The Cement Industry Committee shall establish and from time to time revise delivered prices for cement. No manufacturers shall deviate from or revise or change such delivered prices once determined and published by the Cement Industry Committee." *Aetna* v. *FTC,* Pet.Br., App. A, Vol. 2, p. 633. This proposal did not receive official approval. Moreover, as adopted and approved the cement code, unlike the steel code, made no specific provision for basing point pricing.

price cutting. The five-day waiting period deprived a price cutter of the chief advantage in a price reduction—the chance to attract business before rivals could meet the lower price.

NRA Helps the Institute Solve Trucking Problem

But perhaps more helpful to price stabilization under the basing point system than any of the foregoing provisions was paragraph (g) in Article X of the code. This made it illegal to "knowingly ship cement by any transportation agency which, for the purpose or with the effect of inducing or influencing the sale or purchase of cement, makes payments or concessions by rebates or otherwise."[71] This provision was apparently aimed primarily at the practice, long repelled but never entirely stamped out, of selling cement for delivery by truck. With truck delivery specified, the delivered price might be less than the nearest base mill's price plus railway freight to destination.

The trucking of cement on a fairly large scale had begun about 1920. According to the testimony of cement manufacturers, loading costs are greater when trucks are used, because the mills are designed to load into railway cars.[72] Nevertheless, the use of trucks increased rapidly. Trucking had two advantages over rail shipment. Cement frequently could be moved directly from the mill to the job, thereby eliminating intermediate handling and reducing costs. Again, when trucking first came into use it was the general practice to sell cement f.o.b. trucks at the mill, the price being computed by simply deducting the rail freight element in the delivered price applicable to the buyer's location. So whenever trucking charges were less than rail freight, the buyer got cement for a lower delivered price. While this was a gain to the dealer, and through increased sales might bring some advantage to the manufacturer engaging in the practice, it disrupted the industry's price structure. Since trucking rates were neither standardized nor published, cement manufacturers were unable to quote identical destination prices for truck delivery.[73]

71. *Ibid.*, Vol. 3, p. 2112. Mr. Reiter, general manager of the Institute, testified that this provision referred to water and truck transportation agencies, whose rates were not, at that time, on file with a public regulatory body. *Ibid.*, Comm.Br., p. 157.

72. *Ibid.*, Pet.Br., App. A, Vol. 3, pp. 1430-50.

73. Representatives of the indicated companies expressed the following opinions on the effect of trucking on price stability.

Lehigh: "The manufacturer, striving to figure his prices on indeterminate and

Competition in pricing was intensified. Lehigh, replying to the Clark-Burns questionnaire circulated among industry members in 1935, stated that "By 1932 it was clear that trucking practices were one of the chief contributory causes of the state of chaos and demoralization in which the industry found itself." [74]

Railroads Aid in Drive to Eliminate Trucking

Manufacturers were not alone in opposing delivery by trucks. Many dealers recognized that truck delivery disturbed prices, intensified competition. Railroads recognized it as a threat. These three groups saw the spread of trucking as a common problem and they cooperated in trying to solve it.[75] Although they did not succeed in eliminating trucking entirely or in standardizing trucking practices, they apparently brought it so nearly under control that by the middle 1930's it no longer constituted a serious threat to price stability.[76]

Institute Continues Effort to Stabilize After NRA

After the demise of NRA the industry did not abandon its collective effort to stabilize cement prices. The Institute amended its articles of association on December 11, 1935 and adopted a "Compendium of Established Terms and Marketing Methods." [77] The

---

fluctuating trucking rates and to meet the equally fluctuating and indeterminate rates from his competitor's plant, quickly found himself engaged in blind, reckless and destructive competition."

Alpha: "We could not control the deliveries and the many trucking prices disrupted our entire marketing and price structure."

Lawrence: "Our business has been built on a delivered price basis, and when we were selling to buyer's trucks at the mill our whole price structure within a trucking radius of the mill was jeopardized."

Many other cement producers testified to the same effect. See 37 FTC, p. 192; and *Aetna* v. *FTC,* Comm.Br., pp. 130-61. See also *ibid.,* Pet.Br., App. A, Vol. 3, pp. 1401-694, *passim.*

74. *Ibid.,* p. 1414.

75. Cooperation took the form of conferences attended by railway traffic executives and representatives of the Institute and of dealers' organizations. In 1931, following one such conference, a large number of railroads undertook each to check up on truck deliveries from every cement plant served by its lines. In this checkup the great majority of the mills cooperated. See 37 FTC, pp. 191-95.

76. Evidence presented before the Circuit Court of Appeals indicated that in 1937, of 138 mills east of the Rocky Mountains reporting, 88 had discontinued trucking entirely, 14 had never permitted it; 36 mills and 15 packing plants permitted trucking. Trucking was generally either (a) localized, (b) subject to a price penalty, (c) permitted only at full rail freight rates, or (d) performed by the cement plant itself and hence subject to control. About one third of the mills and packing plants east of the Rockies that permitted trucking were located in Michigan. *Aetna* v. *FTC,* Pet.Br., App. A, Vol. 3, pp. 1415-30. For similar data for 1936, see 37 FTC, p. 198.

77. *Aetna* v. *FTC,* Pet.Br., App. A, Vol. 3, pp. 1834 and 1851.

Compendium paralleled in a general way the provisions of the NRA code. It embodied certain rules governing pricing methods, product standardization, terms and conditions of sale, and trade practices, which the president of Universal Atlas testified the industry's experience had proved to be "good, sound and fair." [78] But it dropped the price-filing requirements of the NRA code.

Although experience had convinced the leaders of the industry of the essential fairness and soundness of the Compendium rules, collective effort was necessary, still, to insure their general observance. Moreover, the assumption behind the rules was that unrestrained business rivalry would wreck the industry. John Treanor, president of the Riverside company and a trustee of the Institute, clearly set forth this view to a fellow trustee in 1934. Mr. Treanor, while defending the basing point system of delivered prices, objected to the arguments offered by the industry to support it. He wrote:

> Do you think any of the arguments for the basing-point system, which we have thus far advanced, will arouse anything but derision in and out of the government? I have read all recently. Some of them are very clever and ingenious. They amount to this however: that we price that way in order to discourage monopolistic practices and to preserve free competition, etc. This is sheer bunk and hypocrisy. The truth is of course—and there can be no serious, respectable discussion of our case unless this is acknowledged—that ours is an industry above all others that cannot stand free competition, that must systematically restrain competition or be ruined.[79]

How Collaboration Works: The Aetna Example

One striking episode will illustrate how the industry's leaders have collaborated to assure compliance with the code of business behavior that cement producers have elaborated over the years and in particular with the rules covering the basing point method of pricing. In the 1920's and early 1930's Aetna, with a plant at Bay City, Michigan, had a general manager, Lingeman, and a sales manager, Cree, schooled in the old-fashioned ways of free competition. They went after business wherever they could find it, even if

78. *Ibid.*, p. 1865. For full text of the Compendium, see *ibid.*, pp. 1852-60.

79. 37 FTC, p. 248. The occasion for Mr. Treanor's remarks was a proposed advertising and good-will campaign to dissipate public hostility. Mr. Treanor criticized it again in a letter of July 31, 1934 to E. J. Mehren, president of PCA, stating, "This is not a subject which can be presented to the public through advertising, or in any way. It is an argument that has to be made and can be made in special places where it may be calculated to do some good." *Ibid.*

they had to cut prices to get it. In doing so they apparently transgressed the industry's Code of Ethics. Aetna's competitors resented these aggressive tactics and on several occasions they retaliated by sharply reducing the Bay City base price.[80] Repeatedly they protested against Aetna's sales methods to its president, F. R. Johnson, who although not active in the management of the company could exercise a veto over its business policies.

Mr. Johnson apparently tried earnestly to make his managers conform to the business practices to which the industry generally subscribed. After a conference in the fall of 1933 with near-by cement producers who had complained about Aetna's sales policies, Mr. Johnson addressed a mild reminder to his general manager.

Referring to the conference which Harold Cree and I attended on Friday last, at which there were also present Mr. Stone of . . . Universal Atlas . . ., Mr. J. B. John of . . . Medusa . . ., Mr. Rooney of . . . Huron . . ., Mr. Lucas of . . . Petoskey . . ., a representative from . . . Marquette . . ., and later we called on Mr. Emil Stroh of . . . Wabash . . . It seems to me that the results of that conference should be a matter of record.

1. We admitted that we had made a blunder when we quoted on the Government . . . jobs, March, 1933, and I promised that this will not happen again.

2. I did admit that while we quoted regularly on the Indiana letting in December, 1932, we did quote irregularly and different from the others in March, 1933, by using the Wyandotte base. The result of that bidding has been rather disastrous, as I see it.

* * *

4. As to the Milwaukee situation and Pipkorn, that was discussed and we agreed that we should not allow a jobber to buy a large amount of cement with an idea that he could use it later on to burst open the market. . . .

* * *

So in summing it all up, I pledged my word and the word of the Aetna Cement Company that we would play the game one hundred per cent—there would be no deviation from this in any way; we would be regular in quotations, fair in speech, in impressions and innuendoes, which we would expect others to be. With that general understanding, all trouble caused by chiseling will be eliminated, and we shall go on in a harmonious way.[81]

This admonition had little effect on Aetna's stubborn and independent managers. In 1935 the old difficulties again cropped out.

80. *Ibid.*, pp. 187-91, sets out FTC's findings on this whole episode.
81. *Ibid.*, pp. 187-88.

This time Mr. Johnson, under pressure of renewed competitor complaints, gave his managers a sterner lecture on their contentious ways.

> I now refer you to our policies, as dated December 6, which were read at the meeting the other day; and for your information I will say there were present at that meeting the following men:
>
> Mr. Ben Calvin and Mr. William Storey, of . . . Consolidated . . .
> Mr. J. B. John and Mr. Harry Lucas of . . . Medusa and . . . Petoskey . . .
> Mr. Burt Rooney of . . . Huron . . .
> Mr. Frank Mooney . . . of . . . Wolverine . . .
> Mr. Archie Conkrite . . . of . . . Universal Atlas . . .
> Mr. Jennings of . . . Wabash . . .
> Mr. D. C. Colburn . . . of Marquette . . .
> Mr. William Russell and Mr. Luck of . . . Peerless . . .
> Mr. F. R. Johnson, Mr. Oscar Lingeman, and Mr. Harold Cree of . . . Aetna . . .
>
> You will remember that at that meeting all things were discussed clearly . . .
>
> Now in the first paragraph, we speak about selling to dealers. It is clearly understood that we sell to a dealer at our regular price . . . he must not deliver that cement, except into his own locality . . .
>
> Now this is a matter of much importance and I want you and your organization to start at once to see these people . . . and explain the matter clearly to them, so that promised we will do, and we will; and it is up to you, Oscar, to see that it is done . . . this should not be allowed to drag . . .[82]

But apparently the Lingeman-Cree team was incorrigibly competitive. Despite this strongly worded warning, after a few months Aetna's competitors were once more protesting to Mr. Johnson that his managers were not abiding by the accepted rules of the game. Accordingly, in July 1936 the harassed Aetna president demanded their resignations; Lingeman tendered his, and on Cree's refusal, Mr. Johnson discharged him.[83] In this way the members of the cement

82. *Ibid.*, pp. 188-89. This letter was dated December 13, 1935, four days after the Cement Institute meeting at which the Compendium of Established Terms and Marketing Methods was adopted.

83. *Aetna* v. *FTC*, Pet.Br., App. A, Vol. 3, p. 2228. Mr. Johnson testified that he asked for Lingeman's resignation on the professional advice of a physician and that he dismissed Cree because he had lost confidence in him. *Ibid.*, pp. 2230 ff. No doubt Mr. Johnson knows better than anyone else what his motives were in getting rid of Cree and Lingeman, but his motives are not at issue here. The point is that business rivals, disturbed about the way Mr. Johnson's managers played the game, complained to him and that he then undertook to persuade his managers to mend their ways. Failing to do so, he found reason to get rid of them.

industry got rid of a source of disturbance that had hindered the development of their market stabilization policy.

The Aetna episode clearly indicates that the "big brothers of the cement industry" actively cultivated a live-and-let-live policy.[84] They were not content to trust to complaisant acceptance of their own example. They were far from indifferent to whether individual sellers of cement conformed to the rules for "orderly marketing."

But their policing of the industry was not always and everywhere effective, of course. Bad times weakened discipline. As conditions grew worse in the early 1930's, the rule of live and let live was often violated. Many manufacturers seemingly accepted as inevitable a struggle for survival with every man for himself. But when the going was the toughest, the government intervened to coerce businessmen into doing what they would not do voluntarily or perhaps could not do without violating the law of conspiracy. By throwing its support, in a period of adversity, behind a set of business practices to which it required the industry to conform, the government reinforced industrial self-discipline. An enlarged and revitalized Cement Institute was in a position to take over its accustomed functions when NRA collapsed.

Basing Point System Requires Collaboration

The history of basing point pricing in the cement industry undermines the "spontaneity" thesis of its origin and operation. Continual concerted action, reinforced at times by law, has been necessary to insure that all producers of cement would systematically and persistently quote identical prices at any point of delivery. And even this has not always been enough. At times—specifically during the Great Depression—genuine price competition in cement has broken out.

Generalization from the record of cement may not be warranted. It is quite possible that in an industry like that described by Clark (standardized product, constant per unit variable cost, heavy fixed costs, heavy freight charges, few sellers, localized production, and inelastic demand), self-interest and self-discipline might insure

84. The quoted phrase is from a letter dated July 9, 1936 that Mr. Crapo of Huron addressed to Mr. Johnson of Aetna. Discussing an allegation that "Cree had hijacked a Wabash contract," he said, "In the previous instance, the big brothers of the Cement Industry interested themselves in the matter, and accomplished a reconciliation which restored the base price." 37 FTC, p. 190.

identical and relatively stable prices by all sellers, persistently calculated from one or more basing points. No convincing example that we know of can be cited to support this thesis. In the four major Federal Trade Commission proceedings involving basing point pricing on which the Supreme Court has ruled, the industries had a long record of concerted action to eliminate competition.[85]

Basing Point Pricing in Steel

The Commission has resumed its proceeding against basing point pricing in another major industry: steel. The respondents are the American Iron and Steel Institute, the United States Steel Corporation, its subsidiaries, and some eighty other companies, together accounting for about 96 per cent of the country's output of steel. The amended complaint as issued on November 13, 1948 charges among other things that the respondents have conspired to suppress competition through the use of basing point pricing and numerous complementary price-fixing devices, including the joint preparation and use of a "common list of charges to be added to base prices in lieu of switching, shipping and freight charges" and of schedules of "extras" and "deductions" by means of which identical prices for

85. See Machlup, *op. cit., passim.* Three industries—cement, rigid steel conduit, and cornstarch—were involved in the four cases: *FTC* v. *Institute; Corn Products Refining Co.* v. *FTC,* 324 U.S. 726 (1945); *FTC* v. *A. E. Staley Manufacturing Co.,* 324 U.S. 746 (1945); *Clayton Mark & Co., et al.* v. *FTC,* 336 U.S. 956 (1949). The proceedings against Corn Products Refining Company and Staley were brought under the price discrimination provisions of the Robinson-Patman Act and did not charge conspiracy. But there is much evidence of persistent attempts to monopolize the cornstarch and glucose industry, not only by mergers and by trade tactics designed to exclude competitors (actual and potential), but also by collusion (overt or tacit). See Myron W. Watkins, *Industrial Combinations and Public Policy,* Houghton Mifflin, Boston, 1927, Chap. 10.

For Federal Trade Commission orders in point, see *In re Anheuser-Busch Co.,* 31 FTC Decisions 986 (1940); *In re Penick & Ford Co.,* 31 FTC Decisions 1494 (1940); *In re Union Starch & Refining Co.,* 32 FTC Decisions 60 (1940); *In re American Maize Products Co.,* 32 FTC Decisions 901 (1941); *In re Hubinger Co.,* 32 FTC Decisions 1116 (1941); *In re Corn Products Refining Co.,* 34 FTC Decisions 850 (1942); *In re Clinton Co.,* 34 FTC Decisions 879 (1942); and *In re A. E. Staley Manufacturing Co.,* 34 FTC Decisions 1362 (1942).

In 1932, the Department of Justice obtained a consent decree in a suit charging restraint of trade by the industry's trade association. See *U.S.* v. *Corn Derivatives Institute, et al.,* in U.S. District Court for the Northern District of Illinois, consent decree entered April 6, 1932, reported in Commerce Clearing House, *Trade Regulation Service,* Court Decisions Supplement (1932–1937), par. 7002.

For the lower court rulings in the Trade Commission cases, see *Corn Products Refining Co.* v. *FTC,* 144 Fed. *2d* 211 (1944); and *A. E. Staley Manufacturing Co.* v. *FTC,* 144 Fed. *2d* 221 (1944). After the Supreme Court decisions in these cases in 1945, the Federal Trade Commission issued, on June 20, 1947, a new complaint, *In re Corn Products Refining Co., et al.,* Docket No. 5502, and on July 12, 1949 entered an order dismissing respondents' motion to dismiss.

each of the thousands of steel products of varying size, shape, composition, and physical properties can be insured.[86] Whether or not the respondents have violated the law is for the Commission and the courts to decide. But that steel prices are the product of wholly independent decision making by oligopolists few observers of the industry would contend. The steel industry, like the others against which the Commission has proceeded, has a long record of concerted action to stabilize prices.

During its first decade the Steel Corporation "concerted with" its competitors "in the expedients of pools, associations, trade meetings" and in the famous Gary dinners, characterized by the lower federal court as "pools without penalties" but more efficient.[87] Until the Federal Trade Commission ordered the Steel Corporation to abandon the practice, the Corporation took the lead in promoting Pittsburgh Plus (pricing all steel as though it were produced solely at Pittsburgh) because, as Judge Gary said, "it was deemed necessary for the orderly conduct of the business to have one basing price . . . so that every user of steel all over the country bought and used his steel on a certain basis, knowing in advance that everyone else who bought steel had to pay exactly as he did, with the addition of the increased freight depending upon where he wanted to use the steel." [88] After the Steel Corporation abandoned Pittsburgh Plus the industry generally quoted delivered prices computed from the same half-dozen or so basing points as those designated by the Corporation. The pricing practices of the industry were formalized and supplemented under NRA. Indeed, the code not only incorporated the basing point system and designated the basing points but also provided machinery for policing the system.[89]

86. *In re American Iron & Steel Institute, et al.*, FTC Docket No. 5508, complaint issued August 16, 1947. On December 5, 1949 respondents filed a novel proposal: the issuance of a "consent order," the terms of which they suggested. The Commission took the proposal under advisement, and in January 1950 the case was still pending.

87. Quoted in *U.S.* v. *United States Steel Corp.*, 251 U.S. 417 (1920), at p. 440.

88. 8 FTC 1 (1927), at p. 33. FTC's findings make it clear that steel producers reached a general understanding to adopt and use Pittsburgh Plus as a method of pricing and that some producers definitely agreed to use it as a specific means of fixing and maintaining prices of certain products.

89. National Recovery Administration, *Codes of Fair Competition*, Washington, 1933, Vol. 1, No. 11, p. 198. Another provision of the code (Section 1, Article V) expressed the view "that the elimination of unfair practices in the industry will automatically eliminate any overproduction therein and any alleged inequities in the distribution, production and sales among its members." *Ibid.*, pp. 184-85.

NRA Steel Code Formalizes Pricing Practices

The code designated the directors of the American Iron and Steel Institute as the code authority and empowered them to interpret and enforce the codified "standards of fair competition." [90] Not only did the code insure concerted action in steel pricing (to violate the code was to violate the recovery statute), but, according to the code, it constituted "a valid and binding contract by and among all members of the Code." [91] The code authority fined those who violated the rules and regulations established under the code $10 a ton for each violation. The Federal Trade Commission in two 1934 reports analyzed evidence from the files of the Institute and its members showing that the producers collaborated in establishing base prices.[92] The code compelled the quotation of delivered prices amounting to not less than the sum of the applicable base price and the all-rail freight rate from basing point to point of delivery, except as otherwise provided by the directors.[93]

After the Schechter decision in 1935 liquidating NRA, steel producers representing 90 per cent of production capacity ratified a resolution declaring their intention to maintain the standards of fair competition set forth in the steel code.[94] How closely the industry has collaborated since 1935 in maintaining the common trade practices enforced by law under NRA, available information does not disclose. But James Brackett of the United States Steel Corporation wrote the executive secretary of the Temporary National Economic Committee on December 18, 1939 that he was aware of no amendment or modification of the 1935 resolution. Moreover, Benjamin Fairless, president of the Steel Corporation, testified before

90. *Ibid.*, pp. 179-208.

91. Sec. 6, Art. XI. *Ibid.*, p. 189.

92. See Federal Trade Commission, *Report to the President in Response to the Executive Order of May 30, 1934, With Respect to the Basing Point System in the Steel Industry,* November 30, 1934, Washington, 1935; and *idem, Report on the Steel Code to the President of the Senate,* pursuant to S.Res. 166, adopted February 2, 1934, Washington, March 19, 1934, pp. 5-8.

93. Because of the great diversity in switching charges, the board of directors found it necessary to prescribe arbitrary rates reflecting a "fair average of actual rates" in order to prevent unequal competition "in selling steel at any basing point." See TNEC Hearings, Pt. 27, Ex. 2206, p. 14435; see also p. 14252; and Walter B. Wooden and Hugh E. White, "An Analysis of the Basing-Point System of Delivered Prices as Presented by United States Steel Corporation in Exhibits No. 1410 and 1418," in *The Basing Point Problem,* TNEC Monograph No. 42, Washington, 1941, p. 94.

94. TNEC Hearings, Pt. 27, pp. 14232 ff. and 14434.

the TNEC that the industry collaborated in cost studies on which the prices of "extras" were based,[95] and in keeping up to date the freight rate book that the Institute compiled and published.[96]

Whatever the legal status of their acts or the effectiveness of their pricing policies, it is clear that the industry members have collaborated in shaping them.

The Law on Basing Point Pricing

Outlawing basing point pricing in the cement and rigid steel conduit industries brought a vehement protest from its practitioners. They immediately initiated a political campaign to change the law. Two days after the Supreme Court's decision in the cement case, Chairman Irving S. Olds, of the United States Steel Corporation, stated that the industry must either get the law modified or "educate the Supreme Court." "I can't believe," he said, "that the country is going to let industry be disrupted by a theory that was developed many years ago by a Princeton professor." [97] The campaign culminated in Senate Bill 1008, which, as amended in its entirety on Senator O'Mahoney's motion, was ostensibly designed to clarify the law on basing point pricing.[98]

95. *Ibid.*, Pt. 19, p. 10560.

96. *Ibid.*, Pt. 27, p. 14222. Mr. Fairless said: "The American Iron and Steel Institute has a traffic committee composed of traffic managers of 10 different steel companies. This committee supervises the Institute's Freight Rate Book . . . and the responsibility of keeping these sections up to date is assigned to different members of the committee. When corrections are necessary—and by necessary I mean when rate changes take place—these committee members have the changes made on supplementary sections or pages, sending these sections or pages to the Institute for distribution to holders of the rate book."

97. *Journal of Commerce* (New York), April 28, 1948, p. 1. The reference is to the late Professor Frank A. Fetter. See also *Congressional Record,* 81st Cong., 1st sess., 1949, Vol. 95, No. 78, Congressman Wright Patman of Texas, in the House of Representatives, May 3, 1949, p. A-2811, and No. 79, May 5, 1949, pp. 2832-33. Congressman Patman quoted an article from the Washington correspondent of the *Rocky Mountain News,* James M. Daniel, indicating that Ketchum, Inc., registered lobbyists, had charge of the campaign to legalize basing point pricing and that Pittsburgh industrialists put up 25 per cent of the expenses. Daniel quotes Walter Megronigle, of Ketchum, Inc., on the extent of the campaign, as follows:

"We don't have a Washington office. We have chapters in Dallas, Houston, Tulsa, Cincinnati, Dayton, Cleveland, Philadelphia, and Pittsburgh. Harold Huycke is in Denver for us now organizing a chapter there. Eventually we will have 25 chapters.

"The National Competition Committee is a one-shot operation. Its purpose is to legalize the uniform delivered price system. When that is done it will be through."

98. On May 20, 1948, Senator Capehart of Indiana submitted S.Res. 241 to authorize the Senate Committee on Interstate and Foreign Commerce to conduct an "inquiry into . . . the activities of the Federal Trade Commission . . . with particular relation to the basing point . . . system of pricing . . . and the status of free enterprise as affected by transportation and Federal trade regulations." The Senate approved an

The central feature of the O'Mahoney bill was a proposal to amend Section 5 of the Federal Trade Commission Act by appending to it the following:

It shall not be an unfair method of competition or an unfair or deceptive act or practice for a seller, acting independently, to quote or sell at delivered prices or to absorb freight: Provided, that this shall not make lawful any combination, conspiracy or collusive agreement; or any monopolistic, oppressive, deceptive or fraudulent practice, carried out by or involving the use of delivered prices or freight absorption.

The bill also provided for amendments to the Robinson-Patman Act to bring it into harmony with Section 5 of the Federal Trade Commission Act as amended, and to change it in other respects.[99]

Proponents of the bill alleged that dicta by the Supreme Court, pronouncements by members of the Federal Trade Commission and its staff, and the Commission's findings and orders on Count II of the rigid steel conduit case had both confused the issues and out-

---

amended resolution on June 12, 1948; and a subcommittee under Senator Capehart's chairmanship conducted hearings from November 9, 1948 to December 8, 1948. See *Study of Pricing Methods,* Hearings before a Subcommittee of the Committee on Interstate and Foreign Commerce, U.S. Senate, 80th Cong., 2d sess., pursuant to S.Res. 241, Washington, 1948.

Some critics have alleged that the Committee's conduct of the hearings reflected a strong bias in favor of basing point pricing. The *Engineering and Mining Journal* (September 1948, p. 101) commented as follows on the Committee's attitude:

"Some idea of the Committee's sympathies may be gained from its actions to date. . . .

"General Counsel for the Committee will be William Simon, member of a Chicago law firm that represented the Salt Producers Association five years ago when it lost a price-fixing case involving identical delivered prices.

"The Committee's advisory council, a 40-man group appointed by Senator Capehart early in August, includes at least seven executives of companies who have lost to the F.T.C. in price-fixing cases in which identical delivered prices figured heavily in the evidence."

On January 5, 1949 Senator Johnson of Colorado introduced S.Res. 236, which would have legalized basing point pricing by statute unless "employed pursuant to an agreement or conspiracy" and would have limited the Commission's power to stop the practice. The Senate referred the bill first to the Interstate Commerce Committee and later to the Committee on the Judiciary. On February 17, 1949 Senator Myers of Pennsylvania introduced S. 1008 providing for a two-year moratorium on the "application of certain antitrust laws to individual, good faith delivered price systems and freight absorption practices." Senator Myers' bill was subsequently replaced by the O'Mahoney bill.

99. The Senate passed the O'Mahoney bill on June 1, 1949, with the amendment to Section 5 of the Federal Trade Commission Act unchanged. Subsequently the House also passed the O'Mahoney bill with this section unchanged (it amended the Senate's changes in the Robinson-Patman Act). Because of disagreement between the Senate and the House on the proposed changes in the Robinson-Patman Act, the bill was referred to a conference committee, which filed its report on October 12. The changes recommended were not acceptable to some of the bill's supporters, and the Senate voted to put over further consideration of the measure until the next session.

lawed innocent practices. The first of these two charges is partly but not wholly justified. In their campaign to modify the law, its critics have thrown up a smoke screen to conceal the real nature of the practices they wish to have legalized. They must share a part of the responsibility for the confusion that exists about the legality of the basing point practices. The truth of the second of these two charges—that the Commission and the courts have outlawed innocent practices—depends on one's point of view. The first step in determining their innocence is to determine their character. What, in fact, have the Commission and the courts outlawed?

The Corn Products and Staley Decisions

As previously indicated, in every case instituted by the Commission in which basing point pricing has been a major issue, the respondent industry has had a long record of concerted action to prevent or restrain competition. In the Corn Products case, however, the Commission did not charge conspiracy. Proceeding under the Robinson-Patman Act, it found that the respondent, by selling glucose from its Kansas City plant at the base price fixed at its Chicago plant plus freight charges from Chicago, had discriminated among buyers. This method of selling involved freight absorption on sales from Kansas City to points freight-wise nearer Chicago than Kansas City and phantom freight on sales from Kansas City to points freight-wise nearer Kansas City than Chicago. It resulted in varying net realized prices on Kansas City sales, depending upon the point of delivery. These mill nets ranged from $2.13 to $2.49 a hundred pounds on actual sales on August 1, 1939.[100] The Commission found that such price discrimination had injured competition among candy manufacturers who bought respondent's glucose, and that it therefore violated the Robinson-Patman Act.[101] Both the Circuit Court of Appeals and the Supreme Court upheld the Commission.[102]

100. *Corn Products Refining Co.* v. *FTC,* 324 U.S. 726 (1945), at p. 733.
101. 34 FTC 850 (1942), at pp. 854-55 and 860-76. The relevant portion of the Clayton Act, Section 2, as amended by the Robinson-Patman Act forbade "any person engaged in commerce . . . either directly or indirectly, to discriminate in price between different purchasers of commodities of like grade and quality . . . where the effect of such discrimination may be to substantially lessen competition or tend to create a monopoly or to injure . . . competition with any person who either grants or knowingly receives . . . such discrimination, or with customers of either of them."
102. 144 Fed. *2d* 211 (1944); 324 U.S. 726 (1945).

The Staley case was a companion case, decided by the Supreme Court on the same day that it decided the Corn Products case. The Staley Manufacturing Company was engaged in the same business as Corn Products and its single plant was located at Decatur, Illinois. It priced glucose, like its rival, on a Chicago base, plus freight from that point to destination. The Commission found that in doing so it (1) absorbed freight on sales to all points freight-wise nearer Chicago than Decatur, (2) charged phantom freight on all sales freight-wise nearer Decatur than Chicago, (3) realized varying mill nets depending on the delivery point, and (4) injured competition among candy manufacturers and other customers. Both the Commission and the Court rejected Staley's defense that its prices, if discriminatory, were made in good faith to meet the prices of its rival. As the Court said:

> Thus it is the contention that a seller may justify a basing point delivered pricing system, which is otherwise outlawed by Section 2, because other competitors are in part violating the law by maintaining a like system. If the respondents' argument is sound it would seem to follow that even if the competitor's pricing system were wholly in violation of Section 2 of the Clayton Act, respondents could adopt and follow it with impunity.
> . . . We think the conclusion is inadmissible . . .[103]

It appears that business generally received these decisions with complacency. What the decisions specifically condemned was the use of basing point pricing, even by a single firm, to deprive some buyers of a product of their freight advantage from proximity to a plant and thereby to injure competition between them and the favored buyer, located more distantly, freight-wise, from a plant. But not only did basing point pricing as practiced by Corn Products and by Staley injure competition among their customers, it afforded a convenient device for eliminating price competition between Staley and Corn Products themselves. Although the issue was not before the Court, the Court recognized that the practice was a convenient method of insuring identical pricing by business rivals. While the Commission could have emphasized the point more than it chose to do, proceeding under the Robinson-Patman Act, the lack of effective competition in the sale of glucose was apparently one of the major grounds for the complaint.

103. *FTC* v. *A. E. Staley Manufacturing Co.,* previously cited, pp. 753-54.

The Cement and Rigid Steel Conduit Cases

It was the Court's decision in the cement case in the spring of 1948 that precipitated the campaign to have the law changed, but the Commission's findings and order under Count II of the rigid steel conduit case were made the scapegoat of the campaign.

In the cement case the Commission charged that the respondents: (1) had conspired to use the basing point system to restrain competition in violation of Section 5 of the Federal Trade Commission Act outlawing unfair methods of competition, and (2) in thus pricing their product, had conspired to discriminate among buyers in violation of the Robinson-Patman Act. The respondents did not question the illegality of the conspiracy charged in either count, but denied both that they had so conspired and that the Commission had, in fact, found either conspiracy. Since the Supreme Court has upheld the Commission, objections to the Commission's orders in the cement case must rest on the ground that outlawing conspiracy among business rivals to use a basing point pricing system is unsound public policy.[104] Believers in competition will not generally take this position.

In the rigid steel conduit case something new was added. In Count I of its complaint the Commission charged that respondents had conspired to use the basing point system to restrain competition. In Count II it charged that each respondent used the basing point system knowing that its rivals also used it and that such practices "have a dangerous tendency to, and actually have hindered . . . and prevented competition in the sale of 'conduit.' "[105] After hearings, the Commission found that the evidence supported its charges and ordered the respondents to quit conspiring or pursuing a "planned common course of action."[106] It also ordered respondents individually to quit quoting or selling rigid steel conduit at prices calculated on a basing point system "for the purpose or with the effect of *systematically* matching delivered-price quotations."[107]

104. Or on the ground that the orders will be ineffective unless the structure and ownership of the industry are changed. Dissolution suits against the major companies might be the remedy.

105. *In re Rigid Steel Conduit Association, et al.*, 38 FTC Decisions 534 (1944), at p. 550.

106. *Ibid.*, p. 593.

107. *Ibid.*, p. 595. Italics supplied. With regard to the section of the order directed against individual respondents, the Circuit Court of Appeals, Seventh Circuit, said:

In the light of all the circumstances of this case, Count II clearly implies collusion although it does not specifically charge it.[108] Moreover, the restrictions imposed on individual respondents are designed merely to prevent the *systematic* use of basing point pricing where the evidence indicated that such use restrained competition.

Meaning of the Decisions

The position that the Federal Trade Commission and the courts have taken in these several cases probably warrants an even firmer conclusion than that "any arbitrary industry-wide system or method of arriving at continued identity of delivered price quotations is suspect." [109] But analysis also confirms the view that neither the Commission nor the judiciary has held that everyone must adopt an f.o.b. mill system of pricing and never absorb freight charges. Businessmen apparently are free to absorb freight to get into, or to hold a segment of, any market in which they wish to sell as long as they do not do so in concert with their rivals for the purpose or with the effect of restraining competition. It requires no uncommon perspicacity for a businessman to tell, without the advice of counsel, whether he is cooperating with his rivals in a pricing plan. If he is not, so long as he does not deliberately or systematically discriminate

---

"As already noted, each conduit seller knows that each of the other sellers is using the basing point formula; each knows that by using it he will be able to quote identical delivered prices and thus present a condition of matched prices under which purchasers are isolated and deprived of choice among sellers so far as price advantage is concerned. Each seller must systematically increase or decrease his mill net price for customers at numerous destinations in order to match the delivered prices of his competitors. Each seller consciously intends not to attempt the exclusion of any competition from his natural freight advantage territory by reducing his price, and in effect invites the others to share the available business at matched prices in his natural market in return for a reciprocal invitation.

". . . In the light of [the opinion in the cement case] we cannot say that the Commission was wrong in concluding that the individual use of the basing point method *as here used* does constitute an unfair method of competition." *Triangle Conduit & Cable Co., Inc.* v. *FTC,* 168 Fed. *2d* 175 (1948), at p. 181. Italics supplied. Affirmed by an evenly divided bench, *sub nom. Clayton Mark & Co.* v. *FTC,* 336 U.S. 956 (1949).

108. Space will not permit even a résumé of the evidence of conspiracy in this case. In the following comment made in January 1948 an agent of one respondent, the Garland company, indicated an awareness of a collusive agreement of some kind. "I attended another meeting of the labeled conduit manufacturers today at the New York Athletic Club. . . . Several projects were discussed as to prices and agreements that had been made but nothing was pinned on to any of those present, which was in accord with our agreement to maintain card 76 on any new projects that might come up after our first meeting." See Corwin Edwards, "The Effect of Recent Basing-Point Decisions Upon Business Practices," *American Economic Review,* December 1948, p. 831.

109. Joseph S. Wright, "Collusion and Parallel Action in Delivered Price Systems," *Georgetown Law Journal,* January 1949, p. 214.

among customers, he is apparently free to sell his products where he can and price them as he will. If he is so cooperating, he'd better quit the practice or consult a lawyer.[110]

Economic Consequences of Basing Point Pricing

An exhaustive analysis of the economic consequences of basing point pricing is beyond the scope of this study. It would involve a case-by-case study of the structure and organization of industries using the basing point system, and a detailed analysis of their pricing policies and techniques, of production policies, of plant location, capacity and utilization, and of similar aspects of their operations. Nevertheless, economists who have studied the basing point method of pricing have reached a fair consensus on some generalizations about its economic significance.

First, they generally agree that it increases distribution costs, and hence prices, by fostering wasteful crosshauling and unnecessary selling expenses. The basing point system tends to withhold from buyers the price advantage inherent in patronizing near-by producers. And at the same time it definitely encourages a seller, especially in periods of slack demand, to seek business outside the territory his mill can serve most economically, despite the disadvantage of such sales because of freight absorption. Thus this method of pricing enhances the tendency for products to move in opposite directions over the same routes at the same time.

The only way a seller can increase his sales outside the market territory adjacent to his plant without offering the distant buyers any price inducement is through more aggressive salesmanship. But more aggressive salesmanship generally means increased selling

110. Some lawyers and economists may regard this as a cavalier dismissal of an issue that greatly disturbs industrial leaders. What industrialists apparently want to know is how far they can collaborate without violating the law. That is a nice question—and a proper one. But obviously only FTC and the courts can authoritatively answer it, and they can do so only by an examination of all the facts and circumstances surrounding a particular case. One of the risks that businessmen must be prepared to take in a free-enterprise economy is the risk that collaboration on pricing policy may run afoul of the law.

Clark objects to the present state of the law because of the discretion FTC now has in applying it, and because he thinks that when the Commission finds basing point pricing unlawful its orders may leave no practical alternative to f.o.b. selling. J. M. Clark, "Law and Economics of Basing Points," *American Economic Review*, March 1949, pp. 430-47. With this conclusion the present study disagrees. Noncollusive delivered pricing with freight absorption at the discretion of the seller is likely to result in such price behavior as to render it immune from attack under the antitrust laws.

expense. With all sellers quoting identical delivered prices, none can improve his position in the market except by adding to his outlays for advertising and salesmen. When Aetna abandoned price cutting and began to sell cement strictly "according to the ethics of the industry," its new manager explained to its president that he was obliged to increase the company's sales force because he was "in the process of getting business on a new basis." [111] With business rivals generally pursuing the same tactics, the inflation of selling costs was no doubt substantial. Intensification of sales effort and increase of advertising expense, with attendant mutual frustration and waste, appear to be normal incidents of a basing point price system.

In the long run consumers bear the burden of these added shipping and selling costs. They pay more for the products sold at uniform delivered prices than they would pay if competition in these markets were less "imperfect." The precise effect of such higher prices on the whole economy is not easy to determine, but they transfer purchasing power from consumers to producers of the products so sold, and they increase the cost of distributing these products.[112] They may also lessen consumption and slow down economic activity by fostering and protecting vested interests in artificial advantages.

Basing Point Pricing Impedes Economic Readjustments

Secondly, probably most professional economists agree that a basing point system impedes competition, and strengthens monopolistic elements in pricing, though there is less consensus here. Perhaps the most serious shortcoming of a basing point system is that it circumvents the free-enterprise pricing mechanism. Prices in free markets guide the allocation of productive factors among the various channels in which they may be used, in response to consumer demands. High prices attract additional resources into an industry from less lucrative uses. Low prices drive productive factors out of an

111. 37 FTC, p. 191.

112. J. M. Clark estimated that "potentially avoidable" waste from crosshauling and duplicated sales efforts amounted to about 8 or 10 per cent of the prices consumers paid for cement under the basing point system. Clark, "Basing Point Methods of Price Quoting," p. 483. In his testimony before the Federal Trade Commission on the cement industry's basing point system, after discussing these wastes, Jacob Viner aptly concluded that "In thinking about the structure, I have not been able to see how you could design any worse one, from the point of view of the national economy, assuming you had free choice." See *Aetna* v. *FTC,* Comm.Br., Pt. 2, p. 70.

industry toward more lucrative uses. Competitive prices tend to establish balance both within an industry and among different industries. Competitive markets are the antithesis of centralized planning and administrative controls.

The basing point system is a market-controlling device for obtaining higher prices than the spontaneous forces of supply and demand in a free market would establish. This is particularly true when demand declines or capacity has been overexpanded. If rivals play the game as prescribed, basing point pricing increases the power of price leaders to dominate a market. If the system is in good working order, usually a price leader can raise prices at basing points with the assurance that he will not thereby lose business. He may reduce the area within which his base price governs delivered prices and hence increase the volume of business on which he absorbs freight. But even this need not happen if he has widely dispersed mills at which his price leadership is recognized or if other basing point mills follow his price advance.[113]

The basing point system tends, in the face of declining demand, to keep prices higher than competition would permit or an effective utilization of resources would justify. When an industry is plagued by surplus capacity because it has overexpanded, the system may prevent the writing down of capital values so essential to the processes of economic readjustment. It tends to keep resources in, or draw them into, an industry when, to serve the interests of the whole economy, they should be driven out.

The basing point system in cement seems to have done just this. It attracted into the industry an excess of productive resources and kept alive, by artificial means, and at the expense of the economy as a whole, the resultant surplus capacity. In only three years between 1913 and 1937 was the production of cement in this country as much as 80 per cent of rated annual capacity; in fourteen years it was less than 70 per cent, in seven years less than 50 per cent, and in 1933 only about 23 per cent.[114]

113. In technical language, basing point pricing may eliminate the kink in the demand curve facing an oligopolist; that is, it may minimize the risk an oligopolist runs of losing business by raising prices. See Paul Sweezy, "Demand Under Conditions of Oligopoly," *Journal of Political Economy,* August 1939, pp. 568-73.

114. *Aetna* v. *FTC,* Pet.Br., App. A, Vol. 1, pp. 69-70. Capacity of an industry is difficult to measure, and in an industry like cement—with seasonal, regional, and cyclical fluctuations in demand—full-capacity operations over a long period are

The basing point system not only made for high cement prices; it made for stable prices. Price leaders generally raised base prices in the second half of 1932 and the first half of 1933 in spite of a drastic decline in demand. They then kept them unchanged through good times and bad to the end of the decade.

Identical Bids on Government Business

Sales by industry members to the government reflect the fidelity with which cement producers adhered to the basing point system in quoting identical delivered prices. Government purchases are ordinarily made on secret bids. When sellers tie for the low bid the government chooses the supplier by lot. Before the Great Depression government buying was relatively unimportant. But as the government appropriated more and more funds for highway construction, flood control, hydroelectric development, and other public works projects in its effort to end depression, its cement purchases became larger than those of any other class of buyers. Indeed, at times government purchases exceeded those of all other buyers combined. Though the statutes regulating government purchases contain many provisions for assuring competitive bidding, procurement agencies frequently had to distribute the business by lot, because all bidders on cement contracts submitted identical bids.[115]

The higher prices that the government was obliged to pay for cement, because of the absence of competitive bidding, came ulti-

---

difficult to achieve. W. S. Mallory, Cement Institute statistician, estimated that owing to shutdowns, repairs, and similar causes practical capacity of the industry in 1934 was only 82 per cent of its theoretical capacity. On the basis of Mr. Mallory's estimate, the industry operated at about 41 per cent of actual capacity in 1934 instead of 30 per cent, as computed on rated capacity.

Basing point pricing has apparently not guaranteed an abnormal rate of return to cement producers on their overexpanded capacity. An analysis of prices, costs, and profits prepared by Price, Waterhouse & Company, auditors, and Ford, Bacon & Davis, engineers, which the respondents offered but FTC refused to accept as evidence in the administrative hearings, showed that the respondents had earned on actual cost of assets an average of less than 3 per cent over the ten-year period 1928–1937. See *FTC* v. *Institute,* Resp.Br., p. 241. That their overexpanded facilities earned anything at all apparently reflects the effectiveness with which the industry's price control mechanism worked.

115. The record is replete with striking illustrations. One will perhaps suffice. In April 1936, eleven companies submitted identical bids of $3.286854 a barrel on 6,000 barrels of cement to be delivered to the United States Engineers' Office at Tucumcari, New Mexico.

The Circuit Court rejected FTC's charge of collusion among cement producers in arriving at such identical bids. In this particular instance the court noted that the applicable freight rate from the nearest basing point was $1.186854 a barrel. *Aetna* v. *FTC,* p. 567.

mately out of taxpayers' pockets. Moreover, relatively high prices tended to defeat the purposes of the government spending program. The purchasing power created by deficit financing could not go so far in putting the unemployed to work as it might have if the government had been able to buy cement at a lower, competitive price. Thus the huge outlay of public funds for counteracting the deflationary spiral and stimulating business recovery was less effective than it might otherwise have been.

Competition Not Effective in Cement

Obviously business rivalry as it has worked out in the cement industry does not conform to this study's standard of "effective competition." [116] Whether it has been "workable competition" within Clark's definition of the term—that is, whether it has worked better than any practical alternative—is a matter of conjecture. Clark's fear is that without such control of prices as the basing point system provides in industries like cement, some less acceptable form of control would inevitably develop.[117] Whether this is true, and if so whether such controls would be less amenable to correction through antitrust procedure, is problematical. The problem seems to be one of preventing concerted action by producers to forestall price changes that would otherwise take place.

The effort to forestall them arises out of one or more of three circumstances: (1) a temporary decline in the demand for the products of an industry while other industries are prospering; (2) a cyclical decline in effective demand during a general business recession; (3) a prolonged imbalance in the demand-supply relationship of a particular industry due to (a) changes in consumer habits, (b) speculative overexpansion of an industry, or (c) technological or geographic changes in production that render obsolete old techniques or sources of supply. If decline in demand is temporary, the effects of the price reduction that effective competition would entail will also be temporary and hence of little consequence. If decline in demand is a reflection of a general decline in effective demand, an industry-by-industry approach that holds up prices and curtails output is likely to aggravate the problem rather than to facilitate a

116. See Chap. 4, pp. 108-09.
117. Clark, "Basing Point Methods of Price Quoting."

solution. Clearly what is called for is a program to expand demand, not a program to restrict output. If the imbalance is occasioned either by a permanent decline in demand for the given industry's product or an enduring change in the conditions of its supply, the obvious remedy, unpalatable though it be, is a reduction in prices, a writing down of capital values, and a shifting of resources to more economical uses.[118]

Conclusions

As judged by the history of its operation, in the absence of concerted action basing point pricing is likely to prove ineffective in keeping up or raising prices. If this conclusion is justified, it suggests that no great change in policy on basing point pricing is called for. In this respect, assuming the aim of policy is to promote effective competition, vigorous enforcement of antitrust policy should suffice.

If, as may be true in some instances, self-disciplined oligopolists systematically follow a price leader and use a basing point system without collusion, or with concerted action so subtle as to place it beyond the reach of law, the choice of policy is not so simple. To protect the public's long-run interest, the government might (1) dissolve the oligopolists into a larger number of units; (2) rely on the "perennial gale of creative destruction"; or (3) regulate prices by administrative procedures.

Under the law as it has been interpreted by the Federal Trade Commission and the courts, sellers are apparently free to absorb freight to get into distant markets if they want to do so, as long as they do not conspire with their rivals in doing so. In these circumstances, they are likely to absorb freight only when it pays to absorb it. Sporadic freight absorption is likely to make for flexible rather than inflexible prices, and it may well tend to protect consumers from exploitation by local monopolists. Because freight absorption is costly, however, price cutting is likely to reduce such sporadic invasion of distant markets and leave buyers dependent upon the plants that can most economically serve them.

118. For a fuller discussion of these principles, see Chap. 4. Defenders of the basing point system have pointed out that without the surplus capacity in steel and cement, the nation would have been seriously handicapped in fighting World War II. This may be true for steel, but not many political scientists and military strategists would want to rely on the fortuities of private business decisions to insure adequate resources for national defense.

Chapter 8

TRADE ASSOCIATIONS AND COMPETITION

NEITHER BASING POINT PRICING nor price leadership is likely, barring collusion, to eliminate price competition except in markets where sellers are large, few, and well disciplined. Self-discipline is rarely to be depended upon. The greater the number of sellers and the more diversified their interests, the more indispensable for the suppression of price competition is group discipline. In virtually all antitrust proceedings where defendant industries have sold on a delivered-price basis or practiced price leadership, the facts have shown that sellers collaborated to stabilize prices.

Collaboration Through Trade Associations

Businessmen may collaborate either formally or informally to eliminate price competition or to make it less severe. When they collaborate formally they usually do so through trade associations.[1] A trade association is an organization to promote mutual interests of firms producing or selling the same or similar products. With changes in public policy the trade association movement has waxed and waned. It suffered a setback when the Supreme Court condemned the activities of the Hardwood Lumber Manufacturers Association in 1921 and those of the Linseed Crushers Council in 1923.[2] When in 1925 the Court found the activities of the Maple Flooring Manufacturers Association and those of the Cement Manufacturers Protective Association consistent with the antitrust statutes, the movement accelerated.[3]

Businessmen organized more trade associations from 1925 through

1. See Charles A. Pearce, *Trade Association Survey,* TNEC Monograph No. 18, Washington, 1941, p. 47.
2. *American Column & Lumber Co.* v. *U.S.,* 257 U.S. 377 (1921); and *American Linseed Oil Co.* v. *U.S.,* 262 U.S. 371 (1923).
3. *Maple Flooring Manufacturers Association, et al.* v. *U.S.,* 268 U.S. 563 (1925); and *Cement Manufacturers Protective Association* v. *U.S.,* 268 U.S. 588 (1925).

1929 than during any previous five-year period.[4] In truth, trade association activities became so widespread and so effective during the 1920's that the head of an industrial engineering firm, active in organizing and managing trade associations, could say:

> Practically, under the Harding, Coolidge, and Hoover Administrations industry enjoyed, to all intents and purposes, a moratorium from the Sherman Act, and, through the more or less effective trade associations which were developed in most of our industries, competition was, to a very considerable extent, controlled. The Department of Justice acted with great restraint and intelligence and only enforced the Sherman Act against those industries who violated the laws in a flagrant and unreasonable manner.[5]

Trade Associations Flourish Under NRA

If trade associations throve in the tolerant political and legal environment of the 1920's, in the NRA hothouse they flourished luxuriantly. Where before, on a voluntary basis, they had been a common device for regulating the market, they now became an ordained and legally sanctified instrument for market control. Although presidential approval was necessary for NRA codes, trade groups representing the industry usually initiated them.[6] This fact encouraged the organization of trade associations in industries that had not previously resorted to them and revived many moribund associations. About 23 per cent of the 1,505 trade associations operating on a national or regional basis in June 1938 were organized during the three years 1933–1935.[7]

Virtually all the NRA codes that trade associations formulated contained one or more provisions designed to stabilize prices.[8] About

4. Pearce, *op. cit.*, p. 12.

5. Charles A. Stephenson, *Price Control and Allotment of Business,* address before the annual convention of the National Association of Cost Accountants, Cleveland, Ohio, June 26, 1934; quoted by Corwin D. Edwards in "Can Antitrust Laws Preserve Competition?," *American Economic Review,* Supplement, March 1940, p. 167.

6. Section 3 of the Act provided that "Upon the application to the President by one or more trade or industrial associations or groups, the President may approve a code or codes of fair competition for the trade or industry or subdivision thereof, represented by the applicant or applicants, if the President finds (1) that such associations or groups impose no inequitable restrictions on admission to membership therein and are truly representative of such trades or industries or subdivisions thereof . . ."

On the customary procedure in drafting the codes, see Leverett S. Lyon and Associates, *The National Recovery Administration,* The Brookings Institution, Washington, 1935, Pt. 2.

7. Pearce, *op. cit.*, p. 2, App. D.

8. Of the first 500 codes approved, 79 per cent provided for "practices tending to effect minimum prices"; 72 per cent for uniform methods of cost finding; 59 per

450 codes provided for open price systems.[9] Clearly, under NRA, the government encouraged business rivals to collaborate on production and pricing policies. Both business ethics and the new law sanctioned such collaboration, and in many industries code rules transformed a price chiseler into a law breaker.

When in the spring of 1935 the Supreme Court struck down the National Industrial Recovery Act, it did not modify the standards of business behavior. In support of price stabilization programs, businessmen substituted the sanction of custom and usage for the sanction of law. Trade associations frequently replaced code authorities or continued, without benefit of statutory permission, as the administrative agency through which business practices were codified.

Trade Associations Do Many Things

Trade associations ordinarily engage in many activities not directly associated with market control, price stabilization, and restraint of trade. They deal with the government on matters affecting the welfare of an industry, advise their members on problems of employment relations, sponsor campaigns to promote public good will toward an industry, and sometimes conduct technical and market research. Many of them establish commercial arbitration tribunals. Except as they may foster the spirit and develop the habits of collaboration, such activities do not directly affect the price and production policies of association members.

On the other hand, trade associations frequently engage in a variety of activities some of which are perhaps innocent or even wholesome when considered separately but which together tend to curb competition and restrain trade. Standardization of products and of cost accounting methods, for example, may eliminate waste and lower costs, but it also helps insure uniform prices among trade rivals. Exchange of information on the credit of customers may help

---

cent for open prices; 43 per cent for specified discount and credit terms; 27 per cent for specified transportation terms; 22 per cent for standard forms or terms of contract; 18 per cent for specified forms or terms of, or conditions surrounding the making of, bids and quotations; 17 per cent for classification of customers. Lyon and Associates, *op. cit.*, p. 570.

9. Leverett S. Lyon and Victor Abramson, *The Economics of Open Price Systems*, The Brookings Institution, Washington, 1936, p. 23. An open price system, broadly conceived, involves the compilation and distribution among business rivals of statistical information on inventories, orders, output, sales, shipments, prices, and like matters necessary for each to make an informed decision on price and output. The filing of prices currently charged by each producer is, however, the heart of the arrangement.

reduce bad debts, but it may also serve as a basis for boycotting "undesirable" customers. Statistical reporting on prices, output, sales, shipment, stocks, and the like may aid producers in independently formulating sound price and production policies, but it may also afford a basis for a tacit understanding to stabilize prices and curtail output. The compiling of freight rates from basing points to shipping destinations may serve the convenience of producers who customarily sell at delivered prices. But it is also an important, if not an essential, element in any plan to stabilize prices among widely scattered producers turning out standardized products with an inelastic demand, heavy transportation charges, large fixed costs of manufacture, and relatively constant variable costs when operating below capacity.[10]

An Escape From Competition

When rival businessmen join in such activities as these, they frequently follow price and production policies that promote group business interests at the expense of consumers and of the economy in general, whether or not they conspire to restrain trade. When they conspire to restrain trade, their associations often provide the mechanism. But whether association activities result in an illegal restraint of trade or merely aid members in reaching sound judgments on how their separate and group interests can best be served, the trade association movement represents an organized effort to moderate the rigors of competition. It reflects a lack of confidence in genuinely free enterprise, a fear of the destructive consequences of uninhibited price warfare. It is based on a belief that the welfare of individual companies may be bought at the expense of the industry and that "rugged individualism" may prove self-defeating. Trade associations promulgate a gospel of live and let live.

Views of Association Executives

But perhaps those who take part in trade association activities can describe their aims and explain their significance as businessmen conceive them better than economists can. The views of association executives are revealing:

> The principal achievement of the association has been the preservation of competition in its original sense of "to strive together for common interests."

---

10. See Chap. 7.

The association has . . . helped to eliminate to a great extent competitive antagonism.

While prices are not discussed, the fact that the members know one another and are friendly has had a stabilizing influence on the price of . . . machinery during the life of the association.

Definite price fixing, as such, is not necessary nor wanted in this industry. Price stability is very essential and will be encouraged.

It is part of the function of the trade association—and this Association has tried to specialize on this particular activity—to bring its members into a clear appraisal of the industry. . . . All too often business, and the business activities connected with industry, are conceived as a fight over the division of wealth. When concentration on the production of wealth is abandoned for a fight over the division of wealth, then the devices of a low order of cunning are likely to be more effective than the high order of intelligence.[11]

One thoughtful businessman sees the controls exercised by a trade association as a middle way that avoids both the wastes of destructive competition and the stultification of excessive regulation. He says:

One of the most perplexing and controversial subjects before the Nation today is that of COMPETITION. Within what limits can and should the competitive principle be maintained as an automatic regulator of our industrial economy?

The members of this Association express their beliefs on this subject as follows:

1. There is such a thing as destructive competition that results in totally demoralized markets and losses to everybody concerned, including consumers of its products. Up to a certain point free and active competition is desirable. Beyond that point it tends to depress wage levels, to lower standards of quality and service, to retard research and development and to destroy capital. It actually becomes a breeder of monopoly.
2. At the other extreme are forms of control that in too great degree restrain the competitive urge. Where these occur they may tend to cause the springs of ingenuity and resourcefulness to dry up and to retard economic progress.

It has been the purpose of this Association to strive for the middle course—to preserve the principle of active competition within the framework of an orderly marketing of its products.[12]

11. Quoted in Pearce, *op. cit.*, pp. 47-48.
12. *Ibid.*, p. 48.

Charles R. Stevenson, of Stevenson, Jordan & Harrison, a firm administering the affairs of some thirty national trade associations, states the case for trade associations more positively and bluntly:

What are these fetishes before which we are all bowing down, these idols of brass and stone into whose fiery maws are being thrown the peace, security, and happiness of all our people? First, the belief that competition is the life of trade. Second, the belief that the individual has the fundamental right to engage in trade in whatever form or manner he desires. . . .

Let us suppose that we are able to overcome these fetishes and that we are willing to admit the advantages which would come from controlled production and the adjustment of hours and wages of labor to the production which we require. How could we go about handling the thing from a practical standpoint?

First of all, then, we must change our laws regulating business, so that each industry will be given the right to form a firm organization and to govern and control itself. This organization of the industry must carry with it compulsory membership on the part of every firm engaged in the industry and must give to a sufficiently large majority, let us say $66\frac{2}{3}$ percent of the capital invested in the industry, the right to control the operations of the industry and to compel the adherence of the minority to the will of the majority. Industry, when so organized, must have the right to schedule and regulate production, to allot production between plants and territories and to determine a fair price at which the products of the industry will be offered to the public. New capital desiring to engage in an industry in which the capacity is in excess of production schedules must first secure a certificate of convenience and necessity.[13]

Mr. Stevenson was not disillusioned by the experience of NRA, for in 1939 he argued that "agreements which are in the interest of industry and therefore of the public, should be binding upon all non-signers." [14] Under such agreements he would permit producers to "allocate production fairly" and fix prices "which would assure a fair margin of profit above cost."

Some Fail, Some Succeed

Should this point of view prevail, self-government in industry would replace competition as a regulator of economic activities. To a large extent it actually did replace competition during the interval

13. Quoted in Clair Wilcox, *Competition and Monopoly in American Industry*, TNEC Monograph No. 21, Washington, 1940, pp. 253-54. The passage is from a pamphlet, "The Way Out," issued by the Stevenson firm.

14. Quoted in *ibid.*, p. 254. The quotation is an excerpt from an article in a trade journal.

between World Wars I and II, particularly during the NRA and post-NRA years. All trade associations were not equally successful, however, in their efforts to bring "order" into their respective industries. Where producers are many and relatively small, where they turn out a diversity of products with substitutes available for most, where they have widely different financial needs and obligations, and where neither legal barriers, such as patents, nor heavy capital requirements bar newcomers—where these factors are present, neither self-discipline nor formal restraints are likely to prove effective as market stabilizers when demand declines and plants operate at partial capacity. One disillusioned business executive has expressed the opinion that 10 per cent of those who operate in every business are incapable of self-discipline and must be subject to legal regulation.[15]

Although after NRA many businessmen abandoned trade associations completely or ignored their rules and principles, most manufacturers continued to support association activities designed to stabilize the market. Of 1,175 national and regional trade associations (excluding those in transportation, public utilities, and insurance) operating in June 1938, 966, or about 81 per cent, engaged in one or more of the following activities: standardization of trade practices; collection and distribution of trade statistics, including price information; and promotion of uniform cost accounting systems and cost studies.[16] Sixty-five associations reported all three among their major activities. In general, the fewer the association members, the greater the importance they attached to gathering and distributing trade statistics. All associations with fewer than twenty members reported this as an activity of major importance.

Trade Associations Tend to Lessen Competition

Such activities tend to lessen the severity of competition and to raise or keep up prices. Where sellers are few, informed, and well disciplined they may need only a common knowledge and interpretation of the market to insure price and production policies akin to those of a monopolist. Where these conditions persist, if sellers behave rationally they will restrict output to maximize their earnings.

15. See Pearce, *op. cit.*, p. 18; and Chap. 5, n. 34, of this study.
16. Pearce, *op. cit.*, pp. 63-64.

Businessmen are learning from experience what cloistered economic theorists have expounded. One prominent trade association administrator has put the case as follows:

> . . . the business leader of today achieves success by managing his individual volume in relation to his industry's volume, *so as to maximize his revenue and not his physical output.* To maximize revenue the individual businessman must formulate his policies in light of their effect *on the industry of which he is a part* as well as in consideration of the facts of his individual enterprise. . . . In the vast majority of instances today, if the rate of growth of an individual producer's volume exceeds the rate of growth of his industry's volume, that growth does not represent a corresponding expansion of the industry's total market; it represents business acquired from a competitor. Every businessman within my hearing knows the inevitable result of a continual loss of volume from one competitor to another. It is for these reasons that businessmen must manage volume so as to share the market, not to monopolize it, and, thus, to safeguard the conditions which maximize revenue.
>
> This new attitude toward volume marks the contrast between the new and the old points of view of management. Fortunately, the new point of view has spread with great rapidity in recent years, and it is interesting to note that the men who held it are, as a rule, the leaders of their industries. . . . The significant fact is that where modern business leadership is found one also finds an understanding of the modern relationship between the individual producer and his industry.[17]

When this "modern" point of view has not, alone, proved sufficient to restrict output, stabilize prices, and maximize earnings, some trade associations have not hesitated to supplement self-discipline with a definite educational program and a formal, systematic plan for sharing business. The program of the National Container Association is an illustration in point.

The Container Plan

Drawing on their seventeen years of experience in managing and advising trade associations, in 1932, Stevenson, Jordan & Harrison developed a price stabilization program for the container industry.[18]

17. Quoted in *ibid.*, p. 182. Italics supplied.

18. A memorandum from the industry's NRA code authority to an NRA deputy administrator gives a brief but cogent review of this experience. According to this account, Stevenson, Jordan & Harrison developed their price stabilization program in three stages. At first they thought that if competitors had accurate knowledge of their costs, developed according to a uniform method of cost accounting, they would compete with such restraint and intelligence as to insure orderly markets. They found, how-

The program was designed "to mitigate the extremely destructive competitive practices which were in vogue in the industry and to try and build some sort of an orderly market procedure." [19] It had three features. Basic to the plan were the "Normal Volume Relationships," which Stevenson, Jordan & Harrison determined through a survey of members' output and sales of fiber packing boxes during the preceding three years. In effect, each manufacturer got a production quota. Two supplementary features of the plan—standard cost-estimating and invoice analysis systems—were apparently designed to help members compare their prices with the average price for their region and to adjust prices to standardized costs.

On August 9, 1939 a federal grand jury indicted the National Container Association, its leading members, and the Stevenson firm for conspiring to restrain trade. The indictment alleged that the Association's business manager employed travelling auditors and engineers to examine members' books, to bring to a member's attention any deviation of output from quota or any deviation in price from the regional average, and generally to promote the plan for "prorationing of business." [20] The criminal proceedings were dropped in the spring of 1940 when the same defendants in a companion civil suit accepted a consent decree that enjoined them from continuing the program and practices described above.[21]

Salt Producers Stabilize

Stevenson, Jordan & Harrison were very active in promoting and administering trade association programs designed to mitigate the

---

ever, that knowledge of costs by business rivals was not enough to stabilize markets. Some companies that were "Volume Minded" tried to reduce their unit costs by cutting prices and increasing sales.

Stevenson, Jordan & Harrison's next step was to inform business rivals on the state of the market by compiling, analyzing, and distributing statistics covering orders, production, shipments, stocks on hand, etc. The firm believed that "the two sets of facts together—that is, the knowledge of costs and the knowledge of the industry picture—would result in policies of management . . . which would make for a stabilized market."

When knowledge of costs plus a knowledge of the market did not eliminate competition, Stevenson, Jordan & Harrison took their final step and developed "the principle of an Equitable Sharing of the available volume of business." *Ibid.*, p. 239.

19. *Ibid.*

20. *Ibid.*, pp. 238-49. It was also charged that regional secretaries continually urged association members to adhere to their quotas and refrain from selling at prices below the average for their group.

21. See *U.S.* v. *National Container Association, et al.*, Civil Action No. 8-318, in U.S. District Court for the Southern District of New York, consent decree entered April 20, 1940.

severity of competition. Typical of such programs is that adopted by the Salt Producers Association in the fall of 1935.[22] Eighteen of the country's leading salt producers, including such well-known companies as Diamond Crystal, International, and Morton, belonged to the Association. Before the Association was formed these companies competed vigorously. With a productive capacity in excess of their sales and with selling expenses comprising a large part of their total cost, their net earnings in relation to investment were small.[23] They therefore employed Stevenson, Jordan & Harrison. With this experienced leadership, the salt producers, without formal collusion, worked out a program under which they could all sell salt at uniform prices and on the same terms and conditions. The program comprised some half-dozen steps—all directed toward sharing the market and stabilizing prices.

Salt Producers' Program

First, the Stevenson firm made a survey for the preceding five years in each of the salt-marketing zones into which the United States had been divided. The productive capacity, annual sales, average selling price f.o.b. plant, selling expenses, and net earnings for each company in every area in which it operated were compiled. For each of these categories the Stevenson firm developed a composite figure, which it supplied to all members of the Association and with which it compared the corresponding figures for the particular member. It did not disclose to any member the figures relating specifically to any other company's operations.

The second step was a meeting of the producers at which representatives of the Stevenson firm called attention to the industry's excess plant capacity and its low rate of earnings. These low earnings resulted, they said, from the "unremitting efforts" of each member "to obtain for himself an increased portion of the total volume of business obtainable without due regard to net return on sales of the product and without due consideration to the sales expense involved." [24]

22. See *In re Salt Producers Association, et al.*, 34 FTC Decisions 38 (1941).

23. According to Stevenson, Jordan & Harrison, based on an industry survey. *Ibid.*, p. 51.

24. This is the language used by FTC in its findings. *Ibid.*, p. 51. In this proceeding, each of the respondents first filed answers denying all the allegations of the complaint,

As a third step, Stevenson representatives conducted personal discussions with each of the Association members to educate them on the "fundamental economic truths" developed by the survey.[25] They advised members that if a company persisted in trying to get more than "its share" of the salt business, it must inevitably resort to uneconomic marketing costs and accept low returns, because other salt producers would be sure to counterattack.

At a subsequent meeting it was agreed that each member would submit to the Stevenson firm monthly data on the value and volume of his production and sales by marketing zones and his selling expenses, from which composite figures were to be computed for the whole group. These composite figures permitted monthly comparison by each member of his production, sales, and selling expense with the record of the group as a whole. To insure accuracy of the data, members agreed to permit the Stevenson firm to audit their records and for this purpose to have access to their offices and files from time to time.

To carry out this program, at regular monthly meetings Stevenson representatives explained the statistics. With the help of charts they analyzed the recent course of sales in each zone, advised members on the trend of demand, and explained the significance of the relation of current production to probable demand.

Finally, to keep members "educated," representatives of the Stevenson firm periodically visited each member of the Association, audited the statistical data submitted by the company, and urged the management to consider unceasingly the dire consequences of trying to improve its relative position in the market. They told each member that it could improve its competitive position only at the expense of the others and that if, trying to do so, any company lowered its prices its rivals would follow suit, with the final result that each would sell substantially the same amount of salt at lower prices and make a smaller return on investment.[26]

---

but later withdrew them, filing briefer answers admitting the facts as alleged by FTC. However, the respondents petitioned the court for a review and modification of the FTC cease-and-desist order, challenging the order's phraseology but not its issuance. The court granted the petition and directed FTC to modify its order.

25. 34 FTC, p. 51. This educational campaign lasted a month.

26. *Ibid.*, pp. 52-53.

Effectiveness of the Program

In brief, Stevenson, Jordan & Harrison strove to convince salt producers that self-interest demanded that they act as economists have said producers, so far as they are rational, will act in markets of imperfect competition. But in trying to harmonize business practice with economic theory, the Stevenson firm supplemented the conceptions of the economists with machinery to get results. They not only supplied salt producers with the knowledge essential for them to harmonize their business practices with imperfect-competition theory, but they exercised constant surveillance to insure that the producers would react to the facts as they were theoretically supposed to react. When statistics showed that any member was producing at a rate greater than necessary to maintain his established position in the industry, he was urged to reconsider the eventual unhappy outcome of such undisciplined behavior.

This plan apparently worked about as well as a formal cartel would have worked had it assigned definite quotas to each producer. The Commission found that the practices of the salt producers not only had a "dangerous tendency" to hinder competition, but that in fact they had prevented effective competition in selling salt. The salt producers did not challenge the Commission's findings of fact.

Maltsters Collaborate

The United States Maltsters Association [27] affords another illustration of how a trade association may coordinate the responses of producers to a given market situation and thereby insure common pricing policies. Before World War II, eighteen leading producers controlled about 64 per cent of the total domestic malting capacity and 75 per cent of the commercial capacity. All but four of their plants were located in Wisconsin or Chicago; of the four, one was in Detroit and three were in Buffalo.

Most of the barley from which domestic malt is made comes from Wisconsin, Minnesota, North Dakota, and South Dakota. The cost

27. Organized in 1930 as the Bureau of Barley and Malt Statistics, it changed its name in August 1933. This account is based on the Federal Trade Commission's findings in *In re United States Maltsters Association, et al.*, 35 FTC Decisions 797 (1942), and on the Circuit Court's opinion in *United States Maltsters Association, et al.* v. *FTC*, 152 Fed. *2d* 163 (1945).

of barley is 80 to 85 per cent of the cost of malt. Maltsters buy most of their barley by sample in the terminal markets—Minneapolis, Milwaukee, and Chicago. Although, no doubt, they generally pay about the same price at any particular time for barley of a given grade, during the period in which the Association was active, malting barley prices fluctuated greatly. Transportation costs, from terminal elevators to malting plants and from malting plants to customers' breweries, also varied greatly for the different producers. Making malt is an art, and production costs differ widely. The Federal Trade Commission found that among Association members differences in net manufacturing costs were sometimes as great as 20 per cent.

Although the number of maltsters was not so great nor their individual output so small that each could entirely ignore the others in making output and price decisions, their costs were so varied and their interests so conflicting that it is extremely unlikely that they could have avoided effective competition without collaborating. The Commission's findings support this view.[28]

Price Uniformity Achieved

Apparently the purpose of the Association was to substitute collaboration for competition. Collaboration took the form of a program to insure that all producers would sell at identical prices and under uniform terms and conditions of sale. To carry out this program they hired Stevenson, Jordan & Harrison. The Association inaugurated a system of price reporting. Each member reported daily, usually by wire, every sale of malt, destination of shipment, grade and quality sold, and price. Each member also reported weekly and monthly on total malt shipped, unfilled orders, orders cancelled, malt stocks on hand, barley inventory and purchases, and similar details. The Stevenson firm compiled this information and made daily, weekly, and monthly reports to members, though without identifying sellers or buyers or disclosing the operations of particular members.

Each member filed his current price list with the Stevenson office and undertook to notify the others promptly of any changes therein. To make certain that all charged identical prices at any delivery

28. In FTC's language, "Prior to 1930 said respondent members were in competition as to price with one another in the sale and distribution of malt . . ." 35 FTC, p. 804.

point, the members reported their prices on an "f.o.b. Chicago basis." [29] This method of price reporting made it easy to determine whether all members were selling at identical prices.

Kept constantly informed on the market situation and supplied with a method of quoting identical prices, the Association members were expected to, and in fact did, regularly charge the same price to all customers at any given delivery point.[30] Despite wide differences in costs among Association members at all times and sharp fluctuations in each member's costs from time to time as the price of barley changed, malt prices became very firm. They remained absolutely constant from November 16, 1938 until March 17, 1941, when the Commission concluded its hearings in the case. The Commission found that the Association's program was responsible for both the uniformity and the stability of malt prices and the Circuit Court sustained the Commission.

Was Uniformity Inevitable?

The Association members argued that "economic factors affecting the malt industry . . . inevitably produce substantial uniformity in the selling price of malt of like grade at any given time," and an economist testified in effect that "the uniformity in the selling price of malt at a particular time was consistent with and a necessary consequence of the normal functioning of competition in such an industry." [31]

On theoretical grounds the economist's position was correct, if taken to signify merely that price uniformity is consistent with competition. But he erred in asserting that it was "a necessary consequence of the normal functioning of competition in such an in-

29. "This represented the price at which the malt would have been sold if the sales had been made f.o.b. Chicago." *Ibid.*, p. 808.

30. Its president testified that members were expected to maintain the prices filed with the Association until they notified it of a change, and a member testified not only that he expected other members to adhere to their reported prices until they filed notice of change, but that his experience had been "pretty general that it happened that way." *United States Maltsters Association, et al.* v. *FTC*, 152 Fed. *2d*, p. 164. The maltsters quoted prices f.o.b. destination and apparently used Chicago as a basing point. Though they denied that they did so, the court, without discussing the basing point system or the details of the freight rate system used, concluded that "The incontrovertible fact is that this freight system enabled them to deliver malt at any given destination at exactly the same price."

The record also indicates that members agreed to use uniform standard contracts in selling malt, to adopt uniform grading standards, to sell malt only to buyers who agreed not to resell it, and not to permit sales agents to handle imported malt.

31. *Ibid.*, p. 165. This is the court's summation of the economist's testimony.

dustry." If competition had been perfect, all sellers would, of course, have sold at a common market price. But competition in practice is rarely perfect and the malt industry is no exception to this rule. Nevertheless, competition might have been effective at least without having been perfect. If it were effective, malt prices would probably have shown some variation at any particular time among the different sellers and from time to time with the same seller. These differences might have taken the form of secret discounts or departures from published prices; or they might have been reflected in the terms of sale. But it is unlikely that prices would have been either stable or uniform. They would have tended, however, to equal a producer's marginal cost in the short run, and his total unit cost in the long run.

The testimony of the witness who testified as an economic expert would have been more accurate had he said, "the uniformity in the selling price of malt at a particular time was consistent with and a necessary consequence of the normal functioning of imperfect competition in such an industry." This statement accords with accepted theory. But as this study has shown, even under imperfect competition collaboration among producers is often necessary to insure that they sell at uniform prices and that they change prices infrequently. The facts in the maltsters' case confirm this reasoning. To make self-discipline effective in controlling prices, the Association members implemented it by concerted action.

Collaboration in Crepe Paper

The crepe paper industry illustrates well the practical necessity for continual collaboration among producers, even when they are few and their product standardized, if they are to stabilize prices. Its record indicates that self-discipline and self-interest alone may not be sufficient to make markets behave in accordance with the theory of imperfect competition. It further shows that even the cohesive influence of a trade association is sometimes inadequate, especially in periods of depression, to prevent effective competition and must be supplemented by formal restrictive agreements. Again, it suggests that sellers are quick to take indirect advantage of rivals even when they presumably follow a common pricing policy, so that stern measures to maintain uniform standards of quality and terms and conditions of sale are necessary. In short, it reveals that eternal vigilance in a cooperative program is the price business rivals may be required to pay to maximize their net returns.

Before World War II, eight manufacturers sold all the crepe paper made in the United States.[32] Although they used similar paper and similar machines to crinkle it, "creping ratios" (the ratio of the length of the paper before and after creping), length and width of a fold, weight of paper, terms of sale, and trade discounts—all of which help determine relative values—were not always uniform. Before NRA the industry had established no facilities for standardizing these variables, and with no basing point system it was not easy to maintain either stable or identical prices for the several paper products that each of the companies sold throughout the national market.

With the advent of NRA, the crepe paper manufacturers set out to remedy this situation. In July 1933 they organized the National Crepe Paper Association and drafted a code. In keeping with the spirit of NRA, they took steps to standardize their products and to insure that all sold at the same price to all buyers at any delivery point. As the minutes of the meeting of the Association's executive committee on July 26, 1933 state:

> In addition to drawing up a Code of Fair Competition, the Committee felt that it would be necessary also to draw up a Trade Agreement which would contain standard practices in reference to terms, datings, contracts, freight allowances, standards of lengths, widths, weights, etc., of Crepe Paper, crepe paper put-ups, bulk and package, also crepe paper accessories, selling prices, etc. . . .[33]

The "Trade Agreement" as finally worked out required discontinuance of the sale of "seconds" (substandard crepe), elimination of the customary 2 per cent trade discount, and standardization of the length of folds, weight of papers, and creping ratios. More crucial to the stabilization of prices was a zoning system of delivered prices. For pricing bulk crepe paper, the Association divided the country into three zones, for pricing packaged crepe, into two zones,

32. American Tissue Mills, Charles T. Bainbridge's Sons, Dennison Manufacturing Company, Fort Howard Paper Company, Papyrus Company, C. A. Reed Company, Reyburn Manufacturing Company, and Tuttle Press Company. Not all of these firms sold all types of crepe paper.

33. *In re National Crepe Paper Association of America, et al.*, 38 FTC Decisions 287 (1944).

and within each zone every company quoted identical delivered prices for any particular product.[34]

Members of the Association have pointed out that the zone system was for the convenience of both the industry and the public. In particular, it permitted chain stores and other companies operating on a national scale to buy crepe paper everywhere in any zone at the same price. But it also helped business rivals quote identical delivered prices at all points.[35] As in the case of many other NRA codes with similar provisions, this apparently was its real purpose.

Collaboration After NRA

After NRA, the crepe paper manufacturers agreed that they would operate under the same labor conditions and fair-trade practices that they had followed under the code, at least until such time as a definite and specific policy was adopted by the government.[36] At Association meetings from 1935 to 1939 voluntary collaboration on prices and trade practices continued, though when prices were under discussion some members consistently withdrew and refused to take part in programs for directly restricting competition. Moreover, even among those who did participate in such activities, concerted action was more difficult to achieve without the backing of NRA.[37] In the recession of 1937–1938 some crepe manufacturers apparently departed from their published price lists and rumors of price cutting prevailed. The situation was particularly unstable in

34. The zone boundaries apparently were drawn so as to place all sellers on an equal footing in each zone. For example, the eastern zone for bulk crepe paper extended from the Atlantic Coast to the Mississippi River, and thus included Wisconsin as well as New England plants. Thus the Wisconsin producers sacrificed all freight advantage they would otherwise have used in selling in the Middle West, and New England manufacturers their advantage in Atlantic Coast markets. See *Fort Howard Paper Co., et al.* v. *FTC,* 156 Fed. *2d* 899 (1946), at p. 904.

35. The code members did not always rely on price filing to achieve price uniformity. At one meeting they agreed to sell bulk crepe to syndicate and chain stores on the "Class Three 100 gross lot of $5.70 for 2½ to 1 ratio, and $5.50 for 2¼ to 1 ratio, in any quantity." 38 FTC, p. 289.

36. *Ibid.,* p. 290. This was done by motion adopted unanimously at a meeting June 11, 1935.

37. Thus at a meeting in November 1936, the executive secretary expressed concern over the failure of some members to conform to the creping standards set up in 1933. He emphasized that "excessive ratios have fully as bad an effect on the market as a violation of each manufacturer's own published price list," and that "the stability of the market would surely be wrecked if steps to correct the situation were not vigorously continued." The minutes recite that each member "promised to take this matter up with his Production Department immediately and see that ratios received adequate and proper supervision." *Ibid.,* p. 291.

the sale of florist crepe, made by only three concerns. A letter of November 12, 1937 from Tuttle Press to American Tissue Mills stated pointedly:

We are getting reports that florist crepe paper is being offered in jumbo rolls at 19¢ per lb. Our price is 20¢ per lb., for you will recall that when we advanced the price of florist crepe paper 2¢ per roll in all brackets that we increased the price [of jumbo rolls] 2¢ per lb. The old price was 18¢ which would make the new price 20¢. Will you kindly advise if this understanding is correct? [38]

American Tissue Mills replied that it was selling at Tuttle's price and that it had lost business because it would not cut to 19 cents.

But similar inquiries kept going out, and similar responses coming back. On April 18, 1938 the president of Bainbridge's addressed American Tissue Mills as follows:

We have just had a man return from the South, and he sold quite a little 7½ ft. crepe paper down there a year or two ago, but he tells us now that three or four of the largest customers tell him that our price of $3.84 is crazy, and they are getting better prices from American Tissue, Fort Howard and Tuttle.

Will you tell me frankly—are you selling it in the South for less than $3.84? I think the salesman is putting up an alibi.[39]

American Tissue denied hotly that it was a price cutter. Said its representative, "Any customer that tells you they are getting a lower price than $3.84 a gross from us is just a plain ordinary liar." He was not so sure, however, about some of the other companies' prices.

. . . I couldn't speak for Tuttle Press, as to how they handle it, as I have heard they will allow a 5 per cent discount to good jobbers, but I am quite sure that Fort Howard would be selling strictly on the price list.

Our list is attached and if all the other manufacturers stick to it as closely as we do, we would all be better off.[40]

In an apparent effort to eliminate price cutting, the Association passed the following resolutions at its meeting of May 17-18, 1938:

1. Each member to telephone or telegraph the Secretary's office simultaneously when he changed his published price list. . . .

38. *Fort Howard* v. *FTC,* cited above, in the Circuit Court of Appeals, Seventh Circuit, Brief for the Commission, p. 19, Comm.Ex. 141A.

39. *Ibid.,* p. 15, Comm.Ex. 80.

40. *Ibid.,* Comm.Ex. 81. The record shows frequent correspondence among some but not all members of the Association on pricing policies during this period.

2. Copies of orders and invoices to be furnished the Secretary's office promptly. . . .[41]

Despite "good resolutions" price competition evidently continued, for the minutes of the May 1939 meeting report an unsuccessful effort to strengthen the Association's hand so as to bring about stricter compliance with the trade practice rules to which members had subscribed. Apparently dissatisfied with the way the Association was working, in November 1939 Dennison withdrew from the group, and about the same time Reyburn dropped out.[42]

Although the Association was not altogether successful in stabilizing crepe paper prices, it apparently had some effect. And even though it has been compelled to abandon its price stabilization activities, the crepe paper market, like so many others that have passed through a similar experience, will continue to bear watching.[43] For in the language of the court, manufacturers of crepe paper have been "indoctrinated with the belief . . . that the elimination of all competition" is desirable.

Antitrust Prosecution Frequent

Price stabilization programs are common among trade associations. The programs discussed in this chapter are unique neither in their features for stabilizing the market nor in having run afoul of the antitrust laws. A TNEC survey showed that from June 1, 1935 to

41. 38 FTC, pp. 291-92.

42. Later a Reyburn officer explained that the company withdrew "for several reasons, one was that we did not believe that we were getting a return value from the money we invested from our dues, or the time it had taken for myself to be away from the office." *Fort Howard* v. *FTC,* Brief for the Commission, p. 33; see Comm.Exs. 37, 38A-E, 161A-H.

In a scrupulous effort to avoid involvement in conspiracy, the Reyburn representative had made it a practice to leave Association meetings when pricing questions were up for discussion. See 156 Fed. *2d,* p. 905. He gave as a second reason for resigning from the Association "there were occasions when I found that I left the room and the meetings, and then afterwards the minutes would come in and it would just appear from those minutes as though I had been in attendance the entire meeting. We thought the best way and the nicest way to handle the situation was to tender our resignation."

43. After hearings, on April 12, 1944 FTC ordered Association members to cease and desist "from . . . any planned common course of action, agreement, understanding, combination, or conspiracy," among other things to: fix or maintain uniform prices for crepe paper; establish or maintain delivered-price zones or price differentials between zones; establish or maintain classifications of customers; or file with the National Crepe Paper Association or any other agency copies of invoices or price lists. In the Fort Howard case, the Circuit Court of Appeals upheld FTC, and on December 23, 1946 the Supreme Court denied a petition for a writ of certiorari.

The quotation in the next sentence in the text is from *ibid.,* p. 906.

October 1, 1939 the Federal Trade Commission filed complaints or reached decisions in 93 cases and that the Department of Justice obtained 18 indictments and instituted 14 civil proceedings, all involving similar concerted arrangements to regulate competition in the interest of the group. Forty-eight of these 125 cases were pending on October 1, 1939. The Department of Justice had instituted 15 of these. In its 17 other cases, it obtained an injunction, a consent decree or a criminal conviction in 14, and lost or discontinued the other three. In 52 cases the Federal Trade Commission issued cease-and-desist orders, of which 35 were not appealed.[44]

The antitrust program initiated under Thurman Arnold's aggressive leadership and carried on by his successor, Wendell Berge, was just getting under way during the period covered by the survey. Between January 1940 and July 1946 the Department of Justice initiated about 100 antitrust suits involving trade associations. The courts have not adjudicated all of these cases and, in those which they have, they did not always uphold the government's contention. Most of the completed cases, however, led to verdicts of guilty or to decrees, many of them by consent, adverse to the defendants.

The Issue Not Legal Restraint

The issue here, however, is not the legality of trade association activities but their significance to the maintenance of competitive markets. Trade association activities theoretically might increase or lessen competition or have no effect on it at all. If they have no effect, no case can be made for permitting trade association activities designed to stabilize markets. If they intensify competition, trade associations will apparently have failed to achieve their objective and they are likely to abandon price stabilization activities of their own accord.[45] Men will not ordinarily continue to subsidize activities that render their businesses more precarious.

Businessmen have frequently resorted to trade associations to

44. Pearce, *op. cit.,* pp. 67-69.

45. Seven hundred and fifty trade associations became inactive or disbanded between 1932 and 1938. Of 278 on which TNEC received reports, 69 gave no reason for quitting. Of the remainder about nine tenths apparently quit because they failed to restrain competition. At any rate, among the reasons given for disbanding the most common was lack of confidence or lack of cooperation (28) and the second most frequent explanation was inability to achieve price stabilization (24). See *ibid.,* Table 24, p. 372.

eliminate the "risks" and "wastes" of competition. Through collective action they have sought economic security. If trade associations do not provide it, they will die for lack of support. Pearce has stated the point effectively in evaluating trade association statistical services:

> Comparisons of individual company with industry performance may intensify competition if there is not a general acceptance by the members of an industry of the desirability of restraint in the market. The figures may serve the function of telling each member how he scored in the competitive struggle of the past month, thus spurring him on to greater efforts in the ensuing month. This possible function, which trade association executives sometimes advance as the reason for such comparative analysis, is scarcely to be regarded as an objective of the association program. Rather, it represents a failure of the program to impress upon its members the message of interdependence that the figures are supposed to convey. If the individual company comparisons actually led to more aggressive competition, these statistics probably would after a time be abandoned, just as one association voted to discontinue its Research and Sales Bulletin, because "certain members were of the opinion that research and sales data created undue competition." Similarly, under N.R.A. some industries found it necessary to abandon open price filing because certain members regarded the filed prices of competitors as targets to undershoot, and competitive price cutting was enhanced rather than deterred.[46]

The Issue Is Control of the Market

If trade associations make competition less effective, they are hardly less objectionable if they discover methods of obliquely doing so that do not violate the antitrust laws. But many of them are trying to do just this. As trade associations have repeatedly run afoul of the law their promoters and managers have sought more subtle ways of eliminating price competition among business rivals. They have sought the fruits of conspiracy while trying to avoid its legal penalties. The reasoning of judges and of economists has sometimes helped them.

46. *Ibid.*, p. 185. That business rivals sometimes lack the self-discipline necessary to insure that trade association activities will promote their group interests is made clear in the following statement from a trade association's annual report: "But it would be idle to deceive ourselves. There are members of this industry who are willing to share available business just as equitably as the lion shares his kill with the gentle house cat. It is my opinion that the trials and preachings of the past few years have gone some distance towards educating the over-greedy units—but the lion is not yet ready to lie down with the lamb, and the little child who was to lead them disappeared in the person of General Johnson and his N.R.A." *Ibid.*

Mr. Justice Stone's opinion in the Maple Flooring case provides an example of such reasoning:

It is not, we think, open to question that the dissemination of pertinent information concerning any trade or business tends to stabilize that trade or business and to produce uniformity of price and trade practice . . . the natural effect of the acquisition of wider and more scientific knowledge of business conditions on the minds of the individuals engaged in commerce and its consequent effect in stabilizing production and price, can hardly be deemed a restraint of commerce, or if so, it cannot, we think, be said to be an unreasonable restraint or in any respect unlawful.

It is the consensus of opinion of economists and of many of the most important agencies of government that the public interest is served by the gathering and dissemination, in the widest possible manner, of information with respect to production and distribution, cost and prices in actual sales, of market commodities, because the making available of such information tends to stabilize trade and industry, to produce fairer price levels, and to avoid the waste which inevitably attends the unintelligent conduct of economic enterprise . . . Competition does not become less free merely because the conduct of commercial operations becomes more intelligent through the free distribution of knowledge of all essential factors entering into the commercial transaction.[47]

The late Professor Seligman of Columbia University expressed a similar view as a witness for the defendants in the Sugar Institute case.[48] He testified that "The nearer we get to the conditions of open competition, the nearer we get to the theory of economic competition with general public beneficial results as understood by economists." Such reasoning is based on a nineteenth-century view of economic processes. Its postulates are not generally applicable to today's economy. They stem from an economy of relatively small-scale production with many enterprises in the field.

Logic of Competitive Price Theory

The economic justification of private, concerted action in gathering, analyzing, and disseminating statistical data on market conditions is based, it is evident, on the logic of competitive price theory. This logic, as implied by Seligman, assumes a rational economic man who follows his selfish interests but who, in an atomistic economy, is presumably compelled by market forces to do those things that

47. *Maple Flooring Manufacturers Association, et al.* v. *U.S.*, 268 U.S., pp. 582-83.
48. *Sugar Institute, Inc.* v. *U.S.*, 297 U.S. 553 (1936).

promote the social welfare. Rational behavior in free markets, with hundreds of competing sellers as well as buyers, presumably leads to the economical allocation of scarce resources, to the maximizing of output, and to the minimizing of cost.

Moreover, under the conditions assumed, costs tend to limit prices. If decisions of businessmen operating in such markets are to be rational, they must be informed. Sellers must know their costs, know the extent of supply, know what offers and bids others are making—in short, know all the vital facts affecting the market. Such knowledge is essential if the decisions of businessmen, each of whom sells only a very small part of the total supply, are to promote the general welfare in a free economy. Only if businessmen understand the conditions of the market will they make intelligent decisions, and only if they make intelligent decisions can society rely on competition as a regulator of economic activity. Rational behavior in this type of free market makes for order in industry; behavior based on ignorance, for confusion.

Nineteenth-Century Logic and Twentieth-Century Markets

Such is the reasoning on which rests the social justification of concerted action among business rivals in disseminating trade knowledge and analyzing facts. Economists and judges have regarded trade associations as good because they provide rival sellers with information on which to make wise decisions. But we do not live in an economy of the sort postulated in such reasoning. Today many markets are dominated by a handful of producers; one, two, or three companies operate on a scale so large that the market is under their control. Not atomistic competition, but imperfect competition, is the rule under modern conditions. Many industrial markets today more nearly resemble monopoly markets than competitive ones.

It is such markets of imperfect competition that confuse interpreters of the law who think in terms of the old-fashioned dichotomy between monopoly and competition. They recognize that when monopoly prevails rational behavior may lead to antisocial consequences. They know that a monopolist is in a unique position, affording him the opportunity to obtain full knowledge of the market and of costs and thus to adjust output so as to maximize his earnings. They fail to recognize, however, that in markets of imperfect competition, when two, three, or a half-dozen companies constituting the major if not the sole sources of supply compile and disseminate among themselves complete, detailed data on their operations and policies, they may lay the basis for a similar antisocial role.

When sellers are few, fully informed, and behave rationally, each will take account of the influence that a price change by any one may exert on the price policies of all and on the response of buyers. Common sense and experience may have taught sellers in imperfectly competitive markets that all sellers will quickly meet the price cut of any one. When price cuts do not increase purchases proportionately, they may result in approximately the same amount of business for all rivals but at a lower price and with smaller profits. Under these conditions rational behavior may result in economic sabotage—restriction of output to maximize earnings.

The Trade Association in Imperfectly Competitive Markets

In sum, in markets of imperfect competition rational behavior based on exhaustive trade information obtained through exchange among a few rivals of the intimate details of their several operations and policies—information that a monopolist acquires in virtue simply of being the sole supplier—is apt to exhibit the same pattern as that of a monopolist. Rational behavior in the one case is no more likely to be socially beneficial than in the other. But it will benefit, at least temporarily, each of a few sellers, just as it benefits a single seller. Herein lies a function of the modern trade association. It may compile and disseminate among trade rivals the exhaustive, detailed information that is essential to rational behavior and that fosters a spirit of camaraderie. In doing so it may transform a relatively free, although imperfectly competitive, market into a more rigidly monopolistic market. No formal agreement by trade rivals may be necessary to turn the trick. In truth, where the number of sellers is very small and knowledge of the market complete, no agreement of any kind may be necessary. Knowledge points the way; self-interest furnishes the drive.

Those with firsthand knowledge of antitrust administration know that where business rivals exchange significant market data to stabilize markets they nearly always resort to collusion, tacit agreement, price leadership, basing point systems, and the like to insure unity of action. But where producers are few, such collusion may be so fine-spun that no outsider can discern it. The association itself and its dissemination of trade statistics may be the most important device in the mechanism of control.

The exchange of market information among a small group that practically compose an entire industry may easily become a combination in unreasonable restraint of trade. This is twentieth-century logic, though not always twentieth-century law. But if a free economy is to prevail, society may be forced to base contemporary law on contemporary logic. This does not mean that businessmen should be kept in ignorance. But it does mean that if society is to preserve free enterprise, it must not permit businessmen to collaborate in standardizing every vital feature of a market transaction and in exchanging all the pertinent information about their operations and policies that will enable them to act like monopoly partners. To discourage its use for illegal or uneconomic ends the government might compile and timely disseminate such basic market information as business rivals may need to make intelligent decisions independently. If the truth is to make us free, perhaps the government has no alternative to thus extending its already enormous responsibility in this field. If businessmen were loath to disclose to an official trade statistics agency some of the information they exchange among themselves, they might reflect that the steady growth of "big government" is one of the penalties of business strivings for market control.

Chapter 9

ANTITRUST POLICY AND THE ECLIPSE OF COMPETITION

THE FIRST STEP toward an explicit national policy on competition and monopoly was taken in 1890, when Congress passed the Sherman Act. Despite serious disagreement about its precise meaning, the general purpose of the law is clear. It was intended to restore competition where it had disappeared, preserve it where it still prevailed, and perpetuate it as a system for controlling the American economy. The Sherman Act reflected a deep-rooted national faith in competition as a regulator of economic activity. Its broad objectives are mirrored in the public opinion of its day, in the congressional debates leading to its passage, and in its own provisions.

What the People Thought About Trusts

The hostility of the American people to concentration of economic power, whether public or private, is profound. The Revolutionary War was in part a revolt against the economic restrictions of an absentee government striving to protect British traders from colonial competition. Thomas Jefferson, apostle of freedom, regretted that the Constitution voiced no prohibition against monopolies and he was doubtful about the limited patent and copyright monopoly grants that the Constitution permitted.

Under Jackson, hostility to monopoly brought the second Bank of the United States to an ignominious end. When businessmen strove to stem the market glut of the depression of 1873 through agreements to limit output and keep up prices, the National Grange, with a farm membership of a half million, adopted the slogan "Down With Monopolies." It also helped organize antimonopoly parties in eleven states.

The formation of the Standard Oil Trust and its half-dozen imitators in the 1880's, which used secret railway rebates and price discrimination in a ruthless war of extermination against all outsiders, provoked a more formidable political upheaval. The National Farmers Alliance, of some three or four million members, and the Knights of Labor, with nearly a million, joined in demanding government regulation of railways and curtailment of private monopoly. The growth of the trusts, aided by special preferences from the railways, led to concentration of wealth, increasing control of the market, and restriction of business opportunities. These developments troubled small businessmen no less than farmers. As early as 1878 the New York Chamber of Commerce demanded an investigation of railway abuses. By 1890 Maine, Michigan, Tennessee, Texas, Iowa, and Kentucky had passed antitrust laws.

Such, briefly, was the political atmosphere that precipitated federal antitrust legislation. George Gunton, writing in 1888, said:

> Indeed, the public mind has begun to assume a state of apprehension, almost amounting to alarm, regarding the evil economic and social tendencies of these organizations. . . . the social atmosphere seems to be surcharged with an indefinite, but almost inexpressible fear of trusts.[1]

With the public aroused by the growing concentration of economic power and its dreaded consequences, both the Republican and Democratic parties affirmed their faith in a competitive economy and their determination to safeguard it. The Republicans in their 1888 platform declared their "opposition to all combinations of capital, organized in trusts or otherwise, to control arbitrarily the condition of trade," and recommended "such legislation as will prevent the execution of all schemes to oppress the people by undue charges on their supplies, or by unjust rates for the transportation of their products to market." The Democrats spoke out as strongly. Their platform declared that "the interests of the people are betrayed when . . . trusts and combinations are permitted to exist," for they

1. George Gunton, "The Economic and Social Aspect of Trusts," *Political Science Quarterly*, September 1888, p. 385. James F. Hudson, Gunton's contemporary, anticipated Berle and Means by forty-four years in characterizing, though with less supporting data, the organization of industry as a "modern feudalism." As he expressed it: ". . . our Modern Feudalism is most apparent in the erection of great and irresponsible rulers of industry, whose power, like that of the feudal barons, burdens the people, and even overshadows the government which gave it existence. The only important distinction is, that in the old days of force, the power of feudalism was measured by thousands of warriors; in the days of modern plutocracy, its power is measured by millions of money." "Modern Feudalism," *North American Review*, March 1887, p. 290.

"rob the body of our citizens by depriving them of the benefits of natural competition." [2]

What Congress Did About Trusts

The Fifty-first Congress lost little time in carrying out what apparently was a mandate of the people to curb combinations in restraint of trade. Senator Sherman of Ohio introduced Senate Bill No. 1 on the day it convened. It was a flat declaration in favor of Adam Smith's obvious and simple system of natural liberty—"free and full competition," as Senator Sherman expressed it.[3]

The debates in Congress suggested no intention to abandon the goal of Senator Sherman's bill: the preservation of free competition.[4] The only serious difference of opinion in Congress was over how to accomplish this purpose without going beyond constitutional limitations on its powers. The Senate Judiciary Committee, under the leadership of Senator Hoar of Massachusetts, preferring legal terminology to loose phrases suggestive of campaign oratory, rewrote the bill entirely. The Senate passed the new measure with a single dissenting vote, that of Senator Blodgett of New Jersey, whose state had just fatefully made it legal for corporations to own stock in other corporations. The House passed the Senate bill without opposition and, unchanged, it became law on July 2, 1890.

2. Thomas H. McKee, *The National Conventions and Platforms of All Political Parties,* Friedenwald, Baltimore, 1906, pp. 241 and 235, respectively.

For a concise review of the political and economic agitation that led to antitrust legislation, see *Mandeville Farms* v. *American Crystal Sugar Co.,* 334 U.S. 219 (1948).

3. Senator Sherman had introduced and the Senate had adopted a resolution in the Fiftieth Congress authorizing the Senate Finance Committee to inquire into and report "such measures as it may deem expedient to set aside, control, restrain, or prohibit all arrangements, contracts, agreements, trusts, or combinations between persons or corporations, made with a view, or which tend to prevent *free and full competition* . . . with such penalties and provisions . . . as will tend to preserve freedom of trade and production." *Congressional Record,* 50th Cong., 1st sess., 1888, Vol. 19, Pt. 7, p. 6041. Italics supplied. Section 1 of Senate Bill No. 1 used similar language and had a similar objective—limited, however, to bring it within the scope of the interstate commerce power.

4. Senator Allison of Iowa said the evil in combinations was their *control of prices* (*Congressional Record,* 51st Cong., 1st sess., 1890, Vol. 21, Pt. 3, pp. 2470-71); Senator Pugh of Alabama said that "the existence of trusts and combinations *to limit the production* of articles of consumption entering into interstate and foreign commerce *for the purpose of destroying competition in production* and thereby increasing prices to consumers has become a matter of public history . . . and the universal inquiry is, What shall be done that can be done by Congress to prevent or mitigate these evils and intolerable exactions?" (*ibid.,* p. 2558; italics supplied). Other comments of like import included those of Senator Morgan of Alabama (*ibid.,* p. 2608) and Senator George of Mississippi (*ibid.,* p. 3147). However, Senator Platt of Connecticut was disturbed over the scope of the bill and argued that it "proceeds upon the false assumption that all competition is beneficent to the country" (*ibid.,* p. 2729).

The Meaning of the Sherman Act

On its face the Sherman Act is comprehensive and tough. Literally applied, it would have branded many businessmen as buccaneers and put them behind bars. Section 1 makes illegal "Every contract, combination in the form of trust or otherwise, or conspiracy, in restraint of trade or commerce among the several States"; and Section 2 prohibits a person from monopolizing or attempting to monopolize, or combining or conspiring with other persons "to monopolize any part of the trade or commerce among the several States, or with foreign nations." [5]

The sweeping language of the statute reflects the contemporary hostility of the American people to monopoly and the concentration of economic power. Congress apparently believed, as did the classical and neoclassical economists, that organization of society along competitive lines more or less automatically protected the public interest and promoted the general welfare.[6] Nearly half a century later, commenting on Senator Sherman's resolution of 1888 for an inquiry as to appropriate measures for getting rid of "all arrangements . . . which tend to prevent free and full competition," the Supreme Court said: "This resolution explicitly presented the economic theory of the proponents of such legislation. The various bills introduced between 1888 and 1890 follow the theory of this resolution." [7] In the Court's view, Congress intended to outlaw all arrangements that tend to suppress competition and centralize control over markets.

Some students think that Congress aimed at something less than

5. U.S. Code, Title 15, c. 1. The Act provides criminal penalties in the form of a fine or imprisonment for not more than a year for each offense. The Act also directs the government to proceed civilly against offenders and authorizes the courts to enjoin violations or to permit seizure of goods shipped in interstate commerce pursuant to transactions that violate Section 1 of the Act. Finally, the Act provides that persons injured in their business by violations of the law may recover treble damages from the offenders.

6. This is not to suggest that congressmen were familiar with the writings of the economists. They may or may not have been, but by 1890 the basic ideas of classical economics had woven themselves into the fabric of everyday thought. Nor is it to suggest that Congress passed a well-considered measure. Congressmen apparently regarded the public demand for relief against the "Moloch of Monopoly" too urgent to be temporized with. Senator Platt of Connecticut ascribed the enactment of the Sherman Act to a desire "to get some bill headed: 'A Bill to Punish Trusts' with which to go to the country." L. A. Coolidge, *An Old-Fashioned Senator: Orville H. Platt*, Putnam's, New York, 1910, p. 444.

7. *Apex Hosiery Co.* v. *Leader*, 310 U.S. 469 (1940), at p. 494. The Court added: "The unanimity with which foes and supporters of the bill spoke of its aims as the *protection of free competition* permits use of the debates in interpreting the purpose of the Act." *Ibid.*, p. 495. Italics supplied.

this. Basing their opinions on isolated statements by Senators Sherman and Hoar and on the judicial interpretation of the antitrust act in the 1911 oil and tobacco cases, they argue that the congressional intent was merely to apply common-law principles to combinations in restraint of trade. Senator Hoar was explicit on this point. Congress, he said, had "affirmed the old doctrine of the common law in regard to all interstate and international commercial transactions, and . . . clothed the United States courts with authority to enforce that doctrine by injunction." [8] And Senator Sherman, at one point in his defense of his bill, said: "It does not announce a new principle of law, but applies old and well recognized principles of the common law to the complicated jurisdiction of our State and Federal governments."

The Common-Law Background of Antitrust Policy

Nevertheless, those who accept this view do not agree on what the common-law principles were. All scholars of the law recognize that the doctrine of "restraint of trade" early acquired a narrow technical meaning. It referred to covenants not to compete, which covenants were subordinate to, and constituted part of the consideration for, a contract such as the sale of a business, on the legality of which there was no doubt. A typical contract in restraint of trade was an agreement by a man selling out his business that he would not later re-enter the trade to compete with the buyer. Such agreements were meant to protect the value of what a buyer had bought and paid for—for example, good will, trade secrets, or technical know-how.

At first, all contracts in restraint of trade were adjudged invalid. They were considered contrary to public policy because, as long as law and custom discouraged transfers of residence or occupation among tradespeople, they tended to deprive a person of the opportunity to earn a living and the community of his skilled services. With the weakening of the rule of status and the growth of freedom in economic affairs, as first the guild system and then the mercantilist system became moribund, legal attitudes changed.

Gradually the courts came to distinguish between reasonable and unreasonable restraints of trade. A covenant not to compete was held valid, under the rule of reason, if the restriction was limited

8. *Congressional Record,* 51st Cong., 1st sess., 1890, Vol. 21, Pt. 4, p. 3146.

in space and time to an extent appropriate to the bona fide interests of the parties. To illustrate: A merchant selling his store in a county seat might perhaps be bound by a covenant to refrain from re-entering the same business within the next ten years anywhere in the county. But if the buyer were to exact a promise that the merchant selling out would never again in his lifetime resume the same line of business anywhere in the state, the covenant would probably be held unenforceable. So much for contracts in restraint of trade in the original, technical sense.

During the second half of the nineteenth century a quite different type of agreement not to compete became increasingly common, and for want of a better term, when such agreements came before the courts, lawyers and judges frequently referred to them as contracts in restraint of trade. When regional, or even nation-wide, markets first opened up, competition was quite severe and businessmen sought refuge from the costly readjustments and losses it entailed through combinations or agreements. In brief, they sought to free themselves from the forces of competitive markets and to subject markets to collective control by mutual promises to restrict output, divide markets, or fix prices.

When the parties sought to enforce such agreements to eliminate competition and centralize control of the market, the courts generally held them contrary to public policy and void. Occasionally, however, when one of these new-style agreements in restraint of trade did not embrace all the firms in the market, and more rarely even when it did, a court, applying the rule of reason, would uphold the contract. Implicit in a judicial finding of reasonableness was an assumption either that the agreement was harmless because ineffective, or that it operated only to protect the legitimate interests of the parties from ruinous competition.

Courts in a few states tacitly accepted the more than liberal doctrine that businessmen should be free in a private enterprise economy to make whatever voluntarily concerted arrangements they considered gainful. But the courts that did so usually inquired into how the combination had used its power. If they found no obvious abuse of power they upheld such agreements, invalidating only those that appeared to have used their collective power to exploit consumers or oppress rivals. Most state courts, however, condemned all agreements to restrict competition among business rivals, regardless of the conditions that prompted them and regardless of how they operated.[9]

Such, briefly, was the state of the common law on contracts in restraint of trade when the Sherman Act was passed.

Did Congress Intend to Apply the Rule of Reason?

Nothing in the history of the Sherman Act or its language supports the view that Congress contemplated that the courts would discriminate between reasonable and unreasonable restraints of trade when the sole object of the combination is restriction of competition among the parties and control of the market. Though a minority of state courts did make such a distinction in applying the common-law doctrine of restraint of trade to collusive agreements for sharing or controlling the market, the debates in Congress indicate that few congressmen were aware of the conflict in common-law decisions on this point.[10]

Apparently the Supreme Court correctly epitomized the objectives of the Sherman Act when, after a third of a century of vacillating interpretation of the law, it said: "The fundamental purpose of the Sherman Act was to secure equality of opportunity and protect the public against the evils commonly incident to the destruction of competition." [11]

9. Among the cases in which agreements to restrict competition were held invalid per se at common law were: *India Bagging Association* v. *B. Koch & Co.*, 14 La. 168 (1859); *Morris Run Coal Co.* v. *Barclay Coal Co.*, 68 Pa. 173 (1871); *Central Ohio Salt Co.* v. *Guthrie*, 35 Ohio 666 (1880); *DeWitt Wire-Cloth Co.* v. *New Jersey Wire-Cloth Co.*, 14 N.Y.Supp. 277 (1890); *Chapin* v. *Brown Brothers*, 83 Iowa 156 (1891); *More* v. *Bennett*, 140 Ill. 69 (1892); *People* v. *Milk Exchange*, 145 N.Y. 267 (1895). For discriminating analyses of this line of cases, consult Judge Taft's opinion in *U.S.* v. *Addyston Pipe & Steel Co.*, 85 Fed. 271 (1899), and Milton Handler, *A Study of the Construction and Enforcement of the Federal Antitrust Laws*, TNEC Monograph No. 38, Washington, 1941.

"Trusts" were held illegal, as contrary to public policy, in *Mallory* v. *Hanaur Oil-Works*, 86 Tenn. 598 (1888); *State* v. *Nebraska Distilling Co.*, 29 Neb. 700 (1890); *People* v. *North River Sugar Refining Co.*, 121 N.Y. 582 (1890); *State ex rel.* v. *Standard Oil Co.*, 49 Ohio 137 (1892). Other combinations in restraint of trade involving transfers of property were condemned in *Richardson* v. *Buhl*, 77 Mich. 632 (1889); *Distilling & Cattle Feeding Co.* v. *People*, 156 Ill. 448 (1895); *Craft* v. *McConoughy*, 79 Ill. 346 (1875); *Emery* v. *Ohio Candle Co.*, 47 Ohio 320 (1890).

10. Since lawyers even today do not agree on this subject, it is unlikely that many congressmen had an informed opinion on it, or that those who did were in agreement. But whatever the legislators may have contemplated doing, the law they passed prohibited *every* combination in restraint of trade.

11. *Ramsey* v. *Bill Posters Association*, 260 U.S. 501 (1923), at p. 512. In applying the law both before and after 1923, the Court has often expressed the same view of

Assuming that such was the fundamental aim of the law, was there any need for, or advantage to be gained from, a rule of reason in its application? In 1897 the Supreme Court in the Trans-Missouri Freight Association case rejected the rule of reason over the vigorous dissent of four justices. And until the Court reversed itself, without explicitly acknowledging such action, in the Standard Oil and American Tobacco cases of 1911, the position set forth in the Trans-Missouri case was the law. In 1909, twelve years after the Supreme Court had rejected the rule of reason, Congress rejected a proposal to amend the Sherman Act so that only combinations in *unreasonable* restraint of trade would be unlawful. In recommending rejection of this amendment the Senate Judiciary Committee said:

> To inject into the act the question of whether an agreement or combination is *reasonable* or *unreasonable* would render the act as a criminal or penal statute indefinite and uncertain, and hence, to that extent, utterly nugatory and void, and would practically amount to a repeal of that part of the act. . . . To destroy or undermine it at the present juncture, when combinations are on the increase, . . . would be a calamity.[12]

Actual Scope of Sherman Act

The historical facts indicate that Congress wanted to go as far as it could in condemning combination to control the market. Congressmen recognized that the courts would have to decide, on the facts in particular cases, whether a contract or combination constituted a restraint of trade at all—that is, whether it substituted control of the market for control by the market, whether it was an expression of freedom of enterprise or a limitation or obstruction of such

---

its purpose. In *American Column & Lumber Co.* v. *U.S.*, the Court said: " . . . it has repeatedly been held . . . that the purpose of the statute is to maintain free competition in interstate commerce." 257 U.S. 377 (1921), at p. 400. In *U.S.* v. *Trenton Potteries Co.* the Court said: ". . . it cannot be doubted that the Sherman Law and the judicial decisions interpreting it are based upon the assumption that the public interest is best protected from the evils of monopoly and price control by the maintenance of competition." 273 U.S. 392 (1927), at p. 397. See, to the same effect, *National Cotton Oil Co.* v. *Texas*, 197 U.S. 115 (1906), at p. 129; and *Fashion Originators Guild* v. *FTC*, 312 U.S. 457 (1941), at p. 464.

Despite the frequent reiteration of clear pronouncements of the foregoing kind, the Court has sometimes seemed to be unaware of their practical implications. See, for example, *U.S.* v. *United Shoe Machinery Co.*, 247 U.S. 32 (1918); *Buckeye Powder Co.* v. *E. I. du Pont de Nemours Powder Co., et al.*, 248 U.S. 55 (1918); *U.S.* v. *United States Steel Corp.*, 251 U.S. 417 (1920); *International Shoe Co.* v. *FTC*, 280 U.S. 291 (1930); and *Appalachian Coals, Inc.* v. *U.S.*, 288 U.S. 344 (1933).

12. *Amending Antitrust Act*, S.Rept. 848, 60th Cong., 2d sess., pp. 10-11.

freedom. In a dynamic economy obviously a court must exercise intelligent discrimination between freedom of contract to facilitate the growth of business enterprise and freedom of contract to eliminate independent enterprise and establish monopoly. Otherwise the Act would itself become a restraint on trade. Perhaps Chief Justice Hughes was right in conceiving the Act as a "charter of freedom" with a "generality and adaptability comparable to that found to be desirable in constitutional provisions." [13]

The Sherman Act was apparently broad enough to catch every arrangement in interstate commerce that undermined the competitive process. If wisely interpreted it should have made a substantial contribution to the preservation of free enterprise. And in some ways it did.[14]

Nevertheless, within a decade after its passage, American industry experienced an epoch-making transformation. Within the brief span of a half-dozen years captains of finance had organized hundreds of combinations with a total capitalization running into billions of dollars. None attained complete monopoly of its market. But virtually all achieved a significant measure of market control or at least weakened competition. On every hand, combinations transformed markets of many sellers into markets dominated by a few. How did this come about? A series of legislative and judicial developments contributed to it.

Intercorporate Stockholding and the Concentration of Economic Power

While congressmen were devising ways and means to prevent business firms from consolidating control of the market, New Jersey in 1888 enacted a law permitting the corporations it chartered to hold stock in other corporations. Though in several states a few corporations had by special charter previously been granted this privilege, New Jersey was the first state to make it freely available to all comers. The significance of this event to the combination movement can hardly be exaggerated.[15]

13. *Appalachian Coals, Inc.* v. *U.S.*, cited above, pp. 259-60.
14. See text, pp. 284-304.
15. Edward S. Mead expressed the opinion that the New Jersey statute "nullified the antitrust laws" of other states. See his *Trust Finance*, Appleton, New York, 1903, p. 39. See also p. 31 of this study.

Without the holding company, fusion of many independent concerns into a single giant business unit towering over all the rest in its particular branch of industry would have been difficult indeed to accomplish. New Jersey had created a legal instrument for centralizing control of rival corporations—an instrument that could serve as a ready substitute for the trustee device, virtually outlawed by the courts in Ohio and New York.[16]

The sugar trust promptly took advantage of the timely opening that New Jersey had blasted in the legal walls against monopoly. It transferred the shares it held in affiliated sugar-refining companies to the American Sugar Refining Company, a New Jersey holding company organized to replace the outlawed trust, and then dissolved these affiliated corporations, which, like the North River Sugar Refining Company, offended the law of other states. Other "trusts" quickly followed the lead of the sugar trust. So easy was it to form consolidations in this way that once the monetary crisis of the early 1890's was past the merger movement went into high gear. That was in 1897 and not until 1904 did it come to a temporary halt, when the Supreme Court ruled that the holding company device, though sanctioned by state law, did not exempt a combination in restraint of interstate trade from the penalties of the Sherman Act.[17]

An Illusory Distinction: Commerce and Manufacture

Another event that helps explain the failure of the Sherman Act to stop the combination movement was the Supreme Court's decision

16. *State* v. *Standard Oil Co.*, 49 Ohio St. 137, 30 N.E. 279 (1892); *People* v. *North River Sugar Refining Co.*, previously cited. In the latter case, the court ordered the forfeiture of defendant's charter because it had exceeded its powers as a New York corporation by exchanging its shares for trust certificates issued by the unincorporated Sugar Refineries Company that H. O. Havemeyer and his associates had organized two years before. The decision turned primarily on the loss of the North River Company's corporate independence, though the court did stigmatize the trust as a conspiracy to monopolize the sugar industry. Eighteen separate refineries had already been united under the trust's control.

17. *Northern Securities Co.* v. *U.S.*, 193 U.S. 197 (1904). The Hill-Morgan interests had organized the Northern Securities Company to centralize control of the Northern Pacific and the Great Northern, and thereby assure their continued domination of the Burlington, of whose voting stock Northern Pacific and Great Northern together held a majority. The primary objective of the maneuver was to thwart Harriman's campaign to gain control of the Burlington road.

About this episode Milton Handler says, "After a study had been made of the corporation laws of the various states, the managers decided to incorporate in New Jersey because the power to purchase, hold and dispose of corporate securities in large amounts could beyond question be legally granted to a corporation." "Industrial Mergers and the Anti-Trust Laws," *Columbia Law Review*, February 1932, p. 187, footnote.

in the first antitrust case to come before it, the Knight case.[18] The government challenged the legality of the American Sugar Refining Company's purchase of a controlling stock interest in four companies with refineries at Philadelphia, whereby it increased its control of the domestic production of sugar to 98 per cent. But these transactions were only the latest steps in a series that clearly revealed a persistent effort to monopolize the sugar industry.[19]

When Claus Spreckels, a leading Pacific Coast refiner and owner of large cane plantations in Hawaii, opened a refinery in Philadelphia, a price war immediately ensued which soon forced Spreckels to capitulate. When he sold out to the trust, the other Philadelphia refiners followed suit, giving American Sugar a virtual monopoly. With a target seemingly made to order for antitrust prosecution, the Department of Justice went into action.

Sherman Act No Bar to Monopoly in Manufacturing

Although the Supreme Court recognized that American Sugar had, in effect, as the government charged, "monopolized the manufacture and sale of refined sugar in the United States," [20] it held that the company had not violated the antitrust law. This anomalous outcome was the result of judicial reaffirmation of a distinction between "production" and "commerce" that had plagued the Court for almost a century in its efforts to draw a sharp line between federal and state jurisdiction over an economy that was progressively becoming more closely integrated in all its parts.[21] Without looking too

18. *U.S.* v. *E. C. Knight Co.,* 156 U.S. 1 (1895).

19. Even before the transformation of the trust from the Sugar Refineries Company into the American Sugar Refining Company, as recounted above, it had acquired control of about 80 per cent of the refined-sugar output of the country.

H. O. Havemeyer, chief promoter of the sugar trust, expressed his notion of corporate responsibility before the U.S. Industrial Commission in the following colloquy: "Q. You think, then, that when a corporation is chartered by the State, offers stock to the public, and is one in which the public is interested, that the public has no right to know what its earning power is or to subject them to any inspection whatever, that the people may not buy this stock blindly? A. Yes; that is my theory. Let the buyer beware; that covers the whole business. You cannot wet nurse people from the time they are born until they die. They have got to wade in and get stuck, and that is the way men are educated and cultivated." U.S. Industrial Commission, Reports, Vol. 1, p. 123. Quoted in Eliot Jones, *The Trust Problem in the United States,* Macmillan, New York, 1921, p. 115.

20. *U.S.* v. *E. C. Knight Co.,* cited above, pp. 3-4.

21. This sophistical distinction continued to bedevil constitutional construction—and the development of the national economy—for half a century. Its ghost was not finally laid until the 1940's. The leading cases repudiating the Knight doctrine are: *U.S.* v. *Darby,* 312 U.S. 100 (1941); *Wickard* v. *Filburn,* 317 U.S. 111 (1942);

closely at the facts, the Court declared that "commerce succeeds to manufacture and is not a part of it."

Moreover, the Court indicated that Congress was helpless to protect the public against a proprietary consolidation like the sugar trust.

> Congress did not attempt . . . to assert the power to deal with monopoly directly as such; or to *limit and restrict the rights of corporations created by the States* or the citizens of the States in the acquisition, control or disposition of property . . . or to make criminal the acts of persons in the acquisition and control of property which the States of their residence or creation sanctioned or permitted.[22]

The opinion appeared to invite businessmen to do what Congress had forbidden them to do. A casuistic construction of the commerce clause smoothed the way for the great combination movement that rounded out the century.

Mr. Justice Harlan, dissenting vigorously, indicated the broad significance of the ruling in these words:

> While the opinion of the Court in this case does not declare the act of 1890 to be unconstitutional, it defeats the main object for which it was passed. . . . This view of the scope of the act leaves the public, so far as national power is concerned, entirely at the mercy of combinations . . .[23]

Responsible public officials and enterprising businessmen expressed their belief—the one in words, the other in deeds—that after this decision the Sherman Act was no barrier to the monopolization of American industry. Attorney General Harmon, replying in February 1896 to a House resolution requesting a report on enforcement of the Sherman Act, told the Congress that the Act

> . . . does not apply to the most complete monopolies acquired by unlawful combinations of concerns which are naturally competitive though

---

U.S. v. *Southeastern Underwriters Association,* 322 U.S. 533 (1944); and *Mandeville Farms* v. *American Crystal Sugar Co.,* previously cited.

22. *U.S.* v. *E. C. Knight Co.,* p. 16. Italics supplied. The judges in interpreting the law so as to emasculate it in its application to corporate mergers may have been influenced less by logic than by their social background and their economic interests as lawyers by profession. Their belief that big business stood for economic progress and could alone assure America its "manifest destiny" to rank with, if not outrank, other great powers is enough to explain their decision. But it does not mean that it was a good reason for emasculating the law. It is not hard for men skilled in dialectics to reconcile general principles with specific factual situations that to the untutored mind appear conflicting. For a discussion of the relations between big business and politics, see Matthew Josephson, *The Politicos, 1865–1896,* Harcourt, Brace, New York, 1938; *idem, The President Makers,* Harcourt, Brace, New York, 1940; and Ferdinand Lundberg, *America's Sixty Families,* Vanguard Press, New York, 1937.

23. *U.S.* v. *E. C. Knight Co.,* pp. 42-43.

they in fact control the markets of the entire country, if engaging in interstate commerce be merely one of the incidents to their business and not its direct and immediate object. The virtual effect of this is to exclude from the operation of the law, manufacturers and producers of every class.[24]

With the chief law officer of the country thus forced to concede the legality of combinations which, to most people, seemed clearly to restrict interstate trade, financiers and promoters launched a combination movement which in intensity and scope has had no equal in American history. When it had spent itself, imperfect competition had replaced effective competition over large sections of American industry.

As the movement gained headway, the Supreme Court indirectly gave further impetus to it by holding in the Addyston Pipe case that a loose association of rival manufacturers that fixed prices in interstate sales was an unlawful conspiracy in restraint of trade.[25] With price fixing among competitors outlawed, business rivals anxious to eliminate competition among themselves sought refuge in outright mergers.

Introduction of the Rule of Reason

The Northern Securities case put an end to the widespread notion, based on the Knight ruling, that the use of a corporation as a vehicle for consolidating control of an industry by buying up competing plants gave immunity to antitrust attack, as long as the corporation kept within the charter powers conferred on it by the state of its incorporation. But the damage done to competition while this notion

24. See Felix H. Levy, "The Federal Antitrust Law and the 'Rule of Reason,'" *Virginia Law Review,* 1913, p. 192. Ex-President Taft, while a professor of law at Yale, evaluated the Court's decision in the Knight case as follows: "The effect of the decision in the Knight case upon the popular mind, and indeed upon Congress as well, was to discourage hope that the statute could be used to accomplish its manifest purpose and curb the great industrial trusts which, by the acquisition of all or a large percentage of the plants engaged in the manufacture of a commodity, by the dismantling of some and regulating the output of others, were making every effort to restrict production, control prices, and monopolize the business. So strong was the impression made by the Knight case that both Mr. Olney and Mr. Cleveland concluded that the evil must be controlled through State legislation, and not through a national statute, and they said so in their communications to Congress." *The Antitrust Act and the Supreme Court,* Harper, New York, 1914, p. 60.

25. *Addyston Pipe & Steel Co.* v. *U.S.,* 175 U.S. 211 (1899). Six independent manufacturers of cast iron pipe, controlling about 60 per cent of the total capacity in their major sales territory, had through a bonus scheme eliminated all price competition among themselves. The Court rejected defendants' argument that the power of Congress to regulate interstate commerce does not include the power to prohibit private contracts even though they directly obstruct commerce.

was current was not easily undone. Six years later another judicial development, the adoption of the rule of reason, had a devitalizing effect on antitrust policy second only to the Knight case fiasco. By declaring in the Standard Oil and American Tobacco cases that only unreasonable restraints of trade violate the antitrust law, the Supreme Court opened the way to legal justification of mergers, no matter how comprehensive or powerful, provided only they act with moderation. These two trusts, typical of the many formed in the last quarter of the nineteenth century, had gained ascendancy by ruthless methods.

As early as 1879 the Standard Oil Trust had centralized in a board of trustees control of most of the petroleum-refining, transportation, and marketing facilities of the country. After the Supreme Court of Ohio struck down this arrangement, Rockefeller and his associates formed the Standard Oil Company of New Jersey, under that state's holding company statute, and continued as they had before to monopolize the industry. Through secret railroad rebates, a spy system to check on the business of its rivals, bogus independents, local price discrimination, and cutthroat competition, Standard Oil drove out competitors and maintained its supremacy.

American Tobacco's control of the tobacco market was about as great as Standard Oil's over the oil market, and American Tobacco's record was about as bad as Standard Oil's. In 1890 James B. Duke and his associates got effective control of the supply of cigarettes by consolidating the five leading manufacturers in the American Tobacco Company. With 95 per cent of the cigarette market thus firmly in hand, American Tobacco used its strategic position—and monopoly profits—in this field to invade and subjugate to its control one after another the markets for other tobacco products. It organized or bought out a big consolidation in every branch of the industry: American Snuff, American Cigar, American Stogie, Continental Tobacco (plug), and McAndrews & Forbes (tin foil and other accessories). Altogether it spent more than $50 million acquiring some thirty corporations, and in all of these transactions it obtained a covenant from the former owners that they would not again engage in the tobacco business.

In carrying out its monopoly program it cut prices where and when needed to ruin or subdue less powerful rivals. It used so-called "fighting brands" and bogus independents to avoid the appearance of discrimination, and required tobacco jobbers to refuse to handle the products of American Tobacco's competitors. In short, it conducted a ceaseless, unrelenting, and effective campaign to dominate and exploit to the hilt the domestic market for tobacco and its products.

In both cases the Supreme Court held that the defendants had conspired to monopolize and restrain interstate trade in violation of Sections 1 and 2 of the Sherman Act. But in condemning them as antitrust-law violators and ordering their dissolution, the Court went out of its way to assure other trusts that if they mended their ways and did not abuse their power they need not fear the penalties of the law. A majority of the Court under Chief Justice White's leadership, and over the vigorous dissent of Mr. Justice Harlan, held out an olive branch to big business. The olive branch was labelled the rule of reason.

Judicial Rationalization

The Chief Justice took pains to deny the generality of the language of Section 1 of the Act. Not every combination or conspiracy in restraint of trade is to be regarded as illegal, he declared, but only those that unduly or unreasonably restrain trade. To harmonize this interpretation with the plain language of the Act, he appealed to common-law principles, which he interpreted as condemning restraints of trade, of whatever kind, only if their terms were unreasonable or if in their operation they injured the public interest. In effect, according to his view reasonable restraints were not, at common law, restraints of trade at all.

On its face such reasoning is acceptable. Its flaw is under the surface: its failure to distinguish between the two kinds of restraint of trade the common law recognized—ancillary covenants and collusive agreements. Congress had certainly not intended that the courts interpret the Sherman law to prevent the sale of good will by prohibiting an engagement by the seller of an established business to stay out of that particular trade for a specified period, or to prevent the formation of an ordinary partnership by prohibiting an engagement by each partner not to compete with the firm as long as the partnership continued. Such arrangements are ordinarily designed to promote, not to restrain, trade. Nor is there any reason to believe that Congress intended always to prevent the merger of two or more business rivals. Congress was concerned solely with the elimination of competition in interstate markets. The merger of two business rivals will, of course, eliminate competition between them. But whether it restrains trade—that is, restricts competition in the market—will depend on whether the combined units produce enough of the total output to be able to set the market price. Without power to control the market, there can be no restraint of trade at all.

Good Trusts and Bad Trusts

The judicial amendment of the Sherman Act by introduction of the rule of reason paved the way for economic as well as legal mischief by subtly shifting the distinction between reasonable and unreasonable restraints of trade to reasonable and unreasonable restrictions on competition. In so doing the courts became more concerned with the manner in which market power was used than with the acquisition of such power itself. But they shied away from testing trade combinations by their economic consequences directly. Instead, they looked to the intent of the parties. As the Chief Justice put it in the Standard Oil case:

> . . . dread of enhancement of prices and of other *wrongs* which it was thought would flow from the *undue* limitation on competitive conditions . . . led, as a matter of public policy, to the prohibition or treating as illegal all contracts or acts which were *unreasonably restrictive* of competitive conditions, either from the nature or character of the contract or act or where the *surrounding circumstances* were such as to justify the conclusion that they had not been entered into or performed with the legitimate purpose of reasonably forwarding personal interest and developing trade, but on the contrary were of such a character as to give rise to the inference or presumption that they had been entered into or done with the *intent to do wrong* to the general public . . .[26]

Likewise, the American Tobacco opinion emphasized the significance of the abuse of monopoly power.

> Considering then the undisputed facts which we have previously stated, it remains only to determine whether they establish that the acts, contracts, agreements, combinations, etc., which were assailed were of such an *unusual and wrongful* character as to bring them within the prohibitions of the law.[27]

The way these trusts acquired and used their power over the

26. *Standard Oil Co.* v. *U.S.*, 221 U.S. 1 (1911), at p. 58. Italics supplied.
27. *U.S.* v. *American Tobacco Co.*, 221 U.S. 106 (1911), at p. 181. Italics supplied.

market was plainly the gist of their offense. Under the new interpretation of the antitrust law, a consolidation that wished to avoid its penalties would have to discover—and conform to—a judicial code of business morality. It was an "ever-present manifestation" of "conscious wrong-doing" that brought judicial condemnation now, not primarily monopoly power achieved through combinations and conspiracies. The rule of reason, in effect, then, distinguished between good and bad trusts.[28]

The Significance of Size

The condemnation of predatory practices in the Standard Oil and the American Tobacco cases afforded no clear guide to the canons of business conduct that the courts would approve. But during the next decade a series of judicial opinions made it increasingly clear that bigness was not to be confused with badness and that obtaining power over the market through combining business rivals did not of itself violate the Sherman Act. For example, in the Keystone Watch case, holding unlawful a merger of rival watch-case manufacturers, the court said:

> Size does not of itself restrain trade or injure the public; on the contrary, it may increase trade and benefit the consumer; but, if the power given by

28. Apparently the rule was dredged up out of the remote and irrelevant past partly to relieve businessmen of uneasiness occasioned by the lower courts' decisions in these two cases. The lower courts had taken a more literal view of the Sherman Act. That Standard Oil and American Tobacco had eliminated competition among business rivals by centralizing control over them was enough for the lower courts. As the trial court said in the Standard Oil case: "The principal company . . . has prevented, and is preventing, any competition in interstate and international commerce in petroleum and its products between its subsidiary companies and between those companies and itself." *U.S.* v. *Standard Oil Co.,* 173 Fed. 177 (1909), at p. 183. In the American Tobacco case the court in expressing a similar view held immaterial the business methods of the American Tobacco Company, the course of prices after the merger, or the way in which the combination had used its power. The essence of law violation as the lower court conceived it was the elimination of competition among business rivals. The court said: "The formation of the original American Tobacco Company, which antedated the Sherman Act, may be disregarded. But the present American Tobacco Company was formed by subsequent merger of the original company with the Continental Tobacco Company and the Consolidated Tobacco Company, and when that merger became complete two of its existing competitors in the tobacco business were eliminated. . . . Each one of these purchases of existing concerns . . . was a contract and combination in restraint of competition existing when it was entered into, and that is sufficient to bring it within the ban of this drastic statute." *U.S.* v. *American Tobacco Co.,* 164 Fed. 700 (1908), at pp. 702-03.

Though these expositions of the law doubtless went beyond congressional intent, the trial courts were on the right track. Congress apparently had intended to prevent markets regulated by decentralized decision making from being transformed by combinations into markets controlled by centralized decision making. Obviously an intelligent application of the Sherman Act requires discrimination in the application of this principle, but in the light of the facts before them in the Standard Oil and the American Tobacco cases the lower courts had certainly not perverted it.

the volume of a particular business is improperly used to injure either a competitor or the public . . . the mischief either done or threatened is condemned by the statute. . . . Competitors must not be oppressed or coerced; prices must not be arbitrarily fixed or maintained; an artificial scarcity must not be produced; moreover, the public is also injured if the quality is impaired . . . if the wages of the laborer be arbitrarily reduced, and if the price of raw material be artificially depressed.[29]

In sustaining the government's charges that the Eastman Kodak Company had unlawfully monopolized the trade in photographic materials, another court declared in 1915:

. . . it is undisputed that the Eastman Kodak Company controlled approximately between seventy per cent and eighty per cent of the entire trade at the time of the filing of the bill, and had accordingly obtained a monopoly thereof.[30]

But this was not enough, by itself, to show a violation of the law, according to the court.

There is no limit in this country to the extent to which a business may grow, and the acquisitions of property in the present case, standing alone, would not be deemed an illegal monopoly; but when such acquisitions are accompanied by an intent to monopolize and restrain interstate trade by an arbitrary use of the power resulting from a large business to eliminate a weaker competitor, then they no doubt come within the meaning of the statute.[31]

Rule of Reason and "Monopoly" in Tin Cans

Though, because of their predatory practices or similar abuses, some combinations that greatly weakened competition fell afoul of the antitrust law, even as interpreted under the rule of reason, better behaved combinations with equal or greater power over the market escaped its penalties. Among the latter was the American Can Company. This company had acquired control of more than a hundred independent makers of cans producing more than 90 per cent of all the cans made in the United States, and in an antitrust suit in 1916 the court found as a fact that the company "was organized to monopolize interstate trade in cans." [32] Nevertheless, the court refused to order its dissolution.

29. *U.S.* v. *Keystone Watch Case Co.*, 218 Fed. 502 (1915), at pp. 510 and 518.
30. *U.S.* v. *Eastman Kodak Co.*, 226 Fed. 62 (1915), at p. 79.
31. *Ibid.*, p. 80.
32. *U.S.* v. *American Can Co.*, 230 Fed. 859 (1916).

The court recognized clearly that the intent of Congress was to preserve effective competition, an economy in which power is diffused. In the words of a singularly penetrating opinion:

> . . . one of the designs of the framers of the Anti-Trust Act was to prevent the concentration in a few hands of control over great industries. They preferred a social and industrial state in which there should be many independent producers. . . . The law wished that industrial and trading corporations shall operate under the checks and balances imposed by free and unrestrained competition . . . Congress wished to preserve competition because, among other reasons, it did not know what to substitute for the restraints competition imposes. . . .
>
> Size and power are themselves facts some of whose consequences do not depend upon the way in which they were created or in which they were used. It is easy to conceive that they might be acquired honestly and used as fairly as men who are in business for the legitimate purpose of making money for themselves and their associates could be expected to use them, human nature being what it is, and for all that constitute a public danger, or at all events give rise to difficult social, industrial and political problems.[33]

Though this is an acute analysis of antitrust policy, the resolution to follow through on its implications was lacking. The court was strongly impressed by the fact that for some time before the filing of the petition American Can "had done nothing of which any competitor or any consumer of cans complains, *or anything which strikes a disinterested outsider as unfair or unethical.*" [34] It observed, also, that "Those in the trade are satisfied with it. They do not want it dissolved." [35] So, in the light of the rule of reason, the court was "frankly reluctant to destroy so finely adjusted an industrial machine as the record shows defendant to be," and it refused to do so.[36]

Big Steel: Another "Good" Trust

The Steel Corporation case drew more distinctly the line between good and bad trusts.[37] The Steel Corporation was organized in 1901

33. *Ibid.*, pp. 901-02.
34. *Ibid.*, p. 861. Italics supplied.
35. *Ibid.*, p. 903.
36. The court offered to retain the bill without ordering the company's dissolution, but "reserving the right to do so whenever, if ever, it shall be made to appear that the size and power of the defendant, brought about as they originally were, are being used to the injury of the public." The government, not satisfied, appealed to the Supreme Court, but on June 6, 1921, moved to withdraw the appeal on the ground that the Supreme Court's decision in the steel case made further proceedings unwarranted.
37. *U.S.* v. *United States Steel Corp.*, 251 U.S. 417 (1920).

as a consolidation of three principal groups of interests—Morgan, Carnegie, and Moore-Gates—comprising twelve independent steel-producing companies. These in turn were consolidations of more than one hundred formerly independent steel producers. When organized the Steel Corporation made about 45 per cent of domestic pig iron, 66 per cent of steel ingots and castings, 66 per cent of Bessemer steel rails, 60 per cent of steel plates and sheets, and about 72 per cent of wire rods. During the first decade of its life it absorbed several more independents and collaborated in one way or another with its remaining rivals to stabilize steel prices. It had given up most of these practices, however, before the government instituted its anti-trust suit.

The trial court gave judgment for the defendant and the Supreme Court affirmed. Mr. Justice McKenna's opinion for the majority was in effect an encomium for the Steel Corporation. He found no fault with its behavior.

> It resorted to none of the brutalities or tyrannies that the cases illustrate of other combinations. It did not secure freight rebates; it did not increase its profits by reducing the wages of its employees—whatever it did was not at the expense of labor; it did not increase its profits by lowering the quality of its products, nor creating an artificial scarcity of them; it did not oppress or coerce its competitors . . .; it did not undersell its competitors in some localities by reducing its prices there below those maintained elsewhere . . .; it did not obtain customers by secret rebates . . .; there was no evidence that it attempted to crush its competitors or drive them out of the market.[38]

As the Steel Corporation had followed a policy of live and let live, the Court was not disturbed by its position in the market. The majority declared flatly:

> . . . the law does not make mere size an offense or the existence of *unexerted power* an offense; . . . [it] *requires overt acts* and trusts to its prohibition of them and its power to repress or punish them. It does not compel competition nor require all that is possible.[39]

International Harvester: Still Another "Good" Trust

International Harvester was organized in 1901 as a combination of the five leading manufacturers of harvesting machinery. At the time the antitrust suit was filed it controlled about two thirds of the

38. *Ibid.*, p. 441.
39. *Ibid.*, p. 451. Italics supplied.

domestic sales of agricultural implements.[40] In rejecting the government's demand in 1927 for a decree that would be more effective in loosening its monopolistic hold on the industry, the Supreme Court again gave its blessing to size and unabused power.

> The law . . . does not make the mere size of a corporation, however impressive, or the existence of unexerted power on its part, an offense, when unaccompanied by unlawful conduct in the exercise of power . . . the fact that competitors may see proper, in the exercise of their own judgment, to follow the prices of another manufacturer does not establish any suppression of competition nor show any sinister domination.[41]

In taking this position the Court noted that International Harvester had not adopted the predatory practices on which some other business consolidations had flourished. Moreover, under the consent decree it had already split off two of its constituent units.

The Rule of Reason and Loose Combinations

In thus applying the rule of reason federal courts gave their blessing to outright mergers, even though the mergers centralized power over the market, provided the companies avoided predatory practices. Meanwhile the courts, with steadfast inconsistency, refused to apply a similar rule to mere agreements among business rivals to fix prices, restrict production, and otherwise rig markets. Both before and for at least two decades after the Standard Oil and American Tobacco cases, judges held that such collusive agreements to stifle competition were outlawed by the Sherman Act, regardless of the reasonableness of the prices fixed or of the proportion of the market controlled by the parties. Here the courts applied no doctrine of reasonableness, or if they did they regarded as unreasonable all contracts fixing prices among competitors supplying a common market.

This viewpoint found classic expression in the Trenton Potteries case in 1927.[42] In the District Court a jury had convicted the de-

40. *U.S.* v. *International Harvester Co.,* 274 U.S. 693 (1927). The government had brought suit under the antitrust statute in April 1912. The District Court upheld the government's allegations. Defendant appealed, but moved to dismiss in October 1918, and consented to a dissolution decree in November 1918. The government petitioned for a modification of the decree in July 1925, on the ground that the decree afforded inadequate relief against the illegal combination. The Supreme Court found for the defendant.

41. *Ibid.,* pp. 708-09.

42. *U.S.* v. *Trenton Potteries Co.,* previously cited. In this case the Supreme Court,

fendants, who together manufactured 82 per cent of the output of vitreous pottery, of combining to fix and maintain uniform prices and to limit sales to so-called "legitimate jobbers." In closing the case the judge advised the jury that if it found the defendants had made the agreements complained of, it might return a verdict of guilty without regard to their good intentions in restricting sales to selected jobbers or to the reasonableness of the prices fixed, as such agreements were of themselves unreasonable restraints. In upholding the verdict the Supreme Court said:

> The aim and result of every price fixing agreement, if effective, is the elimination of one form of competition. The power to fix prices, whether reasonably exercised or not, involves power to control the market and to fix arbitrary and unreasonable prices. The reasonable price fixed today may through economic and business change become the unreasonable price of tomorrow. Once established, it may be maintained unchanged because of the absence of competition secured by the agreement for a price reasonable when fixed. Agreements which create such potential power may well be held to be in themselves unreasonable or unlawful restraints, without the necessity of minute inquiry whether a particular price is reasonable or unreasonable as fixed, without placing on the government in enforcing the Sherman Law the burden of ascertaining from day to day whether it has become unreasonable through the mere variation of economic conditions. Moreover, in the absence of express legislation requiring it, we should hesitate to adopt a construction making the difference between legal and illegal conduct in the field of business relations depend upon so uncertain a test as whether prices are reasonable—a determination which can be satisfactorily made only after a complete survey of our economic organization and a choice between rival philosophies.[43]

Consistency in Application

If this is good law and good economics, as it seems to be, then the doctrines enunciated in the American Can, the United States Steel, and the International Harvester cases were bad law and bad economics. What the courts did not see, or ignored, in those cases is (1) that a company need not have a complete monopoly to have power over prices, and (2) that, if it has such power, it must use it,

referring to the Trans-Missouri Freight Association case, said: ". . . it has since often been decided and always assumed, that uniform price-fixing by those controlling in any substantial manner a trade or business in interstate commerce is prohibited by the Sherman Law, despite the reasonableness of the particular prices agreed upon." *Ibid.*, p. 398.

43. *Ibid.*, pp. 397-98.

for good or ill. It may use its power to promote its own interest, without advancing the interests of society. Unless it abandons its business objectives, a company will use its market power to maximize its earnings over some period, short or long. Though giant combines today probably take a longer-run view of what sound business policy requires than did their forerunners half a century ago, they still have a strong incentive to reap the highest rate of profit consistent with steady patronage and the continuity of the business. To do this they may so restrict output that prices will be above costs —marginal cost in the short run, total unit cost in the long. With giant consolidations dominating industrial markets, society is deprived of the sort of protection competition gives it, and that Congress in enacting the antitrust law apparently wanted it to have.

Equally important, by outlawing loose accords that tend to raise and stabilize prices the courts encouraged the formation of tight combinations that could do the job better. Had the more than a hundred firms that composed the Steel Corporation or the similarly large number that united to become American Can agreed as separate entities to charge identical prices, the courts would unquestionably have struck down such an arrangement, awkward and unenforceable though it might have been. But with United States Steel and American Can controlling the price policies of their subsidiaries, formerly independent companies, it followed that price competition among them was eliminated once and for all. Outright consolidation obviously is a surer method of controlling markets than concerted action by independent companies. The courts by their inconsistent application of the rule of reason as between the tight and the loose combination encouraged, perhaps unwittingly, a movement the Sherman Act was written to prevent.[44]

44. The Supreme Court implied as much when it reversed its traditional position on price-fixing agreements among business rivals in 1933 in the Appalachian Coals case. The Court said: "We know of no public policy, and none is suggested by the terms of the Sherman Act, that, in order to comply with the law, those engaged in industry should be driven to unify their properties and businesses, in order to correct abuses which may be corrected by less drastic measures." *Appalachian Coals, Inc.* v. *U.S.*, previously cited, p. 376.

One of the earlier cases illustrates clearly the significance of the Supreme Court's failure to apply the law alike to combinations in the form of mergers and those in the form of marketing agreements. Soon after the courts had held illegal the pooling arrangement among the makers of cast iron pipe in *Addyston Pipe & Steel Co.* v. *U.S.*, previously cited, four of the defendant companies combined to form the American Pipe & Foundry Company. The United States Pipe & Foundry Company, incorporated in New Jersey, then acquired American Pipe & Foundry Company, the two

Emasculation of Section 7 of the Clayton Act

The Clayton Act, like the Sherman Act, has also been interpreted by the courts in such a way as to promote rather than hinder concentration of economic power. Congress passed the Clayton Act and its companion act establishing the Federal Trade Commission in 1914 in response to a growing recognition of the inadequacy of the Sherman Act to stem the decline of competition.[45] By regulating competition and prohibiting specific devices that corporations used to restrict or eliminate it, Congress sought to reinvigorate competition as a regulator of the economy. Among other provisions,[46] the Clayton Act in Section 7 prohibited the acquisition of stock of one corporation by another in the same line of business, "where the effect of such acquisition may be to substantially lessen competition" between the corporations or "tend to create a monopoly." Although the Act exempted intercorporate stock acquisitions for investment purposes and did not prohibit the purchase of the assets of one corporation by another, it clearly went further than the Sherman Act. Its prohibitions were aimed at preventing the elimination of competition between any two business rivals by stock acquisitions, whether or not they could control an interstate market by combining.

Because it is simpler for a corporation to buy enough of the stock of a rival corporation to obtain working control of its business policies than it is to buy its assets, a rigorous application of Section 7 might have retarded the merger movements that flowered during the 1920's and during and after World War II. It was never applied rigorously, however. And in 1926 the Supreme Court virtually emasculated the law by holding in the Thatcher case that if a cor-

---

remaining defendants in the Addyston case, and a number of other companies. Almost fifty years later the Department of Justice filed suit against the United States Pipe & Foundry Company and four other companies alleging both restraint of trade and monopoly. *U.S.* v. *United States Pipe & Foundry Co., et al.,* Civil Action No. 10772, in U.S. District Court for the District of New Jersey, consent decree entered July 21, 1948.

45. For a discussion of the Federal Trade Commission's work, see Chap. 11.

46. Section 2 of the Act made it unlawful for any person to discriminate in price between different purchasers of a commodity "where the effect of such discrimination may be to substantially lessen competition or tend to create a monopoly." Section 3 forbade any person engaged in interstate commerce to lease or sell or price goods on condition that the lessee or buyer not use or deal in the goods of a competitor "when the effect . . . may be to substantially lessen competition or tend to create a monopoly." Section 8 prohibited a director of a non-banking corporation with a capitalization of more than a million dollars from serving as a director in any other such corporation where an agreement between them would violate the antitrust laws. U.S. Code, Title 15, c. 1, Secs. 12-27.

poration had first purchased the capital stock of a corporate rival and through the voting rights thus obtained had then approved the sale to itself of the former rival's assets, before the Federal Trade Commission instituted proceedings, the transaction was beyond the reach of the law. The Court declared that "The Act has no application to ownership of a competitor's property and business obtained prior to any action by the Commission, *even though this was brought about through stock unlawfully held.*" [47]

Public Opinion Changes

The changes the courts made in the antitrust laws were, of course, not wholly in defiance of public opinion. These judicial changes were partly a reflection of the temper of the times, but they also helped to create it. It is true that Congress in 1909 had deliberately refrained from giving its approval to the rule of reason. It is also true that Congress had demonstrated anew its faith in the competitive process by strengthening the antitrust laws in 1914.

But the mobilization of our national resources for World War I required greater cooperation among business rivals than had been tolerated in peacetime and brought a change of attitude toward business collectivism. The return of peace brought a general demand for the abandonment of the comprehensive wartime governmental controls. The war-born maladjustments in both the American and the world economy, the accompanying intensification of trade rivalries, and the spirit of nationalism led to demands for modification of established antitrust policy. Congress responded to the agitation. In several fields previously subject to the general rule of competition it sanctioned collaboration among business rivals for "stabilizing" their common market.

As early as 1916 the Shipping Act legalized joint rate making by common-carrier steamship companies.[48] In 1918 the Webb-Pomerene Act exempted from the antitrust laws associations among business rivals engaged in export trade provided they did not restrain trade

47. *Thatcher Manufacturing Co.* v. *FTC,* 272 U.S. 554 (1926), at p. 561. Italics supplied.

The ruling in the International Shoe case four years later, 280 U.S. 291 (1930), practically nullified Section 7 by exempting from its provisions the acquisition of the stock of a competitor if the two companies produced and sold articles—in the instant case, shoes—differing in style and quality.

48. 39 Stat. 72 (1916).

within the United States or "the export trade of any domestic competitor of such association."[49] In 1922 the Capper-Volstead Act broadened the Clayton Act exemption in favor of agricultural cooperation.

These were more than straws in the wind. They reflected the drift of public opinion toward acquiescence in collaborative action to avoid what was becoming known as the "wastes of undisciplined competition." They were steps along a road to economic collectivism.

The political environment of the 1920's after the "return to normalcy" under a Republican regime was especially favorable to the concentration of economic power and to the development of collaboration among business rivals in shaping business policies. The Federal Trade Commission through trade practice conferences promoted codes of "fair competition" for industry. In the early 1930's most of the oil-producing states, under the guise of conserving oil resources, sponsored programs for curbing output and stabilizing oil prices. As the Great Depression deepened, the shrinkage of production and national income, the steep decline in prices and wages, and the rise in unemployment to unprecedented levels led Congress to abandon temporarily America's traditional antitrust policy. The substitute it adopted was the NRA program.

A New Judicial Doctrine: Good and Bad Competition

With the coming of the Great Depression the judges, also, changed their minds. They once more reinterpreted the antitrust laws. Up to the 1930's the courts had persistently refused to apply the rule of reason to price-fixing arrangements among business rivals for the protection or advancement of their mutual interests.[50] In the Appalachian Coals case, however, the Supreme Court gave its bless-

49. 40 Stat. 516 (1918).

50. In a strict sense, the Chicago Board of Trade case represents an exception to this general statement. It involved the legality of the "Call Rule" of the Board whereby all traders agreed to buy or sell at a fixed price grain shipments "to arrive" between the closing hour of the exchange on one business day and the opening hour on the next business day. The fixed price in such transactions was the closing bid at the last session of the exchange.

The Supreme Court, applying the rule of reason to these facts, upheld the "Call Rule" as a legitimate trading regulation. In the words of Mr. Justice Brandeis, "the legality of an agreement or regulation cannot be determined by so simple a test as whether it restrains competition . . . The true test of legality is whether the restraint imposed is such as merely regulates and perhaps thereby promotes competition or whether it is such as may suppress or even destroy competition." *Chicago Board of Trade* v. *U.S.*, 246 U.S. 231 (1918), at p. 238.

ing to a joint selling agency set up by some 137 rival companies, which together produced about 75 per cent of the bituminous output of the Appalachian territory.[51] The lower court had held that the plan would eliminate competition among those taking part in it; and that, in doing so, it would "affect market conditions and have a tendency to stabilize prices and to raise prices to a higher level than would prevail under conditions of free competition." [52] Although the court concluded that the selling agency would "not have monopoly control of any market nor the power to fix monopoly prices," it held that the arrangement would violate the antitrust laws and issued an injunction prohibiting it.

The Supreme Court apparently accepted the conclusion that the arrangement would tend to raise and stabilize coal prices in some markets. Nevertheless, it reversed the lower court's decision and ordered a judgment for the defendants. It stated that:

> A cooperative enterprise, otherwise free from objection, which carries with it no monopolistic menace, is not to be condemned as an undue restraint merely because it may effect a change in market conditions, where the change would be in mitigation of recognized evils and would not impair, but rather foster, fair competitive opportunities.[53]

This looks like different law from that which a federal court had applied to a similar arrangement in the coal industry thirty years earlier when it held that the Chesapeake & Ohio Fuel Company could not lawfully act as a selling agency for fourteen rival coal firms. Then the court rejected the defense that the coal produced by the parties to the arrangement was "such a small fraction of the quantity sold, that it cannot affect prices materially," and held that "It is not required, in order to violate this statute, that a monopoly be created. It is sufficient if that be the necessary tendency of the agreement." [54] It appears different also from the law the courts had consistently applied for three decades, from the Trans-Missouri Freight Association case in 1897 to the Trenton Potteries case in 1927. During this interval the courts persistently refused to dis-

51. *Appalachian Coals, Inc.* v. *U.S.*, previously cited. The territory covered by the agreement included central and western Pennsylvania, eastern Ohio, western Maryland, West Virginia, southwestern Virginia, eastern Kentucky, eastern Tennessee, and northeastern Alabama.

52. Quoted in *ibid.*, p. 359.

53. *Ibid.*, pp. 373-74.

54. *Chesapeake & Ohio Fuel Co.* v. *U.S.*, 115 Fed. 610 (1902), at p. 623.

tinguish between reasonable and unreasonable price-fixing agreements among business rivals.

The Appalachian Coals decision reflects a change of public attitude toward competition. The public, the courts, and Congress had come to doubt the efficacy of competition as a regulator of economic activity. The reasons for this skepticism are clear. It was largely a depression phenomenon, although it wasn't competition that brought about the depression.

Competition a Scapegoat for Depression

In 1933 the coal industry, like many others, was in distress. For more than a decade it had suffered from overexpansion induced by World War I and from a shrinkage of demand. Consumption of coal had decreased as more economical sources of power like oil and hydroelectricity emerged and as coal was used more efficiently. The industry suffered from a long-run decline in demand. In addition, demand decreased during the depression as industrial output and national income shrank.

These circumstances intensified competition and led to numerous "destructive" practices, the sale of "distress" coal for what it would bring and "pyramiding" in the sale of coal—a practice whereby a producer's own coal competed with itself by being offered for sale through as many as a half-dozen different commission agents or jobbers. To end such practices, to increase the price of coal, and to relieve their financial distress by capturing a larger share of the national income, producers sought refuge in collective action.

Just as the Supreme Court had previously distinguished between good and bad trusts, it now distinguished between good and bad competition. It gave its approval to "Voluntary action to rescue and preserve . . . [fair competitive] opportunities, and thus to aid in relieving a depressed industry and in reviving commerce by placing competition upon a sounder basis . . ." [55]

With this decision the wheel of law had turned full circle. The Sherman Act condemned all contracts in restraint of trade—that is, unification of the interests of business rivals to control any interstate markets or mutual engagements not to compete or to suppress the competition of others. The law had now been so thoroughly "inter-

55. *Appalachian Coals, Inc.* v. *U.S.*, previously cited, p. 374.

preted" as to sanction the regulation of competition by business rivals to enable them better to meet the distressing exigencies and avoid the losses that frequently accompany the competitive pursuit of gain. Under the doctrine of the Appalachian Coals case, a combining group, even though it might have sufficient power to affect market prices, could rely on judicial approval if it exercised its power circumspectly. Only unrestrained or at any rate unscrupulous—and therefore "unreasonable"—exploitation of a monopolistic position remained in danger of judicial condemnation.

The victory of the economic collectivists as reflected in court decisions during the early 1930's and in the NRA experiment was short-lived. By 1935 the country had had enough of "self-government" in industry under the legalized cartel system of NRA. Beginning with the Schechter decision, which struck down the NRA experiment, a change in the judicial attitude toward monopoly restored to the Sherman Act something of its original content and meaning. Generally, however, when the Supreme Court has, in effect, reversed its earlier decisions it has refused to acknowledge the fact. It has chosen rather to distinguish earlier decisions by reference to their underlying facts.

The Socony-Vacuum Case

In the Socony-Vacuum case[56] the Court not only reaffirmed its pre-1930's condemnation of private price-fixing agreements per se, but went further. It condemned a concerted gasoline-buying program that did not directly involve price fixing and that was an outgrowth of NRA experience.

The National Industrial Recovery Act had put the authority of the federal government behind a voluntary proration program that the major oil companies had devised with the support of the leading oil-producing states.[57] Among other measures taken pursuant to

56. *U.S.* v. *Socony-Vacuum Oil Co., Inc.,* 310 U.S. 150 (1940). At the outset the case was based on two indictments. The first charged the defendants with conspiracy to use uniform contracts in the sale of gasoline to jobbers, to set uniform jobber discounts, to base prices f.o.b. Tulsa regardless of the origin of the gasoline, and to standardize other contract provisions in order to eliminate competition in selling gasoline to jobbers. When the defendants pleaded *nolo contendere* to this indictment and paid fines, these proceedings stopped. *U.S.* v. *Socony-Vacuum Oil Co., Inc.,* Indictment No. 11364, in U.S. District Court for the Western District of Wisconsin, 1936.

57. For a detailed discussion of oil under NRA, see Myron W. Watkins, *Oil: Stabilization or Conservation?,* Harper, New York, 1937.

NRA to stabilize the industry was the prohibition of interstate shipments of oil produced in violation of state proration laws. But "hot" oil continued to be produced and to find its way to the refineries. When cheap gasoline from "hot" oil threatened the stabilization program, major companies, selling 83 per cent of all gasoline in the midwestern area, early in 1935 launched a buying program intended to remove so-called "distress" gasoline from the market.[58] Under this program each company picked or was assigned an independent refiner from which it bought the necessary amount of gasoline to keep the supply on the "spot" market small enough to insure a satisfactory price. The designated refinery became amusingly known as the buying company's "dancing partner." By thus assuming a responsibility for the wallflowers, the major companies assured everybody a jolly time, except perhaps the consumer.

Since the independent refineries were the chief suppliers of gasoline in the spot market, spot market prices moved up when the big companies removed the independents' "distress" gasoline. Higher spot gasoline prices were promptly followed by higher retail prices. According to a witness for defendants, the spot market was a "peg to hang the price structure on." [59]

58. The program embraced two major groups of independent refineries—those of the Midcontinent and East Texas areas—and of major companies that did the buying. The principal buyers from Midcontinent refineries were majors marketing in the Middle West, and the buyers from East Texas refineries included East Coast marketers, along with some of those operating in the Middle West. The major companies in putting up the Midcontinent program "recognized that it would be necessary or desirable to take the East Texas surplus gasoline off the market so that it would not be a 'disturbing influence' in the Standard of Indiana territory." *U.S.* v. *Socony-Vacuum,* 310 U.S., p. 185.

As to the mechanics of the scheme, the Tank Car Stabilization Committee of the code authority (the Planning and Coordination Committee) made a monthly survey, estimating the amount of each independent refinery's "distress" gasoline. It was a special subcommittee's task to see that the major companies bought this gasoline, thus keeping it out of the "spot" market. An intercompany memorandum of one of the major companies throws light on the purpose of the program: ". . . with East Coast refineries having a program to purchase surplus East Texas gasoline over the next four months, we feel that still further advances can be made in the tank car market and a resultant increase in the service station price." *Ibid.,* p. 190.

59. *Ibid.,* p. 192. Throughout the midwestern territory Standard Oil Company (Indiana) was the price leader. Standard computed its retail price by adding to the spot price tank car freight from the Midcontinent field, taxes, and 5½ cents. This last included a customary 2 cent jobber margin and a 3½ cent service station margin.

According to the Supreme Court, "though the arrangement was informal, it was nonetheless effective." *Ibid.,* p. 184. The Court pointed out (pp. 195-96) that the spot price rose 1¼ cents a gallon, or about 33 per cent, within three months after the inception of the program and fluctuated around the level thus reached for the next year and a half—as long as the program continued.

The Program Illegal

The Supreme Court held that this program violated the antitrust laws, thus returning to the position it had taken in the Trenton Potteries case (1927). It declared that "for over forty years this Court has consistently and without deviation adhered to the principle that price-fixing agreements are unlawful *per se* under the Sherman Act and that no showing of so-called competitive abuses or evils which those agreements were designed to eliminate or alleviate may be interposed as a defense." Furthermore, the rule of reason "had not affected this view of the illegality of price-fixing agreements." [60]

This is realistic law and sound economics, but it is not the law or economics of the Appalachian Coals case. Ingenious dialecticians can distinguish between the two cases, and the Court did so. It emphasized that the reason for setting up Appalachian Coals, Inc., was the prevalence of "so-called" injurious practices and conditions in the industry—chief of which was the problem of "distress" coal.[61] But the Court recognized also that the reason for setting up the gasoline-buying program was the presence of similar "so-called demoralizing or injurious practices" in the oil industry. These had become so important politically that the National Industrial Recovery Act gave them special consideration.[62]

60. *Ibid.*, pp. 218 and 213, respectively.

61. The coal industry's plight was similar to that resulting from economic dislocations anywhere, but it was more acute than that commonly experienced. For labor it involved unemployment and low wages. For the mine owners it meant operating losses, or at best meager profits, and reduced capital values. For coal-mining communities it meant heavy relief expenditures and crushing taxes.

But it was not quite accurate to conclude, as the Court did in the Appalachian case, that "Defendants' coal will continue to be subject to active competition . . . The plan cannot be said either to contemplate or involve the fixing of market prices." *Appalachian Coals, Inc.* v. *U.S.*, previously cited, p. 373. Unless Appalachian Coals failed in its purpose it would have increased the price of coal—more in some markets undoubtedly than in others; most in South Carolina, where it supplied 96 per cent; least in the Northeast, where it supplied only 9 per cent. Cf. Merle Fainsod and Lincoln Gordon, *Government and the American Economy,* Norton, New York, p. 547.

62. Though the industry took the lead in setting up the gasoline-buying program, it apparently kept the Petroleum Administrative Board informed of its actions. In rejecting this line of defense the Court said: "As to knowledge or acquiescence of officers of the Federal government little need be said. The fact that Congress through utilization of the precise methods here employed could seek to reach the same objectives sought by respondents does not mean that respondents or any other group may do so without specific Congressional authority. Admittedly no approval of the buying programs was obtained under the National Industrial Recovery Act prior to its termination on June 16, 1935 . . . But even had approval been obtained for the buying programs, that approval would not have survived the expiration in June 1935 of the Act which was the source of that approval." *U.S.* v. *Socony-Vacuum,* 310 U.S., pp. 220-27.

Why Did the Court Change Its Position?

Why then did the Court condemn a collusive buying program for the oil industry and approve a collusive selling program for coal? Since the Court's language does not fully reveal the mental processes of the judges, no one can be sure. The following factors, however, are perhaps relevant to a judgment on the matter:

First, the personnel of the Court changed between 1933 and 1940. Different judges looked at different things, and they also saw things differently.

Then, too, the times changed, and so did the public attitude toward concentration of economic power. By 1938, when the Temporary National Economic Committee was established to investigate the causes of the concentration of economic power, as a result of its own failures the New Deal had grown skeptical of the efficacy of centralized power to correct economic abuses. TNEC reflected a growing skepticism toward collective control of economic activity, whether publicly or privately administered.

In the third place, a half million workers, who were also voters, stood solidly behind the price-raising program in coal because they believed higher prices essential to higher wages, and of the many coal producers who supported the program most represented "little business." The oil-buying program enjoyed no such popular support. It was put through by rich and powerful oil companies which for more than a decade had taken the lead in various output restriction and price-stabilizing programs. Small jobbers who found their profit margins reduced as prices advanced initiated the complaints against the gasoline-buying program.[63]

Finally, the structure of the coal and oil industries affected the two programs in different ways. Left to itself, the coal industry was intensely competitive. Thousands of small producers shared the market for coal. Even Appalachian Coals could not promise wholesale elimination of competition. Implicitly at least, the 1933 decision applied the view that some restriction of competition was not too high a price to pay for helping a depressed key industry get a greater share of the national income. The 1940 decision showed no such tolerance for powerful oil producers.

63. Eugene V. Rostow, *A National Policy for the Oil Industry,* Yale University Press, New Haven, 1948, p. 80.

But whatever the reasons, the Supreme Court took a different view of the oil-buying program from the view it had taken of the coal-selling program. Having sought to distinguish the cases, the opinion in the Socony-Vacuum case went on to apply prohibitions against concerted action more rigorously than ever before, thereby extending the frontiers of the antitrust statutes. The Court declared that:

> Any combination which tampers with price structures is engaged in an unlawful activity. Even though the members of the price-fixing group were in no position to control the market, to the extent that they raised, lowered, or stabilized prices they would be directly interfering with the free play of market forces. The Act places all such schemes [including Appalachian Coals?] beyond the pale and protects that vital part of our economy against *any degree of interference.* Congress has not left with us the determination of whether or not particular price-fixing schemes are wise or unwise, healthy or destructive . . .
>
> Under the Sherman Act a combination formed *for the purpose and with the effect* of raising, depressing, fixing, pegging, or stabilizing the price of a commodity in interstate or foreign commerce is illegal *per se.*[64]

Such is the law as laid down in the Socony-Vacuum case. Barring another change in judicial construction, it will make possible, though it will not insure, more effective antitrust enforcement.

The Aluminum Case

The Aluminum case, also, by holding that monopoly power, even though not abused, is illegal, restored to the law some of the original meaning that had been whittled away by earlier Supreme Court decisions. A distinguished jurist, Judge Learned Hand, speaking in this instance for a court of final jurisdiction, declared that a company may be guilty of monopolizing merely by embracing "each new opportunity" as it opens and by facing "every newcomer with new capacity already geared into a great organization, having the advantage of experience, trade connections and the elite of personnel." [65]

64. *U.S.* v. *Socony-Vacuum,* 310 U.S., pp. 221-23. Italics supplied. In a later passage the Court stated that both purpose and effect are not essential to prove an unlawful restraint of trade. Because of jurisdictional issues the Court treated this case "as one where exertion of power to fix prices . . . was an ingredient of the offense. But *that does not mean that both a purpose and a power* to fix prices are necessary for the establishment of conspiracy under Section 1 of the Sherman Act . . . *it is well established that a person 'may be guilty of conspiracy, although incapable of committing the objective offense.'" Ibid.*, pp. 224-25. Italics supplied.

65. *U.S.* v. *Aluminum Co. of America,* 148 Fed. *2d* 416 (1945), at p. 431. This was an antitrust suit in which the District Court for the Southern District of New York had found for the defendants. The government petitioned for a writ of certiorari. The

This means that neither collusion nor predatory aggression is necessary to monopolizing. One may search the law reports in vain for an earlier judicial recognition that the Sherman Act may be violated without proof of combination or conspiracy. Yet Section 2 of the Act condemns "monopolizing" as such, regardless of whether more than one company shares in the market control, and regardless of whether the power acquired is used to oppress consumers or exclude would-be competitors. By resurrecting Section 2 of the Sherman Act from the judicial oblivion to which it had been relegated, the Second Circuit Court of Appeals opened the way for a reconsideration of the economic and legal significance of bigness per se.

The monopoly power of the Aluminum Company of America dates from 1888 when its predecessor acquired the Hall patent for electrolytic reduction of aluminum. Alcoa tightened its monopoly by acquiring the patents and business of its only competitor when an infringement suit backfired and the competitor's basic patent was adjudged valid and infringed.[66] Before the expiration of its patent monopoly in 1909, Alcoa foresightedly bought up the richest and most accessible raw material (bauxite) deposits and available sources of hydroelectric power, and exacted promises from the sellers not thereafter to compete with Alcoa or to deal with any other aluminum producer. When the government instituted its first antitrust suit against Alcoa in 1911, the company consented to a decree abrogating these agreements and enjoining other unlawful practices.

The main question before the court in 1945 was whether Alcoa's monopoly of ingot production persisted from 1912 to 1938, when the government started the second antitrust proceedings, and "whether, if it did, it was unlawful under paragraph 2 of the Sherman Act."[67] In answering the first question it was necessary first to determine what percentage of market control constitutes a monopoly. The court laid down no hard and fast rule. It stated, however, that 90 per cent "is enough to constitute a monopoly; it is

Supreme Court granted the writ, but because of lack of a quorum of six justices qualified to hear the case, it referred the appeal to the Circuit Court of Appeals for the Second Circuit under a 1944 amendment to the Judiciary Act. See 15 U.S. Code, 6A, par. 29. The Circuit Court reversed in part the judgment of the lower court. (This case will hereinafter be cited: *U.S.* v. *Alcoa*.)

66. For the full story, see *Cartels in Action,* pp. 221-26.

67. *U.S.* v. *Alcoa,* p. 423. For Section 2 of the Sherman Act see p. 259 above.

doubtful whether sixty or sixty-four per cent would be enough; and certainly thirty-three per cent is not." [68]

Basis for Holding Alcoa a Monopoly

Applying these standards, the court found that Alcoa possessed a monopoly in a practical economic sense inasmuch as it controlled about 90 per cent of the aluminum market, according to the court's computation. This figure represented the ratio of Alcoa's output of virgin metal to the total supply thereof, imports accounting for the remaining 10 per cent. It included in Alcoa's share, of course, not only the ingots that it sold to other fabricators but also those it itself converted into aluminum products. The court excluded secondary aluminum from its computation entirely, on the ground that it was derived from primary ingots produced in the main by Alcoa and hence its supply was in the last analysis subject substantially to Alcoa's control.

Having found that Alcoa was a *de facto* monopoly, the court turned to the question, Had Alcoa monopolized the market in violation of Section 2 of the Sherman Act? In answering this question affirmatively it laid down two highly significant doctrines. The first was that retention of monopoly power by persistently expanding capacity to meet anticipated demand and to forestall potential competition violates the antitrust laws. The second was that monopoly power need not be abused to be unlawful.

In arriving at the first doctrine, the court recognized that monopoly may be the product of circumstances over which the monopolist has no control. Did Alcoa's monopoly fall "within the exception established in favor of those who do not seek, but cannot avoid, the control of a market"? The court thought not. "It was not inevitable that it should always anticipate increases in the demand for ingots and be prepared to supply them. Nothing compelled it to keep doubling and redoubling its capacity before others entered the field." [69]

68. *Ibid.*, p. 424. The last two clauses are *obiter dicta,* as the case turned out. But their relevance to the decision lies in the circumstance that the trial court had found by comparing Alcoa's *sales* of *virgin* aluminum ingot with the total sales of aluminum in all forms, including secondary (scrap) and imported metal, that Alcoa controlled only 35 per cent of the domestic market.

69. *Ibid.*, p. 431.

This means, apparently, that a single seller who may have acquired his position legally—for example, by being the first to enter a new industry—may become a law violator by retaining his position in the market through administrative foresight.[70] This would leave little or no room for a producer to achieve and maintain monopoly through sheer managerial ability. As long as he did not dominate the market, he could lawfully expand. Once he became the sole producer, he would break the law if he expanded as rapidly as the market unless, perhaps, he could prove that expansion was necessary to reduce costs or to meet a demand potential competition could not supply.[71] A logical deduction from this phase of the opinion is that it is illegal for a single seller to increase his investment so that he may continue to dominate the market.

This is harsh doctrine, but its effects are likely to be less harsh than at first blush might appear, particularly if the judiciary generally should accept the court's *obiter dictum* that control of 64 per cent of the market may not constitute a *de facto* monopoly. Barring patents, history provides few examples of a producer getting, or at any rate holding for very long, control of broad interstate markets through sheer efficiency and natural growth. Most *de facto* industrial monopolies, no less abroad than in the United States, have been created by combining business rivals.

Control of the Market and Monopoly

In sum, the Alcoa ruling makes the acquisition of control of the market the primary test of "monopolizing." But the court recognized two limitations on this test. First, if businessmen try to monopolize markets and fail, failure to achieve their goal does not relieve them of liability. Secondly, a firm that merely possesses monopoly

70. The court was not unequivocal. It seemed to deny this principle at an earlier point by stating that "The successful competitor, having been urged to compete, must not be turned upon when he wins." *Ibid.*, p. 430.

71. In a speculative passage of the opinion, Judge Hand suggested that in some instances only a plant large enough to supply the entire market might be able to recover full production costs. He was of the opinion that a *de facto* monopoly under these circumstances would not violate the Sherman Act. The court cited no illustrations, though there may be cases in point. Unfortunately, not even the economists are able to help much here because too little is known about comparative production costs. It is obviously important when a single producer dominates the field to make certain that great size is the result of efficiency and not of the pursuit of monopoly power.

power has not violated the law if monopoly has been thrust upon it. A monopoly position achieved unwittingly—as an unsought by-product, so to speak, of forthright competition—is beyond the reach of antitrust attack. For the law does not forbid monopoly as such; it merely outlaws monopolizing. But the outstanding development of the law in the Alcoa case was the new significance, the increased importance, assigned to size per se. As Judge Hand expressed it:

> It is possible, because of its indirect social or moral effect, to prefer a system of small producers, each dependent for his success upon his own skill and character, to one in which the great mass of those engaged must accept the direction of the few. These considerations, which we have suggested only as possible purposes of the Act, we think the decisions prove to have been in fact its purposes.[72]

The intuitive fear that Congress and the public seem to have had that big concerns will dominate markets at the expense of the public finds support in the theory of imperfect competition. When concerns are few in number, when they are so large that each must take account of its rivals' reaction to its price policies, when each by its individual output policy may influence price, each can exert power over the market similar to that of a monopolist. Under such circumstances rational behavior without any collusion whatever may result in antisocial business policies—restriction of output and noncompetitive pricing.[73]

The elevation of the importance of size, or market control, as a criterion of unlawful monopoly carries with it some diminution of the significance of intent, or at least of motives. Intent, as evidenced for instance by presence or absence of predatory practices, may concededly be of genuine value in determining whether a firm has monopolized the market and of greater value in determining whether it has tried to do so. But motives are, technically, beside the point. The law judges men's intentions by their actions. So, in

72. *Ibid.*, p. 427.

73. It would be difficult on a basis of theory alone to draw a line between firms so small that they have no control over the market and those so large that they can control it. But it is safe to say that any firm holding as much as 33 per cent of a national market may be a menace to competition. In borderline cases the courts might well look to all of the circumstances that are relevant to an alleged violation of the antitrust laws—economic as well as psychological. A consideration of intent and the existence of predatory policies may help, but they are not enough. All the economic tests of market control should be applied, including number of producers, rate of profit, plant mortality. Cf. Clair Wilcox, *Competition and Monopoly in American Industry,* TNEC Monograph No. 21, Washington, 1940, pp. 19-20.

the Alcoa case, the court disregarded the voluminous evidence that the government presented to show "specific intent," that is, an intent that went "beyond the mere intent to do the act" that was done.[74]

The second doctrine—that monopoly power need not be abused to be unlawful—upsets a widely held view of the applicability of the antitrust law to giant corporations. But it is economically sound and perhaps the most significant aspect of the Alcoa ruling. A monopolist has power to control prices. When he decides on any pricing policy, he exercises that power. As Judge Hand put it, as soon as a monopoly begins to sell, "it must sell at some price and the only price at which it could sell is a price which it itself has fixed . . . Therefore [monopoly] power and its exercise must needs coalesce." [75] This leaves little or no room for the earlier distinction between good trusts and bad trusts. Congress really forbade all.

The New American Tobacco Case

The Alcoa ruling makes clear that the monopoly power of a single seller may violate the Sherman Act regardless of how tolerantly it is exercised. A monopoly, even though not ruthlessly exploited, may be an economic sin—and a legal offense. In the American Tobacco case the Supreme Court tightened the law in another way. It in effect concluded that when several sellers *jointly* hold monopoly power they may violate the law if they use their power to promote their mutual interests even though they do not formally conspire to fix prices or exclude rivals. None of the Big Three tobacco companies produced as much as one third of the total domestic output of small cigarettes. The Court, nevertheless, was impressed by the magnitude of each. "The marked dominance enjoyed by each of these three, in roughly equal proportions, is emphasized by the fact that the smallest of them at all times showed over twice the production of the largest outsider." [76]

In 1939 the Big Three together produced 68 per cent of the domestic output of small cigarettes. Their total assets less current

74. *U.S.* v. *Alcoa,* p. 432.
75. *Ibid.,* p. 428. Again, it is rather difficult to reconcile this position with the dictum that "The successful competitor . . . must not be turned upon when he wins."
76. *American Tobacco Co., et al.* v. *U.S.,* 328 U.S. 781 (1946), at p. 796. The term "small cigarettes" refers to a classification of the product for excise-tax purposes, based on the amount of tobacco in each unit. All popular-brand cigarettes are small cigarettes.

liabilities had risen from $277 million in 1912 to $551 million in 1939; their net annual earnings, before interest and dividends, from $28 million to $75 million. In each of the years 1937, 1938, and 1939 they together spent more than $40 million for advertising. "With this background of substantial monopoly," the Court was of the opinion that "the jury could have found from the actual operation of the petitioners that there existed a combination or conspiracy among them not only in restraint of trade, but to monopolize a part of the tobacco industry." [77] According to the Court, "their practices included a clear course of dealing" indicating "the existence of a combination or conspiracy to fix and control prices and . . . to establish a substantially impregnable defense against any attempted intrusion by potential competitors into these markets." [78]

Community of Interest Among Big Three

The record disclosed no evidence of written or oral agreement on common policies or practices, and economists testified that an identical "course of dealing" was consistent with independent, noncollusive decisions. Yet among themselves the Big Three seem to have recognized a community of interest. Apparently they had learned from experience what economists teach in the schoolroom: that where sellers are few, rational, and informed, each will take account of the impact of his policies on those of his rivals. By paying less for leaf tobacco and charging more for cigarettes during the first three years of the depression they made more money than during any other consecutive three years in their history. When the makers of 10 cent cigarettes made significant inroads into their markets, the Big Three increased their purchases of cheaper grades of tobaccos and lowered their cigarette prices, thereby putting the 10 cent manufacturers in a price squeeze.

By such tactics American Tobacco, Reynolds, and Liggett & Myers

77. *Ibid.*, pp. 797-98.

78. *Ibid.*, p. 800. Chapter 6 of this study has sketched this "course of dealing." Each of the Big Three refrained from participating in tobacco auctions unless all participated. Each instructed its buyers on the ceiling price to pay for tobacco and on the proportion of the total crop to buy. And all paid the same price in any market on any day and bought their "predetermined percentages" of the total crop. With minor exceptions each had the same wholesale list price for its cigarettes and when one changed its list price the others promptly followed. Each insisted that the retailers sell Big Three cigarettes at the same price, which was to be not more than 3 cents above what they charged for the "10 cent" brands.

made business conditions difficult for the small companies. That they had not in fact driven out their aggressive rivals the Court held irrelevant.

> Actual exclusion of competitors is not necessary . . . A correct interpretation of the statute and of the authorities makes it a crime of monopolizing, under Paragraph 2 of the Sherman Act, for parties . . . to combine or conspire to acquire or maintain the power to exclude competitors from any part of the trade or commerce among the several states or with foreign nations, provided they also have such a power that they are able, *as a group*, to exclude actual or potential competition from the field and provided they have the intent and purpose to exercise that power.[79]

By charging all that the traffic would bear in the short run, the Big Three lost business in the long run. When they cut prices to thwart the new competitors, they again overstepped themselves. They found that price competition might cost more than it was worth, so they raised their prices. Though the Big Three failed to oust their rivals,[80] an unwise use of monopoly power does not prove that it does not exist.

Significance of Aluminum and Tobacco Decisions

The decisions in the tobacco and aluminum cases raised the hopes of those who believed that wise use of the judicial power could do much to restore and preserve competition.[81] Some students of antitrust policy see in these decisions an acceptance by the courts of the economists' doctrine of imperfect competition. According to this view, when a few sellers dominate a market they violate the law whether or not they agree to act in concert, because each tends to behave more like a monopolist than like a competitor. As Professor Rostow says of the tobacco decision:

> When three companies produce so large a percentage [68 per cent] of market supply, that fact alone is almost sufficient evidence that the statute

79. *Ibid.*, p. 809. Italics supplied. The consistency of this passage is dubious. If the Big Three were able as a group to exclude potential competition and decided to do it, they would have done it. They no doubt were able, but apparently found the cost greater than they cared to pay. Power over the market is a menace to public welfare, whether the monopolists follow a policy of live and let live, or use their power to exclude.

80. Between 1931 and 1939, the Big Three's proportion of total domestic production of small cigarettes declined from 90.7 per cent to 68 per cent.

81. See, for example, Wendell Berge and Estes Kefauver, "The Sherman Act and the Enforcement of Competition," *American Economic Review*, Papers and Proceedings, May 1948, pp. 172-202.

is violated. Ruthless and predatory behavior need not be shown. The actual elimination of small competitors is unnecessary. . . . Parallel action, price leadership, a reliance on advertising rather than price competition as a means of inducing changes in each seller's share of the market, and, above all, size—the market position of a small number of large sellers or buyers—these are now key points to be proved in a case of monopoly, or of combination in restraint of trade. . . . Painstaking search for scraps of evidence with a conspiratorial atmosphere are no longer necessary. . . . The decisive elements are the power to assert a degree of control over price and output *in the market as a whole* . . .[82]

If this interpretation should be borne out, the tobacco and aluminum decisions would mark a sharp break in antitrust policy. For it ignores the significance of intent and thus would jeopardize a concern that through pioneering enterprise and outstanding efficiency might hold a large share of its market. But it would have the salutary effect of facilitating dissolution of combines that dominate a whole branch of industry and of hindering the further concentration of economic power through mergers. Such a rule, properly qualified and rigorously applied, could lead to sufficient decentralization of economic power to preserve free enterprise against private collectivization, and ultimately nationalization, of business. In short, it would help greatly to make antitrust policy effective.

The Checker Cab Case

For a brief period, indeed, before the Court again began zigzagging, it looked as though this was in substance what the tobacco and aluminum decisions actually signified. Within a year the Court once more broke new ground by bold application of antitrust policy.

In the Checker Cab case the Department of Justice charged that, beginning in 1929, the defendants had conspired to get control of the leading cab-operating companies of Chicago, New York, Pittsburgh, and Minneapolis with the aim of assuring a market for the taxicabs made by the Checker Cab Manufacturing Corporation.[83] The government alleged that eventually Checker Cab through sub-

82. Rostow, *op. cit.*, pp. 136-37. Italics supplied.
83. *U.S.* v. *Yellow Cab Co.*, 332 U.S. 218 (1947). Yellow Cab was a subsidiary of Checker Cab, top unit of a corporate pyramid organized by one Markin.

sidiaries and affiliates got control of 86 per cent of the cab licenses in Chicago; all those in Pittsburgh; 58 per cent in Minneapolis; and 15 per cent in New York.

The District Court dismissed the complaint on the ground, in effect, that it did not state a cause of action. In reversing this ruling the Supreme Court said:

> . . . the amount of interstate trade thus affected by the conspiracy is immaterial in determining whether a violation of the Sherman Act has been charged in the complaint. . . . it is enough if some appreciable part of interstate commerce is the subject of a monopoly, a restraint or a conspiracy.[84]

The implication of this ruling is more than a mere prohibition of regional monopolies. If they involve interstate commerce, local restraints and monopolies have consistently been held to infringe the Sherman Act.[85] The distinctive feature of Checker Cab's vertical integration setup that made it subject to judicial scrutiny under the antitrust laws was that it might prevent operating subsidiaries and affiliates from buying cabs in a competitive market. It did not matter how such a "monopoly" was acquired. The Supreme Court rejected the argument that only one business was involved and that a parent company could not conspire with its subsidiaries. It stated that unlawful restraint "may result as readily from a conspiracy among those who are affiliated or integrated under common ownership as from a conspiracy among those who are otherwise independent. . . . The corporate interrelationships of the conspirators, in other words, are not determinative of the applicability of the Sherman Act. That statute is aimed at substance rather than form." [86] The Court pointed out that the theory of the complaint was that Checker's power over the cab-operating companies "was not obtained by normal expansion to meet the demands of a business growing as a result of superior

84. *Ibid.*, p. 225. See also, to the same effect, *ibid.*, p. 226.

85. In the first recorded proceeding under the Sherman Act, the court enjoined the Nashville Coal Exchange, an association of dealers in a single city, from fixing prices in local sales through collaboration with Kentucky mining companies. *U.S.* v. *Jellico Mt. Coal Co.*, 43 Fed. 898 (1890); and *ibid.*, 46 Fed. 432 (1891).

Later cases adhering to the same principle include: *Gibbs* v. *McNeely,* 118 Fed. 120 (1902); *Montague* v. *Lowry,* 193 U.S. 38 (1904); and *Indiana Farmers Guide Co.* v. *Prairie Farmers Co.*, 293 U.S. 268 (1934).

86. *U.S.* v. *Yellow Cab Co.*, previously cited, p. 227. Among recent cases applying the doctrine set forth in this quotation, probably the clearest and most significant ruling was in *U.S.* v. *Crescent Amusement Co.*, 323 U.S. 173 (1944).

and enterprising management, but by deliberate, calculated purchase for control." [87]

Significance of Checker Cab Case

On their face the two doctrines—(1) that the amount of interstate commerce affected is immaterial in determining a violation of the Sherman Act, and (2) that control through vertical integration does not absolve from guilt a monopolist of an appreciable segment of the market—have great significance with respect to the legality of corporate mergers. Some commentators hold that in this decision "the Court has adopted a uniform standard for determining the application of both Sections 1 and 2 of the Sherman Act." [88] In applying Section 1, the Supreme Court has consistently held that price-fixing agreements among business rivals are unreasonable restraints on trade, regardless of the amount of trade controlled by the price fixers and regardless of whether or not the agreement is effective.[89]

These same commentators conclude from the Checker Cab case that "it is no longer necessary in order to show a violation of either Sections 1 or 2 of the Act to demonstrate the relative importance of the defendants and the business they control." [90] If this interpretation were correct, any merger—horizontal or vertical—would violate the law if it involved an "appreciable" volume of business. It is unlikely to prove correct.

Neither the commentators nor the Supreme Court appear to have understood the economic implications of Checker's setup. A vertical

87. *U.S.* v. *Yellow Cab Co.,* pp. 227-28. When the case was remanded to the District Court for trial, that court held that the evidence did not support this theory. *U.S.* v. *Yellow Cab Co.,* 80 Fed.Supp. 936 (1948).

On appeal to the Supreme Court a second time, the government was unsuccessful. With only two members dissenting, the Court ruled that the evidence was adequate to sustain the findings of fact by the trial judge. On the crucial issue of *intent* to restrain trade, the majority accepted the view of the lower court that "the Government, at the trial, has failed on all the evidence to prove its case." 338 U.S. 338 (1949).

88. Sergei S. Zlinkoff and Robert C. Barnard, "The Supreme Court and a Competitive Economy: 1946 Term," *Columbia Law Review,* September 1947, p. 928.

89. See, for example, *U.S.* v. *Paramount Pictures, Inc., et al.,* 334 U.S. 131 (1948), at p. 143, where the Court said: "We start, of course, from the premise that so far as the Sherman Act is concerned, a price-fixing combination is illegal *per se.*"

90. Zlinkoff and Barnard, *op. cit.,* p. 929.

merger between companies specializing in two successive stages of production of a good or service—for example, making cabs and supplying transportation—can have little or no effect on the price of either product unless the merging units at one or both stages have independent power over the market. That Checker Cab obtained a controlled outlet for its cabs was important only if it had obtained effective control of the market for cab services in certain localities. If it had not done so it could have got no higher prices for its cabs nor sold more of them than it could have done without having integrated. Integrated or unintegrated, it must offer cabs at prices that would enable its buyers to compete with other cab-operating companies in the sale of transportation service. Otherwise it could not protect its market position by acquiring control of a cab-using company.

But whatever percentage of control of local taxicab service a cab-operating company may possess, its market power is strictly limited by the licensing and rate-making powers of public service commissions. If Checker Cab's operating companies paid more for their cabs than they would otherwise have paid, the municipal authorities might have permitted them to increase their fares. But unless a particular operating subsidiary could persuade the regulatory agency to raise its rates, to cover the costs of operating high-priced cabs, Checker Cab's control of that subsidiary was in the long run of little significance to either competing cab manufacturers or the public. In any event, the significant fact under the Sherman Act was the power that Checker Cab operators might exert over the market for taxi transportation services, not the fact that Checker Cab by controlling certain operating companies pre-empted a large share of the market for cabs in some cities. Whatever control Checker Cab operating subsidiaries exercised over local markets for cab services was derived from the policies of municipal cab-licensing authorities.

The Motion-Picture Cases

The motion-picture cases lend support to the view that there may be a judicial trend toward the more rigorous application of the antitrust laws. On a single day in 1948 the Supreme Court handed down three decisions condemning, as attempts to monopolize, the activities of three groups of defendants operating in various phases of this branch of the entertainment business.[91]

The motion-picture industry consists of three divisions, production, distribution, and exhibition, in each of which are some companies that operate solely in that particular division. Only five concerns are completely integrated, operating studios in which they make pictures, booking offices which rent films for exhibition on specific dates, and theatres in which to show them to the general public. In the Paramount case, defendants were these five integrated companies—Paramount, Loew's (MGM), RKO, Warner Bros., Twentieth Century Fox; two others, Columbia and Universal, that produced and distributed films but owned no theatres; and an eighth, United Artists, that confined its activities exclusively to the distribution field. Though a score or more of other companies produce motion-picture films, the seven producer-defendants make almost all the popular "feature" pictures.

The Issues in the Paramount Case

The Paramount case turned on two main issues: (1) the legality of certain trade practices, and (2) the lawfulness of integrating distribution and exhibition, that is, of combining the booking business and the operation of theatres.[92] On the first issue, involving all eight defendants, the trial court held that it unreasonably restrained trade to follow, even though not concertedly, such practices as fixing the price of theatre admissions when leasing films, agreements to pool the revenue derived from exhibition of one or a series of films in a number of theatres, formula deals basing rental rates on the amount of gross revenue that a picture might yield, block booking, or the leasing of a number of pictures as a unit, and so-called master agreements which in effect made of a theatre not owned by a distributor a joint enterprise of the distributor and exhibitor making such a contract. Another, and by all odds the most important, trade practice at issue was that of imposing run and clearance restrictions on the leasing of films for exhibition in particular theatres.[93]

91. *U.S.* v. *Griffith,* 334 U.S. 100 (1948); *Schine Chain Theaters* v. *U.S.,* 334 U.S. 110 (1948); and *U.S.* v. *Paramount,* previously cited.

92. The original complaint also charged that defendants had monopolized the *production* of pictures. But the District Court found no monopoly in production and the government did not appeal from this part of the judgment. See 70 Fed.Supp. 53 (1947), at p. 60.

93. "Run" is the name given to the playing position of particular theatres (as a rule

The trial court concluded that some such method of protecting the interests of prior exhibitors was legitimate, indeed, commercially indispensable. But the established system was so inflexible and, given the large stake of the principal distributors in early-run theatres, so clearly tended to prejudice the interests of independent exhibitors that the court prohibited its continuance. In its stead, the court decreed a system of competitive bidding for pictures.

The Supreme Court sustained the judgment of the lower court on the trade restrictive effect of all these practices, but it overruled that court on the competitive-bidding provision of its decree. In the view of the majority, as expressed by Mr. Justice Douglas, competitive bidding was quite "unworkable," and in any event inadequate. It was inadequate because of the dominating position of the Big Five, alike in the exhibition field and in distribution. The position taken by the Court on this phase of the first issue stems from, or at least is closely connected with, its ruling on the second issue.

Legality of Vertical Integration

Regarding integration of picture distribution and exhibition, the trial court concluded that the defendants "do not and cannot, collectively or individually, have a monopoly of exhibition," and as each distributed only its own films the court found nothing illicit in the integrated organization.[94] Focussing attention mainly on the national market, the court saw nothing to be disturbed over in the Big Five's ownership of 17 per cent of the country's theatres—3,137 out of a total of 18,076 in 1945.[95] But even the higher concentration of theatre ownership (in their hands) in certain urban centers was not an indication of monopolizing.

---

classified on the basis chiefly of seating capacity and location) on a time scale measured (usually in weeks) from the initial release date of a picture. "Clearance" refers to the interval, stipulated in the lease of each picture, that must elapse after its exhibition in the lessee's theatre before the distributor is free to lease the picture to any other exhibitor within a specified (surrounding) territory. Runs and clearances were highly standardized, but the government offered no evidence of collective action among distributors to fix the run and clearance "protection" of specific theatres.

94. 70 Fed.Supp., p. 68.

95. See 66 Fed.Supp. 323, at pp. 353-57. On the basis of film rentals from theatres the interests of the integrated companies were larger, their theatres having paid 45 per cent of all rentals received by the principal producers. Moreover, their theatre interests were concentrated in the larger cities and in the best theatres. In the 92 cities with more than 100,000 population, they had an interest in 70 per cent of the first-run theatres. In 38 of these cities they controlled all the first-run theatres. Note, however, that these figures lump the theatre holdings of five separate companies.

> In localities where there is ownership by a single defendant of all the first-run theatres, there is no sufficient proof that it has been *for the purpose* of creating a monopoly and has not rather arisen from the inertness of the competitors, their lack of financial ability to build theatres comparable to those of the defendants, or from the preference of the public for the best-equipped houses and not from "inherent vice" on the part of these defendants.[96]

The root of the evil, the court felt, lay not in theatre ownership by producer-distributors but in their arbitrary and discriminatory trade practices.

The Supreme Court thought otherwise. While, like the District Court, it rejected the government's contention that vertical integration is unlawful per se,[97] it reasoned that if the starting point is conspiracy "it is relevant to determine what the results of conspiracy" are, even if they fall short of monopoly.[98] This reasoning is unexceptionable, but its applicability to the instant case is questionable in view of the explicit findings of the trial court that no conspiracy among the defendants had been proved, whether in respect to production, distribution, exhibition, or trade practices.[99] The Court was

96. 70 Fed.Supp., p. 70. Italics supplied. However, the court condemned *joint* ownership of theatres by the defendants, whether with one another or with an "outside" exhibitor, because it eliminated potential competition between the parties.

97. Integration may facilitate the exercise of monopoly power or expand its application, but it does not of itself necessarily increase it. The evil lies in monopoly, not in the linking of successive industrial stages under a common ownership. For example, if an industry with one hundred independent firms in each of its two successive phases is competitive, it will remain competitive in its ultimate consumer market if each of the one hundred firms at phase one links up with a firm operating in phase two. On the other hand, if the linkage takes place between two firms either of which has power over the market, it may facilitate the use of monopoly power, or it may eliminate potential competition, but it will not in and of itself have changed the power which the firms separately exercised over the market.

98. *U.S.* v. *Paramount,* previously cited, p. 171. And contrariwise, of course, if the starting point is not conspiracy, even though the result is the achievement of a single-seller position in some market, this monopoly in a popular sense would not, by itself, constitute a violation of Section 2 of the Sherman Act. As the Court said, the owner of the only theatre in a town is not necessarily an antitrust-law violator.

But steering clear of conspiracy is not enough to keep a single seller from being a monopolist in a legal sense. As the text below shows, he must also avoid business practices that restrain trade.

99. It is possible that the Court had in mind at this point an application of the doctrine of "constructive conspiracy" as in the American Tobacco case. But this seems doubtful, because in that case the Court was merely holding that a jury "could have found" what it *did* find, namely, conspiracy without direct evidence of collusion, whereas in the Paramount case the District Court had held that the evidence disclosed no conspiracy, constructive or actual. It seems more likely that in referring to the "results of conspiracy" the Court may have been thinking in terms of the "intra-company conspiracy" doctrine of the first Yellow Cab case. On this premise, of course, whenever the several subsidiaries or affiliates in a single business unit follow a common

on firmer ground when, in a later passage of the opinion, it shifted the basis for its condemnation of integrated theatre ownership from the "results of conspiracy" thesis to one that might be called the "results of restrictive trade practices." Here it declared that:

> It is the relationship of the unreasonable restraints of trade to the position of the defendants in the exhibition field (and more particularly in the first-run phase of that business) *that is of first importance* on the divestiture phase of these cases.[100]

Grounds for Dissolution

This apparently means that if an enterprise acquires a dominant position in any market (in this case, especially, first-run motion-picture exhibition in urban centers) by restrictive practices (such as block booking and arbitrary allotment of run and clearance positions) an injunction against the practices themselves is unlikely to afford adequate relief. The retention of a dominant position acquired by trade-restraining methods is a continuing menace to effective competition, even though those methods be specifically interdicted by decree. As the Court declared, "the existence of power 'to exclude competition when it is desired to do so' is itself a violation of Paragraph 2 [of the Sherman Act], provided it is coupled with the purpose or intent to exercise that power." [101]

In line with well-established precedents, however, the Court made it plain that the existence of an "intent" to monopolize does not turn on the outcome of an inquiry into personal motives. It turns, instead, on an interpretation of market behavior, that is to say, of the course of conduct of a business. Thus, an intent to monopolize was inferred

---

policy or accept a unified direction (and how could they do otherwise?) they "conspire," forsooth, to restrain trade among themselves! The Schine and the Griffith opinions contain some implications of this line of reasoning, but the main basis for those rulings appears to be the sound doctrine that monopolies (even partial monopolies, or preferential positions in a trade) obtained by unlawful means—restrictive trade practices—are subject to dissolution. See text below.

100. *U.S.* v. *Paramount,* p. 172. Italics supplied.

101. *Ibid.,* p. 141. In the same passage the Court reiterated the doctrine laid down in the American Tobacco case that "monopoly power, whether lawfully or unlawfully acquired, may violate Paragraph 2 of the Sherman Act though it remains unexercised." The logic of this statement is open to question, unless by a failure to exercise monopoly power is meant only the nonuse of a power to exclude others. But if "unexercised" monopoly power be taken to mean foregoing price control, then the statement flies in the face of reality. For as Judge Hand said in the Alcoa case, "A monopolist must sell at some price and the only price at which it could sell is a price which it itself has fixed. Therefore the power and its exercise must needs coalesce." *U.S.* v. *Alcoa,* p. 428.

in the Paramount case from the restrictive practices of the defendants in leasing their films. In the Griffith and Schine cases, involving theatre circuits, it was inferred from the misuse of their buying power.[102] Selecting films for all its affiliated theatres and negotiating as a unit with distributors, each could and did obtain runs, clearances, and film-rental terms that gave it preferential advantages over independent theatres.

On the judicial test of intent, the opinion in the Griffith case was clear and outspoken.

> When the buying power of the entire circuit is used to negotiate films for his competitive as well as his closed towns . . . [a man] is using monopoly power to expand his empire. And even if we assume that a specific intent to accomplish that result is absent, he is chargeable in legal contemplation with that purpose since the end result is the necessary and direct consequence of what he did.[103]

Monopolists, in short, are not sleepwalkers. If business firms become monopolies through obstructive or predatory tactics, it is to be assumed that they knew where they were going. Similarly, if they try to monopolize through conspiracy with others, even though they fail to reach the goal, it is to be assumed that they would have gone there if they could. In either case, evidence of "conscious wrongdoing" is quite unnecessary. The motion-picture cases marked some progress in judicial construction of the antitrust laws by their uniform insistence that actions are the test of intent.

The New Steel Merger

The Columbia Steel case was a setback for those who hoped the Supreme Court was ready to use its authority to prevent concentrations of economic power that threaten free markets.[104] It was bitterly

102. The Griffith circuit embraced four affiliates which together held an interest in theatres in 85 towns in Oklahoma, Texas, and New Mexico. The Schine circuit operated theatres through five affiliates in 76 towns in New York, Ohio, Kentucky, Maryland, Delaware, and Virginia. There was evidence in the Schine case, but not in the Griffith case, of direct coercion of rival independent theatres to force them to sell out to the chain, which may account for the fact that in the District Court the government won its case against Schine and lost its case against Griffith.

But the gist of the offense charged in both cases was the same: obtaining special terms and privileges from distributors, in renting their films, by using the leverage made available through combining the buying power of the whole chain, both of the theatres located in towns in which the circuit operated all theatres (closed towns) and of those located in towns in which the circuit met competition (open towns).

103. *U.S.* v. *Griffith,* previously cited, p. 108.

104. *U.S.* v. *Columbia Steel Co.,* 335 U.S. 495 (1948), Transcript of Record, p. 453, Plaintiff's Exhibit No. 1. (This case will hereinafter be cited: *U.S.* v. *Columbia,* with such abbreviations as Rec. for Record, PX for Plaintiff's Exhibit, etc.)

disillusioning for those who thought that with the first Yellow Cab case the Court had abandoned the distinction between loose and tight combinations in applying the rule of reason. The Columbia Steel decision suggests that the Court is not ready to accept fully the view of many economists on the economic significance of imperfect competition. Domination of a market by a few sellers, according to this view, may restrain trade, and lead to results almost indistinguishable from those of outright monopolization, even though the sellers do not overtly conspire. Such centralization of private economic power is wholly incompatible, according to these economists, with the avowed goals of antitrust legislation.

In the Columbia Steel case the government sought under the antitrust laws to enjoin the United States Steel Corporation through its subsidiary, Columbia Steel (Columbia), from buying the assets of the largest steel fabricator on the West Coast—the Consolidated Steel Corporation (Consolidated).[105] The Steel Corporation contracted to buy the assets of Consolidated and four subsidiaries on December 14, 1946. Six months earlier it had bought the Geneva steel plant from the government for $47.5 million, with the understanding that it would spend not less than $18.6 million for additional facilities, including among other things a hot-rolled coils mill with an annual capacity of 386,000 tons, and that it would construct at Pittsburg, California, a $25 million mill in which to use the hot-rolled coils from the Geneva plant and would produce there 325,000 tons annually of cold-reduced sheets and tin plate.[106]

In buying the Geneva plant the Steel Corporation increased its ingot capacity to 32.7 per cent of the total domestic capacity (from 31.4 per cent), to 39 per cent of Pacific and Mountain states capacity, and to 51 per cent of Pacific Coast states capacity.[107] Before buying

105. 74 Fed.Supp. 67 (1947). The District Court denied the injunction, and the government appealed. The Supreme Court affirmed the District Court's judgment by a five-four decision. Justices Black and Murphy joined Mr. Justice Rutledge in a vigorous dissent, and Mr. Justice Douglas filed a separate dissent.

106. *U.S.* v. *Columbia,* Rec., DX 64, p. 659. The Steel Corporation "designed, constructed and operated, without fee or charge, for the United States Government the Geneva steel plant, a war project at Geneva, Utah, for the production of ship plates and ship structurals." Finding No. 39 of the District Court, Rec., p. 47. The plant cost the government nearly $200 million. *U.S.* v. *Columbia,* p. 503.

107. The Attorney General in approving the sale of the Geneva plant to the Steel Corporation presented the above figures. See *U.S.* v. *Columbia,* Rec., DX 66, pp. 681-82. In doing so he quoted with approval the Circuit Court's opinion in the Aluminum case that Alcoa's control of 90 per cent of the domestic production of virgin aluminum "is enough to constitute a monopoly; *it is doubtful whether sixty or sixty-four per cent*

the Geneva and Consolidated plants the Steel Corporation did business in the Pacific Coast area through Columbia, which was an integrated producer with blast furnaces and byproduct coke ovens at Ironton, Utah, and steel mills and finishing facilities at Pittsburg and Torrance, California. Columbia was the only tin plate producer on the West Coast. In buying Consolidated, the Steel Corporation's avowed objective was to provide a backlog of business for the Geneva plant that would enable it to operate on a break-even basis.[108]

Steel Corporation at Disadvantage on Pacific Coast

The Steel Corporation had no plants in the Pacific Coast area for fabricating structural steel. Its subsidiaries with plants in the East supplied, through Columbia, its structural steel customers in this area. Although the war-stimulated industrial expansion of the Pacific Coast had greatly increased the demand for fabricated structural steel, three factors threatened to handicap the Steel Corporation in getting "its share" of future business in this field.

First, war-built government plants gave to this area a capacity for producing plates and structural shapes far beyond the area's probable peacetime consumption of these products.[109] Surplus capacity threatened severe competition in the structural steel market. Second, the expansion of steelmaking capacity in general in the Pacific Coast area had led to a public demand that steel producers modify their established pricing system by introducing a western basing point so as to give western consumers the normal advantages of location in

---

would be enough; and certainly thirty-three per cent is not." Italics supplied. He called attention to the fact that the Supreme Court in the American Tobacco case quoted the aluminum opinion extensively and commented on it favorably. He neglected to note that the Supreme Court did not refer to the passage above quoted, and that the Court held that the jury was justified, even in the absence of evidence of collusion, in finding that the Big Three had conspired to monopolize the cigarette business although together they produced in 1939 only 68 per cent of the total domestic output of cigarettes.

108. See the testimony of Bertram H. Lawrence, vice-president of U.S. Steel of Delaware, and of Benjamin F. Fairless, president of the Steel Corporation. *Ibid.*, pp. 319 ff.

109. The Geneva plant's annual capacity of 250,000 tons of structural shapes compares with an estimated total postwar market in the seven western states of about 213,000 tons. In rolled plates its capacity exceeded prospective demand by more than 200 per cent. *Ibid.*, DX 64, p. 652.

The Geneva plant was a fully integrated steel plant equipped with iron ore deposits, coal-mining and coking facilities, blast furnaces, open-hearth ingot furnaces, and rolling mills to produce plates and structural shapes. Report of the Surplus Property Administration to Congress on *Disposal of Government Iron and Steel Plants and Facilities*, October 8, 1945, pp. 26-27.

proximity to the new plants. Their expanded productive capacity virtually assured that western producers would be obliged to meet this demand, which would lead to lower delivered prices for all rolled and fabricated steel products. Third, as rail freight rates increased, the Steel Corporation found itself with a greater freight disadvantage in competition with western producers than it had had before the war.[110]

These several handicaps put the Steel Corporation at a disadvantage in competing for business on the Pacific Coast, particularly in heavy fabricated structural steel.[111] But the western market was too important for the Steel Corporation to relinquish. Before buying Consolidated it tentatively planned to build plants for making structural steel products in Los Angeles and San Francisco.[112]

110. Freight rates from Gary, Indiana, to Pacific Coast ports on fabricated structural steel had increased from $20.10 a ton in 1937 to $25.54 at the time of the hearings in the Columbia case. This compared with a rate of $9.89 from the Geneva plant and, with allowance for the $3 higher base price that was established at the Geneva plant, this gave the Geneva plant an advantage of $12.65 a ton. See *U.S.* v. *Columbia,* Rec., pp. 45, 200, and 588.

Another aspect of the rise in rail freight rates was the abolition of land-grant railroad rates on materials shipped for the government. To encourage the building of transcontinental railroads, the federal government during the second half of the nineteenth century gave these carriers large tracts of land in the public domain. In partial return for these subsidies, the railroads agreed to carry government property (and personnel, including troops) at reduced rates. After World War II Congress relieved the roads from this obligation.

This action placed the Steel Corporation at a disadvantage in getting government business in competition with western plants. Its importance is indicated by the fact that in 1937–1946, of the 499,605 tons of fabricated structural steel the Steel Corporation sold in eleven western states, 306,488 tons, or 62.5 per cent, were shipped to government agencies at land-grant freight rates. *Ibid.,* pp. 194-95.

111. Fabricated structural products are sold on specification for specific jobs—bridges, buildings, and the like, generally on competitive bids. Bethlehem is the Steel Corporation's chief competitor in the heavy structural field. With reference to the Steel Corporation's position Mr. Obbard testified as follows: "Well, the records that we have just gone through show that we can participate in Western business to any degree only when in the past we have had either some advantage by the way of an extremely specialized product or some freight . . . concession . . . For instance, in railroad bridges in which the carriers supply their own transportation at reduced rates we have been competitive." *Ibid.,* p. 199.

112. American Bridge Company recommended this before World War II. After the war the project was revived, but the Steel Corporation had not yet authorized it when it had the opportunity to buy Consolidated's plants. See *ibid.,* pp. 375-76.

Consolidated was the second or third largest seller of fabricated steel products on the Pacific Coast. During 1937–1942 it booked 5 per cent of all the orders for such steel placed in the eleven states in which it operated. During the same period the Steel Corporation booked 17 per cent. But Consolidated's business grew more rapidly than that of its rivals during World War II, and by 1946 it booked 11 per cent of the fabricated steel products ordered in its marketing area. Bethlehem booked the same amount, while the Steel Corporation's share had fallen to 13 per cent. *U.S.* v. *Columbia,* p. 512. The Steel Corporation contended that these figures did not reflect accurately the extent of competition between it and Consolidated because its business

Effect of Merger on Competition

A mere recital of these facts suggests that the Steel Corporation's acquisition of the Geneva plant and the plants of Consolidated would tend to lessen competition, actual and potential, in the sale of steel products in the Pacific Coast area. Nevertheless, the Supreme Court affirmed the District Court's judgment for the defendants. In rejecting the government's contention that the purchase of Consolidated restrained trade by eliminating competition in the business of supplying Consolidated with its rolled steel requirements, the Court clarified or modified its position in the Yellow Cab case. It stated:

> Exclusive dealings for rolled steel between Consolidated and United States Steel, brought about by vertical integration or otherwise, are not illegal, at any rate until the effect of such control is to unreasonably restrict the opportunities of competitors to market their products . . . It seems clear to us that vertical integration, as such, without more, cannot be held violative of the Sherman Act.[113]

As to the elimination of the competition between the Steel Corporation and Consolidated in the sale of fabricated steel products, the Court found this competition was not "substantial" and therefore, on the authority of the International Shoe case, that the consolidation was not illegal. "We do not undertake to prescribe any set of percentage figures by which to measure the reasonableness of a corporation's enlargement of its activities by the purchase of the assets of a competitor," the Court said. "The relative effect of percentage command of a market varies with the setting in which that factor is placed." [114]

---

was largely in products heavier than those produced by Consolidated. And the facts seem to support the Corporation's position.

113. *Ibid.*, pp. 524 and 525. This position is difficult to reconcile with the Court's position in the first Yellow Cab case. There it ruled that vertical integration excluding competitors from an annual replacement market for 5,000 cabs constituted a prima facie cause of action under the Sherman Act. The Court did not even inquire about, let alone state, the proportion that the replacement market controlled by Checker Cab constituted of the whole market available to cab manufacturers. It merely declared that 5,000 cabs is an appreciable part of the total. Consolidated's purchases of plates and shapes amounted to about 13 per cent of the total purchases in eleven states and 21 per cent in seven states. Are these "appreciable" amounts? The Supreme Court accepted the District Court's finding that Consolidated's requirements represented "a small part" of the total in its marketing area and that Consolidated was not a "substantial market" (cf. the Supreme Court's "appreciable") for rolled steel producers selling in competition with U.S. Steel. *Ibid.*, p. 511. The Court did not explain the difference, if any, between "substantial" and "appreciable."

114. *Ibid.*, pp. 527-28.

On the issue of whether the acquisition represented an "attempt to monopolize" the trade in fabricated steel products in the Pacific Coast market, the Court found it only "an appropriate business expansion by the Corporation." As in 1920, the Court acknowledged that the Corporation's size was impressive, but it declared that the "steel industry is also of impressive size and the welcome westward extension of that industry requires that the existing companies go into production or abandon that market to other organizations." [115]

The Court failed to see, or if it saw, ignored, the difference between the Corporation's "going into production" by building new plants in which to fabricate steel products (a move it was apparently prepared to make) and buying out plants already in operation. It is extremely unlikely that the Corporation would have abandoned the booming Pacific Coast market. By buying out Consolidated it buttressed its position as the largest seller of fabricated structural steel and it eliminated Consolidated's competition, actual and potential.

Mr. Justice Douglas Dissents

Mr. Justice Douglas, speaking for the minority, pointed to the basic significance of the acquisition when he said:

> We have here the problem of bigness. Its lesson should by now have been burned into our memory by Brandeis. *The Curse of Bigness* shows how size can become a menace—both industrial and social. It can be an industrial menace because it creates gross inequalities against existing or putative competitors. It can be a social menace—because of its control of prices . . .
>
> United States Steel, now that it owns the Geneva plant, has over 51 per cent of the rolled steel or ingot capacity of the Pacific Coast area. This acquisition gives it unquestioned domination there and protects it against growth of the independents in that developing region. That alone is sufficient to condemn the purchase. Its serious impact on competition and the economy is emphasized when it is recalled that United States Steel has one-third of the rolled steel production of the entire country. The least I can say is that a company that has that tremendous leverage on our economy is big enough.[116]

A consideration of the Steel Corporation's role in setting steel prices since 1902 lends support to this view of the Consolidated transaction. The Steel Corporation for nearly half a century has

115. *Ibid.*, p. 533.
116. *Ibid.*, pp. 535 and 539-40.

been the recognized price leader in the industry. Until 1948 it vigorously defended and followed the basing point system of pricing, which helped make its leadership effective.[117]

On the whole, the organization and the structure of the steel industry, with one corporation overshadowing the field, have not been consistent with effective competition. Sellers are so few and their power so great in the steel market that, if they are rational, fully informed, similarly minded, and self-disciplined, they will set prices like a monopolist. Such a condition contributes to the development of a business morale, a live-and-let-live attitude, a unity of purpose, which are essential to pricing policies that maximize returns for the few.[118] Prices are apt to remain consistently above costs—marginal in the short run and total unit in the long.[119] A situation such as that in steel may enable companies to reap the fruits of conspiracy without paying its penalties. Industrial history and economic logic suggest that approval of the Steel Corporation's purchase of Consolidated was contrary to sound public policy.

No Requirement of Divestiture in Titanium Decree

The outcome of the National Lead case[120] illustrates again the judicial failure to accept the principle that it is difficult to have effective competition with only a few sellers in the market. National Lead and du Pont were partners in a world cartel and patent pool so

117. Also, it has collaborated with other steel producers in determining costs, without which uniform pricing for steel "extras" would have been virtually impossible. Mr. Fairless, in testifying before the TNEC on how the price of extras was determined, said: "We arrive at these extras by anticipating in some instances our costs. . . . We have technical committees, manufacturing committees, in our Institute that make studies of various phases . . . They don't fix the price charged for these special services rendered, but they do make analyses of the costs and studies of the costs, and since our motive is only to charge cost for services rendered, then obviously it is our duty to develop the best cost that exists, not only within our own company but within this industry." *Investigation of the Concentration of Economic Power*, Temporary National Economic Committee, Hearings pursuant to Pub.Res. 113 (75th Cong.), Pt. 19, p. 10560. (These hearings will hereinafter be cited: TNEC Hearings, Pt. —.) Cf. Chap. 6.

118. Sellers of steel in following the lead of the Steel Corporation defend their policy in the name of competition. Eugene Grace, for example, testified as follows before the TNEC: "Our general policy as to prices is to be competitive, and when the Steel Corporation announces a set of prices it is the best guide that we have as to what our competition may be." TNEC Hearings, Pt. 19, p. 10601.

119. Perhaps the best reason for believing that effective competition has not determined prices in the steel industry is the industry's general policy during the 1930's of pricing steel so high that it could make a profit when operating at about 40 per cent of capacity. *Ibid.*, Pt. 5, p. 2194.

120. *U.S.* v. *National Lead Co.*, 332 U.S. 319 (1947). Titanium pigments are used in making paints, to make them whiter or to give them a lighter tint.

tightly knit that "It was more difficult for the independent outsider to enter this business than for a camel to make its proverbial passage through the eye of a needle." [121] They controlled 100 per cent of the domestic output of titanium when they entered into this arrangement.

Both the District Court and the Supreme Court found the arrangement unlawful, cancelled the agreements by which it had been effected, and ordered the defendants to license their titanium patents at a reasonable royalty to any applicant. But both courts refused the government's plea that du Pont and National Lead each be ordered to transfer one of its two plants to a new and independent corporation.

Effective Competition in Titanium Unlikely

Under the circumstances mere cancellation of the unlawful agreements and compulsory patent licensing at reasonable royalties are unlikely to insure effective competition. Having pooled their patents and technical knowledge, and having insulated the American market from foreign competition, National Lead and du Pont controlled the "manufacture and sale of titanium pigments and compounds in the United States to the exclusion of all actual or potential competition." [122]

During the operation of the unlawful combination, National Lead

121. *U.S.* v. *National Lead Co.,* 63 Fed.Supp. 513 (1945), p. 521. The District Court further stated: "When the story is seen as a whole, there is no blinking the fact that there is no free competition in titanium. Every pound of it is trammelled by privately imposed regulation. The channels of this commerce have not been formed by the winds and currents of competition. They are, in large measure, artificial canals privately constructed. The borders of the private domain in titanium are guarded by hundreds of patents, procured without opposition and maintained without litigation. The accumulated power of this private empire, at the outbreak of World War II was tremendous. . . . the newcomer is confronted by a veritable jungle of patent claims through which only the very powerful and stouthearted would venture . . . These patents, through the agreements in which they are enmeshed and the manner in which they have been used, have, in fact, been forged into instruments of domination of an entire industry. The net effect is that a business, originally founded upon patents which have long since expired, is today less accessible to free enterprise than when it was first launched." *Ibid.,* p. 532.

122. *U.S.* v. *National Lead Co.,* Record and Briefs, U.S. Supreme Court, October Term, 1946, District Court's Findings of Fact, No. 95, par. 7, pp. 71-72. In 1943 National Lead made and sold 76.5 per cent of the composite and 46.4 per cent of the pure TiO_2 made and sold in the United States (Findings of Fact, No. 3), while du Pont made and sold 23.5 per cent of the composite and 45.1 per cent of the pure (Findings of Fact, No. 9). The remaining 8½ per cent of pure TiO_2 was made and sold by two companies, American Zirconium and Virginia Chemical. American Zirconium operated under licenses from du Pont and National Lead and 10 per cent of its stock was owned by National Lead. Virginia Chemical operated under restrictive licenses from du Pont. Findings of Fact, 31, 32, 84, 85.

and du Pont confined their competition to sales efforts and differentiation of products. Though each produced titanium pigments having special uses, they tried to match each other's major (standard) products, which they sold at identical prices. There was no evidence of direct collusion in fixing prices.[123] But specific agreements on prices were apparently unnecessary to insure common pricing policies.

Occupying the field virtually alone, du Pont and National Lead would have been shortsighted indeed to engage in a competitive price struggle that might have left their relative positions in the market unchanged and would surely have greatly reduced their earnings.[124] Schooled as they are as monopoly partners, disciplined in the policy of live and let live, they are unlikely to engage in forthright price competition after the dissolution of the combination. And so far as competition from other quarters is concerned, any rival in the business must start with the handicap of paying monopoly tribute in the form of royalties to du Pont or National Lead on patents which they used illegally to establish control over the industry.[125] Even divestiture would not have guaranteed, but it would have made more likely, effective competition in the sale of titanium.

Present Plight of Antitrust Policy

This review of the Supreme Court's varying attitudes in recent antitrust cases shows the Court's distinct reluctance relentlessly to adapt its interpretation of the Sherman Act to the requirements of an effectively competitive economy. Congress in passing the Act declared in favor of free competition in trade and industry. It expected the courts to determine in particular cases what constituted restraints on trade or attempts to monopolize, but it laid down a general policy that should be clear and it used language broad enough to permit the courts to carry out that policy.

Recent decisions have shown a new judicial appreciation of the

123. *Ibid.*, Findings of Fact, No. 78.

124. This is particularly true inasmuch as a general objective of their unlawful cartel arrangements had been to insure "friendly and cooperative" rather than "hostile" competition. *Ibid.*, Findings of Fact, No. 79, par. 3.

125. As Mr. Justice Douglas said in a critical dissenting opinion concurred in by two other justices (out of a seven-man bench), "Each dollar of royalty adds a dollar to the costs of the new competitor and gives the established licensor another dollar with which to fight that competition." *U.S.* v. *National Lead*, 332 U.S., p. 338.

Even National Lead joined the government in urging royalty-free licensing of the illegally used patents, contending that du Pont would have a significant cost advantage if National Lead were forced to pay royalties to du Pont.

significance of corporate size and market power for the maintenance of free enterprise. They have recognized that in determining whether there has been a violation of the Sherman Act the possession of monopolistic power is more important than the subjective purpose, or "specific intent," of those who exercise such power. At the same time, the courts are apparently unwilling to follow this line of reasoning to its logical end. If a corporation does not attain absolute monopoly, if its acquisition of competitors springs from genuine business requirements, the courts still adhere to the rule of reason, even though economic theory and industrial history teach that, in markets where sellers are few and large, well informed and disciplined, effective competition is unlikely. The Sherman Act was designed, not primarily to punish monopolists (those having 100 per cent control of some market), but to prevent all restraints of trade that stifle competition.

Chapter 10

TRADE PRACTICES AND THE DECLINE OF COMPETITION

FOR COMPETITION to work effectively, sellers must conduct their business according to recognized rules. Otherwise the competitive process is apt to degenerate into a Donnybrook fair. The rules establish a plane of competition, a set of standards for business behavior.

While the basic principles of fair dealing in trade derive from custom and rest on moral sanctions, governments have generally found it necessary to spell them out in considerable detail and make their observance obligatory. And this process of definition and enforcement poses a problem. For the rules must not be so rigorous as to restrict initiative unduly. Nor may they be so lax as to defeat their ultimate objective—the creation of a business environment hospitable to independent enterprise. In sum, they must at the same time repress vicious rivalry and foster vigorous rivalry; and, properly conceived, these aspects are complementary. In repressing vicious rivalry, they foster vigorous rivalry, thus enabling market prices to perform their proper functions of guiding consumer choices, directing resources into the channels of most economical use, and promoting economic progress.

The specific content of appropriate rules as well as suitable procedures for their enforcement vary directly with the size and complexity of the economy. Quite simple rules enforceable by ordinary criminal proceedings and civil suits in the courts sufficed, a century ago, for a relatively homogeneous society producing a few staple commodities and tools by handicraft methods for exchange in local trade. Buyers and sellers knew each other, as a rule, and therefore could appraise—and keep a check on—each other's integrity. Merchandise was open to inspection and it required no laboratory tests to determine its composition nor extraordinary technical skill to judge its quality. In such circumstances, a few plain rules giving rights of action to persons injured by fraud, theft, defamation, or deceptive diversion of patronage (for example, by simulating another's trade-mark or name) were generally enough to protect the interests of both buyers and sellers.[1] Not in vain did the law admonish buyers to beware and sellers to give honest measure.

Times changed, and trade practices changed with them. But the development of law is notoriously sluggish, so that adjustment of the rules to the radically altered market conditions was slow. Indeed, the adjustment is still incomplete, despite the belated prohibition of "unfair methods of competition," establishment of an administrative agency to stamp them out, and vigorous efforts in recent years to raise the standards of business behavior.[2] Meanwhile the virtually undisciplined pursuit of business advantage by sellers led to the widespread adoption of marketing techniques and sale policies that provided powerful tools for market control. By weakening either consumer defenses or the ability of rival sellers to stay in the market if they depend simply on the quality of their wares and the attractiveness of their prices, these aggressive selling methods have frequently impaired competition.

Causes of Changes in Markets

The basic cause of the revolution in markets that made traditional rules of the game obsolete was the advance in technology. The harnessing of steam power and the use of machines in manufacture played a significant part in the transformation of markets.

But it was the application of steam power to transportation and the use of electricity for communication that played the leading role in the revolution of marketing.[3] The railroads knit together all sections of the country in an interdependent economy. National markets replaced local markets. In communication the telegraph and telephone annihilated distance. Air transport and radio later facilitated still further the conduct of business on a nation-wide scale.

1. Myron W. Watkins, *Public Regulation of Competitive Practices,* 3d edition, National Industrial Conference Board, New York, 1940, Chap. 2. The reference in the text is to the American situation. In Europe, a good many of the long-standing statutory (and assize) regulations of the composition, price, and mode of sale of staple commodities, like bread, ale, and cloth, survived into the nineteenth century.

2. See discussion of Federal Trade Commission record in Chap. 11.

3. See Chap. 2. In effect, this is simply a recognition of the validity of Adam Smith's basic tenet: the division of labor is limited by the extent of the market. Economic history has fully confirmed his insight, though it is contrary to popular opinion, which is inclined to put the cart before the horse.

In many industries these developments led to a drastic reduction in the number and a prodigious increase in the size of sellers.

Along with widening of markets came change in the nature of market transactions. Purchase and sale ceased, in large part, to be a matter of direct bargaining between buyer and seller. With steady improvement in the means of communication, personal solicitation of patronage gave way to broadcast appeals through the mails and, above all, through magazine, newspaper, and radio advertisements. Except for some kinds of industrial equipment and supplies, under the new dispensation ordinarily a manufacturing concern initially determines the composition and quality of its products. Although it ignores consumer needs and tastes at its peril, and in fact makes strenuous efforts to anticipate them, it generally makes up the goods on its own initiative in standard sizes and styles and relies more and more on salesmanship to sell them.

Changing Role of Merchants

Today, the common run of retailers rarely qualify as expert judges of merchandise. Whereas formerly merchants acted in effect as agents of consumers, prescribing the quality of goods, selecting suitable varieties, and bargaining for low prices, increasingly they have become mere adjuncts to or outlets for manufacturers. While this has worked to the detriment of consumers in some important respects, it has been compensated for in many markets by a counter-development, the rise of the mass distributor. Chain stores, mail-order houses, department stores, and in recent years chain department stores have taken over an increasing share of distributive trade.[4] Mass distributors have gone a long way toward restoring the balance in wholesale markets. They have confronted manufacturers with large-scale buying power, expert scrutiny of merchandise, and demands for price concessions and frequently even for goods made to their own specifications—sometimes for sale under their own house brands.

The resultant evening up of bargaining power in wholesale markets probably works out to the advantage of consumers—at least as long as the mass distributors continue to face the stubborn competition of so-called independent merchants. (The real "indepen-

4. See Chap. 2.

dents" vis-à-vis the giant manufacturing companies are the chains, mail-order houses, and the like.) But at the same time the development of large-scale distribution has contributed to the increasingly impersonal character of merchandising. Even more than the transformation of erstwhile independent merchants into adjuncts of manufacturers, it signalizes the emergence of a conveyor-belt system of distribution. The typical market transaction has become quite impersonal. Ordinarily the manufacturer (and increasingly the retailer, too) is a corporation, with a "personality" compounded of legal fiction and advertising fantasy.

This depersonalization of marketing operations has both advantages and disadvantages. On the one hand, it eliminates waste of time and energy in higgling over prices. It also reduces risks of fraud, protects the more gullible consumers from the wiles of unscrupulous charlatans. Giant corporations with millions invested in nation-wide markets cannot afford to operate on fly-by-night principles. On the other hand, in cultivating an impersonal market comprising a widely assorted group of potential customers, manufacturers must offer a standardized product at a price that will attract mass purchasing power. This may reduce the emphasis on product superiority as a means of increasing sales. Thus, as consumer welfare becomes more dependent on market forces and less on personal factors, it becomes more imperative that market forces be such as to adequately protect consumer interests.

Changes in the Character of Goods

Another important factor in transforming markets—one that handicaps consumers in buying intelligently—is the change in the character of goods. Instead of staple commodities—flour, lard, salt, woolens, cottons, hammers, nails, stepladders—made of a few common and well-known materials, markets now offer a wide array of complex mechanical devices, obscure chemical concoctions, intricate electrical appliances, and synthetic materials.

What looks like soap may be a detergent. What appears to be cotton may be rayon. The casual buyer cannot distinguish a chromatic film from an ordinary photographic film, or an AM from an FM radio receiving set. Even a trained technician would have difficulty in determining by inspection the relative merits of two or more weed killers, antifreezes, or insulating materials. He is obliged to rely on what the manufacturer says the stuff is made of and will do. Buyers are at a disadvantage in such markets.[5] Moreover, they are so much more numerous than sellers that their individual bargaining power is slight, diluted. Scattered, unorganized, usually ignorant of merchandise qualities, consumers are easily swayed by artful salesmanship. In fact, a big sales campaign usually enlists science—represented by a trained psychologist—as well as art.

Significance of Market Transformation

The dwindling possibility of intelligent purchase set at nought one of the basic assumptions of perfect competition. Correlatively, the growing disproportion between the number and size of sellers and of buyers weakened the incentives of the former to offer better bargains. In short, it tended to devitalize competition. The line of least resistance and most profit for each of a comparatively few sellers in a given branch of trade was to make buying automatic—to eliminate sober comparison of the qualities and prices of goods.

If buyers shift their patronage at will from one to another of a few sellers, it leads to spasmodic changes in demand for each seller's product. And that, in turn, may spell ruin when sellers are engaged in mass production *in anticipation of demand.* To stabilize the demand for its products in the continental markets it must reach, a large-scale manufacturing concern feels compelled to identify its products and cultivate the good will of ultimate consumers through advertising. Consequently, brands and trade-marks have multiplied.[6] These symbols serve, at the same time, to differentiate goods from different sources, though the several branded products may be of

5. S. P. Kaidanovsky, *Consumer Standards,* TNEC Monograph No. 24, Washington, 1941, p. 338.

6. Cf. Paul W. Stewart and J. Frederic Dewhurst, *Does Distribution Cost Too Much?,* Twentieth Century Fund, New York, 1939, pp. 302 ff.; and H. von Beckerath, *Modern Industrial Organization,* McGraw-Hill, New York, 1933, pp. 196 ff.

In food industries, particularly, the custom of packaging products has developed rapidly, along with branding. For many such products the adoption of branding makes packaging necessary. Ordinarily the direct costs of branding and packaging are not high; but the indirect costs are substantial. Associated as they are with pervasive changes in sellers' pricing policies, with the increasing emphasis on nonprice forms of competition, and with the growth of advertising, branding and packaging have become a potent influence in raising the costs of marketing food. See William H. Nicholls, *Imperfect Competition Within Agricultural Industries,* Iowa State College Press, Ames, 1941, pp. 233 ff.; and *idem,* "Imperfect Competition in Agricultural Processing and Distributing Industries," *Canadian Journal of Economics and Political Science,* May 1944, p. 161.

the same kind and of substantially the same quality. If buyers can be made sufficiently brand-conscious, they may make purchases by brand as a matter of carefully conditioned habit instead of deliberate choice.

The drive by manufacturers to create consumer preference for their branded products has had four important consequences: (1) it has tended to drive out the old-fashioned independent manufacturer; (2) it has tended to suppress price competition among rival manufacturers selling substantially similar products; (3) it has led to resale price maintenance and the restraint of competition at the retail level; and (4) it has tended to reduce the effectiveness of quality competition.

Decline of the Independent Manufacturer

In the face of the trend toward national advertising, companies that had customarily concentrated on *manufacturing,* making a good product and making it efficiently, while depending on merchants to distribute it, increasingly found their market outlets drying up. Products unbranded, or branded but unadvertised, will seldom sell themselves, however high their quality in relation to price. They generally require sales promotion by merchants. Hence, with the eclipse of the independent merchant, makers of such products met increasing difficulty in disposing of them.

True, the lone-wolf manufacturer might have learned that it pays to advertise. Some of them did learn. But many of them learned also that it costs to advertise. The financial resources of many companies, even among those big enough to achieve all the technical advantages of large-scale production, did not permit such large expenditures as an effective national advertising campaign requires.[7]

Just as the rise of the mass distributor has compensated in part for the decline of the independent merchant, so it has also counteracted in part the tendency for the independent wholesaler to be eliminated. The mass distributor who frequently prefers to sell an unbranded or his own branded product has become a powerful agency

7. Cf. Federal Trade Commission, *Report on Resale Price Maintenance,* Washington, 1931, Pt. 2, p. 32.

Though advertising costs per unit of sales may not represent a high proportion of the retail price, in fact may be less than the per unit cost of other methods of selling, this circumstance in no way detracts from the significance of the fact that "an effective national advertising campaign" may be beyond the financial reach of small manufacturers.

in making competition effective at both the retail and the wholesale level.

Monopolistic Competition

While mass distribution has insured a continuing place for some manufacturers of unbranded products, it has not effectively checked the tendency for large-scale manufacturers to rely primarily on product differentiation and the cultivation of consumer good will rather than on price inducements to retain consumer patronage. Trade rivalry by manufacturers producing consumers' goods has become increasingly an effort to so differentiate a product that consumers will continue to buy it even though rival products may sell for less.[8]

To business rivalry aimed at insulating the demand for a particular product through advertising in such a way that its market cannot be captured by a rival even at lower prices, economists have given the name "monopolistic competition." While they are not agreed as to the effectiveness of such rival efforts, they generally hold that competitive advertising directed to such ends tends to be self-defeating by increasing average costs. Although it thus forces prices to higher levels, it does not insure monopoly earnings, particularly where potential rivals are free to enter the industry and engage in similar practices.[9]

Advertising outlays, of course, also reflect other ends than product differentiation. Advertising is a means of communication, a way of acquainting potential customers with the merits of new articles that they may learn to value highly. Without such advertising, it might

8. As the Federal Trade Commission has said, "The more brand-conscious the consumer can be made . . . the better it is from the viewpoint of the manufacturer, to whom advantage often accrues from placing a fanciful trade mark or brand name on a well-known article . . . to obscure the fact that identically the same thing may be purchased under another name, and often for less money." *Ibid.*, p. 8.

9. Cf. Edward Chamberlin, *The Theory of Monopolistic Competition*, Harvard University Press, Cambridge, 1933, Chaps. 5-7; Arthur R. Burns, *The Decline of Competition*, McGraw-Hill, New York, 1936, Chap. 8; and Neil H. Borden, *The Economic Effects of Advertising*, Irwin, Chicago, 1942, Chap. 6.

Advertising has many functions and its forms are protean. Its various types and purposes can be, and have been, classified in scores of different ways. One useful classification distinguishes defensive from aggressive advertising. Defensive advertising tries to persuade buyers to "let well enough alone." Aggressive advertising seeks to persuade them that something different is synonymous with something superior. Defensive advertising tries to forestall, and aggressive advertising to induce, a sense of lacking. The differences between these two basic types of advertising correspond to differences in the trade position of advertisers and in the nature of products advertised.

be difficult to sell enough to achieve the economies of scale. On the other hand, competitive advertising may so decentralize production as to preclude the economies of scale. It is not always possible to differentiate precisely between socially economic and uneconomic advertising, but indicative of the trend toward "monopolistic competition" is the rise in advertising expenditures in the United States from $1.5 billion in 1927 to $2 billion in 1937, and a further rise in the next decade to $3.9 billion.[10]

Resale Price Maintenance

Not only has the manufacturer's effort to differentiate his product in the mind of the consumer from those of his rivals, however similar in fact they may be, tended to make price competition less effective at the manufacturer's level. It has tended also to make price competition less effective at the retail level. This has come about through the manufacturer's practice of setting a price at which the retailer shall sell his product and insisting on adherence to it. The original impulse to limit the freedom of dealers in pricing a branded product appears to have sprung from the desire of manufacturers to make their advertising more effective, in short, to reap its full potential benefits.[11]

10. Data on total advertising expenditures are unofficial, and no continuous series of estimates covering a long period is available. The sources of the figures cited are, respectively: National Bureau of Economic Research, *Recent Economic Changes*, McGraw-Hill, New York, 1929, Vol. 1, p. 402; Stewart and Dewhurst, *op. cit.*, p. 226; and H. Zeisel, "1947 United States Advertising Volume Sets New Record," *Printers Ink*, April 30, 1948, p. 28. The methods of computation used in these several studies differed radically. The evidence suggests that estimates for 1927, 1937, and 1947 made on the same basis would show a rate of growth substantially higher than that reflected in the figures quoted, which roughly approximate changes in national income expressed in terms of current dollars.

Borden (*op. cit.*, p. 54) estimated the total cost of advertising in 1935 at $1.7 billion. A comparison of Borden's estimates of expenditures on various media in 1935 with Zeisel's breakdown of the 1947 total shows that: (1) the share of newspapers contracted from 34 to 31 per cent; (2) the share of magazines expanded from 13 to 20 per cent; and (3) radio's proportion expanded from 7 to 16 per cent. The greatest change was in direct-mail advertising, which accounted for 32 per cent of the 1935 total but for only 9 per cent in 1947.

These statistics suggest that mass appeals are taking the place of personal solicitation and that the fostering of undiscriminating good will—which is about all that sponsorship of a radio program can accomplish—is rapidly displacing the informative function of advertising. The spectacular decline in direct-mail advertising points up the atrophy of the traditional function of advertising: to acquaint potential buyers with what sellers have to offer. However, both the volume of advertising and its distribution by types of media vary greatly from year to year. See *Tide's* index of national advertising, for example in the issue of February 15, 1945, p. 36.

11. Cf. E. R. A. Seligman and R. A. Love, *Price Cutting and Price Maintenance*, Harper, New York, 1932, Chaps. 2, 10, and 11. See also Federal Trade Commission,

The primary purpose of manufacturers' advertising was to persuade consumers to insist on a particular product. The advertisers' appeal was a substitute for dealers' advice to retail buyers in the selection of merchandise. Unable to control merchants' choice of brands on which to push sales, manufacturers solicited patronage of the ultimate buyers directly—through advertising.

When the practice arose about a half century ago, the notion prevailed that it was not enough to cultivate a favorable attitude toward the advertiser's branded product. If a manufacturer spent millions on advertising he naturally expected to get results in terms of sales. In other words, to justify their cost, advertisements must stimulate buying.[12] But few consumers intend to buy anything *regardless of price.* One of the most important elements in any market transaction is the price. To eliminate bargaining—to induce prospective buyers to decide on buying the advertised brand before they enter a store—many national advertisers thought it necessary to announce a definite price.[13] Manifestly, the announced price had to be uniform. Hence the effort to enforce resale price maintenance.

Significance of Resale Price Maintenance

Depriving dealers of discretion in the pricing of merchandise obviously restricts competition at the retail level. An efficient merchant cannot, so handicapped, get the full competitive advantage of his lower costs. Equally important, resale price maintenance has facilitated price stabilization at the manufacturers' level, particularly among the few big companies that have been able by aggressive selling to pre-empt the lion's share of the national market for certain important lines of consumers' goods.[14] With leading advertisers

---

Report on Resale Price Maintenance, Washington, 1945, p. 5. (This report will hereinafter be cited: FTC, 1945 RPM.)

12. For a more detailed discussion of the origins of resale price maintenance, consult *Public Regulation of Competitive Practices,* cited above, p. 90.

13. See Roy W. Johnson, William H. Ingersoll, and G. H. Montague, *The Control of Resale Prices,* Dartnell, Chicago, 1936, pp. 139 ff. Where disparity in delivery costs between near and remote sections of the market was too great, some modification of price uniformity was admissible. Before World War I, when price quotation in national advertising was common, Pacific Coast or trans-Mississippi prices were frequently set higher than those for the rest of the country.

14. Summarizing the results of its recent extensive investigation of the practice, the Federal Trade Commission declared that "Application of resale price maintenance . . . has been fostered in certain industries where production is largely concentrated in the hands of a few manufacturers, as in the case of surgical dressings, . . . some soap products, cooking oils, and firearms." FTC, 1945 RPM, p. lvi.

controlling not only the wholesale but also the retail marketing of their branded products, no single one of them could escape responsibility for spoiling the market. If a company in such a position should venture to set its fixed retail price at a figure out of line with those set by other members of the dominant group, it would invite reprisals. As Galbraith says:

> The extent to which monopolistic competition involves a complicated structure of resale price maintenance is a phase of this problem which has . . . been somewhat neglected. The manufacturer . . . of an unadvertised and undifferentiated product has no concern with the margin absorbed by the retailer . . . When the product is differentiated, however, the retail price becomes a matter of concern. It is in part to avoid price competition that he expends money to differentiate his product.[15]

Resale price maintenance effectively places responsibility for price cutting on the manufacturer. He has an implicit obligation, if not an express commitment, to withhold supplies from any distributor who fails to respect the advertised price. As a result, therefore, the practice of resale price maintenance relieves each of a few large sellers of a nationally advertised commodity of uncertainty about its rivals' price policies and of the continual pressure for price reductions that competitive distribution brings. In the words of the Federal Trade Commission, "The essence of resale price maintenance is control of price competition." [16]

Each such manufacturer, furthermore, has an interest in maintaining a relatively high wholesale price—one high enough to permit recovery of heavy advertising expense plus some monopoly revenue from a particular brand. And each also has an incentive for preserving a retail price correspondingly high. The high cost of national advertising makes it imperative that the advertiser get the greatest possible number of retail outlets to stock his brand. And a wide retailers' margin is an effective device for encouraging distributors to carry it. Thus the maintenance of stipulated resale prices by manu-

15. J. K. Galbraith, "Monopoly Power and Price Rigidities," *Quarterly Journal of Economics,* May 1936, p. 468. It was probably the failure to recognize the connection between resale price maintenance and oligopolistic conditions in many manufacturing industries that led some strong supporters of antitrust policy to join with manufacturers in advocating legalization of the practice. Louis D. Brandeis, for instance, before he became a member of the Supreme Court favored such legislation, because he believed the practice was quite consistent with the maintenance of effective competition among producers in marketing their several rival brands. See his essay on this subject in *The Curse of Bigness,* Viking Press, New York, 1934, pp. 125-28.

16. FTC, 1945 RPM, p. lxi.

facturers works in two ways to stifle competition: (1) by putting high- and low-cost distributors on the same level and (2) by fostering monopolistic pricing among producers of nationally advertised brands.

Miscarriage of Resale Price Maintenance

In the past twenty-five years several things have combined to make many manufacturers who once were boosters of resale price maintenance less enthusiastic about the policy. By and large, manufacturers have shown growing skepticism of it, while organized dealers have become its enthusiastic supporters.[17]

One reason for the modified attitude of manufacturers was the confusing course of public policy. Most of the questionable trade practices that grew out of the radical structural change in industry around the turn of the century violated no law. Only after more recent legislation, usually belated and often inadequate at the outset, did the law frown on them. But resale price maintenance had just the opposite history. From the beginning, the courts declined to enforce price maintenance contracts.[18] As time passed, the judicial attitude stiffened: the courts condemned the practice as a violation of the antitrust laws.[19] Until the 1930's, neither Congress nor the Supreme Court showed any disposition to tolerate the practice in any form that businessmen considered workable.[20]

17. *Ibid.*, pp. 5, 142-249, 396-98, and 424-27.

18. *Bobbs-Merrill Co.* v. *Straus,* 210 U.S. 339 (1908). This was the first case involving the issue to reach the Supreme Court. In three lower-court decisions, price maintenance provisions affecting the sale of patented articles had earlier been upheld. In effect, the Bobbs-Merrill case overruled these decisions. See *Public Regulation of Competitive Practices,* cited above, p. 97; cf. FTC, 1945 RPM, p. 23.

Later cases confirming the doctrine applied in the Bobbs-Merrill case include: *Dr. Miles Medical Co.* v. *Park,* 220 U.S. 373 (1911); *Bauer* v. *O'Donnell,* 229 U.S. 1 (1913); *Straus* v. *Victor Co.,* 243 U.S. 490 (1917); and *Boston Store* v. *Gramophone Co.,* 246 U.S. 8 (1917).

19. *U.S.* v. *Schrader's Sons Co.,* 252 U.S. 85 (1920).

20. In the Colgate case, the Supreme Court held it was not illegal for a manufacturer to refuse to deal with distributors who failed to maintain his announced resale price. *U.S.* v. *Colgate & Co.,* 250 U.S. 300 (1919). But in the Beech-Nut case the Court made it plain that the law condemned any such plan that involved cooperation between dealers and the manufacturer. *FTC* v. *Beech-Nut Co.,* 257 U.S. 441 (1922). Since enforcement of resale price maintenance is practically impossible without the cooperation of retailers, this decision amounted to a virtual condemnation of the practice per se.

The persistent efforts over two decades of manufacturers of nationally advertised brands to obtain legislative sanction for resale price maintenance were as futile as their efforts to circumvent the judicial proscription of the practice. See FTC, 1945 RPM, pp. 39-45. Not until groups of organized dealers, politically more powerful because

Then retail trade associations, among which those in the drug trade were most active, got behind the movement and the picture changed rapidly. Within five years proponents of the policy succeeded in legalizing it.[21] They used a new strategy—working first on state legislatures and then seeking congressional exemption of resale price maintenance from antitrust-law prohibitions within the states that authorized the practice. The final consummation came in 1937 with the enactment by Congress of the Miller-Tydings amendment to the Sherman Act.[22] This law, which opened the way to effective application of resale price maintenance, owed much to the aggressive lobbying of the National Retail Druggists Association.[23] Even so, it passed Congress only in the form of a rider to an appropriations bill, which the President signed under protest.

The state "fair-trade" acts and the Miller-Tydings amendment were not responses to agitation of manufacturers. By the time organized dealers succeeded in reversing public policy on the issue, the manufacturers, the Federal Trade Commission found, were generally lukewarm.[24] In part this change may have been traceable to difficulties and disappointments connected with attempts to enforce price maintenance during the years when the law was hostile. But it probably also reflected growing fear that the practice might boomerang, that it might become a means whereby strong dealer organizations could exert more control over the retail price of a manufacturer's branded product than could the brand owner. Solid grounds, the sequel shows, exist for such a suspicion.

---

of their greater numbers and vote-swinging influence, got behind the drive for such legislation did Congress succumb to the lobbyists.

21. The first state law specifically approving resale price maintenance was a 1931 California statute. It was amended in 1933 to make a fixed resale price binding even on dealers that had not voluntarily contracted to observe such a price limitation—the nonsigner clause—and other states quickly followed suit. When the Supreme Court upheld the constitutionality of the so-called "fair-trade" statutes, all modelled on the California measure, and Congress exempted from the antitrust laws interstate sales contracts stipulating resale prices in states having "fair-trade" legislation, the way was clear at last for legalized minimum retail price fixing. See *Old Dearborn Co.* v. *Seagram Corp.*, 299 U.S. 183 (1936); and *Pep Boys* v. *Pyroil Sales Co.*, 299 U.S. 198 (1936).

Before these decisions, thirteen states had legalized resale price maintenance. Within a year, twenty-eight additional states adopted similar legislation, and by 1945 resale price maintenance was lawful in all but three states. See FTC, 1945 RPM, p. xxviii and Chap. 4.

22. U.S. Code, Title 15, c. 1, Sec. 1.

23. FTC, 1945 RPM, pp. 64-66.

24. *Ibid.*, pp. xxvii and xxxiii.

Another Factor: Decline of Price Advertising

Manufacturers discovered, too, that effective promotion of brand good will did not require them to give price information to consumers. Indeed, they sometimes found that announcing prices was a handicap. Buyers often suspected that the "maintained" prices were not bargains. And sellers experienced difficulties in adjusting their announced prices to rapidly changing costs during the deflationary 1930's and, especially, during the inflationary 1940's. At any rate, in recent years there has been a marked change from the earlier custom of quoting prices in manufacturers' advertisements—either f.o.b. factory for heavy items like automobiles or over-the-counter figures for small articles like soap or toothpaste.[25] Instead, in soliciting buyers, manufacturers increasingly appeal to noneconomic motives, such as pride, snobbery, prejudice, fear, or envy. Experience seems to have dispelled the early notion that the efficacy of national advertising hinged on price information that would enable the consumer at once to make up his mind to buy.[26]

In such circumstances, manufacturers have found less advantage in resale price maintenance than it once seemed to promise. Accordingly, all but "a small proportion" of them, the Federal Trade Commission states, have stopped promoting the practice.[27] Among different branches of trade, the use of price maintenance contracts by manufacturers varies widely. It is most common in the drug and cosmetic industries and least common in hardware and food.[28] Adoption of

25. Not even Wrigley emphasizes the price of chewing gum in magazine advertising. Price is seldom mentioned in radio broadcasting. In the main, only in newspaper advertising and counter displays are prices still quoted.

Because of the high proportion of the cost of materials to total cost of some branded products, their prices are more variable than those of others in which processing and selling costs predominate. For this reason chiefly, cured meats and most grocery items are sold, as a rule, without resale price protection. See *ibid.*, p. xxviii.

26. Doubtless the emergence of radio as a big advertising medium helps explain why price information has become much less common and conspicuous in national advertising. Audiences "tune in" for entertainment mainly and are impatient of direct persuasion to buy products. Yet the rapid growth of this kind of advertising attests to the sales-promotional efficacy of hypnotic repetition. Enveloping a brand in a nebulous aura of synthetic prestige appears to be all that is necessary to induce people to buy it.

27. *Ibid.*, p. xxvii.

28. The Trade Commission found that "relatively few food products have been placed under minimum resale price contracts" and that "resale price maintenance in the hardware trade has made little progress." On the other hand, "minimum resale price contracts have been more generally adopted in the drug-store trade than in any other trade." *Ibid.*, at pp. xxix, xxxv, and xxxiv, respectively.

In the tobacco industry a great difference obtains in the extent of price maintenance as applied to cigars and to cigarettes. Very few cigarettes are sold subject to resale

the policy by manufacturers apparently hinges less on their independent calculation of its advantages to them than on the extent of the pressure organized retailers can exert.[29]

Influence of Chain Stores

But probably the most important influence in the disillusionment of manufacturers with resale price maintenance has been the tremendous growth of mass-distribution enterprises. As previously indicated, the rise of department stores, mail-order houses and, above all, chain stores wrought a veritable revolution in merchandising, particularly after World War I.[30]

The chief means used by chain stores to increase sales was price reduction. Cut prices became a symbol of chain store merchandising —in groceries, drugs, notions, shoes, automobile accessories, and other lines. The chains, in fact, throve on the high-price policy that resale price maintenance encouraged. Even if a manufacturer of some brand of soap, hair tonic, mustard, or automobile tires refused to supply a cut-price chain and vigilantly policed the channels of trade to prevent delivery of his product into the chain's hands, he could

---

price restrictions, but in some states such restrictions apply to as much as 75 per cent of cigar sales. A similar situation exists in the beverage industry, with soft drinks and beer generally free of resale price restrictions and distilled liquors commonly subject to them. *Ibid.,* at pp. xxxvii and xxxix-xliv, respectively.

29. For example, in Ohio retail grocery trade associations put on an aggressive drive to line up manufacturers and succeeded in persuading "approximately 55 manufacturers" to place "roughly 200 items under minimum resale price contracts." Elsewhere, however, "not enough food products are under [minimum resale price] contract to be significant with respect to the competitive situation among food retail dealers." And this reflects, in part, "the reluctance of manufacturers . . . to adopt resale price maintenance." *Ibid.,* at pp. xxix-xxx and xxxi, respectively.

30. Though no precise data are available on the growth of chain store merchandising before 1929, Paul H. Nystrom estimates that "In the ten-year period ending 1929 retail trade increased probably 40 or 50 percent, but chain stores spread so fast that their sales must have quadrupled in these same years." Article on "Retail Trade," *Encyclopaedia of the Social Sciences,* Macmillan, New York, 1934, Vol. 13, p. 352.

Since 1929, the inroads of the chains on the business of independent merchants have been less spectacular. Chain store taxes were a powerful factor retarding their rate of growth in the 1930's. See G. J. Feldman, "Legislative Opposition to Chain Stores and Its Minimization," *Law and Contemporary Problems,* Spring 1941, p. 347. During the war, OPA price regulation and the general scarcity of commodities also discouraged chain store expansion. See *Survey of Current Business,* October 1945, p. 16.

In spite of these obstacles, the share of chains in total retail trade rose from 21.5 per cent in 1929 to 22.8 per cent in 1939, and increased further to 24.4 per cent in 1942. See *ibid.,* February 1944, p. 12. Data for postwar years are not available, but indications point to a resumption of the increase in the chain store proportion after a slight decline in 1943–1945. See, for example, *Weekly Digest,* American Institute of Food Distribution, New York, August 16, 1947, p. 5. The figures quoted above do not tally exactly with the Census of Business data given in Chap. 2, n. 85; but they are taken from a continuous series of the Department of Commerce.

not stop the growth of the chains. And if he had he would only have been cutting off his nose to spite his face. For, attracted by the sales volume of the big chains, some rival manufacturers of nationally advertised brands were almost certain openly or covertly to disregard the principles of resale price restriction and enable the chains to stock their brands.

Only a "united front" of the manufacturers of price-maintained brands—not merely of a certain commodity, say crackers, but of grocery items generally—could have effectively thwarted the growth of chain stores. In practice, such a united front would have been impossible—and illegal to boot. Furthermore, even such a "united front" might not have blocked the growth of the chains. Once the chains achieved regional market coverage—not to mention a nationwide reach, like A & P's in groceries, Liggett's in drugs, and Woolworth's in notions—they were in a position to introduce their own brands. With the great number of their outlets, such house brands as Liggett's Rexall remedies and A & P's White House condensed milk were assured of profitability. Their success, furthermore, did not depend on manufacture of the goods by the chain. It was no less profitable (sometimes more so) to use the chain's buying power to induce some manufacturer, who might even be the owner of a nationally advertised brand, to supply the chain's house brand on very favorable terms.

Manufacturers' Dilemma: For or Against?

The upshot was that manufacturers reconsidered their views on resale price maintenance. And second thoughts apparently led many of them to conclude that continued insistence on price maintenance involved greater risk of loss of sales volume than its abandonment.[31] Price maintenance did not necessarily eliminate their brands from the shelves of chain store outlets. But it did involve the risk of loss of sales from direct competition with the chains' house brands as well as rival manufacturers' nationally advertised brands not subject to price maintenance.

Yet abandonment of resale price protection risked loss of the good will of independent retailers, most of whom ardently favored price maintenance. Disgruntled dealers might put non-price-main-

31. FTC, 1945 RPM, pp. 6-9.

tained brands "under the counter" and push the sale of rival brands. But as a rule the risk of loss of sales volume through this second policy was small compared with that of the first. In general, the popularity of nationally advertised brands—particularly among people habitually patronizing independent dealers—insured against undue dealer discrimination among rival brands.[32] Dealers could hardly afford to insist on the purchase of brands of manufacturers more friendly to price protection lest they lose trade to dealers eager to please the customer.

Abandonment of resale price maintenance involved no serious threat of increasing competition from house brands, as did continuation of the policy. Unlike the chain stores, few independent dealers were able to introduce private brands that could effectively challenge nationally advertised brands. So, with the rise of the chains, resale price maintenance lost much of its appeal to manufacturers.

Price Maintenance Boomerangs

But independent retailers refused to give up price protection. Having had a taste of monopolistic pricing, they craved more. Though the manufacturers who first introduced it were generally indifferent, if not opposed, to the practice, most merchants favored it, and they did not propose stoically to forego its advantages. Their strenuous campaign for price maintenance succeeded beyond the expectations of its most ardent sponsors.

Together with the Miller-Tydings amendment, the "fair-trade" acts in many of the states did more than convert the law's frown into an indulgent smile. These statutes put in the hands of merchant groups the power to enforce a minimum resale price for any brand of merchandise, even contrary to the manufacturer's wishes.[33] They went even further. For they apparently made it possible for organized distributor groups, through wholesaler-retailer deals, to fix the minimum retail price of a particular brand according to their own ideas of what the traffic would bear.[34]

32. Cf. M. G. Reid, *Food for People,* Wiley, New York, 1943, pp. 355-64 and 452-56.

33. Such appears to be the rule in at least 25 out of the 45 states authorizing resale price maintenance. In 19 states, however, the law definitely limits the privilege of establishing a fixed minimum resale price to the owner of the brand or his agent. See FTC, 1945 RPM, p. 70.

34. Although all the "fair-trade" acts condemn the fixing of resale prices by agree-

Thus a question has arisen whether the device of resale price maintenance has not boomeranged on those who introduced it, the large-scale manufacturers of nationally advertised brands. The intention of its originators was to stop price cutting; in other words, to restrict competition in the distribution of branded products and thereby stabilize markets.[35] With changes in advertising techniques and the rise of chain and department stores, however, resale price maintenance threatened manufacturers with restricted market outlets and loss of sales volume. Recently the practice has been promoted by independent retailers. In their eager hands, resale price maintenance remains a device to prevent price cutting. Whereas manufacturers used it to defend their quasi-monopolistic positions as popular-brand owners against price-cutting distributors, formidable organizations of distributors now use it to defend their own positions, to preserve the status quo. Originally price maintenance was designed to prevent price-cutting dealers from exploiting the brand good will of manufacturers at the manufacturers' expense; currently it is used to prevent price-cutting dealers from upsetting the rigged market for price-maintained goods to the detriment of organized retailers with a vested interest in noncompetitive distribution.

From the standpoint of the public interest in revitalizing competitive forces, resale price maintenance is objectionable whatever group sponsors it. It deprives low-cost distributors of the competitive advantage of superior efficiency, and thereby deprives consumers of their full share of the benefits from improved business organization and less costly merchandising methods. In many manufacturing industries it restricts opportunities for the launching of new enterprises, or the expansion of old ones, by fostering trivial differentiation of products, irrational choice of goods by consumers, and uneconomic allocation of resources.

---

ments among dealers, as they also condemn so-called "horizontal" resale price fixing by joint action of brand owners, conspiracy within or between dealer groups is really unnecessary. For example, the active propaganda of national and local retail druggists' associations for a standard markup of 33.33 per cent is enough, taken with the enforceability of resale price agreements on nonsigners, to make a contract between a single wholesaler and a single retailer an effective means of fixing the minimum retail price within an entire state. Naturally, such a contract would fix the retail price at a figure acceptable to all, or most of, the "legitimate" members of the trade. See *ibid.*, pp. 74, 80-81, and 131-35.

35. Cf. Seligman and Love, *op. cit.*, Chaps. 10 and 11.

Product Differentiation and Quality Competition

As manufacturers shifted their reliance from competitive pricing to product differentiation as a means of getting and holding customers, advertising became more and more a means of concentrating buyers' attention on trivial values or unverified claims of excellence.[36]

This change in the character of advertising is not unusual, of course, and it in no way reflects on the motives of sellers. Sellers are generally confronted with two choices. They may either emphasize superlative quality and cater to a restricted clientele that is either indifferent to prices or attaches great prestige value to high prices; or they may offer a standardized product at a price that will attract mass purchasing power. Experience and observation may have taught them that although good quality may help sell a product, advertising is more important in mass distribution. Expediency may force them to sacrifice improvement in quality for advertising expenditures.

Mass production itself puts emphasis on cheapness, in order to reach a wide market. But cheapness is seldom a good theme for an effective advertising campaign. Generally, advertising tends to emphasize style, fashion, novelty.[37] Innovation, however inconsequential, may serve better to fix attention and stimulate interest than familiarity, however wholesome or reliable an old product. Dollars spent on a clever advertising campaign to play up some unique but trivial feature of a product may go further—in winning and holding patronage—than the same amount spent on improving the basic quality of the product.[38]

36. As the Commission on Freedom of the Press declares, referring especially to radio advertising, "Sales talk relies heavily on sheer repetition of stimuli, presents favorable facts only, exaggerates values, and suggests a romantic world part way between reality and a materialistic utopia. It does not discuss a product. It 'sells' it." *A Free and Responsible Press,* University of Chicago Press, Chicago, 1947, p. 64.

Furthermore, in this field the influence of advertisers is not restricted to the actual sales talk, the so-called "plug." It extends to radio programming as a whole; and the control thus exercised is extremely concentrated, through powerful advertising agencies. The Commission says (p. 63) that "Fewer than a hundred and fifty advertisers now provide all but 3 or 4 per cent of the income of the radio networks . . . ten advertisers [provide] 60 per cent of N.B.C.'s income. . . . The large advertisers on the air use a small number of advertising agencies . . . These agencies . . . determine what the American people shall hear on the air." And their ideal is strictly noncontroversial broadcasting, "all of it in the 'formula groove.'" *Idem, The American Radio,* University of Chicago Press, Chicago, 1947, pp. 93-100.

37. Cf. Von Beckerath, *op. cit.,* pp. 191-95; and Kaidanovsky, *op. cit.,* p. 316.

38. This may be true even though much present-day advertising merely neutralizes the selling efforts of rivals, and even of rival industries, in quest of the consumer's dollar. And when the efficacy of A's advertising expenditures is not exhausted in cancelling out the sales-promoting power of B's and C's similar expenditures, no solid

Though clever advertising frequently wins patronage for a product that would not readily attract buyers through its merits alone, there are limits to the effectiveness of any type of advertising and these limits vary from trade to trade. Demands for different products are subject to different influences, responsive to different appeals. Some are more susceptible than others to manipulation by suggestion or by crude emotional appeals to fear, pride, or prejudice.[39] Therefore sellers cannot always rely on such advertising campaigns to boost sales regardless of quality. Unless the standardized output of mass-production industries meets certain minimum quality standards, buyers will not continue to buy. Consumers might rely more on local shops or direct their demand to other *types* of products, if the Big Two—or the Big Four, as the case may be—were to put on the market products much below conventional standards. Though good-will values in modern, depersonalized markets may rest more on advertising suggestion than on product performance, there are limits to the efficacy of even the most lavish advertising program for generating consumer satisfaction.[40] Hence the branded products of

---

ground exists for assuming that the advertisement-induced shift of sales from D and E to A leads to any net social advantage. Neither theory nor experience suggests that the bigger the advertising appropriation the greater the productive efficiency and the better the quality of the product. This is not to say, of course, that all advertising is uneconomical. It is to say that when and in so far as advertising goes beyond its informative function, ceases to facilitate a more intelligent use of purchasing power by consumers, and becomes simply an investment in freedom from effective competition, it loses its economic justification.

"During the past twenty-five years, the effects of . . . advertising have probably spent themselves largely in shifting demand from one firm to another within any given industry," or from one industry to another. Nicholls, *Imperfect Competition Within Agricultural Industries,* p. 259. It may well be true, as Nicholls concludes, that "the tremendous growth in consumer advertising has . . . tended to curtail the total volume [of sales] rather than to increase it." The grounds for such a judgment are the added costs of supplying the goods and, even more important, the price inflation from the monopolistic pricing that advertising protects and encourages.

39. Drugs, cosmetics, soap, and personal accessories (for example, safety razors and watches) are easily adaptable to sales promotion by affective stimuli. Such goods are representative, according to Borden, of the "areas in which price competition has been least effective, in which advertising and aggressive selling have been most intense, and in which [profit] margins . . . have been widest." *Op. cit.,* p. 861.

40. In the early 1930's the American Tobacco Company spent $2 million a year trying to popularize a machine-made 5 cent cigar under the brand name Cremo. Although George W. Hill, president of American Tobacco, was a shrewd advertiser with a successful record in the promotion of Lucky Strike sales, the Cremo campaign was an expensive failure. See *ibid.,* p. 554.

The Cremo advertisements said little about the quality of the product. Instead, they emphasized alleged advantages of a machine-made cigar from the sanitary standpoint, the allegation being that in rolling handmade cigars workmen used spittle to make the wrapper fast. The advertising fraternity dubbed the Cremo program a "spit" campaign. The technique was similar to that of the Lucky Strike drive a couple of years earlier, under the slogan "Reach for a Lucky instead of a sweet." Expressive of the

highly centralized industries must be dependable, in the sense of having a uniform quality not too high to prevent pricing within the reach of the many yet high enough to insure—with the help of advertising—general consumer acceptance.

That monopolistic competition tends to subordinate product quality to product differentiation does not mean that manufacturers catering to consumers in national markets can refrain indefinitely from improving quality. While monopoly influences as such, whether due to bigness or to advertising, may tend to weaken the incentive to improve quality, they have not been sufficiently widespread and powerful in the American economy to kill it. Few firms have had such a secure hold on the market that they could ignore the possibility of their position being undermined if they did not discover better ways of making better products. And business is spending millions of dollars in the research laboratories to do just this, reflecting the basic spirit of genuine competitive enterprise. It is evident in better automobiles, better refrigerators, better radios, and hosts of other improved products that have made for modern convenience and comfort. Competition, while far from perfect and not always effective, remains potentially a powerful agency for regulating economic activity.

Quality Deterioration in Markets of Few Sellers

To the extent that the competitive urge to maintain and improve quality standards under conditions of industrial concentration and imperfect competition has been weakened it can be traced in part to commercial considerations associated with product differentiation and advertising strategy. In some lines, however, quality deterioration reflects, also, the influence of technical factors.

---

general condemnation the Cremo program encountered, Cox appraised it as one "which for brazen vulgarity exceeded anything even 'Lucky Strike' cigarettes at their worst had produced." Reavis Cox, *Competition in the American Tobacco Industry, 1911–1932,* Columbia University Press, New York, 1933, p. 237.

When the candy industry vehemently protested the slogan "Reach for a Lucky instead of a sweet," Mr. Hill was reported to have said to a representative of the industry: "It is up to your industry to sell its own products. Anyone who does not recognize that our campaign merely acknowledges that competition for the consumer's dollar today is industry against industry, quite as much, or more than, within industries, is not up on the trend of modern advertising." *United States Tobacco Journal,* January 5, 1929, p. 18. Nevertheless, denunciation of the Lucky Strike slogan as scurrilous and defamatory continued unabated, and nine months after the interview quoted above American Tobacco Company abandoned it in favor of a less objectionable advertising theme. See the full-page Lucky Strike advertisement on the back cover of *Tobacco,* September 12, 1929.

In the flour-milling and the baking industries mass production made it necessary to extract some of the most nutritive elements of the wheat so that the flour, bread, and cakes would not spoil in the long process of production and distribution. As local flour mills were displaced by such giant mergers as Pillsbury, General Mills, and International Milling, and neighborhood bakeries by huge combines like Ward, Continental, General, National, and Loose-Wiles, the interval between grinding of grain and delivery of baked goods to the consumer was so lengthened that only a denatured, "white" flour and only bakery products made therefrom would keep in salable condition.[41]

Large-scale, intensive advertising by the big flour and baking companies long distracted consumer attention from the inferiority of their products as compared with the nutritional values of the unbleached products resulting from decentralized milling and baking. But even the most spellbinding advertisement could not forever obscure the deleterious effects on the health and vigor of the populace. According to one report:

> Both in cities and on farms, families of low income depend largely on bread. This has been true for many generations. Only since the bread has been made of roller-mill flour does this dependence upon it seem to have resulted in serious nutritional deficiencies. Cummings (1940) points out the chronological sequence of the change of milling methods and . . . the appearance of pellagra in many parts of the United States.[42]

41. See Reid, *op. cit.*, pp. 35-36; A. C. Hoffman, *Large-Scale Organization in the Food Industries,* TNEC Monograph No. 35, Washington, 1940, Chap. 5; C. L. Alsberg, "Starch and Flour Quality," *Wheat Studies,* Food Research Institute, February 1935, pp. 229-54; and *idem,* "The Stale-Bread Problem," *Wheat Studies,* Food Research Institute, February 1936, pp. 221-47.

The statement in the text is not quite exact with respect to bread and crackers. Large wholesale bakeries can and do market whole-wheat bread and graham crackers, because their scale of operations permits direct dealing with flour mills and enables them to reduce the relative volume—and the average length of the holding period—of unbleached-flour inventories. Moreover, the addition of so-called "rope inhibitors" to the dough helped the big baking companies to make their loaves widely available without incurring prohibitive losses from returns of stale bread or unduly high costs from multiplication of branch plants. Rope inhibitors retard bacterial growth, or mold. The chemicals generally used for this purpose (propionates) appear to have no adverse effect on the nutritional values of bread. See M. B. Jacobs, *The Chemistry and Technology of Food and Food Products,* Intersciences, New York, 1944, pp. 713 ff.

42. Henry C. Sherman and Constance S. Pearson, *Modern Bread From the Viewpoint of Nutrition,* Macmillan, New York, 1942, p. 80. On the limitations of food fortification, see also an article by a member of the U.S. Public Health Service, W. H. Sebrell, "The Public Health Aspects of the Fortification of Foods With Vitamins and Minerals," *Milbank Memorial Fund Quarterly,* July 1939, pp. 241-47.

Significance of Bread Enrichment Program

Enrichment restores to white flour, in concentrated form, some of the vitamins and minerals that are removed in centralized milling operations. The Food and Drug Administration sponsored a voluntary program for fortifying flour, and since 1941 many commercial millers have embraced the idea.[43] Under current regulations, to qualify for the designation "enriched," each pound of flour must contain a stipulated amount of four nutrients: thiamine, riboflavin, niacin, and iron.[44]

Enrichment unquestionably enhances the wholesomeness of bleached-flour bread. But it restores only a fraction of the original nutrients of wheat and leaves the nutritive value of "enriched" flour still far below that of unbleached, whole-wheat flour. As Brody says:

> To characterize a seriously impoverished food as "enriched" is in a sense misleading. Even the short-time rat-feeding experiments by Morgan . . . and others demonstrate that "enriched" white flour is no substitute for whole-wheat flour.[45]

In short, "enriched" bread is a devitalized product only partially brought back to par.

More specifically, Sherman points out that:

> . . . the thiamine content required of enriched flour is . . . about four fifths of the average thiamine content of whole-wheat.

And about the mineral deficiency he says:

> The "enrichment program" provides restoration of iron to something approaching whole-grain levels, leaving the white product still impoverished in all of these mineral elements except iron.[46]

43. See Reid, *op. cit.,* Chap. 4; also A. E. Taylor, "Why Enrichment of Flour?," *Wheat Studies,* Food Research Institute, November 1941, pp. 77-108.

44. Federal Security Agency, Food and Drug Administration, *Definitions and Standards for Food,* July 1944, p. 7. See Code of Federal Regulations, Title 21, Chap. 1, Pt. 15, Sec. 15.10 (a). The minimum specifications are: thiamine, 2 milligrams; riboflavin, 1.2 milligrams; niacin, 16 milligrams; and iron, 13 milligrams. Practically all "white" flour requires the addition of a certain amount of the designated nutrients in order to meet these standards.

45. Samuel Brody, "Science and Dietary Wisdom," *Scientific Monthly,* September 1945, p. 224.

46. Henry C. Sherman, *Foods: Their Values and Management,* Columbia University Press, New York, 1946, pp. 23 and 24. Calcium is the most important of the minerals for which the enrichment program makes no provision. Calcium deficiency could readily be overcome by using milk instead of water in mixing the dough. But milk costs more than water. Though the use of skim-milk powder in making bread is increasing (*ibid.,* p. 14), the extent to which it is used is not known.

The Federal Trade Commission reports that in 1945 the use of milk solids among

McCollum, another recognized authority on biochemistry, says:

> The primary objective . . . should be to make the bread supply as nearly complete nutritionally as is practicable on the basis of materials which we have available and their cost. This objective will not be achieved by the continuance of the present bread enrichment program.[47]

Nevertheless, advertising has probably succeeded in creating a widespread illusion that "enriched" bread is of superior quality, up to scientific dietary standards.

Use of Irradiation Patents

In certain related food industries, big consolidations were able to exploit even more effectively the food enrichment program to "fortify" not only their products but also their dominant trade position. Fleischmann (Standard Brands) obtained an exclusive license under the Steenbock patents for the irradiation of yeast.[48] With the help of an aggressive promotion campaign Standard Brands used

---

wholesale bread bakers varied from none to ten pounds per hundred pounds of flour. But the weighted average was only four pounds per hundred pounds of flour. See Federal Trade Commission, Report on *Wholesale Baking Industry,* Washington, 1946, Pt. 2, p. 34. (This report will hereinafter be cited: *Wholesale Baking Industry.*)

47. E. V. McCollum, "Bread Enrichment," *Maryland Health Bulletin,* March 1945, p. 2. A preferable program, Dr. McCollum declares, would be "bread improvement achieved by a legal requirement concerning the minimum skim milk solids to be included in bread." He adds that there are "other means at hand for markedly improving the nutritive value of bread at low cost," and gives several examples. In other papers, McCollum has opposed state legislation to make bread enrichment (according to current standards) compulsory, pointing out that the agitation in its favor springs largely from self-serving commercial interests. See his letter of March 20, 1945, to Governor Thomas E. Dewey (on file in the records of the New York State legislative committee that held hearings on the bill), where he says that "the bread enrichment program as now publicized creates a false sense of security among consumers." See also his discussion of the subject in *Science,* August 17, 1945, p. 181; and his Remsen Memorial Lecture, delivered before the American Chemical Society on May 28, 1948, as reported in the *New York Times,* May 30, 1948. James Rorty, in "Bread, and the Stuff We Eat," *Harper's Magazine,* March 1950, reports some of the results of the enrichment program and argues for compulsory labelling.

48. See *Vitamin Technologists, Inc.* v. *Wisconsin Alumni Research Foundation,* 146 Fed. *2d* 941 (1945); certiorari denied, 325 U.S. 876 (1945). The license was originally granted to Fleischmann and assigned to Standard Brands after their merger. It covered the manufacture and sale not only of irradiated yeast but also of "antirachitically activable unsaponifiable lipoids"—in plain words, unpatented yeast. The Steenbock patents covered the activation by irradiation of ergosterol and yeast for increasing the vitamin D content of foods. The courts finally invalidated these patents because their claims were too broad, amounting to an attempt "to patent sunlight." *Ibid.,* 146 Fed. *2d,* p. 947. But the court found that the patentee, the Research Foundation, had for twenty years successfully prevented activation of "the butter of the poor" by deliberately and persistently refusing to grant licenses to oleomargarine manufacturers. The court roundly denounced this policy as an abuse of the patent privilege, contrary to the public interest, and it took judicial notice of the fact that the patentee's sole purpose in thus restraining trade was to protect the Wisconsin dairy industry from competition. *Ibid.,* pp. 943-46.

this special privilege still further to "differentiate" its product from ordinary yeast and to strengthen its virtual monopoly in this field. Similarly, a few large companies, the dominant advertisers in the canned-milk industry, prevailed on the Wisconsin Alumni Research Foundation to limit its Steenbock licenses in that field to them.[49] With the fillip that "irradiation" gave their advertising, they succeeded in regaining the dominance over the market—about 75 per cent of total sales—that their high-price policy during the depression had impaired.[50]

Wasteful Selling Practices Under Monopolistic Competition

The growth of uninformative advertising and the weakening of incentives to improve the quality of products are not the only manifestations of the failure to adapt rules of the game quickly enough to changed market conditions during the past half century. In the absence of suitable legal standards of competitive behavior, many other uneconomic trade practices developed that helped establish and maintain the rule of monopolistic business units in particular markets. True, some of the less defensible and formerly quite common preclusive practices have been condemned by federal law since 1914. Practices outlawed, at least in their more flagrant forms, include price discrimination, exclusive dealing arrangements, and tying contracts.[51] But other trade practices of similar purport have

49. See William H. Nicholls, "Some Economic Aspects of University Patents," *Journal of Farm Economics*, May 1939, pp. 494-98; and *idem*, "Imperfect Competition in Agricultural Processing and Distributing Industries," p. 161. According to Nicholls the "dominant advertisers were the sole assignees in the canned milk industry." This is not quite accurate, because the Wisconsin Alumni Research Foundation made no assignments of the Steenbock patents; it only granted licenses thereunder. The Big Three brands in the canned-milk industry are Carnation, Pet, and Borden. See Hoffman, *op. cit.*, pp. 25-29.

50. See Nicholls, "Imperfect Competition in Agricultural Processing and Distributing Industries," p. 161.

51. Exclusive dealing is an arrangement whereby a supplier closes the channels of distribution to the products of other manufacturers by requiring dealers to handle only the supplier's line. Tying contracts involve the sale or lease of specified articles or equipment solely on condition that the purchaser or lessee buy or use therewith certain other goods that the seller or lessor offers to supply. Obviously, for effective use, both devices depend on the manufacturer's possession of a strong leverage with respect to at least part of the line of goods offered for sale. If the distributor agrees not to handle competing products or to buy some goods he would not otherwise buy—at least from the given supplier—he must have some compelling inducement so to restrict his freedom of action. A monopolistic hold on the supply of some particular product will ordinarily provide the supplier with the needed bargaining power.

Because of the outlawing of these practices by the 1914 and subsequent amendatory legislation, it seems preferable to discuss them in connection with the review of trade practice regulation in Chapter 11. But this procedure does not warrant any inference

continued to enjoy legal immunity, some because their use is less widespread, some because of the difficulty of devising an effective rule for coping with them.

Consignment Selling

An example of a wasteful selling practice peculiarly adaptable to monopolistic ends in a few lines of trade is so-called consignment selling. In the food industries this device has been especially effective in building up and reinforcing the market position of the big companies.

In consignment selling retailers are granted the privilege of returning unsold goods. Frequently deliveries on consignment exceed the amount either party has any expectation of selling. The supplier may overstock the retailer primarily for display purposes, to give customers an exaggerated impression of the popularity of the supplier's brand.[52] The Federal Trade Commission reports that of the amount of bread they deliver the giants of the baking industry take back as much as "thirty per cent from some individual retailers" and that the amount returned "averages fifteen per cent in certain important markets." [53]

So wasteful is this practice that the government strictly prohibited it during the war in the first food conservation order issued under Executive emergency powers.[54] Though enforcement was never completely successful, violations of the order were only sporadic and local as long as hostilities continued.[55]

During this period the profits of the big bakery combines reflected substantial savings as a result of this government order. Despite fixed

---

that the legal prohibition of price discrimination, exclusive dealing arrangements, tying contracts, and other unfair trade practices has entirely eliminated them. In subtle forms, they continue to bolster monopolistic positions in certain industries.

52. See *Wholesale Baking Industry,* Pt. 1, p. 1.

53. *Ibid.* See also *ibid.,* p. 22. The baking companies dispose of the returned product in various ways; about half is sold to processors of animal feeds. *Ibid.,* pp. 16-17.

54. War Food Order No. 1, issued December 29, 1942, effective January 19, 1943. Code of Federal Regulations, Title 7, Chap. 11, Sec. 1404.1.

55. The baking companies generally supported the order. Here and there organized groups of grocers fought it. See *In re Kentucky Food Dealers Association,* 41 FTC 44 (1945). But in certain areas the bread-truck drivers' union was the medium for resistance to enforcement. In Cleveland, for example, some drivers, compelled by employers to take more bread than their retailer customers could sell, accepted "returns" and dumped them in a river rather than lose the retailers' patronage. *Wholesale Baking Industry,* Pt. 1, pp. 5 and 17.

prices for flour and bread and rising labor costs, the 1943 profits of one large company increased "nearly 66 per cent" over its 1942 profits.[56] But the elimination of the practice of overstocking retailers severely limited the power of the big baking companies to displace local, independent bakers.[57]

Continuing Waste From Unsold Bread Returns

Enforcement of War Food Order No. 1 became more and more ineffective after the fighting stopped. The government finally rescinded the order on October 25, 1946, over the strong opposition of the Federal Trade Commission.[58]

Consignment selling, since then, has reappeared in aggravated form, reflecting the strenuous efforts of the bread-baking combines to strengthen and consolidate their semimonopolistic positions. As the Federal Trade Commission summarized the consensus of the trade, the quantities of bread taken back are

> . . . limited only by the wholesale baker's ability and willingness to assume the financial responsibility for disposing of returned goods. Local bakers . . . maintain . . . they are in a weak position in absorbing such losses in competition with large baking companies operating in many markets who can offset losses on excessive "returns" in some highly competitive areas against profits made in other, less competitive markets.[59]

56. *Ibid.*, p. 11.

57. The Federal Trade Commission found that the use and abuse of consignment selling had helped the Big Four to achieve and hold their dominant position in the wholesale baking industry. *Ibid.*, pp. 18-19. But this selling method was ineffective against the competition of the bakery departments of grocery chain stores. Apparently the growth in sales of their own bread by chain stores more than offset the gains of the Big Four at the expense of independent wholesale bakers and neighborhood (retail) bakers. Although total sales of the Big Four increased from $172.8 million in 1925 to $284.1 million in 1944 and the amount of bread they sold increased over the same period from 1.7 billion pounds to 2.2. billion pounds, their share of the entire commercial bread production in the country declined from 20 per cent in 1925 to 14 per cent in 1944. Undoubtedly, the rise of grocery chain bakeries was the main cause of this shift in the relative position of the Big Four in the bread-baking industry. See Federal Trade Commission, *Bakery Combines and Profits*, Washington, 1927, pp. 7, 10, 19, and 94; *idem, Competition and Profits in Bread and Flour*, Washington, 1928, p. 19; and *Wholesale Baking Industry*, Pt. 1, p. 20.

58. See Commerce Clearing House, *Reconversion Business Control Law Reports*, 1948, par. 20101; and *Wholesale Baking Industry*, Pt. 1, p. 25.

59. *Ibid.*, p. 2. For FTC's endorsement of these views, see *ibid.*, p. 18. These statements refer to the practice before the adoption of War Food Order No. 1; but they are equally applicable to the practice as resumed since 1946.

On introducing a bill in May 1948 that would, in effect, put War Food Order No. 1 on the statute books, Representative Ellsworth B. Buck emphasized the need "to call a halt to this improvident practice," which he estimated to involve "an annual loss of approximately 600 million loaves of bread." As he declared, "This shocking

The Commission quotes approvingly the testimony of an independent wholesale baker:

> The whole practice is a device of the large bakers . . . for invading markets remote from their factory base and to crowd out the local bakers . . .[60]

Though independent, local bakers in self-defense usually grant retailers the privilege of returning unsold bread, the Commission makes it clear that the big interstate baking companies are the principal offenders, primarily responsible for this uneconomic practice.[61]

The Commission concludes:

> Probably in no other important industry is there a greater opportunity for small and medium-sized business to efficiently serve the consumer than in the baking industry. To be insured an opportunity to do so requires the elimination of [this selling method, among other "uneconomic practices"] . . . which threatens the existence of many small bakers, foredooms new ventures to failure, and promotes regional monopolistic control of the wholesale bread-baking industry.[62]

Bread is a fundamental symbol of life. What has happened to it in the centralized, mass-production scheme is what has happened to a large variety of foods and other household articles. The passage of the Food, Drugs and Cosmetic Act of 1938 indicates that people are gradually becoming aware of the menace to public welfare from lack of adequate standards and rules of competition. Probably competitive abuses are no worse in the fields to which this legislation applies than in many other fields, ranging from sewing thread to paint, and from nursing bottles to coffins.[63] Only the circumstance that these abuses, when they relate to food and drugs, directly affect the public health can account for the more rigorous regulation in those fields.

None of this argues that there is no proper place for mass production in the economy of a democratic commonwealth. But it would

---

waste of wheat and flour, at a time when the American public is being asked to conserve food and peoples abroad are in dire want, is inexcusable . . ." See *Bakers Weekly,* May 17, 1948, p. 38.

60. *Wholesale Baking Industry,* Pt. 1, p. 10.

61. *Ibid.,* pp. 18-19.

62. *Ibid.,* Pt. 2, p. 137. The FTC investigation also disclosed local price discrimination in this industry as part of a general pattern of what it called "predatory competition," but what some economists would term "monopolistic competition" or merely "imperfect competition." See *ibid.,* Pt. 1, p. 18, and Pt. 2, pp. 93 and 119.

63. For a summary review of the enforcement of the Food, Drugs and Cosmetic Act by the Federal Security Administration and of the administrative record of the Federal Trade Commission in this and other fields, see Chap. 11.

seem to argue that mere bigness is no boon to the consumer. When bigness becomes a fetish and competition a taboo, the consumer stands to lose. Much of the monopoly element in American big business is far from a logical outgrowth of mechanization. In some instances it has apparently been bought at the cost of efficiency.

Squeeze Pricing: Another Monopolistic Trade Practice

Among the competitive tactics that obsolete rules of the game still sanction despite their manifestly uneconomic results probably few are more effective than squeeze pricing in circumscribing business opportunities and hamstringing independent enterprises. Squeeze pricing consists of holding firm or increasing prices in markets in which a rival buys—usually markets for materials or equipment—while depressing prices in the markets in which he sells.

A large company may be able, through the great volume of its own transactions, to influence prices in one or both of the areas mentioned. However, if it has such power in both areas, its ability to control the prices other producers must pay for raw materials, semifinished parts, or equipment may rest on something besides mere size. In practice, such power to influence its competitors' buying prices seldom stems solely from the scale of a single large company's own parallel purchases in an open market.

Even though centralized control is highly developed in the meatpacking industry, the largest buyer, Swift & Company, cannot singlehandedly set the prices in the principal livestock markets.[64] But the Big Four—Swift, Armour, Wilson, and Cudahy—can. At any rate, by market-sharing arrangements, they have determined the buying prices of independent packers, which Nicholls describes as "small local firms existing at their sufferance." [65]

Likewise, the big dairy products combines have kept independent milk distributors in line by a rigid control of the margin between their buying and selling prices.[66] In its recent report on fluid-milk dis-

64. See Burns, *op. cit.*, p. 140.

65. Nicholls, *Imperfect Competition Within Agricultural Industries*, p. 303. See also *ibid.*, pp. 127-30; and *idem*, "Market Sharing in the Packing Industry," *Journal of Farm Economics*, 1940, pp. 225-40. For a list of the numerous judicial decisions and reports of official investigations indicating the persistence of market-sharing arrangements in one form or another among the big meat-packing companies, see Chap. 3 of the present study, p. 71, n. 25.

66. As Nicholls describes the situation, "in milk-pricing, the oligopsonists [small group of large buyers, of which Borden and National Dairy Products are the largest]

tribution, the Federal Trade Commission put special emphasis on

> . . . the growth of large-scale milk manufacturing and retail distribution organizations by mergers and consolidations which have reduced the number and increased the size of business units dealing, on the one hand, with the farmer and, on the other, with . . . consumers. For many years these developments have been replacing former direct personal relations in the trade with indirect contracts between corporation executives . . . and leaders of producer groups.[67]

And the Commission concluded that, from the standpoint of public policy for regulation of the industry,

> The changed situation points to the need for a . . . shift of emphasis from minimum producer price to the giving of more attention to the reasonableness of wholesale and retail prices for both fluid milk and manufactured milk products.[68]

Strategic Advantages of Vertical Integration

Vertical integration increases the power of a big company—or a group of monopoly partners—occupying a dominant position in its selling markets to apply a price squeeze on the business of independent rivals. Competition cannot be vigorous when all competitors but one in a market for finished products are dependent on a single producer, or a tightly knit group of the industry's leaders, for supplies of essential materials, parts, or equipment. The independent, nonintegrated producers under such circumstances exist only by sufferance of the company able to determine the spread between their selling prices and an important element of their costs.

Such situations are fairly common in American industry, especially in those many spheres in which oligopoly prevails and a tradition of price leadership is firmly established. In the steel industry, a few big combinations, fully integrated, like United States Steel and Bethlehem Steel, supply sheets, bars, rods, and other semifinished products to a score or more of nonintegrated finishing mills with

---

do not act independently in bargaining with the cooperative [organized milk producers], but instead bargain collectively through a 'dealers' association.' In such an association one of the dominant firms usually assumes the role of leadership in the negotiations with the cooperative." *Imperfect Competition Within Agricultural Industries,* p. 192. On the organization and pricing practices of the fluid-milk industry generally, see *ibid.,* pp. 190-96; and J. M. Cassels, *A Study of Fluid Milk Prices,* Harvard University Press, Cambridge, 1934, particularly Chaps. 6 and 10.

67. Federal Trade Commission, *Report on Distribution Methods and Costs,* Pt. 6, "Milk Distribution, Prices, Spreads, and Profits," Washington, 1945, p. 20.

68. *Ibid.,* p. 23.

which the integrated suppliers themselves are nominally in competition in the sale of finished products.[69] Plainly, this involves heavy risks for the nonintegrated mills making such products as galvanized sheet, tin plate, wire, and nails. In such a situation competition is likely to be weak and ineffective.

A similar situation exists in the copper industry. The formally integrated Big Three—Anaconda, Kennecott, and Phelps Dodge—and the effectually integrated market leader, American Smelting & Refining, are the principal suppliers of metal to fabricators, yet these four companies themselves control more than three fourths of domestic fabricating capacity.[70]

In aluminum, Alcoa was for half a century the sole, and is still the chief, metal refiner. It also operates rolling mills and manufactures utensils and other finished products. Taking advantage of this position, it applied a price squeeze, as occasion demanded such tactics, to keep independent rolling mills and fabricators "in line." [71]

Control of essential equipment also makes easy the use of pincers on the business of overaggressive competitors. The American Can Company immediately after its organization made contracts with all the principal manufacturers of can-making machinery which, by binding them to sell only to American Can or to give it preferential terms, severely handicapped independent can manufacturers in buying their equipment.[72] Hartford Empire took pains to see that no independent bottle manufacturer could buy or lease bottle-making machinery except on terms that safeguarded the market position of its confederates in the glass container monopoly.[73] The American Telephone & Telegraph Company maintains its unified control of

69. *Investigation of the Concentration of Economic Power,* Temporary National Economic Committee, Hearings pursuant to Pub.Res. 113 (75th Cong.), Pt. 19, p. 10490 and pp. 10502-04.

70. *Ibid.,* Pt. 25, pp. 13091-100, especially p. 13099; *To Amend Sections* 7 *and 11 of the Clayton Act,* Hearings before a Subcommittee of the Committee on the Judiciary, on H.R. 2357, House of Representatives, 79th Cong., 1st sess., Washington, 1945, pp. 108-20; and Clair Wilcox, *Competition and Monopoly in American Industry,* TNEC Monograph No. 21, Washington, 1940, p. 129. See also *Cartels or Competition?,* pp. 126-31. Since its organization in 1899, primarily as a merger of smelters, AS & R has expanded its operations greatly, first in mining, later in fabricating, but generally by stock acquisitions, rather than by consolidation.

71. See *U.S.* v. *Aluminum Company of America,* 148 Fed. *2d* 416 (1945), at pp. 436-38; also *Cartels in Action,* pp. 225-26. The court enjoined this practice, in one provision of the decree.

72. See *U.S.* v. *American Can Co.,* 230 Fed. 859 (1916), at pp. 874-75.

73. See *U.S.* v. *Hartford Empire Co.,* 46 Fed.Supp. 541 (1942), at pp. 550-51 and 599.

the telephone industry chiefly by means of its public franchises and its formidable collection of patents. But it does not trust exclusively to these devices to keep out competition.[74] Through its manufacturing subsidiary, Western Electric, it can make it extremely difficult to establish competitive telephone service anywhere—which might or might not be economically advantageous to the public.[75] Though Western Electric possesses no public franchise, and though its pricing policies are not subject to regulation by any public administrative agency, as the sole manufacturer of much of the telephone equipment that any operating company must have it exercises virtual control over entry to the industry.

Need for New Rules of the Game

Preservation of effective competition requires continual scrutiny of trade practices and unwearying examination of the rules that govern business conduct. The problem is to so regulate business tactics that competition will not give way to monopoly and the venture spirit will not be killed. While the line between regulation that stifles competition and regulation that frees it is not always clear, it must somehow be approximated if free enterprise is to survive. Clearly such business practices as exclusionary price squeezing, wasteful overstocking of dealers, and covert reduction of quality exemplify an undesirable kind of business rivalry that impairs effective competition. These practices may not be amenable to correction under existing laws. To find the right laws is a challenge to the democratic process. If competition is to perform its function in a private enterprise economy, selling methods that are competitive in appearance but monopolistic in reality must be ruled out no less than those that are obviously monopolistic. If competition is to be made effective it is equally imperative promptly to amend rules of the game that, like the state "fair-trade" legislation and the Miller-Tydings law, sanction practices that, as experience shows, serve only to "featherbed" monopoly in one or another of its protean forms.

74. See N. R. Danielian, *A.T. & T.*, Harper, New York, 1940, Chap. 7 and *passim.*
75. *Ibid.*, pp. 365 ff.; and Federal Communications Commission, *Proposed Report, Telephone Investigation,* pursuant to Pub.Res. 8, 74th Cong., Washington, 1938, Pt. 2, Chap. 10, and pp. 632-75.
Since the original draft of this paragraph the Department of Justice has filed a civil suit charging AT & T and Western Electric with conspiracy to monopolize the production and sale of telephone equipment, *U.S.* v. *AT & T,* complaint filed January 14, 1949, in U.S. District Court for the District of New Jersey, Civil No. 17-49.

Chapter 11

TRADE PRACTICE REGULATION

PUBLIC STANDARDS to rule business conduct, experience shows, are as necessary as the prohibition of monopolies and restraints on trade if competition is to survive and be effective. The social functions of competitive pricing, as we have pointed out earlier, are to direct limited economic resources among their various uses in accordance with consumer preferences, to insure an efficient organization of productive factors, and to promote orderly progress. A competitive price system necessarily implies and requires rational behavior, informed decision making, free choice. Rules that permit the rewards of trade to go to sharpers who discriminate, coerce, misrepresent, cheat, or defraud undermine the very foundations of a competitive economic order and pave the way for a centrally controlled economy.

The legal standards governing market behavior appropriate for a competitive society serve three primary ends: (1) to eliminate practices directed toward arbitrary exclusion of others from any industry or trade—in short, to nip monopolies in the bud; (2) to prevent unscrupulous traders from winning patronage from business rivals through deception and fraud; and (3) to aid consumers in making rational choices by giving them reliable information and by suppressing false and misleading claims.

Although the law has long provided some such standards, the rapid growth in size and complexity of modern business enterprise makes it necessary recurrently to revise them, supplement them, and provide new and better ways of enforcing them. Strict enforcement of an adequate code of commercial standards and rules would help keep the channels of trade open to truly competitive enterprise.

Background of Trade Practice Regulation

Before the Clayton and the Federal Trade Commission Acts of 1914, commercial practices were subject mainly to state law.[1] The

1. Some federal measures regulating commercial methods antedated even the Sher-

common law provided a few rules for regulating competition, among them the doctrine of implied warranty of merchantability, protecting buyers, and the rule against misappropriation of trade secrets, protecting rival sellers. But the most important common-law rule bearing on commercial practice gave an injured competitor a right of action for deceitful diversion of patronage.[2] Thus if one trader, A, imitated the trade-mark of B and took business away from him, then A became liable to B for damages.

These common-law rules became increasingly inadequate as railroads replaced canals, steam and electricity replaced water and animal power, factories replaced workshops, and national markets replaced purely local markets. With a complex organization of middlemen, agents, district representatives, and local managers standing between primary producers and ultimate consumers, opportunities for sharp practice multiplied. As great consolidations came to dominate manufacturing, and as chain stores and mail-order houses with a nation-wide scope of operations replaced independent distributors, merchandising became increasingly an impersonal, partly mechanized routine. Petty mendacities and the slander of rivals were no longer serious evils, for in such a system of trade they bring their own penalties within a period brief enough for most businessmen to include in their reckoning. On the other hand, more subtle methods of imposing on consumers and more artful methods of disposing of business rivals may find a place in the lexicon of trade, in such circumstances, before they come within the purview of legal regulation.

---

man Act but most rested on provisions of the Constitution other than the commerce clause. The most noteworthy was the prohibition against using the mails to defraud. What application there was of the commerce clause before 1890 was confined almost exclusively to means of transport such as railroads. See Myron W. Watkins, *Public Regulation of Competitive Practices,* 3d edition, National Industrial Conference Board, New York, 1940, Chaps. 2 and 3.

2. Such was the meaning of the doctrine of "unfair competition." The courts rigorously limited the right to recover damages to instances in which a trader could prove that he had lost customers to a rival because the rival had "passed off" his products as those of the plaintiff. But if a manufacturer sold aluminum washboards as zinc washboards without imitating a rival's mark or name, though he might deceive many buyers, neither a prosecutor nor any rival manufacturer who lost sales by such a practice could stop it. *American Washboard Co.* v. *Saginaw Manufacturing Co.,* 103 Fed. 281 (1900). A consumer could have sued, charging fraud, but in practice such a procedure offered no public protection because an individual buyer had too little at stake to make litigation worth while. In effect, the common law limited remedial action against unfair competition to instances in which a trader trespassed on some property interest of a competitor. See "A Symposium on the Law of Unfair Competition," *Iowa Law Review,* January 1936, pp. 175-486; and Leverett S. Lyon and Associates, *Government and Economic Life,* The Brookings Institution, Washington, 1939, Vol. 1, Chap. 9.

Common-law rules, originally intended to regulate transactions among individuals with about equal bargaining power, proved inadequate to the task of regulating the complex relations among giant corporations, medium-sized and small businessmen, and millions of scattered consumers. The radical changes in the organization of trade and industry that the machine technique fostered led to a lusty scramble for power and an ardent pursuit of the main chance. In the general unsettlement, resort to devious tactics became all too common and competition degenerated into a demoralizing and destructive race for market supremacy. Empire building put a discount on business scruples and a premium on catch-as-catch-can methods of trading.

Trade Practice Regulation by States

During the last quarter of the nineteenth century, business methods became so unsavory with competition ineffectively regulated, that many people came to believe monopoly not only inevitable but desirable. Darwinian theory was misapplied to rationalize the "survival of the fittest" in trade and to justify extermination of the "weak" by the "strong." Fitness in Darwinian doctrine implied nothing honorific but merely adaptability of a species—not members of a species—for purposes of survival. Crocodiles no less than doves were Darwinian "survivors." As it became apparent that the test of survival-fitness under jungle rules of business life was not productive of efficiency so much as of commercial ruthlessness and eventually monopoly, many states undertook to interfere with "Darwinian" economics and to raise the standards of business competition.[3] Not only did they outlaw monopolistic tactics, but they established commodity standards for the protection of consumers.

The more progressive states set minimum requirements of wholesomeness and of labelling for specific kinds of products, such as milk, meats, and medicines.[4] In a few jurisdictions monopolistic trade

3. See Joseph E. Davies, *Trust Laws and Unfair Competition,* Bureau of Corporations, Washington, 1914, pp. 184-94. Davies reports (p. 187) that between 1900 and 1915 the legislatures of twenty-three states outlawed local price discrimination. In the same period a smaller number of states prohibited exclusive dealer contracts and a variety of other unfair practices, such as commercial bribery and malicious interference with a rival's business.

4. *Ibid.,* pp. 521-26; and S. P. Kaidanovsky, *Consumer Standards,* TNEC Monograph No. 24, Washington, 1941, Chap. 4.

practices were spelled out in considerable detail and prohibited. But the great diversity in state laws and their inapplicability to interstate transactions, which were constantly growing in importance, made this way of regulation ineffectual. If the plane of competition was to be raised, it was up to Congress to shoulder its constitutional responsibilities under the interstate commerce clause.

Federal Commodity Standards Legislation

Indignation over the flagrant frauds committed against the government itself in its purchases of food and other army supplies during the Spanish-American War and public alarm over Chicago packing-house conditions depicted in Upton Sinclair's popular novel *The Jungle* inspired the first federal legislation on trade practice regulation adapted to the new industrial conditions and applicable to nation-wide markets.[5] It took the form of the Food and Drugs Act and the Meat Inspection Act of 1906,[6] which established minimum standards of wholesomeness and purity. They required accurate labelling—so far as they required labelling at all. Curiously, food mixtures and medicines sold under brand names were exempt from any requirement of disclosure of their ingredients.[7]

Though the Food and Drugs Act forbade false and misleading statements *on labels* regarding the quality, strength, or curative properties of label-bearing products, the prohibition did not apply to *advertisements.* Hence the law could hardly be said to have interdicted, even with respect to food and drugs, the practice of building up a strong market position on a basis of consumer deception. For products not intended for human consumption these measures left in full force and effect the maxim, Let the buyer beware.

Nevertheless, this early legislation did limit the extent to which

5. See C. C. Regnier, "The Struggle for Federal Food and Drug Regulation," *Law and Contemporary Problems,* December 1933, Vol. 1, p. 3.

6. Act of June 30, 1906, 34 Stat. 768. The Food, Drugs and Cosmetic Act of June 25, 1938 (52 Stat. 1040) repealed the original act but incorporated many of its important provisions. See U.S. Code, Title 21, c. 1.

The original Meat Inspection Act was attached as a rider to an appropriation act that became law on the same day as the Food and Drugs Act. In a slightly revised form, the next Congress re-enacted the measure: Act of March 4, 1907. This statute is still part of the basic law. U.S. Code, Title 21, c. 4.

7. For analyses of the achievements and limitations of this legislation, see: Kaidanovsky, *op. cit.,* Chaps. 7-10; M. G. Reid, *Consumers and the Market,* Crofts, New York, 1938, Chap. 3 and *passim;* Lyon and Associates, *op. cit.,* pp. 343-45; and *Public Regulation of Competitive Practices,* cited above, Chap. 8.

businessmen could with impunity use deceptive and unfair competitive tactics in interstate markets, and it paved the way for later measures, which have substantially raised standards and tightened regulations. Much of the subsequent commodity standards and labelling legislation has related to agricultural products—for example, grain, tobacco, cotton, and perishable fruits and vegetables—or to products mainly used by farmers, such as seeds and insecticides.[8]

The federal government also finally exerted its authority in other fields—turpentine and resin, caustic poison, alcoholic beverages, and wool products—to protect consumers from imposition.[9] The laws in these fields now not only make labelling compulsory but also require specification of the proportions of various elements or constituents in the products named.[10]

Undoubtedly such regulations have aided consumers in more intelligent selection of merchandise and have made them less dependent on unverified advertising claims.[11] In these ways commodity standards and labelling legislation have helped to make competition more effective than it would otherwise have been.

New Regulations for Food, Drugs, and Cosmetics

The Food, Drugs, and Cosmetic Act of 1938 was a significant statutory advance. First, it extended regulation to a great variety of articles not previously subject to the law, such as hair dyes, depilatories, obesity cures, and mechanical and electrical therapeutic devices. Secondly, it authorized the Food and Drug Administration to establish standards of identity (in effect, minimum standards of quality) for food products. The law also authorized the Food and Drug Administration to fix standard grades for specific kinds of food

8. The statutes covering these and similar commodities are assembled in U.S. Code, Titles 7 and 21. See Lyon and Associates, *op. cit.*, pp. 346-60.

9. In the order named, Act of March 3, 1923, 42 Stat. 1436, U.S. Code, Title 7, c. 4; Act of March 4, 1927, 44 Stat. 1406, U.S. Code, Title 15, c. 11; Act of August 29, 1935, 49 Stat. 978, U.S. Code, Title 27, c. 8; and Act of October 14, 1940, 54 Stat. 1128, U.S. Code, Title 15, Sec. 68.

10. The Wool Products Labeling Act requires the manufacturer of any fabric *or garment* "which contains . . . wool" to label it, showing (1) the percentage of total fiber weight consisting of (a) virgin wool, (b) reprocessed wool, (c) reused wool, and (d) each fiber other than wool; (2) the maximum percentage of total weight consisting of nonfibrous "loading," or "filling"; and (3) the manufacturer's name. The Naval Stores Act makes no provision for compound products, but the label must specify the identity and/or grade of the product, as classified by the Secretary of Agriculture.

11. See Kaidanovsky, *op. cit.*, pp. 25 and 335-54.

products, and that body has issued many grade definitions, including, for example, those for a long list of canned fruits and vegetables.[12] A manufacturer of such foods must either mark the correct grade on his product or plainly label it as ungraded.

A third innovation in the 1938 act was the requirement that branded foods, drugs, and cosmetics that are compounds must be plainly labelled to show all the principal ingredients. The revised law also introduced several new public health safeguards. Among the more important were: (1) administrative inspection and certification of all coal-tar dyes and flavors used in foods, drugs, or cosmetics; (2) official testing and certification of new drugs; and (3) labelling of dietary foods and drugs containing habit-forming narcotics not only to specify their contents but to warn of the dangers attending their nonprescribed use.

The most radical revision related to misbranding. Under the original act, false statements on labels were subject to penalty but similar statements in advertisements were exempt, no matter how exaggerated or deceptive.[13] To overcome this defect, Congress prohibited false and misleading advertising no less than labelling.[14] The definition of such advertising covered not only overt misstatements but also the omission of material facts concerning the properties or effects of the product when used "under such conditions as are customary or usual."

Today the failure to disclose significant information in advertise-

12. See Federal Security Agency, *Definitions and Standards for Food,* Washington, 1944, reprint revised to November 1946. Failure to use the official grades in marketing a product for which grade standards are available does not relieve the manufacturer of the obligation to maintain quality at least as high as the identity standard.

Until 1943 the administrator of the food and drug laws was the Secretary of Agriculture, of whose department the Food and Drug Administration was a subdivision. The reorganization of executive departments in that year transferred the Food and Drug Administration to the Federal Security Agency.

13. In the case of drugs, false statements, *even on labels,* did not of themselves constitute misbranding. It was necessary to show not only that the statements were untrue but that the manufacturer made them fraudulently. This meant that a successful prosecution required proof that the manufacturer knew the statements were false, that he intended to deceive the buyer, that the buyer was deceived, and that the deception resulted in injury to the buyer. Manifestly, these requirements virtually nullified the misbranding provisions of the law as applied to drugs. Cf. U.S. Department of Agriculture, *Outstanding Requirements for a New Federal Food and Drug Law,* Washington, no date, published apparently in 1935–1937.

14. This prohibition is not in the Food, Drugs, and Cosmetic Act itself, but in the Wheeler-Lea Act of March 21, 1938, which delegated to the Federal Trade Commission responsibility for enforcement of higher standards in advertisement of food, drugs, and cosmetics. 52 Stat. 115, U.S. Code, Title 15, Secs. 52-58.

ments of food, drugs, and cosmetics is as great an offense as actual misrepresentation of their composition or qualities.[15]

Enforcement of these new standards of advertisement for food, drugs, and cosmetics now constitutes a large share of FTC administrative activities. Of 53 proceedings instituted in the fiscal year 1947, 26 complaints charged false and misleading advertisement. In 1945–1946, the proportion was two thirds of the 101 complaints issued. Not all of these false-advertisement proceedings related to food, drugs, cosmetics, or therapeutic devices. FTC's method of classifying its proceedings does not permit an accurate segregation of the cases in these four industries invoking its special powers under the Wheeler-Lea amendment; however, a safe estimate would be that at least half of all the complaints charging false or misleading advertisement in each of the years specified related to food, drugs, cosmetics, or "devices." [16]

If comparable standards of "truth in advertising" were laid down and strictly enforced for other kinds of merchandise, it would make a further significant contribution to more intelligent buying by the consuming public and thereby to the effectiveness of competition.

Premises and Objectives of 1914 Legislation

The Clayton and the Federal Trade Commission Acts of 1914 were the first statutes broadly applicable to all industries in which Congress recognized its responsibility for regulating trade practices in interstate commerce.[17] Experience had shown the deficiencies of com-

15. See, for example, *Aronberg* v. *FTC,* 132 Fed. *2d* 165 (1943); and *Gelb* v. *FTC,* 144 Fed. *2d* 580 (1944). However, the Second Circuit Court of Appeals has held that the definition of false advertisement in the Wheeler-Lea Act is applicable only in the criminal prosecutions for which that act provides, and not in administrative proceedings under Section 5 of the FTC Act. *Fresh Preserves Corp.* v. *FTC,* 125 Fed. *2d* 917 (1942).

16. See Federal Trade Commission, Annual Report, Washington, 1947, pp. 47-48, and 1946 Report, pp. 28-29.

17. The Clayton Act of October 14, 1914, 38 Stat. 730, U.S. Code, Title 15, c. 1, Secs. 12-27. The Federal Trade Commission Act of September 26, 1914, 37 Stat. 717, U.S. Code, Title 15, c. 2, Secs. 41-51.

In the Interstate Commerce Act of 1887 Congress outlawed railway rebates and other forms of rate discrimination. Undoubtedly special favors to big shippers were one of the most important devices by which many industrial trusts had gained their ascendancy. Suppression of this practice helped to keep open opportunities for competitive enterprise, and this was one of the main objectives of the Interstate Commerce Act. Cf. John D. Clark, *Federal Trust Policy,* Johns Hopkins University Press, Baltimore, 1931. But the railroads were responsible at least equally with shippers for this competition-destroying practice, and in fact the Act of 1887 provided penalties only for granting rebates, not for receiving rebates. Thus, while prohibition of railway

mon-law rules and state legislation for maintaining standards of business conduct compatible with effective competition. These rules did not prevent the notorious practices by which such giant trusts as Standard Oil and American Tobacco achieved mastery of whole industries. Though the Sherman Act condemned monopolies, it said nothing about the business methods (other than connivance with trade rivals) by which monopolies grow.[18] The primary aim of the 1914 legislation was to nip monopolistic organizations in the bud.[19] As Mr. Justice Brandeis put it dissenting in the first Supreme Court review of a Federal Trade Commission order, the establishment of the Commission was a "prophylactic" measure.[20]

There were five significant substantive provisions in the 1914 legislation. Section 5 of the Trade Commission Act declared unlawful "unfair methods of competition." Sections 2 and 3 of the Clayton Act prohibited price discrimination and so-called exclusive-dealing or tying contracts—that is, the sale or lease of goods on condition that the buyer or lessee "shall not use or deal in the goods" of a competitor or competitors of the seller or lessor. Section 7 of the Clayton Act forbade the acquisition of stock in a competing corporation, and Section 8 prohibited interlocking directorates among corporations engaged in the same line of trade. The Clayton Act provisions applied only "where the effect . . . may be to substantially lessen competition or tend to create a monopoly." [21]

---

rebates affected business methods in all lines of trade, it related to a single specific practice—like the earlier mail-frauds law—and falls on the border of trade practice regulation proper.

18. One of the circumstances prompting the 1914 legislation was the Supreme Court's introduction of the rule of reason in applying the Sherman Act. *Standard Oil Co.* v. *U.S.*, 221 U.S. 1 (1911); and *U.S.* v. *American Tobacco Co.,* 221 U.S. 106 (1911). The sudden assumption by the judiciary of power to discriminate between reasonable and unreasonable restraints of trade implied, or at least suggested to many members of Congress, that the courts would undertake to define what business practices or market policies make a trust "good" or "bad." Jealous of its legislative prerogatives, Congress did not propose to leave to the courts such a lawmaking power. See S.Rept. 1326, 62d Cong., 3d sess.

19. Senator Cummins, the chief senatorial sponsor of the Trade Commission bill, said in explaining the kind of conduct it would prohibit: "It is that competition which is resorted to for the purpose of destroying competition, of eliminating a competitor, and of introducing monopoly." *Congressional Record,* 63d Cong., 2d sess., 1914, Vol. 51, Pt. 11, p. 11104.

20. See his dissenting opinion in *FTC* v. *Warren, Jones & Gratz,* 253 U.S. 421 (1920), at p. 436.

21. The wording of this qualification is slightly different in Section 8. But the difference has no practical significance, particularly because the entire section is a dead letter.

Introduction of Administrative Regulation

The procedural provisions were hardly less important than the substantive. The Trade Commission Act established an administrative agency to police the channels of trade. It empowered the Commission to file complaints, hold hearings, and issue orders "to cease and desist" from the practices outlawed in the substantive provisions mentioned above. An order of the Commission carries no penalty, itself, but if respondent fails to comply the Commission may petition any Circuit Court of Appeals to enforce its order. If the court upholds the Commission's order, further disregard of its terms exposes the respondent to penalties.[22] Congress also endowed the Commission with extensive investigatory powers coordinate with, but independent of, its administrative responsibilities.[23] The basic aim of its economic studies is educational: to focus publicity on market arrangements and trade practices that hinder competition and imperil the general welfare.

FTC Administrative Record—Deceptive Practices

The statutory source of the Commission's authority to suppress deceptive practices as distinguished from monopolistic practices is Section 5 of its organic act, as amended by the Wheeler-Lea Act of 1938.[24] If a seller deceives buyers concerning the identity of the

22. The Wheeler-Lea Act of 1938, cited above, modified the requirements for getting a judicial enforcement order. Violators of a "final" FTC order are now subject to a civil penalty of $5,000 for each offense, *without judicial review of the Commission's proceedings.* The circumstances in which an order becomes "final" depend on the legal steps that the Commission or the respondent may take after issuance of the order. But if neither party takes any action, an order becomes "final" sixty days after its issuance. Even now, however, only a court, not the Commission, can impose a penalty.

23. FTC took over this fact-finding function from the old Bureau of Corporations, established in 1903. The Bureau had made penetrating studies of trade practices in a dozen or more basic industries, and its reports had contributed greatly to the reinvigoration of antitrust policy. FTC's Economic Division has carried on the Bureau's traditions. But it has hardly improved on its predecessor's standards. FTC has in several instances brought to light a mass of detailed facts, only to lose the forest in the trees. The public utility, the chain store, and the trade association reports illustrate the deficiency in organization and interpretation of data. But in recent years, with the reorganization of the Economic Division, this deficiency is gradually being overcome.

24. Section 5 of the FTC Act forbids "unfair methods of competition." As interpreted by FTC and the courts this phrase covers monopolistic as well as deceptive practices. Some monopolistic practices may also be attacked under the Clayton Act, and ordinarily FTC, in such circumstances, grounds its complaint on both Section 5 and, as the case may be, Section 2 or Section 3 of the Clayton Act. But the FTC Act is not technically a part of the "antitrust laws." So while competitors injured by a violation

producer, a competitor injured by the practice has a common-law right of action to stop the deception and to recover damages.[25] The Commission may also proceed against this kind of trading tactics, known technically as "unfair competition," and if a substantial public interest is involved the courts will enforce its orders.[26]

The statutory outlawing of "unfair methods of competition" hits many more deceptive practices than come under the common-law doctrine of "unfair competition." Section 5 comprehends, besides trade-name or trade-mark simulation, other types of misrepresentation, notably the misbranding of a product.[27] The courts have also sustained the Commission's efforts to stamp out misrepresentation of the geographic origin of goods,[28] of the nature of a sellers' busi-

---

of Clayton Act rules may sue and, if successful, recover treble damages, no private right of action exists for a violation of Section 5 of the FTC Act.

25. An illustrative case is *Standard Oil Co. of New Mexico* v. *Standard Oil Co. of California,* 56 Fed. *2d* 973 (1932).

26. In the famous Shade Shop case, the Supreme Court set aside an order requiring a disputant to stop using that name for its business. *FTC* v. *Klesner,* 280 U.S. 19 (1929). The grounds for this ruling were that the controversy arose out of a local squabble between two retailers, each of whom was in a position to defend his rights in the courts, and that the general public had no substantial interest in the outcome.

But in later cases the courts have sustained FTC's power to prevent "unfair competition" when a specific public interest was at stake. See, for example, *FTC* v. *Real Products Corp.,* 90 Fed. *2d* 617 (1937); and *FTC* v. *A.P.W. Paper Co.,* 328 U.S. 193 (1946), affirming 149 Fed. *2d* 424 (1945). Though the courts modified FTC's order in the latter case, they affirmed its jurisdiction. How the public interest may be involved in trade-name or trade-mark simulation cases is perhaps most clearly shown in a recent proceeding in which FTC ordered a California manufacturing concern to differentiate itself plainly on labels, packages, advertising, stationery, etc., from Mayo Brothers Clinic of Rochester, Minnesota. *In re Mayo Bros. Vitamins, Inc.,* 40 FTC 116 (1945).

27. The leading cases are: *FTC* v. *Winsted Hosiery Co.,* 258 U.S. 483 (1922); and *FTC* v. *Algoma Lumber Co.,* 291 U.S. 67 (1934). Both these cases involved the sale of merchandise as and for something different from what it was. In the Winsted case, the order required the respondent to stop calling its partly cotton textile products woolen or worsted. In the Algoma case the respondent was required to discontinue the use of the term "white pine" to describe a different kind of wood.

In both cases the Supreme Court held that it was of no importance that dealers who bought the misbranded products from the respondents were not deceived. The crucial fact was that the misrepresentation of the products confused ultimate buyers and tended to make some of them accept what they did not want. As Mr. Justice Cardozo said in the Algoma case (p. 78), "In such matters, the public is entitled to get what it chooses."

Under the spell of his vigorous defense of the consumer's interest in honest information, lower federal courts have since then generally upheld FTC's orders against misbranding. In a recent case in which the Commission stretched the Algoma doctrine to its extreme limit, the Second Circuit Court of Appeals sustained the order but remarked, "We strongly think that the order is far too harsh." *Siegel & Co.* v. *FTC,* 150 Fed. *2d* 106 (1945), at p. 755. The Supreme Court agreed. 327 U.S. 608 (1946).

28. See, for example, *FTC* v. *Walker's Mining Co.,* 79 Fed. *2d* 457 (1935); and on the misuse of the name Havana on cigars, *N. Heusner* v. *FTC,* 106 Fed. *2d* 596 (1937), and *El Moro Cigar Co.* v. *FTC,* 107 Fed. *2d* 429 (1939). Misleading representations that perfumes manufactured in the United States are of French origin have

ness,[29] and of professional or official endorsement, certification, guarantee, or approval of products [30]—not to mention false allegations or misleading implications that a seller's business is run by some branch of government, federal, state, or local.

Basis for Administrative Suppression of Misrepresentation

The Wheeler-Lea amendment strengthened the Commission's authority to prevent these and other kinds of deceptive practices [31] by eliminating the requirement of proof of injury to competitors. In the Raladam case in 1931 the Supreme Court had invalidated the Commission's order requiring respondent to stop representing its obesity cure as "a scientific remedy" that ordinary purchasers could safely use without a physician's prescription.[32] The Court did not deny that respondent's misrepresentation of its product deceived the public, but it held that the record disclosed no evidence of injury

---

also encountered administrative and judicial disapproval. See *Parfums Corday* v. *FTC,* 120 Fed. *2d* 808 (1942); *Etab. Rigaud* v. *FTC,* 125 Fed. *2d* 590 (1943); and *Houbigant, Inc.* v. *FTC,* 139 Fed. *2d* 1019 (1944). But cf. *California Apparel Creators* v. *Wieder of California,* 162 Fed. *2d* 893 (1947).

29. The leading case is *FTC* v. *Royal Milling Co.,* 288 U.S. 212 (1933). A recent case applying the same rule is *Herzfeld* v. *FTC,* 140 Fed. *2d* 207 (1944).

30. See *FTC* v. *Army & Navy Trading Co.,* 88 Fed. *2d* 776 (1937); *FTC* v. *Standard Education Society,* 302 U.S. 112 (1937); *Educators Association* v. *FTC,* 108 Fed. *2d* 470 (1939); and *Bockenstette* v. *FTC,* 134 Fed. *2d* 369 (1943).

Naturally, the more flagrant frauds of this kind that FTC uncovers do not reach the courts. For example, an order to cease and desist was enough to put out of business the Consumers Bureau of Standards. This one-man enterprise purported to be a "national, non-profit consumers' research and educational organization" engaged in making "scientific tests" of branded merchandise and grading it for the information of "members." Actually the Bureau neither owned nor hired the services of any testing laboratory. It derived most of its income from the sale of its "Reports" to manufacturers, whose products the Bureau—for a fee—listed favorably therein. The "approved" manufacturers thereupon distributed the Reports free to prospective customers. *In re Albert Lane,* 32 FTC 1330 (1941). A better-known device for soliciting advertisers' good will is the Good Housekeeping Institute. The Commission ordered a correction of its alleged "guarantee" of products advertised in Hearst magazines. *In re Hearst Magazines, Inc.,* 32 FTC 1440 (1941). See also *Federal Civil Service Training Bureau,* 25 FTC 444 (1937).

31. The degrees and varieties of fraud are legion. It would require a volume by itself to describe in detail all the different kinds of dishonest trading tactics against which FTC has issued orders. The courts have sustained orders to cease and desist the following (perhaps borderline) types of deceptive practices, besides those listed in the text above. Lottery sales methods: *Jaffe* v. *FTC,* 139 Fed. *2d* 112 (1943), certiorari denied, 321 U.S. 791 (1943); and *Brewer & Co.* v. *FTC,* 158 Fed. *2d* 74 (1946). Exaggeration of value of product: *FTC* v. *Standard Education Society,* cited above; and *Consumers Home Equipment Co.* v. *FTC,* 164 Fed. *2d* 972 (1947), which brought to light the age-old fraud of delivering merchandise that did not conform to the samples on the basis of which salesmen took orders.

32. *FTC* v. *Raladam Co.,* 283 U.S. 643 (1931), affirming 42 Fed. *2d* 430 (1930). The trade name of respondent's remedy was "Marmola."

to rival manufacturers—all of whom, apparently, used equally deceptive selling methods.[33]

Misrepresentation could not be an "unfair method of competition," in the Court's view, unless *some* competitor were offering comparable goods, without deceitful claims, and thus subject to loss of trade to his less scrupulous rival. When Congress finally got around to dealing with this casuistry, seven years later, it made short shrift of it. The Wheeler-Lea Act amended Section 5 of the Trade Commission Act by adding a prohibition of "unfair and deceptive practices in commerce." [34]

Since 1938, under this new rule, the Commission has encountered a more sympathetic judicial attitude toward its campaign to raise the ethical standards of business by eliminating selling methods that give consumers a misleading impression of the qualities of merchandise.[35]

Outside the special field of foods, drugs, and cosmetics, the courts have also quite regularly sustained the Commission's orders to stop deceptive trade practices. And the respondents in these cases are by no means all fly-by-night enterprises. Thus the Gulf Oil Corporation unsuccessfully resisted enforcement of an order to stop misleading advertisement of its insecticide spray for cows; and General Motors and Ford were required to discontinue a misleading representation of their deferred-payment plans as "6 per cent plans," when they actually involved charges of "approximately 11.5 per cent simple annual interest." [36]

33. The record does not show whether FTC tried, and failed, to find other manufacturers of obesity cures for self-prescription who sold their products without adequate warning of the dangers from use of such products without a physician's prescription. But the Commission did make a "finding of fact" to the effect that physicians themselves were in competition with respondent. The Supreme Court gave a short but debatable answer to this line of argument. Said Mr. Justice Sutherland (p. 653), "Of course, medical practitioners . . . are not in competition with respondent. They follow a profession and not a trade."

34. This legislative "answer" to the Supreme Court's ruling in the Raladam case was one of the two main features of the Wheeler-Lea Act. The other was the new definition of "false advertisement," discussed above, which related solely to foods, drugs, cosmetics, and therapeutic devices. The prohibition of "unfair and deceptive practices," on the other hand, applied to dealings in all commodities.

35. See, for example, *Justin Haynes* v. *FTC,* 105 Fed. *2d* 988 (1939), certiorari denied, 303 U.S. 616 (1940), upholding an order to discontinue using "Aspirub" as the name of an ointment and claiming it would relieve muscular aches and pains. See also *Charles of the Ritz* v. *FTC,* 143 Fed. *2d* 676 (1944), upholding an order to discontinue representing that a face cream would "rejuvenate" the complexion; and *Associated Laboratories* v. *FTC,* 150 Fed. *2d* 629 (1945), requiring respondent to stop overstating the curative properties of "Kelp-a-Malt."

36. *Gulf Oil Corp.* v. *FTC,* 150 Fed. *2d* 106 (1945); *General Motors Corp.* v.

Beyond doubt the Commission's efforts have strengthened competitive forces in trade by helping consumers to make more intelligent purchases. But current regulation of trade practices shows clearly the continuing need, if competition is to be effective, for vigilant and vigorous repression of all selling methods that mislead consumers and handicap honest sellers.[37] Despite the stiffer standard of fair competition that the Wheeler-Lea Act laid down, the courts have recently shown some disposition to give renewed emphasis to the long-standing judicial precedents that regarded "puffing" as innocuous.[38]

FTC and Collusive Monopolistic Practices

Monopolistic trade practices undermine competition in the market much more directly than deceptive practices. Two distinct types of monopolistic practices come within the scope of the Federal Trade Commission's regulatory powers: those that are collusive and those that are discriminatory. Restrictive trade agreements among competitors are subject to suppression under Section 5 of the FTC Act. Discriminatory attacks on competitors to exclude them from the market are forbidden by Sections 2 and 3 of the Clayton Act, and they are also forbidden by Section 5 of the FTC Act. The Commission alone bears primary responsibility for the enforcement of Section 5 of its basic statute. But it shares responsibility for the enforcement of Clayton Act provisions regulating trade practices with the Attorney General and the business community—firms injured by illegal practices may sue for treble damages.

The Commission early in its life adopted the policy of attacking

FTC, 114 Fed. *2d* 33 (1940), certiorari denied, 312 U.S. 682 (1941); and *Ford Motor Co.* v. *FTC*, 120 Fed. *2d* 175 (1941).

37. Cases dealing with false advertisement of foods, drugs, cosmetics, and devices fill a large part of the administrative record in recent years. Illustrative proceedings are *In re Automatic Electric Devices Co.*, 40 FTC 476 (1945), involving a "Homozone" device for relieving asthma; *In re Solon Co.*, 41 FTC 38 (1945), involving an alleged obesity cure; *In re Frontier Asthma Co., Inc.*, 43 FTC 1 (1946), involving a medicine for "curing" asthma; and *In re Oxford Products, Inc.*, 43 FTC 1 (1946), involving a hair tonic alleged to prevent gray hair.

38. In *Carlay Co.* v. *FTC*, 153 Fed. *2d* 493 (1946), for example, the court set aside an order requiring respondent to stop representing its candy, "Ayds," as an "easy" fat-reducing agent that, if used according to respondent's "plan," obviated the necessity of adhering to a restricted diet. FTC found as a fact that the candy contained nothing to prevent fat accumulation and that its only "virtue" from that standpoint was one it had in common with all candy, namely, that if eaten before meals it reduced one's appetite for fattening foods. The court held that no substantial evidence supported the finding that such advertisements were misleading.

restrictive trade agreements as unfair methods of competition, notwithstanding that such collusive arrangements are clearly subject, as unreasonable restraints of trade, to the much heavier penalties of the Sherman Act.[39] And the courts have consistently supported the Commission in so interpreting its mandate.[40] From the standpoint of efficient law enforcement, on its face it is difficult to justify this overlapping jurisdiction between the Federal Trade Commission and the Department of Justice. But occasionally, as in its vigorous attack on the basing point system, the Commission has succeeded in making a significant contribution to the effective application of antitrust policy.

The collusive trade practices that the Commission has challenged are of two kinds: those establishing uniform rules or policies for members of the group, and those directed, not primarily at collective self-discipline, but at imposing some rule of conduct on others. Of the first kind the most common is the simple price-fixing agreement. Other collusive practices of this sort include agreements on sales territory, output, discounts, pricing methods, accounting procedures, and trade statistics.[41] But the object is always the same: suppressing competition *among the confederates.*

39. The first volume of FTC reports of administrative proceedings listed at least four cases of simple price fixing among competitors. *In re Book Paper Manufacturers,* 1 FTC 38 (1917); *In re Association of Flag Manufacturers,* 1 FTC 55 (1918); *In re Gold Leaf Manufacturers Association,* 1 FTC 173 (1918); and *In re Blakely Printing Co.,* 1 FTC 277 (1918). Later volumes report many similar cases. A recent case involved collaboration on pricing in the same industry as the first case cited above—this time under a basing point system. *In re Allied Paper Mills,* 40 FTC 696 (1945).

Of the approximately 250 cases reported in the latest two volumes of FTC reports, at least eight involved conspiracies in restraint of trade. Each of these eight cases could have been prosecuted with equal likelihood of success under Section 1 of the Sherman Act. Of course, FTC has no jurisdiction in violations of the Sherman Act, as such. But no reason is apparent, other than bureaucratic jealousy, for FTC's not having turned over to the Department of Justice the evidence it had accumulated, in every one of these price-fixing cases, for prosecution under the Sherman Act. The stiffer remedies afforded by the Sherman Act are much more appropriate to an offense like collusive price fixing than FTC's merely admonitory orders to cease and desist. Cf. *Public Regulation of Competitive Practices,* cited above, pp. 229-33; and R. R. Guthrie, "Federal Trade Commission Price Conspiracy Cases," *George Washington Law Review,* January 1940, pp. 620-38.

40. The leading case is *FTC* v. *Pacific States Paper Trade Association,* 273 U.S. 52 (1927). On failure of the respondents to obey the order sustained in this case, a federal court later assessed heavy fines. 88 Fed. *2d* 1009 (1937). Recent lower-court rulings applying the doctrine of the Pacific States Paper case include: *California Rice Industry* v. *FTC,* 102 Fed. *2d* 716 (1939); *Salt Producers Association* v. *FTC,* 134 Fed. *2d* 354 (1943); *E. Dietzgen Co.* v. *FTC,* 142 Fed. *2d* 321 (1944); *United States Maltsters Association* v. *FTC,* 152 Fed. *2d* 161 (1945); *Milk & Ice Cream Can Institute* v. *FTC,* 152 Fed. *2d* 478 (1946); and *Keasby & Mattison* v. *FTC,* 159 Fed. *2d* 940 (1947).

41. See the cases listed in the preceding footnote.

The aim of the second kind of collusive trade practice is to limit the trading opportunities of those not parties to the agreement. In its extreme form it tries to force some competitor or class of enterprises out of the market.[42] The most common technique in this class of cases is the boycott. The collective pressure of a cohesively organized group, acting either as buyers or sellers, provides a powerful leverage for "bringing to heel" competitors inclined to be too independent, or even for eliminating obnoxious elements from the trade. But the well-authenticated tendency of trade confederacies to favor vested interests and block competitive enterprise has made the courts exceptionally resolute in their opposition to boycotting.[43] They have generally supported the Commission in its efforts to repress collusive trade practices of this kind.

FTC and Discriminatory Monopolistic Practices

Discriminatory trade practices are at once a cause and an effect of imperfect competition. Without some monopolistic control of the market no enterprise can afford to charge some customers less than others or to show other preferences. In a freely competitive market a firm so behaving would lose trade to its rivals. Those discriminated against would look elsewhere for supplies, and transferring their patronage would place them under no competitive handicap. The products of rival sellers would be as salable and as satisfactory in use as those of the discriminating producer.

It is otherwise when a manufacturer or dealer holds a commanding position in some section of the market, in the supply of some

42. For example, to restrict the channels of trade to "legitimate" dealers, *In re Pittsburgh Plate Glass Co.*, 25 FTC 1228 (1937) and *In re Motor Equipment Association*, 32 FTC 587 (1941); to compel manufacturers not to sell to mail-order houses, *In re N.W. State Roofing Association*, 25 FTC 1150 (1937); or to force manufacturers to restore privileges withdrawn pursuant to federal wartime food conservation orders, *In re Food Dealers Association*, 41 FTC 44 (1945).

43. The leading case supporting FTC action against trade boycotts is *Fashion Originators Guild* v. *FTC*, 312 U.S. 457 (1941). Leading dress and cloak manufacturers organized the Guild to stop so-called "pirating" of their original designs. In condemning the combination Mr. Justice Black declared (p. 468) its "aim . . . was the *intentional* destruction of one type of manufacture and sale which competed with Guild members . . . Nor can the unlawful combination be justified upon the argument that systematic copying of designs is itself tortious . . . even if copying were an acknowledged tort under the law of every state, that situation would not justify petitioners in combining together to regulate and restrain interstate commerce in violation of federal law." Italics supplied.

For recent cases applying the same principle in Sherman Act prosecutions, see *U.S.* v. *Frankfort Distilleries*, 324 U.S. 293 (1945); and *Associated Press* v. *U.S.*, 326 U.S. 1 (1945).

essential material, or in the production of a particular item in a line of merchandise. In whatever way a firm may have obtained such a partial monopoly—whether by merger with rivals, by patent accumulation, managerial foresight or efficiency, extensive advertising, preclusive buying, or luck—it can use its power as a lever to pry trade away from competitors in other parts of the market. In effect, it can say to buyers, "To get product A, which we alone can supply, you must also buy from us products B and C." Or it can achieve the same end by cutting to a nonprofit level the prices on B and C, which rival firms produce, while exacting a high price for A, which rival firms do not produce.[44] In either case, the partial monopolist is using his dominant position in one part of the market to bolster or increase his power in other parts. Discriminatory trade practices thus promote domination of the market and industrial monopoly.

Barring the elimination of patent rights, prestige values nurtured on advertising, tariff preferences, and a variety of special privileges in trade, legally free markets left unpoliced cannot overcome this process of monopoly strengthening itself by using discriminatory tactics. Only legal sanctions can curb it. Congress recognized this in the Clayton Act by explicitly providing such sanctions for regulation of two outstanding types of discriminatory trade practice. Section 2 made price discrimination illegal except in specified circumstances. Section 3 forbade exclusive dealing arrangements and tying contracts.[45]

Exclusive Dealing and Tying Contracts

Neither of the trade practices forbidden by Section 3 oppresses competitors in all circumstances. For example, if Studebaker, through an exclusive dealing arrangement, limits a local distributor to sales

44. Similarly, it can lower the prices of all its products (A, B, and C) in territories where rivals sell, while maintaining profitable prices wherever it alone operates.

45. In the words of the statute, it was henceforth unlawful "to lease or make a sale" of property "on the condition . . . that the lessee or purchaser thereof shall not use or deal in the goods . . . of a competitor or competitors of the lessor or seller."

This language covered two fairly distinct discriminatory practices. A typical exclusive dealing arrangement is one in which a finished-goods manufacturer selling merchandise to a dealer binds him not to handle similar products made by any other firm. A typical tying contract is one in which a machinery manufacturer selling or leasing equipment to another manufacturer or to a business firm for use in its own offices or stores binds the buyer or lessee to use in or with the machine only materials or auxiliary devices supplied by the machinery manufacturer.

In either case, the seller or lessor forces *others*—his customers—to discriminate against the products or supplies made by competitors of the seller or lessor.

of Studebaker cars, that does not prejudice the interests of competing automobile manufacturers. It assures Studebaker of its local representative's single-minded concentration on promoting the sales of one line of cars. Yet it does not close, or appreciably restrict, the opportunity of Nash, Hudson, Chrysler, or any other automobile manufacturer to obtain comparable marketing facilities in the same territory. Effective sales promotion for bulky or intricate products of great unit value, requiring costly demonstration and repair services, demands undivided efforts and close cooperation with the manufacturer. Similarly, it does not obstruct competitors for either a manufacturer or a distributor of chinaware to "tie" sales of cups and saucers—to offer to sell a gross or a dozen cups only "on the condition" that the buyer shall also take a gross or a dozen saucers.[46]

Doubtless such considerations influenced Congress in limiting the prohibition of exclusive dealing and tying contracts to circumstances in which "the effect . . . may be to substantially lessen competition or tend to create a monopoly." In what circumstances "may" the effect specified reasonably be anticipated? Though it would be difficult to frame a precise rule covering all cases, at least one condition appears to be a prerequisite: possession by the seller of monopolistic power over one or more of the products affected. An analysis of the cases supports this view. In the first two proceedings in which FTC orders for the enforcement of Section 3 reached the Supreme Court, the decisions went against the Commission.[47] In both cases the Commission based its order on the "bare bones" of a tying contract: the sale or lease of one kind of goods on condition that the buyer solely use therewith, or deal in, another kind of goods supplied by the seller or lessor.

The Gratz case dealt with the sale of steel ties for baling cotton on condition that buyers also purchase enough bagging to cover the number of bales that the ties purchased would ordinarily bind. Though the respondent was the exclusive sales agent of a subsidiary of U.S. Steel, which was the principal manufacturer of steel ties,

46. Such a condition is, of course, tantamount to a requirement that the buyer shall not buy the complementary goods (the saucers) from "a competitor of the seller." And the courts have so held. *Lord* v. *Radio Corp. of America*, 24 Fed. *2d* 565 (1928); certiorari denied, 278 U.S. 648 (1928).

47. *FTC* v. *Warren, Jones & Gratz*, previously cited; and *FTC* v. *Sinclair Refining Co.*, 261 U.S. 463 (1923). The Sinclair case represented a consolidation of twenty-seven separate proceedings involving the same issue.

the Federal Trade Commission failed to stress this important feature of the situation in its pleadings.

The Sinclair suit was one of twenty-seven in which the Commission issued orders directing oil companies to stop requiring service station operators, whom they severally provided with gasoline pumps bearing their respective distinctive markings, to handle only one supplier's brands. Here again the Commission neglected to make a point of whatever monopolistic elements there may have been in the market position of each of the major oil companies. But another factor was probably decisive in these cases: the advantage to the public and the refiner alike of identification of each service station with a particular brand and the ease with which competitors could find market outlets, simply by encouraging the opening of new service stations.[48]

Circumstances Alter Cases

Yet these setbacks did not mean that the courts had emasculated Section 3 of the Clayton Act. For sandwiched between the Gratz and the Sinclair decisions was the United Shoe Machinery case, holding the defendant's tying contracts illegal.[49] The defendant violated the law in two respects: (1) by leasing some machines of which United Shoe Machinery held a tight monopoly solely on condition that the lessee (shoe manufacturer) also lease from United Shoe Machinery other machines that competitors could have supplied; (2) by leasing some machines that United Shoe Machinery monopolized solely on condition that the lessee use therein materials (eyelets, for example) that competitors were in a position to supply. But in its attack on the discriminatory practices of the shoe machinery company the Department of Justice took pains to emphasize that the company's marketing methods were destructive of competition because of the leverage that its monopoly on certain types of machines gave it.[50]

48. FTC's case was weaker still when it ordered the Curtis Publishing Co. to cancel provisions of its contracts with newsboys requiring them not to handle other magazines. These distributors were Curtis agents, and the Supreme Court held that such restrictions in agency contracts are wholly outside the scope of the Clayton Act provisions. *FTC* v. *Curtis Publishing Co.*, 260 U.S. 568 (1923).

49. *United Shoe Machinery Corp.* v. *U.S.*, 258 U.S. 451 (1922). The Department of Justice instituted this suit; its powers to enforce Clayton Act provisions are coordinate with those of FTC.

50. A similar requirement exists in the application of Section 3 to exclusive deal-

Taking its cue from the successes of the Department of Justice and private litigants, the Commission became more cautious in the selection and preparation of cases under Section 3.[51] When the Commission confined its administrative action to suppress exclusive dealing and tying contracts to situations in which the seller's possession of a partial monopoly makes these practices destructive of competition, the courts have consistently upheld its orders.[52] In Department of Justice prosecutions and in private suits the judges have been equally vigilant to prevent monopolistic power from being used as a lever to obtain greater monopolistic power, in violation of Section 3.[53]

---

ing arrangements, as shown by another Supreme Court decision in the same year as the Shoe Machinery case. *Standard Fashion Co.* v. *Magrane-Houston Co.,* 258 U.S. 346 (1922). This was a private suit, but it supports the view that for a successful attack on exclusive dealing a necessary element is proof of the seller's possession of some monopolistic power to force dealers to refuse to handle the goods of the seller's competitors. Standard Fashion and two affiliated companies controlled two fifths of the 52,000 pattern "agencies" in the country. As the Supreme Court said (p. 357), "The restriction of each merchant to one pattern manufacturer must in hundreds, perhaps in thousands, of small communities amount to giving such single pattern manufacturer a monopoly of the business . . ."

In this case the Supreme Court first ruled (pp. 356-57) that the verb "may be" in the qualifying clause "where the effect may be to substantially lessen competition . . ." means "will probably be." A "mere possibility" of a lessening of competition is not enough to make the prohibitions of the law applicable. Cf., however, *Corn Products Refining Co.* v. *FTC,* 324 U.S. 726 (1945), where the Court gives (p. 742) a slightly different construction to the same clause in Section 2.

51. As shown, for example, by its findings in the case against the Butterick Co., 6 FTC 310 (1923). The facts were substantially identical with those in the Standard Fashion case, and FTC did not neglect to bring to light the respondent's market domination. On the case thus made out, the courts fully sustained the order. *Butterick Co.* v. *FTC,* 4 Fed. *2d* 910 (1925); certiorari denied, 267 U.S. 602 (1925).

52. See, for example, *Q.R.S. Music Co.* v. *FTC,* 12 Fed. *2d* 730 (1926), in which respondent controlled over half the business; *FTC* v. *Eastman Kodak Co.,* 274 U.S. 619 (1927), in which respondent was defending a virtually complete monopoly; *Carter Carburetor Co.* v. *FTC,* 112 Fed. *2d* 722 (1940), where the court pointed out (p. 733) that "Petitioner occupies a dominant position in the . . . business"; *Signode Co.* v. *FTC,* 132 Fed. *2d* 48 (1942), holding illegal the use of tying contracts in the lease of tying machines. In this case the respondent, with two other companies that also used tying contracts, controlled two thirds to three quarters of the industry. In the most recent case, *Judson Thompson* v. *FTC,* 150 Fed. *2d* 952 (1945), the record showed, according to the court (p. 954), that out of "approximately 19,000 [riveting] machines outstanding on leases" in the United States, respondent was lessor of 8,000. Petition for certiorari denied, 326 U.S. 776 (1945).

53. In the first category, leading cases are: *International Business Machines Corp.* v. *U.S.,* 298 U.S. 131 (1936); and *International Salt Co.* v. *U.S.,* 332 U.S. 392 (1947).

In the second category, private suits, leading cases are: *Carbice Corp.* v. *American Patents Corp.,* 283 U.S. 27 (1931); *Oxford Varnish Co.* v. *Ault & Wiborg,* 83 Fed. *2d* 764 (1936); and *Leitch* v. *Barber Co.,* 302 U.S. 458 (1938).

All the foregoing cases involved tying contracts. An unsuccessful private suit for treble damages, based on exclusive dealing arrangements that came clearly within the doctrine of the gasoline-pump cases, was *Pick* v. *General Motors Corp.,* 299 U.S. 3 (1936).

Price Discrimination Under the Clayton Act

The wording of the original statutory prohibition of price discrimination left many loopholes. To make out a case of unlawful discrimination a complainant was obliged to prove that a price difference in sales to different customers (1) was not made "on account of differences in the grade, quality, or quantity" of the goods sold, (2) represented more than a "due allowance for difference in the cost of selling or transportation," (3) was not "made in good faith to meet competition," and (4) would probably serve "to substantially lessen competition or tend to create a monopoly." These were formidable hurdles to successful prosecution.

The statute did not require that a quantity discount should be *in proportion to* any savings in the cost of manufacture. If, in accordance with custom, a manufacturer granted wholesalers a greater trade discount than it granted retailers buying in the same quantity, would this be an unlawful price discrimination? Or would such a price difference be exempt as not tending substantially to lessen competition either among wholesalers or among retailers? Moreover, if wholesalers *generally* bought in larger quantities than retailers, would it violate the law to make a single sale of a small amount to a wholesaler at a lower price than that in some larger transaction with a particular retailer?

In its initial efforts to obtain a clarification of the ambiguous terms of Section 2 of the Clayton Act the Trade Commission concentrated on the question of the lawfulness of price differences among buyers occupying a different trade status: wholesalers, retailers' buying clubs, chain stores, independent retailers, and so forth. When its orders challenging pricing policies that undoubtedly involved price differences on sales of similar quantities reached the courts, the Commission suffered a setback.[54] The courts held, in effect, that price discrimination based on the commercial status of buyers was outside the scope of the statute.[55] So from 1924 to 1933 the Commission made no further attempts to enforce the Clayton Act prohibition.

54. See *Mennen Co.* v. *FTC,* 288 Fed. 774 (1923), certiorari denied, 262 U.S. 759 (1923); and *National Biscuit Co.* v. *FTC,* 299 Fed. 733 (1924), certiorari denied, 266 U.S. 613 (1924).

55. In the Mennen case the Circuit Court of Appeals indicated that in its opinion the statutory prohibition applied only to a price discrimination that lessened competition between the seller and others engaged in the same line of trade, in the instant case, between Mennen and other *manufacturers* of toilet articles.

Meanwhile, private litigation had shown that Section 2 of the Clayton Act carried more "teeth" than the Commission supposed.[56] In the Van Camp case the issue was not the granting of different discounts to wholesalers and retailers, but discrimination between different buyers of the same trade status. The American Can Company, the defendant, had sold cans to a competitor of Van Camp at a lower price than it charged Van Camp, in fact at a lower price than it had offered to supply cans to Van Camp even on the same volume of purchases. Van Camp sought treble damages, claiming that the discrimination hurt it in competing with rival canners. The defense relied on the dictum in the Mennen case that price discrimination was unlawful only when its intent and effect were to hamper or restrain competitors of the concern granting the discrimination.

In giving judgment for the plaintiff, the Court, through Mr. Justice Sutherland, stated:

> The fundamental policy of the legislation is that . . . competition is desirable and that whatever lessens it . . . is an evil. Offense against this policy, by a discrimination in prices exacted by the seller from different purchasers of similar goods, is no less clear when it produces the evil in respect of the line of commerce in which they are engaged than when it produces the evil in respect of the line of commerce in which the seller is engaged.[57]

Sharper Teeth for Clayton Act

This decision stimulated renewed interest in the possibility of abating discriminatory pricing practices.[58] In 1933 the Federal Trade Commission again entered the lists in this popular cause. It took action against what had become a fairly common form of discrimination: the grant by manufacturers of an exceptionally low price to mail-order houses and other mass-distribution agencies under long-term contracts for supplying them with goods bearing the distributor's brand but otherwise indistinguishable from the product sold

56. *Van Camp* v. *American Can Co.*, 278 U.S. 245 (1929).

57. *Ibid.*, p. 254.

58. As shown, for one thing, by the filing of several suits by private parties to recover treble damages for injuries inflicted on them by such practices. See, for example, *Story Parchment Co.* v. *Paterson Paper Co.*, 37 Fed. *2d* 537 (1930), 282 U.S. 555 (1931); and *American Can Co.* v. *Ladoga Canning Co.*, 44 Fed. *2d* 763 (1930), 282 U.S. 899 (1930). In both of these suits the plaintiffs were successful.

(through other channels) under the manufacturer's own brand name.[59]

The Goodyear case led to a long controversy over the character and extent of the advantages a manufacturer obtains from having an assured outlet for a large volume of production.[60] The Commission denied, and Goodyear asserted, that the savings effected in manufacturing and overhead costs justified the lower prices to Sears, Roebuck.[61] But the legal issue was narrower: whether Section 2 of the Clayton Act required that a price difference based on differences in quantities purchased must correspond fairly closely to demonstrated cost savings. On this issue, the courts finally agreed with the respondent and vacated the Commission's order.[62]

Robinson-Patman Amendments to Clayton Act

Meanwhile, the long depression of the 1930's put increasing pressure on businessmen in all fields and of all ranks to get trade on whatever terms they could. Many people suspected that in this

59. *In re Goodyear Tire & Rubber Co.,* 22 FTC 232 (1936). The complaint, issued September 13, 1933, charged that respondent had for seven years been selling tires to Sears, Roebuck under a "cost plus 6%" contract at prices from 11 to 22 per cent below prices charged "regular" dealers for tires of similar quality bearing the Goodyear brand.

60. When the petition for review first came up, the court held the issue moot, because of the enactment, the year before, of the Robinson-Patman amendment. *Goodyear* v. *FTC,* 92 Fed. *2d* 677 (1937). On appeal, the Supreme Court reversed this ruling and remanded the case to the Circuit Court of Appeals for trial on the merits. 304 U.S. 257 (1938). After trial, the Circuit Court of Appeals vacated FTC's order, and the Supreme Court denied certiorari. 101 Fed. *2d* 620 (1939); 308 U.S. 557 (1939).

FTC found that from 1926 to 1933 Goodyear sold Sears more than 19 million tires, for which net payments amounted to $116.3 million. The Commission computed Goodyear's net profits on this business at $7.7 million, and found that on a comparable volume and assortment of tire sales to "regular" retailers its net profits were $20.4 million. The difference of $12.7 million represented, in FTC's view, "the aggregate net price discrimination not accounted for by differences in cost of transportation and selling." 101 Fed. *2d,* pp. 621-22.

61. In general, accountants for FTC rejected cost deductions claimed by Goodyear to be attributable to the Sears sales, unless they were *directly* derived from the Sears contract. The distribution of Goodyear's advertising expense and administrative costs presented thorny problems. But the most serious difference of opinion was over the question of allowance for reduced hazards to the Goodyear business from price and output fluctuations.

62. In technical terms, the courts held that the first two exceptions provided in the statute were mutually exclusive. This meant that price differences "on account of differences in . . . grade, quality, or quantity" are not to be tested, for their legality, by the standard specified for the second exception: "or that make only *due allowance* for difference in the cost of selling or transportation." Italics supplied. Rather, price differences based on differences in the "quantity" of goods ordered may be legally justified though they are unrelated to any provable differences in the cost of *manufacture.*

struggle giant corporations held a great advantage by reason of their ability both to give and to obtain discriminatory prices.[63] In response to popular agitation for a tightening of the Clayton Act restrictions on discriminatory pricing, Congress in 1936 passed the Robinson-Patman Act.[64] Of the six main sections of the Robinson-Patman Act the last five are new. The first represents a revision of the controversial Section 2 of the Clayton Act, and it is by all odds the most important.[65]

Section 2(a) made four significant changes in the original Clayton Act provisions:

1. It provided an alternative to the required showing of likelihood of a substantial lessening of competition or tendency toward monopoly: a likelihood that price discrimination will injure a particular competitor.[66]
2. It ended the unqualified exemption of price differences based on quantity of purchases and subjected them to the same limitation ("which make *only due allowance* for differences in the cost of manufacture") that had previously applied only

63. Probably chain store organizations were the chief focal point of this suspicion. The voluminous FTC report of its chain store investigation reflects at many points the dread of their growing power among thousands of independent dealers. The FTC chain store report is comprised of a long series of Senate Documents and FTC releases over a three-year period, 1931-1934. For the complete list, see *Public Regulation of Competitive Practices,* cited above, pp. 301-02. The most significant reports in the present connection are S.Docs. 86, 89, and 94, 73d Cong., 2d sess., 1933; and S.Doc. 4, 74th Cong., 1st sess., 1934.

64. Act of June 19, 1936, 49 Stat. 1526, U.S. Code, Title 15, Sec. 13.

65. The U.S. Code designates the several subdivisions of the Robinson-Patman Act by lower-case letters. These lettered subdivisions of Section 13 of Title 15 of the Code correspond to Sections 2(a)-2(f) of the Clayton Act *as amended.* To avoid confusion with the section *numbers* of the Robinson-Patman Act as enacted, instead of referring to Section 1, Section 2, and so on, of the Act, the subdivisions will hereinafter be cited Section 2(a), Section 2(b), etc.

66. Congress inserted this provision because of a general impression that, without it, the law condemned only a price discrimination that tended to eliminate competition *generally* either in the seller's industry or in the buyer's branch of trade. The House and Senate Committee reports on the bill used identical language in explaining this provision. They said that Section 2 "has in practice been too restrictive in requiring a showing of general injury to competitive conditions . . . , whereas the more immediately important concern is in injury to the competitor victimized by the discrimination." H.Rept. 2287, 74th Cong., 2d sess., p. 8; S.Rept. 1502, 74th Cong., 2d sess., p. 4.

In the light of the Van Camp decision, cited above, it is at least doubtful whether this congressional impression of the meaning of the Clayton Act provision was valid. Cf., on this point, H. T. Austern, "Competitive Injury and Permitted Meeting of Competition," in *N.Y. State Bar Association Symposium on the Robinson-Patman Act,* Commerce Clearing House, Chicago, 1947, pp. 65-66. (These symposia are held annually; they will hereinafter be cited: Bar Ass'n Symposium, followed by year.)

to price differences based on differences in selling methods and transportation costs.[67]

3. It authorized the Commission to "fix . . . quantity limits . . . as to particular commodities . . . where . . . purchasers in greater quantities are so few as to render differentials on account thereof unjustly discriminatory." [68]
4. The amendment added a proviso that exempts price differences resulting from "changing conditions affecting the market." [69]

Robinson-Patman Supplements to Clayton Act

Section 2(b) is procedural. It casts on the respondent the burden of proof of any justification he sets up in rebuttal of a prima facie case of price discrimination. On what amounts to a prima facie case of price discrimination, Section 2(b) is by no means clear. It would be a *reductio ad absurdum* to contend that all price differences are price discriminations. In ordinary usage the word "discrimination" implies differentiation in an invidious or culpable sense. As one of the principal sponsors of the Robinson-Patman Act declared in the House debate: "In its meaning as simple English a discrimination is more than a mere difference. Underlying the meaning of the word is the idea that some relationship exists between the parties . . . which entitles them to equal treatment, whereby the difference granted to one casts some burden on the other." [70]

67. Italics supplied. Logic plainly dictated such a change and the demonstrated impossibility of effective enforcement of the statute, otherwise, made it urgent. See discussion of the Mennen and National Biscuit cases above.

68. The wording of this proviso leaves much to be desired from the standpoint of grammatical accuracy, but its meaning is plain. The phrasing "quantity limits" is ellipsis, which would be obscure, to say the least, without the final clause.

Apparently, FTC has taken no action to "fix quantity limits" in any trade. However, in one proceeding, it did specify what amounts to a maximum price differential of 5 cents a case in sales of table salt. *In re Morton Salt Co.,* 39 FTC 35 (1946). But this limitation applied solely to the respondent's price terms. It was not fixed, as the statute requires, "after due investigation and hearing to all interested parties."

69. Though this proviso is new it is extremely doubtful that it changes the law. Nothing in the Clayton Act suggested that different prices to different customers *buying at different times* amounted to price *discrimination* in violation of the Act.

70. Remarks of Rep. Utterback, *Congressional Record,* 1936, p. 9416, quoted in H. L. Schniderman, "The Tyranny of Labels," *Harvard Law Review,* 1947, p. 586.

The language of Section 2(a) makes no distinction between a price discrimination and a price differential. It appears to use the two terms indiscriminately. Reason and common sense both suggest, however, that a prima facie case of price discrimination requires a positive showing of a probable *substantial* lessening of, or injury to, competition or a tendency toward monopoly. This was, in fact, the assumption on which

Limitations on Brokerage Fees and Advertising Allowances

Section 2(c) forbids sellers to pay brokerage fees, in any guise, to buyers, to buyers' agents, or to intermediaries subject to the direct or indirect control of buyers. The only circumstance in which a seller may lawfully pay brokerage fees is when the intermediary acts *solely* as the seller's agent, or representative.[71]

The primary objective of subdivisions (d) and (e) of Section 2 is to put an end to the abuses connected with a widespread trade practice—the granting of advertising allowances—that were insidiously undermining competition. In many fields such allowances were so preferential as to amount to secret rebates.[72]

Sections 2(d) and 2(e) forbade, respectively, the payment for and the furnishing of services or facilities "in connection with the . . . handling . . . or . . . sale of any products" except "on pro-

---

FTC itself proceeded for almost ten years. See W. B. Wooden in Bar Ass'n Symposium, 1947, pp. 37-43. Nevertheless, when FTC switched its position, the courts upheld it in the Moss and the Morton Salt cases. *Moss* v. *FTC,* 148 Fed. *2d* 378 (1945), certiorari denied, 326 U.S. 734 (1945); and *FTC* v. *Morton Salt Co.,* 334 U.S. 37 (1948), reversing 162 Fed. *2d* 949 (1947).

The practical effect of the rule the Supreme Court applied in the Morton Salt case is to impose on respondents the burden of proving justification for *any* price difference that FTC chooses to challenge. As Mr. Justice Jackson said of this rule in his dissent in that case (Advance Print, p. 3), it "is fatal to any discount the Commission sees fit to attack . . . The law of this case, in a nutshell, is that no quantity discount is valid if the Commission chooses to say it is not."

On the desirability of amending Section 2(b) to make it clear that proof of a mere price *difference* does not constitute a prima facie case of price *discrimination,* but requires in addition proof of a reasonable *probability* of a lessening of, or injury to, competition, see P. McCollister, "Suggestions as to Certain Amendments," Bar Ass'n Symposium, 1948, pp. 133-40; and Austern, *op. cit.*

71. Abuses to which the practice had led probably justified this absolute prohibition of payments to buyers on account of, or in lieu of, brokerage. But the courts, while uniformly upholding FTC's strict construction of this section, have repeatedly recognized that it imposes great hardships when, as often happens, an intermediary acting above board and in good faith renders services of real value to *both* the buyer and the seller.

See *Biddle* v. *FTC,* 96 Fed. *2d* 687 (1938), certiorari denied, 305 U.S. 634 (1938); *Oliver Bros.* v. *FTC,* 102 Fed. *2d* 763 (1939); *A & P* v. *FTC,* 106 Fed. *2d* 667 (1939); *Webb-Crawford Co.* v. *FTC,* 109 Fed. *2d* 268 (1940), certiorari denied, 310 U.S. 638 (1940); *Quality Bakers* v. *FTC,* 114 Fed. *2d* 393 (1940); *Modern Marketing Service* v. *FTC,* 149 Fed. *2d* 970 (1945); and *Southgate Brokerage Co.* v. *FTC,* 150 Fed. *2d* 607 (1945).

72. For example, in the grocery trade advertising allowances appear to have been far from uniform. They were generally fixed by "close-in" bargaining, in which the biggest buyers obtained special advantages. See *U.S.* v. *A & P,* 67 Fed.Supp. 626 (1946), particularly pp. 649-50. This was a Sherman Act prosecution, but the applicability of the Robinson-Patman Act to discriminatory pricing policies subject to condemnation under the Sherman Act, as here, cannot be doubted. The Circuit Court of Appeals sustained the judgment of the District Court on February 24, 1949. 173 Fed. *2d* 79 (1949).

portionally equal terms to all . . . customers." The statute left to the Commission and the courts the task of defining "proportionally equal terms." [73]

Finally, Section (f) makes it no less unlawful "to induce or receive" a price discrimination than to grant one.[74]

Problems in Enforcing the Robinson-Patman Act

However incautious may be the language in some other passages in his opinion in the A & P case, Judge Lindley's remark on the ambiguities of the Robinson-Patman Act certainly did not exaggerate them. "I doubt," he said, "if any judge would assert that he knows exactly what does or does not amount to violation of the Robinson-Patman Act in any and all instances." [75] However, the "process of judicial inclusion and exclusion" is gradually clearing up some of the uncertainties.

By itself, refusal to deal does not constitute price discrimination.[76] But when such refusal is part of a concerted plan to drive rival distributors out of business, the practice comes within the prohibitions of Section 2(a).[77] Again, prices may be discriminatory even though they are identical, if other terms of sale give a preferential advantage

73. FTC has taken the position, and the courts have sustained it, that a respondent does not make special sales promotion allowances available on proportionally equal terms when he imposes such strict conditions for the grant of such allowances that only a small number of dealer-customers can qualify for them. See *Elizabeth Arden* v. *FTC,* 156 Fed. *2d* 132 (1946); certiorari denied, 331 U.S. 806 (1947).

The decision of the Second Circuit Court of Appeals in this case is in accord with an earlier ruling of the Ninth Circuit Court in a private suit, which also involved the question of discrimination through giving "free" demonstration services in the stores of certain dealer-customers. *Elizabeth Arden* v. *Gus Blass,* 150 Fed. *2d* 988 (1945). There, however, the court went even further. It said (p. 994), "The furnishing of a service or facility which cannot be proportionalized for the benefit of competing purchasers or, in the alternative, the failure or refusal to proportion the terms upon which services or facilities are granted, so as to make it reasonably possible for competing purchasers to avail themselves of such services or facilities if they desire to do so, constitutes a failure to accord such services or facilities upon proportionally equal terms."

74. See *Kentucky-Tennessee Power Co.* v. *Nashville Coal Co.,* 37 Fed.Supp. 728 (1941); affirmed, 136 Fed. *2d* 12 (1943).

75. *U.S.* v. *A & P,* 67 Fed.Supp., p. 677.

76. *Jarrett* v. *Pittsburgh Plate Glass Co.,* 42 Fed.Supp. 723 (1942), affirmed on this point, 131 Fed. *2d* 674 (1942); and *Sorrentino* v. *Glen Gery Brick Co.,* 46 Fed.Supp. 709 (1942).

77. *Hershey Chocolate Corp.* v. *FTC,* 121 Fed. *2d* 968 (1941). This case involved the pricing of small chocolate bars for distribution in automatic vending machines. The three largest vending-machine operators instituted the boycott of other distributors, but the chocolate manufacturers, Hershey and Peter Kohler, collaborated in it. The absence of any evidence of collusion between Hershey and Peter Kohler did not save their pricing policies from condemnation as discriminatory.

to some buyers. Such concessions as longer options or longer periods in which to take deliveries may violate the Act.[78]

As before the Robinson-Patman amendment, local price discrimination by a manufacturer operating in a wide market to drive out a competitor selling only in the narrower market area affected by the cut prices clearly violates the law.[79] But to charge one price for a product when it is sold separately and another when it is sold in combination with another product does not infringe the statute if identical terms are offered all buyers.[80]

The most troublesome issues raised by the Robinson-Patman Act, in some respects still not fully resolved, concern geographic price discrimination and quantity discounts, particularly in relation to classification of the trade status of buyers. The courts finally upheld the Federal Trade Commission in its contention that when the use of a basing point system regularly involves freight absorption on sales to some buyers, coupled with phantom freight charges to other buyers, with a resultant lessening of competition, it constitutes illegal price discrimination regardless of whether in adopting the system a company acts independently or in concert with rival sellers.[81]

A zone-pricing plan involving similarly indefensible geographic price differentials is likewise subject to condemnation.[82] The same rule applies to a freight equalization scheme.[83]

Status of Quantity Discounts

As to quantity discounts, neither the Commission nor any court has yet ruled that they are *ipso facto* unlawful. On the contrary, certain passages of the majority opinion in the Bruce's Juices case

78. *Corn Products Refining Co.* v. *FTC,* 144 Fed. *2d* 211 (1944); affirmed, 324 U.S. 726 (1945).

79. *Muller & Co.* v. *FTC,* 142 Fed. *2d* 511 (1944). The respondent in this case had completely monopolized a small industry, the chicory business. Chicory, used as coffee "filler," is produced in the Thumb district of Michigan and sold largely in the South and the West. When a small competitor appeared in the New Orleans market, respondent severely reduced prices in that area but continued to sell at profitable prices elsewhere.

80. *Package Closure Corp.* v. *Sealright Co.,* 141 Fed. *2d* 972 (1944). The court held that sale of milk-bottle caps separately and sale of such caps with hoods, in combination, were sales of different "commodities."

81. *Corn Products Refining Co.* v. *FTC,* cited above; *FTC* v. *A. E. Staley Manufacturing Co.,* 324 U.S. 746 (1945); *Triangle Conduit Co.* v. *FTC,* 168 Fed. *2d* 175 (1948), affirmed by an equally divided court, *sub nom. Clayton Mark & Co.* v. *FTC,* 336 U.S. 956 (1949).

82. *Salt Producers Association* v. *FTC,* previously cited; *Fort Howard Paper Co.* v. *FTC,* 156 Fed. *2d* 899 (1946), certiorari denied, 329 U.S. 795 (1947).

83. *Milk & Ice Cream Can Institute* v. *FTC,* previously cited.

strongly support the legality of quantity discounts, as such.[84] The implication of this ruling was to create a presumption in favor of price differences based on volume of purchases, a presumption that only a positive finding by the Commission of substantial injury to competition could overthrow. But the Morton Salt decision put a different face on the matter.[85]

The doctrine for which that case appears to stand is that quantity discounts may be excessive and that the Commission may properly treat any difference in prices on a quantity basis as discriminatory.[86] All the Commission need do, apparently, is to "prove" a price difference in sales to purchasers buying different amounts, and this should not be difficult. The burden of proof then passes to the respondent to justify the price difference under Section 2(b), if he can, by demonstrating a saving, comparable to the price difference, in costs of manufacture, selling, or delivery.[87]

But the Morton Salt decision left unresolved all questions about cost allocation, allowance for commercial risks, and the like, that the Goodyear case raised.[88] It also left unanswered the vexing ques-

84. In *Bruce's Juices, Inc.* v. *American Can Co.,* 330 U.S. 743 (1947), Mr. Justice Jackson, speaking for the majority, said (p. 746): "The economic effects on competition of such [quantity] discounts are for the Federal Trade Commission to judge . . . It would be a far-reaching decision to outlaw all quantity discounts. Courts should not rush in where Congress feared to tread."

85. *FTC* v. *Morton Salt Co.,* previously cited.

86. The majority opinion in the Morton Salt case held that a price difference of 10 cents a case in favor of carlot orders as compared with less-than-carlot orders required justification by detailed cost analysis. It so ruled despite the facts: (1) that this differentiation between carlot and less-than-carlot shipments corresponded to a long-established and practically universal trade custom; (2) that the discount on carlot orders amounted to only 6 per cent; and (3) that in actual practice the nondiscounted price applied to less than one per cent of respondent's business.

87. Not quite so heavy a burden rests on the respondent when the price difference challenged by FTC was made to meet competition. The courts held in the Moss case, previously cited, that to justify such a price difference the respondent need prove only that he reduced the price in good faith to hold the trade of customers. If he undercuts a competitor's price, however, apparently he must show that he did so unwittingly. The Second Circuit Court of Appeals said in that case: "We agree that he must prove that he did not mean to undercut his competitor's price; but when he has in fact undercut that price, we reserve the question whether it is necessary, as part of the proof, for him to show that he did not know what that price was."

The Supreme Court, in accordance with its usual custom, did not indicate why it denied respondent's petition for certiorari. But it is conceivable that it was simply applying the doctrine of the Shade Shop case, previously cited. For the existence of a substantial public interest in the settlement of the private controversy out of which the proceedings arose is at least questionable. The facts were in many respects analogous to those in the Shade Shop case: a squabble between a local trader and a former employee about the pricing of rubber stamps, with evidence of personal pique and vindictiveness on both sides.

88. As Mr. Justice Jackson, here one of the dissenters, pointed out (pp. 2 and 3), the practical effect of the majority's ruling in the Morton Salt case is to throw back

tion of the legitimacy of cumulative quantity discounts: whether it is permissible to base such discounts on the amount bought over a period of time.[89]

The practical upshot of the Morton Salt decision is to obliterate the distinction between a price difference and a price discrimination. The *ipse dixit* of the Federal Trade Commission is enough to make any quantity discount, no matter how small, presumptively a violation of Section 2(a) of the Clayton Act.

This rule may result in the elimination of quantity discount terms by many sellers even though after long and expensive litigation the courts might hold the resultant price differentials nondiscriminatory. Such an outcome would probably mean that the higher prices to quantity buyers will be passed on to consumers. The social desirability of this is questionable. The economies of large-scale buying handicap the small buyer, but if mass distributors share their advantages of this kind with consumers the public gains—immediately, at least.

The ruling tends to prevent effective competition in the short run. It rests on one or both of two questionable assumptions: (1) that preventing effective competition in the short run may prevent monopoly in the long run; or (2) that the preservation of small business is in and of itself desirable.

Conditions Affecting Legality of Trade Discounts

In general, the Commission has taken the position that discounts based on trade status (so-called functional discounts) are legitimate.[90] But it has insisted that classification of customers for this purpose must conform strictly to the nature of each customer's operations.[91] This position has led the Commission into a bewildering tangle of administrative difficulties where the same customer performs differ-

---

into the courts these intricate and involved questions, which they are technically ill-equipped to settle.

89. The majority opinion made no distinction between discounts based on the size of the individual order and those based on cumulative purchases. But the minority opinion did.

90. See, for example, *In re Simmons Co.*, 29 FTC 727 (1939); *In re Standard Brands*, 30 FTC 1117 (1940); and *In re Caradine Hat Co.*, 39 FTC 86 (1944).

91. See *In re American Oil Co.*, 29 FTC 857 (1939); and *In re Sherwin-Williams*, 36 FTC 25 (1943).

ent trade functions—for example, operates as both a retailer and a wholesaler.[92]

The attempt to disentangle the integrated business of split-function dealers and to insure that different prices for different parts of a single order, shipment, or delivery shall correspond strictly to the seller's functional discount plan is bound to lead to unmanageable administrative difficulties. Not only would the Commission be obliged to prescribe an accounting system for such dealers; it would need to employ an army of accountants to see that thousands of merchants scattered over the country kept their books accurately.[93] Plainly, no solution of the knotty problem of enforcing a nondiscriminatory pricing policy is yet in sight.

92. As in *In re Standard Oil Co. (Ind.)*, 41 FTC 263 (1945). In this case respondent sold gasoline to four customers in Detroit at less than its regular tank wagon prices. It classified these four customers as jobbers, though at the time the complaint was issued three of them resold part of their supplies at wholesale and part at retail, and one resold only at retail. Respondent made no attempt to show that the special price to the four dealers was justified on the basis of lower costs. Its main defense was that it had granted these price concessions in good faith to meet equally low prices of competitors; that is, the prices were set no higher than was necessary to prevent other suppliers from taking away these accounts from respondent. FTC, finding that the lower price granted the four distributors had "injured" the competition of other retail outlets supplied by Standard of Indiana at higher prices, held that the "good faith" test did not constitute an adequate defense. So, in effect, FTC ordered Standard of Indiana to discontinue selling to the four distributors at lower prices than it charged to its regular retail outlets, or to take steps to see that the distributors did not resell to the public at lower prices than those charged by its less favored dealers. The Circuit Court of Appeals, although modifying the Commission's order, sustained its findings. *Standard Oil Co. (Ind.)* v. *FTC,* 173 Fed. *2d* 210 (1949).

The soundness of FTC's position in this case is debatable on economic grounds. The four distributors who bought gasoline from Standard of Indiana at lower prices than those at which Standard of Indiana (and other suppliers) supplied other retail filling stations in the Detroit area could, and did, undersell their competitors. As a result, the four favored distributors greatly increased their share of the business of retailing gasoline in Detroit. But their customers benefited by getting their gasoline for less.

It is true that the price differential in favor of the four distributors resulted in diversion of patronage to their (lower-price) stations from those stations that adhered to the general posted retail price. In this sense it "injured" the majority of service station operators—as, of course, any price reduction by one of a group of competitors hurts the others. That is what makes competition "hard." But whether, simply because the lower retail prices of the four favored distributors hurt the business of other service station operators, Standard of Indiana's policy making those lower prices possible "injured" *competition* is by no means clear or certain. Obviously not everything that "injures" (hurts) competitors "injures" (hinders) competition. FTC's ruling appears to lend official encouragement to "soft" competition and to frown on "hard" competition.

93. For example, in the Sherwin-Williams case many customers classified as jobbers also sold at retail. They were required to report monthly the volume of their sales in each category, and the prices Sherwin-Williams charged them were adjusted accordingly. How many of these concerns made accurate reports? How insure the accuracy of reports when each such customer had a strong interest to inflate the relative volume of its wholesale transactions?

Conclusions

Trade practice regulation is still an experiment. But experience has justified these efforts to raise the standards of competitive market conduct. The bludgeoning tactics by which the trusts rose to power a generation ago have virtually disappeared. Predatory practices are no longer defensible simply by invoking the axiom, Business is business. Commodity standards unquestionably could be improved to advantage, but at least a beginning has been made in establishing suitable minima in crucial lines. And positive requirements for dependable information to guide consumers in the selection of merchandise are in force in a few markets. If discriminatory trade practices have proved less amenable to administrative regulation than deceptive trade practices, at least discrimination is less prevalent than it would otherwise have been, and hence opportunities for competitive enterprise are greater.

But this review of trade practice regulation shows that wide disparities in the size of business units, with a few large firms dominating a field, complicate the administrative task of preventing discrimination. The obstacles to the enforcement of rules that promote effective competition are, in such circumstances, out of proportion to the resources of the regulating agencies. Greater equality in the size and power of rival business firms and an increase in their number would greatly simplify the administrative regulation of trade practices. For the rules of the game would then become more nearly self-enforcing.

Chapter 12

POLICIES BEARING INDIRECTLY ON COMPETITION

COMPETITIVE MARKETS do not operate in an economic or a political vacuum. Many customs and slow-changing social institutions affect the forms of competition and determine its vigor. So do general governmental policies. Such institutions as bank credit permeate the whole process of production and condition the responsiveness of supply to demand in practically all markets.

General governmental policies, though not directly related to productive organization and commercial practice, are important in shaping the environment in which businessmen conduct their affairs. They may be favorable or unfavorable to effective competition. Tax policies, for example, may deter businessmen from starting new enterprises in some fields while facilitating them in others. Again, tariff policies may induce investors to withhold or withdraw capital from certain industries, while encouraging investment in others. Plainly, the capacity of competition effectively to regulate the allocation of resources, the relative supply of various goods, the prices of commodities, and the incomes of producers depends greatly on a host of governmental measures outside the sphere of trade regulation proper.

The increasing recognition since the Great Depression of the function of government as an economic stabilizer reflects growing awareness of the impact of governmental policies on the national economy. But it is still not generally realized that, apart from such deliberate interventionist policies as RFC pump priming and WPA unemployment relief, long-range governmental policies on banking, labor, agriculture, and other subjects vitally affect the performance and prospects of a system of—supposedly—competitive markets.

Need for Coordination of Governmental Policies

Failure to take notice of this aspect of general governmental policies has worked out, willy-nilly, to impair competition. Some decline in competition, it may be conceded, was unavoidable under modern conditions of large-scale industry. But analysis has shown that the concentration of economic power and the weakening of competitive markets have been much greater than they need have been. Coordination of other public policies with antitrust policy would unquestionably have helped sustain competitive forces.

The lack of such coordination has affected competition adversely in two important ways. First, it has narrowed the area of the economy subject to the rule of competition, even according to the intent of the law. When the fields in which competition is supposed to rule are steadily cut down by deliberate legislative measures—such as the antitrust exemptions applying in coal mining, petroleum extraction, marine shipping, and agriculture—the efficacy of competitive forces to maintain a balanced economy is seriously impaired.

On the other hand, deliberate displacement of competitive pricing by public administrative controls in some fields may help preserve competition elsewhere. Most observers agree that the regulation of railroad rates and services by the Interstate Commerce Commission was necessary to prevent discriminatory practices destructive of competition among shippers. Though the Commission faced, and still faces, baffling problems in framing rate structures that assure equality of opportunity among rival producers and among different industries, its record, on the whole, vindicates the supporters of authoritative control in this field.

In other industries with similar characteristics—heavy fixed costs, large joint costs, and quite inelastic demand—commission regulation may operate, for all its shortcomings, to provide fairer opportunities for competitive enterprise in the industries these public utilities serve. Such public utility industries as telephone, gas, and electricity plainly require administrative control to prevent the spread of their monopolistic influence to other areas of the economy. The vital question of public policy is to define the boundaries of the utilities field with due regard to the distinctive economic characteristics of such industries and to confine administrative regulation to the appropriate area.

Moreover, in excluding certain economic areas from the rule of competition, Congress has not always provided adequate assurance that regulatory controls will be coextensive with the areas excluded. For example, although the Maritime Commission in approving common-carrier rate agreements (exempt from the antitrust statutes) exercises its authority to prevent discriminatory rates, it has established no effective control over the level of rates, which is in practice determined jointly by the common carriers. Similarly, the rate-making bureaus of rival railway lines have in practice jointly determined most of the rates at which competing lines carry commodities.[1] In this way a sort of no man's land has been created within which neither market forces nor regulatory authority protects consumer interests.

In the second place, the extensive development of governmental policies antithetical to, and largely uncoordinated with, antitrust policy has increased the rigidity of industrial costs. Control of public utility rates, encouragement of industry-wide collective bargaining, support of agricultural prices, and many similar policies have frozen important cost elements and made the whole cost structure less flexible and therefore less responsive to the play of competitive forces. However worthy may be the specific objective of each of these policies, taken as a whole they have reduced the scope of managerial discretion, obstructed competitive experimentation, and "frozen" large sections of the economy in a relatively rigid matrix.

Thus governmental policies collateral to antitrust policy have in recent decades hampered effective competition. To understand how this happened, to what extent it has weakened competition, and how the decline of competition might be arrested requires some examination of concrete manifestations of inconsistency in public economic policy.

MONETARY AND FISCAL POLICIES

Spasmodic changes in the general price level and in the level of national income are incompatible with the orderly functioning of a competitive, private enterprise economy. Though monopolies do

1. Under the law individual carriers may initiate rates, subject to protest by shippers and review by the Interstate Commerce Commission. The burden of rate regulation is so heavy that in practice the Commission formally acts on only 1 or 2 per cent of the rates filed with it. After the Department of Justice brought suit against the western carriers alleging that joint rate making by private carriers violated the antitrust statutes [*U.S.* v. *Association of American Railroads,* complaint filed August 23, 1944, in the District of Nebraska, 4 F.R.D. 510 (1945)], Congress, in June 1948, passed the Reed-Bulwinkle bill (Public Law 662, 80th Cong.) exempting rate bureaus from the antitrust laws. For a more detailed discussion of the significance of the scope of segmental controls, see Corwin D. Edwards, *Maintaining Competition,* McGraw-Hill, New York, 1949, Chap. 7.

not escape the effects of violent fluctuations in the general price level and business activity, their broader base of assets may give them greater survival power than the ordinary independent business has.[2] Financial security is one of the objectives of the continual efforts to monopolize markets. By restricting output monopolists can keep their prices well above their marginal costs even though in depression they may not operate at a profit. Competitors, on the other hand, may be forced to sell at prices that cover only their marginal costs during business recessions and so become the victims of ruinous competition. To avoid this, business rivals are quick to devise control schemes, and where they cannot execute them autonomously they are apt to turn to the government for aid. Experience indicates the government is likely to come to their rescue. Witness, for example, the NRA.

Competitive markets readily effect those marginal, piecemeal, compensatory readjustments in the allocation of resources, relationship of prices, and distribution of income that technological advances, changing living standards, and even fickle fashion demand. But they cannot stop, let alone reverse, the alternating tides of debt-financed investment and speculation and of debt liquidation and hoarding that spell fluctuating business and rising and falling price levels. Indeed, the feverish scramble of competitors to ride the whirlwind of inflation as prices go up and to find a bit of solid ground in the deflationary swamp as prices go down increases the general instability. A mechanism such as the competitive market, while it counteracts disturbances in price *relationships,* provides no adequate means for damping fluctuations in the price *level.*

Price Stability and Competition

A competitive economy requires for effective performance stability of the general price level and flexibility of specific prices. Prices cannot keep order in a free economy if their general level is subject to violent disturbances while some prices are frozen. Such conditions produce tensions and distortions in the price structure inimical to full employment and stable national income. Unless they are elimi-

2. Giant business consolidations depend relatively less on credit, in particular on bank credit, than do independent enterprises. But the rigidity that monopolistic controls foster in the structure of production and prices is one of the principal factors behind economic imbalance and maladjustment. See *Cartels or Competition?,* Chap. 7.

nated, it will be hard to avoid market control schemes—if not under business then under governmental sponsorship.

No one has yet isolated a sole cause of business cycles.[3] Yet few economists would dispute that monetary stability is a necessary condition for making general price level movements less erratic—and thereby enabling competitive markets to work more effectively.

How to achieve monetary stability is a problem beyond the scope of the present study.[4] But the nature of the problem is clear: how to control the supply of money so as to remove it as one of the sources of disturbance of the general price level. Probably monetary measures can never be fully effective in stabilizing the price level and thereby lessening the violence of trade fluctuations. For actual money supply is only partly a function of the quantity of circulating media. It depends partly, also, on the velocity of circulation. And that is beyond the reach of any authority, though monetary and fiscal policies may indirectly influence the disposition of people to hoard or spend cash.

The Task for American Government

No government can guarantee perpetual prosperity. If it could it might take some of the wind out of the sails of monopoly. But a prudent government will use its full monetary and fiscal powers to check the ruinous phenomena of recurrent inflation and deflation. And it can do much, if it will, to keep the economy on a reasonably

3. And probably no one ever will. Even assuming the possibility of defining the phenomena that pass under the term "business cycle," it is by no means clear that any single cause generates such periodic alternations in the economic climate.

4. Writings on monetary policy are numerous and controversial. Some of those most relevant to the problem of economic stability are: Henry C. Simons, *Economic Policy for a Free Society,* University of Chicago Press, Chicago, 1948, Chap. 7; Harold L. Reed, *Federal Reserve Policy, 1921–1930,* McGraw-Hill, New York, 1930; *Banking Studies,* Members of the Staff of the Board of Governors of the Federal Reserve System, Washington, 1941; *Federal Reserve Policy,* Post-War Economic Studies, No. 8, Board of Governors of the Federal Reserve System, Washington, 1947, especially the first paper, by Carl E. Perry, and the third, by Karl R. Bopp; Lauchlin Currie, *The Supply and Control of Money in the United States,* Harvard University Press, Cambridge, 1934; Irving Fisher, *100% Money,* Adelphi, New York, 1935; Alvin H. Hansen, *Fiscal Policy and Business Cycles,* Norton, New York, 1941; *idem, Monetary Theory and Fiscal Policy,* McGraw-Hill, New York, 1949; Milton Friedman, "A Monetary and Fiscal Framework for Economic Stability," *American Economic Review,* June 1948, pp. 245-64; Seymour E. Harris (Ed.), *Saving American Capitalism,* Knopf, New York, 1948; D. H. Robertson, *Essays in Monetary Theory,* P. S. King & Son, London, 1940; *idem, Banking Policy and the Price Level,* P. S. King & Son, London, 1926; Charles R. Whittlesey, "Federal Reserve Policy in Transition," *Quarterly Journal of Economics,* May 1946, pp. 340-50.

even keel. By taxing heavily and at the same time curtailing expenditures, it can create budget surpluses in time of expanding business, and by thus restricting buying power it can check inflationary forces.[5] Similarly, by reducing taxes and increasing expenditures in times of business recession it can check deflationary forces.

The Fiscal Disturbances of Wars

To achieve these ends without unduly curbing private investments or narrowing the scope of private enterprise requires great wisdom and political courage. The task for American government, moreover, has been greatly complicated by its heavy dependence on borrowing to finance two world wars in a generation. Drawing on public credit for the huge funds to prosecute World War II alone increased the public debt by more than $200 billion, much of it immediately monetized through bank purchases "on credit" and still more of it subject to monetization in the same way.[6] Debt service alone in 1946 took $5.7 billion, or more than 12 per cent of total federal expenditures.[7]

Inflationary war finance has seriously damaged the price system through distorting the distribution of income and the relationships of prices. And that is only a part, perhaps a transitory part, of its economic ill effects. It has also greatly weakened the government's power to pursue monetary and fiscal policies appropriate for counter-

5. Debt retirement in prosperity is no less essential than deficit financing in depression. Cf. Harold M. Groves, *Postwar Taxation and Economic Progress,* McGraw-Hill, New York, 1946, pp. 356-62; and Mabel Newcomer, "A Tax Policy for Postwar America," in New York University Institute on Postwar Reconstruction, *Postwar Goals and Economic Reconstruction,* New York University Press, New York, 1944. See also *The Economic Report of the President to the Congress,* Washington, January 14, 1948, pp. 84-85.

Some advocates of a liberal government spending policy during depression would not stop deficit financing as business begins to recover. Convinced of the reality of a secular stagnation trend, they hold that "full employment" requires an indefinite continuance of public debt increase. But if a government wants to keep budget deficits an effective instrument for retarding a spiral decline of the price level and restoring business confidence and investment activity, it must offset them with budget surpluses. Otherwise it will lose its grip on the value of money, its power to influence the public's valuation of the tokens it supplies them. Cf. Hansen, *Fiscal Policy and Business Cycles,* especially Chap. 15.

6. Or indirectly through Federal Reserve open-market operations—to support the government bond market—and loans to member banks on government bond collateral.

7. See U.S. Department of Commerce, *National Income,* Washington, July 1947, pp. 19 and 23.

acting the business cycle. With a large part of the huge public debt held by banks, the government feels obliged to maintain low interest rates in order, for one thing, to maintain the value of bank assets.

The government also feels obliged to maintain low interest rates in order to keep down the costs of government financing. Therefore it no longer feels free to pursue the contracyclical monetary policies of increasing interest rates during inflation and of lowering them in depression. On the contrary, it feels compelled to keep interest rates low at all times. Its obligations to bondholders (particularly the banks), and to itself as a borrower of funds, conflict with its responsibility to businessmen—and to producers generally—to provide a monetary foundation for economic stability.

Though the task of reforming monetary and fiscal policies so as to lessen the severity of business fluctuations is especially difficult in these circumstances, it is perhaps not beyond achievement. But unless such reform is soon undertaken with resolute determination and great wisdom, it will be difficult if not impossible to preserve private enterprise and effectively competitive markets.

TARIFF POLICY

In one sense, tariff policy is simply a branch of fiscal policy. But its primary purpose is to regulate imports—not, ordinarily, to provide public revenue. Ever since the tariff act of 1824, one of the principal aims, avowed or implicit, of American tariff policy has been "protection of the home market." [8]

Tariff policy bears a twofold relation to the maintenance of competition. The direct effect of a tariff schedule is to limit competition in domestic markets. Customs duties restrict the entry of foreign products and thus reduce the sources of supply. If the duty on a particular class of goods is high it may exclude imports altogether.

The indirect, long-run effect of a high tariff is to hinder geographical division of labor and the growth of international commerce. This indirect effect of a protective tariff is not less injurious to a competitive, private enterprise economy than its direct effect on domestic markets. For competition within a national economy can-

8. See Leverett S. Lyon and Associates, *Government and Economic Life,* The Brookings Institution, Washington, 1940, Vol. 2, Chap. 20.

not flourish in a static, shrinking, or disintegrating world economy. This was the sobering lesson of the feverish period between World Wars I and II. Competition thrives only in an environment characterized by widening markets, advancing technology, and increasing investment. And experience, particularly during the nineteenth century, strongly suggests that all these conditions go together and are mutually sustaining.

Tariffs as Direct Restrictions on Competition

Proponents often argue, correctly, that a protective tariff, no matter how high, does not interfere with or prevent competition among domestic producers. A tariff does, however, interfere with or eliminate the competition of foreign suppliers in domestic markets. Unless a foreign producer has a cost advantage over the domestic producer he cannot successfully compete in the domestic market, regardless of a tariff barrier—unless government bounties or cartels facilitate dumping. The erection of a tariff wall, then, means a limitation on the competition of low-cost producers with high-cost producers. Competition among high-cost producers may be keen, but it is not the kind of competition that leads to an economical allocation of resources and promotes the interests of consumers.

Even more important, a protective tariff is a standing invitation to monopoly or restraint of trade in domestic industry.[9] Shutting out foreign rivals very greatly simplifies the job of restraining competition in the domestic market. It is easier either to consolidate a relatively homogeneous and compact group of domestic rivals or to get them to act in concert than it is to do the same things with a more heterogeneous and widely scattered group of foreign and domestic producers. This is what the founder of the sugar trust meant when he said: "The mother of all trusts is the customs tariff . . ."[10]

The rayon industry apparently illustrates how a tariff works in both these ways. Although managerial efficiency and an advancing technology greatly reduced the cost of making rayon in the United

9. See C. L. James and Associates, *Industrial Concentration and Tariffs,* TNEC Monograph No. 10, Washington, 1940, pp. 2-3, 27, and *passim.*

10. *Report of the United States Industrial Commission,* Vol. 1, p. 101, Washington, 1901. A similarly candid disclosure of their paternity would have been welcome.

States during the 1920's, foreigners made rayon much more cheaply than Americans. According to Markham, as late as 1935 it cost Americans 177 per cent more a pound to produce rayon than it cost the Japanese; 93.5 per cent more than it cost the Italians; 40 per cent more than it cost the Germans; and 20 per cent more than it cost the British.[11] Before 1930 tariffs had kept out some but not all foreign production.[12] As late as 1929 Americans got about 12 per cent of their rayon from abroad. But the 1930 tariff act shut out all imports.[13] It guaranteed relatively high-cost American producers the entire American market without the necessity of struggling for it. Freed from foreign competition, American producers were not content to let prices fall to a competitive level as the Great Depression made it harder to get business. In 1931 the ten largest domestic yarn manufacturers agreed to a price-fixing and output-restricting scheme, and hired Price, Waterhouse and Company to police it. Obviously the fight to get and keep a tariff necessitates teamwork. Teamwork is teamwork: rivals who work together on the political front to insure their survival are apt to work together on the economic front to insure their good health. This the rayon producers did. Apparently they did not abandon the illegal arrangement until the price decline had been halted.[14]

With the help of NRA and under American Viscose's price leadership, rayon prices were relatively stable throughout the latter part of the 1930's. Although far below the predepression level, they were higher than foreign prices from mid-1935 to 1940. However, foreign rayon could not surmount the tariff wall.

11. Jesse Markham, *Price and Output Behavior in the Domestic Rayon Industry* (unpublished doctoral dissertation, Harvard University).

12. The tariff on imported rayon was 35 per cent *ad valorem* from 1913 to 1922; 45 cents a pound but not less than 45 per cent *ad valorem* from 1922 to 1930.

13. It provided for a 45 per cent *ad valorem* tariff with a minimum duty of 45 cents a pound on standard yarns, and 45 per cent to 50 per cent *ad valorem* plus 45 cents a pound with a minimum duty of 90 cents a pound on all high-twist yarns. The decline in domestic prices and the increase in the tariff put the American market out of reach of foreign producers.

14. After hearings, the Federal Trade Commission found that the price-fixing agreement violated Section 5 of the FTC Act and ordered the respondents to cease and desist. *In re Viscose Corp. of America, et al.*, 25 FTC Decisions 421 (1937). Markham concludes that the price-fixing arrangement broke down not because of Federal Trade Commission action but because some firms, confronted with the keen competition of natural-fiber yarn, were cutting prices. Recovery in the yarn market shortly after its breakdown made resumption of the agreement less urgent. NRA, of course, came to the rescue in 1933.

Indirect Effects of High Tariffs on Competition

A competitive system thrives best in unfettered and expanding markets. An economy whose growth is retarded by tariffs strangling world trade is inhospitable to competition. Such an environment weakens or retards competition for three basic reasons.

First, a static economy severely limits opportunities for new enterprises. True, even though the economy may be static, thanks to the prospect a tariff offers of sharing in a kind of tax-gathering license, it may attract new firms into industries that are not economically self-supporting. But by and large, outside this protective fold, the major prospect for a new company is to replace an old one, and this is seldom possible. With comparatively few new entrants to challenge established firms, competition loses much of its vigor.

Second, rivalry among established firms tends to slacken in a static market. Price cutting loses its attraction when the only resultant added sales are at the expense of well-entrenched rivals. Though price cutting may win new customers, it brings retaliation. Hence producers in an industry that has stopped growing usually settle down to cultivate their vested interests. They find cooperation more profitable than competition, defense better than aggression.

Third, a static economy is a deterrent to new investment, and hence to competition. Economists in recent years have increasingly recognized the investment process as the mainspring of a capitalist economy.[15] When investment outlets are scarce, savings pile up unused, demand for capital goods slackens, employment falls off, national income declines, and markets become disorganized. With fear prevailing, retrenchment becomes the watchword. Competitive enterprise falters. Instead of starting new ventures, businessmen prefer to salvage old ones, following the line of least resistance: monopolistic restriction. It takes more than legal penalties to keep businesses competitive in a slump.

Tariffs are not the only obstacles to a dynamic economy, it is true. But they are among the most important. If American industries producing capital goods are to expand, therefore, most of them will

15. See John Maynard Keynes, *The General Theory of Employment, Interest, and Money,* Harcourt, Brace, New York, 1936, particularly Book IV; and Norman S. Buchanan, *International Investment and Domestic Welfare,* Holt, New York, 1945, Chaps. 8, 9, and 10.

need to increase exports steadily.[16] In the capital-starved postwar world this can be accomplished only by sustained American investment abroad. Foreign investment cannot be sustained, however, without a reciprocal flow of imports. A country that does not buy abroad cannot long sell abroad. By restricting imports it defies the law of comparative advantage—that it pays a nation to specialize in the production of those things in producing which its cost advantage over other countries is greatest. And it cannot escape the penalty of such a violation of economic law. Ultimately, exports buy imports.[17]

Again, imports create the demand for exports. Fluctuating exchange rates and changes in the volume or direction of indebtedness may obscure for a time the necessity of balancing trade. But, in the end, a nation with capital goods industries geared to world market demand can be prosperous only in so far as it opens its domestic markets to the competition of foreign sellers. Tariff walls that make it onerous or impossible for foreign countries to pay for what they buy here strangle America's economic growth and thereby greatly weaken competitive forces in the domestic economy.

CONSERVATION POLICY

Monopoly has thrived in recent years under the guise of conservation. Both the federal government and state governments have supported output-restricting and price-raising programs as conservation

16. Though technological advance and population growth may offset the checks to economic expansion that come from obstructions to international trade and geographical division of labor, they are not so dependable stimuli as are open markets. Cf. George Terborgh, *The Bogey of Economic Maturity,* Machinery and Allied Products Institute, Chicago, 1945. Inventions sometimes make it possible to produce the same or a greater volume of goods with less capital, instead of leading, as they ordinarily do, to an increased use of capital—along with a more than proportionate increased output of goods. In short, they are sometimes capital-saving rather than capital-using. Hence they may upset the balance between capital accumulation and investment. Moreover, despite the development of highly organized and intensive industrial research, inventions with a significant expansive power do not follow one another in orderly succession. They occur erratically and stimulate investment spasmodically.

So far as population growth is concerned, the postwar rise in the birth rate seems less significant when examined in the light of the long-run trend toward smaller families. The impact of modern living conditions and habits of thought on the family institution gives slight reason for banking on population growth to provide a continuing spur to economic expansion. On the whole, developing the "frontier"—now made up of the economically backward countries of the world—still offers the best prospect of making the American economy expansive and competitive. Cf. Norman S. Buchanan and Friedrich A. Lutz, *Rebuilding the World Economy,* Twentieth Century Fund, 1947.

17. As England discovered barely in time. By 1947 it was faced by the need to "export or expire." See *Cartels or Competition?,* Chap. 10.

measures, ignoring the fact that a genuine conservation program means merely the prudent husbanding of exhaustible resources. Genuine conservation can be effected in either one, or both, of two basically distinct ways. One way is to reduce *losses* by increasing *efficiency* either in production, whereby the amount *recoverable* from the limited reserves is increased, or in consumption, whereby a given amount recovered is made to go further in use. The other way is to avoid *waste* by regulating (i.e., timing) recovery more *economically* (balancing current demands against prospective needs).

In evaluating governmental conservation policy account must be taken of two basic tendencies: the exhaustibility of resources and the advance of technology.

The Exhaustibility of Resources

People generally are not greatly interested in the problem of resource conservation. As long as their present household needs are met they show little concern over the needs of future generations. On the other hand, government officials, daily concerned with national security, cannot ignore the problem of assuring adequate future supplies of strategic materials. The serious inroads that World War II made on domestic reserves of scarce resources apparently increased the significance of conservation. At the end of the war, according to an official estimate, domestic reserves of only nine minerals—including iron ore, bituminous coal, magnesium, and nitrogen—were large enough to supply domestic demand for a hundred years. For each of twenty-two minerals—including petroleum, copper, lead, zinc, nickel, and bauxite—proven domestic reserves would be exhausted in thirty-five years or less, at a normal rate of use. Of some metals important in making alloys, such as manganese, vanadium, and tungsten, domestic reserves could meet domestic requirements for only seven years or less.[18]

On their face such appraisals of raw material supplies are disturbing; but they are also somewhat misleading. They assume a "normal" rate of use and a static technology. Neither assumption is accurate. Moreover, an easy but unwarranted inference from such estimates is that all reserves are known.

18. Annual Report of the Secretary of the Interior, Washington, 1945, pp. v ff.

Any realistic concept of "natural resources" must be dynamic. Natural resources are raw materials that have taken on economic significance as man has learned to use them. The natural resources of yesterday may become today's museum exhibits—amber, for instance. And useless materials of one day, like uranium, may become the natural resources of a later time. An advancing technology changes the demand for and the supply of "natural" resources. It does not invalidate the law of diminishing returns, but it does much to overcome the "niggardliness" of nature.

Relation of Technology to Resource Scarcity

Nowhere is the role of technology better illustrated, in raising or laying the specter of resource exhaustion, than in the oil industry. The discovery in 1859 of how to tap underground petroleum "pools" quieted the fears of a shortage of lighting oils because of the extinction of whales. Seventy-five years later, at the end of 1934, estimated proven oil reserves in the United States were about 12 billion barrels. In the next twelve years the industry produced nearly 17 billion barrels of crude oil. Yet estimated reserves at the beginning of 1947 were 21 billion barrels.[19] Meanwhile atomic fission has opened a potential reservoir of energy resources the social and economic significance of which not even scientists fully comprehend.

Domestic supplies of magnesium a few years ago were limited by the amount of byproduct magnesium chloride the Dow Chemical Company produced from Michigan salt brine. Today the ocean affords an inexhaustible supply.

Such facts, comforting as they are, do not justify the view that

19. Oil shortage scares are as old as the industry. In 1882 a certain Dr. Wrigley, Pennsylvania State Geologist, calculated unmined domestic oil reserves at 96 million barrels, or less than four years' production at the current rate. "Some day," he said, "the cheque will come back endorsed, 'no funds,' and we are approaching the day very fast." Quoted from Wallace E. Pratt, vice-president of the Standard Oil Company, New Jersey, "There Will Be Enough Oil," address before Oil Heat Institute of America, New York, May 12, 1944, p. 2. Pratt points out that only half the potential oil-producing lands of the United States have been thoroughly explored and that we have recovered only about 40 per cent of the underground deposits in exploited fields. Assuming that the unexplored potential producing area will prove as rich in oil as the explored, Pratt estimates that, under past methods of recovery, the yield would be about 50 billion barrels. Improved secondary methods of recovery from this area and from lands already exploited would permit recovery of much of the estimated unrecovered 70 billion barrels. From natural gas, oil shale, and coal "we can obtain supplies of liquid fuel hundreds of times greater than those from petroleum." Wallace E. Pratt, "Are We Running Out of Oil?," *Liberty Magazine,* June 3, 1944.

conservationists are Cassandras. All things may not work together for good, even with those who love the Lord. Because of the uncertainties of the future, prudence may sometimes demand foregoing actual needs to avoid potential disasters. It is at least doubtful whether an unrestrained competitive market will always force, or even permit, the several independent producers exploiting an exhaustible natural resource to adopt methods and rates of production that adequately safeguard society's long-run interests in these materials. Certainly if, by taking thought, we can add to the life of resources without working undue hardship on present owners or users, it would pay us to do so.

Although not consuming today in order to assure adequate supplies of scarce resources for tomorrow may or may not be rewarding, it is always economical to eliminate waste by increasing efficiency.[20] More efficient recovery means that a given reserve of any natural resource will go further than it otherwise would. Both present and future users may have more of it.[21]

Oil: Conservation or Monopoly?

Recognition of these two conflicting factors of exhaustibility and advancing technology helps in evaluating governmental policy toward oil conservation.

The oil conservation program was born in time of surplus. Started in the late 1920's by the major oil companies, it was intended to raise prices, not to increase the future supply of oil. As developed in Texas and Oklahoma, the program was one of straight output re-

20. Economy expresses a value concept. Its opposite is waste. As an equation it may be expressed as: $\text{Economy} = \frac{\text{Returns}}{\text{Cost}}$. A process is never economical unless returns exceed cost. When they do not, the operation is wasteful. Efficiency is a technical concept. Its opposite is loss. It may be expressed as the equation: $\text{Efficiency} = \frac{\text{Output}}{\text{Input}}$. Since a mechanical process always involves some loss, efficiency is always less than 100 per cent. Where economy is increased by increasing efficiency and reducing costs, society always gains. See Myron W. Watkins, *Oil: Stabilization or Conservation?*, Harper, New York, 1937, Chap. 4.

Strictly from his own private viewpoint, a monopolist might increase the economy of his operations by restricting output and thereby increasing his returns. On the other hand, consumers would not immediately gain, because they would pay more and receive less. But future users might gain by having more available. If a monopolist's aim is to maximize his returns, any long-run gains to society from his restriction of current production would be incidental.

21. But this is not a certainty. Increased efficiency in recovery might so lower cost as to increase consumption in the present and reduce the future supply.

striction. In Texas, the State Railroad Commission approved production quotas agreed on by the producers and acted as an umpire to settle disputes. At first the courts struck down state proration orders on the ground that commissions had no authority to issue them because they were intended to stabilize prices, not to conserve oil.[22] But the legislatures and the commissions gradually developed standards for determining allowable production that were not wholly inconsistent with the goals of conservation.[23]

But the oil-producing states have repeatedly turned down proposals to authorize their respective commissions to require the unified operation of oil pools—the starting point for a genuine conservation program. Instead, under the guise of conservation and at the behest of the oil companies, these states have in effect set themselves up as regulators of the nation's supply of oil, primarily to insure "reasonable" prices to the producers within their respective boundaries. In doing so they have incidentally increased efficiency in the production of oil.[24] The aim of proration has consistently been to restrict output to what the market can absorb at prices satisfactory to oil producers and to oil-producing states.

Just as the major oil-producing states put their authority behind proration when the industry's voluntary restriction program broke down, so the federal government came to the rescue of proration

22. See R. E. Hardwicke, "Legal History of Conservation of Oil in Texas," in *Legal History of Conservation of Oil and Gas, A Symposium,* American Bar Association, Chicago, 1938, p. 231. In *Constantin* v. *Smith,* 287 U.S. 378 (1932), the United States Supreme Court held that in declaring martial law and ordering the militia to enforce the proration orders the Governor of Texas exceeded his constitutional powers.

23. In *Champlin Refining Co.* v. *Corporation Commission,* 286 U.S. 210 (1932), the Supreme Court upheld the Oklahoma regulatory statute and proration orders issued thereunder. It declared that the limitation of production to reasonable market demand was a proper method of preventing waste and that its effects on price were incidental.

After this decision the Texas legislature enacted a new regulatory statute that defined the waste, which it authorized the Commission to prevent, to include "the production of crude petroleum in excess of transportation or market facilities or *reasonable market demand.*" Hardwicke, *op. cit.,* p. 239. Italics supplied.

24. For general discussion of the conservation problem in the oil industry, see George W. Stocking, *The Oil Industry and the Competitive System,* Houghton Mifflin, Boston, 1925; Watkins, *op. cit.;* Eugene V. Rostow, *A National Policy for the Oil Industry,* Yale University Press, New Haven, 1948; Roy C. Cook, *Control of the Petroleum Industry by Major Oil Companies,* TNEC Monograph No. 39, Washington, 1941; *Review and Criticism . . . of Monograph No. 39 With Rejoinder . . . ,* TNEC Monograph No. 39-A, Washington, 1941; W. J. Kemnitzer, *Rebirth of Monopoly,* Harper, New York, 1938; and Joe S. Bain, *The Economics of the Pacific Coast Petroleum Industry,* University of California Press, Berkeley, in three parts, Pt. 1, 1944; Pt. 2, 1945; Pt. 3, 1947.

when state authority proved inadequate.[25] The proration program has operated in the last fifteen years approximately as follows. The United States Bureau of Mines makes monthly estimates of the market demand for motor fuel and from this estimate computes the necessary rate of crude-oil production.[26] Its breakdown by states of the indicated total crude-oil requirement for the month guides the several state proration authorities in determining allowable production.[27] An Interstate Oil Compact Commission develops general policies and coordinates the "conservation" program among the several states.[28] A committee of economists paid by the oil industry advises the Compact Commission.[29] The Commission publishes a quarterly bulletin and its staff of technicians has made significant contributions to the study of prevention of waste in oil extraction.

Unit Operation Essential to Genuine Conservation

In spite of signal gains in efficiency of oil recovery under proration, only operation of oil pools as a unit, with the production unit corresponding to the geological unit, would meet the two requirements of a genuine conservation program. First, unit develop-

25. The NRA made violation of the oil code a crime. The Connally Act (Act of Feb. 22, 1935, c. 18, 49 Stat. 35, 15 U.S. Code, Sec. 715) made it unlawful for an oil producer to ship oil in interstate commerce if it had been produced in violation of state proration orders.

26. The Bureau makes its estimates without specific statutory authority. They serve very much the same function as the statistical services of various trade associations that the Supreme Court has condemned. See, for example, *American Column & Lumber Co.* v. *U.S.*, 257 U.S. 377 (1921); *Sugar Institute, Inc.* v. *U.S.*, 297 U.S. 553 (1936).

27. Alfred G. White, Chief of the Division of Petroleum Economics in the Bureau of Mines, has made the forecasts for the past twelve years. He testified that "over a period of years the State production tends to follow the forecasts, due fundamentally to the fact that the information in these forecasts is so nearly the actual demand that develops." *Problems of American Small Business,* Hearings before the Special Committee of the U.S. Senate, pursuant to S.Res. 20, 80th Cong., 2d sess., Pt. 27, p. 3140.

The chairman of the Texas Railroad Commission supported Mr. White's testimony. He said: "Texas has always produced all of the oil that has been indicated as needed by the Bureau of Mines in its monthly certified estimate of crude needed for the current month, month by month." *Ibid.*, p. 3156.

Two important oil-producing states have no official regulatory commission to prorate output. In California a committee of the oil industry acts as the prorating agency. Illinois has taken no part in the program, and when Illinois produced 145 million barrels in 1940 it endangered the program. Only a rapid decline in the potential output of Illinois fields removed the threat.

28. Congress authorized the Compact, to which six states were initially parties. 49 Stat. 939 (1935). Originally authorized for two years, Congress has extended the Compact from time to time, most recently in 1947 for four years. Hearings on *Problems of American Small Business,* 2d sess., Pt. 27, p. 3177.

29. *Ibid.*, pp. 3181-82.

ment would make possible a tremendous increase of efficiency in producing, greatly lower the cost of production, and increase ultimate recovery. Secondly, with unit development it would be practicable, as it is not now, to postpone recovery in times of overproduction and thereby conserve oil for the future.

Moreover, the operation of each oil pool as a unit could be readily adapted to a private enterprise economy. If the states or the federal government required each pool to be operated by a single corporation or cooperative association on behalf of the owners or lessees of the overlying tracts, competition among rival pools could be relied on to protect consumers. The government need only lay down general conservation standards to which every operating unit must conform.

Not only would such unit operation increase the long-run output and reduce cost, but it would make the price structure of oil more flexible, a better regulator of the industry, and would lead to a more economical use of resources. Competition among unit-operated pools would also tend to bring about a closer relationship between prices and costs and thereby permit price to perform more effectively its function as a guide to the use of resources and distribution of income. Whether publicly or privately administered, monopoly in any part of the economy leads to inequities in income distribution and tends to create maladjustments in the economy as a whole.[30]

AGRICULTURAL POLICY

By 1900 in many American industries the number of sellers had become so small, or the dominant position of a single firm so great, that centralized decision making had superseded free markets in determining output, prices, and investment. In agriculture, however, competitive forces still ruled and do so today, except in so far as governmental curbs impound them or governmental subsidies distort them.

Although agricultural technology was the chief factor underlying

30. This may be a serious matter, particularly in times of depression. For example, the oil proration program under NRA substantially increased the prices of crude oil and gasoline. It thereby transferred purchasing power from 30 million users of automobiles to the oil industry. Since the oil industry was already suffering from overinvestment, it is extremely unlikely that the increase in earnings or the decrease in losses that higher prices brought merely shifted effective purchasing power from the many to the few. More likely it decreased total effective purchasing power. In short, it was deflationary.

small-scale farming, public policy toward agriculture has been partly responsible. Congress opened the public domain to small farmers on easy terms, through a series of laws covering more than half a century and culminating in the Homestead Act of 1862. The family-size farm became the customary unit and the farmer was free to choose the type of farming best adapted to the land and to his limited supplies of capital and labor. Except for those areas in the South where the plantation system prevailed, small-scale farming characterized American agriculture throughout the nineteenth century.

Early in the twentieth century the government started a reclamation program. Where the land required large expenditures to fit it for farming, the government supplied the capital, recapturing part of it by selling the reclaimed land in relatively small blocks and charging for water rights. It would be easy to exaggerate the importance of the reclamation program to competition, but by creating new opportunities for farmers and increasing the supply of tillable soil its tendency was to intensify competition in agricultural markets.

Because small-scale farming cannot underwrite sustained scientific research, the government also developed an extensive research program to improve soil, plants, animals, and farm practices.[31] It also established advisory services to help the farmer. Under the Morrill Act of 1862 and subsequent legislation, many states founded land-grant colleges and experiment stations, financed in part by federal funds. The "extension services" of these colleges, introduced after the Civil War, grew impressively after 1900 with direct government support.

Because commercial banks could not adequately meet the credit needs of farmers, Congress passed the Farm Credit Act in 1916 to provide long-term loans at low interest rates. After the postwar collapse of farm prices, the Agricultural Credit Act of 1923 provided the means for intermediate and short-term borrowing to finance the growing and marketing of crops and the feeding of livestock.

Collective Action Encouraged

Congress also encouraged collective selling by farmers. To bring about more orderly marketing of farm products, eliminate waste,

31. For a more detailed discussion of government policy toward agriculture, see Lyon and Associates, *op. cit.*, Vol. 2, Chap. 23.

and stabilize agricultural prices, several states had passed laws encouraging farm cooperatives even before 1900. In 1914 Congress supported this movement by declaring, in Section 6 of the Clayton Act, that farm cooperatives as such are not conspiracies in restraint of trade under the Sherman law.

The Capper-Volstead Act of 1922 broadened the exemptions of agricultural associations under the Sherman Act.[32] In effect this act applied the rule of reason to restraints of trade by farm cooperatives and gave the administration of the law to officials sympathetic to agriculture. The Cooperative Marketing Act of 1926 authorized official research and educational work in this field. It also authorized farm cooperatives to conduct statistical services of a type that the Department of Justice has attacked when trade associations conduct them.

Cooperative marketing enables farmers to bring their products into the market in a more orderly—and less competitive—manner. It tends to iron out seasonal fluctuations in the prices of some products, as the laws contemplated. It may lower costs of assembling and processing, and many local cooperatives have established a better balance in bargaining between producers and local dealers or terminal-market buyers. But farmers, farm product distributors, and farm product processors have occasionally joined hands and used their cooperative privileges to obtain monopoly power. In citrus fruits, control of some markets has been completely centralized. At times the leading citrus fruit cooperatives and auctions have apparently aimed not so much at orderly marketing as at market rigging.[33] But in a recent antitrust action a federal district court held that, in the

32. A proviso in the Act reads: ". . . if the Secretary of Agriculture shall have reason to believe that any such [farm cooperative] association monopolizes or restrains trade to such an extent that the price of any agricultural product is unduly enhanced by reason thereof, he shall serve upon such association a complaint stating his charge in that respect . . ."

33. For example, in December 1941 a federal grand jury indicted the California Fruit Growers Exchange and some fifteen other corporate defendants, including the leading fruit auctions in cities from coast to coast, for conspiring to fix prices and restrain trade in citrus fruits. The corporate defendants entered pleas of *nolo contendere* and paid fines of $80,000. *U.S.* v. *California Fruit Growers Exchange.* See Commerce Clearing House, *The Federal Antitrust Laws,* Chicago, 1947, p. 270. In a civil proceeding based on the same facts the defendants consented to a decree enjoining them from conspiring to fix prices, from coercing buyers to conform to designated marketing practices, from granting secret preferences, from threatening competitors, from interfering with distribution of fruits by motor truck, and from engaging in other monopolistic practices. *U.S.* v. *California Fruit Growers Exchange,* complaint filed November 16, 1942 in U.S. District Court for the Southern District of California, consent decree entered November 18, 1942.

absence of conspiracy with outsiders, farm cooperatives are exempt from the Sherman Act even when they acquire a monopoly.[34]

Farmers and middlemen, when they have had the opportunity, have used collective power to promote their special interests at the expense of the public. Nevertheless, there are few instances in which farm groups either alone or in collaboration with middlemen have been able to rig the market on a purely voluntary basis. They have been confined largely to fluid milk and perishable crops, and even here, farmers have sometimes needed government support to make their schemes work, particularly during depressions. Farmers are too numerous and the spirit of individualism among them is too strong to make cooperative restriction of output and control of prices generally effective.

Political Strength Exerted in Bad Times

But while economically weak, farmers are politically strong. They have accordingly looked to the government to help them escape the rigors of unrestrained competition when the going has become really difficult. While they have not abandoned self-help entirely, they have turned to politics, particularly in recent years. In response to their pressure, public policy has been revolutionized. Except during periods of extreme prosperity (such as 1946–1948), when actual prices rise above support levels, central planning and governmental controls have largely displaced impersonal market forces in determining the pattern of farm production and the level of farm prices. The Great Depression and the New Deal accelerated this change, but stagnation of agriculture during the 1920's initiated it.

World War I had greatly increased the domestic output of farm products as agricultural prices soared, along with, and even above, prices generally. The resumption of European agricultural production after the war bit deeply into the war-expanded foreign markets of American farmers. With the onslaught of deflation in 1920 the prices of farm products fell first, fastest, and furthest. Throughout the decade they never recovered the relative position they held in 1918–1920.

34. *U.S.* v. *Dairy Cooperative Association,* 49 Fed.Supp. 475 (1943). Apparently the courts are inclined to apply the same doctrine to concerted action among farmers that the Supreme Court has applied to labor. See *Allen Bradley Co.* v. *Local Union No. 3, IBEW,* 325 U.S. 494 (1945), discussed in the next section of this chapter.

During the Coolidge Administration the farm bloc tried to put through Congress two measures designed to help American agriculture—an export debenture plan and the McNary-Haugen bill. Congress rejected the export debenture plan, but twice passed the McNary-Haugen bill. Both times, President Coolidge vetoed it. The Hoover Administration set up the Federal Farm Board in 1929 and supplied it with a half billion dollars to lend to cooperative associations, formally to enable them to finance orderly marketing but actually to keep farm products off the market and thereby raise prices. When farm prices declined rapidly during the 1930's, the Farm Board's operations proved futile and its funds soon ran out.

New Deal Measures

At the inception of the New Deal in 1933 the depression had deepened and agricultural income had shrunk spectacularly. Relief to agriculture was accordingly one of the most important parts of a program designed to increase employment and national income. Paradoxically, the new agricultural policy was essentially restrictive. It adopted techniques usually associated with cartels and monopolies.

The Agricultural Adjustment Act of May 1933 had two immediate objectives: to regulate the flow of agricultural products into the market and to restrict production and increase farmers' incomes. The marketing provisions, as amended from time to time, required farmers to join in cooperative arrangements when approved by two thirds of the growers. The law also provided that processors and distributors should share with producers the power to determine prices and manipulate supplies, but it subjected their decisions to approval by the Secretary of Agriculture. In practice specific prices have not generally been fixed under the marketing agreements, but flexible price "goals" have been established and supplies have been manipulated to achieve them.

More significant is the production and income control program of the Act. Its broad objective was to make farmers as prosperous relative to other groups as they had been immediately before World War I. This was to be done by restricting the output of agricultural products so as to re-establish the 1910–1914 relationships between the prices farmers received and the prices they paid. To encourage farmers to abide by their production allotments, the government distributed cash benefits to those who cooperated in the program.[35]

The basic features of the AAA program are unchanged to this date. The Supreme Court ruled in the Hoosac Mills case that "purchasing submission to federal regulation" by distributing to producers the proceeds of a tax levy (the processing tax) was unconstitutional.[36] But Congress promptly enacted a Soil Conservation Act granting benefit payments to farmers who collaborated in a similar output restriction program, effected this time through agreements to rotate crops and rest the soil. Under this measure AAA allotted each farmer who wished to produce soil-depleting crops a certain acreage based on the amount of land he owned.

Price Support by Legislation

The Soil Conservation Act also provided for the support of farm prices by authorizing the Commodity Credit Corporation to lend farmers specified percentages of parity prices in order that they might hold crops off the market without great risk. To dispose of crop surpluses that its program tends to create, the government resorts to the monopoly technique of price discrimination. It sells accumulated stocks at different prices in domestic markets, depending on the use buyers intend to make of the commodity. It also discriminates between domestic and foreign markets.

Perhaps the most important surplus diversion programs were those for cotton and wheat. American farmers have always sold part of these crops abroad. Since the adjustment program raised domestic prices, the government had to choose between subsidizing exports or losing foreign markets. It chose to subsidize. In August 1938, as announced in a departmental press release, the Department of Agriculture inaugurated a "wheat and flour export sales policy for the 1938–39 marketing season, designed to enable United States wheat farmers to maintain their share of the world export trade." There-

35. Under the AAA program cooperation was voluntary, but the Bankhead Act of 1934 provided for a practically prohibitive tax on cotton ginned in excess of individual quotas, the national total of which was set at 10 million bales. Later the Kerr-Smith Tobacco Control Act placed a heavy tax on tobacco that farmers sold in excess of their allotments.

36. *U.S.* v. *William Butler, et al.*, 297 U.S. 1 (1935), at p. 72.

after the government bought wheat at domestic prices and sold it abroad for what it would bring. To keep exporting flour it subsidized flour exporters directly.

As government-supported cotton prices forced American cotton out of world markets the carry-over of cotton by 1939 rose to 14 million bales, more than 11 million of which the government held. According to the Department of Agriculture, to dispose of this surplus and "to assure the United States its fair share of the world trade in cotton—by restoring the normal competitive position of American cotton in world markets" required a subsidy on export cotton of 1.5 cents a pound. Though the abnormal demands occasioned by World War II eliminated the cotton surplus, a succession of big crops after the war brought the price in mid-1948 almost down to the parity-support level.

Disadvantages of Price Supports

If agriculture is depressed while the economy generally is prosperous, as in the 1920's, resources are not being used economically. The problem is, then, to transfer resources, primarily labor, from agriculture to other industries, where the market value of their services is higher. Raising incomes by raising prices in the depressed industry—agriculture—is not the way to do this. It can only perpetuate the uneconomical use of resources at the expense of the economy generally and, in some instances, unfortunately, at the expense of agriculture itself.[37]

The price support program brought temporary prosperity to the American cotton farmer; but before World War II it had priced American cotton out of world markets. It threatened to price cotton out of domestic markets, too, as the cost of producing synthetic fibers rapidly fell. What was needed to save American cotton was lower costs, not higher prices. Resources would have been used more efficiently if some of the less productive land and labor employed in growing cotton had been transferred to other lines.

If agriculture is depressed while the economy generally is also depressed, as in the 1930's, the problem is not to reapportion a

37. The problem of inefficient use of resources in agriculture is more serious than many people realize. Professor Conrad Hammar quotes data showing that of 5,070,000 of the nation's farms that were classified, only 1,370,000 were recorded as efficient; 2,750,000 were classified as marginal or inadequate. See Conrad H. Hammar, "Agriculture in an Expansionist Economy," *Journal of Farm Economics,* February 1943.

shrunken total. The problem is to increase national income. A fiscal policy that shifts purchasing power from those who will not spend or invest to those who will do so might help. But the farmers were not the only poor in the 1930's. The city masses also had small incomes. Diverting inadequate buying power from one set of poverty-stricken buyers to another did not help.[38]

Finally, if agriculture becomes highly prosperous while the whole economy is booming, as happened after World War II, the proper course is to put a damper on inflation. Agriculture is no less subject to speculative excesses than are other branches of industry. The purchase of farms at exorbitant prices, based on a temporary worldwide shortage of farm products, was a main factor in the collapse of agriculture in the 1920's. In so far as agricultural policy guarantees a market for surpluses, thereby encouraging farmers to increase production without regard to the probability of a shrinkage of foreign demand for American crops as agriculture abroad revives, it promotes the sort of speculative excesses that ruined farmers after World War I.

Guaranteed prices at excessive levels and collective output restriction are conducive neither to an efficient use of resources nor to economic progress. In a progressive society agriculture tends in the long run to decline in importance. As productivity and the level of incomes in general rise, people spend relatively less on foodstuffs and relatively more on products and services that cater to comfort, recreation, health, cultural interests, or perhaps mere ostentation. As economists express it, the income elasticity of the basic necessities of life is low. Agriculture is therefore foredoomed to lag behind in a generally advancing economy.

When agriculture is relatively profitless, surplus labor is eventually squeezed out of agriculture and into industry and commerce. Subsidizing farmers prevents this long-run adjustment. Subsidies for any particular group are always made at the expense of the rest of society. The only economic defense for a subsidy is that it may give

38. In practice the wealthy states and the wealthy farmers fared better than the poor states and the poor farmers under the agricultural adjustment program. In fiscal 1940, 362,479 farmers in Illinois received $60,645,000 in benefit payments under the agricultural adjustment program, while 507,010 farmers in Kentucky and Tennessee received only $19,624,000. During the two fiscal years 1940 and 1941, benefits for each payee averaged $182 in Iowa and $140 in Illinois, but only $44 in Kentucky and $34 in Tennessee. See *ibid.*, pp. 36-37.

the subsidized strength to stand on their own feet. But this defense cannot be made for agricultural subsidies. There is no prospect of a diminishing need for them, only a prospect of a steadily growing need—if the same proportion of the population continues indefinitely to seek a living from farming.

Defense of Farm Subsidies

Proponents of farm subsidies resort to another defense. Farming, they say, is more than an industry; it is a way of life. It can be argued—and at least since Cato it often has been argued—that only a nation with roots deep in the soil has the vitality and stamina to meet every crisis. A mode of life cut off from direct dependence on and cooperation with natural forces, the argument runs, is too artificial. It is not adapted to the biological and psychological needs of people. Attachment to the "good earth" is more than a poetic sentiment; it is a condition of the "great society."

In so far as these contentions have merit, the uneconomical character of agricultural subsidies does not dispose of the issue. True enough, other-than-economic values are worthy of cultivation. The economic man is far from being the whole man. And an economic society is not the great society, either in Graham Wallas' meaning of the phrase or in history's lesson book. But a society that disregards economic principles would be well advised to do so only after careful deliberation.

One of the menacing consequences of opening the public treasury to the economic support of any group—on noneconomic grounds—is that it encourages other special-interest groups to seek similar treatment. In a democratic polity few vested interests will magnanimously forego the implied invitation to come and get it when the government starts dispensing largess. In the pull and tug of politics some groups may win bigger bounties than others. But no matter which special interest wins in such a scramble for plunder, society loses.

LABOR POLICY

Unionism and collective bargaining have doubtless brought concrete gains both to labor and to the community. But the power of unions may be abused. Unions sometimes do more than put employees on a par with employers in settling the terms of employment. Often they coerce unorganized labor and impose on employers monopolistic restraints and exactions at the expense of farmers, white-collar workers, small businessmen, and professional people. The public interest is jeopardized no less by monopoly power in the hands of organized labor than in the hands of organized business.

It does not follow, however, that labor organization is as likely to achieve monopoly power as is business consolidation, or that the measures appropriate for dealing with monopoly abuses in the one field are appropriate in the other. Because the threat to the public interest from the aggrandizement of trade unions was not so clearly apparent fifty years ago, when labor organization on a national scale was in its infancy, the Sherman Act was aimed primarily at industrial monopoly. It was an *antitrust* law. Nevertheless, as the strength of organized labor increased, the courts came more and more frequently to apply the prohibitions of the Sherman Act to labor organizations. The fact that Congress made no attempt before the 1930's to enunciate a federal policy specifically regulating unions helps explain this judicial development. Moreover, in spite of the differences between self-help organizations of labor and of business, they have some similarities.[39]

Antitrust Laws Versus Unionism

The judicial application of the antitrust law to labor unions grew steadily more rigorous between 1890 and 1930, while judicial policy in applying the law to business groups became more and more lax. For four decades the trend of decisions was toward accommodating the law to the growing concentration of control in business—the very development it was aimed to stop. Yet these were also the years in which the courts stretched the statutory prohibitions so as to curb the growing power of unions. In particular, boycotts were strongly disapproved by judges.

39. Two differences are striking. (1) Concerted action by business, whether through loosely knit or closely knit combinations, does not generally tend to more nearly equalize bargaining power between buyers and sellers; whereas this was clearly an objective and consequence of trade unionism. Trade unions, however, have no doubt in some cases gained greater power than that possessed by those with whom they deal. (2) Many of the aims of organized labor are consistent with the welfare of society. Trade unions aim to improve living standards and reduce inequalities in income; whereas concerted action among rival firms generally leads to output restrictions and higher prices. Unfortunately, labor unions sometimes work toward similar ends.

A boycott is a potent weapon, striking directly at market demand for an employer's product. Usually unions have used it to coerce nonunion employers. In an economy with national markets, nonunion wages anywhere constitute a threat to union rates everywhere, and hence to the union. If the proportion of a company's employees belonging to or sympathetic to the union is not very large, a strike may be ineffectual. To unionize a plant in such circumstances, withdrawal of labor's purchasing power is likely to be more effective than withholding its (unionized) productive power. Hence the secondary boycott.[40]

The first labor case under the Sherman Act to reach the Supreme Court, the Danbury Hatters case, involved a boycott.[41] The hat workers' union had organized most of the domestic plants manufacturing felt hats. When Loewe, a manufacturer at Danbury, Connecticut, refused to deal with it, the union organized a nation-wide boycott of Loewe's hats. It enlisted the support of members of other American Federation of Labor unions as well as of its own members in other locals scattered over the country. Loewe sued the members of the Danbury local for treble damages under the Sherman Act. The lower court gave judgment for the defendants, but the Supreme Court reversed, holding that the secondary boycott, by reducing out-of-state orders for Loewe's hats, was a conspiracy in restraint of trade within the meaning of Section 1 of the Act. Three years later the Court took a similar stand in the Buck's Stove case, even though in this instance no penalty was laid on the boycotters.[42]

Unionism had too firm a foothold to be dislodged by these adverse decisions, but many labor leaders believed that further development

40. A primary boycott would never work. Refusal of employees of a company to buy its products would not appreciably affect its sales. But the refusal of union members generally to buy a particular employer's products is a different matter. The boycott is useful as a rule, however, only against manufacturers of consumers' goods.

41. *Loewe* v. *Lawlor,* 208 U.S. 274 (1908). This ruling was reaffirmed on a second appeal. 253 U.S. 522 (1915).

42. *Gompers* v. *Buck's Stove & Range Co.,* 221 U.S. 418 (1911). This was a contempt proceeding growing out of a boycott. The AF of L placed the Buck's Stove Company on the "We don't patronize" list in its monthly journal because of a local labor dispute in the company's St. Louis foundry. At the solicitation of the company a federal court ordered the AF of L to drop the company from its "unfair" list. When Gompers and other AF of L officials refused to obey the order, the court held them in contempt and ordered them jailed. Although the Supreme Court set aside the jail sentence, on appeal, it clearly indicated that the AF of L boycott was illegal. Two years later the Court dismissed the suit entirely, on a technicality. 233 U.S. 604 (1913).

of the law along the same line would imperil the whole labor movement. On the basis of these precedents the courts might even hold, some suggested, that collective bargaining itself was a restraint of trade and therefore unlawful. The growing use of court injunctions to deprive unions of the use of economic coercion reinforced these fears.[43] Organized labor therefore turned to Congress for relief from what it regarded as judicial oppression. It urged legislation curtailing the power of the courts to interfere with union self-help activities.

The Clayton Act and Labor

Congress responded in 1914 by incorporating in the omnibus Clayton Act two sections on labor. Section 6 declared:

> The labor of a human being is not a commodity or article of commerce. Nothing contained in the antitrust laws shall be construed to forbid the existence and operation of labor . . . organizations . . . or to forbid or restrain individual members of such organizations from lawfully carrying out the legitimate objects thereof . . .[44]

Section 20 limited the use of injunctions in labor disputes to cases where "necessary to prevent irreparable injury to property . . . for which injury there is no adequate remedy at law." [45]

The meaning of these provisions is far from clear. Did Section 20 limit the discretion of federal courts? Or did it merely restate the rules governing the exercise of their equity powers? And did Section 6 leave unions where they stood before? Or did it exempt them entirely from the antitrust laws? Labor leaders thought it exempted them and hailed it as labor's Magna Charta. But the Supreme Court thought otherwise.

In the Duplex case, the Court held that union activities as such were not exempt from the prohibitions of the Sherman Act nor put beyond the reach of injunctions by the provisions of Section 20 of the Clayton Act.[46] Because the Duplex case was not a dispute be-

43. See Felix Frankfurter and Nathan Greene, *The Labor Injunction,* Macmillan, New York, 1930.

44. 38 Stat. 731, U.S. Code, Sec. 17.

45. 38 Stat. 738, U.S. Code, Sec. 52.

46. *Duplex Printing Press* v. *Deering,* 254 U.S. 443 (1921). This suit arose upon a petition by the Duplex company for an injunction against the International Machinists Union. The union had organized three of the four major companies making printing presses, and after an unsuccessful campaign to organize Duplex employees the union

tween an employer and his own employees, Section 20 was inapplicable, according to the majority view. Mr. Justice Brandeis dissented, saying:

> The conditions developed in an industry may be such that those engaged in it cannot continue their struggle without danger to the community. But it is not for judges to determine whether such conditions exist, nor is it their function to set the limits of permissible control and to declare the duties which the new situation demands. This is the function of the legislature which, while limiting individual and group rights of aggression and defense, may substitute processes of justice for the more primitive methods of trial by combat.

The Duplex decision appeared to undermine the labor provisions of the Clayton Act, particularly Section 20, so far as boycotts were concerned. But would the same construction of the law be applied when the activities in question related simply to direct efforts to obtain union recognition and a collective bargaining agreement?

The answer came in the second Coronado Coal case.[47] Here the Supreme Court reaffirmed that unions are liable under the Sherman Act for injuries to an employer's business from deliberate interference with the shipment of goods in interstate commerce. The United Mine Workers of America, District 21, had struck a Coronado mine. The strike stopped production. Some strikers, with or without union sanction, burned tipples and coal cars, dynamited the mine, and wrought general havoc. In a suit for treble damages against the union, the Court first held there could be no recovery because interstate commerce was not directly involved.[48] In the second suit, however, judgment went for the plaintiff (against the local union, but not District 21) on the basis of new evidence indicating that a specific objective of the strike was to prevent the shipment of nonunion coal to markets in other states where it would compete with union-mined coal.

---

instituted a secondary boycott. Members of the union not only refused to install or repair Duplex presses, but tried to coerce other workers—teamsters and the like—to have nothing to do with them.

47. *Coronado Coal Co.* v. *United Mine Workers of America*, 268 U.S. 295 (1925).

48. *United Mine Workers of America* v. *Coronado Coal Co.*, 259 U.S. 344 (1922). Reasonable people might well contend that the company was entitled to damages for the property destroyed, and indeed the company could have sued under state laws. But the issue before the Supreme Court was far broader: Is a strike which directly interferes with the interstate shipment of goods a conspiracy to restrain trade within the meaning of the Sherman Act?

The practical effect of the foregoing decisions and others of like tenor was to restrain unionism.[49] This development is in striking contrast to the evolution of antitrust policy as applied to business organizations, as in the Standard Oil, the United States Steel, and the Appalachian Coal cases.

Legislative Protection for Labor

The depression of the 1930's changed public sentiment toward trade unionism so sharply that neither the courts nor Congress could ignore it. Even before the Roosevelt Administration undertook the Herculean task of eliminating unemployment and making the economic system work, Congress passed the Norris-LaGuardia Act under the Hoover Administration.[50] This act prohibited the use of injunctions in "labor disputes." It broadly defined a labor dispute as "any controversy concerning terms or conditions of employment, or concerning the association or representation of persons in negotiating, fixing, maintaining, changing, or seeking to arrange terms or conditions of employment, regardless of whether or not the disputants stand in proximate relation of employer and employee." This was an anti-injunction law with teeth so firmly implanted that not even the Supreme Court could easily extract them. But it was more than that. To help labor obtain equality it deprived organized employers of aid from the courts.

The NRA went still further. For Congress decided that collective action by business groups was necessary to reverse the downward trend in economic activity and that collective bargaining by unions was necessary to obtain for labor a fair share of the national income. The premise was that the power of organized labor should match that of organized industry. NRA did not positively reinforce labor's right to organize, but it limited the rights of employers and created

49. See, for example, *Bedford Cut Stone Co.* v. *Journeymen Stonecutters,* 274 U.S. 37 (1927); and *Hitchman Coal Co.* v. *Mitchell,* 245 U.S. 229 (1917). The Hitchman case did not directly involve the Sherman Act.

50. 47 Stat.L. 70. The Norris-LaGuardia Act prescribes, more explicitly than Section 20 of the Clayton Act, the circumstances under which a court may issue injunctions. It prohibits injunctions to prevent laborers, regardless of any promises they may have made to the contrary, from striking; from extending financial aid to strikers; from aiding a person interested in a labor dispute who is being sued; from publicizing a labor dispute whether by advertising, speaking, patrolling, or by any other method not involving fraud or violence; from assembling peacefully to promote their interests in a labor dispute; from stating an intention of doing the above things and "advising, urging, or otherwise causing or inducing without fraud or violence" the above things.

an environment favorable to unionism. Union leaders had a voice in formulating and administering the labor provisions of the codes. The government encouraged labor to exercise its right to organize.

When the Supreme Court struck down NRA in the Schechter decision, Congress more than restored to unions the protection NRA had afforded them by passing the National Labor Relations Act, which not only encouraged labor to organize but also pledged government aid to labor's efforts to organize.[51] By enumerating specific unfair labor practices Congress virtually ordered management to stop resisting labor organization and to bargain collectively.

The Courts Favor Labor

Meanwhile the courts had modified their position on the applicability of the antitrust laws to labor. A precedent-breaking case was that of the Apex Hosiery Company.

To force a contract upon Apex some employees seized its plant, damaged its properties, and refused to let it ship finished goods from stocks to out-of-state customers.[52] When the case reached the Supreme Court, Mr. Justice Stone, speaking for the majority, declared that, although the Sherman Act was applicable to labor, here the union members were not liable because they had not conspired to control the market for hosiery. They had merely brought organized pressure on Apex to force it to recognize the union and bargain with it. While recognizing that "successful union activity . . . may have some influence on price competition by eliminating that part of such competition which is based on differences in labor standards," the Court found in this incidental restriction of competition nothing culpable. It declared that such an "effect on competition has not been considered to be the kind of curtailment of price competition prohibited by the Sherman Act." This is quite different from the doctrine set forth in earlier labor cases.[53]

51. The Supreme Court upheld the National Labor Relations Act in *NLRB* v. *Jones & Laughlin Steel Corp.*, 301 U.S. 1 (1937).

52. *Apex Hosiery Co.* v. *Leader*, 310 U.S. 469 (1940). Apex first asked for an injunction and when it was refused, Apex sued the union for treble damages under the Sherman Act. The District Court recognized Apex's claim as valid and awarded the company damages in the amount of $750,000. The Circuit Court reversed the trial court and the Supreme Court affirmed.

53. For a penetrating criticism of the Court's attempt to reconcile its position in the Apex Hosiery case with its position in the earlier cases, see Charles O. Gregory, *Labor and the Law*, Norton, New York, 1946, pp. 255-69.

The Hutchinson case went even further in freeing labor organizations from the restrictions of the antitrust laws.[54] This case involved a jurisdictional dispute between carpenters and machinists. Both had contracts with Anheuser-Busch, under which they received identical wages for substantially the same hours of work. Each claimed control over the installation of certain machinery. The AF of L had awarded the work to the machinists, and the carpenters had at first accepted the decision. Later they repudiated it, and demanded the transfer of such work to them. When Anheuser-Busch refused, they inaugurated a nation-wide boycott of its beer. They went so far as to call a strike against a contractor building a plant for another company on land leased from Anheuser-Busch.

In its decision in this case the Court came close to accepting the questionable principle that the end justifies the means.

> So long as a union acts in its self-interest, and does not combine with non-labor groups, the licit and the illicit . . . are not to be distinguished by any judgment regarding the wisdom or unwisdom, the rightness or wrongness, the selfishness or unselfishness of the end of which the particular union activities are the means.

In short, under the Sherman Act, employees may promote their interests by collectively coercing employers or unorganized workers even through force or fraud, so long as they do not conspire with business groups in doing so.[55] It matters not that a union may be powerful enough to control the market without conniving with management. If it relies on its own strength it is free, under the antitrust laws as now interpreted, to exercise the most flagrant control of the market in defiance of the interests of other labor groups and of consumers generally.

The recent Bradley case emphasized this new construction of the law.[56] Local No. 3 of the International Brotherhood of Electrical Workers, restricting its membership and operating under a closed-shop agreement with New York employers, refused to handle any

54. *U.S.* v. *Hutchinson,* 312 U.S. 219 (1941).

55. Until the Taft-Hartley Act a union was free to coerce an employer to prevent his dealing with another union even though under the National Labor Relations Act the employer was obligated to deal with the rival union.

56. *Allen Bradley Co.* v. *Local Union No. 3, IBEW,* previously cited. The plaintiffs, electrical manufacturers outside New York, sought an injunction to stop the union from excluding them from the New York market.

equipment made by out-of-state shops, union or nonunion. By eliminating the competition of out-of-state manufacturers the union made it possible for local producers to charge monopolistic prices and increase union wages. On the basis of evidence indicating connivance with the employers, the Supreme Court approved a limited injunction against this union-made barrier to interstate commerce. At the same time, however, the Court made it clear that the Hutchinson doctrine is here to stay and that as long as a labor organization acts independently it may use its coercive power to control the market.

Dangers of Labor Monopoly Practices

Even when trade unions do not use their power directly to control output and prices, they may interfere with the effective operation of a competitive economy. Featherbedding, blocking the introduction of laborsaving devices, and limiting output are among the more flagrant monopolistic abuses to which organized labor sometimes resorts. The public, however, quickly recognizes the waste in such practices and this in itself serves as some check on their use.

But even pure and simple collective bargaining by a powerful union negotiating wages on an industry-wide basis may prevent effective competition.[57] This is a disagreeable fact for all trade-union sympathizers, but one they must face. With the leverage that a union obtains from disciplined organization of all employees in an industry, collective bargaining tends to make rigidly uniform one of the most important elements of cost. It thereby tends to narrow the area within which competition can be effective and to prevent the readjustments in the use of resources that competition must make if it is to perform its proper functions.

Collective bargaining of industry-wide scope also increases the likelihood that business rivals will follow an identical pricing policy. When union officials and business executives representing an entire industry meet to fix wages they are not likely to conclude their nego-

57. Few unions negotiate with industry on a nation-wide basis; coal and railway transportation are notable exceptions. But where bargaining is done on a company-employee basis, the strong unions and a major company may set the pace and the pattern of wage adjustments for the whole industry. According to Dunlop, the number of really key bargains on a basis of which wage adjustments are generally made is from twenty-five to fifty. See John L. Dunlop, "American Wage Determination: The Trend and Its Significance," in *Wage Determination and the Economics of Liberalism*, Economic Institute, Chamber of Commerce of the United States, Washington, 1947, p. 42. Wage leadership and price leadership may both be handmaidens of monopoly.

tiations unless the businessmen have reached some understanding about their pricing policies.[58] And there is nothing to guarantee that wages as determined by industry-wide collective bargaining—and prices, to the extent that they depend on wages or that employers set them by mutual agreement—will be fixed at levels that serve the public interest. There is every reason to believe that they will not be. For both monopoly wages and monopoly prices limit investment opportunities. They interfere with an effective use of the community's resources and an economical distribution of the community's income.

Moreover, standardization of wages in the various sections of the country may have the same retarding effect on economically backward areas as would a tariff wall around the more industrially advanced communities that shuts out the products of the backward areas. If wage rates are standardized geographically regardless of differences in labor productivity and the ratio of labor costs to total costs, living costs, and relative labor supply, the backward industrial areas will be handicapped. Setting wage rates in that fashion is neither economical nor humanitarian. However, this is no argument against standardization of wage rates if differences of the sort enumerated do not in fact exist. Many economists believe that regional differences in the United States have been greatly exaggerated as factors in determining wage rates.[59]

58. Employers may even sometimes accept the union as an agency for controlling the market. *Fortune* presents the following illustration of how the teamsters' union has established arbitrary controls over commercial markets for the benefit of employees and employers at the expense of the public: ". . . Beck's teamsters have created in Seattle a very close approximation of the dictatorship of the proletariat, but not along Soviet lines. For Beck is considered by many potent businessmen to be a force for stability and profits, since, when he signs up with a group of employers, his teamsters act to stamp out competition from any 'independent' who may try to cut prices, employ non-union labor, or otherwise deviate from the terms of the contract. He is a potent force in many industries. For example, laundry prices are high in Seattle on account of the Teamsters' union. The Associated Laundries of Seattle audits the books of the laundries. In charge of the Associated Laundries is William H. Short, one of Beck's right-hand men. But Beck justifies the setup by pointing out that before the Teamsters' organized the laundries there were a great many bankruptcies in the industry." "The I.B.T.C.W.H. of A.," *Fortune,* May 1941, pp. 99-100.

59. See Richard A. Lester, "Diversity in North-South Wage Differentials and in Wage Rates Within the South," *Southern Economic Journal,* January 1946; *idem,* "Wage Diversity and Its Theoretical Implications," *Review of Economic Statistics,* August 1946; *idem,* "Results and Implications of Some Recent Wage Studies," in Richard A. Lester and Joseph Shister (Eds.), *Insights Into Labor Issues,* Macmillan, New York, 1948; "Differences in Living Costs in Northern and Southern Cities," *Monthly Labor Review,* July 1939; "Estimated Intercity Differences in Cost of Living, June 15, 1939," *Monthly Labor Review,* November 1939; John T. Dunlop, "Productivity and the Wage Structure," in *Income, Employment, and Public Policy: Essays in Honor of Alvin H. Hansen,* Norton, New York, 1948; Lloyd G. Reynolds, "Wage Differences in Local Labor Markets," *American Economic Review,* June 1946.

The Line Between Defensible and Indefensible Union Policies

Nor is the discussion intended to imply that labor unions may not bring economic benefits to the community generally. Competition is never perfect and collective bargaining may either force wages up to competitive levels or give wage earners a share in monopoly profits. In the first case the benefits to society are unmixed; historically this was the common situation. In the second, collective bargaining may alleviate an economic evil. Moreover, unions may play a constructive role in determining internal wage structures, promoting democratic procedures in settling grievances, and establishing fair working rules. But the position that some progressive unions have taken that they must regulate both wages and prices in the public interest is inimical to effective competition.[60]

If society is to rely on private enterprise to serve it, all obstacles to its competitive operation must be clearly recognized and rigorously repressed, however sacred may be the vested interests at stake. In its own interest, the public cannot tolerate private groups—either labor or business—strong enough to control markets and disrupt the economy. Monopoly power, in labor's hands or capital's or jointly exercised, is inimical to the general welfare and to democracy.

To prevent the abuse of labor's rights to collective bargaining, it may be necessary to regulate trade unions or limit their power. The Taft-Hartley Act, whatever may be its defects, was a recognition of this necessity.[61] The Act recognizes the right of employees to organize for purposes of collective bargaining or to refrain from doing so (Title 1, Sec. 7). It prohibits certain unfair labor practices of employers (Title 1, Sec. 8a) and certain others of labor organizations (Title 1, Sec. 8b). It restricts union boycotts and jurisdictional disputes and prohibits excessive or discriminatory union fees. It outlines procedures for collective bargaining and limits the use of the closed shop. It authorizes the National Labor Relations Board to petition federal courts for injunctions for the enforcement of its orders and for relief against boycotts and jurisdictional disputes. To obtain the benefits of the Act, it requires unions to file reports with the Secretary of Labor disclosing facts about the organization's

60. See, for example, "Purchasing Power for Prosperity," economic brief submitted by Walter Reuther in contract negotiations with General Motors, October 1945.

61. Labor-Management Relations Act, 1947, Public Law 101, 80th Cong.

finances, fees, officers, constitution and by-laws, etc. (Title 1, Sec. 9).

The government's failure to curb the power of big business during the fateful forty years following the passage of the Sherman Act may have justified the New Deal labor policy and provided extenuation for the ensuing abuses to which the Taft-Hartley Act was a corrective reaction. But a continual struggle between big labor and big business over the division of monopolistic spoils hinders the effective functioning of a private enterprise economy. And that kind of "competition" surely bodes ill for democracy.

CONCLUSIONS

It is not easy to create an environment within which a competitive, private enterprise economy can flourish. Both economic and political obstacles block the way. Economists are not agreed on the measures essential to stabilizing the general price level and preventing violent contractions in the level of employment and national income. Nor is there a consensus among the experts on the sort of monetary controls and fiscal policies that would put an end to the boom-and-bust sequence without lessening the incentive to private investment.

The political obstacles to the creation of an environment favorable to competition are even more serious than the economic. For a century Congress has used tariffs to protect vested interests rather than to promote competition, and despite the recent change in policy under the Reciprocal Trade Agreements Act, Congress shows no great enthusiasm for subjecting American industry to vigorous foreign competition. States have lent the use of their police powers for the promotion of monopoly interests of business groups engaged in exploiting natural resources. Legislative and judicial policy has encouraged the growth of monopoly power among labor unions and sanctioned control of farm prices to insure farmers greater returns than they could get in competitive markets.

Many public policies such as these have had the effect, whether or not so intended, of curbing competition and weakening its power to allocate resources and distribute income economically. It will be very difficult to revise or reverse these policies so as to foster independent business enterprise and reinvigorate competition. Policies that hinder and discourage competition are fast becoming so characteristic and integral a part of the institutional framework of contemporary America that any political party seriously opposing them may find it hard to gain or hold power.

It is possible, of course, to exaggerate the importance of these collateral policies as obstacles to the maintenance of effective competition in industrial markets. But to deny that they are in fact obstacles would only intensify their obstructive effects. It is equally true that a democracy has the power to shape its own political and economic destiny. The problem is to use that power wisely. If the people, acting as an organized community, do not subordinate their several special interests to the general welfare they may lose in the long run what they thought to gain in the short run. Isolationism is likely to prove as futile in domestic affairs as it did in foreign affairs.

Chapter 13

INCORPORATION POLICY AND INDUSTRIAL CONCENTRATION

THE STRUCTURE OF MARKETS is not wholly or even mainly shaped by the deliberate designs of business "architects." It is, rather, determined to some extent by the means at their disposal. Just as the form of a state does not depend preponderantly on the ideas and energies of "great men" (Carlyle notwithstanding) but to some extent on the qualities, traits, and usages of the citizens as well as on accidents of climate and geography, so the form of a market depends at least as much on the tools and materials available to businessmen as on their own ideas and capacities.[1]

Custom and legislation provide the "tools"—the legal devices for organizing and transacting business. The public provides most of the "materials" from which to fashion a going concern—the basic fund of technology, the capital for investment, and the purchasing power that makes demand effective. The rest, consisting mainly of organizing, managerial, and technical abilities and usually also part of the capital, is supplied by the businessmen themselves.

Obviously, the size, weight, complexity, sharpness of an artisan's tools and their adaptability to various uses broadly determine the kinds of things he can produce with them. They limit the quantity and quality of his output. To get desired results the tools must be

1. Comparison of the patterns of markets and of states suggests some instructive analogies. Analogous to the single-party, monolithic structure of a totalitarian state is the single-seller structure of a monopolistic market. In both, power is highly concentrated at the top, and the populace—as subjects in the one case, as consumers in the other—take what they are offered or go without. Analogous to the pyramidal structure of a caste-stratified state is the similar structure of an "imperfectly competitive" market, with the leading firm and a few satellite producers forming the top layers and beneath them a series of subordinate orders of dependent distributors and inadequately protected consumers. Analogous to the rambling, loose-jointed, but nonetheless interlocking structure of a democratic state is the multi-celled, organically integrated structure of an "effectively competitive" market. Interspersed among these major types of governmental and industrial structures are many subspecies, such as oligarchic states and oligopolistic markets; and of course innumerable compromises or blends may be distinguished within or between the several types and subspecies.

adapted to the worker and to the materials at his disposal. A scythe with too long a blade or a hammer with too light a handle may lead not only to waste but to danger—and danger not alone to the artisan using the tool but to fellow workers and innocent bystanders as well.

In the same way, the legal instruments for organizing production and exploiting markets have much to do with the kind of business units enterprisers create. If the forms of business organization are not well adapted to the capacities and limitations of the men who organize business, someone is likely to get hurt.

Forms of Business Organization Affect Market Behavior

Business units ill-adapted to the primary function of a business enterprise—the production and distribution of goods and services—reflect their maladaptation in market behavior. For the way markets work, like everything else, depends, at least in part, on how they are made up—on their structure. How competitive a market is does not, of course, depend solely on the number, size, and pattern of organization of the companies operating in it. But if these factors weaken the incentives to commercial rivalry and foster restrictionism, the market may be—indeed, is apt to be—monopolized regardless of the presence or absence of the objective conditions technically favorable to monopoly—heavy fixed costs, joint costs, inelastic demand, and so forth. Ultimately the structure and the behavior of markets simply reflect the structure and the behavior of the business firms that compose them.

Administratively business enterprises differ widely in their patterns of organization. No two firms assign quite the same powers to their several executive officers or follow quite the same procedure in determining what to do and how to do it. But with respect to legal accountability the forms of business organization of practical significance are limited to a few well-defined types. Incorporated enterprises handle most of the country's business today, even though they comprise only about 10 per cent of all business units. Individual proprietorships and partnerships are still common in neighborhood retail and service trades, but such businesses operate on the fringe of the economy.[2]

2. Of the 3.5 million business firms that the Department of Commerce estimates

Practically all manufacturing, mining, transportation, and trade of more than local significance is organized and conducted by corporations. The 363,000 corporations that filed balance sheets for tax purposes with the Internal Revenue Bureau in 1944 reported aggregate assets of $418 billion.[3] Not all corporations, to be sure, are large-scale enterprises. Although assets of the 363,000 corporations averaged over a million dollars a company, nearly half of them (176,000) had assets of less than $50,000 and 92 per cent (334,000) had assets of less than a million dollars.

Corporation Now Typical Form of Business Enterprise

It is the universal use of the corporate device for organizing large-scale enterprises that emphasizes the importance of incorporated business in the national economy. The 29,000 corporations with assets of more than a million dollars, though constituting only 8 per cent of the 363,000 corporations filing balance sheets in 1944, held no less than 89.5 per cent of the assets of the entire group, transacted 75 per cent of the aggregate business, and obtained 85 per cent of the aggregate net profit of *all* (412,500) active corporations in the country.[4] Evidently, incorporated big business provides most of the capital income, wage income, investment opportunities, and goods for consumption. Certainly from the standpoint of its bearing on the

---

were operating on June 30, 1946, more than two thirds were engaged in retail and service trades. In addition, construction and transportation accounted for more than 10 per cent, and more than three quarters of the "firms" in these two lines were probably individual proprietorships, because their employees, if any, numbered three or less. See *Survey of Current Business,* January 1947, p. 10, and May 1944, p. 4.

3. *Statistical Abstract of the United States,* 1948, p. 361. The revenue laws require all business corporations to file an income report annually but not a balance sheet. In 1944 about 50,000 of the 412,500 corporations did not submit balance sheets. The assets figure contains a large amount of duplication, partly because of parent-subsidiary and debtor-creditor relationships among companies filing returns. On the other hand, omission of the assets of corporations that did not file balance sheets partly offsets the overstatement resulting from duplication. But after making liberal allowance for duplication and for other deficiencies in the assets figure—for example, use of book values—it may be compared with a total national wealth in 1944 of perhaps $600 billion. (Computed on the basis of the National Resources Planning Board's estimate of national wealth in 1935, amounting to $365 billion, account being taken of changes in the value of the dollar and the growth of real investment between these dates. See National Resources Committee, *The Structure of the American Economy,* Washington, 1939, p. 377.) Probably agricultural and urban real estate and government-owned property—including public schools—make up a large part of the difference between corporation assets and national wealth.

4. *Statistical Abstract,* 1948, pp. 351 and 362. Moreover, the 3,874 largest corporations (those with assets of more than $10 million), constituting barely one per cent of the entire group, held nearly three quarters (74 per cent) of the assets, did more than half the business, and garnered 60 per cent of the net profits of all corporations.

economic fortunes of the community, it is the characteristic type of enterprise organization today.

The privilege of incorporation is not, of itself, inimical to a competitive economic order. On the contrary, the advantages of limited liability and subdivision of capital into small shares doubtless stimulate investment and make it easier to assemble the funds required for large-scale production. Freedom to incorporate, if adequately protected from abuse by governmental safeguards, would tend to spur business enterprise and invigorate competition. For it would tend to increase the number of independent sellers in every market, and to force each of them to try to improve his competitive position by eliminating waste, reducing costs, and offering better products at lower prices.

The widespread liberalization of incorporation laws during the nineteenth century was doubtless partly in response to the demands of some business leaders for a freer rein in their quest for market mastery. But it also reflected a popular belief that competition could take care of itself, that privileges formally available to all would not become special privileges in practice, and that there was no longer any need for governmental safeguards against corporate abuses. Moreover, the rapid expansion and the ebullient spirit of the period probably held to a minimum the adverse effect of abuses resulting from lax incorporation laws on business investment and enterprise. However that may be, by the end of the century the accumulation of vested interests and the solidification of centralized corporate control had in many lines reached a stage that apparently weakened individual initiative and tended to frustrate the competitive urge.[5] But paradoxically, the social justification and defense of liberal incorporation laws still ran in terms of their supposed stimulus to private enterprise.

Beginnings of Business Incorporation

The original adaptation of corporations to business purposes—as distinct from ecclesiastical and political purposes—was in public service enterprises: waterworks, turnpikes, canals, insurance companies, and banks. Indeed, until the nineteenth century these were

5. See National Resources Committee, *op. cit.*, Pt. 1, Chap. 2, and Pt. 2, Chap. 6.

practically the only incorporated enterprises in America.[6] Without exception, they were public utilities. Because they required large capital and served community purposes, legislatures granted them charters that relieved of unlimited liability for corporate debts those who contributed to their capital. But as the price of limited liability, colonial and state governments imposed certain conditions, such as a restricted field of operations, standards of service, and a limitation on indebtedness.[7] Railroads were later chartered on the same grounds and subject to similar conditions.

As manufacturing developed, businessmen increasingly sought incorporation privileges. Machine production usually required more capital than one person possessed or could borrow. To promote new enterprises or to expand old ones it was frequently necessary to combine the funds of several persons. If the funds were to be assembled and the undertaking to succeed, not all the investors could be saddled with unlimited liability for the venture and given a veto power in its management, as in an ordinary partnership. An unincorporated association of private persons for a joint venture of any great magnitude was, and is, cumbersome and unwieldy. Moreover, only through incorporation could the continuity of the enterprise be preserved, despite disagreements, defections, or deaths among the owners. And without continuity long-term investment would be impracticable. So legislatures were prevailed upon to endow such associations with certain legal attributes and privileges, such as the right to contract and to sue and be sued in the corporate name and to adopt by-laws for their internal government.

Early Model of a Business Corporation

The pre-Civil War model of a corporation was, in effect, an extended partnership, with limited liability and unlimited life. It was essentially and distinctively an instrument for the organization of production. Industrial corporations whose stock was subject to speculation among a heterogeneous array of widely scattered owners seldom directly acquainted with its operations were comparatively un-

6. Joseph S. Davis, *Essays in the Earlier History of American Corporations,* Harvard University Press, Cambridge, 1917, Vol. 1, pp. 75-103, and Vol. 2, pp. 3-33.

7. See Samuel Williston, "History of the Law of Business Corporations Before 1850," *Harvard Law Review,* 1888, p. 105; and John P. Davis, *Corporations,* Putnam's, New York, 1905, Vol. 2, pp. 280 ff.

known. The stockholders of the business corporations that these early state incorporation laws contemplated formed, typically, a small compact group. The members contributed their funds to the venture primarily with a view to its prospects as a long-term investment.[8] They were seldom interested in "trading on the equity." Commonly the majority stockholders were the active managers, devoting full time to the business. Outside stockholders were few, mostly men of wealth personally acquainted with the management or, as residents in the vicinity, in a position to observe how the business was being conducted.

Under such circumstances the grant of the privilege of incorporation generally fostered vigorous competition for trade, as the main highway to profits. But while the promotion of profit-seeking enterprise in manufacture and trade in this way was of public interest, it was obviously not of the same order of importance as the promotion of public utilities. Legislatures, therefore, at first granted the incorporation privilege to ordinary business ventures reluctantly, and subjected such grants not only to the usual conditions attached to corporate charters but also to additional limitations.[9] Of these the most common and significant were limitations on authorized capital and indebtedness, restrictions on the fields and methods of corporate activity, and a prohibition on the investment of corporate funds in the stock of other corporations.

Liberalization of Incorporation Laws

With the rapid spread of general incorporation laws, after the middle of the nineteenth century, these standards were progressively relaxed as the states vied with one another in trying to attract the business of chartering new companies. To make incorporation in a particular state more attractive to corporate promoters than incorporation elsewhere, and thus obtain charter fees and franchise taxes for the state treasury, legislatures found that removing the limitations on corporate activities and powers was more effective than reducing charter fees.

8. E. Merrick Dodd, Jr., "Statutory Developments in Business Corporation Law, 1886–1936," *Harvard Law Review*, November 1936, p. 27.

9. For a succinct review of the development of incorporation statutes, see Mr. Justice Brandeis' dissenting opinion in *Liggett Co.* v. *Lee*, 288 U.S. 517 (1933), at pp. 541-80.

Realizing that most of the corporations they chartered would never do much business within the state, state legislatures in drafting their statutes often ignored the effect on business structure and practices of conferring wide powers on incorporated groups to write their own charters and make their own by-laws.[10] Pennsylvania showed its complete disregard for the interests of other states when it chartered the New York–California Vineyard Company, empowering it to do business anywhere except in Pennsylvania! The legislature of Delaware framed its incorporation laws, not to meet the needs or promote the interests of Delaware business enterprises, but to induce enterprises in other states to apply for Delaware charters—and pay Delaware franchise taxes.

State charter mongering inevitably resulted in extremely broad powers and narrow responsibilities for corporate managers. As Mr. Justice Brandeis observed:

> The removal by the leading industrial states of the limitations upon the size and powers of business corporations appears to have been due, not to their conviction that maintenance of the restrictions was undesirable in itself, but to the conviction that it was futile to insist upon them; because local restriction would be circumvented by foreign incorporation [i.e., by incorporation in other states] . . . The race was one not of diligence but of laxity.[11]

Even before the end of the nineteenth century several states had already eliminated practically all restrictions on the amount or the pattern of capitalization of their corporate creatures, on the variety of business activities in which such corporations might engage, and on their power to acquire and hold stock in other corporations. In some states even the purposes for which corporate income might be used and the ways it might be distributed were subject to such meager limitations that "control groups" could profit at the expense of a mass of passive, inarticulate stockholders.

The lax incorporation laws invited abuses. Business organizers used the broad license these state statutes gave them to consolidate industrial power on a national plane. The corporation became something more than a device for organizing productive enterprise; it became a device for financial aggrandizement and market mastery. Acute contemporary observers recognized the significance of this

10. See William Z. Ripley, *Main Street and Wall Street,* Little, Brown, Boston, 1927, p. 23.

11. *Liggett Co.* v. *Lee,* cited above, pp. 557 and 559.

transformation. Fifty years ago, in a penetrating and prophetic passage, Arthur Twining Hadley declared:

If the managers of an enterprise are allowed to use other people's money while they risk comparatively little of their own, a number of serious evils will inevitably follow. They will persuade the public to engage in enterprises which are doomed to failure in advance, in the hope that they may themselves make a temporary profit out of their management, either in the form of large salaries or of lucrative personal contracts. Or they may so manipulate the finances of the companies which they control, as to make a personal profit out of fluctuations in the value of their securities. These possibilities form a temptation to waste the investors' private capital and, what is far worse, to misuse an appreciable part of the public capital. . . . The latter affects the whole community . . . by preventing the national resources from being properly utilized. This danger is most inadequately met in the United States.[12]

Modern State Incorporation Statutes

In recent decades this inadequacy has become more marked. As Dodd says, the change in incorporation laws since 1890 has been characterized "by the abandonment of any attempt to limit the size of corporations, by the willingness to allow incorporators a very large measure of freedom to determine the character and internal government of their organizations, by the relaxation of earlier restrictions on the consideration for which stock may lawfully be issued." [13] He concludes a detailed survey of this development with the assertion that "the general tendency of our present-day corpora-

12. Arthur T. Hadley, *Economics,* Putnam's, New York, 1896, p. 179. It was hardly an overstatement to add, as the distinguished author did, "Perhaps the most serious among all the evils under which American business suffers is the lack of clear understanding as to directors' responsibility."

Hadley compared American incorporation law with the laws of certain foreign countries, to the disadvantage of the former. Of course, nowhere was the legislation perfect, then or later; but at least national governments abroad recognized their responsibility for establishing standards for the organization and internal administration of corporations that operated throughout the national realm, and beyond. The law-making bodies of such highly industrialized countries as Great Britain and Germany were alert to plug loopholes and correct deficiencies in company law. For example, Parliament undertook thoroughgoing revision of this branch of English law in 1907 and again in 1929. Recently, after a searching investigation of the whole subject by a special committee of the Board of Trade (Cohen Committee), Parliament adopted the major part of its recommendations. These embodied drastic amendments with respect to such matters as disclosure of beneficial ownership of shares, corporate transactions in which directors are interested parties, and especially accounting procedures and the form of financial statements. See *Report of the Committee on Company Law Amendment,* Cmd. 6659, London, 1945, in particular pp. 43-63; also a series of three articles on "The New Companies Act" in *The Economist* (London), March 6, 20, and 27, 1948, at pp. 386, 464, and 513, respectively.

13. Dodd, *op. cit.,* p. 38. Professor Dodd is a leading authority on the law of corporations.

tion statutes is to give permission to promoters to shape articles of incorporation in almost any way that they may desire, and, by means of the language of such articles or that of the statutes themselves, to grant extremely broad powers to the management." [14]

Mr. Justice Rutledge has listed the "outstanding common tendencies" exhibited in recent incorporation statutes as:

> . . . the diminution of visitatorial powers and administrative supervision in the incorporation process, coupled with the introduction of a very large amount of freedom of contract in drafting the articles of incorporation; the general abolition of the old restrictive provisions in regard to capitalization and the authorization of new types, and almost universally unlimited amounts, of security issues; the broad scope of the powers of amendment of the articles with consequent restriction, if not elimination, of the fixed contractual and "vested" rights of the shareholders; the delegation of vastly greater power to the corporation . . . [and] a correlative increase in the powers of the directors . . .

He says that "the principal failure of the modern statutes has been to devise controls adequate for the new powers which they create" and likens the situation to a contemporary high-powered Packard "equipped only with the brakes of a covered wagon." In sum:

> . . . the new incorporation laws follow the lead of Delaware in abrogating the old statutory limitations upon corporate organization and substituting therefor large authorization for incorporators to create their own types of security structures, powers, and limitations . . . They have created a system which . . . is liable to great abuse.[15]

Results of Legislative Laxity

With the states in effect renouncing responsibility for the conduct of their corporate creatures, these fictitious "persons" have become an undisciplined motley of giants and pygmies, bearing little resemblance to their nineteenth-century prototype. At the one extreme

14. *Idem,* "American Business Association Law," in *Law: A Century of Progress,* New York University Press, New York, 1937, Vol. 3, p. 275.

15. Wiley B. Rutledge, "Significant Trends in Modern Incorporation Statutes," *Washington University Law Quarterly,* April 1937, pp. 310, 313, 327, and 337. This article was written shortly before the author's appointment to the Supreme Court. Among many specific examples the author pointed out that "California allows directors to fix or alter dividend rate or redemption value of any class of stock, or the number of shares of any class of stock, in respect of shares then unissued"; and Delaware permits payment of dividends out of annual net profits "even though capital is impaired prior to the payment." Many states sanction charter or by-law provisions expressly authorizing business transactions between the corporation and one or more of its directors, or companies in which one or more directors are personally interested.

are the thousands of closed corporations, personal holding companies, and transitory corporate entities frequently serving some devious purpose.[16] But lax incorporation laws have spawned giants as well as pygmies, and for present purposes this phase of the development is of major interest because it is more directly and integrally related to the concentration of industrial control.

One of the distinctive features of the large modern corporation is the wide diffusion of stockholding, with an attendant divorce of ownership from control. The 200 largest nonfinancial corporations had at the end of the 1930's more than 7 million common-stock holders of record, an average of more than 35,000 per company.[17] The American Telephone and Telegraph Company headed the list with 641,308 shareholdings, followed by Cities Service with 488,988 and General Motors with 363,005.[18] At the bottom of the list stood the Ford Motor Company with only seven common-stock holders; but, as usual, Ford is an exception. For the 200 companies, the average value of the individual shareholdings slightly exceeded $4,000, but half of these 7 million shareholdings had a value per stockholder of less than $500, while two thirds of them had a value of less than $1,000 and represented altogether only 5.6 per cent of the aggregate value of all common-stock issues of the 200 companies.[19] Yet so great is the total capital invested in many of these giant corporations that even the largest block of shares held by any one person or family group amounts to only a small fraction of the equity securities outstanding. Among the 20 largest shareholdings of record in

16. For example, a leading tax authority has recently said: "It is common knowledge that many corporations are organized solely in anticipation of liquidation, so that [accumulated] earnings can escape the surtax. . . . And we have been recently told that liquidation is no longer required. A sale of stock to a subsidiary corporation can defeat the surtax. [He cites *Trustees of the Common Stock of John Wanamaker,* 11 T.C. #48 (1948).] *It is not surprising, therefore, that there are rumblings of dissatisfaction on the ground that the corporate form is being abused."* Jacob Rabkin, "Capital Gains—A Gloomy Introduction," *Proceedings of the New York University Seventh (1948) Annual Institute on Federal Taxation,* Bender, New York, 1949, p. 287. Italics supplied.

17. *The Distribution of Ownership in the 200 Largest Nonfinancial Corporations,* TNEC Monograph No. 29, Washington, 1940, p. 28. The 7 million-odd separate shareholdings in the common stocks of these 200 companies do not mean, of course, that their stockholders comprised that many individuals. Some individuals held stock in more than one of these companies; and some held shares in different classes of common-stock issues of the same company. Included, also, are the shareholdings of other corporations (some within, some outside, the group) in the common stocks of these 200 companies.

18. *Ibid.,* App. III, pp. 206-31.

19. *Ibid.,* Table 72, p. 337.

each of the 200 largest nonfinancial companies, the proportion of the aggregate common-stock holdings of individuals and family groups (as distinct from holdings of other corporations) to the total of such issues outstanding had a median value of 5 per cent.[20] And commonly, of course, the shareholdings of officers and directors in these giant corporations are relatively even smaller. They amounted altogether to only 5.5 per cent of the equity securities of the 200 largest nonfinancial corporations, and the median holding of individual officers and directors was less than half of one per cent of the outstanding stock of the companies they managed.[21]

Corporations having one or more issues listed on a national stock exchange are probably more representative of current American business organization as a whole than the 200 giants. Though diffusion of ownership is less marked, stocks of these "listed" corporations are likewise commonly split up into many small—and some large—holdings. Total shareholdings in 1,710 such corporations at the end of the 1930's were 14 million; of these, 11.5 million were holdings of common stock.[22] The value of the average holding of common stock slightly exceeded $3,000, but 56 per cent of the 11.5 million shareholdings had a value of less than $500. Holdings of a hundred shares and less—with an average value of less than $750—made up 86 per cent of all shareholdings, but only 20 per cent of the total value of common stocks.[23]

Diffused Stockholdings and Rationale of Business Incorporation

A situation in which thousands of small, scattered stockholders provide much of the equity capital but otherwise have no direct connection or intimate acquaintance with the huge corporate enterprises in which they invest their funds greatly weakens the pressure from "owners" for a rigorous accounting from corporate executives and

20. *Ibid.*, p. 89. The average (arithmetic mean) of such large individual (i.e., noncorporate) shareholdings in these 200 giants would be much higher, because of the high proportion of the common stocks of some of these companies closely held by family groups, such as the Mellons, the du Ponts, and the Fords.

21. *Ibid.*, pp. 57-62. The median value of stockholdings of the 2,500 persons in the management group of the 200 largest nonfinancial corporations was only $20,000. These men exercised managerial power over total assets amounting to $70 billion. *Ibid.*, p. 23.

22. *Survey of Shareholdings in 1710 Corporations With Securities Listed on a National Securities Exchange*, TNEC Monograph No. 30, Washington, 1941, p. 7. On the distinction between "shareholdings" and "stockholders," see footnote 17 above.

23. *Ibid.*, pp. 20 and 68.

directors for the way they exercise their delegated powers. And this undermines a basic assumption of a business enterprise system: that those who make the vital decisions on investment, operating, and market policies shall take the consequences. In the corporation, it is true, the direct link between taking risks and making decisions is deliberately broken—to get the advantages of capital funding and large-scale investment along with those of managerial specialization. But the premise of liberal incorporation laws, so far as genuine concern for the public interest had any place in their drafting, was that the connection between taking risks and making decisions could and would be preserved, indirectly, through the regular and full accountability of officers and directors to stockholders and through the stockholders' vigilant supervision of their agents' activities.

The development of giant companies with widely dispersed stockholdings nullified this premise. And the removal of the earlier limitations on the size, structure, and activities of corporations was in large part responsible for wide diffusion of stock ownership. But in part, also, the causal relationship ran the other way: the liberalization of incorporation laws was partly in response to the agitation of the organizers of big business for more autonomy in their industrial empires. Whether as cause or as effect, the emergence of big corporations within a legal environment lacking adequate statutory standards and rules applicable to their internal relationships and methods of operation has created a challenging problem. If incorporation policy and the public policy that relies on free enterprise and competitive markets for running industry are in conflict, they must somehow be reconciled.

Companies like General Motors, United States Steel, Standard Oil, American Sugar, National Biscuit, General Foods, Anaconda Copper, American Telephone, and General Electric are private enterprises in the narrow technical sense that private investors, rather than governmental bodies, "own" their securities and on this basis can claim the residual income, if any, resulting from their operations. But such organizations, with both stockholders and employees frequently numbered in hundreds of thousands and customers in the millions, exercise a coercive power akin to that of sovereign states within their respective domains.[24]

24. Cf. Sigmund Timberg, "Corporate Fictions," *Columbia Law Review,* 1946, p. 535; and *idem,* "International Combines and National Sovereigns," *University of Pennsylvania Law Review,* May 1947, particularly pp. 578-83.

The public cannot afford to ignore such a situation, even though the corporate officers and directors may be exceptionally scrupulous and public-spirited men. To the extent that the income, livelihood, and welfare of large segments of the population depend on how such companies conduct their affairs, manifestly the public has a vital interest in the methods by which, and the standards according to which, directors and top corporation executives exercise their great power. Mr. Justice Douglas declared shortly before his appointment to the Supreme Court:

> Enterprises . . . which command tremendous resources, which hold the fate of whole communities of workers in their hands, which have a virtual or actual monopoly, which dominate markets and control vast resources tip the scales on the side of prosperity or on the side of depression, depending on the decisions of the men at the top. This is tremendous power, tremendous responsibility. Such men become virtual governments in the power at their disposal. In fact, if not in law, they become affected with a public interest. The impact between their stockholders' interest and the public interest at times becomes acute. Incompatibility is often in evidence. This does not necessarily mean that they are enemies of the democratic system. But it does increase the duties of government to police them, at times to break them up, to deter their further growth. And it also means that if their growth continues at the rate of the last few decades capitalism will be eclipsed. For the inherent characteristic of capitalism is competition, individual initiative, freedom of opportunity.[25]

Diffused Ownership and Concentrated Control in Giant Corporations

To safeguard the public interest in a competitive organization of industry, it is manifestly necessary to limit the inducements to concentration of private capital in the corporate form to those that spring from the economic advantages of large-scale production. But charter-mongering states have no compelling interest so to limit corporate privileges and define corporate responsibilities as to facilitate the maintenance of competition, especially outside their borders. Despite the increasing subdivision of corporate stockholdings and the virtual divorce of corporate management and control from ownership,[26] state incorporation laws have continued, in effect, to trust to

25. William O. Douglas, *Democracy and Finance,* Yale University Press, New Haven, 1940, p. 15.

26. In ordinary usage—indeed, even in economic literature—the precise meaning of such terms as "management," "control," and "ownership" is not always clear. In this study, ownership refers to the proprietary relation of those possessing, collectively, the power to liquidate a joint enterprise and a residuary claim on its assets and income. Control refers to the function of *determining* basic operating policies of an enterprise

the presumptive self-interest and vigilance of stockholders to limit the range of a company's activities and the powers delegated to officers and directors and to assure the pursuit of vigorous competitive policies in line with the long-run interests of the enterprise. This unbounded faith overlooks the practical disfranchisement of the mass of small stockholders, and it ignores their qualifications for assessing risks and passing sound judgment on business policies.

In the first place, there is no evidence to suggest that stockholders, large or small, are any less interested in enlarging the field and scale of a company's operations and in acquiring monopoly profits than are corporate officials. Secondly, probably the great majority of the thousands of small stockholders in these industrial giants have neither the aptitude nor the training that would qualify them intelligently to weigh the record or the policy proposals of corporate managers. Even if they were given the appropriate information and a reasonable opportunity, it is doubtful that many of them would have the time to scrutinize closely the conduct of corporate affairs or participate actively in shaping corporate policies. They are, for the most part, typical "absentee owners," interested primarily in dividends or an increase in the value of their capital. Some of them are sheer speculators, "long" on a company's stock today, "short" tomorrow. Such persons are not apt to be the best judges of the long-run interests of an enterprise, and management's loyalty to those interests is not easy to sustain when conflicting private interests are present, as they frequently are.

Courts Improvise a Remedy: Stockholders' Derivative Suits

In the absence of adequate statutory provisions establishing rules of corporate procedure and standards of managerial responsibility, wide latitude was left for misuse of the corporate device. Legislative laxity in this sphere was offset in some small measure by judicial

---

and inheres in those who actually *exercise* the function, regardless of whether they are vested with legal authority to make such decisions. Management refers to the function of *executing,* or carrying out, the basic policies determined by those *in control* of an enterprise, and though the discharge of this function may involve the making of independent decisions on minor details or specific issues, the authority so to act is in logic always a subordinate authority and in practice it is frequently delegated. Of course, management and control may reside in the same person or group. Indeed, management, control, and ownership may all be unified—as they commonly were in early business corporations. But it is the separation of ownership, directly from control and indirectly from management, that works against responsible administration of large corporate enterprises.

alertness. The courts on their own initiative applied the doctrine of trusteeship to the relations of corporation executives to the enterprises they direct.[27] They invoked a fiduciary obligation on corporate directors and officers and afforded relief, through stockholders' derivative suits, for some of the more flagrant corporation abuses that were traceable, at bottom, to lax incorporation laws.[28] But the costliness of such litigation, the formidable technical defenses that severely limit the chances of recovery, the inaccessibility of vital infor-

27. Mr. Justice Douglas outlined the legal duties of corporate managers as follows in a case condemning sequestration of corporate property to defraud creditors: "A director is a fiduciary. So is a dominant and controlling stockholder or group of stockholders. Their powers are powers in trust . . . He who is in such a position cannot serve himself first and his *cestuis* second. He cannot manipulate the affairs of his corporation to their detriment and in disregard of the standards of common decency and honesty. He cannot by the intervention of a corporate entity violate the ancient precept against serving two masters. He cannot by the use of a corporate device avail himself of privileges normally permitted outsiders in a race of creditors. He cannot utilize his inside information and his strategic position for his own preferment. He cannot violate rules of fair play by doing indirectly, through the corporation, what he could not do directly. He cannot use his power for his personal advantage and to the detriment of the stockholders and creditors . . . *no matter how meticulous he is to satisfy technical requirements.*" *Pepper* v. *Litton,* 308 U.S. 295 (1939), at pp. 310-11. Italics supplied.

Mr. Justice Cardozo expressed a similar conception of corporate managerial responsibility in another case involving a comparatively small-scale "inside deal." See *McCandless* v. *Furlaud,* 296 U.S. 140 (1935), at p. 156. In practice, however, the difficulties of enforcing such a legal standard are great, particularly as applied to the administration of large corporate networks. See cases reviewed in the text below.

28. A stockholders' derivative suit is an action in equity, on behalf of the corporation, seeking an accounting for an alleged breach of trust by one or more officers or directors of the company. In principle, the courts of all forty-eight states and the federal courts recognize a fiduciary responsibility of corporate management to the owners of the enterprise. The officers of a corporation are not supposed to make a private, personal profit at stockholders' expense through the use of corporate funds or inside information—at least without full disclosure of their adverse interest. Yet when technical defenses collapse, as they sometimes do, and the decision of a case turns on the merits, the courts frequently condone what looks to the ordinary layman like a plain breach of trust. The reason usually given for a judgment of no cause of action, in such circumstances, is that the officers' action represented simply the exercise of "a sound discretion" or "good business judgment" in the circumstances.

For critical discussions of the nature and limits of stockholders' derivative actions, see: George D. Hartstein, "Rights of Stockholders in the New York Courts," *Yale Law Journal,* June 1947, pp. 942-58; and R. S. Rubin, "Statutory Inhibitions Upon Unfair Use of Corporate Information by Insiders," *University of Pennsylvania Law Review,* March 1947, pp. 468-504, especially p. 469, where the author says that "Contrary to the general impression, apart from the public utility field [where the federal Public Utility Holding Company Act applies], the financial affairs of sizable publicly-owned companies are largely unregulated, leaving the absentee owner-stockholders largely unprotected, except to the extent that the corporation managers *voluntarily* abide by their fiduciary obligations." Italics supplied.

See also a symposium by H. D. Lasswell, A. H. Dean, and D. L. Podell in *Columbia Law Review,* November 1943, pp. 1036-48; M. Koessler, "The Stockholder's Suit: A Comparative View," *Columbia Law Review,* March 1946, pp. 238-54; and Victor House, "Early Exoneration for Delinquent Directors in New York," *Columbia Law Review,* May 1946, pp. 377-90.

mation, and the feeble incentives for eligible complainants to institute remedial proceedings, all combine to make derivative suits a most inadequate method of enforcing fiduciary responsibility on the insiders who control vast corporate networks that they do not own.[29]

With the penalties of disregarding fiduciary obligations so uncertain, stockholders' derivative suits have proved an ineffective deterrent to business policies calculated perhaps to increase the size of a company and the prestige of its executives regardless of their effect on the competitive strength of the enterprise. Occasionally minority stockholders succeed in obtaining sufficient inside information early enough to permit them to intervene to enforce their fiduciary responsibility on corporate directors and officers.[30] But the relief thus obtained is usually small, out of all proportion to the amounts diverted from the company's owners—which diversions may or may not represent monopoly exactions.

Relation of Lax Incorporation Laws to Industrial Concentration

To permit corporation directors and executives, in effect, to define their own powers and responsibilities in the management of other people's money jeopardizes the public interest in several ways.[31] It

29. For a detailed survey of the inadequacy of such suits, see E. Merrick Dodd, Jr., "Is Effective Enforcement of the Fiduciary Duties of Corporate Managers Possible?," *University of Chicago Law Review,* February 1935, particularly the summary, pp. 197-98.

30. See F. S. Wood, *Stockholders' Derivative Suits,* a "Survey and Report" submitted to the Special Committee on Corporate Litigation, Chamber of Commerce of the State of New York, February 5, 1944. Apparently the main object of this report was to show that most such suits are unwarranted and represent an attempt to blackmail wealthy men. See especially pp. 20-25. Notwithstanding this biased approach [cf. House, *op. cit.,* p. 390; George D. Hartstein, "Directors' Expenses in Stockholders' Suits," *Columbia Law Review,* May 1943, p. 315; and the opinion by J. Rifkind in *Brendle* v. *Smith,* 46 Fed.Supp. 522 (1943), at p. 525], the author assembled some valuable data on the frequency and outcome of such litigation. Excluding duplicating actions based on the same facts, he found that in the eleven years 1932–1942 inclusive, 1,266 stockholders' derivative suits, an average of 115 a year or 10 a month, were filed in the Supreme Courts of New York County and King's County, New York, and in the United States District Court for the Southern District of New York (the principal courts having jurisdiction over such actions in New York City). Of these, 597 cases were either still pending or had been discontinued with no record of disposition. Of the 669 cases disposed of, 45, or 6.7 per cent, resulted in recoveries; 287, or 42.9 per cent, were ended by settlement; and 337, or about half, were dismissed. *Ibid.,* pp. 3-7 and App. D. This record is far from suggesting the groundlessness of derivative actions, taken as a class.

31. On the broad social and political issues to which this separation of ownership interests and controlling powers gives rise, see in particular: Adolph A. Berle, Jr., and Gardiner C. Means, *The Modern Corporation and Private Property,* Macmillan, New York, 1932; National Resources Committee, *op. cit.,* Pt. 1, especially Chaps. 7 and 9; and Marshall Dimock and others, *Bureaucracy and Trusteeship in Large Corporations,*

enables them, and even outside groups with which they are affiliated, to benefit personally from corporate transactions out of proportion to their ownership stake in the enterprise, and sometimes even from transactions involving loss to the company and its stockholders. The moral implications of the temptation to chicanery when men occupy such an ambiguous position are not the least of the resultant evils. A community can ill afford to encourage in this way the development of a habit among its leading members of professing one thing and doing something else or of cloaking a self-serving action with a righteous purpose.

But the economic implications of too liberal incorporation laws are of more direct concern to this study. Basically, legislative laxity in this sphere has permitted business corporations to be used not merely as a means of organizing the production and distribution of goods but as a device for strategic financial maneuvers and control of the market.[32] In four principal ways the failure of the states to provide adequate standards and rules for the organization and inter-

---

TNEC Monograph No. 11, Washington, 1940. For analyses of the implications of such a situation more specifically from the standpoint of business administration, consult Paul E. Holden and others, *Top Management Organization and Control,* Stanford University Press, Stanford University, 1941, and Robert A. Gordon, *Business Leadership in the Large Corporation,* The Brookings Institution, Washington, 1945.

The limitations of the strictly business approach, as distinct from the economic, are more evident in Holden's study than in Gordon's. But neither study is realistically addressed to the issue of managerial *responsibility.* Each virtually disregards the question of how the conjunction of large powers of control with small ownership stakes tends to affect the quality or character of business administration from the standpoint of the public interest, that is, as an economic function. They recognize the conflict between the fiduciary and the private interests of management in such circumstances, but they fail to recognize it as an insistent economic problem. Cf., for example, *ibid.,* pp. 49, 57-58, 71 ff., 108 ff., and *passim.*

Moreover, both authors in effect treat the existing business structure as a datum of their investigations. They are preoccupied with how to make it function smoothly, the types of business executive it calls for and pushes forward, and the kinds of managerial incentives it fosters and that are appropriate in the premises. See, for example, Holden, *op. cit.,* Pt. C, but cf. *ibid.,* p. 17; and Gordon, *op. cit.,* Pt. 3. But in the main they ignore the reciprocal relationship between the concentrated—and complicated—pattern of enterprise organization that corporation finance so effectively molds and the way "business leadership," or "top management," functions.

32. Of course, abuse of the incorporation privilege in this way is not universal. Probably most corporations still function primarily as a means of funding private capital for productive enterprise under a management responsible to stockholders and operating in conformity with principles of public policy for the competitive regulation of trade. But looking at the problem from a different vantage point—considering the proportion of corporate-owned assets, rather than the proportion of incorporated business units, that are subject to heavy risks of corporate abuses—one gets a different impression. It is in giant corporations that one sees most clearly the uneconomic consequences of tolerating separation of control from ownership *without providing adequate standards or rules to govern management in lieu of that regular accountability and full responsibility to stockholders* that "liberal" incorporation laws must have contemplated.

nal government of the corporations they charter has weakened competition. It has (1) facilitated industrial consolidation, (2) discouraged venture capital, (3) made it difficult to trace responsibility for monopolistic arrangements and restrictive practices, and (4) provided managerial incentives that tend to deflect business management from the pursuit of competitive advantages.

Mergers Made Easy

The most obvious way in which virtual renunciation by the states of responsibility for the structural pattern or procedural practices of their corporate creatures works to undermine competition is by withdrawing practically all limits on their capitalization, extent of indebtedness, fields of operation, methods of expansion, or types of intercorporate relationships.

When New Jersey in 1889 legalized intercorporate stockholding without restriction on the scope or purpose of such transactions, it opened the way to a combination movement of unparalleled intensity. Corporate consolidation in the technical legal sense of merging the identities of two separate companies by transferring all the assets, either of one to the other or of both to a third (newly incorporated) company, is a slow and cumbersome process. It requires affirmative action by the whole body of stockholders of each of the companies being consolidated. Statutory or charter provisions may require for such approval advance notification of the terms of the proposed transaction and a waiting period between notice and meeting, the assent of more than a majority of one or more classes of stock outstanding, provision for the settlement of creditors' claims, and many other technical formalities. All these steps and attendant delays are obviated when the corporation, whether an operating or a holding company, can simply go into the market and buy up a sufficient number of shares to give it control of another company.

Such stock acquisitions may proceed so quietly that even the directors and officers of the company being taken over may be unaware of what is going on until the company has lost its independence. But the biggest advantage in concentrating control or extending integration through the holding company device is that it costs less. For example, du Pont got control of United States Rubber by buying only 19 per cent of its common stock and of General Motors by buying some 23 per cent of its common stock. These investments were placed in separate holding companies owned jointly by the du Pont family and E. I. du Pont de Nemours & Company, which the family controlled through trust funds and personal holding companies owning, altogether, only a fraction of its outstanding stock. The du Pont family in this way gained control of an industrial empire with aggregate assets of nearly $5 billion.[33] Yet their personal investment in this financial pyramid could not have exceeded 10 per cent of all the capital and was probably less than 5 per cent.

An indirect but important way in which charter-mongering states facilitated the development of giant industrial combines was by authorizing the formation of subsidiaries without limit. By incorporating sales companies, service companies, research companies, trucking companies, and any number of other subsidiaries, each with a comparatively small capitalization, a big company can reduce to a minimum its tax burden and the risks of civil liability suits for the tortious acts of its agents or employees. State incorporation laws place no limits on the number of different corporate guises in which what is for all practical purposes a single business enterprise may operate. If a company could not thus evade or whittle down its tax load and civil liability damages, the rising costs and risks as it increased in size would, in most lines of industry, check expansion long before it approached nation-wide monopoly.

Discouragement to Venture Capital

Since Keynes, economists have generally recognized the importance of a free and unobstructed flow of savings into investment.[34] In a business enterprise regime that relies on competition to regulate economic activity it is especially necessary to encourage investment in equity securities. Venture capital is the lifeblood of a free-enterprise system. Yet if the risks of investment in "equities" are needlessly magnified by adding to the normal, inescapable commercial hazards the risks of mismanagement and diversion of corporate funds by irresponsible insiders,[35] it may make venture capital hesitant and slow up the investment process.

33. See *U.S.* v. *E. I. du Pont de Nemours & Co.*, complaint filed June 30, 1949, in U.S. District Court for the Northern District of Illinois, Civil No. 49C-1071. Whether these transactions constituted a violation of the antitrust laws is the issue raised by this proceeding; but it is beside the point here, where the sole object is to show how the holding company device facilitated industrial combination.

34. See *Cartels or Competition?*, Chap. 7.

35. As used here, the term "irresponsible" means simply that those who make the

The record is replete with instances of abuse of the discretionary power vested in corporate directors and officers, for their own enrichment. And the reference here is not to ordinary peculation by men whose stealthy operations clearly disclose conscious guilt—as in the McKesson & Robbins affair.[36] Rather the abuses in question involve simply the inside manipulation of corporate affairs to the private advantage of controlling groups by methods that comply, or at least appear to comply, with the technical formalities of the applicable incorporation statutes and corporate by-laws. If they infringe the law at all it is only those nebulous standards of fiduciary obligation that a court of equity may invoke at the instance of some disaffected stockholder. As already indicated, any redress obtained through a derivative suit is apt to be small; so insiders busily engaged in feathering their own nests incur a minimum of legal risk.

It would serve no useful purpose here to relate all the details of the many cases in which officers and directors controlling vast properties that they do not own have disregarded stockholders' interests in order to obtain personal rewards commensurate with the extraordinary value they have placed on their own services.[37] It will suffice merely to list some of the outstanding cases of this kind and to give a thumbnail summary of the salient facts and judicial comments. Among the well-known companies involved in such proceedings are American Tobacco, Bethlehem Steel, General Motors, Warner Broth-

---

decisions on corporate business policy neither take the consequences of bad decisions nor are obligated to make a full and regular accounting for their stewardship to those who do take the consequences, that is, the stockholders. The mere fact of the possession of power to make decisions and to carry them out does not make management responsible, as the word is used in this chapter.

36. See Securities and Exchange Commission, *Report of Proceedings in the Matter of McKesson & Robbins,* Docket No. 1-1435, Washington, 1939.

37. Though many directors and officers of giant corporations put their obligations to society at the head of the list and try, doubtless sincerely, to identify self-interest with the abiding interests of their companies and of the community, in the labyrinthine structure of these corporate networks the opportunities for putting a cloak of business expediency on fiduciary dereliction are so great that to resist them unflaggingly takes a sterner and more resolute will than many men possess. Indeed, probably in most cases corporate directors and officers who give short weight to their trusteeship duties and full measure to their private purses are not conscious of wrongdoing. They simply place a high value on their own services. And from one standpoint their appraisal may be sound enough. They commonly "deliver the goods." But even if, by ordinary standards, the "left-over" profits of the corporate empires they rule are high, as they frequently are, that circumstance in no way mitigates the economic evils of irresponsible corporate management. Instead, it underscores those evils. For it indicates the high price the community is paying for sanctioning (or at least not providing adequate measures to prevent) such corporate abuses, through lax incorporation laws.

ers Pictures, National Cash Register, American Metals, and United States Rubber.[38] These are leading enterprises in their respective

38. Through various "Stock Allotment" plans, "Executive Bonus" schemes, and "Special Credits," the president of American Tobacco, who dominated the board of directors, obtained total compensation on a generous scale, amounting in 1930 to $1,283,978 and in 1931 to $2,220,910. *Rogers* v. *Guaranty Trust Co.,* 288 U.S. 123 (1933), held that the court had no jurisdiction to pass on one of the plans; and *Rogers* v. *Hill,* 289 U.S. 582 (1933), held on another bonus scheme that the amounts involved conceivably might be "so large as in substance and effect to amount to spoliation or waste of corporate property." The second decision led to a modification of the plan and an out-of-court settlement after certain new facts came to light, including the payment of a bribe by American Tobacco Company's advertising agency to the federal judge (Judge Manton) before whom the case was being tried. See *In re Levy,* 30 Fed.Supp. 317 (1939); *Rogers* v. *Hill,* 34 Fed.Supp. 359 (1940); and *Heller* v. *Boylan,* 29 N.Y.Supp. 653 (1941).

The directors of Bethlehem Steel distributed over a period of two decades some $36 million of the company's income to its executives, over and above their regular salaries. The leading beneficiaries were also directors of the company, and as the court declared, "The administration of the bonus system has been sedulously suppressed from the stockholders . . ." *Berendt* v. *Bethlehem Steel Corp.,* 108 N.J.Eq. 148 (1931), at p. 150; *Cwerdinski* v. *Bent,* 256 App.Div. (N.Y.) 612 (1939), affirmed, 281 N.Y. 782 (1939); *Zwerdling* v. *Bent,* 264 App.Div. (N.Y.) 195 (1942), affirmed, 291 N.Y. 654 (1943). In *Lyon* v. *Holton,* 172 Misc. (N.Y.) 31 (1939), affirmed, 259 App.Div. (N.Y.) 877 (1940), affirmed in part, 286 N.Y. 270 (1941), a stockholder unsuccessfully challenged the action of Bethlehem directors in offering to repurchase from executives, at the price they had paid for it, stock they had acquired under special option though the repurchase price was 50 per cent higher than the current market price.

After du Pont acquired control of General Motors, the board of directors adopted in 1923 an officers' bonus scheme under which, up to 1930, certain favored executives realized profits amounting to $235 million without risking a dollar of their own funds. Recovery of any part of this huge gift of corporate funds was held in 1942 to be barred by the statute of limitations. *Winkelman* v. *General Motors Corp.,* 44 Fed.Supp. 960 (1942). A modified plan adopted in 1930 had a broader coverage and a more equitable basis, but gave certain special concessions to the original beneficiaries. Regarding this phase of the modified plan, the court said: ". . . the so-called equalization payment of 36,071 shares on February 11, 1931, in which many of these executives shared, was without any legal or moral basis whatsoever and constituted an illegal gift of corporate assets . . . Directors who act for a corporation cannot justify the payment to themselves and other executives of $1,540,830 in Treasury stock on the basis of a 'gentlemen's agreement' *which they have made with themselves.*" *Ibid.,* pp. 970 and 978. Italics supplied. The court also severely criticized certain features of the administration of the modified plan and held the defendant directors legally liable therefor, whereupon they negotiated a voluntary settlement. 48 Fed.Supp. 485 (1942).

When Warner Brothers Pictures, Inc., made a contract with three of its officer-directors, the Warner brothers themselves, to pay them salaries of $520,000 a year, plus an allotment of 90,000 shares of stock with a current market value of $12 million, a timely (for once!) stockholders' derivative suit led to cancellation of the stock allotment and dismissal of the bill. *Koplar* v. *Warner Brothers Pictures, Inc.,* 19 Fed.Supp. 173 (1937).

A voluntary settlement likewise terminated a derivative suit charging that the extra compensation allotted to the chief executive of National Cash Register Co. represented a misappropriation of the corporation's funds. *McQuillen* v. *National Cash Register Co.,* 112 Fed. *2d* 877 (1940).

The American Metal Co. is an offshoot and affiliate of the great German nonferrous metals house, Metallgesellschaft. The American unit appears to have concentrated its operations in the Western Hemisphere. "Through ownership of stock in subsidiary corporations it controlled and had a substantial interest in mining properties, refining plants, oil and gas land leases, coal mines, ships, railway equipment, and other properties in the United States, Peru, Chile, and Mexico . . ." *Turner* v. *American Metal Co.,* 36 N.Y.Supp. *2d* 356 (1942). In 1916 it acquired a "business opportunity" in

fields. All are industrial companies, a class still untouched by federal regulations in respect to corporate powers and corporate setup.[39]

Colorado and in the course of the next year spent, including the option price, about $500,000 on its development. Then, in the words of the court, "a most amazing incident" occurred. A group of officer-directors of American Metal formed a corporation to exploit the new "business opportunity," which was the fabulously profitable Climax Molybdenum Co., holder of a natural monopoly on this rare metal. American Metal, which had thus far put up all the money and assumed all the liabilities, was allotted a 10 per cent interest in Climax, the remaining 90 per cent going to the controlling clique of American Metal officer-directors. But the statute of limitations saved all but one of this group when a stockholder brought suit in 1938, even though he acted promptly on learning of the directors' dereliction of duty.

The United States Rubber Co. likewise suffered from the depredations of its senior executives. And its globe-encircling investments and complex corporate structure afforded ample room for inside manipulation. The court summarized its corporate ramifications as follows: "The company . . . a parent . . . of subsidiaries at one time numbering 35 . . . had 14 subsidiaries located in Canada, 7 . . . for export, and one, U.S. Rubber Plantations, Inc., . . . comprised of 5 corporations; there also were 21 corporations . . . which were carried as an investment." *Diamond* v. *Davis,* 62 N.Y.Supp. *2d* 181 (1945), at p. 188. Shortly after du Pont acquired working control of this corporate network, the board of directors adopted a "Managers' Share Plan," and in 1936 the stockholders, voting mostly by proxy, approved the board's action, previously taken, in granting one of its members, the president of the company, a five-year option to purchase 25,000 shares of the company's stock at $20 a share. This option price was about two thirds the current market price and barely two fifths of the market price in December 1938, when the holder of the option exercised it to the extent of 5,000 shares. The option on the remaining 20,000 shares was later extended to 1946. Meanwhile, a stockholders' derivative suit challenging the deal on the ground that the board of directors could not lawfully divert the corporation's assets to one of its own members resulted in dismissal of part of the charges and voluntary settlement of the remaining causes of action.

39. The discussion here and throughout this chapter refers solely to the use of the corporate device in the industrial field. If it were within the scope of this study, an analysis of corporate management in other fields would show that elsewhere the corporate pyramid builders have been no less active and their cryptic operations no less important.

In fact, among public utilities the art of corporate financial manipulation reached its highest development and led, as is well known, to corrective legislation, the Public Utility Holding Company Act of 1936. In upholding the constitutionality of the "death sentence" provision of this act (Section 11, b, 2), Mr. Justice Murphy recently summarized its background. Speaking of the pyramiding device specifically, he said: "In many instances this created *financially irresponsible managements* and unsound capital structures. Public investors . . . found themselves the innocent victims . . . *Prudent management of the operating companies became a minor consideration,* with pressure being placed on them to sustain the excessive capitalization to the detriment of their service to consumers . . ." *American Power & Light Co.* v. *SEC,* 329 U.S. 90 (1946), at p. 102. Italics supplied. And Mr. Justice Douglas, referring to another public utility holding company reorganization case—*Taylor* v. *Standard Gas & Electric Co.,* 306 U.S. 307 (1939)—approved the Court's drastic ruling because it was "based on . . . the history of spoliation, mismanagement, and faithless stewardship of the affairs of the subsidiary by Standard to the detriment of the public investors." *Pepper* v. *Litton,* 308 U.S. 295 (1939), at p. 308. See also *In re Van Sweringen Co.,* 119 Fed. *2d* 231 (1941); certiorari denied, 314 U.S. 671 (1941).

In the field of banking, also, Congress has provided some regulation, however inadequate, of corporate setups. The Banking Act of 1933, Section 20, prohibits Federal Reserve member banks from being affiliated with securities companies. See Board of Governors of the Federal Reserve System, *Banking Studies,* Washington, 1941, p. 285. This very limited response to the revelations of the Pecora Investigation [*Stock Exchange Practices,* Hearings before the Committee on Banking and Currency, U.S. Senate, 73d Cong., 1st and 2d sess., on S.Res. 84 (72d Cong.) and S.Res. 56 and S.Res. 97

They are not fly-by-night promotions. By accepted standards their chief executives are respectable businessmen.

That, in companies like these, investors run the risk of losing a substantial part of the gains realized by the enterprises they have financed may help explain the growing dearth of venture capital. Apparently people with small incomes who might otherwise invest their savings in equity securities are coming more and more to prefer the guaranteed returns, even at a lower rate, that bonds, savings bank accounts, and life insurance policies offer. It may well be that the spectacular abuses of the corporation as a business institution, rather than the oft-blamed tax structure, have accelerated the shift in popular sentiment from opportunity seeking and risk taking to the quest for security that has been so often remarked in recent years. Incidentally, among the many and varied manifestations of this signal social phenomenon is the widespread adoption of pension and retirement plans by self-perpetuating groups of corporation executives—the reputed archetypes of modern adventurers.

Obstruction of Antitrust Enforcement

The proliferation of corporate entities, including corporate subterfuges, that lax incorporation laws have tolerated, if not indeed fostered, has contributed to the decline of competition by making it difficult to trace the real offenders and hold them responsible. The complicated corporate structure of huge combines provides broad opportunities, not only for manipulating corporate affairs to the private advantage of controlling groups, but also for restraining trade and winning monopoly profits without detection. Antitrust enforcement officials need the ingenuity of Houdini and the persistence of Sisyphus to penetrate to the ultimate seat of authority in many an industry today.

(73d Cong.)] left untouched such abuses as those disclosed in *Gallin* v. *National City Bank of New York,* 273 N.Y.Supp. 87 (1934). The record in that case showed that the bank executives not only received enormous bonuses, kept secret from stockholders, but in computing their bonuses made accounting "adjustments" that greatly increased their "take," by eliminating certain heavy bank losses, without even troubling to get the approval of the board of directors. See *ibid.,* 281 N.Y.Supp. 795 (1935); and George T. Washington, *Corporation Executives' Compensation,* Ronald Press, New York, 1942, pp. 280-84.

A later case, involving syndicate operations of officers and directors of Industrial Finance Corp., holding company for the chain of Morris Plan banks, indicates the inadequacy of the 1933 remedial measures. See *Hauben* v. *Morris,* 255 App.Div. (N.Y.) 35; 5 N.Y.Supp. *2d* 721 (1938); affirmed, 281 N.Y. 652 (1939).

The Swedish Match Company (Svenska Tandsticks Aktiebolaget) provides a good example of the complexity of intercorporate ties, some contractual, some proprietary, and some resting on more shadowy bases that develop as byproducts of charter mongering. The Department of Justice has attempted to unravel this tangled corporate network, with what success remains to be seen.[40] The following companies are among the score or more of corporate entities, subsidiaries, affiliates, and dummies the defendants are alleged to have used to cover up secret transactions, siphon off profits without income-tax liability, deter competitors, restrict investment, and in many devious ways restrain trade.

Berst-Forster-Dixfield Co.	Lion Match Co.
British Match Corp.	New York Match Co.
Bryant & May, Ltd.	Ohio Match Co.
Diamond Match Co.	Swedish Match Co.
Eddy Match Co.	Transamerican Match Corp.
Federal Match Corp.	Universal Match Co.
William Gordon Corp.	Vulcan Match Co.
International Match Co.	West Virginia Match Corp.

The list omits some of the more obscure investment affiliates, banking affiliates, voting trusts, and general agencies of the combine, such as the defunct Kreuger & Toll Co., A. B. Transfer Co., Export A. B. Svalen, and Enskilda Bank (all Swedish enterprises), and Nymco Investment Co. (a Prince Edward Island corporation, subsidiary of New York Match, a subsidiary of Swedish Match), American Far Eastern Match Co. (a Shanghai corporation, subsidiary of Transamerican Match, a subsidiary of Swedish Match), and Agencia de Fosforos Suecos, S. A. (a Guatemalan corporation, another Transamerican Match subsidiary, the combine's key outpost for Central American countries and controlling stockholder in Nile Match Co., an Egyptian corporation).

But who, in the final analysis, pulled the strings in this puppet show? It is a fair question, and it indicates the obstacles to antitrust policy enforcement springing from the unhindered creation of corporations not subject to adequate structural standards, operative rules, or visitatorial powers. Only one who has tried to find his way through one of the labyrinthine corporate structures so characteristic

40. See *U.S.* v. *Diamond Match Co., et al.,* complaint filed May 1, 1944, in U.S. District Court for the Southern District of New York, Civil No. 25-397, consent decree entered April 9, 1946.

of industrial monopoly nowadays can appreciate either the misdirected skill of corporation lawyers or the Herculean task of antitrust enforcement in such situations.

Walton Hamilton has picturesquely but nonetheless realistically stated the problem as follows:

> It is not on record that the dominant intent of the Pharaohs was to enlighten international lawyers; but the pyramiding of corporations has today become a fine art. A large mine in Timquay is owned and operated—not by a Timquayan but—by a Delaware corporation, which is "a wholly owned subsidiary" of a Panamanian corporation, which is a wholly owned subsidiary of a French corporation, which is a wholly owned subsidiary of a Nevada corporation, which is a wholly owned subsidiary of a British corporation, which is a wholly owned subsidiary of a Brazilian corporation. . . . Nor is the phrase "wholly owned" of any real significance. It can be materially compromised without putting corporate dominions in serious jeopardy. In fact the best legal taste condemns the merging of corporate identities in so crude a way. Said an empire builder, new style, to his legal staff, "Forge these corporate ties in so intricate and circuitous a way that no court in the world can unravel the network." [41]

Lax Incorporation Laws and Managerial Incentives

Giving virtually free rein to businessmen to write their own terms into corporate charters assumes that they will have to compete among themselves for investors' dollars and therefore promise—and give—fair treatment to stockholders. It takes for granted the loyalty of corporation executives to stockholders' interests. It also assumes that competition for consumers' dollars, not an altruistic concern for the public welfare, will restrain stockholders' endeavors to maximize profits.

The course of events has undermined these assumptions. The fact is that the complex corporate structures, widely ramified interests, and widespread operations of the giant industrial enterprises fostered by lax incorporation laws have presented continual conflicts between the private interests and the fiduciary duties of those who control but do not own them.

The illustrative cases briefly reviewed above show that, in the absence of adequate legal standards and rules, corporation executives will not always voluntarily adhere to the high moral standards that

41. Walton H. Hamilton, "The Economic Man Affects a National Role," *American Economic Review*, Papers and Proceedings, May 1946, pp. 740-41.

a trusteeship demands. Doubtless the motives of corporation officers and directors in general are as exemplary as those of ordinary men, if that be commendation. But the position executives occupy in the typical large corporation today is not ordinary. It is difficult at best to serve two masters faithfully. It is especially difficult where one master is an inarticulate mass of absentee stockholders, with constantly changing membership, and without cohesive organization or coherent purpose. In such circumstances the habit of listening to the other master's voice develops all too readily.

The significance of all this for the maintenance of competition is not that corporation executives characteristically covet monopoly profits either more or less than do stockholders. It is rather that the opportunities for easy gain from inside manipulation of corporate investment policies, corporate transactions, and corporate accounts deflect the energies of the managers of these corporate networks from ordinary competitive channels. The drive for improving productive techniques, enlarging markets, and increasing real wealth suffers approximately in proportion to the increasing preoccupation with financial maneuvers and inside deals.

At the same time, the bigger and more complex the corporate structure, the larger the body of stockholders, and the fewer the firms constituting an industry, the greater—and safer—are the opportunities for financial manipulation; also, the bigger are its rewards—out of monopoly profits. When two, three, or four corporate giants dominate whole branches of trade, their executives and directors usually find that collaboration pays and competition doesn't. They may have no need for secret understandings, gentlemen's agreements, or conspiratorial arrangements.[42] Self-interest and mutual interest may be so nearly identical—and so clearly so—that collaboration is virtually automatic. None wants, perhaps none dares, to upset the applecart. Each dreads getting a reputation of being a nonconformer, a lone wolf, a "chiseler."

In such an environment forthright competition is taboo. Resolute independence is not good business. It doesn't maximize net revenue. Where small groups of top management officials and bankers con-

42. In *American Tobacco Co., et al.* v. *U.S.,* 328 U.S. 781 (1946), the Supreme Court recognized this fact, probably for the first time. At any rate, it upheld a conviction of the Big Three cigarette manufacturers on a charge of their having conspired to restrain trade, though the jury inferred conspiracy "entirely from circumstantial evidence," as the Court found. See Chap. 6.

trol large corporate enterprises in which their ownership stake, individually or collectively, is small, personal ambition turns easily toward skillful financial maneuvering. Getting big rewards in this way is often easier than through aggressive marketing and unremitting cultivation of productive efficiency. Moreover, it may involve less risk of disesteem among similar cliques of insiders in other corporations, that is to say, among members of the social class to which such business leaders belong. Henry Ford took a different, an unconventional, route to success and reached his goal. But for that very reason, he was anathema to the big-business fraternity in general and to the bankers in particular. There are few Henry Fords.

The further the process of industrial concentration and corporate pyramiding goes, the nearer it approaches to monopoly power, the stronger become the incentives for carrying it still further—and the weaker the incentives for vigorous competition. It is under the lush conditions of noncompetitive trade that the arts of corporate legerdemain can be most safely indulged. Without some protection from the continual threat of commercial displacement, nest-feathering corporation executives might soon have no nests to feather. Nest feathering flourishes in that commercial security most readily achieved by cultivating the status quo in trade and tacitly cooperating in restrictive business policies.

Opportunities for Financial Manipulation a Stimulus to Mergers

Corporate mergers beget more and bigger corporate mergers, partly through imitation and partly as a ready-to-hand means of maintaining the strategic position. The attractive opportunities for playing both ends against the middle that abound in intricate corporate networks have undoubtedly spurred their creation. Likewise, the weakening of competitive impulse by the diversion of the primary interest of corporate management from productive efficiency to financial manipulation has unquestionably stimulated the persistent extension of such corporate networks. A recent case pointedly illustrates both propositions.

Three promoters holding options on the six dry-dock and ship repair plants on New York Harbor devised a plan for merging these properties.[43] After consulting with an "originating group" of three

43. See *Laird* v. *United Shipyards, Inc.,* 163 Fed. 2d 12 (1947). (The case will hereinafter be cited: *Laird* v. *United.*) The District Court's opinion (U.S. District

bankers who approved the project, they organized United Dry Docks in December 1928. The chief promoter, one Powell, who became president of United Shipyards, testified that:

> The whole idea [was to] get all of the large companies into one consolidation. . . . The basis of the whole entire consolidation was that we had to get everybody or the plan fell of its own weight, because any one of the companies operating as an independent could have broken down the [drydock] rates.[44]

The bankers were interested in the project partly as underwriters. They underwrote the sale of 450,000 shares of United Shipyards common stock, for which the public paid $22 a share and the company received $20 a share, leaving $900,000 for bankers' fees. However, two of the "originating group" of bankers had other irons in the fire. One was John E. Aldred. His firm, Aldred & Company, owned a one-half interest in the New York Harbor Dry Dock Company, which was one of the plants United Shipyards acquired. This company had sustained heavy losses for several years. The other was Albert Wiggin. The Chase National Bank, of which he was chairman of the board, held notes payable of another constituent company amounting to about $700,000. This concern was in receivership at the time.

After the organization of United Shipyards but before the issuance of the stock, the bankers formed a syndicate and sold to private investors interim certificates issued by the Chase Bank, which acted as trustee for the subscribers, from whom the syndicate collected $9,900,000. After turning over to United Shipyards $9,000,000 of this sum in exchange for the 450,000 shares, but before distributing the stock to the subscribers against their interim certificates, the Chase Bank gave Powell, Rogers, and Morse, directors of United Shipyards, a proxy to vote the stock at a "stockholders' meeting." Under this authority the promoters and Morse accepted the promotors' offer to turn over to United Shipyards the six options that

---

Court for the Southern District of New York, Civil No. 10-404) sets out the facts more fully. Rendered on August 14, 1943, it is unreported, but the Appendix to Appellant's Brief on appeal to the Circuit Court of Appeals (2d Circuit) reproduces it in full: Vol. 2, pp. 1230-50. United Dry Docks, Inc., became United Shipyards, Inc., in 1936 after reorganization under Section 77b of the Bankruptcy Act.

44. *Laird* v. *United*, Transcript of Record, pp. 210-11. Powell's lawyer, one Rogers, was also one of the promoters. He became counsel of United Shipyards. The third promoter was one Farley, a business associate of E. P. Morse, president of one of the companies merged in United Shipyards.

they held. Part of the consideration for this deal was the issuance to the promoters of 4,400 shares of United Shipyards preferred stock, with a par value of $440,000.[45] This emolument was in addition to their promoters' fees of $60,000 and their share of the commissions, as minor participants in the banking syndicate and selling group, amounting to $34,895. The prospectus for the public sale of the shipyard company's stock "when, as, and if issued" not only made no mention of the contemplated issuance of this preferred stock to Powell and Rogers but clearly implied (contrary to fact) that United Shipyards itself already owned the options.[46]

Shortcomings of Derivative Suits Illustrated

When, ten years later, a stockholder who was one of the original subscribers to the stock learned about the secret deals attending the formation of the company, he brought a derivative action seeking an accounting.[47] The District Court gave judgment for the defendants, on the merits, and on appeal to the Circuit Court of Appeals that court affirmed the judgment but placed its ruling on a different ground.[48] It held that the ten-year rule of the New York statute of limitations barred the action, there being no fraud because, forsooth, the "stockholders" in 1929 had been fully apprised of all the facts and had approved the transactions of which the plaintiff complained.[49] But the "stockholders" who were informed of the facts and who approved the transactions were not the equitable owners of the stock, the people who had put up the money, the holders of the interim certificates. They were the officers and directors of the

45. These shares were nominally issued to Powell and Rogers because they took over underlying mortgages of two of the constituent companies. But these mortgages, being prior liens on properties United Shipyards acquired, presumably had a value approximating the amount of the debts they secured. Even the common stock of United Shipyards sold at a 10 per cent premium over the book value of the merged properties. Moreover, apparently these mortgages eventually paid out in full. See *ibid.*, Ex. 58, Appendix to Appellant's Brief in the Circuit Court of Appeals, Vol. 2, p. 880.

46. *Ibid.*, pp. 711-13, which contain a facsimile reproduction of the prospectus (Ex. 17). See also Appellant's Brief in the Circuit Court of Appeals, pp. 10-11.

47. He complained, also, of certain later transactions, wherein Rogers, he alleged, profited to the extent of more than $100,000 at the expense of the company. See *ibid.*, paragraphs 75-78 of amended complaint, reproduced in Appendix to Appellant's Brief in the Circuit Court of Appeals, Vol. 1, p. 46.36.

48. *Laird* v. *United.* Certiorari denied, 332 U.S. 842 (1947).

49. On the authority of *Old Dominion Copper Co.* v. *Lewisohn,* 210 U.S. 206 (1908), and of *Reno* v. *Bull,* 226 N.Y. 546 (1905). But in the Old Dominion case the promoters held the stock in their own right at the time of the transaction complained of. In the instant case, the Chase Bank held the stock as a trustee for the ultimate, beneficial owners.

Chase Bank, which held the stock as a depositary, a trustee for the real stockholders. And, of course, the Chase Bank was itself a party to the promotion and organization of United Shipyards.

With all the scheming and inside manipulation, it is not surprising that United Shipyards did not prosper. Its business was unprofitable from the beginning.[50] After its reorganization in 1936 under Section 77b of the bankruptcy law it was "saved" by the negotiation of a new consolidation with the Bethlehem Shipbuilding Company. It became, thus, part of a much larger corporate enterprise, the Bethlehem Steel Corporation, linked to an even more comprehensive network of financial and industrial power.

Remedial Programs for Perversion of Corporation Device

The simplest and most effective way to put a stop to manipulation of corporate affairs for the benefit of insiders would be to impose definite—and far more rigorous—statutory standards on the eligibility, powers, and obligations of corporate officers and directors. Rules relating to their "eligibility" would deal, among other things, with executives' affiliations with banking houses. Rules relating to executives' "powers" would severely limit, among other things, their rights to negotiate transactions between corporations they control and themselves, as individuals or private groups. Rules relating to their "obligations" would prescribe, among other things, a full and frank periodical accounting for their stewardship, if not directly to all stockholders at least indirectly to visitatorial committees independently elected by, and representing, each class of stock—as Mr. Justice Rutledge and others have proposed.[51] These suggestions merely indicate the wide scope for corrective legislation.

The difficulty with such a program is that it is impracticable as long as forty-eight different states continue to compete for the "business" of chartering corporations that operate mainly on an interstate basis and are largely owned by stockholders resident in other states than the one that grants the charter. Every state has a "hip-pocket"

50. *Laird* v. *United,* Brief of Appellees (Rogers and Powell) in the Circuit Court of Appeals, p. 13.

51. See Rutledge, *op. cit.,* p. 342. A slightly different suggestion is to set up a quasi-public, disinterested research bureau, voluntarily financed on a cooperative basis, to keep a check on corporate management and to report directly to nonmanagement stockholders. See Harold D. Lasswell, "A Non-Bureaucratic Alternative to Minority Stockholder Suits," *Columbia Law Review,* November 1943, p. 1036.

interest in getting charter fees and corporation franchise taxes. As long as some states, such as Delaware and Nevada, have virtually no direct, local interest to serve by stipulating more definite and higher standards of management for the hundreds of corporations they charter to do business elsewhere, it would do other states little good to adopt such measures. For corporate promoters would simply go to the states offering the widest latitude for corporate executives' discretion, as in fact they generally do now. State charter mongering, therefore, effectively blocks any real progress toward ending such evils as corporate financial manipulation, corporate pyramiding, and the like.

In these circumstances, the only promising approach to the problem of checking corporate abuses and restricting the corporation device to its legitimate uses is through an exertion of the dormant federal power to prescribe conditions for the structure and administration of business corporations engaged in interstate commerce.[52] The government might establish appropriate standards of corporate organization and corporate management directly by means of a federal incorporation law. Or it might reach the same goal indirectly, by requiring that charters and by-laws of companies incorporated under state laws and engaged in interstate commerce should measure up to specified standards. Congress has already taken some steps in the latter direction by subjecting corporations with securities listed on "national stock exchanges" to certain statutory rules and to administrative regulations of the Securities and Exchange Commission promulgated thereunder.

SEC Regulation of Corporate Financial Practices

In four principal matters the Securities and Exchange Act either establishes definite standards of corporation practice or authorizes

52. Not absolutely "dormant," of course, but relatively so in the fields here under discussion: manufacturing, mining, and trade. Congress has used the commerce power for this purpose most extensively in the comparatively narrow field of public utilities (including railroads). The Transportation Act of 1920, as amended, gives the Interstate Commerce Commission wide powers over corporate consolidation, financial operations, and accounting practices of carriers. See Interstate Commerce Commission, *Interstate Commerce Commission Activities, 1887–1937,* Washington, 1937, pp. 168 ff. The Public Utility Holding Company Act of 1935 establishes strict standards for the corporate structure and financial methods of companies subject to the Act and empowers the Securities and Exchange Commission to promulgate suitable accounting standards. See Securities and Exchange Commission, Tenth Annual Report, *A Ten-Year Survey, 1934–1944,* Washington, 1945, Pt. 3, pp. 83-119.

the Securities and Exchange Commission to issue rules for the purpose. These matters are: (1) disclosure of ownership by corporation executives and large stockholders; (2) penalization of in-and-out trading in the corporation's securities by such persons; (3) solicitation of proxies; and (4) use of manipulative or deceptive devices in securities trading.

Section 16 of the Act covers the first two subjects. The requirement of regular reports to the Commission on changes in the stockholding position of the persons specified has the main purpose of facilitating enforcement of the ban on short-term trading in corporate securities by insiders. The Commission summarizes the background and the result of these regulations as follows:

> Prior to the enactment of the Securities Exchange Act, profits from "sure thing" speculation in the stocks of their corporations were more or less generally accepted by the financial community as part of the emolument for serving as a corporate officer or director notwithstanding the flagrantly inequitable character of such trading. . . . There is no doubt but that short-term trading by insiders has become very much less common than formerly.[53]

The Commission's rules concerning proxy solicitation have undergone a steady, progressive development since 1935. These rules have substantially modified the traditional practice of keeping proxy machinery firmly in the hands of existing management and soliciting blanket authority from stockholders to vote on virtually anything and in any way that the proxy holder might choose. The existing rules give nonmanagement stockholders fair access to proxy machinery, require detailed specification of, and adequate information on, each matter on which the proxy may be used and an opportunity for the stockholder to stipulate how his vote shall be cast on each question. Probably recent years have witnessed comparable improvement in no other aspect of corporate administration. The Commission does not exaggerate in stating that "the rules have already made a contribution to a revitalization of the democratic process in the conduct of corporate affairs."[54]

The outstanding case applying the rule against the use of manipulative and deceptive devices in stock trading illustrates both the need for such a rule and its salutary effect. It involved the Ward

53. *Ibid.*, p. 50.
54. *Ibid.*, p. 53.

LaFrance Truck Corporation. The Commission has neatly summarized it.

In that case, two officers who were in control of Ward LaFrance entered into negotiations with another corporation with a view to selling their interest and merging Ward LaFrance with the purchasing corporation. The two officers, after it appeared probable that the deal would be consummated, and well aware of the figures at which it probably would be made, authorized a broker to buy the Ward LaFrance shares in the over-the-counter market for Ward LaFrance's account. Shares were obtained from the company's stockholders at prices ranging from approximately $3 to $6 a share. None of the stockholders who sold their shares was advised that Ward LaFrance was the ultimate buyer. Nor were they told of the negotiations to sell the controlling shares at approximately $45 a share, or of the proposal to liquidate Ward LaFrance at a figure which would give shareholders $25 a share on liquidation. Also withheld from them was the fact that the company's earnings had improved since the last published statement from $2.75 to $15.75 a share. . . .

When the Commission brought these facts to the attention of the parties involved, arrangements were made to pay the stockholders who had sold their shares the difference between $35.98 per share and the price they had received in selling their shares.[55]

Gaps in Regulation of Corporate Financial Manipulation

Notwithstanding the notable advance made under the Securities and Exchange Act toward checking the perversion of the corporation device, serious deficiencies remain in the existing system of regulation. First, the SEC regulations apply solely to corporations having securities listed on a registered stock exchange.[56] Thousands of corporations are wholly exempt from these rules. Some exempt corporations are among the 200 largest corporations in the country.[57] The fact that a corporation's stock may be closely held, so that list-

55. *Ibid.*, p. 82.

56. See "New Civil Liability Under Securities and Exchange Act Rules," *University of Chicago Law Review,* April 1947, pp. 471-79. After noting that Sections 19(b) and 16(a) of the Securities and Exchange Act (1934), respectively prohibiting "manipulative" or deceptive "devices" and requiring an accounting for profits from "in-and-out" trading in a corporation's securities by its officers or directors, apply only to corporations with securities listed on national stock exchanges, the author points out (p. 472) that "Only in a minority of [state] jurisdictions is a duty of disclosure and fair dealing placed on directors in their transactions in the corporation's securities with its stockholders."

57. Outstanding examples are Ford, Alcoa, and A & P. SEC is reported to be studying means of extending its jurisdiction over such companies. If the project materializes, it would probably bring under regulation several somewhat smaller (but by no means diminutive) companies, including American Optical Co., Ideal Cement Corp., and Time, Inc. See *Wall Street Journal,* April 29, 1949, p. 1.

ing is considered useless, does not prevent dereliction of duty among its officers and directors.

Secondly, because of the nature and limited objective of its organic act, the scope of SEC rules and regulations is confined to matters relating to corporation *securities.* Managerial powers of corporation executives are much broader in scope than that. It would be difficult to distinguish, in principle, between in-and-out trading in tin on the commodity exchanges by an official of a large tin can company and in-and-out trading by the same official in his company's stock on the stock exchange. Yet the former type of manipulative dealing on the basis of confidential information is wholly beyond the reach of SEC rules and regulations.

Thirdly, even within the sphere in which the Commission has jurisdiction and exercises its administrative powers, the opportunities for evasion of existing rules are many. For example, the requirement that insiders must forfeit to the company any profit realized from short-term trading in securities of the company in which they occupy a fiduciary position does not, on its face at least, apply to profits that such an insider's brother or cousin may make from speculative operations based on confidential information obtained from the same source. Nor does the SEC rule, as it stands, forbid an officer of corporation A from giving to an officer of corporation B timely hints on the still unpublished earnings of corporation A in exchange for like information about corporation B. Each of these officers may then speculate with impunity in the stock of a company with which he has no direct connection but about the financial affairs of which he has more and later information than any of its long-standing stockholders.

The foregoing exposition suggests the advantages of a federal incorporation law, obligatory on all business enterprises above a specified size engaged in interstate commerce. Congress would then be responsible directly for enforcing a simplified structure and responsible management on the giant corporate enterprises that draw their capital funds from, and sell their products in, all parts of the country—enterprises, in short, that are the warp and woof of the national economy. And Congress would be in a position to discharge that responsibility, as neither federal nor state government is under the existing scheme of hit-or-miss regulation.

Chapter 14

PATENTS AND MONOPOLY

PUBLIC POLICY has long recognized the intimate relation between a dynamic technology and a well-adjusted economy. Without experiment, industrial arts stagnate. Rightly understood, invention is synonymous with improvement in the industrial arts, and invention comes about only from experimenting. Not every inventor finds what he is looking for, true enough, or is looking for what he finds. But unless, consciously or unconsciously, he is seeking a new way to do something or a new "combination of matter" he will never discover anything.

To encourage experiment and thus foster technical improvement is the avowed purpose of the American patent system. The men who wrote the Constitution did not mention "patents," but they did authorize Congress "To promote the Progress of . . . useful Arts." The Constitution, moreover, specifies how this power, alone among the enumerated powers of Congress, shall be exercised. It limits congressional discretion in the choice of means for accomplishing the stated end to "securing for limited Times to . . . Inventors the exclusive Right to their . . . Discoveries." [1]

1. Art. I, Sec. 8, par. 8. A common mistake is to associate the constitutional authorization to promote the progress of "Science" with the grant of patents to "Inventors." But the branch of knowledge now called science was in the eighteenth century termed natural philosophy. As the men who drafted the Constitution used the term, "Science" embraced all knowledge. If the eighth paragraph of Sec. 8, Art. I, had been divided into two paragraphs, instead of covering both copyrights and patents in a single paragraph, these would have read:

"8a. To promote the Progress of Science, by securing for limited Times to Authors the exclusive Right to their Writings.

"8b. To promote the Progress of useful Arts, by securing for limited Times to Inventors the exclusive Right to their Discoveries."

In his dissenting opinion in *U.S.* v. *Line Material Co.*, 333 U.S. 287 (1948), p. 332, Mr. Justice Burton makes a comparable division but limits it, unfortunately, to the instrumental phrase beginning "by securing . . ." No reason is suggested, and in fact none exists, for not carrying the same division straight through the substantive clause itself, as in the paraphrase of this section (8a and 8b) above. Even so discriminating a scholar as Walton H. Hamilton missed this point. See his pamphlet, *Patents and Free Enterprise,* TNEC Monograph No. 31, Washington, 1941, p. 1. (This monograph will hereinafter be cited: Hamilton, *Patents.*)

Origins of Patent System

England for more than a century and a half prior to the writing of the United States Constitution had recognized the great advantage for industrial development of encouraging inventors with limited-term monopolies. The famous Statute of Monopolies of 1623 explicitly exempted from its sweeping proscription of exclusive privileges those patents given inventors for introducing "any manner of new Manufacture within this Realm." [2] Parliament, it is clear, made the grant of monopoly privileges to inventors an exception to the general rule.

Free access to all technological methods of established trades was made inviolable. Not subject to the let or leave of anyone was the right of an Englishman, if entitled to practice any trade, to practice it as others customarily practiced it. Such was the meaning of the Statute of Monopolies. But so important was it thought to be for innovators to discover new ways of making things or new things to make that Parliament undertook to stimulate such activity by offering to traders, for devising a novel "manner of manufacture," what immemorial experience indicated they most coveted: freedom *from* competition.

Lest the monopoly privileges of inventors become an obstruction to the general freedom of trade and a drag on progress—in short, lest the exception become the rule—the statute limited the life of patents for invention to fourteen years.[3] Parliament apparently reasoned that such a period was sufficient to enable infant industries to acquire strength to stand on their own feet without benefit of a public franchise.

Changes in the Nature of Invention

The distinctive features of the American patent system derive from the circumstances surrounding its origin. Since it originated

2. 21 James I, c. 3, Sec. V (1623).

3. Until the middle of the nineteenth century, both in England and America, grants of exclusive privileges, whether in the form of patents for invention or of copyrights, were always for a period representing some multiple of 7 years. The original copyright statute, 8 Anne, c. 19 (1709), specified a term of 14 years, renewable for the same term. In the United States, the 14-year term applied to both copyrights and patents at first, though copyrights were subject to renewal for another 14 years. In 1831, the initial copyright period was extended to 28 years. The 17-year term of patents was adopted in 1861. It represented a split-the-difference compromise between those who wanted a flat extension of the term to 20 years and those who wanted simply to eliminate the discretionary 7-year extension that Congress had authorized in 1836.

when handicraft was characteristic of technology, it was adapted to the discovery and improvement of tool-using techniques.[4] For this purpose it looked to the initiative and resourcefulness of *individuals*. And it did not look to them in vain. Under then existing conditions, invention involved tinkering with tangible things. Commonly, it was not a full-time job. Rather, it was a side line, often a mere pastime.

The patent system contemplated that the artisan at his bench or the manufacturer familiar with certain productive processes would from time to time hit upon a short cut, or perhaps devise some new method.[5] It was presumed that he would himself make commercial use of his discovery and, armed with a patent, prevent others from using it.

At the same time, in view of the comparatively slow advance in a technology still dominated by manual skill, improvements subject to patent seemed unlikely to be frequent or radical enough to enable an inventor to monopolize an entire branch of industry. Others, it was assumed, would continue to make and sell the same product in the traditional way, or to make and sell conventional products for which a patented product was only a substitute. Thus competition would not disappear, and "going concerns" would be in a position to utilize the invention when the patent expired. In the days of slow, costly transport and local markets, this was not an unjustified assumption. Under such conditions there was no anomaly in offering a public reward to a "true and *sole* inventor."

The growth of corporate enterprise and the prodigious development of physical science in the nineteenth century led to a gradual eclipse of the independent inventor. In the first place, ready access

4. The explanation of the original selection of a 14-year term for patents in 1623 is found mainly in the circumstance that the conventional period of apprenticeship for most crafts under the guild system as regulated by the Statute of Apprentices (1563) was seven years. Parliament probably considered that the introduction of a new trade and its establishment on a sure footing required training in the new art of more than a single complement of artisans. With two "classes" of full-fledged journeymen from which to recruit a corps of workers, there would be opportunity for an enterprising master to set up shop for himself and provide effective competition in the practice of the invention.

5. See J. C. Stedman, "Invention and Public Policy," *Law and Contemporary Problems*, Autumn 1947, especially p. 678. It is significant that the patent system first appeared in an era when the only resources on which inventors could draw, other than the knowledge derived from practice and observation, were those of a "natural philosophy" which was an avocation, chiefly, of schoolmasters and clergymen. When the United States patent system was established even the atmosphere was still empty space, except for Priestley's "phlogiston."

to current technological usage was blocked by the concentration of production in most industries under the control of comparatively few large corporations representing a heavy capital investment. Such enterprises do not usually open their facilities to the experiments of outside "inventors" with a roving curiosity.

The change in the qualifications and equipment necessary for significant invention also restricted the opportunity for casual experimentation by individuals. The progress of science made available for technological adaptation a bewildering assortment of obscure chemical reactions, subtle biological processes, invisible electrical phenomena, and elusive kinetic forces. The mastery of these varied and cumulatively complex scientific advances, to subdue them to industrial application, was not a task for lone inventors, however versatile. It called for well-financed, systematically organized, and highly specialized research in elaborately equipped laboratories.

Invention in the twentieth century became, therefore, characteristically a group process.[6] It is a misleading legal fiction to assume, as do the patent laws, that some "true and sole inventor" can be found who alone is responsible for every discovery issuing from the highly articulated experiments of a great industrial laboratory employing scores, even hundreds, of technicians.

Safeguards Against Patent Perversion

Radical changes, both in technology and in the organization of industry, have so altered the nature of invention and the economic position of inventors as to cast strong doubt on whether patents are a suitable stimulus to individual experimentation and innovation under modern conditions. Though the patent system today still serves this basic purpose, it tends to funnel the major benefits of the monopolistic privileges it creates into the hands of large corporations, which find these grants useful as an adjunct and aid in restraining competition.

Quite apart from these fundamental changes in the institutional environment, patents are a rather awkward way of stimulating and

6. See Alfred E. Kahn, "Deficiencies of American Patent Law," *American Economic Review,* September 1940, especially pp. 478-82; James B. Conant, "The Place of Research in Our National Life," *Harvard Business Review,* January 1948, especially pp. 50-51; Sylvester Petro, "Patents: Judicial Developments and Legislative Proposals," *University of Chicago Law Review,* December 1944, and June 1945, especially pp. 352-81 of Pt. 2; and Hamilton, *Patents,* pp. 43-44.

rewarding inventors, even in an economy made up mainly of small-scale enterprises using handicraft techniques and catering to local markets. The founders of the American patent system were aware of the dangers inherent in governmental grants of monopoly privileges in any economy that depends on free enterprise and competition to protect the public interest. They tried to guard against those dangers.

The most obvious safeguard was the limitation of patent grants to fourteen years. Another was the requirement of disclosure; the law required a patent applicant to specify exactly what he claimed to have discovered "to the end that the public may have the full benefit thereof after the expiration of the patent term." [7]

A third safeguard was the restriction of the subject matter of patentable invention to technological devices. The words of the original patent act of 1790 clearly reflect congressional intent to limit in this way the discoveries or contrivances eligible for patents. The statutory definition embraced any "useful art, manufacture, engine, machine or device, or any improvement therein, not before known or used." [8] These terms connote technological advance; they

7. For citations of the early patent statutes and general information on the development of legislative policy and administrative practice, see "Outline of the History of the United States Patent Office," *Journal of the Patent Office Society,* 1936. The Society published this useful study serially on the centenary of the basic statute still in force, the Act of July 4, 1836.

Both the first (1790) and second (1793) patent acts required enough disclosure to distinguish the alleged invention from the prior art. The third (1836) went further. It required the specification of "claims," a detailed differentiation from the elements "before known or used" of "the part, improvement, or combination which he claims as his own invention or discovery." Thus it put the responsibility on the inventor to winnow the grain from the chaff. If he "claims" as his invention more than what is novel, the Patent Office may reject his application, or require its amendment. And if a patent issues with a claim broader than the invention, the courts may invalidate it. "The claims measure the invention." *Continental Paper Bag Co.* v. *Eastern Paper Bag Co.,* 210 U.S. 405 (1908), at p. 419. See also *General Electric Co.* v. *Wabash Appliance Corp.,* 304 U.S. 364 (1938); and *Funk Bros. Seed Co.* v. *Kalo Inoculant Co.,* 333 U.S. 127 (1948), reversing 161 Fed. *2d* 981. The majority opinion in the Wabash case and the concurring opinion by Mr. Justice Frankfurter in the Kalo case held the particular patents invalid on the ground that the patentee failed clearly to specify the novel elements in his invention.

8. The second (1793) patent act substituted "composition of matter" for "device." This change was apparently designed to cover new chemical compounds. It did not modify the emphasis of the original definition on novel technological contributions. Subsequent judicial and administrative interpretations of the definition have broadened the scope of patentable subject matter to embrace contrivances of every kind—even consumable commodities—provided they are "new and useful." See J. B. Waite, *Patent Law,* Princeton University Press, Princeton, 1920, pp. 25-26.

The only subsequent changes in the statutory scope of patentable subject matter were an amendment of 1842 authorizing patents for designs and an act of 1930 that included new varieties of botanical plants. The propagation of hybrid plants is doubtless

carry no suggestion of permitting monopoly privileges for new toys, medicines, or other consumable commodities. Finally, the law authorized administrators to issue patents only for inventions that were, in their judgment, "sufficiently useful and important" to warrant a monopoly grant.

Broadening the Scope of Patentable Invention

Congress later abandoned this prerequisite for a patent. In 1793 it adopted the so-called registration system, under which the patent issues as a matter of course if the application is in proper form.[9] The issuance of the patent is merely a ministerial act, not conditioned by any examination for novelty or judgment on utility. Among the leading industrial countries, France alone still follows this procedure.

The registration system continued until 1836, when Congress restored the examination system. "Examination" in the Patent Office means simply review of the prior art (as disclosed nowadays chiefly in technical publications) to determine whether the alleged invention has been *anticipated*. The courts, moreover, have upheld the

---

a "useful Art," but mere ornamentation is in a different category. Nevertheless, a Supreme Court solicitous of property rights and tolerant of their rapid extension into the public domain upheld the design-patent law. *Gorham Manufacturing Co.* v. *White*, 14 Wall. 511 (1872). It did so notwithstanding an express finding that the act was "plainly intended to give encouragement to the *decorative* arts" and that "giving certain new and original appearances to a manufactured article *may enhance its salable value.*" *Ibid.*, p. 524. Italics supplied. It apparently escaped the notice of the Court that, however laudable such an object may be, it does not lie within the constitutional powers of Congress, or, if so, at any rate not within the specific grant in Art. I, Sec. 8, par. 8.

Decorative designs are still subject to patent, though even those who want design protection recognize the anomaly and have long sought eligibility to copyright, instead. See, for example, *Design Protection*, Hearings before the Committee on Patents, House of Representatives, on H.R. 5859, 74th Cong., 1st sess., 1935. The same situation exists in England. See *Patents and Designs Acts*, Final Report of the Departmental Committee, Board of Trade, Cmd. 7206, London, September 1947.

9. Jefferson was mainly responsible for the adoption of the registration system, but he favored it, not because he thought the test of usefulness was unnecessary, but because as Secretary of State, charged with the chief responsibility for applying the test, he found it took too much time from more important duties. He said, "I know well the difficulty of drawing a line between the things which are worth to the public the embarrassment of an exclusive patent, and those which are not." He had seen "with what slow progress a system of general rules could be matured." To relieve the heads of executive departments of this burdensome task he suggested it be "turned over to the judiciary to be matured into a system." Even so, he expressed misgivings about the efficacy of this procedure. He considered lawyers poorly qualified for such a function, which "is more within the information of a board of academical professors, and a previous refusal of patent would better guard our citizens against harassment by lawsuits." The characterization of "Sage of Monticello" was well earned! See *The Writings of Thomas Jefferson*, memorial edition, Washington, 1904, Vol. 13, pp. 335-37.

practice of the Patent Office in basing the test of "sufficient" usefulness and importance merely on the absence of inutility. Justice Story's dictum in an early case has become settled doctrine: ". . . the word 'useful,' therefore, is incorporated into the act in contradistinction to mischievous or immoral." Consequently, for over a century the Patent Office has gone on issuing patents on frivolous inventions, in this respect continuing the same practice that developed under the registration system.[10]

Original Safeguards Against Abuses Weakened

The designers of the original patent system, then, plainly sought to provide one that would conform closely to its constitutional mandate: to promote, and not obstruct, "the Progress of . . . useful Arts." Each of the specified safeguards recognized by implication that patent monopolies are in some respects anomalous in a predominantly competitive, free-market economy and recognized that the practical problem is one of balancing the advantages of promoting invention against the disadvantages of restricting competition.[11] The first Congress showed determination to limit such special privileges to the minimum consistent with encouragement of technological experimentation. Later Congresses have not hewed so closely to the constitutional line. Every one of the four safeguards mentioned

10. *Lowell* v. *Lewis,* 15 Fed. Cases 1018 (1817), at p. 1019. See the testimony of Dr. Waldemar Kaempfert, science editor of the *New York Times,* in *Pooling of Patents,* Hearings before the Committee on Patents, House of Representatives, on H.R. 4523, 74th Cong., 1st sess., 1935, pp. 874 ff. As an example of frivolous patents, he mentioned the pedal calorificator, a device for warming one's feet by exhalations of the lungs conducted from the nostrils through tubes!

11. The short-run problem is complex; the long-run problem is even more so. No one can be sure to what extent patent monopolies accelerate technological advance and the investments required to make its fruits available to society. Schumpeter thinks patent monopolies may lure risk capital into enterprises that otherwise would not be launched. See Joseph A. Schumpeter, *Capitalism, Socialism, and Democracy,* Harper, New York, 1942, Chaps. 7 and 8. Veblen, Ogburn, and Ayres hold that the cumulative nature of technology makes technological innovations practically inevitable. See Thorstein Veblen, *The Place of Science in Modern Civilization,* Huebsch, New York, 1919, "On the Nature of Capital," pp. 324-86; William Fielding Ogburn, *Social Change,* Huebsch, New York, 1922, particularly Pt. 2, Chaps. 4 and 5; Clarence Ayres, *The Theory of Economic Progress,* University of North Carolina Press, Chapel Hill, 1944, particularly Chaps. 6 and 7.

Whoever is correct, one thing is certain, patent policy affects, for good or ill, the rate of the commercial introduction of technological innovations. As to what its precise effects may be, it is hazardous to generalize. But the record clearly indicates that business has used the monopoly privileges that patent policy bestows to obtain controls over industry that antitrust policy prohibits. See text below.

has been weakened in the course of a century and a half of intermittent statutory amendment.

Even if legislative policy had adhered to the original constitutional prescription, the patent system as we know it today would still tip the scales heavily in favor of promoting invention as against fostering competition in trade and industry. It would still be a bulwark of industrial monopoly because judicial interpretation and administrative practice gradually modified the original safeguards until by the first decade of the twentieth century the patent system had become a special sanctuary for trusts, pools, and trade confederacies. With the protection of patent franchises, big business has been able to circumvent the basic law prohibiting monopoly.[12] Armed with a patent—still better, with a whole arsenal of patent rights and patent licenses—a consolidation or restrictive trade pool was almost immune to antitrust action.[13]

Evils of Multiplicity

If the patent system has in some important respects miscarried, the government shares responsibility with business. If in the quest for industrial hegemony giant corporations have used patents to

12. Cf. Hamilton, *Patents,* pp. 57-85, especially p. 62; and pp. 134-43, especially p. 141, where the author says: "The 'exclusive right' of the patentee became 'the patent monopoly,' and this was converted into a one-way street along which no trespassers might go."

13. For notorious examples see *Bement* v. *National Harrow Co.,* 186 U.S. 70 (1902); the second Continental Paper Bag case, 210 U.S. 405 (1908); *Leeds & Catlin* v. *Victor Talking Machine Co.,* 213 U.S. 325 (1909); *Henry* v. *A. B. Dick Co.,* 224 U.S. 1 (1912); the Shoe Machinery cases, *U.S.* v. *Winslow, et al.,* 227 U.S. 202 (1913), and *U.S.* v. *United Shoe Machinery Co.,* 247 U.S. 32 (1918); *U.S.* v. *General Electric Co.,* 272 U.S. 476 (1926); and *Standard Oil Co.* (*Ind.*) v. *U.S.,* 283 U.S. 163 (1931).

The rule was not always thus. In the 1880's a federal court held that a patent, far from representing an absolute property right, was invested with such public significance that a patentee "is bound either to use the patent himself or allow others to use it on reasonable or equitable terms." *Hoe* v. *Knap,* 27 Fed. 204 (1886). And in the 1890's, the Supreme Court itself showed some concern to keep patent monopolies subservient to the public interest. *Morgan* v. *Albany Paper Co.,* 152 U.S. 425 (1894); and *Keeler* v. *Standard Folding-Bed Co.,* 157 U.S. 659 (1895). Occasionally, moreover, even in the heyday of the patents-as-private-monopoly doctrine, the courts stripped patent-pooling schemes of their subterfuges and condemned them (or their practices) as restraints of trade. *Standard Sanitary Manufacturing Co.* v. *U.S.,* 226 U.S. 20 (1912); *U.S.* v. *New Departure Manufacturing Co.,* 204 Fed. 107 (1913); and *Motion Picture Patents Co.* v. *Universal Film Co.,* 243 U.S. 502 (1917). Thus the path to legal sanctuary for industrial monopoly, through patents, has not been entirely smooth and free from risk. Moreover, since the Great Depression and the New Deal, which brought great changes both in the personnel and the outlook of the Supreme Court, judicial interpretation of the patent laws has undergone a revolutionary change. And this judicial revision of patent policy is still in progress. See text below.

stifle competition, even in matters outside the scope of letters patent, the laxity of Congress, the Patent Office, and the courts has abetted such practices.

Congress could easily have checked one abuse—patent multiplicity—that has contributed to the promotion of ends the patent system was never designed to serve. Amendment of the definition of "invention" to narrow the scope of patentable subject matter would have reduced the flood of specious claims for special privilege. A rigorous limitation of "invention" to new technological expedients would bring the patent system closer to the constitutional specification: promoting progress in the "useful Arts." Perhaps the outstanding illustration of congressional indifference to limitation of competition through the liberal application of the patent laws is the continued authorization of patents on foods and medicines. The evil of a government grant of monopoly in things necessary for health and even for human life is underscored both by recent experience and by the opposite practice abroad.[14]

Even without any statutory changes, the Patent Office in the first instance, and the courts on review, could have checked the proliferation of patent rights. But the Patent Office has a bureaucratic stake in a liberal patent policy—the greater the number of patent applications on file and of patents granted, the longer its civil service list. Naturally the Patent Office welcomes all grist to the patent mill. Naturally, too, the longer the list of "patent numbers" and "patents pending" that a company can stamp or print on each of its products, the more effectively it can frighten off easily intimidated competitors.[15] Hence "supply" and "demand" for patents are both under inflationary pressure. The channels of trade are consequently cluttered with a multitude of extremely dubious patent claims, many of which represent invention only by a great stretch of the imagination.[16]

14. Great Britain specifically excludes from patent privileges "substances . . . intended for food or medicine." See *Patents and Designs Act,* cited above, p. 21. For recent American experience, see a discussion of the Steenbock patents on "enrichment" of food by irradiation in Chap. 10, pp. 336-37.

15. To obtain protection of a patented article, the statutes require a patentee so to mark it plainly and in a suitable place to specify the number and date of each patent involved. But the law does not require differentiation between patents for invention and design patents. Only by a search of Patent Office records can a person tell whether it is the ornamental design on a patented product or its structure that cannot be copied without risk of a suit for infringement. See U.S. Code, Title 35, c. 2, Sec. 49.

16. See, for example, *Investigation of the Concentration of Economic Power,* Temporary National Economic Committee, Hearings pursuant to Pub.Res. 113 (75th

In the fifty years from 1890 to 1940, the annual average number of patents issued increased progressively from decade to decade. The rate of issuance in the 1930's—48,520 a year—was more than double the rate in the 1890's, as the following annual averages per decade show:[17]

1890–1899	23,475
1900–1909	31,448
1910–1919	39,754
1920–1929	44,394
1930–1939	48,520
1940–1947	35,078

Even after making allowance for the growth of population, the rate of issuance increased nearly 20 per cent between the decade of the 1890's and the decade of the 1930's. On annual average, patents issued per million of population were as follows:

1890–1899	308.9
1900–1909	341.9
1910–1919	376.1
1920–1929	361.6
1930–1939	368.5
1940–1947	245.9

That the increase is more a reflection of judicial and administrative policy than of the rate of technological advance is suggested by the sharp decline since 1940. In 1947 only 22,433 patents were granted, less than half the number issued in 1939. This decline apparently reflects the response of the Patent Office to the increas-

Cong.), Pt. 2, pp. 369-70. (These hearings will hereinafter be cited: TNEC Hearings, Pt. —.) The pages cited give testimony of James McEvoy, head of the patent department of General Motors Corporation. He illustrated "a perfectly silly patent" and declared: ". . . there are thousands and thousands of patents just like that . . . Of course, I think that most patents like that are utterly invalid." On the reasons for this situation, he said: "I think one difficulty, sir, in the Patent Office is the pressure that they are under to get out patents. . . . I understand in a great many divisions the head of the division has given orders to the men that they have to get out so many patents every week . . . and in many cases there is no proper investigation, sometimes no investigation whatever." For a collection of "silly patents," see A. E. Brown and H. A. Jesscott, Jr., *Beware of Imitations,* Viking Press, New York, 1932.

17. Data on patents from *Index of Patents,* issued annually by the United States Patent Office, Department of Commerce. The data cover not only patents for inventions but also design patents, plant patents (since 1931) and reissues. The following data for 1947 show how total issues are currently distributed among these four categories:

Inventions	20,149
Designs	2,102
Reissues	130
Plants	52

ingly vigilant scrutiny of patents by the courts in recent years whenever they have had an opportunity to rule on patent validity.[18]

Worthless Patents a Hindrance to Competition

The multiplicity of patents and the large proportion of patents issued on trivial, often worthless, innovations [19] obstruct enterprise and hinder competition in several ways. They lengthen and complicate the search to find out whether a particular technique or product feature is within the public domain or a possible infringement of a valid patent. Thus they increase the overhead costs—and the risks—of every manufacturing enterprise. They also make more costly the litigation necessary to settle patent claims, even when there is an honest difference of opinion. New and small-scale enterprises in particular seldom have funds to expend in legal contests that, by delaying tactics, can be prolonged for three, five, seven years or more.[20] Such firms usually find it more profitable to capitulate and negotiate a license or accept a trade agreement that will give them an assured, though minor, position in the market in return for ending competition.[21]

On the other hand, in some industries large and small firms alike

18. For surveys of the results of patent litigation before and after the radical change during the 1930's in the views of the Supreme Court on the question of patentable invention, see W. H. Kenyon, Jr., "Sore Spots in the Patent System," *Journal of the Patent Office Society,* 1942, p. 469, and J. M. Cole, "Patent Law Trends," *Journal of the Patent Office Society,* 1944, pp. 252-55. Whereas from 1900 to 1930, the Supreme Court invalidated 35 out of 62, or 56.5 per cent, of the patents challenged in cases reaching that tribunal, from 1930 to 1943 it invalidated 30 out of 37, or 81 per cent. Cole found a similar trend, though with a lag, in the decisions on patents by lower federal courts. *Ibid.*

19. The late Frederick P. Fish, former president of American Telephone and Telegraph Co., general counsel of United Shoe Machinery Co., and a leading member of the patent bar, testified that "My personal view is that not one patented invention in ten is worth making." *United States Patent Office,* Hearings before the Committee on Patents, House of Representatives, on H.R. 5011, 5012, and 7010, 66th Cong., 1st sess., 1919, p. 63.

20. For example, the Aluminum Company of America liquidated the Cowles Bros. enterprise after ten years of patent litigation. Even though the Cowles' patents were eventually upheld and their process found not to infringe Alcoa's patents, the drain on their resources was too great for them to continue competition. They became discouraged and sold out. See *Cartels in Action,* pp. 221-22.

The United Shoe Machinery Company affords another classic example of how a giant industrial consolidation can tie up and wear down competitors by patent infringement litigation. For a discussion of tactics that have enabled United Shoe Machinery to reverse the roles of Gulliver and the Lilliputians in the fable, see Hamilton, *Patents,* pp. 59-60.

21. See cases discussed on pages 472 ff. of this chapter, in particular the glass container, wallboard, salt, gypsum, and electric circuit breaker monopolies.

have tried to rid themselves of the nuisance and expense of continual patent litigation and negotiation by reciprocal, royalty-free cross-licensing agreements. But as the automobile industry has found, to try to by-pass the patent system in this way and free a developing technology from its restrictions cannot eliminate heavy expense for "patent protection." Such cross-licensing arrangements are not wholly successful, because they leave the manufacturers exposed to a steady barrage of shake-down demands by outsiders who collect patents and patent applications for this specific purpose. Since the contents of patent applications are secret, and it is so easy to get patents even on meretricious claims, these tactics are hard to combat. After describing the experience of the Ford Motor Company in this connection its patent counsel declared, in response to the question whether he thought the patent law served a useful purpose:

> . . . we feel at times that, viewing the matter from the standpoint of being made the defendant in all sorts of harassing litigations, our general feeling is that the system has got to the point where the tail is wagging the dog, and that it isn't acting 100 percent to promote progress, but in many instances is used to impede progress.[22]

Abuses of Procedure

In procedural matters, also, the patent system, as it has actually operated, has helped to throttle competition and frustrate the advancement of "useful Arts." An astute patentee can prolong the legal monopoly in an invention far beyond the seventeen-year term of the patent itself simply by keeping the application "alive" for many years in the Patent Office. The law permits an applicant to file amendments to his claims, to divide applications in which the claims cover more than a single invention, and to take three months, if he chooses, to revise an application in response to objections of Patent Office examiners.

By judiciously stringing out a series of such formal changes, some of which could and should have been anticipated while others may be quite inconsequential, the applicant may keep the essential "invention"—if there is one—out of the public domain almost indefinitely. In one instance, an inventor succeeded in maintaining for fifty-three years an exclusive right in his novel device—for sound-recording

22. TNEC Hearings, Pt. 2, p. 279. See also *ibid.*, pp. 256-376.

on films.[23] Moreover, a "slumbering" application in the Patent Office can be used, if drafted in broad and nebulous terms, as a convenient sponge for absorbing new developments in the particular industrial art as they unfold, from whatever quarter they may come.[24] And such pending applications can be used most effectively, as experience shows, to block improvements of which competitors may be the real originators.

H. R. Smith, secretary-treasurer of Hartford Empire, the patent-holding company dominating the glass container industry, succinctly and frankly described the patent policy of his company as follows:

> In taking out patents we have three main purposes: (a) To cover the actual machines which we are putting out and prevent duplication of them. . . . (b) To block the development of machines which might be constructed by others . . . using alternative means. . . . (c) To secure patents on possible improvements of competing machines so as to "fence in" those and prevent their reaching an improved stage.[25]

Interference Aggravates Delays

The procedure technically known as an "interference" aggravates the evils of delay in completing patent applications. When the Patent Office receives two or more applications covering substantially the

23. Patent No. 1,203,190 issued to one Fritts in 1916 after the application had been pending thirty-six years. The Patent Office itself computed the permissible term of protection under the rules in force in 1938 as forty-four years. See testimony of the Commissioner of Patents, TNEC Hearings, Pt. 3, pp. 860 and 1133.

24. See testimony of G. H. Willitts, a patent attorney and secretary of a "group of 50 large manufacturing concerns," in *Patents,* Hearings before the Committee on Patents, House of Representatives, on General Revision of Patent Laws, 72d Cong., 1st sess., January 25-28 and February 16-17, 1932, pp. 69-72. "There is another angle of the long-pending case that is particularly grievous . . . There are some companies that carry patent practice to extremes, and one of their favorite stratagems is this: They file large numbers of patent applications; they keep them in the Patent Office as long as they can—perhaps they are already established in their field . . . They are afraid a competitor may come along with something just as good. . . . As a competitor comes out with a new machine . . . they look through all their pending applications, which may run into several thousand, and see if they can't find some similarity, no matter how far-fetched, but some similarity between the competitive machine and this matter that is in the pending application, then they will write claims into the pending application covering this competitor's machine, and in a short time come out with a patent, make charges of infringement, and bring suit. That is not accidental. . . . It is a policy of certain companies. . . . Now, that thing has happened to industry after industry. . . . [These difficulties] have affected . . . most of the major industries in the United States. . . . You are led into a trap. . . . and then the trap is sprung on you."

25. *U.S.* v. *Hartford Empire Co.,* 46 Fed.Supp. 541 (1942), at pp. 611-12.

In carrying out this policy the company found it convenient to acquire licensing control over more than a thousand patents, 717 of which it owned outright. See *ibid.,* p. 618; and TNEC Hearings, Pt. 2, p. 380.

same invention it declares them in interference, sets a date for a hearing, and requires the applicants to submit evidence in support of their respective claims to priority. The examiners who conduct the hearings possess no powers to subpoena witnesses and demand that specific documents be submitted for the record. The evidence offered customarily consists of *ex parte* depositions. The contestants not appearing in person, the examiner has no alternative but to assume their veracity. In any case, the proceedings afford no opportunity for a public prosecutor to examine or cross-examine witnesses under oath; the public interest, lacking a champion, goes by default.

Not only are interference proceedings costly and long drawn out, frequently lasting three or four years or longer,[26] but their very nature encourages fraud and collusion.[27] The Commissioner of Patents himself testified as follows in 1939:

> There is no question that the interference procedure has been greatly abused and that in some instances it has been invoked for unworthy purposes, as, for example, to delay a competitor's application in the Patent Office. . . . it is the unanimous opinion of the officials of the Patent Office and virtually the consensus of the patent bar and the public that the interference practice should be reformed.[28]

Nine years later it remained, nevertheless, essentially unchanged, despite minor improvements introduced in 1940 to overcome obstructive delays.

26. Hamilton states (*Patents,* p. 128) that the average pendency of interference proceedings in the Patent Office is three years, and of those that are carried into court, four and a half years. On the costliness of interference practice and the handicap it imposes on small concerns trying to compete with companies that command "large resources," see the testimony of Dr. Vannevar Bush, TNEC Hearings, Pt. 3, p. 880. The "large resources" to which Dr. Bush referred were financial resources, not technical resources.

27. For an exceptionally spectacular example in confirmation of this statement, see *Precision Instrument Co.* v. *Automotive Maintenance Co.,* 324 U.S. 806 (1945). The Supreme Court directed the dismissal of Automotive's suit for infringement because, though it was the owner of a valid patent, it had connived with its competitor, Precision, to settle an interference proceeding involving a patent application by one of Precision's founders *after* it had learned that that application was founded on fraud and perjury. By negotiating a settlement, Automotive obtained a patent on the perjured application and thus fortified its hold on the market. At the same time it granted Precision a license, allotting its unscrupulous competitor a small share of the market, and got a promise from that company never to question the validity of any Automotive patent—not even the one that both parties knew was tainted with fraud. Precision's perfidy in disregarding its license restrictions was the occasion for the instant suit. But because Automotive did not come into court "with clean hands," the Court declared, "That the actions of . . . Precision may have been more reprehensible is immaterial." *Ibid.,* p. 819.

28. TNEC Hearings, Pt. 3, p. 861.

The Abuse of "Reissues"

Another procedural abuse that has helped business erect patent barricades against competition is the enlargement of the scope of "reissues"—in nontechnical terms, amended patents. On application, the Patent Office may substitute for an outstanding patent another running for the same period but with modified claims.

In authorizing reissues Congress expressly limited the privilege to the correction of mistakes. In practice, however, the Patent Office and the courts permitted patentees not only to disclaim some elements of the alleged invention, and thus save "claims" stated in such broad terms that a court would probably hold them invalid, but also to add new elements to the claimed invention.[29]

As in the case of the amendment of applications, reissues may bring under patent protection features of the general advance in the industrial arts that might not themselves amount to patentable invention and for which, in any event, the patentee may not be primarily responsible. In this way, an alert and aggressive corporation can fortify its patent position and continually reinforce its dominance of the market.

Infringement Suits and Threats

The most effective weapon in the patents arsenal for harassing competitors and thwarting the development of new rivals is the infringement suit. As *Fortune* magazine has said:

> The most versatile of all devices . . . is the infringement suit, one of the most expensive forms of litigation. The infringement suit can be used not only as a simple legal action to stop someone from stealing your invention, but also as a controlling device with a wide range of action all the way from the veiled threat to the punitive war. A competing product, process, or machine is challenged . . . If both patents and the patent-owning corporations seem to be of equal weight, the dispute is likely to be settled out of court with a cross-licensing agreement between the two. If the challenged

29. See, for example, *Topliff* v. *Topliff,* 145 U.S. 156 (1892); *Corbin Lock Co.* v. *Eagle Lock Co.,* 150 U.S. 38 (1893); *Crown Cork & Seal Co.* v. *Aluminum Stopper Co.,* 108 Fed. 845 (1901); and *Perfection Bed Co.* v. *Murphy Bed Co.,* 266 Fed. 698 (1920), certiorari denied, 254 U.S. 652 (1920).

The more vigilant scrutiny that the Supreme Court has given to Patent Office procedure and to patent restrictions generally in recent years has narrowed greatly the permissible changes in patent specifications and claims on reissue. See, for example, *U.S. Industrial Chemicals, Inc.* v. *Carbide & Carbon Chemicals Corp.,* 315 U.S. 668 (1942), reversing the Circuit Court of Appeals decision, 121 Fed. *2d* 665 (1941).

company is fairly small, but its patent sound, it is likely to be forced, in lieu of incurring . . . [heavy] expense . . ., to accept a license under the challenger's patent setting rigid price and production limits. This may continue . . . all the way out to an open reign of terror not only against the alleged infringer but against all of his customers . . . More time, money, and energy have sometimes gone into this kind of warfare than ever went into the original technological development.[30]

A large company with a formidable collection of patents and ample financial resources can impose an insupportable burden on a small enterprise by forcing it to defend its right to use techniques or to manufacture products that, as it eventually turns out, may be entirely in the public domain. Even the most scrupulous care to avoid invasion of existing patent rights cannot render the small company immune from infringement litigation. For it costs as much —if not more—to defend an infringement suit as to prosecute it. A small competitor can stand the financial strain only so long before it succumbs to its more powerful rival.

Even though the principal issue may be whether the government granted the patent improvidently, and even though the benefits of successful defense accrue to the public, a private business must bear the entire cost of defending an infringement suit. In this way the patent system plays into the hands of monopolies. It also imposes a one-sided and unfair handicap on competitive enterprises by obliging them, at their own expense, to defend the *public* interest in keeping an advancing technology open to common use—except for exclusive rights in bona fide inventions. If an inventor himself, or an alleged infringer, could obtain at public expense a judicial determination of the validity of any of the thousands of patents issued almost promiscuously by the Patent Office, it would deprive monopolies founded on patents of much of their power to perpetuate themselves.

A company that sedulously uses patents to strengthen its monopoly may fear to challenge an upstart competitor directly, lest some or all of the patents allegedly infringed be held invalid. But in that case it can proceed indirectly, with less risk, by threatening the competitor's customers with suits for contributory infringement. Seldom will customers regard continued commercial relations with a particular supplier so important as to make it worth while for

30. From "War and Peace and the Patent System," *Fortune*, August 1942, pp. 105 and 132.

them to contest such a challenge.[31] Thus, the patentee-monopolist can, in effect, create a boycott against a fledgling rival. At the same time it can keep intact its imposing array of letters patent, even though these may amount to nothing more than a paper façade, and it can use them later against new rivals.

Licensing Aids Monopoly

If multiplicity of patents and procedural loopholes have indirectly facilitated the use of patents to stifle competition, the broad scope of licensing privileges has directly and substantially helped attain the same end. The power of a patentee to assign his "exclusive rights" to others rests on explicit statutory authorization, and the courts have construed the patent grant as in the nature of a property right.[32] And, as an incident of such a right, they have accorded the patentee the privilege of splitting up his patent through license contracts, pretty much as he may choose.

In virtual disregard of the origin of the grant as a government franchise [33] and of its strictly defined constitutional purpose, judicial

31. In practice the customer ordinarily takes the precaution of stipulating that his equipment supplier must defend contributory infringement suits brought against him, if there is any question of conflicting patent rights. But when, as often happens, the customer also buys or leases some of his equipment from the dominant patent-holding company with which the independent is trying to compete, the defense of invalidity of the patents allegedly infringed may be blocked. The customer's renunciation of any right to challenge the validity of such patents may foreclose the independent's best defense. The Hartford Empire Company used this strategy to cripple its smaller rivals. In this way it eventually eliminated Amsler-Morton from the annealing oven business in the glass industry. For details, see text below. Recently, however, the Supreme Court has severely limited the enforceability of convenants not to contest the validity of patents. See *Sola Electric Co.* v. *Jefferson Electric Co.,* 317 U.S. 173 (1942); *Scott Paper Co.* v. *Marcalus Manufacturing Co.,* 326 U.S. 249 (1945); *Katzinger Co.* v. *Chicago Metallic Manufacturing Co.,* 329 U.S. 394 (1947); and *MacGregor* v. *Westinghouse Electric Co.,* 329 U.S. 402 (1947). Cf., however, *American Cutting Alloys, Inc.* v. *General Electric Co.,* 135 Fed. *2d* 502 (1943).

32. See the second Continental Paper Bag case, 210 U.S. 405 (1908), where the Court says (p. 425) that "patents are property, and entitled to the same rights and sanctions as other property." This dictum ignores, incidentally, the numerous and widely differing limitations that both common and statutory law impose on the use and disposition of different kinds of private property.

See, also, for a more recent case in the same vein, *General Talking Pictures* v. *Western Electric,* 304 U.S. 175, and, on rehearing, 305 U.S. 124 (1938). Cf. Mr. Justice Douglas, dissenting in *Special Equipment Co.* v. *Coe,* 324 U.S. 370 (1945), at p. 382: "It is a mistake therefore to conceive of a patent as but another form of private property. The patent is a privilege 'conditioned by a public purpose' *Mercoid Corp.* v. *Mid-Continent Investment Co.,* 320 U.S. 661 [(1944), at p.] 666 . . ."

33. The public franchise conception of a patent had its clearest and most forceful judicial enunciation in *Bloomer* v. *McQuewan,* 14 Howard 539 (1852), at p. 549. It began to lose ground, in favor of the private property concept, in the last quarter of the nineteenth century—see, for example, *March* v. *Nichols,* 128 U.S. 605 (1888),

opinion in patent cases has stretched to the limits of a barren logomachy the doctrine that "a man can do with his own as he likes." [34] Corollaries of this doctrine have been the doctrines that a patentee could suppress his invention altogether if he wished,[35] and that, because in his discretion he could refuse to grant licenses under the patent, the patentee could impose such conditions on licensees as he might think fitting.[36]

The discretionary power of patentees to restrict the use of inventions by, and to control the business policies of, licensees has not always been allowed. It was a distinctive feature of the development of patent law in the fifty years after 1890.[37] But even during this period, when the licensing privilege gave a patentee almost complete immunity from the law forbidding "monopolizing," the courts now and then hesitated to go to the full extreme in applying the doctrine. In 1911 the Supreme Court held a patent-licensing scheme for controlling the output and price of sanitary pottery ware a violation of the antitrust law.[38] It interpreted the scheme as practically a fraud on the public. Also, the Court sometimes backtracked from an advanced position on patent-licensing freedom. Five years after it approved, in the A. B. Dick case, a restriction imposed by a patentee on the commercial source of unpatented materials to be used in the patented device, it withdrew that approval in the Motion Picture Patents case.[39]

Nevertheless, the courts continued in general to look with toler-

---

at p. 608—and for a half century after 1890, or until its renascense in *Morton Salt Co.* v. *Suppiger*, 314 U.S. 488 (1942), and the Mercoid cases, *Mercoid* v. *Mid-Continent Investment Co.*, 320 U.S. 661 (1944), and *Mercoid* v. *Minneapolis-Honeywell Co.*, 320 U.S. 680 (1944), judicial opinions showed only slight traces of it. Cf. G. Rich, "Patent Practices and the Anti-Monopoly Laws," *Journal of the Patent Office Society*, 1942, p. 85, where he says (p. 88) that the patent law "went on a spree from 1896 to 1917." But if the Motion Picture Patents case (previously cited) ended the "spree," it did not eliminate a hang-over. See, for example, *U.S.* v. *General Electric Co.* and the General Talking Pictures case (1938), previously cited.

34. Cf. Hamilton, *Patents*, pp. 57-64.

35. Second Continental Paper Bag case.

36. *Leeds & Catlin* v. *Victor Talking Machine Co.* and *Henry* v. *A. B. Dick Co.*, previously cited.

37. The outstanding cases that exhibit the evolution of the idea of patent-licensing freedom are the Heaton-Peninsular Button-Fastener case, 77 Fed. 288 (1896); and the Bement, the Leeds & Catlin, the A. B. Dick, and the General Electric cases, previously cited.

38. *Standard Sanitary Manufacturing Co.* v. *U.S.*, previously cited. Although this decision did not expressly overrule the Bement case, much the same elements that the Court condemned in the Standard Sanitary case it had earlier sanctioned in the Bement case.

39. Previously cited. The opinion expressly repudiated the A. B. Dick ruling.

ance, if not complacency, on the tactics of patentees in drafting license contracts so as to fortify and even extend their monopoly privileges. As late as 1926 the Supreme Court could find nothing to condemn in General Electric's patent-licensing policy that limited the output of its licensees and required them to sell at prices identical with its own.[40]

The General Talking Pictures Case

Such a broad licensing privilege was an open invitation to use patents to establish unified, arbitrary control over entire branches of industry. If a patent-holding producer could persuade or coerce other producers to accept licenses, every member of the group could be lawfully bound to pursue a common price and production policy. In fact the law as interpreted permitted such a scheme to divide whole branches of industry, assigning to each licensee a designated field. In the General Talking Pictures case the Supreme Court upheld the right of a licensor to restrict the uses to which either a licensee to manufacture or his vendees might put the patented device. Stated abstractly, the proposition may appear quite innocuous. But its concrete application disclosed its oppressiveness.

The actual licensor in the General Talking Pictures case was Western Electric, a subsidiary of American Telephone and Telegraph (AT & T). AT & T in turn was a member, along with Radio Corporation of America and General Electric, of the electronics pool.[41] The significance of the General Talking Pictures case was, therefore, that it sanctioned the allocation of fields among these three giants. At any rate, it gave judicial blessing to an arrangement whereby one member of the group (AT & T) reserved to itself the trade in radio tubes (amplifiers) for use in sound reproduction equipment in theatres. The principle of the case would similarly sustain the allotment to the other members of the pool of other "uses" for, or parts of the trade in, this patented device.

40. And as late as 1936 a Circuit Court of Appeals upheld a provision of a patent license, uniform for the several manufacturing licensees, requiring them to sell at a price fixed by the licensor patent-holding company unpatented products made on a patented machine. *Straight Side Basket Corp.* v. *Webster Basket Co.*, 82 Fed. *2d* 245 (1936), affirming 10 Fed.Supp. 171 (1935).

41. On the structure and status of the electronics pool, see Petro, *op. cit.*, pp. 372-80; F. C. Waldrop and J. Borkin, *Television: A Struggle for Power*, Morrow, New York, 1938; and L.I. Wood, *Patents and Antitrust Law*, Commerce Clearing House, Chicago, 1942, pp. 128-45.

Other Cases

Two important byproducts of the extremely broad licensing privilege were those permitting a patentee (1) to stipulate that his licensees should under no circumstances challenge the validity of the patents involved and (2) to require reciprocal licensing. The judicial doctrine of estoppel was sometimes invoked to block any effort of a licensee to attack the validity of the patents under which he was licensed, even without any express contractual limitation on his right to set up such a defense in an action for infringement.[42] But it was safer to bind the licensee not to question a licensor's patent rights than to trust to invocation of the principle of estoppel.[43]

Apparently the legality was never questioned of a patentee's making it a condition of a license that the licensee reciprocate by granting him a cross-license under whatever patents the licensee might possess in the same field. The extension of this assumed right to cover not only a licensee's improvements in the licensed process but whatever future patents he might acquire in the same general field was easily made.[44] By stipulations of reciprocal licensing, patentees with a strongly fortified patent position sometimes undertook to establish prior claims on all patents in a broad field of technology.

The Cases of Rubber and Electric Lamps

When the Standard Oil Company of New Jersey obtained from I. G. Farbenindustrie an assignment of IG's Buna rubber patents, Standard Oil submitted to rubber manufacturers a draft of a uniform licensing agreement that would have made almost impossible the development of any synthetic rubber technique outside its control. The provisions of the proposed contracts required each rubber company to license reciprocally to Standard Oil not only all its existing

42. The leading case is *U.S.* v. *Harvey Steel Co.,* 196 U.S. 310 (1905).

43. As mentioned before, the enforceability of such covenants has lately come into question, particularly since the Sola decision in 1942. But see Mr. Justice Frankfurter's vigorous protest against this overthrow of a "century-old" precedent, in his dissenting opinion in *Altvater* v. *Freeman,* 319 U.S. 359 (1943).

44. The first clear-cut decision on this issue by a court of final jurisdiction was in *Transparent-Wrap Machine Corp.* v. *Stokes & Smith Co.,* 329 U.S. 637 (1947). The Supreme Court upheld the reciprocal licensing covenant here involved, but the licensee had an exclusive license.

patents on Buna-type synthetics and all improvement patents but also whatever patents it might subsequently acquire on alternative processes. Standard Oil's patent attorney described this provision as follows:

> The agreement as it is now drafted will lead to the centering of all patent rights of licensees in the hands of licensor, with no outflow of those rights except to customers of licensor . . .
>
> All manufacturing patent rights of licensees will help to build up licensor's dominating position . . . In other words, this is not a cross-licensing agreement, but one in which patents are piled on patents in the hands of one centralizing company.[45]

A patent-licensing privilege so broad that it permits the use of one or a few patents to tie up all other patents in a certain field of technology obviously promotes domination of whole branches of industry by patent-holding companies. By the use of this device a company can perpetuate an industrial monopoly obtained through the leverage of a seventeen-year patent grant. And once it attains a dominant position, it may be less urgent for it to continue vigorously to subsidize technical research. In practice many such companies—for example, AT & T, General Electric, United Shoe Machinery, Hartford Empire, and du Pont—do persevere in research. A company can achieve the greatest security if it combines leadership in technological development with a system of license contracts, whereby the "leader" shares its patents with smaller companies and requires its licensees continually to reinforce its dominant patent position by handing over to it control of all advances in that branch of the industrial arts.

The electric lamp industry illustrates how broad licensing privileges may retard technological progress by restricting the research efforts of licensees. In the recent antitrust suit against General Electric the government charged that defendant's cross-licensing contracts as such had deterred licensees from expanding research. The court thought this was a matter of conjecture because the evidence showed that the licensees had in fact spent substantial sums on research. But it declared that:

> . . . the vice lies in the clause establishing a quota on sales of the incandescent lamp. This placed "B" licensees in such a position that with their

45. *Investigation of the National Defense Program,* Hearings before a Special Committee of the U.S. Senate, 77th Cong., 1st sess., pursuant to S.Res. 71, Pt. 11, Ex. 383, p. 4605.

income circumscribed to a given fraction of General Electric sales, they could not support expenditures necessary to operate extended research and engineering development projects.[46]

The restrictive influence that cross-licensing provisions have exerted on research has not been confined to the electric lamp field. As Mr. Justice Reed has said:

> Where two or more patentees with competitive, non-infringing patents combine them and fix prices on all devices produced under any of the patents, competition is impeded to a greater degree than where a single patentee fixes prices for his licensees. The struggle for profit is less acute . . . *The stimulus to seek competitive inventions is reduced by the mutually advantageous price-fixing arrangement.*[47]

Evils of Patent Accumulation

The simplest and most obvious way of using patents to suppress competition is by concentrating in one organization control of all or most of the patents in a particular field. One method of doing this is for a company to accumulate as many patents as it can lay hold of, either by assignment from its own research staff or by purchase from outside persons. The accumulation of patents in the hands of a single company has attained fantastic proportions in some industries. In the mid-1930's AT & T owned more than 9,000 patents and held licenses under 6,000 others, General Electric controlled more than 8,000 patents, and United Shoe Machinery more than 6,000.[48] Such formidable aggregations of "exclusive rights" amount in practice to much more than a seventeen-year grant of monopoly. They tend to assure a perpetual monopoly.

The fallacy that "the whole is only the sum of the parts" has few more striking demonstrations than here. If Mr. Justice Holmes had been fully aware of the implications of his own dictum that "the

46. *U.S.* v. *General Electric Co.,* 82 Fed.Supp. 753 (1949). See Advance Print, p. 203.

Counsel for Tungsol, a General Electric licensee, expressed the position this way: ". . . a lamp licensee has no inducement to develop new inventions if General Electric can freely take whatever they develop." Government Exhibit 197, reproduced in part in Opinion of Court. And a General Electric official expressed it as follows: "Westinghouse has never done and probably will never do their real share of the work in these fields. They can't afford to because we would reap three-fourths of their purely creative work." Government Exhibit 1854, reproduced in *ibid.*

47. *U.S.* v. *Line Material Co.,* previously cited, p. 311. Italics supplied.

48. See Federal Communications Commission, *Telephone Investigation* (Proposed Report), Washington, 1938, p. 267; and Hamilton, *Patents,* p. 60.

life of the law is experience, not logic," he could hardly have made the following statement in the first Shoe Machinery case:

It is said that from 70 to 80 per cent of all the shoe machinery business was put into a single hand. . . . But taking it as true, we can see no greater objection to one company manufacturing 70 per cent of three non-competing groups of patented machinery collectively used for making a single product than to three corporations making the same proportion of one group each.[49]

With this reasoning the Supreme Court upheld the lawfulness of a combination that brought together the business and patents of four distinct groups of companies, all making shoe machinery but none producing a complete line. Yet the monopoly power of the several constituents of United, based on their respective patent holdings, was certainly increased under the consolidation's policy of making available to shoe manufacturers any particular type of machine only on condition that they also lease or purchase United's patented, and even unpatented, equipment of other types. Under this "full-line forcing" policy, the patent-monopoly powers of Goodyear, McKay, Consolidated, and Eppler were raised to an industrial monopoly level.[50]

Barricades Against Competition

Multiplicity of patents greatly facilitates the raising of formidable patent barricades against competition. As Judge Clark tersely put it:

Clearly, in the multiplicity of patents lies the opportunity for pooling, for unfair competition, and for in terrorem suppression. . . . Multiplicity of trivial patents furnishes the field in which the trust operates.[51]

The ease with which patents can be obtained from the Patent Office is only one factor contributing to the erection of barricades.

49. *U.S.* v. *Winslow*, previously cited, p. 217. The explanation of Mr. Justice Holmes' reference to three companies instead of four is that the fourth group of companies was acquired shortly after the organization of United Shoe Machinery Corporation. The original combination brought together the Goodyear companies, the McKay companies, and the Consolidated Shoe Machinery Company. With the Eppler companies, which came in almost immediately afterward, the consolidation controlled—and still controls—about 90 per cent of the shoe machinery produced in the United States. These four groups of companies operated independently before the merger and their business was competitive to the extent that the lines of machinery each group manufactured overlapped to some extent the types of machinery one or more of the other companies produced, as they did in the past.

50. Full-line forcing was outlawed by decree after the passage of the Clayton Act. See *United Shoe Machinery Corp.* v. *U.S.*, 258 U.S. 451 (1922).

51. From his testimony in *Pooling of Patents,* Hearings before the Committee on Patents, House of Representatives, on H.R. 4523, 74th Cong., 1st sess., 1935, Pt. 1, pp. 1077-80.

Supplementing it is the ease with which a giant consolidation can buy patents from free-lance inventors. When a single company controls through patents most of the equipment used or the different types of products manufactured in a certain branch of industry, it severely restricts the opportunity of independent inventors to dispose of their inventions, and (except in the rare case of a basic patent) it practically extinguishes their opportunity to exploit them independently. The only possible purchaser of patent rights applicable in that field can in effect dictate the terms on which it will buy them.[52]

Facing a single buyer, and that buyer fortified with financial resources far exceeding those at his own disposal, the independent inventor is under a severe handicap. He has practically no alternative but to assign his patent, and so he hands it over on such terms as the single buyer may offer. Of the 715 patents that Hartford Empire accumulated prior to 1939, more than half represented assignments from outside parties.

The continual accumulation by a single dominant company of patents for new techniques invented by outsiders is in many ways comparable to the steady absorption of independent producers through mergers. The purchase of such patents is in one sense tantamount to acquisition of potential competitors. Not every patent, of course, affords a basis for new enterprise. But if, out of the many patents issuing to independent inventors, those bearing on the technology of a certain industry were beyond the reach of its dominant patentee, then new inventions would soon make competitive enterprise possible. The pre-emptive and preclusive rights that a dominant patentee in fact holds over new technological developments in its field greatly facilitate indefinite continuance of monopolistic control.

Furthermore, such a combination as United Shoe Machinery eliminates the incentive each of the constituents would have, as an independent producer, to round out its line of patented techniques or products. The Goodyear companies, with a special interest in welting machines, would have had a strong competitive interest, had there been no merger, to introduce and perfect a line of lasting

52. On the handicap that concentration of patent ownership imposes on the independent inventor, see *ibid.*, pp. 1075-76. After quoting corroboratory statements by such experienced inventors as Edison and Baekeland and such distinguished lawyers as Brandeis and Fish, Judge Clark said that the aggregation of patents by industrial monopolies gives them "an unfair advantage in bargaining for patents for improvements" and "automatically closes the market to outside inventors."

machines that would not infringe the patents on such equipment of the Consolidated and the Eppler companies. But after the merger United Shoe Machinery was obliged only to buy up any new technical developments in lasting machines—or any other type of shoe machinery—that might threaten its exclusive control of the industry. And this it apparently has done as occasion demanded.[53]

Cross-Licensing Abuses

Another method of using patents to block competition is for a group of companies to pool or cross-license their respective patents, so that all licensees operate under restrictions mutually arranged. Cross licensing may be justifiable in some instances. An invention is seldom the work of one inventor. Usually many technicians are experimenting in the same field, at the same time, trying to solve the same problems. Different experimenters working independently may, and frequently do, simultaneously find different ways of achieving the same objective. Some features of a device or some steps in a process worked out by different inventors may be identical. More commonly, one process or device will supplement another. Each may represent a genuine invention and so be patentable. If patents are issued in such circumstances one may block the other: the commercial use of one depends on its exploitation in conjunction with the other. Cross licensing enables both patentees, very often, to take advantage of each other's inventions, while avoiding the expense of infringement suits. Such was plainly the object of the royalty-free cross-licensing agreement in the automobile industry and apparently, also, of that in the aircraft industry with its provision for arbitration of royalties.[54]

Historically, then, the reason for cross licensing is found in efforts to overcome reciprocal blockages; and even today it is used in some industries for a similar purpose: to free a rapidly developing technology from the trammels of monopoly privileges. But in other industries cross licensing has come to serve other purposes. Currently a cross-licensing agreement is often a result of connivance among a group of competitors to circumvent—legally—their obligation to

53. "But Business Is Always Good," *Fortune,* September 1933, pp. 34 ff. See also *Fortune,* November 1944, pp. 214 ff.

54. For a review of the operation of various cross-licensing agreements, see *Pooling of Patents, passim.* The committee listed (p. 1145) a score of such agreements then (1935) in existence having an industry-wide compass.

avoid restraining trade. The cross-licensed patents may have no technical interdependence and no one of them may be so important that its use is indispensable. The main purpose of such cross-licensing agreements is not to make technology available; it is to make competitive pricing and competitive expansion of production impossible.

Before the drastic revision of patent law interpretation wrought by the New Deal appointees to the Supreme Court, the leading case on patent pooling was that of the Standard Oil Company (Indiana), decided in 1931.[55] Several of the major oil companies had independently developed various methods of increasing the proportionate output of gasoline from the refining process by distillation of crude oils under pressure, that is, by "cracking." Numerous patents covered these improvements, and though at least some of them might have been exploited independently the patentees believed that elimination of competition in their use would facilitate commercial exploitation. They therefore formed a patent pool. By mutual agreement they fixed royalties on the several cross-licensed processes, established conditions for license eligibility, and divided the royalty revenues among the members in predetermined proportions. Primarily on the ground that members of the pool produced only a small percentage of the entire volume of motor fuel manufactured in the United States, so that refiners using the pooled cracking patents faced effective competition from refiners producing only straight-run gasoline, the Supreme Court sanctioned the arrangement when the government assailed it as a violation of the antitrust laws.

Courts Hit Monopoly Use of Patents

In a series of twelve cases beginning in 1939, however, the courts have consistently outlawed the use of patents to monopolize trade or stifle competition. The first case in the series involved the same industry and many of the same defendants as the cracking-patents case. Standard Oil Company of New Jersey acquired, jointly with General Motors and du Pont, patents on a tetraethyl lead compound for mixture with gasoline to improve its octane rating. The three partners organized Ethyl Gasoline Corporation, which sold the antiknock fluid to licensed refiners under a restrictive covenant that they would supply lead-treated gasoline only to Ethyl-licensed jobbers

55. *Standard Oil Co. (Ind.)* v. *U.S.*, previously cited.

and retailers. Ethyl required its dealer-licensees to sell the gasoline only at prices fixed by it, and refused licenses to distributors known as price cutters. The Supreme Court condemned this industry-wide licensing system as a price-fixing scheme.[56]

Two years later, the Court struck down two attempts by patentees to extend their respective monopolies on patented devices by monopolizing unpatented materials used in conjunction therewith.[57] In these cases the Court for the first time took the position that an appropriate remedy for such a misuse of the patent was judicial withholding of equitable relief for infringement. This amounted, in effect, to forfeiture of the patents involved.

In the same year, the Court also held illegal two schemes closely comparable to that condemned in the Ethyl case.[58] The Univis case involved a regimentation of the distributive trade under a licensing system, with resale price restrictions. The Masonite case involved a *del credere* "agency" arrangement that not only tied up the dealers but also divided the market among the various hardboard-manufacturing concerns.

In 1944, a patent-licensing scheme for uniting under the domination of a single holding company all manufacturers of thermostatic control devices met a similar fate.[59] The following year witnessed the partial dissolution of the patent pool in the glass container industry.[60]

The titanium pigments cartel, in which National Lead and du Pont played leading roles, cross-licensed their respective patents with foreign producers, and suppressed all competition in the domestic market, encountered judicial disapproval in 1947.[61] In the same year International Salt's patent-licensing system ran up against the same legal barrier that the Court had erected to block a similar arrangement in the Morton Salt case.[62] Finally, in 1948 the Supreme Court

56. *Ethyl Gasoline Corp.* v. *U.S.*, 309 U.S. 436 (1940).
57. *Morton Salt Co.* v. *Suppiger*, previously cited; and *B. B. Chemical Co.* v. *Ellis*, 314 U.S. 495 (1942).
58. *U.S.* v. *Univis Lens Co.*, 316 U.S. 241 (1942); and *U.S.* v. *Masonite Corp.*, 316 U.S. 265 (1942).
59. *Mercoid* v. *Mid-Continent Investment Co.* and *Mercoid* v. *Minneapolis-Honeywell Co.*, previously cited.
60. *Hartford Empire Co.* v. *U.S.*, 323 U.S. 386 (1945). For a detailed account of this proceeding, see text below.
61. *U.S.* v. *National Lead Co.*, 332 U.S. 319 (1947).
62. *International Salt Co.* v. *U.S.*, 332 U.S. 392 (1947).

applied the ax to two more patent-licensing schemes that involved combinations among otherwise competitive manufacturers mutually to fix prices. The first involved a series of license agreements that after 1937 embraced all manufacturers of gypsum wallboard and required them to sell at uniform prices. The second arose out of a simple cross-licensing agreement on drop-out fuse cutouts (for use in electric circuits) to settle an interference proceeding in the Patent Office and to enable the patentees to use two mutually inhibitory, or "blocked," patents. But this cross-licensing agreement led to a concerted price-fixing arrangement among all the principal producers. This, said the Court, "is more than an exploitation of patents. There is the vice that patentees have combined to fix prices on patented products." [63]

Most of these cases involved licensing or cross-licensing arrangements that went much further than those judicially sustained in the cracking-patents case, and some even went beyond the limits set down in the General Electric case. Without exception the license restrictions condemned involved attempts to fix prices, to limit output, or to control channels of distribution. In these twelve cases, in other words, the patent-holding groups were trying to push to its logical extreme the doctrine of the cracking-patents case. The outcome indicates that the courts have in late years greatly narrowed the scope of patent licensing and cross-licensing arrangements. Though the General Electric and the Standard Oil Company of Indiana decisions have never been overruled, it is at least doubtful that either still represents a valid and binding precedent.

Patent Abuses in Glass

The practices of no single company—indeed, the business arrangements of no single industry—illustrate all the abuses to which the patent system is subject. Misuse of patents apparently is so widespread and takes so many different forms that it would require almost a comprehensive survey of American manufacturing to cover the subject exhaustively. Nevertheless, a single recent case—concerning the Hartford Empire Corporation—gives a fairly clear picture

63. *U.S.* v. *U.S. Gypsum Co.*, 333 U.S. 364 (1948); and *U.S.* v. *Line Material Co.*, previously cited. The Court, with only eight justices sitting, split three ways. Four of the eight, speaking through Mr. Justice Douglas, favored explicitly overruling the General Electric case; but the majority opinion, by Mr. Justice Reed, rejected that step as unnecessary.

of the concrete circumstances and specific results of various methods of using patents to restrain trade.[64] This case is noteworthy, not only as a striking example of the consequences of patent abuses in terms of market control but also as a landmark in the integration of patent law and antitrust law.

The glass industry is composed of two major parts, organized as distinct branches of trade. These are the sheet-glass and the glass container industries.[65] Two companies dominate the sheet-glass industry: Pittsburgh Plate Glass and Libby-Owens-Ford. Their operations are closely interlocked through patent cross-licensing agreements resembling those in the glass container field.[66]

The glass container branch of the industry manufactures bottles and bulbs for electric lamps. The Corning Glass Works completely monopolizes the electric lamp bulb business, and it is also an important producer of such speciality products as heat-resistant ware and glass tubing.[67] In the bottle field proper five producers practically

64. *U.S.* v. *Hartford Empire Co.,* 46 Fed.Supp. 541 (1942); judgment for defendants affirmed on appeal but certain features of the decree modified, 323 U.S. 386 (1945); on the government's petition for a clarification of the judgment, directives to the trial court amended in minor respects, 324 U.S. 570 (1945).

The case began with a complaint filed December 11, 1939. After a trial lasting 112 days and resulting in a printed record running to 16,500 pages, the trial judge gave an exhaustive summary of the evidence in 628 findings of fact. He also filed 89 conclusions of law, and the Supreme Court set a modern record by allowing 19½ hours for argument. Both courts held that the defendants had clearly violated the antitrust laws. The only significant difference in their views related to the severity of the penalty to be imposed. The majority of the Supreme Court refused to sanction the provision of the lower court's decree requiring royalty-free licensing of defendants' patents. Instead, the Supreme Court directed the trial court to enter a decree stipulating compulsory licensing with reasonable royalties. The Supreme Court also directed the trial court to terminate immediately the involuntary receivership that it had imposed on Hartford Empire as a means of insuring compliance with the terms of the decree. The revision of the District Court's decree in these two important respects encountered vigorous dissents from Justices Black and Rutledge.

65. Several other branches of the industry contribute in a small way to the total output of glass products. The oldest of these branches of the industry makes pressed ware such as table tumblers. Another makes specialty ware such as optical lenses, photographic lenses, and ornamental figures. In recent years many new types of glassware have appeared on the market such as fiber glass for insulation and glass blocks for building construction.

On the historical development and the structural peculiarities of the glass industry, see Myron W. Watkins, *Industrial Combinations and Public Policy,* Houghton Mifflin, Boston, 1927, Chap. 8.

66. In an antitrust complaint, Civil No. 5239, filed in U.S. District Court for the Northern District of Ohio, on May 23, 1945, and amended March 19, 1946, the government charged that these arrangements formed the basis for a cartel in restraint of domestic and international trade in plate glass, window glass, and other types of sheet glass. This case was settled by a consent decree on September 5, 1946. See Commerce Clearing House, *Trade Regulation Service,* 1946–1947, par. 57489, p. 58216.

67. Most of the data in this section refer to the situation at the end of the 1930's, as presented in the evidence submitted in the government's antitrust case against Hart-

blanket the field. They are Owens-Illinois, Hazel-Atlas, Thatcher, Ball Brothers, and Anchor-Hocking. These companies produced in 1937 about 70 per cent of the total domestic output of glass containers. The 35 other manufacturers in the field were to all intents and purposes not competitors of the Big Five. For their output of such staples as medicine, beer and milk bottles, fruit jars, and packers' ware for food products such as ketchup, meats, and coffee was insignificant. Their main trade consisted of specially shaped bottles for perfumes, soft drinks, hair tonics, and the like.

Of the Big Five, Anchor-Hocking, the third largest, appears to have operated independently; it was early dismissed as a defendant. The other four were all intimately interconnected through patent license agreements with Hartford Empire, which itself manufactured no glassware. The largest member of the group was Owens-Illinois. Its shipments in 1938 were more than the combined shipments of the others. In fact, Owens-Illinois shared with Hartford Empire virtually a dictatorship of the whole industry.

This combination dominating the glass container field was the result of a series of maneuvers directly or indirectly related to the exploitation of patent privileges.

A Seven-Point Monopoly Plan: Hartford Empire

There were innumerable individual transactions and piecemeal mergers, all of which fitted into the general plan.[68] But to indicate

---

ford Empire and affiliated manufacturing companies. The weakening of patent controls as a result of that case may eventually bring about some changes in the relative position of various members of the industry. However, as of the beginning of 1948 sufficient time had not elapsed for any significant alteration in the general picture to make its appearance. In any event, Corning's quasi-monopoly of electric lamp bulbs and of heat-resistant ware, marketed under the trade name of Pyrex, was not materially disturbed by the Hartford Empire decision.

68. For example, Owens-Illinois reached its towering position in part as a result of mergers with some thirteen other glass container manufacturers at intervals over a period of thirty years. The largest of these acquisitions was that of the Illinois Glass Company in 1929. One of the principal factors behind all of these mergers was the strong patent position of the Owens company. In some cases the acquisitions clearly reflected Owens' desire to strengthen its patent position, but more frequently the company absorbed probably found its independent position untenable against the steady pressure that Owens could exert through the exploitation of its accumulated patents.

In addition to such piecemeal mergers, another development that helped cement the glass container industry into a monolithic structure was the organization of the Glass Container Association. The trial court considered the operations of this trade association so integrally connected with the patent pool that it listed it as one of the eight major steps in the evolution of the monopoly. Undoubtedly, as the court found, the Association acted in the role of a policeman to enforce the license restrictions that Owens and Hartford Empire imposed on the rest of the industry. Nevertheless, such

the main lines of development it will suffice to distinguish seven major steps in its evolution. These were:

1. The founding of the Owens Glass Company about 1906 to exploit Owens' basic invention in automatic glass-bottle-blowing machinery
2. The negotiation in 1916 of a contract between Hartford and Empire, a Corning subsidiary, for the concerted exploitation of patents relating to an independent development in the automatic glass-bottle-blowing art
3. The consolidation of Hartford and Empire in 1922 and the concurrent agreement dividing the field between Hartford and Corning
4. The negotiation of an offensive and defensive alliance between Hartford Empire and Owens in 1924
5. The negotiation of a tripartite agreement among Hartford Empire, Owens, and Hazel-Atlas in 1932
6. The signing of a contract between the Hartford Empire–Owens consortium and Ball Brothers in 1933
7. The signing of a contract between the Hartford Empire–Owens consortium and Lynch Machinery Company in 1933

The significant details of these events were as follows:

1. The introduction of automatic glass-bottle-blowing machinery revolutionized a trade that had previously consisted of small shops dependent on skilled artisans. As a single Owens machine displaced more than a score of hand "blowers" and "gatherers," a strong centralizing tendency in the organization of the industry was inevitable. But the tendency was strengthened by Owens' policy of persistent accumulation of improvement patents and the acquisition of competing plants, some of which had grown to substantial size by the use of semiautomatic machinery. The basic feature of the Owens invention was a suction-feed device that drew the molten glass into the mold, where pneumatic pressure "formed" it to the desired shape. The major difficulty in this process was to overcome the tendency of the molten glass to harden at the point where its flow into the mold

activities are not necessarily an adjunct of cross-licensing arrangements. Many trade associations perform comparable functions with respect to stabilization programs that have no connection with a network of patent cross-licenses.

was cut off. The original Owens invention left room for many subsequent improvements in this part of the machinery.

2. A major step forward in the bottle-blowing art came with the invention in 1912 of an automatic machine using the gob-feed process, which differed radically from the Owens process. Instead of drawing molten glass into the mold by suction out of a continuous stream, the new process used pneumatic pressure to propel into the mold a previously separated globule, or gob, of molten glass. Hartford acquired the patent on this process and made it the basis for promotion of a scheme of industrial control that ultimately at least matched that of Owens. Corning also acquired some patents in the gob-feed field, and in 1916 Hartford and Empire reached an agreement for the exchange of rights under their respective patents and the elimination of competition in their exploitation.

3. After six years of cooperation under this contract Hartford and Corning merged their interests in the bottle machinery field. They formed the Hartford Empire Company, in which Corning held 40 per cent of the stock. Hartford Empire agreed with Corning to stay out of the electric lamp bulb field in return for Corning's promise to stay out of the bottle field. A Hartford official told of the goal sought by the merger and accompanying agreement. He said that "working as one unit properly financed and properly organized, this unit . . . would, within reasonable time, dominate the entire glass industry." [69]

4. The 1924 contract between Hartford Empire and Owens brought under unified control the only commercially workable techniques for the automatic production of glass bottles. Owens gave Hartford Empire an exclusive license under all of its patents adaptable to gob feeders and forming machines, with rights to sublicense others. Hartford Empire gave Owens a nonexclusive, unrestricted, royalty-free license under its patents for forty gob-feeder units. This license was the only "unrestricted" license that Hartford Empire ever granted.[70] Owens retained exclusive control of suction-type machines.[71] In addition, Owens obtained a 50 per cent share in all

69. 46 Fed.Supp., p. 553.

70. In fact, the license was not wholly unrestricted because, whether by express provisions of the contract or by mutual understanding, Owens was bound not to use the Hartford Empire patents in Corning's field of electric lamp bulb manufacture. For a summary of the terms of the agreement, see *ibid.*, pp. 549-50 and 564.

71. The agreement did not mention suction-feed patents. But the court found that

royalties above $600,000 annually collected by Hartford Empire from its licensees. Finally, Owens obtained veto power over all licenses that Hartford Empire might negotiate.[72]

Stacking the Cards Against Competitors

Correspondence among the parties reveals the essential character of this contract, which on its face was simply a cross-licensing agreement. Soon after the conclusion of the agreement a Hartford Empire official addressed a letter to an Owens official saying that he hoped they would "soon have an opportunity for putting the cards on the table and properly stacking them for use against our common adversaries." [73]

5. The Hazel-Atlas Glass Company was the second largest bottle manufacturer in the country. At first it refused to join the Hartford Empire–Owens patent-pooling scheme. It possessed some patents of its own on feeder devices and had applications on file for important improvements. After long, fruitless negotiations, in which Hazel-Atlas showed that it preferred independence to submission, Hartford Empire eventually brought suit for infringement. Hazel-Atlas was convinced that Hartford Empire had obtained by fraud the principal patent on which it based the charge of infringement. Hazel-Atlas hired detectives to trace the origin of certain statements submitted to the Patent Office in support of the application for this Hartford Empire patent, but it could not prove the suspected fraud.

"it was the . . . understanding of the parties that there would be no undue competition between the suction and the gob-feed processes and that Owens intended to guard [against] any invasion of the suction field by anyone, including Hartford." *Ibid.*, p. 549. By a supplemental agreement in 1932, Owens obtained an option on all present and future Hartford patents relating to the suction-feed process. *Ibid.*, p. 570.

72. Owens never had occasion to use its veto power, because Hartford Empire had the same interest as Owens in rigidly restricting its licensees in order to strengthen the joint patent monopoly. In 1931, at the urgent solicitation of Hartford, Owens agreed to cancel this provision of the 1924 agreement (Section 22). Hartford's interest in obtaining an annulment of Section 22 was avowedly based on the desire to make the basic 1924 agreement less vulnerable to attack under the antitrust laws.

Cooperation between the senior monopoly partners after Hazel-Atlas joined the consortium shows that the cancellation of Section 22 did not alter Hartford Empire's practice of consulting Owens before issuing licenses and obtaining its approval of the proposed provisions thereof. A Hazel-Atlas official admonished Hartford not to reveal the influence of its *manufacturing* partners (Owens and Hazel-Atlas) on its licensing policy. He said: "It seems to me that when people like the Maywood Glass Company take up with the Hartford Empire Company about the extension of licenses, that Hartford should certainly not write them and tell them they are referring it to the glass companies for decision; that is what they did in this case. This makes a lot of hard feeling among the competition." *Ibid.*, p. 591.

73. *Ibid.*, p. 611. The "common adversaries" were apparently the remaining independents.

Though Hazel-Atlas obtained a judgment in its favor in one Circuit Court of Appeals in 1932, another Circuit Court of Appeals in the same year held one of Hartford's most important patents valid and infringed by Hazel-Atlas.[74] Rather than incur continuing heavy expenses of litigation and risk eventual defeat, Hazel-Atlas took advantage of its still favorable position to effect a settlement.

By the terms of the agreement Hazel-Atlas obtained a one-third interest in Hartford Empire's royalty income above $850,000 a year. At the same time Owens agreed to accept a reduction in its share of Hartford's "excess" royalty income from one half to one third. Unlike Owens, however, Hazel-Atlas was obliged to grant Hartford licenses, with power to sublicense, under all glass machinery patents it had accumulated or might henceforth acquire. Again unlike Owens, Hazel-Atlas was obliged to pay Hartford royalties on all its feeder machines—even though at least some of these machines were Hazel-Atlas machines constructed before the agreement, independently of Hartford Empire patents.

Ten years after this settlement, Hazel-Atlas discovered for the first time that its suspicions were well grounded regarding the circumstances under which Hartford Empire had obtained the principal patent at issue in the infringement suit that led to the 1932 settlement. It therefore brought suit to have vacated the 1932 decree adjudging it an infringer. The Supreme Court upheld Hazel-Atlas's contention and directed the Circuit Court to annul the patent.[75]

74. These decisions were, respectively, *Hartford Empire Co.* v. *Nivison-Weiskopf Co.*, 58 Fed. *2d* 701 (1932); and *Hartford Empire Co.* v. *Hazel-Atlas Glass Co.*, 59 Fed. *2d* 399 (1932). In the former case, Hazel-Atlas was defending a suit for contributory infringement brought against one of its customers.

75. *Hazel-Atlas Glass Co.* v. *Hartford Empire Co.*, 322 U.S. 238 (1944). Though the Court split 5 to 4 on this decision, the minority, for whom Mr. Justice Jackson wrote a dissenting opinion, did not question the appropriateness of some relief from the 1932 decree in view of the disclosures regarding the disreputable means by which Hartford Empire had obtained it—and the patent. The minority simply sought to have the case sent back to the District Court for a "more orderly procedure."

For the majority Mr. Justice Black wrote an opinion vehemently denouncing the tactics Hartford Empire had employed to subdue the largest independent producer in the industry. The evidence showed that Hartford Empire had paid a former president of the glass workers' union $8,000 to sign an article, which officers and attorneys of Hartford Empire and Owens had prepared, representing that the invention in question was a substantial advancement in the art, and had used this article both in the Patent Office, to support its application for the patent, and in court, to defend the patent's validity.

After summarizing the facts, Mr. Justice Black said: "Every element of the fraud here disclosed demands the exercise of the historic power of equity to set aside fraudulently begotten judgments. . . . This matter does not concern only private parties. . . . It is a wrong against the institutions set up to protect and safeguard the public, insti-

Meanwhile the infringement suit had served its purpose. It had brought Hazel-Atlas into the patent fold and had given the tripartite consortium virtually unrivalled mastery of the industry.

6. In one special part of the field, however, the dominant group still faced the competition of a well-entrenched independent. Ball Brothers was the largest maker of fruit jars, in the manufacture of which it used Owens suction-type machines under an exclusive license granted nearly a quarter century earlier. Fortified by this contract, Ball at first rejected Hartford Empire's invitation to give up its suction machine rights and accept a restricted share of the market under the gob-feed patents umbrella. Ball took the position that it had nothing to gain from a nonexclusive Hartford license as long as Hartford had outstanding four licenses for the manufacture of fruit jars in unlimited quantities.[76] After some reshuffling of these licenses, including concessions from Owens and Hazel-Atlas to limit their output of fruit jars, Ball eventually accepted a Hartford license. The agreement recognized Ball's paramount position in the fruit jar field and, in return for an agreement to pay Hartford Empire stipulated royalties, practically guaranteed to Ball a major share of the market. Moreover, Ball received assurance that in accordance with Hartford Empire's traditional policy no new licenses would be issued in this special field.

Last Independent Brought in Line

7. Finally the Lynch company, the largest independent manufacturer of glass-making machinery, joined the patent consortium in 1933. By the terms of a cross-licensing agreement Lynch received the right to make and sell forming machines embodying Hartford patents. But Lynch was required to exact discriminatory terms of buyers other than Hartford licensees. According to the court, "the

tutions in which fraud cannot complacently be tolerated consistently with the good order of society." *Ibid.*, pp. 245-46.

After this decision disbarment proceedings were instituted against several of the attorneys representing Hartford Empire in the 1932 infringement suit and these led to an order of disbarment. See P. Marcus, "Patents, Antitrust Law, and Antitrust Judgments Through Hartford Empire," *Georgetown Law Journal*, November 1945, pp. 1-63.

76. Owens, Hazel-Atlas, Knox, and General were the four such licensees. The latter two were eventually eliminated as factors in the negotiation. With the help of Owens and Hartford, Ball bought out Knox. In return for $100,000 cash, General relinquished its unlimited fruit jar license and agreed to stay out of the domestic household trade in this line of products. These transactions were all part of the 1933 deal that brought Ball into a more precisely defined relation to the glass container pool. See *U.S.* v. *Hartford Empire,* 46 Fed.Supp., pp. 582-84.

result of the agreement was that Lynch could sell no narrow neck forming machines except to persons who had first obtained a forming machine license from Hartford." [77]

The Lynch deal closed the last opportunity for independent bottle manufacturers to obtain the more important kinds of glass-making machinery without paying toll to the patent monopolists. One or two concerns still manufactured such minor elements in glass-making equipment as the lehrs, or ovens, for tempering the ware. In 1934 a Hartford representative approached one such manufacturer, the Amsler-Morton Company of Pittsburgh, with an offer of a merger. Amsler-Morton was to receive a one-third interest in the Hartford Empire lehr business. In view of the volume of business it had developed in this field, Amsler-Morton considered these terms too harsh. But the Hartford representative left no doubt that the patent consortium was in no mood to brook continued competition. "If you do not go on with us," he said, "you are going to be sued, and continue to be sued until you are out of business . . . It is our plan that nobody in the glass industry is going to be allowed to own one piece of equipment." [78]

Amsler-Morton rejected the Hartford offer and rashly elected to try to continue as an independent manufacturer. Hartford Empire thereupon threatened to bring suit against Amsler-Morton's customers, thus avoiding the risk of having its patents declared invalid in a suit directly against Amsler-Morton. In one such suit, after the District Court had held that the Amsler-Morton lehr did not infringe any of Hartford's patents, the Circuit Court of Appeals reversed the judgment.[79] Without adequate funds to continue the fight, Amsler-Morton withdrew from the field, its glass container equipment business ruined.

77. *Ibid.,* p. 550. In the sequence of processes used in making bottles, "forming" is the next step after "feeding," that is, after placing the "gob" of molten glass in the mold.

78. *Ibid.,* p. 599. The reference to the ownership of glass-making equipment is explained by the fact that Amsler-Morton sold its lehrs while, as in the case of its other glass-making equipment, Hartford Empire only leased its lehrs. The advantages of a leasing arrangement for keeping glass manufacturers in line are obvious.

79. *Hartford Empire Co.* v. *Swindell Bros.,* 18 Fed.Supp. 191 (1937); reversed, 96 Fed. *2d* 227 (1938). Amsler-Morton was required by contract to defend this suit. As the trial court in the antitrust action said, "It was limited in its defense of the suit, because Swindell was under license and lease from Hartford and had agreed not to contest the validity of Hartford's patents." *U.S.* v. *Hartford Empire,* 46 Fed.Supp., p. 551. On this whole episode, see TNEC Hearings, Pt. 2, pp. 596-602.

Hartford Empire: Monopoly Through Patent Abuse

The ruthless policy that the Hartford Empire–Owens combination pursued in building up its patent monopoly was not a chance outcome of practical exigencies or of casual consideration. It was part of a deliberate plan to monopolize the entire industry. Evidence of this may be found not only in the combination's persistent efforts to eliminate competition [80] and in its steady accumulation of hundreds of patents in all branches of the glass-making art, but also in the explicit statements of members of the combination. Thus the secretary-treasurer of Hartford Empire outlined the company's policy as follows:

> It has always been our ambition to obtain patents which related to furnace, melting and refining, feeding, delivery, forming, automatic handling, carrying, stacking, and annealing. Conceivably we might lose patent domination of one or more important links, but still retain practical control of the whole chain by means of control of the most efficient form of the other links. . . . we adopted the policy which we have followed ever since of restricted licensing. That is to say,
>
> (a) We licensed the machines only to selected manufacturers of the better type, refusing many licensees whom we thought would be price-cutters, and
>
> (b) We restricted their fields of manufacture, in each case to certain specific articles, with the idea of preventing too much competition.
>
> (c) In order to retain more complete control of the situation, we retained title to the machines and simply leased them for a definite period of years, usually 8 or 10 years.[81]

The record contains further evidence of the resolute determination of the chief architects of this "glass house" to control the entire industry. A 1924 Hartford memorandum referring to the basic agreement between Hartford Empire and Owens declares that "the com-

80. The instances of absorption or expulsion of competitors mentioned in the text are merely illustrative of a long list of similar maneuvers. To add only one more example, when Hartford discovered in 1925 that a rival, Federal, had developed a feeder machine that was "successful" and "a distinctly different type from those developed by Hartford and Owens," according to the words of a Hartford official, it paid $1,600,000 to get rid of this competitive threat.

A Hartford memorandum analyzing the risk of antitrust prosecution on account of this transaction stated: "Of course, the court might order that we transfer the entire Federal licensing business to some other party and turn over to that party the Federal patents. . . . I do not see much danger of having any of these deals upset. . . . If they are upset, I still believe that by that time we will be in a better position, even with such dissolution, than we would be otherwise." Quoted by Mr. Justice Black in his dissenting opinion, *Hartford Empire* v. *U.S.*, 323 U.S., p. 437, to show that the majority's "watering down" of the District Court's decree amounted to a confirmation of the Hartford official's shrewd forecast.

81. *U.S.* v. *Hartford Empire,* 46 Fed.Supp., pp. 611 and 593.

mercial considerations involved . . . are of greater importance than the relative patent values controlled by the two companies. By 'commercial considerations' is meant the domination of outside feeders, the stabilization of the industry tending against irresponsible price-cutting." [82]

When the case reached the Supreme Court that tribunal unanimously agreed that the evidence disclosed a clear violation of the antitrust law. But the majority regarded as too severe the terms of the District Court's decree and refused to uphold the provision requiring compulsory, royalty-free licensing of the formidable array of patents that Hartford Empire had accumulated in the course of its long climb to ascendancy in the industry.[83] The court pointed out that the antitrust laws provided specific penalties for violations thereof and that the specified penalties did not include forfeiture of defendants' assets otherwise than by way of a cash fine. In the opinion of the majority a requirement of royalty-free licensing was tantamount to cancellation of the patents.

In vigorous dissents Mr. Justice Black and Mr. Justice Rutledge denounced the majority's "watering down" of the District Court's decree. After reviewing the facts Mr. Justice Rutledge declared:

> When the patent-holder so far overreaches his privilege as to intrude upon the rights of others and the public protected by the antitrust legislation, and does so in such a way that he cannot further exercise the privilege without also trespassing on the rights thus protected, either his rights or the other person's and the public's rights must give way. It is wholly incongruous in such circumstances to say that the privilege of the trespasser shall be preserved and the rights of all others . . . shall continue to give way . . . this is substantially what the defendants have sought . . . so inverted an idea of equity, or of the law, cannot stand . . . The court's major modifications, in my opinion, emasculate the [District Court's] decree.[84]

Patents and the Antitrust Laws

As the patent system has actually developed, it has in various ways provided legal cover for practices that undermine a competitive economic system. Any governmental grant of exclusive patent rights limits, at least in the field the franchise covers, freedom of enterprise and competitive regulation of the market. Yet, on a broad

82. *Ibid.*, p. 561.
83. *Hartford Empire* v. *U.S.*, 323 U.S. 386 (1945).
84. *Ibid.*, pp. 452-53.

reckoning, such grants need not be incompatible with the rule of competition in the economy as a whole. Public utility franchises probably help conserve competition in the industries that depend on the franchise holders for transportation, power, or other services. Similarly, the patent system could be remodelled so that, even under modern conditions, it would provide an adequate stimulus to technological advance while at the same time imposing fewer limitations and less severe handicaps on competitive enterprise than it now does.

In view of the opposition of strong vested interests, such a remodelling will require a determined, coordinated drive by the three major branches of government, backed by an informed public opinion. Despite the impressive line of twelve recent cases in which the Supreme Court has heroically struggled to adapt the patent system to the needs of a competitive industrial order and release technology from oppressive restraints,[85] correction of patent abuses will be a slow process at best unless Congress lends a hand. Since Congress has sanctioned patent rights, it is for Congress to define the correlative patent obligations—a logical step that legislatures have taken as a matter of course in reference to all other franchise holders. Without such legislative definition, judicial precedents hardened by a century of established usage cannot easily be overthrown.

Even after the Hartford Empire, United States Gypsum, and Line Material cases, it is still questionable whether a single corporation may not lawfully accumulate a formidable array of patents by buying up every important invention applicable in a particular industry and by means of restrictive licenses control the quantity and quality of output, the geographic and industrial field of sales, and even the prices of most, if not all, producers in that field.[86] The tendency of the Supreme Court in the past ten years to scrutinize more closely the standards of invention in use by the Patent Office has plainly had a salutary effect in reducing the multiplicity of patents, but it will take a long time to bring administrative practice into conformity

85. As Judge Learned Hand has suggested, "perhaps the system is outworn." *D. & A. Chemical Co.* v. *Mimex,* 124 Fed. *2d* 986 (1942), at p. 990.

86. Though the twelve recent cases listed in footnotes 56-63 represent a radical change in patent law, all of them, except those involving restriction on the use of unpatented materials in or with patented devices, turned on the issue of conspiracy. In the two most recent cases decided in March 1948, for example, the decisive factor was the concerted action among a group of competing manufacturers, both licensors and licensees.

with enlightened judicial conceptions of what constitutes genuine invention.

Legislation Needed to Preserve Competition

If the goal of public policy is to preserve competition—to make it effective—a prompt and thorough legislative reconsideration of the patent problem appears essential. Otherwise relief from patent abuses may be too little and too late. The increasing demand for patent reform in recent years provides a good omen for early action in this direction. The Temporary National Economic Committee placed revision of the patent laws in the forefront of its recommendations, and in response thereto Congress adopted four minor amendments to accelerate Patent Office procedure.[87] Shortly thereafter, on December 12, 1941, President Roosevelt appointed a National Patent Planning Commission. This Commission could find little to criticize in the American patent system, which it considered "the best in the world." [88] Its only significant recommendations were (1) establishment of a single Court of Patent Appeals and (2) a requirement that patent agreements be filed in the Patent Office.

Congress was not satisfied that these measures touched the heart of the problem. After extensive hearings on technological mobilization before the Senate (Bone) Committee on Patents and the (Kilgore) Subcommittee on War Mobilization of the Senate Military Affairs Committee, Senator Kilgore and others in 1945 and 1946 introduced five bills having as their main object the release of technology from stifling restraints founded on patent abuses.[89] These bills, together with the proposals put forward by Dr. Vannevar Bush, head of the Office of Scientific Research and Development, in his report to the President in July 1945, *Science: The Endless Frontier,* formed the basis for the projected National Science Foundation.[90]

87. 34 U.S. Code, Secs. 52, 57, 59a, and 63 (1940). See TNEC, *Final Report and Recommendations,* S.Doc. 35, 77th Cong., 1st sess., Washington, 1941, pp. 36-37.

88. *The American Patent System,* Report of the National Patent Planning Commission, H.Doc. 239, 78th Cong., 1st sess., Washington, 1943, p. 1.

89. See *Scientific Research,* S.Doc. 92, 79th Cong., 1st sess., November 1945; *ibid.,* S.Rept. 1136, Pt. 2, 79th Cong., 2d sess., May 1946; and *Science Legislation,* Appendix to Report of the Subcommittee on War Mobilization to the (Senate) Committee on Military Affairs, 79th Cong., 1st sess., Subcommittee Monograph No. 5, December 1945.

90. See *National Science Foundation,* Report to accompany S. 526, S.Rept. 78, 80th Cong., 1st sess., March 26, 1947. Though Congress passed the National Science Founda-

The major thrust of the congressional program has been toward subsidizing scientific research with public funds. The sponsors of the program have not squarely faced the issue of the impact of such subsidized research on the patent system. Agitation for direct reform of the patent system has continued, however, and in April 1945 the President appointed an interdepartmental Patent Survey Committee.[91] If this committee can avoid falling into the rut that made the work of the National Patent Planning Commission an exercise in futility, it has a rare opportunity to prepare the way for a remodelling of the patent system that will bring it into greater harmony with the objectives of antitrust policy.

Suggestions for Revision of Patent Laws

It is beyond the scope of this chapter to explore possible ways to reconstruct the whole framework of the American patent system in order to make it a more efficient instrument for achieving the constitutional objective of promoting "the Progress of . . . useful Arts." But it will be useful to canvass briefly less drastic remedies for making the patent system less of a hindrance to the competitive process of industrial regulation. A convenient procedure will be to follow the outline of patent abuses already considered.

To abate patent multiplicity two measures immediately suggest themselves. The first is to raise the standard of patentable invention. Recent Supreme Court cases indicate clearly how Congress could make a beginning in this needed reform.[92] The Court has increasingly

tion Act, the President vetoed it in September 1947. On May 10, 1950 the Act became law. Public Law 507, 81st Cong., 2d sess. In preparation for the contemplated establishment of the Foundation, whenever the Executive and the Congress could agree on a suitable administrative plan, the President appointed a Science Research Board in 1947. Its report, *Science and Public Policy,* in five volumes, was published in 1947. About the same time, on request of the President, the Attorney General undertook an investigation of *Government Patent Practices and Policies.* See Report and Recommendations of the Attorney General to the President (under above title), 3 vols., Washington, 1947. This report was confined, except for certain monographic studies in Volume 3, to policies and procedures of various governmental agencies in relation to patents.

91. This committee, under the chairmanship of William H. Davis, is still (spring 1950) engaged in its survey and has submitted no report. See the chairman's statement of the problem, "Proposed Modifications in the Patent System," *Law and Contemporary Problems,* Autumn 1947, pp. 796-806.

92. See, for example, the opinion of Mr. Justice Douglas in *Cuno Engineering Co.* v. *Automatic Devices Corp.,* 314 U.S. 84 (1941), at pp. 90-92; the opinion of Mr. Justice Murphy in *Dow Chemical Co.* v. *Halliburton,* 324 U.S. 320 (1945), at pp. 328-29; the opinion of Mr. Justice Jackson in *Sinclair & Carrol Co.* v. *Interchemical Corp.,* 325 U.S. 327 (1945), at p. 335; and the opinion of Mr. Justice Douglas in *Funk Bros. Seed Co.* v. *Kalo Inoculant Co.,* 333 U.S. 127 (1948).

emphasized that to be patentable an invention must be not only "new and useful" but must exhibit a degree of novelty that rises higher than mere skillful adaptation, and a degree of utility that amounts to more than commercial profitability. Were Congress to lay down the rule that a patentable invention must represent a genuine technological advance, it would materially help the Supreme Court in its efforts to raise the standard of invention.[93]

A second way to abate the evils of patent multiplicity would be to eliminate food and medicine from patentable subject matter. In the interests of public health and nutrition it is anomalous still to permit private corporations to monopolize such products. Patent medicines are an anachronism, peculiar to the United States. In England, as already noted, the public is not dependent on the chance error of a patentee in overstating his claims to achieve freedom of access to health-building vitamins.[94] Monopoly profits are surely an unnecessary incentive for the experimental research leading to genuine advances in medical science. To permit commercial groups to derive monopoly profits from such research appears contrary to the public interest.

Procedural Reforms

Of the many procedural reforms that would improve the patent system, three are noteworthy. The first is to make applications a matter of public record and to forbid reissues. The second is to provide for the intervention of a disinterested public agency or official in interference proceedings. If this can be accomplished only by transferring interference proceedings to the courts, perhaps to a special patent court, Congress might well consider doing so.

The record reviewed in this chapter plainly shows that in one way or another the public interest must have a defender in the settlement of a contest over priority of invention between two private parties if the channels of trade are not to be cluttered with a large number of invalid patents. The opportunity for fraud and the invita-

93. Cf. Stedman, *op. cit.*, pp. 664-67.

94. Referring to *Vitamin Technologists, Inc.* v. *Wisconsin Alumni Research Foundation*, 146 Fed. *2d* 941 (1945); certiorari denied, 325 U.S. 876 (1945). The case is discussed in Chap. 10. See also in this connection, FTC Complaint No. 5070, order entered March 19, 1948, against American Dietaids Company directing the respondent to cease and desist from false and misleading advertising of its patent medicine, "Enrich," a vitamin preparation.

tion to collusion under the existing procedure encourage the parties to sink their differences and share the spoils.

Finally, Congress might well consider the advantages of a measure for promptly establishing the validity of patents by judicial process at public expense. No good reason has been advanced for throwing upon independent competitors the burden of determining whether the Patent Office has improvidently taken out of the public domain some technique that rightfully belongs there and given the exclusive right to use it to a private monopolist.[95] One way to accomplish this end would be to empower the Department of Justice, either on its own initiative or at the request of an inventor with an adverse interest or of any enterprise threatened by an infringement suit, to institute actions in the courts to test the validity of patents.

To meet patent-licensing abuses Congress could make a significant beginning, at least, by heeding the dissenting opinions in recent Supreme Court cases. It is not apparent that any advantages attend awaiting some possible change in the personnel of the Bench, or in the opinion of one or two of its members, to clear up the present muddled situation regarding the extent of a patentee's licensing power. It is the responsibility of Congress, as the supreme lawmaking body, definitely to settle such an issue, for example, as that of whether a patentee is entitled, entirely apart from questions of collusion or conspiracy, to restrict by license agreement the output and prices, or the market territories, of his licensees.

Feasibility of Compulsory Licensing

Beyond this, Congress might well consider the relief of competitive industry from oppressive licensing policies by providing for compulsory licensing on payment of reasonable royalties. One of the objections most frequently raised in opposition to this proposal is the difficulty of determining a reasonable royalty. But this objection will not withstand critical analysis.[96] The courts have had no particular difficulty in solving essentially the same problem in cases

95. Consult in this connection the penetrating and perspicacious article by W. R. Woodward, "A Reconsideration of the Patent System as a Problem of Administrative Law," *Harvard Law Review,* April 1942, especially p. 977.

96. See J. Borkin, "Patent Abuses, Compulsion to License and Recent Decisions," *Columbia Law Review,* 1943, p. 720; and M. Feuer, "The Patent Privilege and the TNEC Proposals," *Temple Law Quarterly,* February 1940, especially pp. 192-93.

involving the assessment of damages for patent infringement. That the damages judicially assessed in such cases have generally been reasonable would seem a fair inference from the absence of any suggestion, much less any agitation, for modifying established standards and procedures for recoupment of damages from infringement. In such cases, once the fact of infringement is established, the aim is to redress the injury, or as the saying goes, "make whole" the patentee. The proper measure of damages, therefore, is the market value of the privilege of using the patent for the period of the infringement. And this is equivalent to a fair royalty.

Whether or not such a measure were made applicable to all patents, Congress could at least give statutory sanction for compulsory licensing of patents that (1) have been used to accomplish a violation of the antitrust acts, (2) have been suppressed, and (3) are subject to discriminatory licensing by patent holders other than the inventor.

Perhaps the statute should specify a fourth situation in which compulsory licensing would be in order, namely, when a patent holder other than the inventor exploits the patent but does not license it. The object of such a provision would be to limit the privileges of corporations that accumulate a great number of patents as a barricade against competition.[97] At the same time, it would reserve for inventors, if they choose to exploit their inventions, the "exclusive right" to do so.

The foregoing measures might not be wholly effective in restoring the patent system to its constitutional function. But they should help materially to stop its use in circumventing the antitrust laws. They would provide constructive steps toward reform long overdue. A patent system thus revised would *complement,* instead of obstructing and hampering, a public economic policy designed to foster free enterprise and preserve effective competition.

97. Only a natural person can "invent" anything. Corporations are ineligible, now, to apply for patents. They can acquire patents only by assignment.

Chapter 15

PAST, PRESENT, AND FUTURE OF COMPETITION

IT IS DIFFICULT to describe with minute accuracy of detail the organization and structure of the American economy or to indicate to what precise extent competition still governs it. It is even more difficult to indicate precisely the changes in economic control that time has brought about. Trends and tendencies have been discontinuous, fluctuating, and inconsistent. And crosscurrents and countertrends have intervened. It is possible, nevertheless, to outline broadly the course of American industrial development for the past century.

The factory system ultimately destroyed most local, handicraft monopolies, and a network of waterways and railroads enlarged regions within which the products of factories competed. Mass-production techniques at first intensified competition. Large-scale producers not only competed with hand producers, but after driving them out of business competed vigorously among themselves for consumer favor. During the third quarter of the nineteenth century the trend was toward competitive control of industry. Competition intensified and markets broadened.

Early Trust Movement

Beginning about 1879 (with the organization of the Standard Oil Trust) the trend was reversed.[1] The new trend rapidly became defined as a full-fledged historical movement and reached a climax with the combination movement of 1897–1903. Never before or since have the structure and the method of control of an economy been so suddenly changed as during this brief period. Enterprising promoters and investment bankers put together scores of combina-

1. This is merely a convenient date. Historical trends are not reversed with the suddenness that such a precise date suggests. Adam Smith's comment on the persistent disposition of businessmen to convert convivial conversation into trade conspiracies finds ample illustration in early American economic history. Moreover, before 1879 businessmen had frequently resorted to such formal but loose arrangements as trade associations and pools to control markets.

tions embracing nearly every branch of American industry. Light and heavy industries alike were engulfed.

When the movement temporarily halted in 1903 it had transformed the character of industrial markets. Many of the combinations operated nationally, others only regionally. In both regional and national markets the combination movement greatly reduced the number of sellers. In no industry, of course, did it create pure monopoly. But many combinations controlled so much of their respective markets that they affected prices directly by their production policies; others collaborated readily with their rivals, big or little, to stabilize the market in ways that might or might not amount to illegal conspiracy. Moreover, so great was their power that smaller sellers could ignore their price policies only at great risk. Price leadership became the order of the day. In steel the United States Steel Corporation set the pace; in electrical appliances, General Electric. National Lead, Pittsburgh Plate Glass, International Harvester, American Woolen, United States Rubber, American Optical, American Window Glass, and many similar industrial giants led in their respective fields.

Trade Associations and the "New Competition"

After 1903 a countertrend set in. A few of the giant consolidations of the earlier period disintegrated; the government dissolved a few more; many others, by failing to grow as fast, lost ground relative to their smaller rivals. By World War I, United States Steel, Standard Oil of New Jersey, American Tobacco, American Sugar, International Harvester, American Can, Corn Products Refining, and a score of other consolidations, while still the leaders in their respective fields, shared control of the market with lusty rivals.

The countertrend was ruffled by crosscurrents. Businessmen, both in industries where concentration of control had gone far and in those where control was relatively decentralized, sought ways to soften the rigors of old-style competition and found a solvent in the program of "New Competition." Starting from the premise, based on familiar trade experience, that unrestrained competition might easily become ruinous, this program called for a live-and-let-live policy to replace the "law of the jungle," and promised greater security for all producers through collaboration in trade associations.

World War I accelerated the trade association movement, and

Congress brought it to flood tide by passing the National Industrial Recovery Act during the Great Depression. While the Schechter decision invalidated the Act it did not banish the trade association as a device for softening competition. Many of these organizations, operating on a national or regional basis, continued to conduct activities designed to stabilize markets.[2] Not all succeeded, but the movement undoubtedly tempered competition as a regulator of the economy.

Interwar Merger Movement

As business groups took to the trade association, a second merger movement—less spectacular than that of 1897–1903—got under way, achieving its greatest momentum during the decade after World War I. Except in younger industries such as chemicals, rayon, motion pictures, and in fields in which the combination movement had not previously made much progress, such as bread, bottles, dairy products, few new market leaders emerged. The movement was, however, pervasive.[3] Many concerns, both large and small, strengthened their market position by combining with other firms to extend either their vertical or their horizontal scope of operations, or both. In this process of amalgamation and expansion, although established market leaders kept pace with smaller concerns, few industrial giants were displaced.

In some instances this merger movement tended to centralize market control or redistribute it, facilitating centralized decision making. By buying out rivals the four leading copper producers increased their share of domestic production from about 20 per cent in 1920 to about 80 per cent in 1940. In other instances, mergers exerted a contrary influence—temporarily at any rate. National Steel became a fully integrated concern by merging several independent producers and apparently achieved enough power to unsettle the steel market.[4] Its aggressive policy, chiefly manifested by price cutting, provoked competition all around—although here as elsewhere revived competition also owed much to the Great Depression.

2. See Chaps. 7 and 8.
3. See Chap. 2.
4. See Chap. 5.

Data are not available to show exactly the net effect of the interwar merger movement on industry as a whole. However, it probably weakened competitive forces. It certainly reduced or held down the number of competitors in many markets. It enhanced the market influence of those sellers supplying, either alone or together with two or three others, a preponderant part of the goods offered in a particular market. Above all, it created an environment friendly to a live-and-let-live policy.

Although they do not accurately measure the extent to which competition was effective in determining prices in domestic markets, available statistics do throw some light on the extent to which the concentration of industry had progressed on the eve of World War II. In each of seven industries one corporation controlled the entire domestic output; in five others one company accounted for from 60 to 95 per cent; in twelve others two companies accounted for from 62 to 100 per cent. Industries in which four producers or less accounted for from 75 to 100 per cent of the total value product produced one third of the value of all manufactured products. Industries in which four producers or less turned out more than half the total value product accounted for 57 per cent of the value of all manufactured products.[5]

In manufacturing, concentration had gone furthest in industries producing heavy semifinished materials, durable goods subject to intricate belt-line assembly techniques, and products fabricated by patented or complex technical processes. In some fifty industries where style and consumer taste played a more important role, where capital requirements were relatively small, and where patents were unimportant, the four largest concerns produced less than a fourth and the eight largest concerns less than a third of the total output.[6]

In the extractive industries the location of sources of supply largely determined the extent of concentration. Where the resources were dispersed or where chance played a large role in discovery, control was generally decentralized. Agriculture, lumber, bituminous coal, crude-oil production, and fisheries remained highly competitive, except as the state intervened to prevent competition, or col-

5. See Chap. 2.
6. Clair Wilcox, *Competition and Monopoly in American Industry,* TNEC Monograph No. 21, Washington, 1940, p. 29.

lusive agreements temporarily stifled it. In sulphur, anthracite coal, and practically all metals, control was more centralized.

Retail distribution and service trades—aided by the growth of chain stores—remained for the most part competitive, in urban centers at any rate. So did the construction industry, where capital requirements are relatively small and access to the market is easy, although concerted action, frequently involving trade unions, restricted competition in many localities.

After World War II: More Mergers

It is too early to evaluate definitively the influence of World War II on the control of industry. Forces working toward and away from concentration were both at work. The armament program made the going tough for many small independents producing nonessentials and not in a position to convert their plants to war production. On the other hand, the government's liberality in financing defense facilities made it easy for a going concern to adapt its organization to the requirements of a war economy. But the little man was at a disadvantage in obtaining contracts and supplies, and the government found it convenient to allocate its war orders primarily among the big companies.

The Smaller War Plants Corporation's report on *Economic Concentration and World War II* throws some light on the problem and reveals important trends. Most of the primary contracts went to big business, as did also the leases of government-built plants and the subsidies for research.[7] In surveying the postwar outlook for competition, the report recognized that the government, in disposing of war plants, might exert a powerful influence in breaking up control of markets, but the Corporation concluded that big business was likely to "acquire a greater proportion of the . . . publicly owned facilities which it operated" than would small business. Many of the government-built plants consisted of "scrambled facilities," that is, additions to existing plants, of use only in conjunction therewith.

7. Thirty-two companies received over half (specifically, 50.5 per cent), by value, of all prime war contracts. *Economic Concentration and World War II,* Report of the Smaller War Plants Corporation to the Special Committee to Study Problems of American Business, U.S. Senate, 79th Cong., 2d sess., S.Doc. 206, Washington, 1946, pp. 30-33. The sixty-eight companies that were the top beneficiaries "received nearly two-thirds of the values of Federal research and development contracts and the top ten received nearly two-fifths of the total."

Moreover, many contracts for the private operation of government-built plants carried an option to buy the plant after the emergency. Finally, despite the fact that the Surplus Property Act was intended to "strengthen and preserve the competitive position of small business [and] to foster the development of new independent enterprise," the War Assets Administration sometimes found that only the dominant concern in the industry was in a position to make an acceptable offer. That, at least, was the reason advanced for the sale of the government's fully integrated western steel plant to a subsidiary of the United States Steel Corporation.[8]

Events appear to have justified the Smaller War Plants Corporation's forecast. Up to January 1, 1947 the government had either sold or leased plants having about one third the value of all usable government-built defense facilities. In these transactions sixteen corporations, all except one of them among the country's 250 largest manufacturing corporations, obtained 53 per cent by value of the total facilities disposed of.[9] On the basis of such data the monopoly subcommittee of the House Committee on Small Business concluded that "surplus plant disposals have actually improved the relative position of the 250 largest manufacturing corporations over their 1939 position." [10]

Moreover, World War II engendered a merger movement the scope and extent of which were still not clear four years after hostilities ceased. According to the Federal Trade Commission, more than 2,450 manufacturing and mining firms with assets totalling $5.2 billion, or roughly 5.5 per cent of the total assets of all manufacturing companies, were absorbed by other corporations between 1940 and 1946.[11] Corporations with assets of more than $50 million acquired one third of the companies merged. One hundred and

8. On the significance of this transaction to competitive conditions in the steel industry, see Chap. 9.

9. Harrison F. Houghton, "The Progress of Concentration in Industry," *American Economic Review,* Papers and Proceedings, May 1948, pp. 87-88.

10. *United States Versus Economic Concentration and Monopoly,* an investigation pursuant to H.Res. 64, 79th Cong., of the Effectiveness of the Government's Efforts to Combat Economic Concentration, Washington, 1946, p. 8.

11. Federal Trade Commission, *Report on the Merger Movement,* Washington, 1948, p. 17. Because the compilation does not generally indicate the relation of a given merger to market control, it is easy to exaggerate the significance of these data. If, for example, a cannery decides to print its own labels and buys out a local printing establishment, the "consolidation" has only the slightest, if any, bearing on the development of concentration in the control of industry.

twenty of the country's 200 largest nonfinancial corporations accounted for 27 per cent of these mergers.

The pent-up demand for consumer goods created great opportunities for new business enterprises after the war, however, and for about three years the total business population increased, more than compensating for the wartime reduction. But the increase of about 20 per cent over the prewar level in the number of active business units does not warrant the conclusion that the control of industry has been decentralized since the end of World War II. The great majority of the additions to the business population were in the retail and service trades, in which control was always decentralized.

On the whole, the war has not greatly changed the prewar picture, which was one of imperfect competition, with a few large concerns dominating the market in many important sectors of the economy.

Causes of Economic Concentration

Four major kinds of forces were responsible for limiting competition and concentrating control of industry: technical, commercial, financial, and strategic. Chapter 3 deals with this topic.

The growth of big business reflects in part a quest for the technical gains of large-scale production. The optimum scale of operations in many industries is relatively large, the optimum scale of organization even larger. Large-scale production pays; it is advantageous both to businessmen and to society.

Obviously, the advantages of size set minimum limits to the scale on which productive units can economically operate. These limits will vary from industry to industry, but in many manufacturing and extractive industries the economical scale of production is large, absolutely and relatively—too large to permit pure competition to work. Modern technology decrees an organization in some industries so large that a few sellers may supply the market (regional or national) at a lower average cost than many sellers each operating on a smaller scale could supply it. This is probably true in the manufacture of electric light bulbs, for example, of which the entire prewar domestic output was produced in only four plants.[12] Though little authentic information is available on costs, and in particular on the influence of plant capacity on unit cost, it would be reason-

12. U.S. Tariff Commission, *Incandescent Electric Lamps,* Report No. 133, Ser. II, Washington, 1939, p. 14.

able to suppose that a similar situation prevails in many other industries in which concentration of control is marked.

The advantages of size set maximum as well as minimum points to the scale on which production can be economically organized. Increasing the scale of operations, the facts indicate, does not continue indefinitely to yield lower unit costs of production. Available evidence suggests that the consolidation movement has carried the expansion of many big business units beyond the size essential for economical operation.[13]

Commercial Factors and Industrial Consolidation

Analysis and experience point to a similar conclusion with regard to the commercial advantages derived from industrial combination. Economies in selling have undoubtedly been a potent factor in the development of giant combines. A single sales force can in some lines cover a given market territory as effectively—obtain as large orders—as three or four representing different manufacturers. Consolidation also permits larger expenditures for advertising, which, up to a point, reduce not only selling costs per unit but also, indirectly, total unit cost. Without advertising it might be impossible to sell enough of either a new product or a new brand to attain the optimum scale of production. Of course many producers are big enough to advertise, even to advertise nationally, without merging with others to increase the size of the business unit. It is the incentive to advertise and the scale of advertising that mergers tend to increase. A reduction in the number of sellers tends to change the principal leverage on which sellers rely in competing for patronage from price to prestige and propaganda. So the importance of advertising as a factor in selling rises as more and more independents disappear in bigger and bigger mergers. On the other hand, this carries no implication that either selling or total costs per unit rise as the number of sellers declines. The available data on costs are too fragmentary to support or refute any general conclusion on this point.

Financial Factors in Merger Movement

The quest for lower costs does not fully explain the growth of big business and the trend toward concentration of control. Financial

13. See Chap. 3.

and strategic factors also played important roles. Many of the consolidations of the 1897–1903 period were promoted to make money for the promoter, or to stabilize or enhance security values by restricting competition.

Bigness in business, unfortunately, does not encourage risk taking. Man's urge to achieve and to hold power is great. In a private enterprise economy it may reflect itself in consolidating ownership and control in giant corporations.

The modern corporation, with its limited liability, its perpetual existence, and its legal personality, while providing a remarkably efficient device for raising funds needed for mass production, also provides a remarkably effective instrument for the creation and exercise of market domination. The holding company greatly broadened the scope for the exercise of private power and made it easier for ambitious men to acquire monopoly. It was a convenient instrument for centralizing control over previously independent enterprises, themselves incorporated. Having acquired dominion over vast segments of American industry by combining business rivals, the managers of these corporate giants were naturally more interested in perpetuating their control and preserving capital values than in risking losses by launching new ventures or by exposing their businesses to the vigorous competition of trade rivals. Stabilization of markets was unquestionably an important objective of the combination movement.

Strategic Factors in Merging Business Rivals

Many mergers were designed to make more secure the position of a firm by freeing it from dependence on others for raw materials. Companies were integrated not merely to reduce costs by eliminating some operations but to reduce their dependence on others for basic supplies. Both of these are good business reasons to integrate; but both are not of equal significance in evaluating the concentration movement.

The technical gains from integration are reflected in lower costs and, if competition survives, are passed on in lower prices to consumers. The gains from control of raw materials are of a different order. Control of exhaustible raw materials may make a company's position more secure; but if raw materials are available at competitive prices, acquiring control of them will not ordinarily lower a company's costs. If the supply of raw materials is closely held, acquiring one's own source of supply may redistribute control but it will not eliminate monopoly earnings.[14] It is, of course, strategically advantageous for a company to own its own sources of supply.

Summary of Causes of Industrial Concentration

Only a detailed study of the history of particular consolidations would reveal the relative importance of these several factors in the merger movement. Such facts as are readily available, however, bear out the conclusions of this study that financial and strategic factors have been more immediately decisive than commercial and technical factors. In the initial phase of the consolidation movement, the circumstances of the wave of trust building that swept the country and the tactics employed to hold or extend power clearly indicate that such archetypical trusts as Standard Oil, American Sugar Refining, American Tobacco, and United States Steel were bent on market control rather than on reducing production costs.

There is little evidence, indeed, to suggest that the great combination movement was directed toward accomplishing anything but the elimination of competition. Its scope and spread could scarcely support any other conclusion. It took place on a scale and at a tempo inconsistent with a genuine quest for cost reduction. In a competitive economy reductions in production costs are achieved piecemeal. The short but rapid phase of indiscriminate consolidation that so revolutionized the pattern of business control about 1900 took place without any special new development in the field of technology, indicating that consolidation was prompted primarily by strategic and financial considerations.

The merger movement of the 1920's cannot be so simply explained. It was compounded of the several factors already analyzed in this study, but commercial considerations were more conspicuous than in the earlier phase of the trust movement. However, financial and strategic factors seem to have played a more important role than either technical or commercial ones. What the merged companies and their bankers apparently sought was to improve the position of the merged companies in the market by gaining control of raw products and market outlets.

14. Discovery of new sources of supply, of course, would tend to intensify competition.

In the merger movement of the 1940's strategic considerations were apparently decisive. Companies with large war profits sought security in postwar markets. They fortified their positions by rounding out their operations. It was more prudent to buy out established concerns than to launch new enterprises. In a period marked by severe shortages of materials, it was also an easier and quicker way to expand.

However, government tax policies added new force to the postwar merger movement by providing an incentive to small concerns to sell out. Corporations must pay a combined normal and surtax of, ordinarily, 38 per cent of their earnings. To avoid a tax penalty, they must also redistribute not less than 70 per cent of their net income as dividends or prove they have a special need for the funds. As the stock of most small corporations is ordinarily closely held and the stockholders may be subject to high surtaxes on their individual incomes, the owners of a small business frequently found it more profitable to sell out and pay the capital gains tax (ordinarily 25 per cent) on the increased value of their business than to run the risks and continue the responsibilities of enterprisers.

Strategic and financial factors have unquestionably carried combination in many fields far beyond the point where the economies of large-scale production cease. But it is important for policy makers to remember that the economies of large-scale production nevertheless provide a ground for business units larger than contemplated in the economists' theory of pure competition. In some industries the most efficient scale of production is so large that, if every producer attained it, a small number of sellers could supply the market at the lowest unit cost.

Markets Not Perfect

It is also important to remember that competition does not generally work out in the business world in accordance with abstract formulas. A real economy is not frictionless. Buyers and sellers are not fully informed about the market, and cannot hope to be. Knowledge of market conditions must remain imperfect; information available to some is not always accessible to all. Custom and habit may have more influence than reason on economic behavior. The movement of capital and labor between industries and firms may be sluggish. Consumers are far more ignorant of market conditions than sellers. They have neither the technical skill nor the time to inform themselves on relative values and prices. People do not buy as cautiously today as their grandparents did. They seem to know less about goods, whereas they should know more; for goods themselves are more complex than they used to be. It is therefore easier for sellers to deceive consumers than was once the case.[15]

Indeed, it is common knowledge that with such market imperfections competition does not guarantee that the consumer will always get his money's worth. Both anonymous manufacturers with no reputation at stake and giant combines with only ineffective competition to worry about may exploit the ignorance of consumers. Even big department stores and chain stores competing vigorously for patronage by offering recognizable bargains, or loss leaders, may at the same time exploit ignorance. Loss leaders attract both the wary and the unwary into a store, but they do not guarantee that when the consumer buys unbranded goods he gets his money's worth. Loss leaders may serve as a screen behind which to mulct the consumer.

It is essential in shaping policy with respect to such business practices to recognize that the alleged shortcomings of competition may reflect a failure to achieve it rather than a defect in competition itself. The so-called wastes of competition are generally, nowadays, the wastes of quasi-monopoly or imperfect competition. In order to eliminate or reduce them it may be necessary to change the rules of the game, but hardly to abolish the game entirely.

While competition as it works out in the market is not always adequate to protect the public interest, neither is quasi-monopoly always as detrimental to the public interest as the writings of some economists might lead one to conclude. In the first place, pure

15. Many studies reveal both the inability of consumers to pass intelligent judgment on relative qualities of goods and the lack of correlation between prices and quality. A laboratory analysis of cotton sheeting at Teachers College, Columbia University, some years ago showed a complete lack of correlation between price and quality. The sheeting eighth in quality was second in price; of two sheetings identical in quality one sold for two and one half times the other. The best quality sheeting sold for less than the second-to-poorest. The cheapest sheeting was sixth in quality, and the most expensive third. Without benefit of the laboratory tests consumers failed utterly in their effort to rank the sheetings on a quality basis. A group of trained salespeople did no better. From the article by Cook, "Do Your Customers Really Know Your Product?: A Scientific Study of the Consumers' Buying Judgment," in *Cotton and Its Products*, January 1926; cited by Stuart Chase and F. J. Schlink, *Your Money's Worth*, Macmillan, New York, 1931, pp. 85-86.

A more recent study of gasoline grades and prices by the University of Texas Bureau of Industrial Chemistry showed similar lack of correlation between quality and price.

monopoly, like perfect competition, is a theoretical concept. It is never found in the market. Substitute goods, potential competition, business standards, a sense of social responsibility, and, in the United States, the fear of government intervention and public opinion, limit the power of big business relentlessly to exploit the market. These are often effective checks.

Substitute Goods Limit Monopoly Power

There are few commodities for which no substitutes are available. Although modern technology with its heavy capital requirements and its emphasis on specialization has introduced some rigidities into the making and using of specific goods, it has also made for flexibility by increasing the variety of goods. Many metals with different properties have common uses. Aluminum is interchangeable with copper in electrical transmission lines, with magnesium in a score of other uses. Moreover, magnesium and aluminum compete with each other, at least in a technical sense, and perhaps also in a commercial sense, since the antitrust judgments condemning their joint control. They also compete with light steels, plywood, and more recently with plastics, in the making of furniture, household appliances, and other products. Plastics compete with leather, rubber, and glass. Silk competes with rayon and nylon, and all three compete with each other; and, wonder of wonders, they also compete with fine-spun glass for milady's expensive gown. In truth, synthetic fibers have virtually revolutionized the textile industry.

In both the making and the using of goods buyers thus have many choices despite the reduction in the number of sellers of many specific kinds of products—fabricated from a particular material or in a particular way. These possible choices limit greatly the influence a seller might otherwise exert over the market. Not only do different products compete for the same uses; different processes compete in the making of identical or nearly identical products. Solvay-process alkalies compete with electrolytic alkalies. Plastics emerge from cellulose and from coal or petroleum; rubber from trees and chemicals. Commercial nitrogen is obtained as a byproduct from coke ovens and meat-packing plants, as a natural product from the Chilean deposits of *caliche,* as a synthetic product from the air by a half-dozen variants of the Haber-Bosch process.

Potential Competition and Respect for Public Opinion and Law

Potential competition, as well as substitutes, checks monopoly power. Where there are no artificial or arbitrary obstacles, such as exclusive control of a limited natural resource or the ownership of exclusive patents, capital may quickly invade a field that promises relatively high returns.[16] The temptation of dominant sellers to exploit an industry may be tempered by this fact.

Finally, monopolists are not always irresponsible. In the United States they live in constant fear of prosecution and exposure under the antitrust statutes. They are under the continual surveillance of public officials. They realize that they may become the football of politics and the object of popular obloquy, jeopardizing large investments. The constant threat of public intervention, combined with a sense of decency and fair play on the part of the managers of a quasi-monopoly, may restrain greed. Big businessmen may realize that traffic will bear less in the long run than in the short, and they are likely to want to preserve their dominant position over the long run, even if it means forbearance in the short.

They may, also, prefer self-restraint to the external restraint that active competition imposes. Federal price regulators during World War II found that industries dominated by a few big sellers offered less resistance to the government's price control program than industries in which sellers were more numerous and smaller.

Moreover, oligopolies often check each other. This they do especially when they confront each other as buyers and sellers. General Motors, with its tremendous requirements for steel, and other industrial giants in the same position, whether or not they follow the example of Ford in obtaining their own source of supply, may exert almost as much influence on the price of steel as does the United States Steel Corporation. Under such circumstances relative bargaining strength determines prices. By playing one steelmaker off against another, big motor manufacturers are able to get steel for very much less than could smaller buyers. And if motor manufac-

16. Where much capital is required and well-entrenched firms dominate a field, as in the steel industry, businessmen are reluctant to launch new enterprises or find it impossible to obtain adequate capital through investment bankers interested in the stability of the industry. Although independent steel companies have grown more rapidly than the United States Steel Corporation, and have improved their position by combining, only a single wholly new major integrated company has come into the industry in about a half century.

turers compete in selling automobiles, the gains are passed on to the consumer in lower prices and improved quality.

How to Foster Effective Competition

As pointed out in Chapter 5, the greater the number of sellers and the more diverse the conditions under which they operate, the more likely they are to behave like genuine competitors if they act independently. Even though every seller follows a price policy designed to maximize his earnings, as the number of sellers increases it becomes increasingly unlikely that they will all follow identical pricing policies. This is true for several reasons.

Business rivals are usually inclined to be suspicious of each other. Even in markets of few sellers, one may cut prices for fear that if he doesn't another will—thereby "getting the jump" on him. The greater the number of sellers, the greater the uncertainty of each about how the rest will behave, and the greater the likelihood of price cutting when demand is slack. Moreover, no two sellers are likely to make precisely the same estimate of consumer response to price cuts. Small firms have more to gain from cutting prices than large ones. And a small seller may believe that the larger sellers will tolerate price cuts in restricted areas without matching them. Again, sellers often differ in their costs and financial needs. Small firms sometimes find it necessary to increase output in order to lower costs, and may decide that to increase sales they must lower prices. As to financial needs, those of some producers may be more urgent than others. If they were guided solely by their short-run interest, these hard-pressed producers might have to close up shop at once. Hence, with several sellers in the market the temptation to cut prices, when they are above marginal cost, may become irresistible.

When demand falls off the result is likely to be secret price discrimination and eventually open price cutting. The lower limit to price reduction by any producer will be the direct costs encountered in producing the added output—that is, his marginal costs. In the absence of concerted action among two or more business rivals there is always the possibility that price may sink to marginal costs. The greater the number of producers, the greater the likelihood that it will. In the long run, total unit costs must be covered or resources will move from the less remunerative to the more remunerative fields.

Thus, the public interest may be as well protected in markets of imperfect competition as in purely competitive markets if sellers are not too few and if they do not resort to concerted action. If this is true, what kind of public policies are most dependable for insuring that competition will be effective, even though imperfect?

Increasing the Number of Sellers

To foster effective though imperfect competition the first requirement is to see to it that the number of producers, industry by industry, is as large as is practical. The ideal presumably would be the largest number consistent with the economies of mass production and distribution. It would, to be sure, be impossible to enforce a law that limited the number of producers by this criterion.[17] Even though suitable standards are lacking by which to determine precisely how many firms the most economical scale of production requires, it is evident that it would be possible, without sacrifice of efficiency, to have far more producers in many industries than at present. Two steps would be necessary to increase the number: first, a broader interpretation and a more vigorous enforcement of antitrust laws; second, a modification of the Clayton Act with a view to preventing the merger of competing businesses.

Antitrust administration since the death of NRA has shown that it is possible to eliminate many collusive trade agreements and to minimize the effectiveness of this method of market control. But the antitrust laws have been far less effective in dissolving concerns formed primarily to control markets, owing largely to judicial hesitancy to disturb big business. Witness the outcome of the recent aluminum, steel, glass container, and titanium cases. But judicial timidity in fact reflects public indifference. Public indifference and the hostility of big business account primarily for the failure of Congress to put teeth in Section 7 of the Clayton Act.[18] Section 7

17. If it were possible, in some instances society might be obliged to choose between too many firms for efficiency and too few for effective competition.

18. Section 7 prohibits the acquisition by one corporation of stock in another where it will substantially lessen competition between the two firms or restrain trade in any line of commerce or tend to create a monopoly. As pointed out in Chapter 9, the Supreme Court by its interpretation has virtually emasculated this section of the Act. But the Act is defective in not applying the same restrictions on the acquisition of assets as it places on the acquisition of stocks. Bills designed to plug these loopholes have been introduced year after year (for example, H.R. 2357, 79th Cong., 1st sess., and H.R. 515, 80th Cong., 1st sess.), but so far none has been passed.

was intended to prevent the birth of combinations in restraint of trade rather than to destroy them. If the American people want effective competition, they must prevent and dissolve such combinations.

This raises an issue which to the undiscriminating is rapidly becoming a bugaboo—the atomization of industry. No sensible person wants to atomize American industry. And no one could if he would, except perhaps an enemy equipped with the H bomb. But because one can't establish pure competition in an industry is no reason for not blocking the further absorption of rival companies by big multiplant combines that have gained, and seek to hold, a dominant market position in that way. Nor is it a reason for not proceeding to separate such combines into as many units as are consistent with the economies of mass production—and distribution—when there is evidence that competition is ineffective.

Federal Incorporation

By less direct means the people might foster an increase in the number and independence of manufacturing enterprises. By centralizing the power of chartering companies doing business in interstate commerce and limiting the use of the holding company they could increase corporate responsibility and eliminate perhaps the most effective instrument for centralizing control. The looseness of state incorporation laws is a standing invitation to business to create giant consolidations so intricate in pattern and so great in power that they afford maximum scope for financial manipulation and market control. In these circumstances the continuing centralization of industrial control in big-business corporations reflects less a shrewd quest for productive efficiency than a strenuous pursuit of power.

Limiting the use of the holding company, raising the standards of responsibility for corporate directors and executives, and general tightening of incorporation laws would contribute greatly to the maintenance of effective competition. For it would discourage the enlargement of business enterprises beyond the size that corresponds to the economic optimum. In the absence of the artificial inducements to centralization of control that lax incorporation laws provide, the number of sellers in markets where imperfect competition now prevails would no doubt have been greater. The simple and obvious means of getting rid of these artificial inducements to corporate giantism is a federal incorporation law for businesses above a specified size if they operate in interstate or foreign commerce.

Commodity Standardization

A second way in which public policy might stimulate effective competition would be by encouraging commodity standardization. In doing so it would be important to avoid trying to standardize wants. Nobody likes to sit always in the same kind of chair, so it would be absurd to forbid furniture manufacturers to make anything but a single type. Nor does effective competition require people to submit to such farfetched standardization. On the contrary, to carry standardization to a point that makes free choice impossible is plainly to kill competition.

How, then, can commodity standardization contribute to effective competition?

First, it can curb fictitious differentiation, which is one of the main props of imperfect competition. If a manufacturer can make people believe that his product, say an ordinary vegetable-oil hand soap, is unique, that it has some special property making it good for the complexion, he can "take it out of competition" with other hand soaps, that is, with the standard or staple commodity. In technical terms, he can make the demand for his product less elastic. In common language, he can sell nearly as much at a high price as at a lower price.[19]

The chief means toward this kind of product differentiation is advertising, which promotes imperfect competition and its attendant quasi-monopolistic pricing. It is difficult, however, to do away with the nuisance of fictitious product differentiation without harm to the economy. A heavy flat-rate tax on advertising, for instance, might be harmful. While discouraging fictitious product differentiation, it would probably also discourage the introduction of new products that could not be profitably sold without extensive consumer education. This drawback might be overcome by exempting from the tax advertisement of a product for a specified period, say two years, after its introduction and graduating the tax thereafter accord-

19. Under "monopolistic competition," using that term to refer to the narrow market resulting from product differentiation, where rivals are free to enter the market with nearly similar substitute goods, prices tend to equal total costs (including sales expense) but total costs tend to be enhanced.

ing to the amount, either absolute or relative, of the advertising outlay thereon. But administrative difficulties would arise in defining "new products" and in applying a limitation on the scale of advertising expenditures—for example, when the advertising is of the producer, instead of a specific product. So it is not entirely clear how to limit advertising without discouraging innovation.

One thing that Congress could advantageously do to discourage fictitious product differentiation, however, would be to overhaul trade-mark law to limit trade-marks and brands to their original and proper function: identification of the commercial source of goods. Long overdue is a law prohibiting the anomalous privilege of asserting monopoly claims in the public domain of language. The recognition of exclusive rights in the common names of articles of merchandise is clearly incompatible with effective competition.

Compulsory Labelling or Grading

The harmful effects of fictitious product differentiation could also in part be overcome by providing consumers with official information with respect to specific characteristics essential to intelligent selection of goods. The government could aid the consumer in making intelligent choices among rival products by requiring sellers to supply information, certified by, say, the Bureau of Standards, on the presence, absence, and extent of specific qualities in nonstaple differentiated products and by encouraging commodity standardization of staple or near-staple commodities.

Second, grading of finished merchandise might be enforced. Grading of raw materials has long been customary in wholesale produce markets. It developed spontaneously from the need of buyers to know what they were buying, and it obviously facilitated the effective competition that in general prevails on produce exchanges.

Grading of finished merchandise presents more difficulties than grading of raw materials, because like products of different manufacturers are seldom indistinguishable. The more complex the article, the less it lends itself to grading. In making electric fans, for example, many different materials may be used to make component parts, and the possible variations in construction are also many. It would be almost impossible to lay down specifications (useful to consumer-buyers) for a list of standard grades of such an article.

A list that provided a sufficient variety of standard grades to meet varying consumer requirements and the reasonable convenience of manufacturers would be too long to be of any use. And nothing would be gained comparable to what would be lost by restricting fan manufacturers to the production of specific parts from an arbitrarily limited range of specified materials or of fans embodying one or another of a few standard types of construction.

But much more could be done than has been done to devise commodity standards that would provide competitive incentives. Many articles of merchandise are neither so complex nor so intricate as to preclude the making of a list of useful and economically advantageous standard grades. Such a list would foster effective competition in industries making simple utensils, such as pots and pans, for example, if the government required manufacturers to grade their products in accordance with certain specifications. For enamelled ware, a metal base of a specified minimum thickness would qualify a product for a certain rating, and a coating of a specified minimum thickness and degree of freedom from flaws would qualify it for rating on another scale. Thus the grades for such an article might vary only among, say, X-A, X-B, and X-C and Y-A, Y-B, and Y-C, with X and Y indicating the thickness, or strength, of the base, and A, B, and C the thickness and quality of the enamel. For uncoated pots and pans of iron, aluminum, copper, magnesium, or some other metal, establishment of a similar limited range of grades, based on thickness and freedom from flaws, would be even more feasible and not less advantageous.

Manufacturers often oppose such grade standardization of ordinary merchandise on the ground that it tends to deprive quality goods of the higher price their added cost of production warrants. They say it drives all producers who manufacture a given grade of a commodity thus marketed to adopt the minimum specifications for that grade, because regardless of actual differences in quality buyers will not pay more for one brand bearing that grade label than for other brands so labelled.

Neither experience nor theory supports this contention. In Canada, for example, grade labelling of canned fruits and vegetables is compulsory, but quality variations within grade limits persist. And with manufacturers continuing to market products under distinctive brand names, no reason is apparent for buyers not to respond to advertising claims of quality if the alleged superiority is real.

In fact, of course, compulsory grade labelling of merchandise only supplements the standardization represented by product branding. Grade standards do not supplant brand standards; they simply give them more meaning. And grade standards place no upper limit on the improvement of quality of any manufacturer's product. What they do accomplish is to make price competition more effective by assuring buyers that, *within certain limits,* what they may gain by a lower price they do not lose by lower quality.

Making Capital More Mobile

As this study has repeatedly emphasized, effective competition requires continual shifting of productive resources from industry to industry and from region to region in response to changes in market conditions, originating sometimes on the side of supply but more frequently on the side of demand. Whenever in a particular industry supply outruns demand, as it is said, it means that so many resources are engaged in production that their yield, measured by the value buyers place on the output, is less than some part of those resources could earn in other industries. Moving the excess resources out of such a field and into more remunerative lines of production is the only sensible and effective way to correct such an uneconomic allocation of resources. But modern technology interposes formidable obstacles to this corrective process.

The development of modern technology, in both its mechanical and chemical aspects, has had opposite effects on the mobility of labor and capital. Labor, except as circumscribed by seniority rules, insurance programs, pension plans, and the like, has become more mobile, capital less mobile. Increasing specialization has meant for labor, on the whole, decreased time requirements for job training and hence less of a deterrent to transfer. On the other hand, increasing specialization of capital equipment has meant more time and expense required for adaptation (planning and constructing a plant and devising and installing equipment) and increased difficulties in the way of conversion to other uses.

It follows, therefore, that a major task in fostering effective competition is to make capital more mobile. Negatively, this requires that in industries of surplus capacity—whether occasioned by changes in demand, speculative excesses, or bad judgment, or by technological innovations that outmode costly ways of making or doing things—artificial barriers to the outflow of capital should not be tolerated.

Industries must be allowed not merely to sicken but to die, that the economy as a whole may be healthy. Propping up sick industries or high-cost producers by artificial control schemes—basing point systems, trade association rules, or less formal devices—does not contribute to the health of an economy. In industries of surplus capacity, prices must be allowed to fall below the total costs of high-cost producers, and under some circumstances even of low-cost producers. This will lead to a reduction of capital values through bankruptcy and the writing down of assets and will encourage the actual disappearance of tangible facilities as they wear out or can be turned to other uses.[20] Such readjustments may be long drawn out and they may be very painful to those on whom the impact of the process immediately falls. They are, however, part of the costs that society must somehow defray to get the benefits of a private enterprise economy. If the market-determined distribution of those costs is regarded as too uneven, society may choose to relieve those upon whom the main burden of competitive readjustments falls. But to prevent the readjustments through price control and output restriction schemes is not only to renounce the competitive process. It is to repudiate the most fundamental of all economic principles: the use of resources to the greatest possible social advantage.

The government can also take positive measures to foster capital mobility. It can use its monetary and fiscal powers to counteract violent changes in economic activity, price levels, and national income. In this way it can facilitate the maintenance of a high level of employment and promote steady growth of the economy. In short, a general increase in demand tends to reduce the surplus capacity of overexpanded industries and it creates new avenues of employment for surplus resources. Thus the government can help to create an environment that will make competition "workable" by reducing the amount of "work" it must do.

The government can also make it easier for new investment funds to flow into fields of comparative underinvestment and underpro-

20. For a discussion of the problems involved, see John M. Clark, *The Economics of Overhead Costs*, University of Chicago Press, Chicago, 1923.

duction. In practice, this means breaking down barriers to new enterprises. Some of the barriers are technological; others are fiscal; still others are financial; and some, finally, are commercial.

There are various possible ways to overcome these obstructions to the flow of capital into fields where marginal rates of return are relatively high. To reduce fiscal obstructions the government could impose differential corporation income-tax rates in favor of new, small, and independent companies as contrasted to old, large, and consolidated concerns. To reduce the commercial obstacles, it could foster commodity standardization. To reduce technological barriers, the government could revise the patent system.

Patents and Capital Mobility

As to patents, the Constitution sets no limits on the power of Congress to define the scope of patent assignment and patent-licensing privileges. Whether Congress has used its power over patents efficaciously, on the whole, to "promote . . . useful Arts" may be debatable. But clearly the patent system as it has developed has enabled corporations to extend monopoly power far beyond those inventions for which they may be in some sense responsible. It is one thing to give *inventors* "exclusive Right" in their inventions "for limited Times" and quite another to accord *corporations*—which can themselves invent nothing—the privilege of accumulating an indefinite number of patents *by purchase* and then imposing an ingenious tangle of restrictions by license on the use of those pooled inventions. Congress could readily open up new competitive opportunities in many lines of industry now subject to centralized control by limiting the transfer of patent rights and by devising a compulsory licensing system for patents that would assure inventors reasonable rewards for their inventions. It could promote the same end, also, by sponsoring technical research at public expense, whether in government laboratories, as it does now for agriculture, or in industrial research institutes.

It is not necessary here to canvass the advantages and drawbacks of various ways for making technological knowledge more easily accessible on less discriminatory terms. It is enough to point out that effective competition requires a deliberate, well-articulated program for putting more nearly on a par technologically big and little, old and new, integrated and nonintegrated enterprises. Though the advancement of technology depends on individual effort, it does not depend on that alone. It is an endless collaborative effort, each contributor building on the achievements of others and in turn opening new doors for still others.

Fundamentally, technology is a social product. It is part, perhaps the most important part, of the community's cultural capital. Manifestly the community cannot afford to permit large segments of it to be taken out of the public domain and appropriated by private groups for their exclusive benefit. To be sure, providing adequate incentives for experimentation and at the same time adequate opportunities for competitive exploitation of the common fund of technological knowledge will test the mettle of democratic statesmanship. But it is a test that cannot be evaded.

Making Labor More Mobile

A minor part of the problem of making productive resources more mobile—and thus weakening the grip of imperfect competition on the economy—is to lower the institutional barriers to changes in employment. Here also the most promising approach is through long-run measures. Just as opening investment outlets is the most practicable way to increase capital mobility, so opening the gates of opportunity for young people just entering industry is the most practicable way to increase labor mobility. If "new" labor has a wide range of choice in the selection of lines of employment or careers, the labor supply will be more easily adapted to the requirements of a balanced economy. Plainly this would make competition more attainable. What it involves, above all, is the provision of opportunities in school and elsewhere for young persons to discover their individual aptitudes, and the nature and prospects of various kinds of jobs. Despite some experiments, the American school system has made little progress in aptitude analysis. Cooperation between industry and the schools would probably overcome the deficiency.

One institutional obstacle to labor mobility is the mutual-aid program of American trade unionism. Once a worker joins the union having jurisdiction in a particular industry he acquires a stake in the organization, or more specifically in its treasury, that he can seldom afford to forfeit by taking a job in some other industry. This circumstance tends to freeze the labor supply of each unionized industry, regardless of changes in technology or in market demand for its products. Leaving a union does not always mean complete loss of benefits under union pension or insurance plans, but it usually involves some sacrifice. After a member has paid heavy fees for several years to a union treasury, he is apt to think carefully before taking a job outside the union's jurisdiction, where his rights in union funds, if any, may be negligible. Another deterrent to transfer is that a worker must again start from scratch to acquire the highly prized seniority rights. While trade unionism offers little obstruction to geographical migration, it does resist interindustry migration.

To lessen this resistance new legislation might safeguard the rights and interests of union members in pension, mutual-aid, strike, and similar funds to which they have contributed and may wish to continue to contribute, notwithstanding a transfer to employment in other fields. Statutes defining the rights and interests of policyholders in life insurance companies are a precedent for such legislation. Similar measures may be appropriate to reduce the obstacles to labor mobility erected by employer-financed pension schemes. The widespread adoption of such schemes latterly, under pressure of collective bargaining, may lead to a more comprehensive government-administered program. But if it does not, measures such as those suggested might help to reduce interference with labor mobility.

Governmental Policy on Labor and Agriculture

To achieve an effectively competitive economy will require drastic changes in governmental policy on labor and agriculture. The details of such policy changes are beyond the scope of this study. The nature of the problem is outlined in Chapter 12. In a democracy it is perhaps inevitable, and from many points of view desirable, that large groups with common interests band together to promote their welfare. Experience shows, however, that if self-help is not adequate they will look to government. Farmers have become accustomed to the idea that price controls are essential to give them a "fair" share of the national income. It is difficult to devise equitable standards for sharing income, and when the judgment is politically expressed whatever a group can get becomes the measure of what it thinks it is entitled to. As price controls without output controls are self-defeating, once the government assumes responsibility for guaranteeing the standard of living of farmers it is necessary to extend rather than reduce controls over agriculture. Until farmers themselves recognize that their long-run interests in freedom transcend their short-run interests in security, it is perhaps oversanguine to expect any abandonment of controls over agriculture. A modification of controls with the intention of accelerating rather than retarding the transfer of resources is essential to making the American economy more effectively competitive.

The growth of group labor power, whether it is reckoned on balance as social gain or loss, is not favorable to a competitive economy. As the power of labor unions grows they demand not only a larger share of industrial income but also standardization of wages both within an industry and among industries producing competitive products. Nor are they likely to stop here. Some labor unions have seized upon the novel idea, based on Keynesian doctrine, that their responsibility in wage negotiations is not merely to their members but to the public. As custodians of their members' welfare they demand higher wages. As custodians of the public welfare they demand lower prices. By trying to keep down automobile prices and to raise workers' wages, the United Automobile Workers, negotiating with General Motors in the fall of 1946, made it evident that they aimed at such a redistribution of income as to keep the economy in balance. Commendable though this goal may be, the means to its attainment obviously cannot be entrusted to a group wielding private power if an effectively competitive economy is to be maintained. For the danger of labor monopoly is real. And ignoring it can only accelerate the decline of competition.

A More Consistent and Effective Antitrust Policy

Not only has antitrust policy been inconsistent in application to labor and agriculture, on the one hand, and to business, on the other, but it has not in all respects been clearly defined or consistently enforced as a rule of conduct for business. The policy laid down in the Sherman Act is at first sight specific. Section 1 prohibits all combinations or contracts in "restraint of trade," regardless of their form. Section 2 prohibits monopolizing or attempts to monopolize, regardless of conspiracy. Although the language seems specific its meaning is actually vague, allowing a wide range of judicial discretion not merely in determining whether a particular arrangement or practice violates the law but also in determining what kinds of arrangements are outlawed.

Interpreting the Act, a court can say, as in the American Can case, that Congress favored an economy of many relatively small business units with decision making decentralized, and yet leave undisturbed a merger that embraced, at its formation, 90 per cent of the manufacturing capacity of the industry. Or a court can say, as in the steel cases, that bigness is no offense under the law, and on this basis exonerate a merger that consummated the consolidation of more than a hundred independent companies and some two thirds of the capacity of this basic industry and later, not content with the impressive size thus achieved, absorbed additional productive units. Or a court can deny, as in the National Lead case, that increasing the number of sellers from two to four is likely to make competition more effective, and on this basis reject the remedy of dissolution. In short, despite the apparently clear mandate of the statute, the courts have found it possible to give their blessing to "good" trusts, and to stigmatize vigorous business rivalry as "ruinous competition."

If Congress wants to create and preserve an effectively competitive economy, one of the first items on its agenda might well be to repeal those laws—such as the Reed-Bulwinkle and the Miller-Tydings Acts—that legalize collective action to control markets.[21] It might also consider modifying the Robinson-Patman Act to make certain that it will not become a means of so standardizing pricing practices as to make prices rigid.

Alternatives to Effective Competition

Unless the American people are willing to establish the conditions in which competition can regulate the economy they must accept some other method of regulating it. Clearly it will not regulate itself—in the public interest. Ridding the economy of monopoly controls and maintaining the conditions essential for effective competition will not be easy. Many obstacles stand in the way of dissolution of huge industrial combinations and drastic revision of public policies on corporations, patents, trade-marks, tariffs, commodity standards,

21. For a discussion of the Miller-Tydings Act, see Chap. 10.

taxation, agriculture, labor, and banking. Perhaps the chief one is popular apathy, rooted in widespread economic ignorance, but a close second is the resourceful opposition of powerful vested interests. It is not always appreciated, however, that alternative systems of industrial control also involve difficulties. Because the outlook for an adequate implementation of effective competition is far from bright, it will be well to review and appraise some of the possible alternatives.

Taking "possible" in a practical rather than a theoretical sense, this review can dispense with a discussion of such extreme proposals as a return to laissez faire or the adoption of total collectivism as represented by communism. For present purposes, putting aside the innumerable quack schemes that litter the forum of politico-economic debate, and ignoring marginal shades of doctrinal variation, two major possibilities merit attention. These are: business syndicalism and administrative regulation (as of public utilities).

Business Syndicalism

Though the proponents of business syndicalism seldom march under its banner, the term aptly describes what some propose. Most frequently described as self-government in industry by majority rule, in its basic outlines it is familiar to Americans as the ill-starred NRA experiment.

To outward appearances business syndicalism signifies merely an elimination of the threat of antitrust prosecution for the conduct of industry according to a concerted plan. "Concert of action" suggests harmony, and "self-government in industry" has the ring of a genuine democratic formula. But appearances are often deceptive; and they are here. To shelve the antitrust laws and authorize business groups to centralize the control of industry is to legalize private monopoly. And this means that the coercive power of law will be enlisted in support of monopoly.

Consumer choice, in such a dispensation, must obviously be limited to whatever the confederated group of dominant producers in each industry finds it in its own interest to offer at whatever price it deems expedient. But coercion does not stop there. A scheme for the planned development and operation of an industry as a unit is meaningless—nothing but a flight of fancy—unless it provides some means for blocking deviations from the concerted program. Recalcitrants must toe the "party line." Although this isn't the basic issue, in practice it means little enterprises must subscribe to the rules that big business lays down—and adhere to them under penalty of extinction. They must, in brief, forfeit their independence. This aspect of the coercion that goes along with self-government in industry is apt to be overlooked in the promotional stages of such a policy. Two years of practical experience under NRA was enough to make it clear, however, that it is an inescapable incident of business syndicalism. For majority rule in industry does not under present circumstances count heads; it counts units of investment, assets, or capacity. So the "majority" consists, in practice, of a few giant companies, almost invariably.

Coercion is not the whole story. Unbalancing of the economy is also involved, no matter who makes intra-industry policy. With each industry a law unto itself, coordination among industries must suffer. A symmetrical development of investment, output, and employment in different lines of production would be utterly fortuitous and highly improbable under such a regime. Effectively competitive markets do at least promote economic equilibrium—such an allocation of resources among various industries as equalizes marginal returns to capital, labor, and management—which is a precondition of economic stability.

Effective competition does this, be it granted, at a certain cost. The chief accusation against effective competition is that from time to time it unstabilizes markets and causes business losses and unemployment. But it would be shortsighted statecraft, indeed, to notice only the short-run costs of competition and not to notice the long-run costs of business syndicalism. A public policy that neglects to make any provision for coordinated development of the economy such as is inherent in competition, and thereby fosters lopsided economic growth, involves long-run risks of the gravest kind for society.

To some people, criticism of business syndicalism as a practical alternative to effective competition amounts to setting up a straw man only to knock it down. Such people easily forget recent history. The courts struck down NRA only fifteen years ago, but on the eve of World War II some business leaders were clamoring for its revival.[22] More recently a war-engendered prosperity that has not yet spent its force has given businessmen renewed faith in competitive enterprise. With the public clamoring for goods in short supply and business generally confronted with unexcelled opportunities for making more money by making and selling more goods, active exponents of business syndicalism have become relatively few and inarticulate. A general depression, however, would quickly change the climate of opinion.

Administrative Regulation

Business syndicalism amounts to *private* administrative regulation. Regulation of industry by government commissions, as with public utilities, is simply *public* administrative regulation. Just as few policy makers are now giving serious thought to authorizing private industries to set up codes of fair competition for their self-government, so are few considering the extension of administrative controls of business by public regulatory bodies. If the scope of administrative regulation is greatly widened, it is likely to be a piecemeal process and it might well go hand in hand with self-government in industry. Should public opinion conclude that competition is no longer effective in basic industries and that the concentrated private controls replacing competition therein do not adequately protect the public interest, an extension of the public utility concept—and administrative regulation—to embrace a much wider industrial area than it does at present would be almost inevitable.

This alternative to effective competition has much in common with business syndicalism, not only in its advantages, but also in its drawbacks. Both promise to do away with the short-run "wastes" of competition—in particular, to eliminate much duplication of facilities and effort and to reduce short-term market risks for employees as well as employers. Both involve coercion, which is inherent in any scheme of centralized control. Finally, both ignore the problem of providing for the articulation of production and marketing policies among separate industries. It is not apparent how a series of independent administrative commissions for the diverse branches of trade could coordinate their development and promote economic balance. Indeed, in this respect public administrative regulation would prob-

22. See Chap. 8.

ably be even worse than private administrative regulation. When it comes to coping with jealousy among administrative authorities, each supreme in its jurisdiction, ties of political homogeneity are weaker than those of community of financial interests.

Differences between private and public administrative regulation of industry are often thought to swing the balance heavily in favor of the latter. Because the administrators who decide on investment, output, and prices answer to a democratic government there is all the difference in the world, some people say, between public administration and business syndicalism. The motives of members of an official commission are no doubt different from those of legalized monopolists. But just how great the difference is one cannot exactly ascertain.

Qualifications and Limitations of Regulatory Commissions

Members of public administrative agencies are sometimes elected, in which case they generally have the qualifications of politicians. Among those qualifications administrative ability is not always outstanding. More commonly, though, the members are appointed. Politicians select them, and politicians establish their standards.

If administrative agencies are not to be hamstrung they must be allowed considerable discretion. No convincing evidence suggests that administrative officials can be found who are wise and courageous enough to regulate investment, output, and prices for whole branches of monopolized industry so that the results will approximate those of effective competition. Even if the politicians authorized them to do so and if they tried to do so, experience suggests that they would not be able to exercise their wisdom without political complications.

In a democracy administrative agencies are constantly subject to the pressure of vested interests, and the exertion of such pressure on public officials is regarded as a basic civic right. When these vested interests are powerful, the pressure is apt to be greater than the majority of administrative officials can withstand. Though long-term appointments protect such officials from the upheavals of party politics, nothing protects them from the strong pressures exerted by the groups whose interests are at stake, groups that are regulated precisely because they possess monopolistic powers. On the contrary, their duties bring administrative officials into continual personal contact with the members of those groups. However zealous they may be to protect the public welfare, administrators are apt eventually to accept the point of view of the regulated, who identify their own with the public interest. As Mr. Justice Douglas has tersely put it: "The regulated groups tend to take over their regulators." [23]

Administrative Regulation in Practice: The Oil Industry

These observations on the shortcomings of the administrative process are based on experience. Recent history is replete with illustrations in point. Under the National Industrial Recovery Act the Petroleum Administrative Board gave unofficial approval to a voluntary price-regulating scheme later condemned by the Supreme Court as a violation of the Sherman Act.[24] Again, the Texas Railroad Commission in regulating oil production has persistently used its powers under the conservation statutes to restrict output and raise prices, in accord with the United States Bureau of Mines "estimates," which in turn reflect the market strategy of the major oil companies.[25]

23. So likely is this to happen that Douglas suggested, "If it were not, of course, impractical, every regulatory bureau ought to be abolished after ten years of life and some new machinery set up in its place." Quoted by Fred Rodell, in "Bill Douglas, American," *American Mercury,* December 1945, p. 663.

It would require quite exceptional independence for commissioners and their staffs to avoid developing a viewpoint tinged with solicitude for the interests they are supposed to regulate. For the entire careers of these men are bound up with the welfare of the specific industry subject to their jurisdiction. They occupy a position closely akin to that of professional management. Many of them expect to, and do, "graduate" into lucrative jobs with the regulated enterprises, for which their administrative experience so well qualifies them. Hence the uncritical assumption that commission regulation of industry will provide effective protection for consumer interests is scarcely justified.

24. *U.S.* v. *Socony-Vacuum Oil Co., Inc.,* 310 U.S. 150 (1940), at pp. 220-27. See also Chap. 9 of this study. The price-regulating scheme challenged in this case was a gasoline-buying pool. The defendants continued with the scheme after the collapse of NRA, and it was the post-NRA operations that the courts found illegal. Whether, in view of the invalidation of part of the National Industrial Recovery Act in the Schechter decision, the pool was unlawful from its inception was not in issue and therefore was not decided.

Three young lawyers and two economists, all able and zealous watchdogs of the public interest, made up the Petroleum Administrative Board. Despite their unquestioned integrity, the Petroleum Administrator found it necessary to restrict them in their social contacts with leaders of the oil industry and to caution them against an intimacy he feared might be insidious. Apparently, however, even this was not enough to prevent their eventually accepting the industry's point of view on prices.

25. See Chap. 12 of this study. The statement in the text does not imply that the Commission has exceeded its authority or that the Commissioners have violated their oath of office. The policies of the Texas Commission are in no essential respect different from those followed by the proration authorities in other oil-producing states—including California, where an autonomous group, representing the oil producers themselves, administers the proration machinery.

When administrative agencies are not sufficiently responsive to pressure groups, politicians are likely to bring the full weight of their influence to bear on them. In the spring of 1942 the enemy submarine campaign in United States coastal waters threatened to cut off the fuel oil supply of the populous and industrially important Northeastern and Middle Atlantic states. To parry this danger, the Office of Price Administration raised the price of gasoline from Maine to Florida, proposing to use the proceeds to subsidize overland shipments of fuel oil from the Gulf Coast to the Northeast.

The rationale of OPA's program was to avoid raising the price of fuel oil, which had a much greater influence on the general price structure than did gasoline. But the political opponent of a senator from Georgia, up for re-election, proclaimed that this was nothing other than a "damn Yankee scheme to make the Southerners pay to keep the Northerners warm in the winter time." Such was the popularity and power of the senator whose re-election was thus jeopardized, that he was able to persuade Congress to outlaw the particular program OPA had suggested. Congress did this in a rider attached to the OPA appropriations bill requiring that price increases should not be confined to the areas of shortage but should be general throughout the country.

Such is the actual process of government. And no doubt much can be said for it. It may prevent administrative boards from abusing their discretion. It may also prevent wise use of it. The remedy, of course, is not to limit truly democratic processes but to limit, as far as may be feasible, reliance on administrative processes to control in detail the operations of the economic system.

Administrative Regulation in Practice: Labor

The settlement of labor disputes under the Railway Labor Act during World War II provides another illustration of how the effectiveness of administrative agencies can be undermined by political influences. After an emergency board recommended a wage increase of eight cents an hour for the nonoperating employees in the spring of 1943,[26] Director of Economic Stabilization Vinson refused to approve the recommendations on the ground that they

26. See *Report to the President by the Emergency Board,* appointed February 21, 1943, pursuant to the Railway Labor Act and Executive Orders 9172 and 9299, May 24, 1943.

violated the government's wage stabilization program. Thereupon the President appointed a second emergency board to review the recommendations of the first, and this board recommended an increase on a sliding scale ranging from four to ten cents an hour. Meanwhile, another emergency board dealing with the wage demands of the operating employees recommended an increase of four cents an hour as the maximum permissible under the formula endorsed by the Economic Stabilization Director.

The railway unions rejected these awards and prepared to strike.[27] Before the strike occurred the President himself offered to arbitrate the disputes. Two of the unions accepted the President's proposal; all of them eventually accepted his award. In the end, the President gave both operating and nonoperating employees wage increases substantially greater than those the regular administrative boards either had originally granted or had been prepared to grant and the President's own special appointee, the Director of Economic Stabilization, had blocked.[28] Thus the unions were right in concluding that "the strike vote did get results." Regardless of the merit or lack of merit in the railway union's position in this episode, it indicates how economic issues are disposed of in the political field.

Commission Regulation and Problem of Economic Balance

Granting to administrative commissions the responsibility for regulating the details of economic activity, each in a particular branch of industry, is unlikely to bring about an economical use of resources and an equitable distribution of income. Only an interlocking system of competitive markets can provide for continual coordination of the activities of separate industries and trades and, in this way, promote balanced economic growth.

The recurrent readjustments that economic progress demands are frequently severe. The benefits are widely diffused throughout the

27. They may have been encouraged to take a defiant attitude by rumors that had "gone around the country" that President Roosevelt—always responsive to the sentiments of voting blocs—had expressed his belief that the eight-cents-an-hour wage increase "was good and that he hoped it would be granted." See *New York Times*, October 17, 1943, p. 1.

On the general attitude of railway employees toward these successive administrative recommendations, see *ibid.*, p. 17; and *ibid.*, December 31, 1943, p. 8.

28. The President's award gave the operating unions an increase equivalent to eleven cents an hour and the nonoperating unions an increase ranging from ten to sixteen cents an hour. These increases were partly in lieu of supplemental compensation some railway employees had previously received. See *ibid.*

whole economy, but the impact of their immediate cost may rest heavily on a single economic or regional group. Those who pay the costs always resist the changes. Under such circumstances, society's obligation is, not to prevent change, but to cushion its impact. If control of industry has been transferred from the market to the political arena, readjustment is not made easier. Resistance to change in such a circumstance is only strengthened. Pressure groups use all the political power they possess to block changes that they would be forced to take for granted in a competitive economy.

Even if administrators were always exceptionally wise and stalwart, the complexity of the problems of regulating investment, output, and prices in manufacturing and trade on a comprehensive, industry-wide basis would deter all but the most foolhardy. Few people realize how great is the difference between the problems involved in administrative regulation of public utilities and in administrative regulation of manufacturing industries. Whereas each public utility unit operates in a separate market, most manufacturing enterprises cater to a common market. Whereas the services that a particular utility sells are essentially homogeneous, simple, and readily subject to standardization, the products of most manufacturing industries are heterogeneous and often complex, varying widely in quality, style, and specifications not only among the several producers but for each company.[29] And whereas most costs of a public utility are either fixed or relatively stable, a major cost element in most manufacturing industries is raw materials, notoriously subject to violent price swings.

In such circumstances, as the analysis in Chapter 8 of *Cartels or Competition?* shows, to fix prices and apportion output of manufactured goods by a time-consuming administrative process superimposed on a highly systematized method of management would be a stupendous and self-defeating task. It would manifestly be impossible to regulate industry satisfactorily in this way.[30] The magni-

29. Some standardization of manufactured products is feasible, of course, and doubtless in many lines of manufacture more standardization than now exists would be economical. But the limits that a reasonable regard for consumer choice sets to the development of standardization of manufactures, particularly of finished goods, are much narrower than those that like considerations set for utility services.

30. It is the well-articulated, highly systematized method of management, of course, that gives rise to the need for administrative supervision. But it should be plain that the remedy for private concentrated economic power, that is, for imperfect competition, is not to be found in highly concentrated governmental control, which only adds fuel to the fire.

tude of the problem as it appears when candidly faced is enough to overwhelm all but the rashest and most quixotic of adventurers. Sensible men will reject a policy that presupposes superhuman powers of instantaneous comprehension and sure judgment for its successful application. To understand the economic process in all its fullness would require time. Yet decisions could not be interminably delayed; and as a result they would probably be either sound but too late or on time but unsound, the product of guesswork. This would hardly do.

The Economic Prospect

Unless policy makers are able to shape a publicly acceptable economic and legal environment conducive to effective competition, competition as a vital social institution may disappear. And if it does, the outcome will probably be an economy more rigid than the American people are used to and more rigid than is consistent with their accustomed living standards. Experience indicates that effective competition withers and eventually dies unless it is nurtured by positive policies. Either the people must call a halt to the concentration—whether in governmental or private hands—of economic power, or they must be prepared to give up a competitive economy, bit by bit, year by year, until it is beyond recall. They will then be obliged to accept some collectivistic alternative that may give more short-run basic security but in the long run will almost certainly provide less freedom, less opportunity for experiment, less variety, less economic progress, and less total abundance.

How can material welfare be advanced without any increase, or at any rate without a proportionate increase, in productive effort? One method that has many advocates nowadays is redistribution of income. In general those who favor this method look to the government to achieve their aim. They believe, probably rightly, that only the coercive powers of sovereignty can level incomes. They are sympathetic, therefore, to the idea of depending on some form of governmental intervention to order the economy.

It is seldom realized how little enhancement of general welfare could be achieved by this method, even in the short run.[31] In 1947,

31. Colin Clark has effectively dispelled the illusion that bad distribution of income is the cause of "poverty in the midst of plenty." See his *The Conditions of Economic Progress,* Macmillan, London, 1944.

when the output of consumers' goods in this country was approaching an all-time peak, had they been evenly distributed among the 60 million wage earners, each would have received only $2,750 worth. On the average, the American workingman's standard of living might have risen 20 per cent in that year, but how soon or how far it would have fallen had the arbitrary enforcement of such a pattern of distribution continued can only be surmised. Plainly, equalizing incomes is no way for Americans to realize their aspirations for an abundance of the material comforts of life. If the nation is to improve greatly the lot of its citizens it must somehow contrive to keep increasing the total production of goods and services faster than the increase of population.

Another method of promoting the general welfare is to stimulate individual initiative and technological advance by making income dependent on competitive effort. Those favoring this method look to the government to establish and enforce suitable *rules* and *standards* for private economic activities, but they would keep to a minimum the direct, authoritative control of industrial operations. They make a sharp distinction between the policy-forming (legislative) and the rule-making (administrative) functions, on the one hand, and the choice of specific courses of individual action consistent with established policies and rules, on the other. As Edwin Cannan put it, the proper province of government is to maintain "hedges" or fences along the avenues of production and enforce traffic rules, not to drive the vehicles or choose the routes they take. According to those holding this view, outside the clearly defined fields of public enterprises, such as postal service, and public utilities, such as telephone service, decisions on investment, output, methods of production, product styles and qualities, prices, and the like should be left to individuals and private groups. The competitive market, registering consumers' choices and evaluations weighted by purchasing power, would impersonally determine the outcome.

Rationale of Competition

In an effectively competitive economy the willingness and ability of consumers to buy goods at prices covering their marginal production costs provide the basic guide to productive activities. Price-cost relationships, profits or losses, measure the degree to which productive resources are being used in accordance with consumer preferences. Actual and prospective losses check the inflow of resources into overdeveloped lines and actual and prospective profits pull them toward underdeveloped lines. Competitive self-interest tends constantly to stimulate economic expansion and change. Risk is inseparable from change, of course, so effective competition leads unavoidably to mistakes and excesses. Far from guaranteeing continuing stability for all business enterprises, competition demands of them the utmost flexibility and adaptability as a condition to the maintenance of stable equilibrium in the economy as a whole. Effective competition involves continual readjustments in the use of productive resources, and these readjustments are by no means painless. They are the price of economic progress. The discovery of new and more economical ways of making things, and of new things to make, implies that old ways must be modified or discarded unless progress is to be stifled.

The two methods of fostering economic progress—by coercive redistribution of income and by stimulating individual initiative through making income dependent on competitive effort—are not mutually exclusive. Nor has public policy in the United States or elsewhere ever relied exclusively on the one or the other. When laissez faire was at the height of its popularity, England still had its Poor Laws. Russia under a communist dictatorship still adjusts wages, to a great extent, on the principle of payment according to results.

In the United States the adoption of social security laws, labor legislation, graduated income taxes, and antitrust laws has not led to abandonment of reliance on profit seeking as a spur to productive energies. Nor do developments that emphasize social responsibility for the maintenance of living standards and economic opportunities appropriate to a democratic society necessarily devitalize the profit motive.

The problem is to find a golden mean between the demands for economic security and those for economic freedom and opportunity. Here lies the great challenge to democratic statesmanship today. The American people can have short-run stability and long-run insecurity. Or they can have short-run insecurity, facing the risks of effectively competitive markets, and long-run stability. But they cannot completely escape short-run risks without incurring grave long-run penalties. If they want to be free, they must pay the price of freedom. And freedom cannot be preserved by concentrating economic power in the hands either of politicians or of oligopolists.

The analysis of this book has shown that ways are available to prevent the further concentration of economic power and to make competition more effective. A people that lacks the will and the cohesiveness to agree on appropriate measures to this end will never, one may be sure, devise effective ways to make either public or private monopoly serve the common welfare.

REPORT OF THE COMMITTEE

The following chapter is a report of the Committee on Cartels and Monopoly appointed by the Trustees of the Twentieth Century Fund. It was prepared with the able collaboration of Professor Clair Wilcox of Swarthmore College, whose help is gratefully acknowledged by the Fund and the Committee. Dr. George W. Stocking and Dr. Myron W. Watkins, with the assistance of a research staff, are solely responsible for the preceding chapters of this book. The Committee itself is responsible for the recommendations for action that are incorporated in the following chapter.

Chapter 16

A PROGRAM TO PROMOTE COMPETITION

THE WHOLE LOGIC of a system of private enterprise rests on the fundamental assumption of active competition in free markets. If such a system is to be preserved, it is essential that competition be kept active and markets free.

This fact has long been recognized in the United States. Since 1887 it has motivated the enactment of antimonopoly laws by state legislatures. In 1890 it led to the passage of the Sherman Antitrust Act by all but unanimous vote of the national Congress, and in 1914 to the adoption of the strengthening provisions of the Clayton and Federal Trade Commission Acts.

The state laws, necessarily limited in scope to intrastate commerce, have proved relatively weak and ineffective. But the federal legislation, extending to commerce among the states, has repeatedly demonstrated its strength. It is with this legislation that discussions of antitrust policy are usually concerned.

For sixty years the antitrust laws have been accepted and maintained by American opinion. Though they have been amended from time to time, even for the purpose of exempting particular groups and practices, no important voice has ever demanded their repeal. Their suspension for two years under the National Industrial Recovery Act afforded an object lesson that served completely to discredit the alternative of cartelization. It is recognized, of course, that in some markets, such as those for services rendered by public utility companies, competition is clearly inappropriate. And it is recognized, too, that competitive methods must not be unfair to actual or potential rivals, to buyers, or to sources of supply. But the maintenance of competition, by and large, may now be taken as a settled objective of national policy.

The antitrust laws have been directed, over the years, toward two developments that have threatened to weaken competition seriously or to destroy it completely. The first has been the conclusion, among independent enterprises, of agreements that have operated, directly or indirectly, to control investment, output, prices, or terms of sale. The second has been the attainment by individual enterprises, through processes of combination or through internal growth, of monopolistic powers that have put them in a position to dominate the markets in which they buy and sell. More recently, the issue raised by the concentration of industry has come to be stated in broader terms and it has been argued that great size, in and of itself, may operate, in certain circumstances, to impair the effectiveness of competition.

These two developments—agreements and concentration—have differed sharply in issues raised, difficulties presented, and solutions required. The policy of antitrust has been applied to them, in consequence, with striking differences in sureness and success.

RESTRICTIVE AGREEMENTS

The problems presented by restrictive agreements are far simpler than those presented by combination and concentration. Great combinations have a long life; agreements among independent enterprises tend to break down. Determination of output and price by a single company appears to be a matter of internal policy; their control through agreement involves overt restraint of trade. In the former case, it may be argued that power has not been abused; in the latter, abuse is open and obvious. Combinations cannot be dissolved without some difficulty; agreements can be cancelled with relative ease. Concerning combinations, the rule of the law is uncertain; concerning agreements, it is relatively clear. Independent enterprises, in general, may not agree to exclude competitors from markets, to curtail productive facilities, to restrict output, to allocate sales, to fix prices, to compel participation in an agreement, or to enforce observance of its terms. In the first case, public opinion is confused by an apparent conflict between the advantages of competition and those of large-scale, low-cost production; in the second, it has no such hesitation: agreements to restrain trade are held, in general, to be undesirable.

This generalization is subject to important qualifications, however. For one thing, restraints may be hidden in a complex of activities that is generally approved: the propriety of cooperation in the work of trade associations, for instance, is unquestioned; the restrictive potentialities of many association activities are not always understood. Similarly, practices that facilitate competition when followed without collusion may eliminate competition when used in a systematic program of restraint. For example, when a line must be drawn between the independent use of freight absorption to make a sale in a distant market and the common use of freight absorption to effectuate a nation-wide pattern of identical prices, public opinion is confused.

Opinion wavers, moreover, when restraints are presented in the guise of efforts to prevent losses by protecting small traders against uncertain markets, unfair methods of competition, or inequality in bargaining power. In such cases, exemption from the provisions of the law has frequently been requested and obtained. It has not been widely appreciated that when injury to a competitor is identified with injury to competition, the basis for destroying, rather than preserving, competition may be laid.

Trade Association Activities

Many of the functions of trade associations are quite consistent with the preservation of competition among their members: cooperative industrial research, market surveys, the development of new uses for products, mutual insurance, the publication of trade journals, the joint advertising of products or services, and the conduct of relations with the government. All these undertakings may be socially desirable, serving a trade without disservice to its customers. But many others may involve the imposition of restraints: the establishment of common cost accounting procedures; the dissemination of statistics on capacity, output, orders, and shipments; the operation of price-reporting plans; and the standardization of products and terms of sale. While these practices often may merely assist the members of an association usefully to adjust their operations to the circumstances of the market, they may be and have been employed, at times, to facilitate restraint of trade.

Prevention of the abuse of such practices does not necessitate any change in antitrust policy or procedure. It does, however, require unceasing vigilance in the enforcement of the law and a high degree of precision in its interpretation.

Delivered Pricing Practices

Since the Supreme Court handed down its decision in the cement case in 1948, public policy on basing point pricing systems has been vigorously debated. Many of the arguments advanced, on both sides, have contributed more to confusion than enlightenment. On certain points, however, agreement seems fairly general. At the one extreme, many agree that f.o.b. mill pricing should not be required by law and that voluntary independent freight absorption should not be forbidden. At the other, it is agreed that overt collusion in establishing and maintaining systems of basing point pricing should be enjoined. But between these extremes, an area of uncertainty remains.

Though they act independently, without evidence of formal agreement, many firms may absorb freight so consistently that their delivered prices are generally identical. Here one may find neither the wholly voluntary behavior of active competitors nor overt collusion among sellers, but merely common and knowing observance of pricing practices through which competition may be effectively restrained.

The issue between the opponents and the defenders of basing point pricing is thus a narrow one: must formal agreement be conclusively proved before such pricing can be enjoined, or may collusion be inferred from the general and continuous observance of a common course of action? If formal agreement is the criterion, many basing point systems might be preserved by placing on the enforcement agencies an impossible burden of proof. If general and continuous action is the criterion, the legal status of delivered pricing in many industries might remain in doubt until further cases were brought before the courts. But if the maintenance of competition is to be the governing objective of public policy, the second course, rather than the first, must be pursued.[1]

Inconsistencies of Government Policy

The policy of enforcing competition embodied in the antitrust laws has never governed all federal legislation. The tariff has always made it difficult for foreign producers to sell in American markets. The

1. If by "common course of action" is meant uniformity of prices, I cannot agree with the conclusion of this paragraph. Under keenly competitive conditions, the dispersion of prices among competing sellers will occur within very narrow limits, if at all.—FRANK M. SURFACE

patent system has conferred upon patentees, over long periods, the privilege of monopolizing particular products and processes. The corporation laws of the several states have promoted combination and concentration by permitting intercorporate stockholdings and facilitating the pyramiding of control. Aside from its regulation of public utility holding companies and railroad consolidations, the federal government has generally not attempted to intervene in this sphere. Under state laws and city ordinances, moreover, outsiders are sometimes denied entry to local markets and newcomers excluded from protected trades.

Although the prohibition of restrictive agreements has been accepted in principle, Congress and the courts have granted a number of exceptions to this rule. The combination of workers in labor unions and of farmers and fishermen in cooperative associations has been explicitly approved. Labor legislation, more recently, has encouraged the development of industry-wide collective bargaining and the conclusion, between organizations of workers and groups of employers, of agreements that influence production and prices as well as wages and conditions of work. Agricultural legislation, likewise, has undertaken directly or indirectly to control the output and sale of farm products and to establish their prices at levels higher than those that would result from the interplay of the forces of demand and supply in free markets. State laws to control the production of petroleum have been enforced through federal action, and minimum prices have been established, for a time, for bituminous coal. Certain group activities of shipping companies, railway traffic officials, interstate motor carriers, and insurance companies, among others, have been removed from the jurisdiction of antitrust.

Each of these exceptions raises particular problems and presents issues of policy that are outside the scope of this report. Whatever their justification, however, it must be recognized not only that the exceptions are inconsistent with the basic philosophy of antitrust, but also that they operate positively to carry the economy away from competition toward monopoly.

Certain other exceptions, broader in scope and impinging more directly on the operation of the antitrust laws, require special mention.

Exceptions to Antitrust

1. Under the Webb-Pomerene Act of 1918, firms engaging in export trade may enter into associations to allocate orders and fix prices on their foreign sales. Such associations are forbidden substantially to lessen competition, to influence prices, or otherwise to restrain trade within the United States. But can their members achieve personalities so divided that they cooperate closely when they sell abroad and compete vigorously when they sell at home? When joint action is permitted in foreign sales, it is quite possible that competition in the domestic market will be impaired.

2. Under the Miller-Tydings Act of 1937, contractual provisions requiring the maintenance of prescribed resale prices, when permitted under state laws, are exempt from the provisions of the Sherman Act. In operation, such contracts prevent all retailers, whether signatories or not, from competing in the prices at which they sell trade-marked goods; sellers and buyers alike thus are denied the advantages that might otherwise flow from superior efficiency and lower costs in the distributive trades.

3. The Robinson-Patman Act of 1936 forbids sellers to fix different prices for "different purchasers of commodities of like grade and quality" unless the differences involved "make only due allowance for differences in the cost of manufacture, sale, or delivery, resulting from the differing methods or quantities in which such commodities are sold or delivered." This rule, of course, should serve merely to place purchasers, as competitors, on an equal footing. But other provisions of the Act are inconsistent with this rule.

Suppliers are forbidden to pass on to distributors savings that result from the elimination of brokerage services in making a sale. They may not render services to distributors or pay distributors for services rendered them unless such services or payments are available "on proportionally equal terms" to all. The Federal Trade Commission may establish quantity limits beyond which differences in price may be forbidden even though they make only due allowance for differences in cost. And finally, any person who shall "sell, or contract to sell, goods at unreasonably low prices for the purpose of destroying competition or eliminating a competitor" may be punished by fine and imprisonment. As a consequence of these provisions of the Act, distributors may be deprived of advantages that could be justified in terms of efficiency and cost, and may be subjected, by law, to an artificial handicap.

4. As the antitrust laws have been interpreted by the courts, the immunity granted to labor extends beyond the market for labor to the markets for other goods and services. Interference with competition in such markets, though forbidden to employers acting alone and to employers and organized workers acting together, is permitted to organized workers acting alone. Labor unions are thus given considerable freedom to restrain trade.

5. Under the agricultural marketing agreements legislation of the 1930's, agreements concluded between the Secretary of Agriculture and the producers, processors, and distributors of agricultural commodities and products thereof are exempt from the antitrust laws. Such agreements, employed principally in the markets for milk, fresh fruits, and vegetables, may divert commodities from commercial channels, restrict sales, and fix prices. They may even be imposed by the Secretary upon sellers who would not voluntarily participate. This legislation, in effect, permits a program of cartelization that may be either permissive or compulsory. And it applies not only to farmers but also to industrial and commercial enterprises engaged in the processing and distribution of agricultural products.

The most important issue of policy raised by the application of the antitrust laws to restrictive agreements relates to the scope and character of these legislatively sanctioned exemptions. Can they be justified? Should they be retained, modified, or repealed? Apart from these questions, the use of antitrust legislation in the case of restrictive agreements appears to be well established. In economics, in law, and in public opinion, it stands on firm ground.

COMBINATION AND CONCENTRATION

Over the past half century there has been a marked increase in the number and variety of goods and services offered for sale in the United States, in the total number of enterprises engaged in production and distribution, in the size of the market for particular goods and services, and in the maximum and average size of individual enterprises, both in industry and in commerce. In some fields the number of concerns has decreased; in others it has increased. In some, the share of the market occupied by the largest concerns has grown;

in others it has shrunk. In many industries, however, there are firms so large in relation to the markets in which they deal as to be in a position to influence output and price appreciably.

The significance of this development depends in each case upon the character of the product involved. The consequences of concentration will be less serious where goods are easily dispensable and close substitutes are readily available, more serious where goods are relatively indispensable and where no acceptable substitutes are at hand. In this respect concentration and agreements among independent concerns do not differ in the problems they present. In both, the power significantly to influence markets is present and the question of public policy is raised.

In the case of concentration, however, opinions as to the desirability and the practicability of the policy of antitrust have differed and the rule of the law, as interpreted by the courts, is neither consistent nor clear. It is in its application to the problems of monopoly and oligopoly that antitrust has encountered the greatest obstacles and achieved the least success. It is in this area that the appropriateness of the policy is still a matter of debate.

Size: Absolute and Relative

In approaching this problem, a distinction must be drawn between the size of an enterprise in absolute terms of employment, assets, or sales, and size in relation to the character of the markets in which it occurs. Small firms may possess concentrated power in limited markets. In extensive markets such power may be beyond the reach of very large concerns. Size is synonymous with concentration only when it is so great in relation to the market that it may operate to deny to buyers and sellers an adequate number of genuine alternatives in making purchases and sales. If the number of firms in a market is so small, or if the strength of these firms is so disproportionate, or if the entry of new firms is so difficult that real independence of action is limited, it is unlikely that such alternatives will obtain. It is only under circumstances such as these that size threatens the freedom of markets and the vigor of competition, and it is in this sense alone that the problem of size and concentration falls within the scope of this report.

The Problem Defined

In analyzing the relation of bigness to the effectiveness of competition, moreover, a number of considerations may be dismissed as irrelevant. It does not matter whether those who were responsible for the growth of an enterprise, through combination or otherwise, were motivated by a desire to bring a market under control; the effect of their efforts, rather than the intent, is important. Similarly, it does not matter whether the methods by which power was obtained or the manner in which it has been exercised may be held to be legal or illegal; again, the consequence of concentrated power, not its legal status, is under discussion.[2] Finally, we do not inquire, in this analysis, whether bigness, as such, is desirable or undesirable; we are here concerned only with the relation of bigness to the effectiveness of competition.

Bigness and Effective Competition

The nature of this relationship will vary from market to market and from industry to industry. Three characteristic situations may be distinguished.

1. There are instances in which large-scale organization has apparently brought with it a more persistent downward pressure upon costs and prices than would have resulted from the competitive efforts of small concerns. The rubber tire and automobile industries and the distributive trades are cases in point.

2. In some instances the power of bigness has clearly been abused; some large firms have been found by the courts to have taken advantage of suppliers, competitors, and customers by engaging in a wide variety of objectionable practices.

3. There are instances in which size itself may carry with it serious liability to abuse, interposing obstacles to the entry of new competitors, promoting the adoption of a live-and-let-live philosophy, holding a protective umbrella over the members of a trade, or otherwise encouraging the development of patterns of behavior that are not effectively competitive.

2. Both the purpose underlying concentration and the means by which it has been achieved are extremely important in determining whether the particular concentration is violative of the antitrust laws. Purpose, if established, is a datum from which future direction and future activity can be gauged. Means are again data from which purpose and directive can be inferred.—JAMES M. LANDIS

The first situation presents no problem for public policy; [3] here size has been so employed that the effectiveness of competition has been increased. In the second, the necessary measures are beyond dispute: objectionable practices must be ferreted out and their continued use prohibited. In the third, however, the proper course of policy is not so clear; a choice must be made among alternatives.

Should the state attempt, at the one extreme, to prohibit the acquisition or retention by one or more large enterprises, in any industry, of a position sufficiently free from competitive pressures to permit the adoption of restrictive price and output policies? Or, at the other extreme, should it acquiesce in such concentration and attempt to protect the public interest by subjecting large enterprises to public regulation or by taking them into public ownership? Or should it pursue a middle course, not undertaking to prohibit concentration, but limiting its extent, checking its growth, and employing administrative regulation or nationalization only as a last resort? Each of these possibilities will be examined in turn.

PROHIBITION OF CONCENTRATION AS A GENERAL POLICY

Not even the most enthusiastic proponents of antitrust would contend that conditions closely approaching the economist's ideal of perfect competition can be or should be achieved in all markets in the United States. The reasons are clear. Industries differ in the character of the goods and services they produce and in the scale of operation that may be required to provide a maximum of service at a minimum of cost. It would be unwise arbitrarily to apply a like policy to situations that are unlike. Distinctions must be drawn among industries with differing characteristics and an appropriate policy must be applied to each.

In some industries, such as those providing postal, telecommunications, power and light, and other public utility services, the very nature of the services provided is such that monopoly is generally held to be necessary and desirable. In other industries, also, it may be found that the scale of operation that will afford the lowest costs is

3. This is not quite accurate. As is wisely observed later, despite concentration that may create downward pressures upon costs and prices, this good may be counterbalanced by limitations imposed upon the freedom of others to enter that particular enterprise. In other words, for the sake of freedom it may be wise to pay high prices.—JAMES M. LANDIS

so large in relation to the size of the markets for their products as to justify substantial concentration of control. But this will not often be so. In each instance judgment must depend upon the relationship between the economic characteristics of the industry and the size of the market it serves.

The line is not an easy one to draw. In the present state of knowledge, it is scarcely possible to distinguish with any certainty between those cases in which the public interest would best be served by limiting the extent of concentration and those in which it would not. If policy is to be enlightened, criteria should be developed for measuring the comparative advantages and disadvantages of operation at sizes involving various degrees of concentration of control. These criteria might set forth such tests of social performance as relative waste and economy in the use of resources; efficiency of production and unit costs of output; expansion of an industry's total output and sales; improvement of quality and service; progress through research, invention, and innovation; and stability of operations over time. If such tests could be applied in exhaustive studies, industry by industry, public policy with respect to concentration could be more adequately informed.

Continuing studies of this kind are not now available. But action cannot be suspended until they have been made. Research takes time and its results are open to debate; in the meantime decisions must be made in particular cases even though knowledge is incomplete. Harm may be done by partly informed action; but harm may also be done by failure to act—a policy of drift is nonetheless a policy. In the absence of greater certainty, however, it would be desirable to proceed with caution.

Indiscriminate Attack Unwise

The structure of many markets in the United States is imperfectly competitive. But competition may operate effectively to serve the public interest even though it is less than perfect. When judged by its performance, against the performance of industry in other parts of the world, rather than by its structure, American industry appears, on the whole, to be remarkably dynamic. It has achieved a steady flow of new products, a continuous cultivation of new tastes, a constant improvement of quality, a progressive development of technology, a repeated reformation of the patterns of production and distribution, an ever-widening provision of goods and services. How far these results were compelled by competition, and whether they could have been bettered by even greater competition, cannot be conclusively demonstrated. But it is clear, at least, that no indiscriminate attack upon the structure of the industrial machine that produced them would be wise.

What is needed is not an arbitrary assault upon size as such, but a vigorous effort to discover those market situations where concentration of control is prejudicial to the public interest. In such situations there is ample scope for the corrective processes of antitrust. But even here it may be well to make haste slowly.[4] The reformation of long-established combinations is a difficult and time-consuming business. If it is to be successful, it must proceed at a pace that permits the careful preparation of cases and the development and application of effective remedies. Where new combinations are proposed, however, these considerations bear with less force. If further concentration in any market threatens to moderate the vigor of competition, preventive action may need to be swift.

ACQUIESCENCE IN CONCENTRATION AS A GENERAL POLICY

It is frequently asserted that the development of modern technology has made the policy of antitrust obsolete. The superior economy of large-scale production and other advantages inherent in great size, it is said, are to be obtained only at the cost of concentration of control over the markets where goods are sold. Concentrated power should therefore be accepted, it is argued, as an accomplished fact and the public interest should be protected either by regulating, in some detail, the manner in which it is exercised or by nationalizing the enterprises in which it may occur. This position must be rejected. The premises upon which it is based are dubious. The conclusion to which it leads is unacceptable.

4. I agree with the thought but I dislike the emphasis. In other words, we cannot be too precipitate because we do not know the facts but that is the only reason for hesitation. As the matter is now phrased, it would indicate that there is some benefit to be derived in engaging in a dilatory approach. Rather, we should recognize that whatever delay is necessary is occasioned merely by our want of knowledge.—JAMES M. LANDIS

Technology and Concentration

It is true that the technology of production, in many industries, is such that, within limits, lower costs will be achieved by a large plant than by a small one. But there are few cases of any importance in which this fact necessitates substantial concentration of control over markets. Such concentration is usually achieved, not through the growth of a single plant, but by uniting several plants under a common ownership. The optimum scale of operation required by the technology of production may necessitate a large plant. The scope of ownership required for the control of markets may necessitate a large firm. But the two cases are not to be confused; the technology of the plant cannot often be said to explain the size of the firm.

This is not to say no advantages are to be realized through the combination of several plants, each producing the same product. Such combination may enable managements to spend more on research, to standardize products, to employ specialists in various phases of administration, to save on transportation, to cut the cost of financing, to buy materials in larger quantities at lower prices, to advertise more widely, and to reduce the expense involved in making sales.

But there are "diseconomies" as well as economies of size. The decisions required of management increase in number and complexity. Administration, remote from actual operations, must obtain information and take action through paper controls. Confusion in organization and overlapping of functions may lead to avoidance of responsibility, conflict in authority, and delay in the determination of policy. Adherence to precedent, reliance on routine, and an accumulation of red tape may result in inflexibility. There is an increasing burden of overhead costs. Decentralization of management may afford a partial offset to some of these disadvantages. But in large-scale undertakings bureaucracy is not to be escaped. Bureaucracy is not peculiar to government; it is a function of size.

There are virtually no definitive studies of the balance of advantage and disadvantage in bigness, either in a single establishment or in multi-plant concerns. Such data as are available can justify no firm conclusion about the relationship that may exist, industry by industry and product by product, between the scale of operations, on the one hand, and the costs of production and distribution, on the other But it may be said, at least, that there is no evidence to support the contention that greater size invariably or usually involves greater efficiency.

Strategic Advantages of Size

A distinction must also be drawn between the technological and the strategic advantages of size. The profits of a firm may be enhanced by reductions in cost achieved through the large-scale performance of the essential functions of management. But they may also be enhanced by such differential advantages as the bargaining power that a firm enjoys in the markets in which it buys and sells, by banking connections that give it a preferred position as a borrower, and by financial resources that strengthen its hand in litigation and in relations with agencies of government. Whether it is in the public interest for any enterprise to enjoy such advantages may be open to argument. But it is clear, at least, that they are to be attained only at a size that can rarely be required for efficiency alone.

The history of the combination movement in the United States, moreover, makes it evident that efficiency was not the only goal. The promoters of corporate combinations have profited, in the past, from the sale of securities; the manipulation of finances; the direction of corporate purchases of equipment, materials, and services; and the monopolization of markets. Without passing judgment on these activities, it need only be remarked that they serve to discredit the view that concentration, in such cases, was impelled solely by the superior economy of great size.[5]

Alleged Failure of Antitrust

Many of those who contend that the concentration of economic power is inevitable go on to assert that the substantial degree of concentration that has actually occurred in the United States clearly dem-

5. Too much emphasis is placed here on efficiency in physical operations, using this term in a strictly engineering sense only. But efficiency in a business organization is a far broader term than that related only to low-cost production. Efficiency certainly should include low-cost marketing, to which no reference is made. Efficiency in any going business organization would include many other things, such as serving the public interest by providing good working conditions, job stability and security, a way of life for employees, and many other things not covered by an engineering definition. It is things of this character that distinguish competent management from the less competent and, by and large, it is the character of management that determines the success or failure of an enterprise.—FRANK M. SURFACE

onstrates that the policy embodied in the antitrust laws was ill-conceived and that the laws, in operation, have failed. The evidence at hand does not support such a conclusion.

Until recent years the policy of antitrust, as applied to the complex problems of concentration, has not been given a real trial. It has been handicapped by the adoption of inconsistent policies in other fields, by inadequate implementation, by sporadic enforcement, and by adverse judicial decisions. It is only possible to speculate about what the consequences of more vigorous enforcement, over the past half century, might have been.

It cannot be said that antitrust, as it has been applied, has been a complete success; it can be said that it has not been a complete failure. It would be useful to have studies made of the effectiveness, in individual industries, of injunctions, dissolution orders, and consent decrees. But even if these remedies were found to be generally ineffective, it would not follow that antitrust had failed. It is impossible to say what the pattern of industrial control and the practices of business would have been in the absence of such a policy. It is not unlikely, however, that the mere existence of antitrust has materially affected business decisions. The more flagrant abuses of the nineteenth century have disappeared. Restraint of trade, where it occurs, generally is less ruthless [6] and more circumspect.

It is certain, moreover, that the situation in the United States is very different from that in countries whose policy has permitted or encouraged cartelization and the concentration of control. American industry is more vigorous, more resilient, more dynamic; it is more hospitable to new blood and new ideas. In most other countries, little or no effort has been made to enact or to enforce laws designed to insure the maintenance of competition. And in such countries, by contrast, industrial progress has been retarded by timidity and lethargy.

It may well be that the greater vitality of American industry is attributable, in large part, to the survival of a wider area of competition in the American economy. And it may well be, in turn, that the wider area of competition is attributable, in large part, to the enactment and the enforcement of antitrust.

6. Perhaps this is true with regard to the means employed. The effect, however, remains the same.—JAMES M. LANDIS

The Alternative of Administrative Regulation

It is unrealistic to pass judgment on the policy of maintaining competition without also considering the nature and the consequences of the possible alternatives. If dangerous concentration of power cannot be prevented or eliminated, it will ultimately be subjected, in one way or another, to public control. Is this to be preferred, as a general solution, to antitrust?

American experience with administrative regulation of railroads and public utilities over the past half century does not suggest an affirmative reply. The commissions established in these fields have suffered from the same handicaps of inadequate implementation, ineffective enforcement, and adverse judicial decisions as has antitrust. The attention of managements has been diverted from internal administration to external lobbying and litigation. The progress of technology has been slower in the railway industry, which is regulated in minute detail, than in many other large-scale industries that have not been regulated at all. Improvements in railway service and desirable modifications of the structure of railway rates have been brought about, not by the Interstate Commerce Commission, but by the competition of motor carriers. Similarly, in electrical utilities, commission regulation has failed notably to develop effective substitutes for competition in promoting efficiency, reducing rates, and encouraging consumption.[7] Expansion of service through the revision of rate structures has been prompted, in recent years, less by the processes of regulation than by the demonstration, partly through the policies adopted by public power projects, that wider sales and higher profits are to be realized at lower rates.[8] Administrative regulation, where it has been applied, has not been so successful as to justify a similar prescription for all industries in which the degree of concentration destroys the effectiveness of competition.

7. I share completely these criticisms of administrative regulation, but two other points should be made. The first is a noticeable decline in the quality of the personnel of the top level of bureaucracy that has the responsibility for this administrative regulation. This fact was commented on again and again in the reports of the Hoover Commission. Whether that is something innate to the processes of government or not, I do not know. But the fact is too patent to be denied. Secondly, reference must be made to what I would call the utter bankruptcy of the Federal Trade Commission. As a practical matter the deterioration of that Commission has gone beyond the possibility of redemption. If duties of this kind are to be thrust on some agency, there is really only one thing to do, and that is to wipe out the FTC completely and start afresh.—JAMES M. LANDIS

8. Cf. *Electric Power and Government Policy,* Twentieth Century Fund, New York, 1948, pp. 244-45, 651, 678, 720, 749, 778.

The task of control in industries other than the public utilities would present even more difficult problems. It would be necessary to deal with numerous enterprises differing in size; in corporate structure; in degree of integration; in diversity and quality of products; in number and location of establishments; and in equipment, processes, and costs; with complicated price structures and pricing practices, and with changing technology and changing tastes. If control were to be effective, it would have to be extended to every aspect of business policy: to entry, expansion, contraction, and abandonment; to volume and quality of output; to prices and terms of sale; to securities and accounts; to expenditures, earnings, and the distribution of dividends. Regulation always advances; it never retreats. Its final stage, as the case of the railways demonstrates, is virtual duplication of managements.

Socialization and Economic Planning

If the state is to take over in large part the function of making managerial decisions, the question arises whether it would not be more efficient and economical to socialize the regulated enterprise. Duplication of functions could thus be avoided, the cost of litigation eliminated, and authority and responsibility combined. Where a high degree of concentration of control over physical operations is an accomplished fact, the most formidable obstacles to socialization have already been overcome. The transfer of control to public officials can be accomplished by the simple process of acquiring a majority of the voting stock. It is noteworthy that proposals for nationalization are more often concerned with industries in which firms are few in number and large in size than with those in which firms are numerous and small. It is a sound instinct that has led socialists consistently to oppose the policy of antitrust.

Where the share of production by publicly owned or regulated industry in the economy is small, the over-all direction of economic activity can be left to the forces of demand and supply operating in the market place. But if the share of production brought under such regulation or ownership were large, the many interrelationships of the industries involved would necessitate coordination of the controls. Resources would have to be allocated among rival claimants, the output of one industry dovetailed with the requirements of another, and the prices established for different industries and different markets brought into some sort of harmony. The policy of detailed administrative regulation or socialization, if consistently pursued, could end only in comprehensive economic planning and the authoritative direction of economic activity. Collectivism, in one form or another, is the logical outcome of acquiescence in a dangerous concentration of economic power.[9]

It is not to be expected, in a democratic society, that highly concentrated power will long go uncontrolled. Administrative regulation or socialization must therefore be accepted, however reluctantly, where no alternative exists. Usually, however, antitrust affords an alternative. Whatever its shortcomings, this policy can be regarded, at the very least, as the lesser of evils.[10]

LIMITATION OF CONCENTRATION AS A GENERAL POLICY

The economic argument for reducing existing concentration and preventing further concentration is a strong one. The smaller the number of sellers, the more likely they are to behave like monopolists. Fewness of sellers facilitates formal agreement or informal understanding on price and production policies. The more sellers there are, the more likely they are to behave like competitors. Where sellers are numerous, the objectives sought in an agreement to suppress competition are more modest, the methods that must be employed in carrying out such an agreement are more elaborate and overt, and the restraints involved are easier to discover and correct. Under such circumstances, collusive behavior is unlikely to be effective and enduring unless it is required by law and enforced by the state. There is thus a strong presumption in favor of limiting concentration if competition is to be preserved.

The standard by which antitrust is to be appraised, however, should not be too exacting. Even though an increase in the number of sellers

9. The thought in this sentence is extremely important. See footnote 10 below.—JAMES M. LANDIS

10. I have always contended that the function of the administrative process is to try to make administrative regulation sufficiently effective so as to enable capitalism to live up to its own pretensions and that if administrative regulation were to fail, collectivism would be the only answer. Wall Street and big business seem to me singularly unaware of this possibility. They build as the German industrialists did—perilously close to collectivism—not only because they build instruments of power which can be so easily seized by the government but also because these instruments of power if inefficiently regulated may be required to be taken over by the government.—JAMES M. LANDIS

in an industry cannot be expected to establish the conditions pre-requisite to perfect competition, it can reduce the likelihood of uniformity in policy and afford to buyers a larger number of alternatives. The circumstances of individual sellers will seldom be the same. There will be differences in the temperaments, attitudes, and judgments of business managers; in cash position and financial needs; in location, techniques of production, efficiency, and methods of computing costs. The more sellers, the more likelihood of differences in opinion on market prospects and elasticity of demand, and resulting differences in price and production policies. It requires only one seller to introduce an innovation in product, quality, or price. The larger the number of sellers, the better is the chance that one or more of them will take an independent line. As a practical matter, therefore, oligopoly is generally to be preferred to monopoly and even as few as six or eight large sellers in a market to only three or four.[11]

Ceilings on Size

We have rejected two extremes of policy: the view that concentration should be completely prohibited and the view that it should be generally accepted as inevitable and brought under public regulation or ownership. We conclude, instead, that policy should seek a middle course, keeping concentration within the bounds of social usefulness by limiting its extent and checking its growth. But it is by no means easy to determine just how this should be done.

The simplest rule to lay down, of course, would be one that placed a ceiling on the size of an individual enterprise in terms of total assets or its share, industry by industry or product by product, of capacity, output, or sales. Such a rule would be arbitrary in character and crude in application: the scale of operation required for maximum efficiency differs from industry to industry; a ceiling appropriate to the conditions in one industry might be so low as to impair effi-

11. It is difficult to agree to all the implications of the preceding two paragraphs. It is certainly not always true that "the more sellers there are, the more likely they are to behave like competitors." One could cite many instances where numerous small retailers have brought pressure upon legislative bodies to outlaw competitive practices which would have operated in the interest of the consumer: for example, the chain store tax laws in Iowa and other states. Again, a great many of the innovations in products, in techniques of production and distribution have originated through the research carried out by large business units. One could cite a number of large industries characterized by large numbers of relatively small firms where innovation and progress have at least been relatively slow.—FRANK M. SURFACE

ciency in a second and so high as to be meaningless in a third. Different limits might be set, of course, for different industries or products, but the information essential to their establishment is lacking and the likelihood of agreement on their enactment is small. Any rule that employed the concepts of "industry" or "product" would be difficult to administer: the words are familiar, but their meaning, in application, would not be easy to define. An absolute ceiling on size, moreover, would be unfortunate in its results: as the established limit was approached, all incentive to industrial progress—to the advancement of technology, the improvement of products, and the reduction of costs and prices—would be removed.[12] The problem of concentration is not to be solved by placing fixed limits on size.

The Rule of Reason

In one case, great size and substantial concentration may serve the public interest. In another, they may not. It is the task of public policy to draw a line between the two. Where size and concentration are in the public interest, existing combinations can be allowed to stand and new combinations approved. Where they are prejudicial to the public interest, existing combinations should be dissolved and new combinations prohibited.

This is the position toward which the law has been groping, under the rule of reason. But the line between what is reasonable and what is unreasonable, in combination and concentration, is still obscure. If the greatest problem facing antitrust is ever to be solved, this line must be drawn more sharply. The task will not be an easy one, but if policy is to be rescued from confusion and futility, a beginning must be made.

The real test of the reasonableness of the position occupied by a large-scale enterprise should be that of its performance in the public interest. This test might be given legislative sanction by writing it into the law itself. But it can be applied, without such sanction, in cases brought before the courts. However the test is handled, the difficulties inherent in its application should be faced squarely. The agencies of enforcement should attempt a painstaking formulation of

12. An absolute ceiling would remove incentives to improvement in so far as improvement required expansion of size. It would not remove incentives to lower costs in so far as such lowering of costs could be achieved without involving an increase in productive capacity.—JACOB VINER

criteria of the public interest and a thorough development of tests of industrial performance. These criteria should be applied and the results of these tests set forth in briefs presented by the government and their validity submitted to the determination of the courts. It should be possible, through this approach, gradually to develop a body of law that would give explicit content to the rule of reason. The process would be a slow one, but it should serve, in time, to bring the decisions of the courts closer to the realities of economic life.

One device that might serve to facilitate this process is worthy of mention. The Sherman Act might be amended to establish a rebuttable presumption that concentration exceeding a specified percentage of the market for any product, or related group of products, was prejudicial to the public interest. Enterprises seeking to retain or attain a size in excess of the limit specified would then be forced to bear the burden of proof. If they could demonstrate to the satisfaction of the courts in antitrust proceedings that greater concentration was in the public interest, they might be permitted to retain or expand their area of control. Otherwise, existing combinations might be dissolved and the right to enter into future ones denied. This device would make it necessary for defendants in dissolution proceedings to prepare and present their own briefs in terms of evidence of performance in the public interest. If industrial concentration is to be permitted to stand, it is not unreasonable to require that it be justified.[13]

13. In my view, the suggested rebuttable presumption serves no useful purpose. Earlier paragraphs have rejected fixed ceilings on size, in part because different limits would be required for each industry, and "the information essential to their establishment is lacking and the likelihood of agreement on their enactment is small." Moreover, "any rule that employed the concepts of 'industry' or 'product' would be difficult to administer." (See above, p. 552.) These objections are not met by establishing a rebuttable presumption or ceiling. Instead, this merely admits that satisfactory ceilings are probably impossible to set and to administer, and then transfers the resulting burden onto the shoulders of business. I agree with the earlier paragraph of the report that "the real test of the reasonableness of the position occupied by large-scale enterprise should be that of its performance in the public interest." I agree that the "agencies of enforcement should attempt a painstaking formulation of criteria of the public interest and a thorough development of tests of industrial performance," and that "these criteria should be applied and the results of these tests set forth in briefs presented by the government and their validity submitted to the determination of the courts." (See above, pp. 552-53.) But I must point out that until this is done, rebuttable ceilings are impracticable; once it is done, they are unnecessary. Without adequate criteria of "performance in the public interest," satisfactory rebuttal cannot be made. With such criteria, the ceilings are irrelevant; "performance in the public interest" is itself the test. Moreover, the development of such criteria by the agencies of enforcement, and their acceptance by the courts, would itself require the defendants in dissolution proceedings to "prepare and present their own briefs in terms of evidence of performance in the public interest." Rebuttable ceilings therefore add nothing, but detract much.—FRANK M. SURFACE

Social Considerations

It is possible, though unlikely, that a policy of reducing and preventing concentration might be carried to a point where the productive efficiency of an industry would be impaired. But this possibility should not necessarily influence the adoption or rejection of such a policy. The issues presented by bigness are not to be resolved on economic grounds alone. Even where the survival of concentration can be justified in terms of the superior economy of large-scale operations, noneconomic considerations may support an effort to reduce the size and increase the number of sellers in the major markets for goods and services.

Human freedom in other areas depends upon the preservation of freedom in economic life. It is more difficult to preserve freedom where power is centralized, whether in public or private hands, and where the scope of individual decisions is broad. It is easier to preserve freedom where power is widely dispersed and where the scope of individual decisions is narrow. It may sometimes be necessary, therefore, to make a choice between lower costs and greater freedom. And it may be wise to accept higher costs as the price of freedom, instead of sacrificing freedom to get lower costs.

Concentration of the power to make vital decisions renders business vulnerable to political attack. Such power may have been acquired without violation of law or unfair treatment of competitors. Its exercise may be motivated, not by a desire to maximize profits, but merely by a desire to maintain solvency and avoid bankruptcy. It may manifest itself in policies that are beneficial to consumers or in policies that are harmful, not positively through curtailment of output and elevation of prices, but negatively through undue caution in innovation and underestimation of elasticity of demand. It is not merely the origin, the motivation, or the abuse of power that can be attacked, but its very existence. Concentration of power gives rise to demands for administrative regulation. It facilitates socialization. It threatens the preservation of private enterprise. Bigness, under these conditions, is bad for business.[14]

14. I agree that bigness has one serious drawback; namely, that it is vulnerable to political attack. There has been much evidence of this in the recent past. However, I do not agree with the implications in this and related paragraphs. I do not agree that large size, as it exists in American industry, necessarily or even usually limits the benefits accruing to the public from competitive behavior. I do not agree that there

Size may, of course, carry with it social as well as economic advantages. It may raise the standards and increase the security of employment. It may contribute to higher levels of living and a wider enjoyment of leisure. It may encourage the advancement of science and the promotion of art. But these advantages will not necessarily preserve it from attack. Hostility to concentrated power is deeply rooted in American tradition. The desire for economic independence is at the basis of the philosophy of antitrust.

ABUSE OF POWER

Sometimes, as we have seen, bigness may exert a more persistent downward pressure on costs and prices than is to be obtained through the competition of many small sellers. Where this is the consequence, public policy is not concerned.[15]

In other instances the power implicit in size may be abused through resort to clearly objectionable practices. Competitors—present and potential—may be handicapped by arrangements that pre-empt resources, equipment, and technology and bar access to existing channels of distribution. Small concerns may be threatened with litigation or harassed by discriminatory price cutting in particular markets or on particular lines. Independents, operating at a single stage of the productive process, may find their margins squeezed by the pricing practices of integrated firms. In all of these ways, potential competition may be obstructed, small competitors disciplined, and a position of dominance extended and re-enforced. Here the need for corrective measures is obvious.

In still other instances, where concentrated power is permitted to persist, there may be no present evidence of its abuse. But even here there can be no assurance that such power will always be exercised in a manner consistent with the public interest. Here, too, the practices of business must be kept under continuing public scrutiny.

If private enterprise is to be really private, it is obvious that it

---

is any evidence which indicates that large business in general is more likely to exert undue caution in innovation or to underestimate the elasticity of demand. In fact, I suspect that, if the facts were available, they might well lead to the opposite conclusion. I do not agree that the existence of large business units in itself threatens the existence of private enterprise. Rather it is the use which some politicians and some demagogues make of the transgression of the law by a relatively small percentage of large firms which is a far greater threat to our enterprise system.—FRANK M. SURFACE

15. This seems to me to contradict much of page 554, where it is argued that power is bad even if it yields these and other benefits.—JACOB VINER

must be left free to make decisions in such matters as innovation, technology, output, and price that might be held to be unwise from the standpoint of the community. Public policy, under the circumstances, must confine itself to the prevention of abuse. To this end, three courses are open. First, the government might attempt to specify, in explicit legislation, those business practices that are to be enjoined. Second, it might undertake, through continuous supervision, to influence the behavior of business from day to day. Or, third, it might outlaw unfair practices in general terms and proceed against such apparent violations as come to light.

Methods of Prevention

Of these three courses, the first and the second are open to serious criticism. Under the complex and changing conditions of modern business it would scarcely be possible to devise a statute that would enumerate known types of malpractice in detail without thereby surrendering the comprehensiveness and the flexibility necessary to prevent novel forms of abuse. Legislation cannot be expected to keep pace in such matters with the ingenuity of enterprise. It is for this reason that recurrent proposals to rewrite the antitrust laws would be likely to create as many problems as they would solve.

Detailed supervision, on the other hand, though it might be comprehensive and flexible, would be exceedingly difficult to administer. If it were not guided by definite standards and kept under steady rein, it would become either irresponsible or ineffective. If supervision were lax, failure to register objections might be interpreted as official endorsement of possible malpractices; if it were rigorous, the authority of managements would be challenged and a protracted struggle between business and government would ensue. More might be lost to the public interest as a result of such conflict than was gained by the possible prevention of abuse.

By comparison, the method of outlawing undesirable practices in general terms and taking legal action against specific violations is greatly to be preferred. This is the policy that is embodied in the antitrust laws, carried out through the procedures provided in those laws, and made effective by orders issued by the Federal Trade Commission, by consent decrees in antitrust cases, and by decisions handed down by the courts. This approach has the merit of comprehensiveness and flexibility. Supported as it is by well-established tradition, it has the additional advantage of general acceptability. The present provisions of the law, if properly administered, appear to be adequate to check the more serious forms of abuse.[16]

WEAKNESSES OF ANTITRUST

If the antitrust laws are to be the instrument for preventing restrictive agreements, limiting combination and concentration, and keeping in check the abuse of economic power, attention must be directed to the organization and the procedures provided for their enforcement. This organization and these procedures have been inherited from the years before the first world war. In many respects, they are ill-adapted to the task for which they were designed.

Weaknesses of Organization

It is a commonplace to remark that the appropriations voted and the staffs provided for the administration and enforcement of the antitrust laws have been too small. But even if budgets and personnel were multiplied, antitrust would still operate under a serious organizational handicap. Major responsibility for the enforcement of the law is divided between an executive department (the Department of Justice) and an independent agency (the Federal Trade Commission). The functions of these two bodies overlap; action in the same case may be initiated either by the Antitrust Division of the Department of Justice, under the Sherman Act, or by the Federal Trade Commission under the Trade Commission or the Clayton Acts. Furthermore, particular segments of jurisdiction have been parcelled out to the Secretary of Agriculture, the Board of Governors of the Federal Reserve System, the Interstate Commerce Commission, the Federal Communications Commission, the Securities and Exchange Commission, the Tariff Commission, and the Civil Aeronautics Administration. No organizational provision has been made to coordinate the activities of these agencies. Nowhere in the government is there an officer, or even an interagency committee, charged with responsibility or given authority to draw up comprehensive plans for administering and enforcing the antitrust laws or for overseeing their execution.

16. This seems to be contradicted by the "Recommendations" (pp. 560 ff.), which urge fairly substantial changes in the law.—JACOB VINER

Weaknesses of Procedure

Antitrust is defective not only in organization but also in procedure. The procedures available for the enforcement of the Sherman Act are ill-adapted to solution of the problems presented by complex patterns of industrial organization and complicated business practices. Availability of the grand jury and the power to subpoena books and records may lead too often to the initiation of criminal actions, since equally effective investigatory procedures are not available in civil suits. Once an indictment is obtained, the trial that follows is concerned, not with determination of policy for the future, but with evidence of wrongdoing in the past. Whatever the substance of the case, the prosecution must seek a conviction and the defense an acquittal; the outcome will be influenced by technicalities of the law. Juries in such cases, mystified by the intricacies of business organization and practice, and impressed by the respectability of the defendants, may be reluctant to subject them to the penalty of imprisonment. If the government loses, it has no right of appeal. And even if it wins, the penalties applied cannot have much force as a deterrent. Imprisonment is rare; the fines imposed are insignificant. The real penalty is to be found in the unfavorable publicity attendant upon indictment and trial.

In private suits for treble damages, far heavier penalties may be imposed. Such suits may at times serve as an effective method of enforcement. But they are brought on the initiative of private litigants; they cannot, therefore, be expected to assure the comprehensiveness or the continuity that are required in the administration of the law. Private suits may supplement, but they cannot supplant, the efforts of enforcement agencies.

In civil suits brought by the government, specific remedies can be proposed. Illegal combinations can be dissolved and illegal practices enjoined. More often, cases will be closed by negotiating a consent decree in which the agreed terms of a settlement may be set forth in considerable detail. No thoroughgoing procedure is provided, however, for the development, consideration, and adoption of civil remedies. And the effectiveness of such remedies is open to question. More study is needed, industry by industry, of the consequences of past decrees. It is clear, however, that observance of their requirements has not, in the past, been systematically policed. Although violators can be punished for contempt of court, this penalty has rarely been applied.

The determinations contained in the verdicts of juries and the decisions of the courts apply only to specific individuals and firms; they do not constitute a generally applicable code to govern business practices. Even though the courts may have repeatedly held a particular practice to be an unfair method of competition within the meaning of the Federal Trade Commission Act, or to be in violation of the specific prohibitions of the Clayton Act, the Commission must obtain an injunction against each new offender before a penalty can be imposed. The law would be more effective if the application of judicial determinations of the legality of specific practices could be more readily generalized.

As the law now stands, moreover, no penalty may be imposed in Federal Trade Commission cases until it has been established in independent proceedings that two successive violations of the Trade Commission Act or three successive violations of the Clayton Act have occurred. Under the Trade Commission Act, if a cease-and-desist order is not appealed to a court, it becomes effective in sixty days; if it is appealed and sustained, it is confirmed by an injunction; in either case, a defendant may then be punished for a single repetition of his offense. Under the Clayton Act, however, the Federal Trade Commission must prove a first violation before it can issue an order to cease and desist, a second before it can obtain an injunction, and a third before an offender will be punished for contempt. There seems to be no good reason why the simpler procedure now provided in the Trade Commission Act should not also apply to the Clayton Act. One repetition of a violation should be enough.

Advantage of Present Antitrust Procedure

The obvious weaknesses of legal proceedings as a method of maintaining competition have frequently led to the suggestion that antitrust enforcement should be brought within the exclusive jurisdiction of an administrative agency. Such an agency would be empowered to issue regulations, industry by industry, forbidding practices in which it found a tendency to restrain trade or promote monopoly contrary to the public interest. The validity of such regulations would be subject to judicial review and their terms, if upheld, would be enforced by legal penalties.

This proposal seeks to remove antitrust from the arena of litigation and to place it in the hands of impartial administrators possessing intimate knowledge of business organization and practices. But administrative agencies also have their weaknesses. They are all too likely to be hedged about with limitations, inadequately financed and seriously understaffed, lacking in vigor and enslaved by routine. Through close and continual association they may come, in time, to reflect the interests of those whom they were originally established to regulate. If complacent, they are ineffective. If active in the public interest, they are peculiarly vulnerable to political attack.

Litigation, with all its faults, has one outstanding advantage: it is familiar, it is understood, it is clothed with prestige; as a consequence it is accepted, if not with enthusiasm, at least with tolerance. The traditional procedures of antitrust are more likely than any others to be permitted to do their work.

RECOMMENDATIONS

If the maintenance of competition is to be accepted as an expression of prevailing policy, the content and consequences of the whole body of relevant legislation should be surveyed so that inconsistencies may be eliminated or at least explicitly recognized and kept within narrow bounds. To this end, the effect of laws relating to tariffs, patents, corporations, labor, agriculture, natural resources, and transportation should be studied and, where it is found that measures operating to impair the effectiveness of competition cannot be justified by overriding considerations of national policy, corrective legislation should be devised.

In recent years there has been a drift toward increasing tolerance of restrictive programs adopted by particular producing groups. If the common interest is to prevail, this trend must be reversed. Monopoly is not to be rendered harmless by making it universal; such a policy can only end in mutual frustration. The preservation of freedom and progress, throughout the whole economy, require that the antitrust laws be vigorously enforced. In so far as antitrust fails to maintain competitive conditions in industry and commerce, the pressure for legalizing the adoption of offsetting restraints in other sectors of the economy will be strong. In so far as it succeeds, the case for such restraints will be weakened and the prospect for resisting such pressure will accordingly be improved.

REPEAL OR MODIFY EXCEPTIONS

A number of the exceptions to the antitrust laws that permit particular groups to enter into agreements that restrain trade should be repealed or modified.

1. This Committee, in its report on "A Cartel Policy for the United States," has already recommended a substantial modification of the exemption granted to export trade associations under the present provisions of the law.[17]

In our opinion, *the Webb-Pomerene Act should be repealed and new legislation should be enacted to take its place.* The new law should limit permissible association in the export trade to groups of small-scale enterprises organized for collective bargaining in accordance with strictly defined cooperative principles and it should subject such associations to supervision under rules that are clearer and stricter than those of the present Act.

2. *The Miller-Tydings amendment to the Sherman Act and the so-called state fair-trade laws should be repealed;* retailers should be permitted to compete in the prices they charge for trade-marked goods; they should be encouraged to pass on to consumers the savings resulting from greater volume and lower costs.

3. *The Robinson-Patman Act should be amended* to delete those provisions that are inconsistent with the general principle that differences in price should not be disproportionate to differences in cost; namely, the provision that forbids suppliers to grant discounts in lieu of brokerage where the services of brokers are not required, the provision that forbids suppliers to render services to distributors or to pay distributors for services rendered them unless such services or payments are proportionally available to all, the provision authorizing the Federal Trade Commission to establish quantity limits beyond which differences in price may be forbidden, and the criminal penalty for selling goods at "unreasonably low prices"; advantages that can be justified by actual savings should not be taken away by law.

17. George W. Stocking and Myron W. Watkins, *Cartels or Competition?*, Twentieth Century Fund, New York, 1948, pp. 436-37.

4. *The Sherman Act should be amended* to confine the immunity granted to labor to those markets in which it sells its services; restraint of trade in other markets should be brought within the scope of the law, whether it is imposed by employers acting alone, by employers and workers acting together, or by workers acting alone.

5. *The agricultural marketing agreements legislation should be revised* to provide for effective consumer representation in the negotiation and administration of such agreements [18] and to afford adequate safeguards against possible abuse; the immunity granted to producers, processors, and distributors of agricultural commodities under the terms of existing agreements should be scrutinized, and agreements found to be operating in a manner contrary to the public interest should be terminated.

PERMIT DELIVERED PRICING, BUT PROSECUTE CONSPIRACY

It is generally conceded, apart from exceptions such as those discussed above, that restrictive agreements among independent enterprises should be prohibited. Antitrust is therefore on firm ground when it moves against conspiracies in restraint of trade. And this is equally true if the substance of an agreement is confined to certain artificial elements in a complicated pattern of market behavior. Elaborate systems of delivered pricing, such as those formerly employed in the cement and steel industries, are a case in point.

The law should not undertake to prevent the voluntary absorption of freight by an independent producer who seeks to compete for sales in a distant market. But delivered pricing has often been implemented by such practices as standardization of contracts and terms of sale, guarantees, extras, and deductions, trade-ins and returns; concerted refusal to sell on any other than a delivered basis; adherence to common basing points; computing freight on an all-rail basis and using a common freight rate book; and policing conformity. Such measures are not intended to promote competition, but to insure that

18. While I favor effective consumer safeguards in the marketing agreements program, I do not see how there can be practical consumer representation when those who presume to speak for consumers are either self-appointed or represent only a small fraction of the consumers. If the consumer safeguards which provide a price ceiling at parity when the agreement is in force and which provide for public hearings are not adequate, they should be strengthened. Collective bargaining between labor and industry, especially when industry-wide, is of more national economic consequence than agricultural marketing agreements; and as far as I know, the negotiations provide for neither consumer safeguards nor consumer representation.—A. S. Goss

it will not occur. *The full force of the law should be brought against those aspects of delivered pricing practices that are collusive in character; adherence to common procedures that inhibit independence of action should be enjoined.*

LIMIT CONCENTRATION

The most difficult problem facing antitrust arises in those industries in which sales have long been highly concentrated in the hands of a few large firms. It is necessary to decide whether to seek the dissolution of such combinations or to permit them to stand. This decision should depend upon an informed judgment on the relationship that exists, in each instance, between size on the one hand and the public interest in active competition and in productive efficiency on the other. Where it is clear that dissolution would involve a serious loss of efficiency, combinations should be allowed to stand. Where the effects of dissolution are uncertain, enforcement should proceed with caution. *Where it is clear that dissolution would enhance the vigor of competition without impairing productive efficiency, suits should be filed.*

As it stands, the Sherman Act does not deal explicitly with the problem of size in business or with the concentration of control over markets that great size may entail. The law approaches this problem obliquely. The charges that may be brought in cases involving size and concentration are those of combination in restraint of trade, monopolization, and attempts to monopolize. In dealing with such cases, the courts have sought to distinguish between those in which great size is reasonable and those in which it is not. But forty years after the enunciation of the rule of reason, the meaning of the statute is still obscure.

If this situation is to be clarified, the law should be brought face to face with the problem of size. *Recognition should be given to the principle that great size, involving substantial concentration, will be permitted if it can be justified in terms of performance in the public interest, prohibited if it cannot.* This principle might be written into the law itself; it might be established through the process of interpretation. In either case, the agencies of enforcement should develop criteria of the public interest and devise tests of industrial performance for submission to the judgment of the courts in future proceedings.

As a possible means of facilitating the establishment of this principle, we propose for consideration the desirability of amending the Sherman Act to create a rebuttable presumption against the retention by any enterprise of a position that enables it to control more than a fixed percentage of the market for any product or related group of products. If an enterprise could then demonstrate, in antitrust proceedings, that a higher degree of concentration would serve the public interest, it might be permitted to retain the necessary area of market control. Otherwise, it might be divided into separate units of more moderate size.[19]

Certain misgivings that may induce caution in breaking up existing combinations do not apply with equal force to the prevention of new combinations. Section 7 of the Clayton Act forbids one concern to acquire the stock of another when the effect would be "to substantially lessen competition" or when it would "tend to create a monopoly." The prohibition does not extend to the acquisition of physical assets. The section has consequently been rendered ineffective by judicial decisions that enable one concern completely to absorb another by first acquiring its stock and then exercising the voting power thus obtained, before the Federal Trade Commission has time to intervene, to acquire title to its assets. *This loophole should be closed by amending Section 7 to cover acquisitions of assets as well as acquisitions of securities.*[20] Cease-and-desist orders could then be issued against all new combinations that threatened substantially to lessen competition or to create a monopoly. In passing on proposed combinations, the criteria of public interest, proposed above, might well be applied.[21]

19. I am not in agreement with this method of facilitating the objective in question. See footnote 13.—FRANK M. SURFACE

20. See p. 506, footnote 18. H.R. 2734 (the Celler bill) extends the prohibition of Section 7 of the Clayton Act to the acquisition of assets. It was passed by the House of Representatives on August 15, 1949, and was reported favorably to the Senate in Senate Report 1775 by the Senate Judiciary Committee on June 2, 1950. As of August 1950 it had been passed over by the Senate three times on call of the calendar and would probably be called again.

21. In a substantial number of the instances in which small firms are acquired by their larger competitors, the initiative comes from the family-owned enterprise, which—for tax or other reasons—must be sold. If the opportunity to make such sales is seriously to be circumscribed, other measures should be adopted to facilitate the distribution of equities in the small concern.

CHECK ABUSE OF ECONOMIC POWER

Where concentrated power is allowed to stand, there must be assurance that it will be exercised responsibly. It is possible, fortunately, to check abuse of power without undertaking to regulate the day-to-day activities of business managements. The present provisions of the law concerning unfair methods of competition, price discrimination, and exclusive dealing and tying contracts are fairly adequate for this purpose, and the provisions made for their enforcement are, in general, appropriate. *The appropriations and the staff provided for the Federal Trade Commission should be made adequate to the task at hand.*[22] *Orders issued under the Clayton Act should be made effective unless appealed within sixty days, as are those issued under the Trade Commission Act.* Further protection might be secured by strengthening the investigatory powers of the Federal Trade Commission and requiring corporations in excess of a stipulated size, when engaging in interstate commerce, to submit periodic reports.[23]

COORDINATE ANTITRUST ENFORCEMENT

Close coordination of the activities of the Federal Trade Commission and the Antitrust Division of the Department of Justice was contemplated by the framers of the Trade Commission Act. Under the provisions of that law, the two agencies were expected to cooperate fully in the enforcement of the Sherman Act. Upon request by the Attorney General or by a federal court, the Commission was to make recommendations regarding the substance of decrees in civil suits, and when such decrees had been entered it was to investigate and report on the manner in which they were being carried out. No such measure of cooperation has ever been achieved. There seems to be no good reason why these provisions, written into the law in 1914, should not be given a trial. This would require no new statutory authority and no new organizational arrangements.

Further provision should be made, however, for coordination in the

22. I disagree with any recommendation that would give more appropriations or staff to the existing Federal Trade Commission. I would agree to a recommendation that would give adequate appropriations and staff to a new Commission.—JAMES M. LANDIS

23. Corporations already are required to file very detailed reports with the Securities and Exchange Commission and the Internal Revenue Bureau, to mention only two. It seems doubtful whether additional reports of this character would perform any useful purpose.—FRANK M. SURFACE

administration of antitrust. To this end, *the Committee recommends that the President establish, by executive order, an executive committee on antitrust policy,* with representation for all interested departments and agencies. It should be the function of this committee to prepare and to recommend to the President a comprehensive program for the maintenance of competition, to make recommendations for the removal of inconsistencies between antitrust and other national policies, to resolve such conflicts as may arise between the programs of different departments and agencies, and to propose further procedures looking toward the coordination of their activities.[24]

INCREASE PENALTIES

Attention should be directed to the penalties that may be imposed upon violators of the Sherman Act. Since the Act is sometimes used to prosecute restraints imposed on trade by petty gangsters and racketeers, the penalty of imprisonment cannot be dropped. But in cases involving complicated problems of industrial organization and business practice, this penalty has seldom been invoked and should not be sought. The other penalties provided in the Act, however, are too light to operate as a deterrent. *These penalties should be increased. The fines imposed on companies found guilty of violating the law should be related to the magnitude of the offense.*

IMPROVE PROCEDURES

In the case of some business practices, the interpretation of the law may be so clear as to justify the institution of a criminal suit. In other cases, however, the rule of the law is not clear; here, civil action is to be preferred. *The subpoena power should be made available in cases where criminal indictments are not sought.* Criminal suits should not be used for the purpose of developing evidence for use in civil actions. They should not be used as a method of obtaining agreement to consent decrees.

Expert knowledge should be brought to bear in the analysis of business organization and practices and in the development and applica-

24. I do not agree that the addition of another committee to coordinate the activities of these agencies would perform any useful purpose. The Hoover Commission has called attention to many similar top-heavy organizations in the federal government with resulting inefficiency. Furthermore, the President's Committee on Government and Business Relations (of the Department of Commerce), which includes several of these agencies, has yet to achieve very positive results.—FRANK M. SURFACE

tion of remedies. In accordance with the provisions of its statute, *the Federal Trade Commission should be called upon to work out the substance of dissolution decrees and to advise upon the provisions of injunctions and consent decrees.*[25]

REDUCE ARTIFICIAL BARRIERS

If enterprise is to be kept free, competition rather than detailed regulation must be relied upon to safeguard the public interest. And if this policy is to prevail, a program that confines itself to the prevention of collusion and combination will not suffice. Further steps must be taken to open the door to new enterprise. The possibility of potential competition must be preserved by lowering artificial barriers to entry into the market for goods and services. To this end, *tariffs that shelter domestic monopolies should be reduced, numerous obstacles to the movement of goods between the states should be removed, state and local licensing requirements that operate to exclude qualified competitors from a trade should be revised, and the provisions of building codes and sanitary regulations that are designed to keep outsiders from entering local markets should be repealed.*

REVISE THE PATENT LAWS

Equally serious and even more difficult are the barriers that can be established under the protection of the patent laws. That these barriers are serious there can be no doubt. Subsidiary patents have sometimes been used to maintain a protected position long after the basic patents have expired. Patent litigation, between parties of unequal financial strength, has been employed as a method of retaining and strengthening a position of monopoly power. Restrictive provisions in patent licenses have likewise been used, in violation of the antitrust laws, to curtail production, fix prices, and allocate markets. These and similar abuses clearly require correction.

That these problems are difficult, there can also be no doubt. For it is necessary to effect a compromise between the interest of the public in maintaining competition and its interest in the development of technology. The issues raised by this conflict of objectives are dis-

25. For the reasons I have already expressed, I would not concur in the recommendation that the Federal Trade Commission should be called upon to work out the substance of dissolution decrees.—JAMES M. LANDIS

cussed in some detail in Chapter 14 of this book. It would appear, from this analysis, that reform of the patent system is long overdue. But, as far as this Committee is concerned, the direction of this reform is not entirely clear.

Certain conclusions seem warranted, however. The Patent Office should be more adequately staffed and financed. *Restrictive provisions written into patent licenses in violation of the antitrust laws have been struck down and should continue to be condemned. Under suitable circumstances, royalty-free licensing has been and should be required. Patentees should also be compelled, after a number of years of nonuse, to grant licenses at reasonable royalties to anyone who may apply.* On such matters as the standards of patentability, the duration of the patent grant, and the procedures involved in patent administration and litigation, the Committee is not prepared to make recommendations.

PROVIDE MARKET INFORMATION

Competition may be safeguarded negatively by preventing collusion, checking combination, and removing artificial barriers to enterprise. It may be promoted positively by facilitating the operation of free markets. One of the major prerequisites of market freedom is the availability to buyers as well as sellers of complete and accurate information concerning the goods in which they deal. *Such information may be provided for, depending upon the particular commodity, by instituting systems of grading and inspection, by forbidding deception and misrepresentation, by compelling the disclosure of significant facts, and by requiring truthful and informative labelling.* Many such measures have long since been written into the laws of the United States. The principle they embody is capable of further extension. To require that sellers tell the truth, the whole truth, and nothing but the truth is not to hamper private enterprise; it is to strengthen private enterprise by insuring its integrity.

AID SMALL BUSINESS

Attention should be directed toward the possibility of promoting competition by removing obstacles to the development of small business. The burden of taxation falls heavily on new and small ventures; the tax structure should be examined with a view to modifying those features that operate to check the growth of such enterprise. Capital is less readily acquired by small undertakings than by large and well-established firms; methods of meeting their financial requirements, including the possible creation of a system of capital credit banks, should be explored. Small enterprises are handicapped by their inability to employ large staffs of experts specializing in various phases of research and administration; encouragement should be given to the further development of facilities to serve them, at a reasonable cost, through market and product analysis, production studies, and guidance in management and merchandising techniques. It is by such means, rather than by imposing artificial handicaps on their larger competitors, that the interests of small enterprises are to be brought into harmony with those of the community at large.

STUDY BUSINESS PRACTICES

In an economy as complex and dynamic as that of the United States, the struggle to maintain the pattern of active competition in free markets can never end in final or complete victory. The problems confronting antitrust keep changing, from industry to industry and from day to day. If competition is to be preserved, *the organization and practices of business, market by market, must be the subject of extensive and continual investigation by both public and private agencies.* Otherwise, for want of knowledge, policy will be misdirected or will go by default. Eternal vigilance is the price of free enterprise.

JAMES M. LANDIS, *Chairman*
A. S. GOSS
MARION HEDGES
DONALD M. NELSON
FRANK M. SURFACE
JACOB VINER
J. RAYMOND WALSH

SUPPLEMENTARY COMMENT

American antitrust legislation, which has no counterpart in other countries, has unquestionably contributed greatly to the remarkable development of our economic system. The principles and policies embodied in these laws should be continued and enforced. But in the hurly-burly of everyday competition there will always be some who overstep the boundaries set by these laws and their interpretation by the courts. It is the proper function of the government to protect the competitive system by preventing such actions and by punishing transgressors.

Unfortunately, however, indiscriminate attacks are being directed against large industry, apparently based on the specious theory that bigness is inherently bad and big companies are guilty of misuse of power until proved innocent. Such attacks are not in the public interest. They represent a purely negative approach to certain important questions about industrial concentration that call for constructive solutions.

It seems to me that much of our theoretical thinking is based on what happened in the latter part of the nineteenth century and the early part of the twentieth. At that time we were, to a large extent, in a pioneering stage with large geographical frontiers to be developed. Business at that time was pretty rough-and-tumble and many things were common practice that would not be tolerated by present-day management. We have passed to a more mature stage where the fierce struggle to conquer a geographical frontier is no longer so insistent. Time and opportunity have become available for more concern with social values and for a consideration of ultimate effects. Modern business management has not lagged so far behind in this as some of its critics think.

The evidence is certainly clear from Department of Commerce reports that, in spite of all the furor raised about big business and monopoly, thousands of new businesses of varying kinds are being established every day and that they are successfully competing with the so-called industrial giants. True, it may be a little difficult for a man with only an urge, but little money, to start in a large-scale mass-production industry such as the oil-refining business or to establish a new make of automobile. But is that necessary? Certainly there are many opportunities for him to go into a business that is commensurate with the finances he has or can obtain, and with his proven ability as a manager.

Furthermore, the existence of relatively large stable units in the mass-production industries, for example, has made it possible for literally hundreds of thousands of independent businesses to come into existence. These include manufacturers supplying parts or materials to larger units and the many thousands of car dealers, repair shops, distributors, service stations, garages, and the like.

True, there are problems to be solved, and there always will be, but there is a big question in my mind whether certain of the remedies proposed in the foregoing Committee report might not prove to be more destructive than constructive in relation to the dynamic quality of our present economy that is the envy of the rest of the world. There are grave dangers in hedging and limiting big enterprises, which have been so large a factor in making our American economy what it is today.

An objective study is urgently needed that will concentrate, not on the shortcomings of American business, but on what it is that has enabled American companies, both large and small, to grow, to achieve commercial success, and to contribute to giving the American people the highest living standards in the world. It would seem to me that such a study might help to harmonize the interests of large and small enterprises, and that it would be more helpful than imposing artificial handicaps on the former.

FRANK M. SURFACE

TABLE OF CASES

A

B

F

G

H

I

J

K

L

M

N

O

P

Q

R

S

T

U

V

W, X, Y, Z

INDEX